T0351544

# THE RELIGIOUS HOUSES OF LONDON AND MIDDLESEX

# THE RELIGIOUS HOUSES OF LONDON AND MIDDLESEX

*Edited by*

Caroline M. Barron and Matthew Davies

Centre for Metropolitan History and Victoria County History

Institute of Historical Research
School of Advanced Study, University of London

2007

*Published by*

UNIVERSITY OF LONDON
SCHOOL OF ADVANCED STUDY
INSTITUTE OF HISTORICAL RESEARCH
Senate House, Malet Street, London WC1E 7HU

© University of London, 2007

ISBN-13: 978 1 905165 12 4

*Cover illustrations*

South-east View of St. Helen's Priory, Bishopsgate, by Frederick Nash (1782–1856), engr. M Springsguth, 1819. *Guildhall Library, City of London.*

Reverse of the Common Seal of the Priory of St. Bartholomew, Smithfield, 13th century, round, *c.*60 mm, impressed in brown-green wax. *The National Archives, UK,* E322/136. Photograph and description by Elizabeth New.

The seal depicts a church with tower and spire on a ship with animal heads at bow and stern, the words NAVIS ECCLIE in the field. Legend: CREDIMVS : ANTE [DEVM PROV]EH I : PER : BARTHOLOMEVM.

The design is most unusual. It is, however, very similar to an earlier seal of office of the Prior of St. Bartholomew's, which depicts what appears to be the Ark, and also to the image of the Ark on the reverse of the 13th-century Common Seal of Coventry Priory. This suggests a fashion for the typology of the Flood. Both Coventry (with the Virgin and Child) and St. Bartholomew's (with one of the Apostles) display New Testament imagery on the obverse of their seals.

The more conventional obverse of this seal depicts an enthroned St. Bartholomew, with the legend SIGILLVM : COMMVNE : PRIOR : ET : COVENTVS : SCI : BARTHOLOMEI : LONDON.

*Typeset by* Olwen Myhill

*Printed in Great Britain by*
Q3 Print Project Management Ltd, Quorn House,
Charnwood Business Park, North Road, Loughborough, LE11 1LE

# CONTENTS

# CONTENTS

Hᴏꜱᴘɪᴛᴀʟꜱ

# ACKNOWLEDGMENTS

The editors would like to take this opportunity to thank those who have been of particular help with the research for this volume and in preparing the text for publication. We are especially grateful to the Victoria County History at the Institute of Historical Research, University of London, for permission to reproduce the accounts of the religious houses originally published for London (1909) and Middlesex (1969). We are grateful to the Vice-Chancellor's Publications Fund, University of London, for supporting the publication of this volume. Bruce Tate, Project Manager of British History Online at the IHR, prepared and supplied the electronic text while Olwen Myhill of the Centre for Metropolitan History prepared the text and images for publication with her customary skill and efficiency. We are grateful to Jeannette McLeish of the Museum of London Archaeology Service for preparing the map showing the locations of the London religious houses, and to Nick Holder of MoLAS for help with this and for supplying details of forthcoming archaeological publications. Elizabeth New provided the photograph of the seal of St. Bartholomew's Priory which appears on the back cover and her description of the seal is to be found on the reverse of the title page. David Smith, editor of the forthcoming third volume of *Heads of Religious Houses: England and Wales* very generously checked our lists against his, and made a number of valuable corrections and additions. We are also indebted to Jeremy Smith and John Fisher of Guildhall Library's Department of Prints, Maps and Drawings for the images of the religious houses used for the cover and elsewhere. Ann Thomson, Archivist of Newnham College, Cambridge supplied us with information concerning the career of Minnie Reddan. Finally, this volume would not exist were it not for the heroic labours of researchers on the Victoria County History, past and present. We are particularly grateful to the staff of the V.C.H. Central Office, and particularly to Alan Thacker and Patricia Croot, for their support of this project.

*Caroline M. Barron*
Royal Holloway,
University of London

*Matthew Davies*
Centre for Metropolitan History,
Institute of Historical Research,
University of London

March 2007

# LIST OF MAPS AND ILLUSTRATIONS

# LIST OF CONTRIBUTORS

## *V.C.H. London,* i. (1909)

John Charles Cox
Helen Douglas-Irvine
Minnie Reddan
Phyllis Wragge

## *V.C.H. Middlesex,* i. (1969)

Helena M. Chew
Marjorie Chibnall
J. L. Kirby
Dom. David Knowles
Marjorie B. Honeybourne

## New Introductions and Revised Lists of Heads of Houses

Caroline M. Barron, Royal Holloway, University of London
Ann Bowtell, Royal Holloway, University of London
Martha Carlin, University of Wisconsin-Milwaukee, USA
Patricia Croot, Victoria County History, Institute of Historical Research, London
Matthew Davies, Centre for Metropolitan History, Institute of Historical Research, London
Lauren Fogle, Royal Holloway, University of London
Christine Fox, Royal Holloway, University of London
Jessica Freeman, Royal Holloway, University of London
Stephanie Hovland, Royal Holloway, University of London
Jennifer Ledfors, Royal Holloway, University of London
David Lewis, Royal Holloway, University of London
Jessica Lutkin, Royal Holloway, University of London
John McEwan, Royal Holloway, University of London
Frances Maggs, Royal Holloway, University of London
Claire Martin, Royal Holloway, University of London
Amanda Moss, Royal Holloway, University of London
Leah Rhys, Royal Holloway, University of London
Jens Röhrkasten, University of Birmingham
Christian Steer, Royal Holloway, University of London
D. Anne Welch, Royal Holloway, University of London
Robert A. Wood, Royal Holloway, University of London

# LIST OF ABBREVIATIONS

This is a combined list of the abbreviations given in *V.C.H. London,* i and *V.C.H. Middlesex,* i. The footnotes to the early volumes were usually very heavily abbreviated, and the tables of abbreviations were consequently very lengthy and included abbreviations for counties and personal names, as well as for documents, archives and libraries and published works. While many are obvious to modern readers, some are less common and so it has been decided to retain almost all the abbreviations in the original lists, where they are found in the accounts of the religious houses. In addition, some of the bibliographical details have been expanded to include fuller titles and dates and places of publication, particularly for the abbreviations from the 1909 volume.

The main modern additions to the list include selected references to works frequently cited in the new bibliographical introductions to the accounts of the religious houses. An example is D. Keene and V. Harding (eds.), *A Survey of Documentary Sources for Property Holding in London before the Great Fire* (London Record Society, 22, 1985), which has been abbreviated as *Documentary Sources*.

## ARCHIVES AND DOCUMENTARY REFERENCES

Since the publication of the two *V.C.H.* volumes, and particularly *V.C.H. London* i (1909) there have been various changes to the organisation of the archives and libraries of London and Middlesex. The London Metropolitan Archives (L.M.A.) has superseded the L.C.C.R.O. and G.L.R.O, while the Guildhall Museum is now part of the Museum of London. Manuscripts formerly part of collections housed in the British Museum (B.M.) are now housed in the separate British Library (B.L.). Finally, the Public Record Office (P.R.O.) is now incorporated under the umbrella of The National Archives (T.N.A). The original references to these archives and libraries have not been changed, but the obsolete abbreviations have been cross-referenced to their modern counterparts or successors, which have been added to this list of abbreviations to help modern researchers.

Original documentary references in the footnotes, particularly to Public Records, have been left unchanged. However, to help modern readers the list below now includes modern classification references where manuscript rather than printed calendar material is being referred to. For instance, 'Chan. Enr. Decree R.' is now explained as 'Chancery Enrolled Decree Rolls (T.N.A. C78)'. Manuscript sources now in the British Library (B.L.), such as the Cotton Manuscripts, have also been identified as such in this list.

| | |
|---|---|
| *Abbrev. Plac.* (Rec. Com.) | *Placitorum in domo capitulari Westmonasteriensi asservatorum abbreviatio* (Record Commission, 1911) |
| *Acts of P.C.* (Rec. Com.) | *Acts of the Privy Council of England* (Record Commission, 1890–1964) |
| Add. | Additional |
| Add. Chart. | Additional Charters (B.L.) |
| Anct. Corresp. | Ancient Correspondence (T.N.A. S.C.1) |
| Anct. D. (P.R.O.) A 2420 | Ancient Deeds (Public Record Office) A 2420 (T.N.A. E40) |
| *Ann. Mon.* | *Annales Monastici*, 5 vols., Rerum Britannicarum Medii Aevi Scriptores, 36 (1864–9) |
| Antiq. | Antiquarian or Antiquaries |
| App. | Appendix |
| Arch. | Archæologia or Archæological |
| *Arch. Cant.* | *Archæologia Cantiana* |
| Archd. Rec. | Archdeacons' Records |
| Archit. | Architectural |
| AS | Anglo-Saxon |

| | |
|---|---|
| Assize R. | Assize Rolls (T.N.A. various classes) |
| Aug. Off. | Augmentation Office |
| Aungier, *Syon* | C. J. Aungier, *History and Antiquities of Syon Monastery, the Parish of Isleworth, and the Chapelry of Hounslow* (London, 1840) |
| Barron, *LLMA* | Caroline M. Barron, *London in the Later Middle Ages: Government and People, 1200–1500* (Oxford, 2004) |
| Bed. | Bedford |
| Beds. | Bedfordshire |
| Bell, *Nuns* | David N. Bell, *What Nuns Read: Books and Libraries in Medieval English Nunneries* (Michigan, 1995) |
| Berks | Berkshire |
| Bdle. | Bundle |
| B.L. | British Library |
| B.M. | British Museum (for which see B.L.) |
| Bodl. Lib. | Bodley's Library (i.e. Bodleian Library, Oxford) |
| Boro. | Borough |
| Brit. | Britain, British, Britannia, etc. |
| *B.R.U.C.* | A. B. Emden, *A Biographical Register of the University of Cambridge to 1500* (Cambridge, 1963) |
| *B.R.U.O.* | A. B. Emden, *A Biographical Register of the University of Oxford to AD 1500*, 3 vols (Oxford, 1957) and *A Biographical Register of the University of Oxford AD 1501–1540* (Oxford, 1974) |
| Buck. | Buckingham |
| Bucks | Buckinghamshire |
| Cal. | Calendar |
| *Cal. of Early Mayor's Court R.* | *Calendar of Early Mayor's Court Rolls Preserved Among the Archives of the Corporation... AD 1298–1307*, ed. A. H. Thomas (Cambridge, 1924) |
| *Cal. Letter Bk.* A, B, C etc. | *Calendar of Letter-Books Preserved Among the Archives of the Corporation of the City of London at the Guildhall*, ed. R. R. Sharpe, 11 vols. (A–L) (London, 1899–1912) |
| *Cal. Plea and Memoranda R.* | *Calendar of Plea and Memoranda Rolls Preserved Among the Archives of the Corporation of the City of London at the Guildhall*, ed. A. H. Thomas and P. E. Jones, 6 vols. (Cambridge, 1926–61) |
| *Cal. of Wills in Ct. of Husting* | *Calendar of the Wills Proved and Enrolled in the Court of Husting, AD 1258–1688*, ed. R. R. Sharpe, 2 vols (London, 1890) |
| Camb. | Cambridgeshire or Cambridge |
| Campb. Chart. | Campbell Charters (B.L.) |
| Cant. | Canterbury |
| Cap. | Chapter |
| Cart. Antiq. R. | Cartæ Antiquæ Rolls (T.N.A. C52) |
| C.C.C. Camb. | Corpus Christi College, Cambridge |
| Certiorari Bdles. (Rolls Chap.) | Certiorari Bundles (Rolls Chapel) (T.N.A. C204) |
| Chan. Enr. Decree R. | Chancery Enrolled Decree Rolls (T.N.A. C78) |
| Chan. Proc. | Chancery Proceedings (T.N.A. C1) |
| Chant. Cert. | Chantry Certificates (or Certificates of Colleges and Chantries) (T.N.A. E301 and L.R.2) |
| Chap. Ho. | Chapter House |
| Chart. R. 20 Hen. III. pt. i. No. 10 | Charter Roll, 20 Henry III. part i. Number 10 (T.N.A. C53/30) |
| Chartul. | Chartulary |
| Chas. | Charles |

| | |
|---|---|
| Ches. | Cheshire |
| Chest. | Chester |
| Ch. Gds. (Exch. K.R.) | Church Goods (Exchequer King's Remembrancer) (T.N.A. E317) |
| Chich. | Chichester |
| Chron. | Chronicle, Chronica, etc. |
| Close | Close Roll |
| C.L.R.O. | Corporation of London Record Office |
| Co. | County |
| Colch. | Colchester |
| Coll. | Collections |
| Com. | Commission |
| Com. Pleas. | Common Pleas |
| Conf. R. | Confirmation Rolls (T.N.A. C56) |
| Cornw. | Cornwall |
| Corp. | Corporation |
| Cott. | Cotton or Cottonian (B.L.) |
| Ct. R. | Court Rolls |
| Ct. of Wards | Court of Wards and Liveries (T.N.A. WARD1–16) |
| Cumb. | Cumberland |
| Cur. Reg. | Curia Regis (T.N.A. K.B.26) |
| D. | Deed or Deeds |
| D. and C. | Dean and Chapter |
| Davis, *Clergy* | Virginia Davis, *Clergy in London in the Late Middle Ages: A Register of Clergy Ordained in the Diocese of London Based on Episcopal Ordination Lists 1361–1539* (London, 2000) |
| De Banc. R. | De Banco Rolls (T.N.A CP40) |
| *Dep. Keeper's Rep.* | *Deputy Keeper's Reports*, 1– (1838–) |
| Derb. | Derbyshire or Derby |
| Devon | Devonshire |
| Dioc. | Diocese |
| Doc. | Documents |
| *Documentary Sources* | *A Survey of Documentary Sources for Property Holding in London before the Great Fire,* ed. D. Keene and V. Harding (London Record Society, 22, 1985) |
| Dom. Bk. | Domesday Book |
| Dors. | Dorsetshire |
| Duchy of Lanc. | Duchy of Lancaster |
| Dur. | Durham |
| East. | Easter Term |
| Eccl. | Ecclesiastical |
| Eccl. Com. | Ecclesiastical Commission |
| Edw. | Edward |
| Eliz. | Elizabeth |
| Engl. | England or English |
| *Engl. Hist. Rev.* | *English Historical Review* |
| Enr. | Enrolled or Enrolment |
| Epis. Reg. | Episcopal Registers |
| Esch. Enr. Accts. | Escheators Enrolled Accounts (T.N.A E357) |
| *Excerptae Rot. Fin.* (Rec. Com.) | *Excerptae Rotulis Finium* (Record Commission) |
| Exch. Dep. | Exchequer Depositions (T.N.A. E134) |
| Exch. K.B. | Exchequer King's Bench (T.N.A. K.B.) |

| | |
|---|---|
| Exch. K.R. | Exchequer King's Remembrancer (T.N.A various classes) |
| Exch. L.T.R. | Exchequer Lord Treasurer's Remembrancer (T.N.A various classes) |
| Exch. of Pleas, Plea R. | Exchequer of Pleas, Plea Roll (T.N.A. E13) |
| Exch. of Receipt | Exchequer of Receipt (T.N.A various classes) |
| Exch. Spec. Com. | Exchequer Special Commissions (T.N.A. E178) |
| Feet of F. | Feet of Fines (T.N.A. CP25) |
| Feod. Accts. (Ct. of Wards) | Feodaries Accounts (Court of Wards) (T.N.A. WARD8) |
| Feod. Surv. (Ct. of Wards) | Feodaries Surveys (Court of Wards) (T.N.A. WARD5) |
| *Feud. Aids* | *Inquisitions and Assessments Relating to Feudal Aids*, 6 vols. (H.M.S.O., 1890–1920) |
| f. or fol. | Folio |
| Gaz. | Gazette or Gazetteer |
| Gen. | Genealogical, Genealogica, etc. |
| Geo. | George |
| Glouc. | Gloucestershire or Gloucester |
| G.M. | Guildhall Museum (for which see M.o.L.) |
| Guild Certif. (Chan.) Ric. II. | Guild Certificates (Chancery) Richard II. (T.N.A. C47/38–46) |
| G.L. or Guildhall MSS. | Guildhall Library, London. This includes bishops' registers (MS. 9531) and diocesan administration (MSS. 9532–60) |
| Hants | Hampshire |
| Harl. | Harley or Harleian (B.L.) |
| *Heads of Religious Houses* | *The Heads of Religious Houses: England and Wales, vol. 1, 940–1216*, ed. D. Knowles, C. N. L. Brooke and V. C. M. London, 2nd edn. (Cambridge, 2001); *vol. 2, 1216–1377*, ed. D. M. Smith and V. C. M. London (Cambridge, 2001); *vol. 3, 1377–1540*, ed. D. M. Smith (forthcoming, 2008) |
| Hen. | Henry |
| Hennessy, *Novum Repertorium* | G. Hennessy, *Novum Repertorium Ecclesiasticum Parochiale Londinense* (London, 1898) |
| Heref. | Herefordshire or Hereford |
| Hertf. | Hertford |
| Herts. | Hertfordshire |
| Hil. | Hilary Term |
| Hist. | History, Historical, Historian, Historia, etc. |
| *Hist. Mon. Com. Mdx.* | *Royal Commission on Historical Monuments, An Inventory of the Historical Monuments in Middlesex* (1937) |
| *Hist. MSS. Com.* | *Historical MSS. Commission Reports*, 1– (London, 1870–) |
| Honeybourne, 'Property' | M. B. Honeybourne, 'The extent and value of the property in London and Southwark occupied by the religious houses' (unpub. Univ. London M.A. thesis, 1929) |
| Hosp. | Hospital |
| Hund. R. | Hundred Rolls (T.N.A. SC5) |
| Hunt. | Huntingdon |
| Hunts | Huntingdonshire |
| Inq. a.q.d. | Inquisitions *ad quod damnum* |
| Inq. p.m. | Inquisitions *post mortem* |
| Inst. | Institute or Institution |
| Invent. | Inventory or Inventories |
| Ips. | Ipswich |
| Itin. | Itinerary |

| | |
|---|---|
| Jas. | James |
| Journ. | Journal |
| Kitching, *Chantry Certificate* | C. J. Kitching ed., *London and Middlesex Chantry Certificate 1548* (London Record Society, 16, 1980) |
| Lambeth (Lib.) MSS. | Lambeth Palace Library |
| Lanc. | Lancashire or Lancaster |
| L.C.C.R.O. | London County Council Record Office (for which see L.M.A.) |
| *L. and P. Hen. VIII* | *Letters and Papers, Foreign and Domestic, Henry VIII*, 21 vols (London, 1862–1932) |
| Lansd. | Lansdowne (B.L.) |
| Ld. Rev. Rec. | Land Revenue Records (T.N.A. L.R.) |
| Leic. | Leicestershire or Leicester |
| Lib. | Library |
| Lich. | Lichfield |
| Linc. | Lincolnshire or Lincoln |
| L.M. | London Museum (for which see M.o.L.) |
| L.M.A. | London Metropolitan Archives |
| Lond. | London |
| Lysons, *Environs of Lond.* | D. Lysons, *The Environs of London* (London, 1792–6) |
| Lysons, *Supplement* | D. Lysons, *Supplement to the First Edition of the Historical Account of the Environs of London* (London, 1811) |
| m. | membrane |
| McHardy, *Church in London* | A. K. McHardy (ed.), *The Church in London 1375–1392* (London Record Society, 13, 1977) |
| *Med. Rel. Houses* | D. Knowles and R. N. Hadcock, *Medieval Religious Houses in England and Wales* (London, 1953). See also 1973 edn. |
| Mem. | Memorials |
| Memo. R. | Memoranda Rolls (T.N.A. various classes) |
| Mich. | Michaelmas Term |
| Midd. | Middlesex |
| Mins. Accts. | Ministers' Accounts (T.N.A. various incl. SC6 and D.L. 29) |
| Misc. Bks. (Exch. K.R., Exch. T.R. or Aug. Off.) | Miscellaneous Books (Exchequer King's Remembrancer (T.N.A. E164) Exchequer Treasury of Receipt (T.N.A. E36) or Augmentation Office (T.N.A. E315)) |
| M.o.L. | Museum of London |
| MoLAS | Museum of London Archaeology Service |
| Mon. | Monastery, Monasticon |
| Monm. | Monmouth |
| M.R.O. | Middlesex Record Office. Became part of Greater London Record Office and then L.M.A. |
| Mun. | Muniments or Munimenta |
| Mus. | Museum |
| *N. and Q.* | *Notes and Queries* |
| Newcourt, *Repertorium* | R. Newcourt, *Repertorium Ecclesiasticum Parochiale Londinense* (London, 1708–10) |
| Norf. | Norfolk |
| Northampt. | Northampton |
| Northants | Northamptonshire |
| Northumb. | Northumberland |
| Norw. | Norwich |
| Nott. | Nottinghamshire or Nottingham |

| | |
|---|---|
| N.S. | New Style |
| Off. | Office |
| Orig. R. | Originalia Rolls (T.N.A. E371) |
| O.S. | Ordnance Survey |
| Oxf. | Oxfordshire or Oxford |
| p. | page |
| Par. | Parish, parochial, etc. |
| Parl. | Parliament or Parliamentary |
| *Parl. R.* | *Parliament Rolls* (Record Commission) |
| Parl. Surv. | Parliamentary Surveys |
| Partic. for Gts. | Particulars for Grants (T.N.A. various classes) |
| Pat. | Patent Roll or Letters Patent |
| Paxton, 'Nunneries' | C. Paxton, 'The Nunneries of London and its environs in the later middle ages' (unpub. Univ. Oxford D.Phil. thesis, 1992) |
| P.C.C. | Prerogative Court of Canterbury (T.N.A PROB) |
| Pet. | Petition |
| Peterb. | Peterborough |
| Pevsner, *London*, ii | N. Pevsner, *The Buildings of England, London except the City and Westminster* (London, 1952). NB for up to date information see recent Greater London volumes in the series |
| Pevsner, *Mdx.* | N. Pevsner, *The Buildings of England, Middlesex* (1951). NB for up to date information, see recent Greater London volumes in the series |
| Phil. | Philip |
| Pipe R. | Pipe Roll (T.N.A. E372) |
| Plea R. | Plea Rolls (T.N.A. C.P.40) |
| *P.N. Mdx.* (E.P.N.S.) | *The Place Names of Middlesex* (English Place-Name Society xviii, 1942) |
| *Pope Nich. Tax.* (Rec. Com.) | *Taxatio Ecclesiastica Angliae et Walliae Auctoritate Papae Nicholai IV* (Record Commission, 1802). |
| P.R.O. | Public Record Office (see also T.N.A.) |
| Proc. | Proceedings |
| *Proc. Soc. Antiq.* | *Proceedings of the Society of Antiquaries* |
| pt. | part |
| Pub. | Publications |
| R. | Roll |
| Rec. | Records |
| Recov. R. | Recovery Rolls (T.N.A. CP43) |
| Rentals and Surv. | Rentals and Surveys (T.N.A. SC11) |
| Rep. | Report |
| Rev. | Review |
| Ric. | Richard |
| R.O. | Record Office |
| Roff. | Rochester diocese |
| *Rot. Cur. Reg.* | *Rotuli Curiæ Regis*, 2 vols (Record Commission, 1835) |
| Rut. | Rutland |
| Sarum | Salisbury diocese |
| Ser. | Series |
| Sess. R. | Sessions Rolls |
| Shrews. | Shrewsbury |
| Shrops | Shropshire |
| Soc. | Society |

| | |
|---|---|
| Soc. Antiq. | Society of Antiquaries |
| Somers. | Somerset |
| *S.P. Dom.* | *Calendar of State Papers, Domestic Series* |
| Staff. | Staffordshire |
| Star Chamb. Proc. | Star Chamber Proceedings (T.N.A. STAC) |
| Stat. | Statute |
| Steph. | Stephen |
| Stow, *Survey* | J. Stow, *Survey of London*, ed. C. L. Kingsford (Oxford, 1908) |
| Subs. R. | Subsidy Rolls (T.N.A. E179) |
| Suff. | Suffolk |
| Surr. | Surrey |
| Suss. | Sussex |
| Surv. of Ch. Livings (Lamb.) or (Chan.) | Surveys of Church Livings (Lambeth Pal. Lib.) or (Chancery: T.N.A. C94) |
| Syon Ho. A | Manuscripts of the Duke of Northumberland, Syon House, Rentals, Surveys, &c. |
| Syon Ho. D | Title Deeds of the Duke of Northumberland, Syon House |
| Thompson, *Women Religious* | Sally Thompson, *Women Religious: The Founding of English Nunneries after the Norman Conquest* (Oxford, 1991) |
| Thorne, *Environs* | J. Thorne, *Handbook to the Environs of London* [alphabetically arranged in two parts], (London, 1876) |
| *T.L.M.A.S.* | *Transactions of the London and Middlesex Archaeological Society* |
| T.N.A. | The National Archives (incorporates P.R.O. and Historical Manuscripts Commission) |
| Topog. | Topography or Topographical |
| Trans. | Transactions |
| Transl. | Translation |
| Treas. | Treasury or Treasurer |
| Trin. | Trinity Term |
| Univ. | University |
| *Valor Eccl.* (Rec. Com.) | *Valor Ecclesiasticus* (Record Commission, 1810–34) |
| *V.C.H.* | *Victoria County History* |
| Vic. | Victoria |
| vol. | volume |
| W.A.M. | Westminster Abbey Muniments |
| Warw. | Warwickshire or Warwick |
| Westm. | Westminster |
| Will. | William |
| Wilts | Wiltshire |
| Winton. | Winchester diocese |
| Worc. | Worcestershire or Worcester |
| Yorks | Yorkshire |

# EDITORIAL PREFACE

## Matthew Davies

This volume brings together for the first time the histories of the religious houses of London and Middlesex that were originally published in the famous red volumes of the *Victoria History of the Counties of England* – the '*V.C.H.*' The sixty-five accounts printed here first appeared in *V.C.H. London*, i, ed. W. Page (London, 1909) and *V.C.H. Middlesex*, i, ed. J. S. Cockburn, H. P. F. King, and K. G. T. McDonnell (1969).[1] The entries are accompanied by newly commissioned bibliographical introductions and by revised lists of the heads of these religious houses.

## THE VICTORIA COUNTY HISTORY AND ITS CONTRIBUTORS

More than 240 volumes have been published by the V.C.H. since the foundation of this ambitious project in 1899, covering (wholly or in part) some forty counties. Early volumes in each county series tended to take a thematic approach, and dealt with topics as diverse as education, ecclesiastical organisation, industry and agriculture, as a preliminary to the detailed studies of the hundreds and parishes which followed in later volumes. Religious houses were covered in great detail by many county volumes, and despite their age, the accounts for the London and Middlesex houses are still of immense value to historians working on London and on the religious life in England. They represent a huge quantity of original archival research and scholarship that still, by and large, stands the test of time. The thorough investigation of records in the Public Record Office (now part of The National Archives) and the British Museum (British Library) was one of the hallmarks of the work of researchers on these early *V.C.H.* volumes, including the first (and only) volume on the City of London, published in 1909. Like other volumes published before the First World War, *V.C.H London*, i relied heavily on the work of relatively unknown researchers, working under the direction of William Page, in the days before the project became attached to the University of London (1932). Strikingly, many of them were young women who had recently completed undergraduate history or classics courses. The majority did not have a degree, however, as it was still the case that women who attended Oxford and Cambridge were not awarded degrees, even though they had completed all the necessary examinations.[2] The most notable such contributor to *V.C.H. London* was Minnie Reddan, who was responsible for no fewer than forty-one of the forty-six articles on the London houses – one of the most significant individual contributions to the early *V.C.H.* volumes. After Notting Hill High School, she attended Newnham College, Cambridge, and completed the History Tripos in 1891. After working on the London *V.C.H.*, Reddan contributed articles on religious houses for county volumes for Hertfordshire (published in 1914) and the North Riding of Yorkshire (1923), both of which were also edited by William Page.[3] In the meantime Reddan continued to pursue her interest in the London houses, and contributed to the Survey of London's volume on the parish and house of St. Helen Bishopsgate, published in 1924.[4] Little else has been discovered of her subsequent career: she died in London in 1952 at the age of 82.[5]

---

[1] The text is reproduced here by permission of the Victoria County History (University of London). The editors are grateful to Bruce Tate of British History Online, the IHR's digital library, for supplying electronic versions of the *V.C.H.* texts. These were created for the online editions of *V.C.H. London,* i and *V.C.H. Middlesex*, i, by scanning and double-keying the original volumes.

[2] See J. Beckett, 'Local History, Family History and the V.C.H.: New Directions for the Twenty-First Century' (The Marc Fitch Lecture 2006), p. 3. [http://www.englandspastforeveryone.org.uk/resources/assets/T/The_Marc_Fitch_Lecture_522.pdf, accessed 25 January 2007]. Women were allowed to take examinations from the 1880s onwards, but were not awarded degrees until 1920 (Oxford) and 1948 (Cambridge).

[3] *V.C.H. Hertfordshire*, iv, ed. W. Page (London, 1914); *V.C.H. Yorkshire, North Riding*, ii, ed. W. Page (London, 1923).

[4] J. Bird and P. Norman (eds.), *Survey of London: Vol. IX, The Parish of St. Helen, Bishopsgate, part 1* (London County Council, 1924).

[5] *Newnham College Register, 1871–1971*, 3 vols. (Cambridge, 1979), i, p. 98.

The remaining five London religious houses were shared between three contributors. Phyllis Wragge, who read history at Somerville College, Oxford, wrote entries on the religious houses for the Dorset, Lincolnshire and Sussex V.C.H.s in addition to London during the first decade of the twentieth century. She went on to be a lecturer at Goldsmiths' College, University of London (1908–12), was Principal of the Women's Hostel, University of Durham (later St. Mary's College) from 1913–15 and then made a career in primary school teacher training. Her publications included several children's history books.[6] Helen Douglas-Irvine, who had an M.A. from St. Andrew's, subsequently published a history of London (1912), various other works of history, poetry and fiction, and was the translator of a French history of medieval English literature published in 1926. She died in Chile in 1946.[7] These three young female contributors can be contrasted with the only male author of the essays on the London religious houses. This was John Charles Cox (1843–1919), an antiquary and ecclesiologist, who was already a leading authority on the medieval English church. In addition to contributing to the accounts of religious houses in thirteen county volumes, Cox was also on the advisory council of the V.C.H.[8]

Better known to modern historians are some of the authors of the accounts of the Middlesex religious houses. Just one volume had been produced on the county before the Second World War, but Middlesex was one of the counties that benefited from the post-war revival of the V.C.H. as a national project, and research on the county re-commenced in 1955. The religious houses were covered by a volume which was published in 1969, chronologically the third to appear, although it was designated as volume 1 in the series because of its thematic content – including its focus on religious life and organisation.[9] Notable contributors to the volume included David Knowles, who brought his unmatched expertise on monastic history to an article on the London Charterhouse,[10] and Marjorie Honeybourne, who was already a leading expert on the estates of the London houses and on the city's hospitals before she contributed her articles on these houses.[11] The other contributors included J. L. Kirby, Helena M. Chew and Marjorie Chibnall, all of whom were established scholars in their fields. Their involvement reflected the growing status of the V.C.H. as an academic project, the rise of 'local history' more generally as a respectable subject within universities, and the growing connections between the V.C.H. counties and regional universities which remain important to it today. The V.C.H. also at this time became something of a 'training ground' for researchers who were at earlier stages in their careers; and the lists of contributors to county volumes published from the 1960s onwards include a number of historians who have since gone on to hold positions at leading universities.

[6] For brief details of Wragge's career, see *Somerville College Register, 1879–1971* (Oxford, 1972), p. 34. Her appointment at Durham was noted in *The Times*, Wednesday, Jul 16, 1913, p. 4. Her later publications included: (with Ethel Spalding) *The Piers Plowman Histories. Junior Book VII* (London, 1913) and *The Nation and its Government From 1485 to the Present Day* (London, 1914); (with Margaret Keary), *Stories from English History, 1066 to 1805* (London, 1923); *The Young Citizen's Social History of Britain* (London, 1949); and (with Edward Carter) *Two Paths to Freedom. Great Britain and the Commonwealth, and the United States of America* (London, 1951).

[7] Her publications include: *The Royal Palaces of Scotland*, ed. with R. S. Rait (London, 1911); *The History of London* (London, 1912); *The Making of Rural Europe* (London 1923); the translation of E. Legouis, *A History of English Literature: The Middle Ages and the Renascence* (London, 1926); *Magdalena. [A novel]* (London, 1935); *Saint Catherine of Genoa. Treatise on Purgatory. The Dialogue*, translated by Charlotte Balfour and Helen Douglas Irvine (London, 1946).

[8] Bernard Nurse, 'Cox, John Charles (1843–1919)', *Oxford Dictionary of National Biography*, Oxford University Press, 2004 [http://www.oxforddnb.com/view/article/41055, accessed 24 Jan 2007]

[9] The first volume to appear was in fact *V.C.H. Middlesex*, ii, ed. W. Page (London, 1911) and the next, *V.C.H. Middlesex*, iii, ed. S. Reynolds, was published in 1962.

[10] In addition to his many books on the monastic orders and religious houses Knowles had already jointly published a book on the Charterhouse: D. Knowles and W. F. Grimes, *Charterhouse: The Medieval Foundation in the Light of Recent Discoveries* (London, 1954).

[11] M. B. Honeybourne, 'The extent and value of the property in London and Southwark occupied by the religious houses (including the prebends of St. Paul's and St. Martin's le Grand), the inns of the bishops and abbots, and the churches and churchyards, before the dissolution of the monasteries', *Bulletin of the Institute of Historical Research*, 9 (1932), pp. 52–7. This was derived from her 1929 London M.A. thesis of the same title. See also *eadem*, 'The Leper hospitals of the London Area, with an appendix on some other mediaeval hospitals of Middlesex', *T.L.M.A.S.*, 21 (1963–7), pp. 1–61.

## NEW SCHOLARSHIP AND THE 'RELIGIOUS HOUSES PROJECT'

Inevitably, the intervening years have seen a dramatic increase in the amount and variety of research into the history of London, and into the religious orders and their houses. While most of the articles still stand up to scrutiny, the many hundreds of books and articles that have appeared since 1909, and even since 1969, have greatly deepened our knowledge of the religious houses through detailed examinations of areas such as material culture and archaeology, economic history, and religious life – a reflection of the specialisation and diversity characteristic of the field as a whole today. New sources have come to light, documentary and material; new and interdisciplinary approaches have been brought to bear on the evidence; and developments in information technology have enabled historians to assemble and interrogate evidence in ever more inventive ways.

This project began with the aim of uniting the accounts for London and Middlesex, published some sixty years apart, in a single, accessible volume. How, then, to take account of this scholarly productivity? So great is the volume and diversity of written material relating to the religious houses that it was obvious that to re-write all sixty-five original articles completely would not be feasible without considerable resources. Yet it was clearly not enough simply to reproduce the original articles without any form of critical commentary or without – perhaps more importantly – providing guidance to readers wishing to find out more. The editors, in consultation with staff at the V.C.H. central office, decided that the best solution would be to print the original text along with a short introduction outlining some of the main printed and electronic sources for each house, particularly on subjects that were poorly covered, if at all, in the original articles. For some of the houses the list of published work is enormous: St. Paul's and Westminster Abbey have been the subject of several thousand books and articles between them. In these cases only the key publications have been listed. Other houses have been less well served by historians and archaeologists, although in almost every case it has been possible to identify several useful recent publications that shed light on aspects of their history.

The new introductions were written by the editors and a team of twenty-one researchers, including postgraduate students as well as more established scholars. Many of these researchers have specialized in the history of particular religious houses or orders, as well as in other aspects of London's history. The introductions note some of the most useful sources for particular topics, such as the personnel, fabric and estates of the houses, as well as one or two more general works on the monastic order as a whole that have appeared over recent years. In the case of the Middlesex Leper hospitals, an additional note was written by Patricia Croot, drawing on recent work undertaken by the V.C.H. on Middlesex, which clears up some of the confusion surrounding these foundations. As the project developed, a number of key works were identified which contain material relating to the London and Middlesex religious houses as a group, notably editions of taxation records and other sources published by the London Record Society, and websites such as the English Monastic Archives project at University College, London.[12] Some of these are discussed in the historical Introduction to this volume, and in the note on abbreviations, above.

## HEADS OF HOUSES

When it came to the lists of the heads of the religious houses, which appeared at the end of each article, the editors felt that this was one area where it was both necessary (and feasible) to revise the original entries. A third aim of the project was therefore to seek out new information about the priors, prioresses, abbots, abbesses and others who headed these institutions before the Reformation. Of enormous assistance were the two published volumes of *Heads of Religious Houses*, ed. Knowles, Brooke et al., and the editors are indebted to David Smith for checking the lists against draft lists for his forthcoming volume in this series, which will cover the period from

---

[12] English Monastic Archives Project, http://www.ucl.ac.uk/history/englishmonasticarchives (accessed 25 January 2007).

1377 onwards.[13] Nevertheless, the London friaries, hospitals and quite a few other institutions lie outside the scope of *Heads of Religious Houses*, vols 1–3. A few other lists are available in works published on individual houses, such as St. Bartholomew's Priory and the Hospital of St. Mary of Bethlehem, and these have been cited as the main source for the lists printed here. Elsewhere, a wide range of other sources, both manuscript and in print, have been consulted by the research team in an attempt to fill the gaps and/or check the original lists. For the friaries, the work of Jens Röhrkasten, one of the contributors, has been invaluable. The revised lists therefore include a significant number of new names, especially for those houses (such as the friaries) that have been the subject of recent archival work.

## MONASTIC SEALS

The original *V.C.H.* entries were accompanied by descriptions of the seals of each religious house, then known to be extant. Much of this work has been superseded, both by print publications and by the increasing amount of material available online, and so for this reason the editors, with the advice of V.C.H. staff, took the decision not to reproduce these small sections of the text. For further information on the seals, see Roger H. Ellis, *Catalogue of Seals in the Public Record Office: Monastic Seals, vol. 1* (London, 1986), to be used in conjunction with T.N.A.'s card index and typescript *Catalogue of Seals*, compiled by P. D. A. Harvey and available at Kew. These cross-reference to the older, but still valuable, *Catalogue of Seals in the Department of Manuscripts in the British Museum*, 6 vols., ed. W. de Gray Birch (London, 1887–1900). A significant number of monastic seals also survive in the archives of the city of London and are in the process of being catalogued.

## FOOTNOTING

New footnotes have been used as sparingly as possible, and only for the lists of heads of houses. Where the lists have been taken from easily accessible printed sources, such as *Heads of Religious Houses*, a reference to the source has been included, and the majority of the original references have been omitted to avoid confusion (e.g. the entry for Westminster Abbey). Other lists have been obtained from multiple sources and so remain fully footnoted: these are generally a mixture of names and references from the original *V.C.H.* accounts and additional information obtained by the researchers on the project (e.g. the entry for Blackfriars). New footnotes have been edited to conform to the V.C.H. 'house-style' as far as possible, although titles of books and articles are generally less heavily abbreviated to aid comprehension.

## NUMBERING OF THE ENTRIES

For consistency, the entries are printed and numbered exactly as they appeared in the original *V.C.H.* volumes, 1 to 46 in the case of London and 1 to 19 in the case of the Middlesex houses. They are grouped together by religious order or 'type', e.g. Augustinian Canons, Colleges, Hospitals. The list of Contents and the running header on each page provide a means to locate individual articles.

---

[13] *The Heads of Religious Houses, England and Wales, Vol. 1: 940–1216*, ed. D. Knowles, C. N. L. Brooke, and V. C. M. London (Cambridge, 1972); *Vol. 2: 1216–1377*, ed. D. M. Smith and V. C. M. London, Cambridge, 2001); *Vol. 3: 1377–1540*, ed. D. M. Smith (forthcoming).

# INTRODUCTION

*Caroline M. Barron*

By the time of the Dissolution of the Monasteries in the 1530s there were some sixty religious institutions in London and Middlesex which are described in this volume: almost all of them were clustered around, or within, the walled city itself. Only seventeen of the houses could be described as 'rural' and of these eight were very small – originally leper – hospitals. In fact several of the religious institutions included in these histories were not, strictly speaking, monastic houses at all: St. Paul's Cathedral was served by secular canons, as was St. Martin le Grand; ten of the institutions were small colleges of secular priests and eight were simply lay hospitals under varying degrees of religious guidance. The almshouse, which became ubiquitous in late medieval England, is represented in this collection only by Whittington's Hospital (in fact an almshouse), the Brentford almshouses and those established by Sir John Milbourne in 1535 for decayed members of the Drapers' Company. By this date there were in fact at least a dozen such establishments in, or near, London.[1] Included here are also some 'oddities': the Domus Conversorum founded to house converted Jews in 1232; St. Augustine Pappey, set up as a retirement home for elderly secular priests in 1442, and Jesus Commons, established as a small college for priests in 1507. The editor in 1909 also chose to include two chapels: St. Peter ad Vincula in the Tower of London and the chapel dedicated to St. Thomas Becket on London Bridge. This idiosyncratic eclecticism of the editor of the 1909 London volume (by 1969 the editors of the Middlesex volume were less idiosyncratic) does, in fact, reflect the diversity and mutability of medieval monastic institutions. Between the foundation of Westminster Abbey in the tenth century and the Dissolution, numerous religious institutions were founded, but the form, governance and purpose of many of them changed over the years. This was not the case with great houses like Westminster itself, or the Friaries or wealthy new foundations such as the Bridgettine house at Syon established at Isleworth in the early fifteenth century: but others changed with changing times.

The houses of St. Thomas of Acre and St. Mary Bethlehem, originally founded in the twelfth century to support work in the Holy Land, found new roles, in the first case as a chapel and school under the wing of the Mercers' Company, and in the other as a hospital for the sick and, in particular, for the insane.[2] The hospital of St. Anthony of Vienne, founded as a cell of the French order in 1254, was taken over by the Crown after the Alien Priories Act of 1414 and later became a notable grammar school. Alien priories were, of course, particularly vulnerable to royal interference: the priory and manor of Harmondsworth, founded as a cell of the Benedictine Abbey of St. Catherine at Rouen by William I in 1069, finally passed into the hands of William of Wykeham and became part of the endowment of Winchester College and New College Oxford. Ruislip priory was the administrative centre of the English lands of the great Abbey of Bec, but it also fell into royal hands and in the fifteenth century formed part of the endowment of King's College Cambridge.

The chronological pattern of foundations in London and Middlesex reflects, in microcosm, the waves of religious enthusiasm that swept over Western Europe. St. Paul's Cathedral, dating back to the time of the conversion of England to Christianity by St. Augustine in the early seventh century, and served by a group of secular canons, represents the early minster pattern of Anglo-Saxon Christianity. The pre-Conquest foundation of St. Martin le Grand by Ingelric, possibly a German immigrant who was attracted to England to work at the royal court, followed this earlier practice in which large churches were served by a group of secular priests who lived

---

[1] Barron, *LLMA*, p. 299.

[2] See Anne Sutton, 'The Hospital of St. Thomas of Acre of London: the search for patronage, liturgical improvement, and a school, under Master John Neel, 1420–1463', in *The Late Medieval English College and its Context*, ed. Clive Burgess and Martin Heale (Woodbridge, forthcoming).

together but were not bound by a monastic rule.[3] This tradition was submerged during the great age of monastic foundations but re-emerged in the fourteenth and fifteenth centuries which saw numerous foundations of small colleges of secular priests attached to parish churches or chapels.

Until the twelfth century, when medieval men and women thought of monks they thought of Benedictine monks: men (and sometimes women) living together in poverty, chastity and obedience, following the sixth-century rule of St. Benedict. Westminster Abbey founded (or re-founded) by King Edgar in the mid-tenth century, represents this older and venerable form of monasticism. Surprisingly, perhaps, the only other Benedictine foundations in London and Middlesex were two houses for nuns: one dedicated to St. Leonard at Stratford, founded in the early twelfth century, and another founded a century later dedicated to St. Helen near Bishopsgate.

The twelfth century was the great age of new monastic orders and new foundations. The Cistercians, who sought out wild and uncultivated land, were not attracted to the urban environs of London (although Edward III did later found a Cistercian house of St. Mary Graces in East Smithfield in 1350), but the two new crusading orders both established their English headquarters in London: the Templars on the Strand in 1128 and the Knights Hospitallers at Clerkenwell a few years later. But the twelfth century was, above all, the century of the Augustinian Canons. The rule of St. Augustine was flexible and allowed for a measure of 'outreach' to the surrounding community. It was also possible to found an Augustinian house with a smaller endowment than a more traditional Benedictine foundation.[4] The new houses of Austin canons were often founded in, or near, the fast-developing towns of Western Europe and nowhere more so than in London and the surrounding area where at least ten houses of the new Augustinian order were established in the twelfth century. Three of these were founded simply as houses for canons (Holy Trinity Priory, Southwark Priory and Bentley Priory) but four had important hospitals associated with them (St. Bartholomew's, St. Katherine by the Tower, St. Thomas Southwark and St. Mary Bishopsgate) and three were houses for women (Haliwell, Clerkenwell and Kilburn). The flexibility of the Augustinian rule meant that it could sometimes be used to accommodate the small groups (sometimes only one or two) of men who ran the small leper hospitals around the city such as St. Giles in the Fields, St. James at Westminster or the Lock Hospital in Southwark.

If the twelfth century was the great age of the Augustinian order, then the thirteenth century was, without doubt, the age of the Friars. The city of London attracted seven different orders of friars and also saw the foundation of a house of Minoresses. Although the communities of the Friars of the Sack and the Friars de Areno (Pied Friars) barely survived into the fourteenth century, the other six houses flourished and played a significant part in the life of the city.[5]

The fourteenth century saw the beginnings in London of the movement to set up groups (or Colleges) of secular priests to pray for the soul of the founder and, sometimes, to perform other social and spiritual functions within the urban community. The wealthy mayor Sir John Pountney attached his College to his parish church of St. Leonard, Candlewick Street, early in the reign of Edward III and this was followed by Adam Frauncey's College at the Guildhall chapel and Sir William Walworth's College at St. Michael Crooked Lane. The foundation of Colleges continued apace in the next century: Richard Whittington's College at St. Michael Paternoster (1424); Leadenhall College set up under the will of Simon Eyre (d. 1459), and the College at the parish church of All Hallows Barking founded by a group of royal civil servants in the later fifteenth century. It seems clear that Edward IV had also intended to set up a College in the church of St. Peter ad Vincula.[6] Colleges and almshouses, or hospitals, were, indeed, the characteristic foundations of the later middle ages in England, but there were also some important new monastic

---

[3] Pamela Taylor, 'Ingelric, Count Eustace and the Foundation of St. Martin-le-Grand', *Anglo-Norman Studies*, 24 (2001), pp. 215–37.

[4] C. H. Lawrence, *Medieval Monasticism* (London, 2nd edn. 1989), pp. 165–9.

[5] See below. The Trinitarian Friars, whose house was founded at Hounslow in the twelfth century, were not strictly speaking friars: they followed an austere form of the rule of St. Augustine and were particularly devoted to ransoming captives.

[6] Below, pp. 214–15.

houses founded in London in this period: the Charterhouse of the Carthusian order (1371) and the Cistercian house of St. Mary Graces (1350) were founded on two hastily-consecrated burial sites for victims of the Black Death of 1348–9. Moreover the great Bridgettine house for women of the Order of St. Saviour was founded by Henry V at Isleworth to form an important link in the girdle of prayer with which he intended to defend his kingdom.[7]

By the beginning of the sixteenth century within the four hundred or so square miles covered by the small county of Middlesex and the populous capital city at its core, there could be found sample houses of almost every religious order. There were the great houses like those at Westminster, or Holy Trinity Priory, or the Greyfriars or the Charterhouse or Syon, and tiny hospitals such as St. Mary Rouncivall or the modest colleges founded in city churches.[8] There is no doubt that the London area was well provided with religious houses but it may be worthwhile to explore the extent to which they interacted with the secular world at (or often within) their gates.

* * *

Not surprisingly perhaps, all the founders of the earliest houses were members of the royal family, or the new Norman aristocracy, both secular and religious: Henry I, for example, together with a clerk named Rahere, founded the priory of St. Bartholomew in Smithfield, and Henry's queen, Mathilda, founded the priory of Holy Trinity. Another queen, Mathilda the wife of Stephen, founded the hospital of St. Katherine. Both the Priory of St. John at Clerkenwell and the house of Augustinian canonesses there were founded in the early twelfth century by Jordan de Bricett (fitz Ralph *alias* fitz Brian), a wealthy Essex landowner. Both his daughter and his granddaughter became nuns in the house at Clerkenwell.[9] The first house founded by a 'Londoner' was the hospital served by Augustinian canons, established outside Bishopsgate and dedicated to the Virgin by Walter Brunus and his wife Roisia in 1197. Walter may have been a mercer who owned the painted Seld in the Mercery in Cheapside and was one of the city's sheriffs in 1202–3.[10] It is possible that Walter acted as the leader of a group of other Londoners who jointly founded and endowed the hospital.[11] The foundation of urban hospitals in this period, it has been argued, can be seen as one of the expressions of a growing urban self-consciousness which, in London, was also to be seen at this time in the development of the commune, the engraving of the magnificent common seal and the building of the stone bridge across the Thames.[12] The example of Walter Brunus was followed by William, son of William the Goldsmith, who founded a Benedictine nunnery dedicated to St. Helen early in the thirteenth century.[13] This house in its early days was almost the 'family' house of the great London dynasty of Basings. In 1247 Simon FitzMary, towards the end of his tempestuous career as sheriff, royal agent and rioter, founded the London house of the crusading order of St. Mary of Bethlehem just outside Bishopsgate. This house later became better known as 'Bethlem' or 'Bedlam'.[14] Although the foundation deed did not specifically enjoin the brothers and sisters to care for the poor and sick, yet a hospice of some kind seems to have been envisaged from the start.[15] But perhaps the most 'London' of all the foundations was the hospital established by the mercer, William Elsing, to provide shelter for the poor and destitute, particularly blind and paralysed priests, who thronged the streets of London in the 1320s. Although at first William's intention

[7] See J. I. Catto, 'Religious Change under Henry V', in G. L. Harriss (ed.), *Henry V: The Practice of Kingship* (Oxford, 1985), pp. 97–115.

[8] The only major orders not represented were the Gilbertines and the Premonstratensian Canons.

[9] Pamela Taylor, 'Clerkenwell and the Religious Foundations of Jordan de Bricett: a re-examination', *Historical Research*, 63 (1990), pp. 17–28.

[10] Below, p. 160; Anne Sutton, *The Mercery of London: Trade, Goods and People, 1130–1578* (Aldershot, 2005), p. 18.

[11] Christopher Thomas, Barney Sloane and Christopher Phillpotts, *Excavations at the Priory and Hospital of St. Mary Spital, London*, MoLAS Monograph Series, 1 (London, 1997), p. 19.

[12] I am grateful to Dr Sethina Watson for sharing with me her ideas on the motivation behind the foundation of early hospitals in English towns.

[13] Below, p. 71.

[14] Below, p. 113; Gwyn Williams, *Medieval London: From Commune to Capital* (London, 1963), pp. 202–7.

[15] Barron, *LLMA*, p. 290.

had been that his house should be run by secular priests, in 1340 he converted his foundation into a house of Augustinian canons.[16] It may be significant that three of the four houses founded by Londoners themselves, had a social as well as a spiritual purpose.

Aristocratic interest in the foundation of London houses continued and this can be clearly seen in the patronage of the friars. Five of the London houses owed their foundation to noble patrons: the Carmelite house in Fleet Street was founded by Sir Richard Grey in the 1240s; the Austin friars by Humphrey de Bohun, earl of Essex, in 1253; the Friars of the Sack were granted 100 marks to purchase their London site by Henry III who also patronised the Pied Friars, and the Minoresses house was established outside Aldgate by Edmund, earl of Lancaster, the brother of Edward I.[17] But Londoners also played a part in the foundation of the great London friaries. The site of the Dominican house was given to the Order by a number of wealthy Londoners: William Viel (sheriff 1247–8); Alice le Brun (possibly related to Walter Brunus who had founded the hospital at Bishopsgate); Ralph Eswy, (mercer, sheriff 1234–5; mayor 1242–3) and Richard Renger (sheriff 1221–2, mayor 1222–7, d. 1238).[18] The support of the Londoners for the Franciscans was even more significant: John Travers (sheriff 1215–16 and 1224–5) provided them with their first temporary accommodation in Cornhill, and John Iwyn, a merchant, William Joynier (sheriff 1222–3, mayor 1238–9) and Joyce Fitz-Peter (sheriff 1211–12), whose son became a friar there, were among several prominent Londoners who provided money, and the land on which the permanent house was built.[19] The involvement of Londoners themselves in religious foundations became more marked as time went on: all the Colleges (Guildhall, Pountney, Walworth, Whittington, Leadenhall, All Hallows Barking) and most of the later almshouses or hospitals (Kingsland Hospital, Whittington's almshouses, and the Drapers' almshouses near the Tower) were all founded by Londoners, and the Brentford Hospital was re-founded in 1498 by Hugh Denys, a royal servant with London connections.[20] But the really large foundations continued to be the work of outsiders: the Cistercian house of St. Mary Graces founded by Edward III in 1350; the establishment of the London Charterhouse in 1371 by Sir Walter Manny, and the foundation of the great Syon Abbey by Henry V in 1415.

Even if comparatively few of the religious houses in London and Middlesex were actually founded by 'locals' this did not mean that they were not valued by the people who lived in their vicinity. Most of these houses interacted closely with their local communities and developed relationships of mutual inter-dependence. Many adapted (or were adapted) over time to respond to local needs and concerns. One way in which their popularity may be gauged is by investigating the extent to which these houses drew their recruits from the city and county.

Several London recruits to the religious houses in the years immediately following their foundation have already been noted. The evidence about recruitment is inevitably patchy and anecdotal. It is particularly hard to trace sons who entered religious houses since, unlike daughters, they were rarely referred to in their father's wills, being in less need of parental subsidies perhaps. In the later fourteenth century Thomas, the son of William atte Hale (possibly a brewer) was a novice canon of Holy Trinity Priory and his sister was a nun at the Minories, and Roger, the son of the draper, Stephen Cavendish, became a Franciscan.[21] William Sudbury, who joined the Westminster Abbey community in 1373, and went on to have a distinguished career there, was the son of a London skinner, Henry Sudbury.[22] The monastery also drew recruits from the more immediate vicinity of Westminster itself, and from its manors largely clustered within

[16] Below, pp. 165–6; W. Dugdale, *Monasticon Anglicanum*, ed. J. Caley, H. Ellis and B. Bandinel, 6 vols. (London, 1817–30), vol. 6, pt. 2, pp. 704–8.

[17] Below, pp. 128–9, 133, 145; Jens Röhrkasten, *The Mendicant Houses of Medieval London 1221–1539* (Münster, 2004), p. 57.

[18] Ibid., 30–3; Barron, *LLMA*, p. 314.

[19] Röhrkasten, *Mendicant Houses*, pp. 44–7, 117–18, 221.

[20] Below, p. 303.

[21] *Cal. of Wills in Ct. of Husting*, ii. 118, 149. Roger's sister Cristina was a nun at the Benedictine house at Cheshunt.

[22] *B.R.U.O.*, iii. 1813. William's sister was a nun at the Minoresses, *Cal. of Wills in Ct. of Husting*, ii. 225.

Middlesex.[23] In 1538 Robert Byggyng gave evidence in a case in the London Commissary court: he stated that he had been born in the parish of St. Mary Aldermanbury and had then become a canon in the local house of Austin Canons – Elsingspital.[24] Hence although it seems likely that most of the London houses would have recruited some London boys, the evidence can only be impressionistic. There is, however, stronger evidence that the London nunneries were filled by the daughters of Londoners. The house at Haliwell seems to have been particularly favoured by London families: Isabella, the daughter of the tailor Robert Westmelne went there as an orphan in 1362, and Agnes, the daughter of Robert Warner, a London mercer and undersheriff of Middlesex, who died in 1439, was also a nun there.[25] When he died in 1460, John Burton, a London mercer, bequeathed his English copy of the *Legenda Sanctorum* to his daughter Dame Katherine Burton who was a nun at Haliwell, 'and after hur decesse, to remayne to the prioresse and the covent of halywelle for evermore'.[26] There is good evidence also that London girls entered the house at Kilburn.[27] For example, Mathilda, the orphan daughter of a London grocer, entered the house with the permission of the mayor and aldermen, and ten years later the prioress, Lady Emma de Saint Omer came to the court to collect the money that had been left to Mathilda under her father's will since, presumably, Mathilda had now accepted the religious habit.[28] Some London girls took their vows at Stratford, and a number of daughters of London merchants as well as Middlesex gentry families entered the house at Syon.[29] The Middlesex family of Muston supplied two abbesses of Syon, a nun and also the lay steward. Mary Newdigate, a nun at Syon who died in 1535, was one of seventeen children of the Middlesex lawyer John Newdigate: her sister Sybil was the last prioress of Haliwell nunnery and her brother Sebastian was one of the Charterhouse monks who died as a martyr.[30] A study of the personnel of six London nunneries (Clerkenwell, Haliwell, Kilburn, St. Helen's Bishopsgate, Stratford and the Minoresses) in the period 1370 to 1540 was able to find the names of 291 nuns from diverse sources. Of these sixty-four could be linked with particular families: twenty-four came from gentry families and thirty-one – the largest social group – were the daughters of urban dwellers. Of these townspeople, twenty-eight were the daughters of London citizens (ten in the Minories; five in St. Helen's; five at Clerkenwell; four at Haliwell; three at Stratford and one at Kilburn).[31]

There is no evidence to suggest a decline in the recruitment to these religious houses in London. For those houses where we can compare the numbers of inmates in the late fourteenth century with the numbers at the time of the Dissolution, it seems clear that most houses were about the same size as they had been 150 years earlier. Some were notably larger: St. Bartholomew's Hospital, St. Mary Cripplegate (Elsingspital) and, of course, the Charterhouse (see Table 1). Some, like St. Thomas of Acre, St. Katherine by the Tower or St. Anthony's had altered their functions and so there had been a rise in numbers.[32] We do not have any late fourteenth-century figures for the friars, but it seems clear that the London houses never regained the buoyant communities they

[23] Gervase Rosser, *Medieval Westminster 1200–1540* (Oxford, 1989), pp. 260–1. There is evidence that although several of the recruits to Westminster in the late eleventh century and early twelfth century appear to have been Londoners, this seems to be less the case later as more religious houses were founded within London itself. I am grateful to Miss Barbara Harvey for discussing this point with me.

[24] G.L. MS 9065/1/1 ff. 12v 13, *ex inf.* Dr. Jessica Freeman.

[25] Below, pp. 271–2; *Cal. Letter Bk. G*, pp. 152–3; Nellie J. M. Kerling (ed.) *Cartulary of St. Bartholomew's Hospital* (London, 1973), no. 1143.

[26] Bell, *Nuns*, pp. 148–9. The book is now Oxford, Bodl. Lib., Douce 372.

[27] Below, pp. 276–7.

[28] H. T. Riley (ed.), *Memorials of London and London Life* (London, 1868), p. 535.

[29] Below, pp. 243–4, 286.

[30] I am grateful to Dr Virginia Bainbridge for information about the family backgrounds of the sisters and brothers at Syon which she will be publishing. Dr Bainbridge estimates that before the Dissolution of the house perhaps 15% of the sisters and brothers at Syon had links with London and Middlesex.

[31] Paxton, 'Nunneries', pp. 15–34.

[32] The only serious decline in numbers occurred in the Colleges, where the endowments would no longer support the original numbers of chantry priests: see St. Thomas on London Bridge, St. Laurence Pountney and the Guildhall College.

## TABLE 1. COMPARATIVE NUMBERS IN SOME RELIGIOUS HOUSES IN LONDON AND MIDDLESEX IN THE LATE FOURTEENTH AND EARLY SIXTEENTH CENTURIES

Figures for the late fourteenth century are from the Poll Tax lists in McHardy, *Church in London*, pp. 1–38; those for the time of the Dissolution can be found in the relevant entries in this volume.

| House | Late Fourteenth Century | | Sixteenth Century | |
|---|---|---|---|---|
| | Year | Personnel | Year | Personnel |
| St. Peter's Westminster | 1381 | Abbot, 28 monks | 1536 | Abbot, 24 monks |
| St. Helen's Bishopsgate | 1379 | Prioress, 11 nuns, 8 chaplains, 1 clerk | 1539 | Prioress, 14 nuns |
| St. Mary de Graciis | 1379 | Abbot, 7 monks | 1539 | Abbot, 9 monks |
| Holy Trinity Aldgate | 1379 | Prior, 17 canons | 1532 | Prior, 18 canons |
| St. Bartholomew's Priory | 1379 | Prior, 15 canons, 7 clerks, 1 other | 1539 | Prior, 13 canons |
| St. Thomas of Acon | 1379 | Master, 6 brothers, 7 chaplains, 1 clerk | 1534 | Master, 6 brothers |
| Minoresses | 1379 | Abbess, 26 sisters | 1539 | Abbess, 23 nuns, 1 novice, 6 lay sisters |
| St. Bartholomew's Hospital | 1379 | Prior, 3 brothers, 2 chaplains, 3 sisters | 1532 | Master, 8 brothers |
| St. Katherine by the Tower | 1379 | Master, 4 chaplains, 3 sisters | 1535 | Master, 3 brothers, 3 sisters, 3 priests, 6 clerks, 10 b'women, 6 children |
| St. Mary Bishopsgate | 1379 | Prior, 11 canons 1 clerk, 6 sisters | 1534 | Prior, 11 brothers |
| St. Mary Cripplegate | 1379 | Prior, 5 canons, 3 chaplains, 1 clerk | 1536 | Prior, 10 canons |
| St. James Westminster | 1381 | Master, 4 celebrants | 1536 | 4 sisters |
| St. Martin le Grand | 1379 | Dean, 12 canons 13 vicars, 4 clerks | 1530s | 1 Prebendary, 6 vicars, 5 clerks |
| St. Stephen Westminster | 1381 | Dean, 11 canons, 11 vicars | 1547 | Dean, 11 canons, 11 vicars, 4 chantry priests, 4 clerks, 7 choristers |
| St. Thomas on London Bridge | 1379 | 6 chaplains | 1538 | 2 priests, 1 conduct |
| St. Laurence Pountney | 1379 | Master, 8 chaplains 1 clerk | 1547 | Master, 3 chaplains, 4 conducts |
| College in Guildhall | 1379 | 6 chaplains | 1547 | 3 chaplains, 1 chantry priest |
| Hospital of St. Anthony | 1379 | Master, 3 chaplains | 1522 | Master, 4 priests curate, schoolmaster, master of song school 7 clerks, usher |
| Priory of Stratford at Bow | 1381 | Prioress, 13 nuns | 1528 | Prioress, 9 nuns |
| Charterhouse | 1379 | Prior, 13 monks, 18 lay brothers | 1530s | Prior, 30 monks, 18 lay brothers |
| Priory of Haliwell | 1379 | Prioress, 10 nuns 2 chaplains | 1539 | Prioress, 13 nuns |
| Priory of Kilburn | 1381 | Prioress, 5 nuns | 1536* | Prioress, 5 nuns 1 priest |
| Priory of Hounslow | 1381 | Minister, 3 brothers | 1537 | Minister, 3 brothers |
| Hospital of St. Giles | 1381 | Master, 1 brother 2 celebrants | 1535–6 | 14 paupers |

* see also T.N.A. SC6/HenVIII/2424

enjoyed before the Black Death. The Dominicans, who numbered seventy in 1316 were reduced to seventeen by 1538, and the Greyfriars who numbered eighty in 1243, and seventy-two in 1315, had shrunk to twenty-one by 1538.[33] Although there is some evidence that the Carmelites and the Crossed Friars were having difficulties in the later fourteenth century in attracting recruits and so resorted on occasion to kidnapping and intimidation, yet a recent study has shown that in fact they were recruiting (perhaps because of their methods?) more strongly than either the Dominicans or Franciscans at this period.[34] In 1538 the Carmelite and Austin Friaries each had thirteen friars and there were six at the Crossed Friars.[35]

Almost all the London houses, and most of the Middlesex ones, were well-endowed by comparison with houses elsewhere in England. Some of the smaller houses in Middlesex were modestly endowed (annual income of Kilburn was £73; Stratford £97 and Hounslow £61) but only Elsingspital (annual income £194) among the London houses had an income of less than £200 and so fell in the first cull of 1536. A very high percentage of the income of the London houses was derived from properties in the city, and although the Middlesex houses had a smaller urban endowment, it was still very considerable.

### TABLE 2. INCOME OF SOME LONDON HOUSES DERIVED FROM CITY ESTATES, BASED ON THE *VALOR ECCLESIASTICUS* OF 1535[36]

| House | Gross Temporal Income | London Income | % |
|---|---|---|---|
| Elsingspital | £224 | £191 | 85 |
| St. Helen, Bishopsgate | £365 | £312 | 85 |
| St. Thomas of Acre | £308 | £249 | 81 |
| St. Mary, Clerkenwell | £245 | £173 | 71 |
| Charterhouse | £614 | £428 | 70 |
| Priory of Haliwell | £319 | £222 | 70 |
| Minoresses | £305 | £202 | 66 |
| St. Bartholomew's Priory | £702 | £451 | 64 |
| St. Mary Bishopsgate | £528 | £278 | 53 |
| St. Mary Graces | £580 | £291 | 50 |

The ten London houses included in Savine's table, together with the six Middlesex houses (Hounslow, Kilburn, St. John of Jerusalem, Stratford, Syon and Westminster) had a gross temporal income of over £11,000, and £4000 of this came from urban (London) revenues. As Savine noted, however, these monasteries 'were in a quite exceptional position'.[37] But these exceptional figures testify to the exceptional generosity of London donors. These endowments were scattered across London parishes: Holy Trinity Priory had tenements in eighty-seven parishes; St. Mary Overy, Southwark, in forty-seven parishes; St. Mary Clerkenwell, in sixty-four.[38] It has been estimated

---

[33] Below, pp. 119, n. 62; 123–4, 126.

[34] Below, p. 130; *Cal. Plea and Memoranda R.*, 1381–1412, p. 182; Virginia Davis, 'Mendicants in London in the Reign of Richard II', *London Journal*, 25 (2000), pp. 1–12.

[35] Below, pp. 131, 135, 141.

[36] Based on Alexander Savine, 'English Monasteries on the Eve of the Dissolution', in Paul Vinogradoff (ed.), *Oxford Studies in Social and Legal History* (Oxford, 1909), pp. 1–303, at p. 117.

[37] Ibid. 117.

[38] Below, pp. 85, 97, 264; M. C. Rosenfield, 'The Disposal of the property of London Monastic Houses, with a special study of Holy Trinity Aldgate' (unpub. University of London Ph.D. thesis, 1966), chapter 8; John Schofield and Richard Lee, *Holy Trinity Priory, Aldgate, City of London*, MoLAS Monograph Series, 24 (London, 2005), p. 157. The Monastic Archives Project at UCL has created an online database of the archives and properties held by the religious houses of England and Wales, and includes entries relating to many of the London houses: URL http://www.ucl.ac.uk/history/englishmonasticarchives/ [accessed 24 January 2007].

that on the eve of the Dissolution one third of all property within the walls of London was owned by the Church.[39] There may also have been deliberate policies on the part of the London houses to concentrate their estates, by exchange or purchase, near to the house in order to achieve more efficient management. The house of Augustinian canonesses at Clerkenwell in the 1190s had properties in seventeen counties; by c.1250 their holdings were in thirteen counties and by 1540 the number was reduced to six, and the bulk of their income (70%) was now derived from their urban estate.[40] But in spite of these measures almost all the houses ran into financial problems in the fifteenth century: in part this was the result of the general slump in the economy when rents were low and tenants in short supply.[41] Some houses, such as Elsingspital, climbed out of their debts by the infusion of new endowments.[42] But other houses spiralled downwards helped by the incompetence or negligence or extravagance of those in charge. At Holy Trinity Priory the profligacy of Prior Thomas Percy (1481–1493) exacerbated a downward trend that could not be reversed. In the end the Crown took over the house in 1532 in order to provide a remedy and prevent its extinction.[43] That is not, of course, how it all turned out in the end.

The original purpose of these endowments, whether in the city or elsewhere, had been to enable the members of these religious communities to live without having to labour for their livelihoods, and thus to free them from worldly concerns so that they could concentrate of the business of prayer. But, in practice, the need to maintain their urban properties, find tenants and collect rents dragged the religious houses into the world rather than saving them from it. By the end of the period many houses – particularly the larger ones – were employing lay stewards as land agents to run their estates for them, and also legal counsel to help them defend their properties in the law courts.[44] The records of the London Possessory Assizes (largely cases of *novel disseisin*) reveal that in the years between 1340 and 1469, 28% of the cases involved one or more religious house.[45] The involvement of the houses in disputes about property seems to have increased during the period (perhaps as their portfolios of London property expanded). And this impression is confirmed by the evidence of the arbitrations in disputes between neighbours in London in the years from 1508 up to the Dissolution. In 36% of the 140 cases which were settled in this way in these years, a London religious house was either a plaintiff or a defendant. In all, twenty of the local houses were involved in these disputes.[46] Since the accounts of the disputes occasionally record that the prior or abbess used an attorney, it would seem to be the case that on most other occasions the head of the house appeared in person in court to argue about inheritances, privies, rents and party walls.[47] Sometimes the religious house was in dispute not with an individual Londoner but with the city corporately. There were, for example, complaints when St. Helen's nunnery c.1260 closed 'St Helen's Lane' which ran from Bishopsgate to St. Mary Axe 'down which men had been used to ride and take carts'.[48] When the Hospitallers took over the lands of the Templars, the prior found himself in dispute with the city over a right of way to the Thames through the Templars' lands.[49] This long-running dispute may, in part, explain the hostility shown to the Hospitallers

---

[39] Honeybourne, 'Property', p. 8; she goes on to write that 'it would be a much nearer estimate to say that two thirds of London was in the hands of religious persons'.

[40] See table in B. Sloane, *Excavations at the Nunnery of St. Mary Clerkenwell, London*, MoLAS Monograph Series (forthcoming, 2007/8).

[41] See Rosser, *Medieval Westminster*, pp. 74–7.

[42] E.g. St. Bartholomew's Priory, below p. 93; Elsingspital, below pp. 166–7; Paxton, 'Nunneries', chapter 5.

[43] Below, p. 87 and see M. C. Rosenfield, 'Holy Trinity, Aldgate on the eve of the Dissolution', *Guildhall Miscellany*, iii no. 3 (1970), pp. 159–73.

[44] Paxton, 'Nunneries', chapter 2.

[45] See Helena M. Chew (ed.), *London Possessory Assizes: A Calendar* (London Record Society, 1, 1965).

[46] See Janet S. Loengard (ed.), *London Viewers and their Certificates 1508–1558* (London Record Society, 26, 1989).

[47] See the case in 1342 when the prioress of St. Mary Clerkenwell was represented by her attorney, as was the prioress of Halliwell in 1400 and the prioress of St. Helen's in 1411, see *Possessory Assizes*, ed. Chew, pp. 6, 75, 84.

[48] Below, p. 72.

[49] Below, p. 106; *Cal. Letter Book G*, xxvi, 126, 322, 324–5 and n.; Riley, *Memorials*, 305–6, 376–7; *Cal. Plea and Memoranda R. 1364–81*, pp. 238–40.

during the Peasants' Revolt.[50] In the mid-fifteenth century the city had protracted disputes with the Hospital of St. Katherine and the Abbot of St. Mary Graces about access to, and ownership of, the Common Soil lying to the east of the Tower, and a common way which the two houses had blocked with stakes.[51] Then, as now, the blocking of rights of way could cause grievances, just as the misuse of such thoroughfares could cause offence to the adjoining properties.[52] For these reasons it may be argued that the extensive London rent rolls of the religious houses came at a price because the houses became 'intricately involved in civic affairs, no less by their material interests and obligations than by the services they rendered for the poor and sick of London'.[53] But not all contacts between the religious houses and lay people were contentious: a Westminster monk, John Wrottyng, who collected the Abbey's important rents in Wood Street, was remembered with a bequest of 6s. 8d. by the widow Mathilda Penne who ran a skinner's shop there for twelve years before her death in 1392. The friendship must have grown up as the monks' rent-collector went about the Abbey's business in that part of London.[54]

Those who founded religious houses were driven by the need for prayer: prayer by those who were professionally trained to intercede with God for the sins of mankind. Prayer and intercession remained the primary objective of founders throughout the six hundred years of the history of religious houses in London. Indeed this desire for intercession probably intensified with the development of the doctrine of Purgatory, which emphasised the obligation of the living to pray for those whose souls were awaiting release. But even if all religious foundations throughout the period were established to facilitate prayer, yet the form of those institutions changed over the years. Only a very few laymen could afford to found a religious house and so lay people developed the idea of chantries in which a secular priest attached to a parish church, or a group of priests gathered together in a College, would be funded to say masses for the soul of the founders and such others as he or she chose to nominate. The chantry was infinitely flexible and so, as time went on, the older religious houses came to incorporate chantries, that is they accepted bequests in return for agreeing that certain monks or canons would say daily masses for the benefactor.[55] It came to be accepted that the prayers of laymen – particularly the poor – were also of value to souls in Purgatory. So the foundation of hospitals or almshouses for the poor became more common. Sometimes these hospitals were served by secular priests or Augustinian canons, but often they were simply charitable hospices providing shelter for the sick and destitute and, in particular, for lepers. St. Giles in the Fields founded by Mathilda, the wife of Henry I, and the leper hospitals in Southwark and St. James Westminster, also twelfth-century foundations, were all lay houses of this kind. Inevitably their informal lay status made them particularly susceptible to outside interference: in form and function they were the least 'stable' of the religious houses. But quite as much as monks, or canons or friars, the inmates of these hospitals were expected to pray for their benefactors whether in the past or present in return for the alms they received. The validity of lay prayer came to be formally acknowledged in the establishment of almshouses, or *maisonsdieu* as they were sometimes called. Here the inmates, usually seven or thirteen in number and old and decayed, rather than sick and leprous, in return for food and shelter, carried out a daily round of prayer for their benefactors which was in many ways quite as taxing as the monastic *opus dei*. The first almshouse in London was established by John Chirchman (d. 1413) under the auspices of the Tailors' company. Although there are no surviving statutes for this almshouse, the elaborate rules drawn up to regulate the daily life of the thirteen inmates of Whittington's

[50] Caroline Barron, *Revolt in London: 11th to 15th June 1381* (London, 1981), pp. 2–3.

[51] L.M.A., Journals of Common Council, 3, ff. 44v., 66v., 98, 116; Journal 4, ff. 32v., 60v.; Journal 5, f. 65v.; Journal 6, ff. 122, 286v., 73v.

[52] E.g. St. Martin's, below p. 201.

[53] Helen M. Cam (ed.), *The Eyre of London 14 Edward II AD 1321*, 2 vols. (Selden Society, 1968), i , cxxxvii.

[54] Elspeth Veale, 'Mathilda Penne, Skinner (d. 1392–3)' in Caroline M. Barron and Anne F. Sutton (eds.), *Medieval London Widows 1300–1500* (London, 1994), pp. 47–54, esp. p. 51. I am grateful to Miss Barbara Harvey for this information.

[55] E.g. at St. Katherine's Hospital, below p. 157; at Elsingspital, p. 167.

Hospital or almshouse in 1424 were to set the pattern for all later London almshouses.[56] Prayer and intercession remained of vital concern to founders and benefactors, but the institutional form had changed. And there was another change: whereas monks and canons, and secular priests in colleges, managed their own estates which, as we have seen, might be a considerable distraction from the work of prayer, hospital inmates and almsmen and women were not distracted in this way because their estates were managed for them by others usually, in London, by one of the city companies newly-chartered by the Crown.[57]

So prayer for the founder, for benefactors and for all Christian souls, whether by monks, or nuns, friars or secular priests, lay brothers and sisters, lepers or hospital inmates, remained the 'core function' of all these religious houses. But, as time went on, some of them acquired other functions and developed these alongside the daily round of prayer. All religious houses, to a greater or lesser extent, accepted a responsibility for charity and almsgiving. This charity could take many forms.

Five of the religious institutions in London seem to have had, or to have developed, a particular concern to care for the sick: St. Bartholomew's, St. Thomas in Southwark, St. Mary Bishopsgate (all houses of Austin Canons), St. Mary Bethlehem and the Savoy Hospital founded by Henry VII in the early sixteenth century.[58] All these hospitals cared for the sick and the help that they received became increasingly professional over the years. The Savoy, for example, following the model of Santa Maria Nuova in Florence, provided a physician, surgeon and apothecary, and from the fourteenth century the insane received special treatment at St. Mary Bethlehem. There seem to have been maternity wards at St. Bartholomew's,[59] and also at St. Thomas's where Richard Whittington funded a room with eight beds for unmarried mothers.[60] Perhaps as an offshoot of their care for pregnant women, it would seem that some houses also provided care for babies and young children. If the mother died, babies who were born there were cared for at St. Bartholomew's Hospital until they were seven years old, and the brothers seem also to have tried to rescue babies from Newgate prison.[61] Children were also received into the Domus Conversorum with their converted parents. There was, however, no orphanage in London until the mid-sixteenth century, and it would seem that, at least in the post-Black Death period, abandoned or orphaned children were welcomed into the labour-starved workshops in the city.

The leper 'isolation colonies' around London took the form of – usually small – religious houses: St. James at Westminster for leprous women, and St. Giles in Holborn, were both founded by pious individuals in the twelfth century and the city of London seems also to have taken some communal responsibility for coping with leprosy: two small houses, the Lock in Southwark and a house at Kingsland near Hackney, were funded and managed by the city from at least the thirteenth century.[62] By the later fourteenth century the city was also managing the hospital at St. Giles.[63] The other small leper hospitals at Knightsbridge, Mile End, Highgate and Hammersmith were all founded in the late fifteenth century, possibly in response to the royal ordinance of 1472 which required lepers to be sequestered from the community.[64] By 1549 all the leper hospitals, except St. Giles and St. James, had passed into the control of the city and were run in association with St. Bartholomew's Hospital.[65]

Religious houses also provided care for the elderly. Wealthier Londoners might make agreements with religious houses to care for them in their old age: Ralph Quatremaras and his wife Aubrey

---

[56] Barron, *LLMA*, pp. 298–9; Jean Imray, *The Charity of Richard Whittington* (London, 1968), Appendix 1.

[57] Barron, *LLMA*, p. 225.

[58] Ibid. 289–95. It may be that Elsingspital also cared for the sick in its earlier years although it may later have become more like an almshouse.

[59] *Cal. of Close*, 1349–54, pp. 414–15.

[60] *The Historical Collections of a Citizen of London*, ed. J. Gairdner, Camden Society, new ser. 17 (1876), p. xi.

[61] *Cal. of Close*, 1349–54, pp. 414–15; N. Kerling, 'A Note on Newgate Prison', *T.L.M.A.S.*, 22 (1968), pp. 21–2.

[62] Below, pp. 175–6; Barron, *LLMA*, pp. 293–5.

[63] Riley, *Memorials*, 510–11.

[64] Carole Rawcliffe, *Leprosy in Medieval England* (Woodbridge, 2006), pp. 281–2.

[65] Barron, *LLMA*, pp. 293–5; we are grateful to Dr Patricia Croot for her help in elucidating the history of the Middlesex leper hospitals.

granted a tenement and orchard in the parish of All Hallows Bread Street to St. Bartholomew's in the late twelfth century and in return the hospital agreed to look after them in their own home or, if necessary, to receive them into the community for care.[66] Arrangements like these were known as corrodies and they could have detrimental financial implications for the religious houses: St. John's Clerkenwell was much burdened with corrodies in the fourteenth century.[67] Corrodies might also bring unsuitable lay people into the religious community. Sometimes the elderly lay poor lived as a group within the religious house: at St. Katherine's Hospital a varying number of bedeswomen lived together in the house and wore special grey caps and cloaks.[68] Such institutionalised groups of poor people were also to be found living at other houses such as Westminster Abbey, in Holy Trinity Priory and at Elsingspital.[69] Corrodians, and others, might lease property within the precinct of a religious house and so benefit from its facilities both material and spiritual. Some of these leases may have been simply commercial transactions such as Sir John Crosby's lease of land in the precinct of St. Helen's in 1466.[70] Many aristocratic widows chose to live in the precinct of the Minoresses' house outside Aldgate including Elizabeth de Burgh, Lady of Clare (d. 1360), Lucia Visconti the widow of Edmund earl of Kent (d. 1424), Elizabeth the dowager duchess of Norfolk (d. 1507) and Margaret, the widow of Edmund de la Pole who was executed in 1513. These women could find refuge, security and companionship within such a precinct. And it was not only aristocratic women: Alice Hampton became a vowess at St. John Haliwell with a cell laid out at the west end of the church and she remained there until her death in 1514.[71] John Clerk, a Chancery clerk from Preston arranged in 1415 for his widow to live at St. Mary's Priory at Clerkenwell and he left 100s. to the Prioress to pay for this.[72] Some houses formalised their provision for the elderly by establishing fraternities. At St. Katherine's Hospital, in return for a down payment of 10s. 4d., brothers and sisters enrolled in the fraternity dedicated to St. Barbara, and who later became enfeebled, could bring their letters of fraternity to the house and receive a pension of 12d. a week, room, bedding, and a woman to wash their clothes and cook for them.[73]

One religious house in London (apart from the almshouses) was specifically founded to care for the elderly and infirm, in this case secular priests who did not benefit from the security of belonging to a religious order. In 1442 three secular priests together founded a house for sixty poor priests in the church of St. Augustine Pappey where they lived a communal life in a house close to the church and received shelter, food and heating. The priests were supported by a fraternity to which many lay Londoners belonged, and they were the recipients of numerous small bequests in return for their prayers.[74] The small house, also for priests, known as Jesus Commons may also have been founded for a similar social and welfare purpose in 1507 by a London shearman, James Fynche, who entrusted its administration to his guild.[75]

At the furthest point on the life cycle, the growing enthusiasm for polyphonic music created a need for young boys to sing the treble parts and this encouraged the growth of song schools attached to religious houses. By the early sixteenth century Holy Trinity Priory maintained 'children of the chapel' and paid wages to their master, and St. Katherine's Hospital was paying £24

[66] N. M. J. Kerling (ed.), *Cartulary of St. Bartholomew's Hospital: a calendar* (London, 1973), no. 726.

[67] Below, pp. 299–300; and see also St. Mary Bishopsgate, below pp. 161–2.

[68] Below, pp. 155–6.

[69] Barbara Harvey, *Living and Dying in England 1100–1540: The Monastic Experience* (Oxford, 1993), p. 18; M. C. Rosenfield, 'The Disposal of the Property…of Holy Trinity Priory', p. 26. Twelve sisters were living at Elsingspital at the time of the Dissolution and received a pension of £10 a year between them thereafter, T.N.A. SC6/HENVIII/2345 *ex. inf.* Ann Bowtell.

[70] Below, pp. 73–4 and see table in Sloane, *St. Mary Clerkenwell* (forthcoming).

[71] Mary C. Erler, *Women, Reading and Piety in Late Medieval England* (Cambridge, 2002), pp. 14–15; G.L. MS 9171/9 ff. 5v–6 *ex inf.* Dr. Jessica Freeman.

[72] G.L. MS 9171/2 ff. 308–308v *ex inf.* Dr. Jessica Freeman.

[73] Barron, *LLMA*, p. 298.

[74] Below, p. 188; Barron, *LLMA*, p. 300.

[75] Below, p. 190.

p.a. for the maintenance of six children and £8 p.a. to their master.[76] The City's Common Clerk, John Carpenter who died in 1442, left money to support the schooling of four boys, attached to Guildhall College, who were to sing in Guildhall chapel.[77] The reorganisation of the house of St. Anthony of Vienne in the mid-fifteenth century led to its development not only as a grammar school but it became notable for training men and boys both in plainsong and polyphonic singing.[78] It is this development which explains the remarkable expansion of the personnel of the house to be observed by 1522 (see Table 1). Simon Eyre, who drew up his will in 1459, envisaged the foundation of three separate schools at Leadenhall chapel, for teaching grammar (i.e Latin), writing (i.e. business studies) and singing.[79] There were song schools for boys at Westminster Abbey and also at St. Bartholomew's Hospital.[80] Girls might also be educated, or at least find refuge, in the London nunneries. There were young women boarding at St. Helen's from the late thirteenth century, and in the troubled times of the London mayor, John of Northampton, his two step-daughters were boarded with the prioress of Kilburn at a safe distance, perhaps, from the city.[81] After the death of their father, Sir Thomas Charlton, royal official and MP, in 1466, his two orphaned daughters 'sojourned' at the nunnery at Haliwell, but they brought with them their own bedding and linen.[82]

Associated with teaching were books. Among the major contributions which the friars made to the city were their vigorous intellectual activities, seen in their dynamic preaching (see below) and their extensive libraries. Although the London friaries did not run grammar schools for boys, they were certainly centres of 'higher education' and study and, in this regard, the Carmelite house seems to have been particularly notable.[83] All the religious houses would have had libraries to which Londoners would have had some access, but the library of the Austin Friars seems to have been particularly notable, and the commitment of Londoners to the friars' libraries can be seen in Richard Whittington's bequest of the very considerable sum of £400 for the funding of a new building to house the library of the Greyfriars.[84] And, of course, the most extensive library in London during the medieval period was that attached to the Cathedral. To the already substantial library at St. Paul's, Bishop Baldock bequeathed a further 150 volumes at his death in 1313 and in the middle of the fifteenth century Walter Sherrington, a prebendary at the Cathedral, left money to build a new library near the north door of the cathedral above the east walk of the Pardon Churchyard cloister. The extensive opening hours specified in the foundation ordinances suggest that the library was to be a resource not simply for those who lived and worked in the Cathedral precinct but also for the clergy of the city more widely.[85] The religious houses for women also had libraries, if not as extensive as those of the male houses. We know something of the libraries at the houses at Kilburn, Haliwell, St. Helen's Bishopsgate, the Minoresses and, above all, at Syon Abbey.[86] There were two libraries at Syon, one for the brothers and one for the sisters, and

[76] Below, p. 158; in 1273 six scholars were provided for at St. Katherine's, p. 525; *L. and P. Hen. VIII*, ii. pt. 1, pp. 38–9.

[77] See Caroline M. Barron, 'Church music in English towns 1450–1550: an interim report', *Urban History*, 29 (2002), pp. 83–91, esp. p. 89.

[78] Below, p. 230; there may have been a schoolmaster at St. Anthony's in the mid-thirteenth century, see p. 218.

[79] Below, p. 224.

[80] Caroline M. Barron, 'The Expansion of Education in Fifteenth-Century London', in *The Cloister and the World: Essays in Medieval History in Honour of Barbara Harvey*, ed., John Blair and Brian Golding (Oxford, 1996), pp. 219–245, esp. pp. 220 and 231. See also Roger Bowers, 'The Musicians and Liturgy of the Lady Chapels of the Monastery Church, c.1235–1540', in Tim Tatton-Brown and Richard Mortimer (eds.), *Westminster Abbey: The Lady Chapel of Henry VII* (Woodbridge, 2003), pp. 33–57.

[81] Below, p. 277; Eileen Power, *Medieval English Nunneries c.1275–1535* (Cambridge, 1922), pp. 576–7.

[82] W.A.M. 6625 m. 3; 5471 ff. 14 and 16v. *ex inf.* Dr. Jessica Freeman.

[83] Below, pp. 118–19, 128; see William J. Courtenay, *Schools and Scholars in Fourteenth-Century England* (Princeton, 1987), pp. 94–5, 102–4.

[84] Below, pp. 134 and 125; see K. W. Humphreys ed., *The Friars' Libraries*, British Academy, Corpus of British Medieval Library Catalogues, 1 (London, 1990).

[85] Nigel Ramsay, 'The Library and Archives to 1897', in St. *Paul's: The Cathedral Church of London 604–2004* (New Haven and London, 2004), pp. 413–25, esp. 413–17.

[86] Bell, *Nuns*, pp. 143–4; 148–52.

the surviving early sixteenth century catalogue is that of the brothers' library. It is possible to identify at least forty-eight books which belonged to the sisters, many of which were written in the vernacular.[87] It seems likely that the libraries at Syon were accessible to the laity, many of whom chose to live in close association with the house.[88]

It is customary to see the giving of alms as the characteristic 'outreach' of religious houses, but it is hard to know to what extent religious houses did distribute alms to the poor at their gates. The evidence seems to suggest that Benedictine monks, where possible, selected the poor whom they helped, preferring 'stable and formal arrangements in almsgiving' and disliked 'the casual and spontaneous'.[89] Over the centuries the Westminster monks became more discriminating in their charitable activities and, as their own resources contracted, they became less generous. It is possible that the friars gave more indiscriminate help to the poor: fifty people were crushed to death in 1322 in the throng that struggled to secure alms at the gate of the Dominican friary when it opened in the morning.[90] The sight of the homeless poor who crowded the streets of the city, provoked William Elsing to found his hospital in 1331, but after the Black Death, which reduced the population so drastically, there were fewer desperately poor people in the city.[91] An insight into the amount spent by some religious houses on alms is provided by the 1535 *Valor Ecclesiasticus* in which houses were allowed to claim tax exemption on the payments which they made to the poor, but only those which they were compelled to make in accordance with the stated wishes of benefactors (Table 3).[92] Those payments which the houses made voluntarily were disallowed. Different commissioners were biased in different ways and, in any case, their purpose was to find as much taxable ecclesiastical wealth as possible. It has, therefore, recently been argued that monastic almsgiving was considerably more generous than the bare figures in the *Valor* might suggest.[93]

TABLE 3. SPENDING ON ALMS OF SOME LONDON AND MIDDLESEX RELIGIOUS HOUSES BASED ON THE *VALOR ECCLESIASTICUS* 1535[94]

| House | Gross Temporal Income p.a. | Alms Spending p.a. | % |
|---|---|---|---|
| Elsingspital | £224 | £10 | 4.5 |
| Westminster Abbey | £3,165 | £104 | 3.3 |
| St. John Clerkenwell | £2,175 | £57 | 2.6 |
| Priory of Haliwell | £319 | £6 | 1.9 |
| St. Mary Bishopsgate | £528 | £4 | 0.8 |
| Charterhouse | £614 | £5 | 0.8 |
| St. Mary Clerkenwell | £245 | £2 | 0.8 |
| St. Mary Graces | £580 | £4 | 0.7 |
| Syon Abbey | £1,500 | £5 | 0.3 |

In this sample these nine London houses on average spent less than 2% of their gross temporal income each year on charity. But as Savine pointed out, it is unlikely that six other London houses (St Helen's, St. Bartholomew's Priory, the Minoresses, St. Thomas of Acre, St. Leonard at Stratford and St. Mary Overy), all of which had incomes of more than £50 p.a., spent nothing at all on

[87] Ibid., pp. 75, 171–210.
[88] See Erler, *Women, Reading and Piety*, chapter 4.
[89] Harvey, *Living and Dying*, chapter 1, esp. p. 21.
[90] *Cal. of Coroners' Rolls of the City of London 1300–1378*, ed., R. R. Sharpe (London, 1913), p. 61.
[91] See note 16 above.
[92] Savine, 'English Monasteries', p. 240.
[93] Neil Rushton, 'Monastic Charitable Provision in Tudor England, Quantifying and Qualifying Poor Relief in the Early Sixteenth Century', *Continuity and Change*, 16 (2001), pp. 9–44.
[94] Table derived from Savine, 'English Monasteries', pp. 236 and 277–8.

charity, although none was recorded by the commissioners who compiled the *Valor*.[95] Indeed Harvey has calculated that the average annual charitable expenditure at Westminster Abbey came to £401, but this figure includes the expenses of Henry VII's new almshouses and the costs of the Grammar and Song schools. Only £210 was spent each year on doles but even this enlarged figure would double the percentage figure derived from the *Valor*.[96] Indeed St. Thomas's Hospital in Southwark claimed in 1535 that it spent over £42 each year (i.e. 13% of its gross annual temporal revenue) on the poor and infirm.[97] Much of the almsgiving by religious houses was probably informal, and often in kind rather than cash. It was, for example, customary to distribute the food and drink left over from the monastic tables to the needy at the gates.[98] In 1535 the priory of St. John of Jerusalem in Clerkenwell claimed that twenty shillings a week was spent on alms given to the poor 'at the door and in the hall of the priory'. This would suggest, perhaps, that there were those poor who may have lived and eaten regularly in the priory and others who received casual alms 'at the door'. The Commissioners in 1535 accepted that the house had had these obligations 'ex antiqua fundacione et consuetudine accustumata'.[99] And there is no doubt that many of the smaller houses, like the hospitals at Brentford and at Charing Cross, were providing casual charity to wayfarers and the poor.[100]

Although many of the smaller religious houses, the wayside hospitals, leper houses and almshouses, would have been barely distinguishable from other houses in the vicinity, yet many of the houses would have dominated their surroundings and none more so than the Cathedral church of St. Paul. But the friars' churches were also very large structures deliberately built to serve as preaching halls. It was their skills as preachers, along with their claims to poverty and alms, which brought the friars into conflict with the secular clergy of the city. Their intellectual skills made them formidable opponents and they retained their popularity with Londoners until the Dissolution. This popularity is attested by the number of Londoners who chose to be buried in their houses. Although it was often members of the gentry or aristocracy who chose burial in the friaries[101] (and the heads of executed aristocrats were often reunited with their bodies in a London friary) yet many Londoners are also to be found there.[102] In the early sixteenth century the Grey Friars compiled a list of those buried in their house: in all some 671 graves are recorded of which, 107 (16%) were certainly those of Londoners because they identified themselves as 'citizen' on their monuments. Many others may have been Londoners, but not citizens.[103] Those buried there include several notable London mayors, including John de Gisors (d. 1282), Gregory de Rokesle (d. 1291), Sir John Philpot (d. 1384), Sir Nicholas Brembre (d. 1388) and Sir Stephen Jennings (d. 1523).[104] The Dominican house was also popular with Londoners: 211 testators between 1376 and 1538 requested burial in the London Blackfriars, and 84 or 40% of these were London citizens.[105]

The friaries, because they were international in organisation, also provided particular services for the alien communities in London. Two fraternities founded by German merchants in London, one dedicated to the Holy Blood of Wilsnak and the other to St. Katherine 'de le stranghers', were

---

[95] Ibid., 239.

[96] Harvey, *Living and Dying*, Appendix 1.

[97] Savine, 'English Monasteries', p. 541.

[98] Harvey, *Living and Dying*, pp. 10–16.

[99] Below. p. 300.

[100] Below, pp. 232–3, 311–12.

[101] E.g. at Austin Friars, see p. 512.

[102] Chief Justice Robert Tresilian and Sir Nicholas Brembre, who were executed during the Merciless Parliament of 1388, were both buried in Greyfriars, see C. L. Kingsford, *The Greyfriars of London* (Aberdeen, 1915), pp. 135, 143.

[103] John Stow, on whom we primarily rely for the names of those buried in the London Friaries, largely used the lists compiled by the heralds who were only interested in armigerous burials. Hence Stow's lists rarely include Londoners. The Greyfriars' own list is more comprehensive and reveals the presence of considerable numbers of Londoners. I am grateful to Christian Steer for help on this point.

[104] Below, p. 124.

[105] Below, p. 118 and see C. F. R. Palmer, 'Burials at the Priories of the Blackfriars', *The Antiquary*, XXIII (1891), pp. 122–6; XXIV (1891), pp. 28–30, 76–9, 117–19, 265–9.

based at Crutched Friars, although the Holy Blood fraternity seems to have moved by the end of the fifteenth century to the Austin Friars.[106] And this is not surprising since it seems to have been the Austin Friary which particularly catered for the needs of aliens, and there were native Italian and German speakers in that house. Before their association with All Hallows developed, the Hanse merchants of the Steelyard usually specified burial in the Austin Friary: Arnald Soderman who died in 1441 left a bequest to his confessor, brother George of the Austin Friars, and Eva van Styberghe, four years later, left 6s. 8d. to each 'Doche' brother of the house.[107] The Italians also showed a marked preference for the Austin Friary: thirty-three of the fifty-two 'London' Italians who died in England and specified a place for their burial, designated the Austin friary, and many of them clearly knew the house well. A fraternity there dedicated to St. James seems to have been particularly favoured by the Italians.[108] It was not only aliens who founded fraternities in the London friaries: some of the fraternities at the friaries were associated with particular crafts: the curriers in the later fourteenth century in the Carmelite house and the waterbearers and the shearmen in the Austin Friars.[109]

Sometimes it seems that 'subversive' groups of journeymen members of a craft would meet under cover of a religious purpose at a religious house while allegedly secretly pursuing policies deemed to be hostile to the interests of their employers. The journeymen cordwainers who met together on the feast of the Assumption at the Blackfriars claimed that they had been encouraged by brother William Barton there who had collected money from them in return for promising to secure for them a papal confirmation of their fraternity.[110] The journeymen of the spurriers' craft were accused of having met secretly in St. Bartholomew's church (probably the hospital church) in Smithfield, to form a confederacy to maintain prices for their work, and the yeomanry of the tailors met at the priory church of the Hospitallers at Clerkenwell, until the mayor and aldermen intervened for fear of disturbances.[111] Although most crafts in London, before they had halls of their own, chose to base their associations, or fraternities, in parish churches, this was not always the case: several chose to meet at religious houses. The carpenters' guild, dedicated to the Virgin and St. John, met at Epiphany at the house of St. Thomas of Acre in Cheapside and then, at midsummer, on the feast of St. John the Baptist, they gathered at the more rural house of the Augustinian canonesses at Haliwell.[112] There were craft fraternities also based at the hospitals of St. Katherine, St. Anthony, St. Mary Bethlehem, St. Mary Rouncivall, and at the London Charterhouse.[113] Doubtless the houses, and the hospitals in particular, wanted the economic and social support of lay people. Some houses seem to have developed their own confraternities in which the members paid a 'subscription' and entered into fraternity with the house and were included in their prayers: for example Elizabeth Kirby in her will of 1488 claimed to be a sister of the London Greyfriars and William Payne who died in 1508 was a brother of the Charterhouse.[114]

[106] Below, p. 140.

[107] S. Jenks, 'Hansische Vermachtnisse in London ca.1363–1483', *Hansische Geschichtsblatter*, 104 (1986), pp. 35–111.

[108] Helen L. Bradley, 'The Italian Community in London c.1350–c.1450' (unpub. University of London Ph.D. thesis, 1992), pp. 16–20; G.L. MS 9171/8 ff. 46, 50v. After the Dissolution the Austin Friary became the Dutch church.

[109] Below, p. 118; C. Barron and L. Wright, 'The London Middle English Guild certificates of 1388–9', *Nottingham Medieval Studies*, 39 (1995), pp. 108–45, esp. pp. 124–5; H. C. Coote (ed.), *Ordinances of Some Secular Guilds of London from 1354–1496* (London, 1871), pp. 47–56; 79–81; Caroline M. Barron, 'The Parish Fraternities of Medieval London', in Caroline M. Barron and Christopher Harper-Bill (eds.), *The Church in Pre-Reformation Society: Essays in Honour of F. R. H. Du Boulay* (Woodbridge, 1985), pp. 13–37, esp. p. 23.

[110] Riley, *Memorials,* pp. 495–6. A fraternity dedicated to the Assumption of the BVM made a return to the guild enquiry of 1388, but there was no mention of the cordwainers, see below p. 118.

[111] *Cal. Plea and Memoranda R.* 1364–81, pp. 291–4; Barron, *LLMA*, pp. 212–13.

[112] R. W. Chambers and M. Daunt (eds.), *A Book of London English 1384–1425* (Oxford, 1931), pp. 41–4.

[113] T.N.A., C47/41/197 (St Anthony's Hospital); C47/42/202 (St Mary Bethlehem); C47/42/215 (Cutlers at the Charterhouse); C47/42/216 (St Katherine's hospital); Coote, 'Ordinances', pp. 33–7 (Glovers at the Charterhouse); Rosser, 'Medieval Westminster', 310–21 (St. Mary Rouncivall).

[114] T.N.A., PROB 11/8 ff. 76v.–77; 11/16 f. 2, *ex inf.* Jennifer Ledfors; Barron, 'Parish Fraternities', pp. 17–18.

There was a similar confraternity at the house at Hounslow.[115] Indeed it would seem that these associative confraternities, in which brothers and sisters received 'letters of confraternity', became more popular in the fifteenth century, perhaps as the religious houses and hospitals sought to alleviate their financial difficulties. The Tailors' fraternity, dedicated to St. John the Baptist, was associated by letters of confraternity, with eight religious houses around London. In this way its members acquired the prayers of 'intercessors par excellence' and, in return, the religious houses might hope to benefit from the bequests of their lay associates.[116]

It seems clear that many of the religious houses with their large precincts and stone buildings provided convenient places in which Londoners might gather for legitimate or nefarious purposes. Some houses, within their precincts, even provided a parish church for the local community. This was the case at St. Giles's Hospital, and at the nunneries at Stratford, St. Helen's Bishopsgate and at St. Mary Clerkenwell. Not surprisingly, where the local parishioners shared a building with a religious community, more of the parishioners made bequests to the house than was the case elsewhere (as many as 50% of testators as opposed to 10%).[117] Where the religious house was responsible for providing a separate parish church for the local people, as in the case of St. Katherine Cree Church within the precinct of Holy Trinity Aldgate, the parent house may have helped to meet extra expenses: the accounts of Holy Trinity reveal that the Priory paid for the hire of the Barking Abbey procession pageants for the Easter celebrations at St. Katherine's church and also for a 'harness for the Resurrection'.[118] Within their walls the churches of the religious houses, as churches elsewhere, could offer sanctuary to debtors and criminals. The most ancient houses of the Benedictines at Westminster and the canons at St. Martin le Grand could offer sanctuary not only within their churches but, more controversially, within their precincts. Here debtors, aliens, foreigners, shoddy workers and refugees from legal proceedings could set up shop and practise their trades immune from prosecution. These sanctuaries perhaps provided crucial safely valves for an over-rigid judicial system, but they were also a source of grievance and vexation to the city's rulers and to the masters and wardens of the craft guilds.[119]

Religious houses were usually well-endowed, and rich by the standards of contemporary Londoners. Within their walls they had men – and women – of education and wealth and they could marshal the financial resources and the technical expertise to create notable and sophisticated buildings. The facilities of these buildings usually included the provision of piped fresh water and this seems to have had 'spin-off' advantages for the Londoners. Although we do not know the precise steps whereby the Londoners came to invest in a piped water supply in the middle years of the thirteenth century, it cannot be unconnected to the arrival of the Dominicans and Franciscans who were laying down water pipes for their new friaries at exactly this time.[120] The water for the hospital at St. Mary Bishopsgate was brought from 'Snekockeswelle' and the elaborate system not only provided drinking water, but the overflow was then used to wash down the kitchens and flush out the latrine in the infirmary.[121] The water supply about which we are best informed is that provided for the London Charterhouse: the surviving maps show the route of the pipes from Islington to the great quadrangle, and the means established within the monastic precinct for the distribution of the water.[122] The advantages to the city of these sophisticated and expensive water supplies can be seen in 1436 when the Priory of St. Bartholomew, and six years later, the Hospital

[115] Below, pp. 292–3; see Jessica R. Freeman, 'The Political Community of Fifteenth-Century Middlesex' (unpub. University of London Ph.D. thesis, 2002), pp. 142–3, 307.

[116] The religious houses were: St. John of Jerusalem, Clerkenwell, St. Mary Graces, Holy Trinity, Syon Abbey, and the hospitals of St. Mary Bishopsgate, Elsingspital, St. Bartholomew's and St. Mary Rouncivall; see Matthew P. Davies, 'The Tailors and their Guild, c.1300–1500' (unpub. University of Oxford D.Phil. thesis, 1994), pp. 13–15.

[117] Below, pp. 267, 315–17; Paxton, 'Nunneries', pp. 150–3.

[118] L. and P. Hen. VIII, ii, pt. 1, p. 38; Rosenfield, 'Disposal of Property', p. 26.

[119] Barron, LLMA, p. 35.

[120] See David Lewis, '"For the poor to drink and the rich to dress their meat": the first London water conduit', T.L.M.A.S., 55 (2004), pp. 39–68, esp. pp. 39–40, 50; Rohrkasten, Mendicant Houses, 35–6; Barron, LLMA, pp. 256–9.

[121] Below, p. 160; Thomas, Sloane and Phillpotts, Hospital of St. Mary, p. 43.

[122] Below, p. 250.

of St. Bartholomew, both agreed to allow the grocer, Thomas Knolles, to siphon off some of their water brought in pipes from Canonbury, and to use it for the relief of the prisoners at Newgate and Ludgate.[123]

The religious houses were also important to the economy of the communities around them because they were employers and customers on a grand scale. Westminster Abbey, in the early sixteenth century may have employed about 100 lay servants at any one time and, in addition, would seek the services of specialists such as physicians and apothecaries.[124] Holy Trinity Priory in 1513 was paying wages to the steward, rent collector, cook, master of the children, laundress, carpenter, bellringer, gardener, butler and porter, and one-off payments, among others, to waits and minstrels, to lawyers, to gardeners and to a man to mow the churchyard of St. Katherine Cree.[125] The much more modest house at Elsingspital in 1536 was employing five servants and a boy and a hundred years earlier had employed three principal servants, a cook's boy and several others on a part-time basis to repair tenements, transport building materials, mend clothing and kitchen equipment and remove rubbish.[126] The rural houses, such as Haliwell, paid men to plough the fields, to harvest their crops and to repair farm implements.[127] As the religious houses became less self-sufficient, and leased their demesnes to produce cash, so they purchased more and more goods of all kinds in the markets and shops of London. The range of goods purchased for the Holy Trinity Priory in 1513 and, in particular, for the Prior's Lodgings, suggests that the 'consumer society' was already alive and flourishing in this period.[128] The cellaress at Syon bought bread locally, beer in London and sheep and oxen in the markets of Oxford and Uxbridge.[129] The religious houses were particularly important customers because, unlike the aristocracy, they were always in residence. Aristocratic town houses might be empty for months at a time, but the religious houses were always there. Moreover, their apparent stability and continuity ensured that, eventually, accounts would be settled.[130] In this way they were more satisfactory debtors than the litigious and battle-prone aristocracy.[131] The flow of business, however, was not only one way. At Westminster surplus food and drink, together with produce from the great 'Covent garden' were sold in the London markets, and at the priory of Ruislip corn and timber were taken to London for sale.[132]

* * *

There is no doubt that in many ways the religious houses served the communities around them: apart from prayer which was clearly valued (and the extensive bequests by Londoners to the friars, and to the Carthusians in particular, demonstrate this), the houses, in their different ways, provided vocations, education, employment; they cared for the sick and for young children, pregnant women and the old. They offered hospitality to travellers and alms to the poor. They met the special needs of outsiders: lepers and aliens. The buildings of the houses were useful for preaching and for large gatherings, and their expertise brought fresh water to the city and provided access in their libraries to manuscripts and printed books. It is clear that the houses were still valued in the sixteenth century. In 1514 London citizens contributed to the costs of paving the Greyfriars' church with

---

[123] Barron, *LLMA*, p. 258.

[124] Harvey, *Living and Dying*, pp. 82–3, 95, 164.

[125] *L. and P. Hen. VIII*, ii. pt. 1, pp. 38–9; Schofield and Lee, *Holy Trinity Priory*, 162; cf. Paxton, 'Nunneries', chapter 2.

[126] T.N.A. SC6/HENVIII/2424; SC6/1257/3 *ex inf.* Ann Bowtell.

[127] Below, p. 191.

[128] *L. and P. Hen. VIII*, ii. pt. 1, pp. 38–41.

[129] Below, p. 284; cf. Rosser, *Medieval Westminster*, pp. 136–7 on the range of food purchased in Westminster and London to feed the monks who, in 1402–3 consumed 40,000 loaves and 80,000 gallons of ale.

[130] C. M. Barron, 'Centres of Conspicuous Consumption: The Aristocratic Town House in London 1200–1500', *London Journal*, 20 (1995), pp. 1–16.

[131] For the relations between the abbey and the citizens, see Barbara Harvey, 'Westminster Abbey and Londoners, 1440–1540', in *London and the Kingdom: Proceedings of the 2004 Harlaxton Symposium* (forthcoming: Donington, 2007).

[132] Below, p. 308; Rosser, *Medieval Westminster*, pp. 135–7.

marble; in 1520 the City accepted the patronage of the Crossed Friars and, two years later granted some of the Common Soil for an extension to the church; and about the same time the mayor, aldermen and citizens of London contributed a total of 300 marks to help with the rebuilding of the Minoresses house after the buildings were destroyed by fire.[133]

But there were also disputes: about the annual fair granted by Henry III to the Abbey of Westminster in the thirteenth century, and about the management and profits of the annual St. Bartholomew's fair in the fifteenth century.[134] All the houses, with their extensive London rent rolls, were constantly in dispute with tenants and neighbours over repairs and access and nuisances of all kinds. There were brawls between the – usually lay – members of the religious houses and the Londoners: in the 1450s the Court of Aldermen took very seriously an attack during the St. Bartholomew Fair on Geoffrey Feldynge (mayor 1452–3) by members of the household of the St. John Clerkenwell priory.[135] Not all members of religious communities were impressive and, of course, they were highly visible within an urban community. The Prior of Holy Trinity was particularly visible since he was, by virtue of his office, also the alderman of the ward of Portsoken. He rarely attended meetings of the Court of Aldermen (except for the annual election of the mayor) although he did preside over the Portsoken wardmoot.[136] The priory fell into dilapidation and debt in the 1430s due to the foolishness of the prior, William Clerk, to such an extent that the king was forced to take over the administration of the house: a move which was to be followed by his namesake nearly a hundred years later, but with more far-reaching consequences. John Sevenoke was elected to replace Clerk, but the mayor and aldermen took the unusual action of objecting to his election on the grounds that he had 'gross faults' which made him unsuitable for office. When Sevenoke turned up for the mayor's election in October 1439 the aldermen only allowed him to take part on certain conditions, and he was not sworn as an alderman until January 1444.[137] It is not known what 'gross faults' were detected in Sevenoke, but the charges against Richard Cressall, the prior of St. Mary Bishopsgate were certainly explicit. When, in 1513, he pursued Robert and Joanna Pellet for debt, they bruited it about that he, and his canons, were 'whoremongers' and 'bawds'.[138]

There were further insidious processes at work: lay intervention in the affairs of the houses was becoming much more common. The king might intervene briefly to reform a foundering house as he did at Holy Trinity Priory in 1439, or he might take over a house that was no longer fulfilling its purposes (e.g. the hospitals of St. Giles or St. James or St. Thomas of Acre) or because it was an alien house and so furthering the war effort of England's enemies (Harmondsworth, Ruislip and St. Anthony). In the same way, but for different reasons, the citizens of London also began to take over religious houses. Indeed the two small leper hospitals at the Lock in Southwark and at Kingsland near Hackney had been administered by Londoners since their foundation in the twelfth century. By the fifteenth century the city seems also to have taken over the running of the St. Giles Hospital and intervened in the administration of the hospital of St. Mary Bethlehem.[139] These interventionist policies formed the blueprint for the city's later 'take-over' of the hospitals of St. Bartholomew and St. Thomas in the mid-sixteenth century. In a similar manner, the Mercers' Company took over the hospital of St. Thomas of Acre in Cheapside and adapted it to serve as their chapel and school.[140] At the same time, lay men and women were evolving religious ways of life, and solutions to social problems, which did not depend upon the founding of costly religious houses. Henry VII established the Savoy Hospital without finding it necessary to place it under the

---

[133] Below, pp. 126, 140, 147.
[134] Below, pp. 57–8, 91–3; Rosser, *Medieval Westminster*, pp. 97–8.
[135] L.M.A., Journal 5, ff. 118v., 126v., 130, 132, 199.
[136] Christine L. Winter, 'The Portsoken Presntments: an analysis of a London Ward in the 15th century', *T.L.M.A.S.*, 56 (2005), pp. 97–161.
[137] Below, pp. 86–7; *Cal. Letter Book K*, p. 230; L.M.A., Journal 3, ff. 3, 24v.; 4, f. 13.
[138] L.M.A. DL/C/206 ff. 107v–109.
[139] Barron, *LLMA*, pp. 291–4.
[140] Below, p. 111; Sutton, *Mercery of London*, chapter 12.

rule or guidance of a religious house. Within the London almshouses lay men and women lived ordered and prayerful lives just as successfully, or perhaps more so, than the vowed members of religious orders.

In stages between 1532 and 1540 almost all the religious houses in London and Middlesex were dissolved, their lands and property forfeited to the Crown, their inmates pensioned off and dispersed. Some houses had, as we have seen, already been appropriated by the Crown, or adapted to new purposes. Some institutions survived because they were closely associated with the Crown (Westminster Abbey or the Savoy hospital) or because it could be argued – as in the case of the almshouses – that they were not primarily founded for 'superstitious purposes', i.e. prayers for those who had died. The Colleges of secular priests lingered on until they too were abolished by the Chantries Act of 1548. But the large houses, with extended precincts and substantial endowments were all swept into the maw of the Court of Augmentations. They were rapidly bought up by ambitious royal servants who converted them into private mansions or sold them on to others. Holy Trinity Priory was converted into the London house of Thomas Audley and then of the duke of Norfolk; St. Mary Clerkenwell became the home of the duke of Newcastle and the Charterhouse was bought by Sir Edward North. Other buildings such as Blackfriars became theatres; and the house at St. John Clerkenwell was used by the Clerk of the Revels to store tents. Some precincts, such as the Crutched Friars and St. Mary Overy in Southwark declined into industrial sites. The City was able to buy the hospitals of St. Bartholomew, St. Mary Bethlehem and St. Thomas's, together with the Greyfriars, to use as civic hospitals. Some of the conventual churches, at St. Helen's Bishopsgate, St. Bartholomew's priory, the Minoresses, Austin Friars and Greyfriars, were adapted for use as parish churches.[141] The precincts of all the dissolved houses were rapidly built over as the pressure for housing and industrial workshops intensified in the course of the sixteenth century. In this way London's 'green lung' was removed and outbreaks of plague became more frequent and more severe.

The fate of the dispossessed inmates of the London houses is difficult to trace. It is generally acknowledged that it was harder for the religious women to find new lives in the secular world.[142] Some of the heads of the female houses received generous pensions: Agnes Jordan at Syon received £200 p.a., but Anne Browne at Kilburn was allowed only £10 p.a.[143] It has been suggested that several religious women chose to continue to live together in 'some type of communal situation'.[144] Displaced monks could find work as chantry priests, and it is sometimes possible to chart their post-Dissolution careers. Thomas Salter who had become a Carthusian monk after a successful career as a London merchant later fell out with the austere Prior John Houghton and left the Charterhouse before the end. He then found work as a chantry priest in the London parish church of St. Nicholas Acon. In Edward's reign he seems to have gone into hiding in Southwark and when Mary came to the throne he was able to work again as a priest in St. Magnus Church until his death in 1558. When he died he was quite a wealthy man.[145] When the London Dominican house was dissolved in 1538, Adam Garrett, who had been a brother there for six years, went to the parish of Owslebury in Hampshire for six months, was then a curate at St. Peter Paul's Wharf in London for three years, then a chaplain for three months in St. Dunstan in the West and finally, in 1544 he was a chaplain at St. Alphege parish church.[146] Such restless careers following the dissolution of their houses must have been common among the displaced clergy of mid-sixteenth century London.

[141] See Schofield and Lea, *Holy Trinity Priory*, pp. 182–3. See E. Jeffries Davis, 'The Transformation of London', in R.W. Seton-Watson (ed.), *Tudor Studies Presented to A. F. Pollard* (London, 1924), pp. 287–314.

[142] See Kathleen Cooke, 'The English Nuns and the Dissolution', in Blair and Golding (eds.), *The Cloister and the World*, pp. 287–301, esp. p. 291.

[143] Below, pp. 278, 288.

[144] Cooke, 'English Nuns', p. 300. See also Mary C. Erler, 'Religious Women after the Dissolution', in *London and the Kingdom: Proceedings of the 2004 Harlaxton Symposium* (forthcoming: Donington, 2007).

[145] See Roger Greenwood, 'The Will of Thomas Salter of London, 1558', *Norfolk Archaeology*, 38 (1983), pp. 280–95; C. J. Kitching (ed.), *London and Middlesex Chantry Certificate 1548* (London Record Society, 16, 1980), p. 31.

[146] G.L. MS 09065A/1 f. 88v, *ex inf.* Dr Jessica Freeman.

Over the years the religious houses had abandoned their separateness: they were no longer points of prayer in a dark and disorderly world. The social functions of caring for the young, the sick and the old could be better carried out by more flexible, more secular, institutions. The extensive landed endowments of the houses had brought them, not relief from the cares of the world, but litigation, expense and administrative worry. Within a generation the religious houses which, for half a millennium, had defined the spiritual, social and physical topography of the city had been almost completely eradicated. Reformist ideas in religion and the pressures of burgeoning capitalism overrode scruples and loyalties. On 22 June 1537 the Court of Aldermen, who had earlier, on hearing of the king's intention to dissolve the Charterhouse, decided to labour for its 'continuance', now 'agreed that no labour shalbe made by thys Cytye yn that bihalf'.[147] The end had come.

[147] L.M.A., Repertory of the Court of Aldermen, vol. 9, f. 255.

# PART I

# LONDON HOUSES

THE RELIGIOUS HOUSES OF MEDIEVAL LONDON AND ITS ENVIRONS
(*Museum of London Archaeology Service*)

Priory of Haliwell

Hospital of St Mary Bishopsgate

Hospital of St Mary Bethlehem

Hospital of St Augustine Pappey

Holy Trinity Priory

St Helen's Bishopsgate

Minoresses

St Mary de Gracis

Hospital of St Katherine

St Peter ad Vincula

Milbourne's Almshouses

Crossed Friars

College All Hallows Barking

Fraternity of Sixty Priests (Leadenhall)

Austin Friars

Hospital of St Anthony

Walworth's College

Chapel of St Thomas

Hospital of St Thomas

Friars of the Sack

College St Laurence Pountney

Jesus Commons

Guildhall College

Hospital of St Thomas of Acon

Hospital of St Mary within Cripplegate

Whittington Hospital and College

Southwark Priory

Hospital of St Giles Cripplegate

St Martin Le Grand

St Bartholomew Smithfield

St Paul's

Grey Friars

Charterhouse

St John Clerkenwell

Hospital of St Bartholomew

Southwark Leper Hospital

St Mary Clerkenwell

Black Friars

White Friars

Domus Conversorum

The Temple

River Thames

Friars de Areno

Hospital of the Savoy

St Stephen Westminster

Hospital of St Mary Rouncivall

St Peter's Westminster

N

1km

0

26

# HOUSE OF SECULAR CANONS

## 1. THE CATHEDRAL OF ST. PAUL

### INTRODUCTION

This entry remains a compact explication of the foundation, building and properties of the cathedral, and of the duties of the Dean and Chapter. This account is now much enlarged by the chapters on the medieval cathedral in Derek Keene, Arthur Burns and Andrew Saint (eds.), *St. Paul's: The Cathedral Church of London 604–2004* (New Haven, 2004). Based on the most recent and extensive research into the cathedral and its role, this book contains a comprehensive index and indispensable bibliography. The volume is richly illustrated and includes chapters updating the archaeology and fabric, foundation and endowment of the cathedral, its estates and income, and relationship with the medieval city. There are accounts of liturgy and music, devotional patterns, the lives and responsibility of the clergy, and the library and archives of the cathedral. The cathedral archives and manuscript collections are extensive and most are held and catalogued at the Guildhall Library, London. Much hitherto uncatalogued material has been recently listed.

*Stephanie Hovland*

The history of the church of St. Paul has tended from its foundation to make it rather the church of a city than a national or even a diocesan church. London was the metropolis of the East Saxons,[1] and the hill on which the cathedral now stands was, in some sort, the central point of London. In Anglo-Saxon times it was the meeting-place of the folkmoot, and the bell which called the people together hung in the place of the churchyard.[2] Such tradition affected later custom: in 1252 the citizens swore fealty to Edward, the king's son, in St. Paul's Churchyard.[3] In 604, when Augustine had ordained Mellitus bishop of London, King Ethelbert made the church of St. Paul;[4] and his choice of a site shows that he meant it to be the metropolitan church of the kingdom.[5] The course of history tended to confine its sphere of influence to London; yet in Anglo-Saxon times it was at least twice the burial-place of royal persons: of Ethelred in 1016[6] and of Edward

Atheling in 1057.[7] The position is illustrated by an incident which occurred in the eleventh century. When Archbishop Ælfheah was murdered by the Danes, in 1012, his body was brought to London. The bishops and the townsfolk received it with all veneration and buried it in St. Paul's monastery; and 'there God made manifest the holy martyr's miracle.' With the permission of Cnut the body was removed, however, to Canterbury, in 1023.[8]

How completely Ethelbert 'made' the church is not known. Earconwald, who was consecrated bishop of London in 675,[9] is said to have bestowed great cost on the fabric,[10] and in later times he almost occupied the place of traditionary, founder: the veneration paid to him is second only to that which was rendered to St. Paul.[11] Much of the Anglo-Saxon history of the cathedral is involved in a like ambiguity; for the early charters have for the most part been condemned as forgeries. Many Saxon kings are, however, traditionary benefactors to St. Paul's. 'I have renewed and restored,' said

---

[1] Bede, *Eccl. Hist.* lib. ii, cap. 3.
[2] Stow, *Surv. of Lond.* (Strype's ed.) iii, 148.
[3] *Chron. of Edw. I and Edw. II* (Rolls Ser.), lib. i, 46.
[4] Bede, *Eccl. Hist.* (Rolls Ser.), lib. ii, cap. 3.
[5] *Liber Albus* (Rolls Ser.), bk. i, pt. i, cap. 8. The municipal position of St. Paul's is shown by the customary attendance at the cathedral, in mediaeval times, of the mayor, his household, and all of his liberty, with the aldermen and the men of the mysteries, on All Saints' Day; and of the mayor, aldermen, sheriffs and all of their liberties, on Christmas Day, the days of St. Stephen and St. John the Evangelist, and the Monday after Pentecost.
[6] R. de Diceto, *Opera Hist.* (Rolls Ser.), i, 168.

[7] *Angl.-Sax. Chron.* (Rolls Ser.), ii, 159.
[8] Ibid. 118.
[9] Newcourt, *Repert.* i, 7.
[10] Dugdale, *Hist. of St. Paul's*, 4.
[11] *Registrum S. Pauli* (ed. W. St. Simpson), 11, 52, 81, 393–5; Newcourt, *Repert.* ii, 7. It is said that on the death of Earconwald there was a struggle between the canons of St. Paul's and the monks of Chertsey as to who should bury him, during which the people of London brought his body to St. Paul's: it was transferred to a shrine in the cathedral in 1140.

Athelstan, in one of the rejected charters, liberty to the monastery of St. Paul in London, where holy Earconwald held his bishopric for long; and all privileges which my ancestors for their souls and for their desires of heavenly kingdom constituted, and which are contained in the writings of the monastery.[12]

The date and the terms of this charter lead further to the supposition that the church had suffered during the Danish occupation of London in the beginning of the tenth century, and the disorder consequent on war with the Danes. In 962 it was attacked by its most persistent enemy: 'in that year Paul's monastery was burnt and was again founded.'[13] But the life of the church appears to have been little interrupted: a grant of land was received from Queen Egelfleda[14] and a confirmation of lands and possessions from Ethelred.[15] In 1012 and 1013, and from 1017 to 1040 the Danes were again in London; and, unlike their ancestors, they worshipped in St. Paul's. A stone has been found in the churchyard which bears the Runic inscription; 'Kina caused this stone to be laid over Tuki.'[16] Cnut confirmed all the lands of the church, and intimated to his bishops, earls, peers and ministers that the priests of St. Paul's monastery were under his protection and their lands free from burdens.[17] Nevertheless their liberties must have been violated during the confusion which followed on his death; for Edward the Confessor not only granted a charter which confirmed them in their lands and possessions,[18] but also 'restored' certain property to them.[19]

It is probable that the influx of foreign ecclesiastics into England particularly affected the cathedral, for Robert of Jumieges, consecrated bishop of London in 1040,[20] and his successor William were both Normans; and it can hardly be doubted that the bishop appointed the clergy of the church at this date as in later times. The Norman names Ralph and Walter are indeed those of two of the four canons of St. Paul's, who are mentioned in the Domesday Survey.[21] Bishop William, according to his epitaph in the cathedral, was 'familiar with St. Edward, king and confessor, and admitted to the councils of Prince William, king of England.'[22] He obtained great and large privileges for London, and was for

many centuries revered by the citizens.[23] It is to be concluded that he took under his protection the cathedral church, with which, of all the institutions of the city, he was particularly connected. Thus circumstances must have combined to prevent the Conquest from occasioning any break in the history of St. Paul's. Several grants of land and two charters were conferred by William I:[24] an instruction for the restoration of ancient possessions, which occurs in one charter,[25] indicates some losses in the times of disorder, or neglect of the like provision of Edward the Confessor. William desired that the church might be as free as he would wish his soul to be on the Day of Judgement. Confirmations of liberties and property were received from both his sons.[26]

In 1087 the Saxon church of St. Paul's was burnt,[27] and Bishop Maurice began the building of that cathedral which was beautified and enlarged by many generations, and stood in 1666.[28] Richard de Belmeis bestowed for some years all the revenues of his office on the work of construction, and yet 'it seemed that nothing had been done.'[29] Richard made St. Paul's churchyard, and enlarged the streets and lanes about the cathedral at his own cost.[30] He obtained from Henry I a grant of as much of the ditch of Baynard's Castle as was needed to make a wall about the church and a way without the wall;[31] and in 1106 Eustace earl of Boulogne renounced all his claim to lands thus surrounded.[32] Henry I helped the builders in another way; he commanded that ships which entered the River Fleet to bring stone for the church should be free from toll and custom.[33] In 1135 the building was injured by a fire which arose at London Bridge and spread to St. Clement Danes.[34]

In the story of a disputed election the attitude of the chapter during the disorderly times of Stephen is discovered. Gilbert Universalis, bishop of London, died in 1134;[35] for two years the see remained vacant; then a meeting of the chapter was held simultaneously with that of a council summoned by the king to Westminster. There were two parties among the canons, that which favoured and that

---

[12] Printed in Dugdale, *Hist. of St. Paul's*, 181.
[13] *Angl.-Sax. Chron.* (Rolls Ser.), ii, 92.
[14] Printed in Dugdale, *Hist. of St. Paul's*, 181.
[15] Ibid.
[16] The stone is preserved in the cathedral library.
[17] Charter printed in Dugdale, *Hist. of St. Paul's*, 181.
[18] Printed in Dugdale, *Hist. of St. Paul's*, 181.
[19] Ibid.
[20] W. Stubbs, *Reg. Sacr. Angl.* 20.
[21] *Dom. Bk.* i, 127, 128.
[22] Stow, *Surv. of Lond.* (ed. Strype), iii, 158.

[23] Dugdale, *Hist. of St. Paul's*, 51.
[24] Cart. Antiq. R. A. 1.
[25] Printed in Dugdale, *Hist. of St. Paul's*, 187.
[26] Cart. Antiq. R. BB. 9; *Hist. MSS. Com. Rep.* ix, App. i, pt. i, 45.
[27] *Angl.-Sax. Chron.* (Rolls Ser.), ii, 188.
[28] Much material was obtained from the ruins of a strong castle called the Palatine Tower, which was burnt with the old church. Dugdale, *Hist. of St. Paul's*, 6.
[29] Will. of Malmesbury, *Gesta Pontif.* (Rolls Ser.), 145.
[30] Dugdale, *Hist. of St. Paul's*, 6.
[31] Stow, *Surv. of Lond.* (ed. Strype), iii, 142.
[32] Dugdale, *Hist. of St. Paul's*, 6.
[33] Ibid.
[34] Matt. Paris, *Hist.* (Rolls Ser.), ii, 163.
[35] Newcourt, *Repert.* i, 11.

which opposed the election to the episcopacy of Anselm, abbot of Bury St. Edmunds.[36] This was a nephew of the late Archbishop Anselm, who had been abbot of St. Sabas in Rome, and had visited England as legate in 1115. In 1116 he had arrived in Normandy bearing letters which conferred on him the administration of the apostolic see in England, and Henry I had been persuaded by the queen, Archbishop Ralph and certain nobles to send him back to Rome.[37] Some of his supporters in this election were deprived of their goods, and Ralph de Diceto says of them that they were wise not in God but in things of the world, and that their action seemed iniquitous to all the council at Westminster.[38] It is evident that they represented the anti-national party in the politics of the church, and the party opposed to Stephen in state politics. Their opponents, who were led by Dean William, underwent a temporary defeat. The treasurer was an adherent of Anselm, and with Anselm, others of the canons and much gold, journeyed to Rome, where, by help of the confusion due to the schism of Leo, an appeal was gained. Anselm was accordingly received in the cathedral by a solemn procession,[39] and was enthroned in 1137.[40] The time was favourable for highhanded administrations; the new bishop's rule was autocratic, and he probably weakened his party in the chapter and the country. In the following year Richard de Belmeis and Ralph of Langford, resident canons, rendered a second appeal to Rome, which was supported by a letter from Archbishop Thurstan of York, and, according to Ralph de Diceto, by the evidence of all the suffragans of Canterbury.[41] As a result Anselm's tenure of the bishopric was declared to be invalid because his appointment had lacked the dean's consent.[42] The succession of Ralph of Langford to Dean William in this year[43] further indicates a change in the disposition of power in the chapter. The cathedral received a charter from Stephen which confirmed its lands and possessions.[44]

In the quarrel between the king and Archbishop Thomas, in the next reign, St. Paul's sided with Gilbert Foliot. When this bishop had summoned a meeting of London clergy in the cathedral, and had publicly appealed to Rome against his excommunication,[45] the dean and chapter wrote to the pope in his support.[46] They received from the archbishop an intimation of the sentence of their bishop, who, both in this year, and, presumably, when he was again under a ban from 1170 to 1171, did not enter the cathedral.[47] In later times an altar and a chapel were dedicated to St. Thomas the Martyr in St. Paul's Church.[48]

In this reign, as in that of Henry I, much care was bestowed on the restoring, and the building and adorning of the cathedral. The bishop of Winchester ordered the inhabitants of his diocese in 1175–6 to afford assistance to those sent to collect money for the building of the church of St. Paul.[49] A system of wandering collectors for the building fund, instituted by the bishop or the chapter or both of them, seems to be indicated.

The dean and chapter gave two palfreys to King John in the year 1200, that he might protect their enjoyment of the liberties contained in their charter,[50] and they received from him an additional charter which confirmed their rights and possessions.[51] Their attitude in the struggle between the king and his barons is definite. At the end of the list of excommunicated rebels, in the bull of 1215, a paragraph is devoted to the sentence of 'Master Gervase de Hobrugge, chancellor of London, who is the most manifest persecutor of the king and the king's friends,'[52] and it is this Gervase who was elected dean in 1216.[53] He and Simon Langton, canon of St. Paul's, and brother of the archbishop, appealed, in the year of the election, against the excommunication of Louis and his followers.[54] Both Gervase and Simon, with Robert de St. Germain,[55] were deprived of their benefices by the legate Gualo,[56] who, in the next year, signified to the bishop and the dean and chapter that he had appointed Henry of Cornhill to the office of chancellor, vacated by the deposition of Gervase of Hobrugge for contumacy and contempt.[57] In detestation of the masses of the excommunicated the altars in London on which they had celebrated were destroyed.[58]

In the reign of Henry III the clergy of St. Paul's took part in that movement of the church towards

[36] R. de Diceto, *Opera Hist.* (Rolls Ser.), i, 249.

[37] *Ann. Mon.* (Rolls Ser.), ii, 215; Roger of Hoveden, *Chron.* (Rolls Ser.), i, 171.

[38] R. de Diceto, *Opera Hist.* (Rolls Ser.), i, 248.

[39] Ibid.

[40] Newcourt, *Repert.* i, 11.

[41] R. de Diceto, *Opera Hist.* (Rolls Ser.), i, 249.

[42] R. de Diceto, *Opera Hist.* (Rolls Ser.), i, 250.

[43] Newcourt, *Repert.* i, 33.

[44] *Hist. MSS. Com. Rep.* ix, App. pt. i, 45.

[45] *Materials for Hist. of Thos. Becket* (Rolls Ser.), iii, 32.

[46] Ibid. vi, 618.

[47] R. de Diceto, *Opera Hist.* (Rolls Ser.), i, 334.

[48] Dugdale, *Hist. of St. Paul's*, 24, 131.

[49] *Hist. MSS. Com. Rep.* ix, pt. i, 58.

[50] *Rot. de Oblat. et Fin.* (Rec. Com.), 63.

[51] Cart. Antiq. R. A. 7.

[52] Rymer, *Foed.* i, 225.

[53] *Ann. Mon.* (Rolls Ser.), iii, 51.

[54] Matt. Paris, *Hist.* (Rolls Ser.), ii, 655.

[55] The wording of the appeal makes it possible that Robert de St. Germain was not a canon.

[56] *Ann. Mon.* (Rolls Ser.), iii, 51.

[57] Ibid.

[58] *Hist. MSS. Com. Rep.* ix, pt. i, 22.

independence which identified itself with the struggle for political liberty. Ranulf le Breton, canon and treasurer of St. Paul's, had been a familiar friend of the king. He incurred the royal displeasure; a messenger was sent to accuse him of treason, and an obedient mayor placed him in the Tower. The chapter would not brook such infringement of the rights of one of its members. In the absence of the bishop, Dean Geoffrey de Lucy 'incontinently' pronounced sentence of excommunication on all who had been concerned in the imprisonment, and placed the cathedral under an interdict. When, in spite of admonitions, the king remained obdurate, the bishop was about to extend the interdict to the whole city, and was supported by the legate, the archbishop, and many other prelates. Such extreme measures were not necessary. Henry commanded Ranulf to be set free, but stipulated that he should be kept in readiness to come forward whenever an accusation should be made against him. The canons refused for him such conditional liberty, and demanded his absolute restoration to the church as its child; and the king gave way.[59] Two years later the chapter elected Fulk Bassett, dean of York, to the see of London, in spite of the king's efforts to procure the choice of Peter d'Aigueblanche, bishop of Hereford. For three years Fulk awaited his consecration; in 1244 he was installed and the chapter had secured another victory.[60] The politics of St. Paul's were not only local. The dean and chapter addressed to Clement II, in 1307, a eulogy of Bishop Grosteste, and a request that his name might be enrolled in the hagiology of the church.[61] In 1269 Henry III granted to them a charter, confirming divers liberties and quittances of which their enjoyment had lately been hindered by the war and tumult in the realm.[62]

In the matter of the election it is likely that the canons sought to resist the power and greed of foreigners as much as to maintain rightful liberties. The cathedral took a prominent part in the resistance to Archbishop Boniface. It claimed immunity from metropolitical visitations. When, therefore, the archbishop would have visited the chapter in 1250, the canons refused to admit him into their church and appealed to the pope; and Boniface excommunicated the dean, Henry of Cornhill, with certain other dignitaries. Afterwards, when he was about to go to Rome, he procured that the dean and canons should be cited to appear at the papal court, and he was supported by a letter of the king to Innocent IV.[63] The chapter asked for the help of all the bishops of England, and sent to Rome, as proctors, the dean and the canons Robert of Barton and William of Lichfield.[64] In 1251 Innocent revoked the sentence of excommunication;[65] but, in the next year, a papal decree obliged the cathedral to submit to an archiepiscopal visitation.[66] It took place in 1253; and Matthew Paris tells that the canons 'kindly' admitted Boniface, and that he bore himself cautiously and moderately.[67]

There were few papal provisions to offices in St. Paul's in this reign. A prebend and canonry were conferred by the pope on Alexander de Ferentino, papal sub-deacon and chaplain, but they were granted in effect to William of Kilkenny, and the dean and chapter contended, in justification, that the papal appointment could not take effect, since the prebends were limited in number, and the collation to all of them belonged to the bishop. A papal chaplain was thereupon ordered to hear the proctors of both parties, and, on his report, a mandate of 1254 granted the disputed prebend to Alexander, and provided William to the next which should fall vacant.[68] In 1256 Alexander is called canon of London.[69] On the death of Richard Talbot, in 1262, Innocent IV attempted to provide John de Ebulo, papal subdeacon and chaplain to the deanery. But the canons were resolute in their resistance; the settlement of the question was delegated by the pope to the cardinal of Sts. Cosmo and Damiano, who arranged a compromise. By virtue of this Ebulo resigned his claim to the deanery and received certain pensions from the goods of the dean and chapter, and the promise of the next prebend that should fall vacant. Yet in the two following years his claim was twice disregarded; canonries were granted to Thomas of Cantilupe, and to Amatric son of Simon de Montfort, respectively; and in 1264 Urban IV wrote to urge that the agreement be fulfilled.[70] The canons sometimes reinforced themselves by the pope's authority when they wished to enjoy a plurality of benefices,[71] and in this way papal power had significance.

Independence was generally maintained until the end of the reign of Edward I. The deans were English.[72] In 1294 Dean William de Montfort fell dead at the king's feet as he was about to plead against excessive taxation.[73]

[59] Matt. Paris, *Chron. Maj.* (Rolls Ser.), iii, 547.

[60] Ibid. iv, 171.

[61] Lambeth MSS. 580, fol. 454.

[62] Cart. Antiq. A 26.

[63] Matt. Paris, *Chron. Maj.* (Rolls Ser.), v, 121, 124–5, 208, 213.

[64] Ibid. vi, 199.

[65] Ibid. v, 212.

[66] *Cal. Pap. Letters*, i, 276.

[67] Matt. Paris, *Chron. Maj.* (Rolls Ser.), v, 322.

[68] *Cal. Pap. Letters*, i, 302.

[69] Ibid. i, 334.

[70] Ibid. i, 417.

[71] Ibid. i, 377, 525, 533.

[72] List of deans in Appendix to *Reg. S. Pauli* (ed. W. S. Simpson).

[73] Wharton, *De Episcopis*, &c., 210.

Much was done to the fabric of the cathedral in the thirteenth century. On St. Remigius' day, in 1241, it was dedicated afresh by Bishop Roger Niger, in the presence of the king and many prelates and magnates.[74] A grant had been received, in 1205, of a market place, to the east of the church;[75] and this was the site of the New Work, begun in 1251.[76] The enterprise was, to some extent, that of the Catholic church. From 1228 to 1255, and again from 1260 to 1276, numerous hortatory letters of the English and Welsh bishops granted indulgences to penitents in their dioceses who should help in the work of St. Paul's church. Eight Irish bishops issued similar indulgences between the years 1237 and 1279. In Scotland only Albinus, bishop of Brechin, attempted thus to direct the liberality of his people, and the benefits he conferred were extended to those who should pray at St. Paul's for the soul of Isabella of Bruce. But in 1252 Henry, archbishop of Cologne, when in England, sent out a hortatory letter to encourage contributions; and Innocent III granted a pardon of forty days' penance for the same purpose.[77] When the Emperor Frederick raised the siege of Parma, in 1248, the inhabitants, in their thankfulness, vowed that they would send to St. Roger, bishop of London, a like sum to that of which they had despoiled him on his way to Rome, for the building of the church in London or for other alms which touched his honour.[78] Through out these years many individuals made donations and bequests to forward the New Work.[79] After 1283 hortatory letters of bishops for the same end were few: 'the main brunt of the work was over.'[80] The dean and chapter became involved in a quarrel with the mayor and commonalty on the question of the boundaries of their precincts. The determination of the way without their churchyard wall, which Henry I had suffered them to make, appears to have been ambiguous, while the completion of the wall was delayed. Further, the chapter had, apparently, an unrestricted power of closing the gates of the churchyard, naturally productive of inconvenience to the citizens. In 1281 an agreement was made by which the mayor and citizens conceded that the southern gates should not be open from curfew to morning.[81] In 1284–5 Edward I granted that the churchyard might be inclosed and have fitting gates and posterns.[82] The bishop, the dean and the chapter pleaded before the king at the Guildhall, in this year, that the proximity of houses to their wall had prevented them from building residences for the ministers of their church, and judgement was given in their favour.[83]

The attitude of St. Paul's in connexion with national politics under Edward II is proved by the honour that was paid to Thomas earl of Lancaster, after his death. The earl had put up a tablet in the cathedral to commemorate the granting of the ordinances, and its neighbourhood acquired a reputation for the working of miracles.[84] An image of Lancaster was erected there, before which, with the sanction of the church of Rome and the bishop, the people prayed and made offerings. The king by letters to the bishop and to the dean and chapter ordered such practice to be discontinued;[85] the tablet, and presumably the statue, were removed by royal writ; but the people still made oblations on the spot which had become sanctified.[86] A form of prayer in honour of Thomas of Lancaster, which was used in St. Paul's, is extant, and it betrays curious popular sympathies on the part of the cathedral clergy. In a hymn the earl is addressed as 'he who, when he saw the common people shipwrecked and in travail, did not spurn to die for the right.'[87] Under the stronger governments of Edward III and Richard II St. Paul's lost individuality and independence. To the first the chapter granted loans and free gifts.[88] In 1379 Richard II exercised with regard to St. Paul's the privilege conceded to him by Urban VI, of nominating two canons in all cathedrals and collegiate churches in England.[89] He presented a minor canon in 1381, a treasurer in 1387, and a prebendary in 1391.[90] In 1393 he again conferred the office of treasurer; the matter was brought before the Court of Chancery, and, in accordance with the decision, Richard revoked his grant.[91]

[74] Matt. Paris, *Chron. Maj.* (Rolls Ser.), iv, 49.

[75] *Trans. of St. Paul's Eccl. Soc.* i, 178.

[76] Stow, *Surv. of Lond.* (ed. Strype), iii, 173.

[77] Dugdale, *Hist. of St. Paul's*, 6 et seq.

[78] Matt. Paris, *Chron. Maj.* (Rolls Ser.), v. 13. In the year 1247 a curious ceremony took place in connexion with St. Paul's. Among the treasures of the cathedral was a vase said to contain the blood of Christ. Apparently it was considered fitting that it should have a yet holier resting place. The king ordered all the priests and clerks of London to assemble in the church on the day of St. Edward in their most ceremonious vestments. Then with highest honour and reverence and fear he received the vase, and, preceded by the clergy in procession, he bore it to Westminster; walking, and in the habit of a poor man. He held it above his head, and always he looked at the sky or at the vase. Ibid. iv, 641.

[79] *Hist. MSS. Com. Rep.* ix, pt. 1; Sharpe, *Cal. of Wills*, &c.

[80] Dugdale, *Hist. of St. Paul's*, 14.

[81] *Hist. MSS. Com. Rep.* ix, App. pt. i, 51.

[82] Dugdale, *Hist. of St. Paul's*, 17.

[83] Sharpe, *Cal. of Letter Bk. A.* 213; *Abbrev. Plac.* (Rec. Com.), 208.

[84] Fabyan, *Chron. of Lond.* 257.

[85] *Cal. of Close*, 1313–18, p. 723.

[86] Fabyan, *Chron. of Lond.* 257.

[87] *Doc. Illus. Hist. of St. Paul's* (ed. W. S. Simpson), 11–14.

[88] *Cal. of Close*, 1333–7, p. 17; 1339–41, pp. 558, 684; 1346–9, p. 384.

[89] *Cal. of Pat.* 1377–81, pp. 328, 329.

[90] Ibid. 1381–5, p. 411; Le Neve, *Fasti* (ed. 1716), 201.

[91] *Cal. of Pat.* 1383–92, pp. 327, 412.

From the accession of Edward II resistance to papal aggression was likewise harder and less effectual; its successes were due to the fact that Roman greed of gold was stronger than greed of power. After Ralph Baldock had been promoted to the bishopric, the deanery was held successively by two Roman cardinals, Raymond de la Goth and Arnald de Cantilupe.[92] It is probable that these deans took little part in the doings of the chapter: thus, in 1309, the year in which he died, Arnald was authorised to appoint attorneys while he was absent for three years at the court of Rome.[93] It was in 1307 that the chapter wrote to the pope on the subject of Grosteste.[94] John Sendale was 'rightly elected dean by the canons' in 1311;[95] yet in 1314 Edward II sent a letter to the pope asking him to grant to John that confirmation without which his tenure was incomplete.[96] The occasion of such a request becomes clear when it appears that, probably in this year or the next, John XXII granted the deanery of London with a canonry to Vitalis de Testa, nephew of William, cardinal of St. Curiac;[97] and addressed him as dean and canon of London until the year 1322.[98] The papal mandate states that the offices are void by the death of Arnald de Cantilupe, and ignores John Sendale. Yet in a list of deans in the archives of the cathedral it is stated that John was dean from 1311 to 1316, Richard Newport from 1314 to 1317, and Vitalis in 1323.[99] In 1316 the pope granted to Vitalis leave to enjoy the fruits of his benefices while he pursued his studies at a university.[100] This, coupled with the fact that he seems to have been chiefly distinguished as the nephew of his uncle, makes it probable that he was very young, and must have rendered necessary the existence of a substitute who can only have lacked the title of his office. Hence must have arisen the confusion which appears in the cathedral list. Vitalis was not protected by the king, who granted his canonry and prebend to Roger of Northburgh.[101] Finally the pope authorised his exchange of benefices with John of Everdon, who became dean in 1322 or 1323.[102] There was another instance of successful resistance to papal aggression in 1317. The pope provided Vitalis, cardinal of St. Martin's in the Mountains, to a prebend in St. Paul's.[103] The dean and chapter obtained from the king a prohibition to publish the grant, and thus incurred excommunication.[104] In the following year they bought from the proctor of Vitalis, with five hundred Florentine florins, a concession that they should not be molested in the matter of the disputed prebend.[105] Again in 1321 the archdeaconry of London, to which Elias Talleyrandi, brother of the count of Périgord, had been provided, was held by Richard of Haston.[106] A papal mandate ordered restitution and was obeyed.[107] At least ten other dignities and prebends were conferred by the pope in the reign of Edward II.[108]

Under Edward III there were certainly eighteen provisions before 1346.[109] In 1328 both the bishop and the pope presented to the prebend of Brondesbury; the nominees collided, and there ensued a brawl which brought the church under an interdict for five days.[110] Many provisions were made at the king's request. In the lifetime of Dean Gilbert Bruere, who is said to have served four cardinals of the Roman church for thirty-four years,[111] the pope reserved to himself the presentation to the deanery, and he appointed Richard of Kilmington to it in 1353.[112] John of Appleby, who became dean in 1364, also owed his office to a papal grant.[113] Under Richard II Thomas of Evrere was provided to the deanery in 1389.[114]

The history of the building of St. Paul's in this century is chiefly concerned with the diocese of London. The pope granted in 1306 a release of certain periods of penance to all who visited the cathedral on the feast of St. Paul and the following days;[115] Bishop John Salmon of Norwich, in 1303, and Bishop Thomas Hatfield of Durham, in 1345,[116] urged contribution to the New Work in letters hortatory; like appeals were issued by Roger Mortival, bishop of Salisbury, in 1316, for the repair of the Old Work; and by Simon, cardinal, in 1371, for repairs in general.[117] But in the diocese of London there was greater activity. It was ordained in 1300 that all offerings in the cathedral should be assigned to the completion of the New Work.[118] Ralph Baldock, while he was bishop of London

[92] Le Neve, *Fasti* (ed. 1716), 183.
[93] *Cal. of Pat.* 1307–13, p. 122.
[94] v. *supra*.
[95] Wharton, *De Episcopis Lond. etc.*, 214.
[96] Rymer, *Foed.* iii, 473.
[97] *Cal. of Pap. Letters*, ii, 124.
[98] Ibid. ii, 155.
[99] *Reg. S. Pauli* (ed. W. S. Simpson), 468–470.
[100] *Cal. of Pap. Letters*, ii, 155.
[101] *Cal. of Pap. Letters*, ii, 188.
[102] Ibid. ii, 225.
[103] Ibid. ii, 155.
[104] Ibid. ii, 169.
[105] *Hist. MSS. Com. Rep.* ix, App. i, 654.
[106] *Cal. of Pap. Letters*, ii, 211.
[107] Ibid. ii, 231.
[108] Ibid. ii, 124–276; Lond. Epis. Reg. Baldock, fol. 21.
[109] *Cal. of Pap. Letters*, ii, 281–410; iii, 50–423.
[110] *Chron. of Edw. I and Edw. II* (Rolls Ser.), i, 340.
[111] *Cal. of Pap. Letters*, iii, 246.
[112] Ibid. iii, 428.
[113] Le Neve, *Fasti* (ed. 1716), 184.
[114] Ibid. 189.
[115] *Cal. of Pap. Letters*, ii, 17.
[116] *Hist. MSS. Com. Rep.* ix, App. i, 42.
[117] Dugdale, *Hist. of St. Paul's*, 14.
[118] Lond. Epis. Reg. Baldock, and Gravesend, fol. 205.

from 1306 to 1313, gave two marks every year to this object;[119] he promised an indulgence to all who contributed to the repairs of the Old Work.[120] His successor, Gilbert Segrave, and all the clergy of London urged on the people the necessity of providing for the restoration of the bell tower.[121] For this purpose exclusively, under Bishop Richard Newport, in 1320, collections were ordered to be made in all churches within the jurisdiction of the see, and on every Sunday.[122] The whole church was elaborately measured in 1313; and Gilbert Segrave dedicated altars in the New Work to the Virgin, St. Thomas the Martyr, and St. Dunstan.[123] In 1327 the choir was moved to the New Work, and mass was first celebrated at the great altar on All Saints' Day.[124] The high altar and two collateral altars were consecrated by Bishop Richard Bintworth to the glory of the saints Paul, Ethelbert, and Mellitus. This bishop loved the church and the City, and was present in the cathedral on all saints' days; in consequence he received great honour.[125] Peter, bishop of Corbavia, consecrated a bell in 1331.[126] In 1332 the mayor and aldermen granted to the master of the New Work exemption from liability to be put on assizes and juries.[127] Towards the end of the fourteenth century the people appear to have grown less careful of their church. The commission issued by Edward III, in 1370, reproaches the bishop with neglect of its buildings.[128] In 1385 Bishop Robert Braybrook complains of the unseemly behaviour of the people. By buying and selling they had made of the cathedral a public market. They threw stones at the rooks and pigeons in the church, and they played at ball and other games, to the detriment of the windows and images. On pain of excommunication the delinquents were ordered to mend their ways within ten days.[129] The same bishop, by letters addressed to the clergy of the City and diocese, conferred an indulgence on all who contributed to the Old Work.[130]

The boundaries of the precincts were still questionable. In 1316–17 Edward II granted that the churchyard wall might be completed.[131] The chapter appears to have taken advantage of his permission, and thus to have become involved in another dispute. In 1321–2 the mayor pleaded before the justices that the dean and chapter had surrounded with a mud wall the ancient meeting-place of the folkmoot, the property of the commonalty; that they had inclosed St. Augustine's Gate and thus obstructed the king's highway through it and the western gate of St. Paul's to Ludgate; and that they had prevented passage through Southgate and 'Dycer's Lane.' In reply the canons produced their various charters.[132]

It is difficult to discover the political attitude of the chapter in the fifteenth century. The privileges of the cathedral had been confirmed by Richard II, and a like benefit was granted by Henry IV and Henry V.[133] In 1464 Dean William Saye, who had been chosen proctor by the clergy of the synod of London, was admitted by Edward IV to secret councils.[134] Another possible indication of policy occurs in 1455, when the commons petitioned that Thomas Lisieux, dean of St. Paul's, might be an administrator of the property of Humphrey, late duke of Gloucester.[135] At all events the cathedral does not appear to have suffered otherwise than accidentally from the changes of dynasty. Charters were confirmed to St. Paul's by Edward IV[136] and Henry VII[137] in the first year of the reign of each; in 1464 the cathedral was exempted from the effects of the Act of Resumption.[138] William Worseley, dean, was implicated in the conspiracy of Perkin Warbeck,[139] but received a royal pardon and was suffered to retain his office.[140]

Twelve prebends in St. Paul's were certainly provided by the pope between 1396 and 1404,[141] and three from 1404 to 1415;[142] but the great period of papal aggression was over.

From the sixteenth century the history of St. Paul's loses much of its interest: when the chapter can be said to have a policy, it is one of consistent servility to kingly government. The cathedral was brought into prominence by the deanery of Colet.[143] After his death, in 1519, it suffered for many years from virtual lack of a dean. Richard Pace, Colet's successor, was prevented, first by his foreign avocations and later by illness, from taking part in the affairs of

[119] Chron. of Edw. I and Edw. II (Rolls Ser.), i, 277.
[120] Lond. Epis. Reg. Baldock and Gravesend, fol. 16.
[121] Ibid. fol. 35.
[122] Ibid. fol. 47.
[123] Chron. of Edw. I and Edw. II (Rolls Ser.), i, 277.
[124] Ibid. i, 338.
[125] Ibid. i, 368.
[126] Ibid. i, 383.
[127] Sharpe, Cal. of Letter Bk. E, 264.
[128] Reg. S. Pauli (ed. W. S. Simpson), bk. 2, iii.
[129] Lond. Epis. Reg. Braybrook, fol. 330.
[130] Lond. Epis. Reg. Braybrook, fol. 340, 341.
[131] Stow, Surv. of Lond. (ed. Strype), iii, 142.

[132] Abbrev. Plac. (Rec. Com.), 354; Hist. MSS. Com. Rep. ix, App. pt. i, 49.
[133] Reg. S. Pauli (ed. W. S. Simpson), vii, cap. 15.
[134] Wharton, De Epis. Lond. &c. 228.
[135] Parl. R. (Rec. Com.), 339a.
[136] Chart. R. 1 Edw. IV, pt. 6, No. 4.
[137] Reg. S. Pauli (ed. W. F. Simpson), v, 2.
[138] Parl. R. (Rec. Com.), v, 421 a.
[139] André, Hist. of Hen. VII (Rolls Ser.), 69.
[140] Letters of reigns of Ric. III and Hen. VII (Rolls Ser.), 375.
[141] Cal. of Pap. Letters, v, 142.
[142] Ibid. vi.
[143] v. infra.

St. Paul's.[144] Richard Sampson was twice appointed his coadjutor in 1526 and 1536. The latter year is probably that of Pace's death, and in July Cranmer licensed Sampson, then bishop of Chichester, to hold the deanery *in commendam*. In 1534 the clergy of St. Paul's formally denied the pope's supremacy, in a declaration so explicit that it became a model for such renunciations.[145] Yet Bishop Stokesley asserted that he had supported its adoption by the chapter, almost singly. In this period the cathedral received Cromwell's visitors,[146] Thomas Legh and John Ap Rhys, who are said to have comported themselves with insolence towards the clergy. During a short time of triumph for Cromwell in 1540, Sampson,[147] who was a conspicuous member of Gardiner's party, lost the deanery of St. Paul's and was sent to the Tower.[148] Cranmer was appointed preacher and reader in the cathedral;[149] and John Incent, a leader of factions in the chapter, became dean.[150]

The iconoclasts began their work in St. Paul's under Henry VIII;[151] but it was under Edward VI, in 1552, that all the chapels and altars and much 'goodly stonework' were demolished.[152] The motives for such destruction were often mixed: thus Somerset used the stone of the chapel and cloister in Pardonchurchhaugh[153] for his new palace;[154] in 1553 all the plate and coin and the vestments and copes of the cathedral were commanded to be given for the king's grace.[155] In like manner the prebend of Kentish Town was appropriated, in 1551, to the furnishing of the royal stables.[156]

In August, 1553, the dean and chapter were cited to appear before Queen Mary's commissioners.[157]

All the great dignitaries of the cathedral, with the exception of the archdeacon of Essex, and the chancellor, resigned, or were deprived; and Bonner collated others to their places. The office of Dean William May, a leading Puritan, was given to John Feckenham.[158] In September Bonner sang mass in the church,[159] and in the next year a 'young flourishing rood' was set up to welcome King Philip.[160] The accession of Elizabeth wrought another complete change in the holders of offices and in the services.[161] May was restored to the deanery,[162] and, on his death in 1530, he was succeeded by Francis Nowell, who had been an exile in the time of Mary.[163]

On 4 June, 1561, St. Paul's steeple was struck by lightning; and a fire ensued which burnt all the tower, the roof, and the timber work.[164] The queen deputed a commission to order the restoration, and directed that it should confer with the lord mayor.[165] On her recommendation a collection for the repairs was made among all the clergy of the province of Canterbury.[166] In or about the year 1590 the ancient dispute between the cathedral and the City was revived. The mayor and commonalty claimed a right of making arrests within the precincts. In reply the dean and chapter stated that the inhabitants of the churchyard were freemen of the City; but that, although they dwelt within a ward, they were not of it, but belonged to a place of exempt jurisdiction. The action of Incent, who had prevented the City's alleged right of way through the churchyard, was defended. Eventually the parties submitted to the arbitration of the lords chief justices. The point of exempt jurisdiction was apparently conceded, and the ancient limits of the churchyard were defined.[167]

The early Stuart kings were careful of the cathedral. In 1620 its ruinous state was urged by the bishop of London, in a sermon preached before the king at St. Paul's Cross.[168] As a result a royal commission was formed for the restoration and maintenance of the church, and the remedy of encroachments on the precincts.[169] For these objects the king laid aside the yearly sum of £2,000, and Prince Charles that of

---

[144] *L. and P. Hen. VIII*, iv, 14, 93, 126, 177, 185, 374, 392.
[145] Rymer, *Foed.* xiv, 493. The declaration was signed by five resident and three other canons, nine or ten minor canons, six vicars, thirty-one chantry priests, and twenty-three persons of unspecified rank.
[146] *L. and P. Hen. VIII*, ix, 622.
[147] Ibid. xi, 125.
[148] Hall, *Chron.* (ed. 1809), 328
[149] *L. and P. Hen. VIII*, ix, 922.
[150] Ibid. viii, 744, 745.
[151] Collection of records in Burnet's *Hist. of Ref.* pt. ii, bk. i, No. 35.
[152] *Chron. of Greyfriars* (Camden Soc.), 75.
[153] The building of the chapel in the western quadrature of Pardonchurchhaugh, which was called Sheryngton's Chapel, and dedicated to the Blessed Virgin and St. Nicholas, was begun by Walter Sheryngton, resident canon of St. Paul's, and chancellor of the duchy of Lancaster, and completed by his executors. Sheryngton died in 1445–6, a licence to found in it a chantry, and his executors therefore endowed two chaplains, and granted the advowson to the dean and chapter. A library and a chamber were annexed to the chapel. (*Hist. MSS. Com. Rep.* viii, App. 634; Sharpe, *Cal. of Wills*, ii, 539.)
[154] *Chron. of Greyfriars* (Camden Soc.), 58.
[155] Ibid. 77.
[156] Letters printed in Strype, *Eccl. Memorials*, pt. ii, 264.
[157] Foxe, *Acts and Monuments* (ed. 1846), vi, 533.

[158] Le Neve, *Fasti* (ed. 1716), 185.
[159] *Chron. of Greyfriars* (Camden Soc.), 84.
[160] Foxe, *Acts and Monuments* (ed. 1846), vi, 553.
[161] Le Neve, *Fasti* (ed. 1716), 185.
[162] Collection of Records in Burnet's *Hist. of Ref.* pt. ii, bk. iii, Nos. 1, 481.
[163] Description of Monuments in St. Paul's in Stow, *Surv. of Lond.* (ed. Strype), iii, 160.
[164] *Doc. Illus. Hist. of Old St. Paul's* (ed. W. E. Simpson), 113–119.
[165] *Cal. S.P. Dom.* 1547–80, pp. 177, 178.
[166] Ibid. 179.
[167] S.P. Dom. Eliz. vol. ccxxx, Nos. 37, 40.
[168] *Cal. S.P. Dom.* 1619–23, p. 131.
[169] Ibid. 409.

£500;[170] and there were many other subscriptions. When Laud became bishop of London he took a very active interest in the work. He obtained a new commission from Charles I,[171] and himself contributed £100 every year.[172] Inigo Jones was made surveyor-general, and was able to exempt those he employed from liability to impressment.[173] The commissioners instituted collections in the City and in every county. In 1636 the king assigned to the repair of St. Paul's all profits of ecclesiastical causes and all moneys compounded for in the exchequer during the next ten years; and forbade that any crimes of ecclesiastical cognizance should be pardoned without the assent of the archbishop of Canterbury.[174] Buildings which were considered to straiten the churchyard or to impair the beauty of the cathedral were demolished, and their owners compensated.[175] Thus St. Gregory's Church was pulled down.[176] Such actions did not tend to make popular a work to which the sympathies of the Puritan party were already opposed[177] because it was earnestly forwarded by Laud and the king, and because its aim seemed to be rather outward show than the care of men's souls.[178] Moreover, Puritan censure was more than once directed against the services and ritual authorized by the chapter.[179] At his trial Laud was charged with having controlled the orders of the king and council board, in the matter of pulling down houses about St. Paul's, against right and equity,[180] and with appropriating to the restoration money intended for other objects.[181] It was declared that the devotion of the profits of ecclesiastical courts to the repair of the cathedral had been instrumental in increasing abuses and augmenting the archbishop's jurisdiction. As the Civil War drew nearer Royalists also were hindered from contributing to the restoration, because they must use all their resources to hinder 'more near approaching mischief.'[182]

Other efforts of the king and archbishop were directed to ensuring more decorous behaviour in the cathedral. Literature and contemporary records prove that men continued to transact business in St. Paul's after the issue of Braybrook's

admonition.[183] In 1561 Pilkington described the condition of the cathedral before the Reformation, and his account appears to have been only slightly exaggerated:

> the south alley for usury and popery, the north for sorcery, and the horse fair in the midst for all kinds of bargains, meetings, brawlings, murders, conspiracies, and the font for ordinary payments of money, are so well known to all men as the beggar knows his dish.[184]

The Reformation brought little or no improvement. In Queen Mary's reign an act of the Common Council ordered that carriers, and such as led horses, mules, and other beasts, should not make a passage through St. Paul's.[185] A royal proclamation, in the year of Pilkington's description, strictly prohibited in the cathedral brawling and fighting, walking, and driving of bargains in time of lectures or services, business appointments, and the thoroughfare of porters.[186] Still in 1600 it was the meeting-place of the gossips of the town.[187] In 1632 a notice was posted in St. Paul's which by royal order forbade that men should walk about the church in time of service, that children should use it as a playground, and that any should carry burdens through it.[188]

Charles I supported the chapter against the City. The claim to exempt jurisdiction can be traced in a summons of Sir Nicholas Rainton, lord mayor, before the council, because he had carried his sword in St. Paul's; an incident which became the subject of an accusation made against Laud at his trial.[189] In 1638 the dean and chapter petitioned that nothing prejudicial to their liberties and privileges might be inserted in a renewal of charters about to be conceded to the City; and the king returned a favourable answer.[190]

In the period of the Civil War and the Commonwealth there is a complete break in the history of St. Paul's. In October, 1642, the cathedral was closed by order of Parliament.[191] The lord mayor and aldermen were appointed sequestrators of the goods of the dean and chapter;[192] the clergy were deprived, and some or them suffered when they were thrown suddenly on their own resources.[193] In 1643 Dr. Cornelius Burges, a member of the committee

[170] Ibid. 1631–3, p. 281.
[171] Ibid. 1631–3, p. 6.
[172] Ibid. 1636–7, p. 400.
[173] Ibid. 1634–5, p. 150.
[174] Ibid. 1635–6, p. 339.
[175] Ibid. 1619–23, pp. 171, 206, 165, 169; 1631–3, p. 281.
[176] Ibid. 1636–7, p. 400.
[177] Ibid. 1640, p. 463.
[178] Ibid. 1644, p. 4.
[179] Ibid. 1617–18, p. 472; 1619–23, p. 449; 1633–4, p. 252.
[180] Ibid. 1641–3, p. 524.
[181] Ibid. 526, 551.
[182] Ibid. 1637, p. 512.

[183] Shakespeare, 2 Hen. IV, i, 2; *Cal. of Close*, 1341–6, p. 546; 1346–9, pp. 275, 364, &c.
[184] *Works of Pilkington* (ed. G. Scholefield), 540.
[185] Stow, *Surv. of Lond.* (ed. Strype), iii, 169.
[186] Wilkins, *Concilia*, iv, 227.
[187] *Cal. S.P. Dom.* 1593–1604, p. 457.
[188] *Doc. Illus. Hist. of St. Paul's* (ed. W. S. Simpson), 13.
[189] *Cal. S.P. Dom.* 1641–3, pp. 550.
[190] Ibid. 1637–8, pp. 551, 552.
[191] *Hist. MSS. Com. Rep.* v, App. 56, 161.
[192] *Com. Journ.* iii, 421.
[193] *Hist. MSS. Com. Rep.* vi, App. 22.

for sequestration, was appointed lecturer in St. Paul's;[194] and an allowance of £400 a year from the revenues of the cathedral was bestowed on him. To this the dean's house was added next year.[195] By the building of a partition wall, part of the choir was arranged for a preaching place in 1649.[196] In 1655–6 an order of council directed that the allowance of the lecturer at St. Paul's should, for the future, be decided by the trustees for the maintenance of ministers.[197] This body, in 1657, conferred the lectureship, with a yearly salary of £120, on Dr. Samuel Annesley.[198] The changing fortunes of parties were reflected in the cathedral: in 1647–8 it was the meeting-place of the provincial Presbytery;[199] later it gave shelter to sectaries. A congregation led by Captain Chillendon obtained leave to meet in the Stone Chapel[200] in 1652–3.[201] Three years later it was dissolved; a riot between soldiers and apprentices had been caused by a sermon against the deity of Christ.[202] In 1657–8 some waste ground at the west end of St. Paul's was allowed as the site of a meeting-house for 'John Simpson's congregation.'[203] The fabric of the church was at best neglected during these years. The cathedral was used as a barrack in 1647–8, and frequently after that time:[204] in 1657–8 800 horse were constantly quartered in it.[205] An order of the council of state, in 1654, devoted the scaffolding which had been set up for the repairs to Cromwell's necessities.[206] Sawpits were dug within the church, many of them over graves; and the choir stalls and part of the pavement were demolished.[207]

The council of state directed, in 1650, that the statues of King James and King Charles should be taken down and broken.[208] In Dugdale's words, St. Paul's presented 'a woeful spectacle of ruin.'[209]

In the year of the Restoration such of the clergy of St. Paul's as were still living returned to their places; and successors to the others were appointed.[210] Dr. Annesley was at first suffered to continue his ministrations; but within a year or two he was removed,

and the duty of providing lecturers returned to the dean and chapter.[211] In 1663 Charles II confirmed the charter of the cathedral.[212] The building, which had needed so grave repairs before the Civil War, was now in want of very extensive restoration. A commission for this end was issued in 1663, and the revenues arising from unappropriated church possessions which remained with government officials after the Act of Indemnity, together with all moneys still in the hands of the trustees appointed in 1649, were devoted to it.[213] In 1666 the great fire of London ended the history of the fabric of Old St. Paul's.[214]

It had been built by the initiative of the bishops of London, and by the efforts of the Church; by enterprise that was, to some extent, more than national. After the fire of 1666 the dean and chapter laid aside a portion of their revenue for the building of New St. Paul's;[215] the bishop exhorted to liberality in an address,[216] and individuals responded by gifts and bequests.[217] But the work was begun and mainly carried through by the secular government. Money was raised by a collection made on letters patent of Charles II, and by a grant of commutations of penances and of fines and forfeitures on the Green Wax.[218] Otherwise, of £427,847 which had been received in 1700, £368,144 was the outcome of the duties on coals.[219] On Midsummer Day, 1675, the first stone was laid. Morning Prayer Chapel was opened in 1690; and the choir on the day of thanksgiving for the Peace of Ryswick, when a special prayer for the New Work was added to the service by the king's order.[220] In 1710 the exterior of the cathedral was completed;[221] Sir Christopher Wren deputed his son to lay the highest stone of the lantern.[222] Within, the work continued: a commission for the finishing of the cathedral was issued in 1715.[223]

The internal history of the house begins with a statement by Bede in his 'Ecclesiastical History' that in the church of St. Paul Bishop Mellitus and his successors 'had their place.'[224] Arguments from analogy make it hardly doubtful that the clergy of St. Paul's were in the first instance the servants of the bishop, who ministered in the bishop's church. But before the

[194] Ibid. 28; *Rep.* vii, App. 49.
[195] *Com. Journ.* iii, 421.
[196] Dugdale, *Hist. of St. Paul's*, 172.
[197] *Cal. S.P. Dom.* 1655–6, p. 192.
[198] Ibid. 1657–8, p. 52.
[199] *Cal. of Clarendon Papers*, i, 375.
[200] Chapel of St. George.
[201] *Cal. of Clarendon Papers*, ii, 267; *Cal. S.P. Dom.* 1652–3, p. 423.
[202] Ibid. 1653–4, p. 204; 1655, p. 224.
[203] Ibid. 1657–8, pp. 109, 280.
[204] *Cal. of Clarendon Papers*, i, 375; Dugdale, *Hist. of St. Paul's*, 172.
[205] *Cal. S.P. Dom.* 1657–8, p. 326.
[206] Ibid. 1654, pp. 114, 163.
[207] Dugdale, *Hist. of St. Paul's*, 172.
[208] *Cal. S.P. Dom.* 1650, p. 261; *Com. Journ.* iv, 413.
[209] Dugdale, *Hist. of St. Paul's*, 172.
[210] Le Neve, *Fasti* (ed. 1716), 185, 194, 197, 198, 201, 204.

[211] *Cal. S.P. Dom.* 1661–2, p. 202.
[212] Ibid. 1663–4, p. 188.
[213] Ibid. 115.
[214] *Pepys' Diary* (ed. 1880), ii, 396; *Diary of J. Evelyn* (ed. 1879), ii, 199, &c.
[215] *Cal. S.P. Dom.* 1667–8, p. 557.
[216] Stow, *Surv. of Lond.* (ed. Strype), iii, 152.
[217] *Wills from Doctors' Commons* (Camden Soc.), 122, 136.
[218] Lambeth MS. 670.
[219] *Statutes of Realm*, v, 673; vi, 15; vii, 205; viii, 173
[220] Lambeth MS. 670.
[221] Ibid. ix, 475.
[222] C. & S. Wren, *Parentalia*, 293.
[223] Dugdale, *Hist. of St. Paul's* (ed. Ellis), 174.
[224] Bede, *Eccl. Hist.* lib. viii, cap. iii.

Norman Conquest they had left such a condition so far behind them that they held the property of the cathedral apart from the bishop; and they had reached that considerably advanced stage in corporate existence which admits of common ownership.

The spurious Anglo-Saxon charters of the cathedral show the probable modification of their position to be traditional. That of King Ethelbert grants land to Mellitus 'to have and to hold that it may remain to the monastery of St. Paul for ever';[225] and Cnut's charter[226] reverts to this old form and confirms to Bishop Aelfwin the lands of St. Paul's. But the charters of Athelstan,[227] Edgar,[228] and Edward[229] the Confessor are addressed to the 'monastery.' Of the accredited charters that of Cnut[230] alludes to the possessions of the priests of the 'monastery'; and that of Edward[231] the Confessor bestows free tenure of their property on 'his priests in the church of Saint Paul.' Finally the Domesday Survey discovers that 'in the time of King Edward' the canons were tenants in chief of the king in seven places, while in thirteen they held of the bishop the lands of the cathedral.[232]

It is certain that in the end of the tenth century the church of St. Paul was served by a body of clergy who were able to hold property in common, and who derived their food from a common source. For there exists a grant of Queen Egelfleda to the 'monastery,' 'for the living of the brothers who there serve God.'[233] There is no evidence that the cathedral clergy ever lived in one building; from 1101 there occur mention of the separate houses of canons.[234] Ralph de Diceto qualifies the canons who procured the election of Anselm in 1136 as 'the domestic clergy of the dean,' 'whom he had with him at meals every day';[235] and hence there arises the supposition that at least some of the canons

had once such common meals as continued among the lesser clergy of the cathedral. It is possible that Ralph has ascribed to the year 1136 an earlier custom; his own constitutions cannot be understood to contemplate any such practice.

A charter of Edward the Confessor forbade the monastery of St. Paul to receive more priests than it could maintain.[236] This may have caused the limitation of the number of canons.

In the twelfth century the possessions of the cathedral consisted of the patrimony of St. Paul and the prebends. The manors which belonged to the first of these divisions were farmed by the chapter, and rendered yearly rents, in money and in kind, to the chamber, and the brewery and bakehouse, respectively. The produce provided for daily distributions of money, bread and ale to all the ministers of the church.[237] There are traces of a like two-fold division of property before the Norman invasion. The explicit grant of Queen Egelfleda makes it probable that some possessions of the church existed for other than common uses. It is stated in Domesday that, in the time of King Edward, the canons held land in three places 'for their living,'[238] while five canons are named who held of St. Paul's individually in 1086.[239] The prebendal system appears to have been established in the reign of William II.[240] Both he and Henry I granted free disposition of their prebends to the canons.[241]

In the most ancient portion of the cathedral archives there is a canonical rule which is almost

---

[225] Dugdale, *Hist. of St. Paul's*, 181.
[226] Ibid.
[227] Ibid.
[228] Ibid.
[229] Ibid.
[230] Kemble, *Codex Dipl.* 1319.
[231] Ibid. 387.
[232] The canons were tenants in chief before the Conquest in Essex, in Chingford, Belchamp St. Paul's, Wickham St. Paul's, and the manor of Aedulvesnesa which lay in Kirby le Soken, Thorpe le Soken, and Walton on the Naze; in Hertfordshire, in Ardeley, Luffenhall in Ardeley parish, and Sandon. They were tenants of the bishop in Twyford, Harlesden, Tottenham, the parish of St. Pancras, Islington, Stoke Newington, Staines, Drayton, Rugmere (the later name of a prebend whose corps lay in the parish of St. Pancras), and Willesden; and as such had two and a half hides in Stepney and ten cottars 'at the gate of the bishop.' The manor of Fulham is entered in Domesday among the lands held of the bishop, but is stated to be an ancient possession of the canons held by them of the king (*Dom. Bk.* ii, 126; i, 127 & 136).
[233] Kemble, *Codex Dipl.* 1222.
[234] *Hist. MSS. Com. Rep.* ix, App. i, 26.
[235] R. de Diceto, *Hist.* (Rolls Ser.), i, 248–9.

[236] Kemble, *Codex Dipl.* 887.
[237] *Dom. Bk. of St. Paul's* (ed. W. H. Hale), Introd.
[238] Two and a half hides in Stepney, and the manors of Willesden and Fulham, v. *Dom. Bk.* i, 127.
[239] In Stepney, in two holdings in Twyford, in Rugmere, and in St. Pancras, v. *Dom. Bk.* ii, 9.
[240] In addition to their ancient possessions the canons held in chief, in 1086, in Caddington in Bedfordshire, in Caddington and Kensworth in Hertfordshire, in Barnes in Surrey, and in Leigh and Norton Mandeville and two manors of Navestock in Essex. They held Wanstead in Essex of the bishop (v. *Dom. Bk.* i, 211; ii, 12b; i, 136, 34; ii, 9). The manors of Islington, Harlesden, Hoxton, Newington, St. Pancras, Rugmere, Tottenham, Willesden, Aedulvesnesa, and Tillingham must have become wholly or partially prebendal. Other property assigned to prebends lay in Shoreditch, and in the parishes of St. Andrew Holborn, and St. Giles without Cripplegate (Newcourt, *Repert.* i, 65, 169, 183). The prebend of Chiswick may not have been formed until after the acquisition of the manor of Sutton in the parish of Chiswick before 1181 (*Dom. Bk. of St. Paul's* [ed. W. H. Hale], 100–21). The names of twenty-eight of the prebends have not varied from 1291 until the present day, if it be accepted that Halliwell is the older name of the prebend called Finsbury or Halliwell (*Pope Nich. Tax.* [Rec. Com.], 362 and 19b, and App. 1 to *Reg. S. Pauli* [ed. W. S. Simpson]). The prebends of Caddington Major and Caddington Minor are not mentioned in the 'Taxatio' of Pope Nicholas, although Le Neve asserts that they existed in 1103 (*Fasti Eccl. Angl.*). They were certainly formed before 1322 (*Cal. of Pat.* 1321–4, p. 222).
[241] *Hist. MSS. Com. Rep.* ix, App. i, 60.

entirely taken from the 'Regula' of St. Chrodogang.[242] It enjoins virtue, dignity of bearing, and due discharge of services in the cathedral and obedience to prelates in the chapter. Whenever it was adopted, perhaps by a continental bishop of the eleventh century, it shows the constitution of the clergy to have been fairly complete, and to have approximated to the mediaeval institute of secular canons. It accords, however, a real pre-eminence in the cathedral to the bishop; while the lack of any allusion to the dean, in this as in other early authorities, in connexion with the chapter and otherwise, goes to prove that his office, if it existed before the Conquest, can only have been that of a subordinate. The traditional history of St. Paul's describes its governing body as consisting originally of the bishop and thirty canons, and dates the foundation of the deanery two hundred years later than that of the cathedral.[243] Hence there have been attempts to argue that the co-operation of the dean was not essential to the chapter's capacity for action.[244]

Under the Norman kings there must have been much definition of the customs of the church and the classes of its clergy, of its offices and the functions of its chapter. Maurice, bishop of London, was a signatory of the 'Institutio' of Osmund,[245] and therefore it is probable that the model of Salisbury directly influenced the growth of St. Paul's. Two fresh developments must be ascribed to this period: the dean acquired the first place in the church; the practice of non-residence, to which there is no allusion in Osmund's 'Institutio,' came into existence.

Detailed information as to the state of the cathedral is first obtained from the story of the disputed election in 1136–8, together with the compilations of statutes which were made by the deans Ralph de Diceto, Henry of Cornhill, and Ralph Baldock. In this picture of the twelfth and thirteenth centuries there are traces of the original position of St. Paul's, that of the church of the bishop and the central church of the diocese;[246] but

it shows it to be actually the church of an exclusive body of clergy who owe to the bishop more respect than obedience.

St. Paul's claimed immunity from metropolitical visitations. Therefore Archbishop Boniface was not suffered to enter the cathedral until after a protracted struggle, and the arrival of a papal mandate. The memory of such real or fictitious privilege continued in the seventeenth century.[247] But the jurisdiction of the bishop over the cathedral, as a church within his diocese, was apparently not questioned. As bishop of London he visited St. Paul's and addressed admonitory letters to the chapter;[248] in this capacity he intervened both in the government of the church and in the management of her property.[249] In 1289, however, all prebends were declared free from episcopal as from archidiaconal jurisdiction.[250] The bishop's ancient and intimate relation to the cathedral resulted in the chapter's function of electing him. And probably because he thus derived his power from the clergy of St. Paul's they appear to have been regarded as its ultimate holders, as able to exercise it when his office was void. During a vacancy of the see of London Ralph de Diceto officiated in the place of the bishop at the coronation of Richard I.[251] Serious disputes were settled in 1262 by an agreement between Archbishop Boniface and the dean and chapter, that whenever there was no bishop of London the dean and chapter should choose two or three major canons, or one minor and one or two major, and that the archbishop should depute one of these to exercise episcopal jurisdiction during the vacancy. The deputy must take an oath of office before the archbishop, and another in the presence of the dean and chapter.[252] In 1273 the first arrangement was somewhat modified by Archbishop Robert Kilwardby, who determined the proportion of the profits and costs of the vacant see which fell to the dean and chapter.[253] Thus the canons received assured possession of a right which they still exercised in 1723.[254] It was confirmed to them in 1594 as the result of an investigation ordered by the lord treasurer.[255]

[242] *Reg. S. Pauli* (ed. W. S. Simpson), 38.

[243] MS. of D. & C. of St. Paul's, W. D. 6, fol. 16, 58.

[244] Ibid. fol. 16, 58.

[245] *Statutes of Linc. Cathedral* (ed. H. Bradshaw). 'Institutio' is signed by 'Martin' of London; Bishop Stubbs conjectures the name to be a clerical error.

[246] Some customs indicate the diocesan position of St. Paul's. At the third hour on Sunday no processions were suffered in lesser churches within the City and archdeaconries, but as many of the people as were able then assembled in the cathedral, and all were obliged to go to St. Paul's in procession, with the archdeacon and other members of their several archdeaconries, on the second, third, and fourth feast days in Pentecost week, respectively. (*Reg. S. Pauli*, [ed. W. S. Simpson], 79.) In 1393 Bishop Braybrook revived an ancient custom by which the parochial clergy repaired to St. Paul's on the days of the Conversion and Commemoration of St. Paul, and the Deposition and Translation of St. Earconwald, and joined in the procession of the choir. (*Hist. MSS. Com. Rep.* ix, App. i, 58.)

[247] v. *infra*.

[248] *Reg. S. Pauli* (ed. W. S. Simpson), 163, 167, 169, 271, 272, 281, 286, 317, 391, 393, and MSS. of D. & C. of St. Paul's, W. D. 22, fol. 69b, &c.

[249] *Reg. S. Pauli* (ed. W. S. Simpson), *passim*.

[250] Ibid. 89. An injunction of Bishop Gravesend in 1387 declared prebends free from all special jurisdiction; MSS. of D. & C. of St. Paul's, W. D. 6, fol. 10.

[251] R. de Diceto, *Hist.* (Rolls Ser.), ii, 69.

[252] Wilkins, *Concilia*, i, 758.

[253] Ibid. ii, 27.

[254] Lambeth MSS. Index to archiepiscopal registers; Wake, pt. i, fol. 48.

[255] Stow, *Surv. of Lond.* (ed. Strype), iii, 157.

The bishop was still in some degree an official of the cathedral. He nominated prebendaries and canons,[256] but he sent all whom he beneficed in St. Paul's, except the chaplain of his own chapel, to the dean and chapter for institution. He appointed the keeper of the Old Work,[257] but it was declared, when Ralph de Diceto was dean, that the supervision of both the old and the new parts of the building belonged to the dean and residents since they must chiefly bear the burden of repairs.[258] The bishop's right to sit in the chapter, mentioned as a matter of course in the early rule, appears to have been the subject of a dispute which ended in his defeat. Pope Alexander IV granted to him that, as a canon, he should enjoy the rights of canons, a concession which included participation in the chapter's property. It was revoked by a bull of Urban IV in 1262.[259]

The bishop held the most honourable place in the services and ritual of the church and chapter; as often as was possible he ministered at the high altar on great feasts.[260]

The province of the dean, who was next to the bishop in dignity,[261] was confined to the cathedral and its property. From William, in the beginning of the twelfth century, the deans were customarily canons.[262] Such qualification does not appear to have been essential, but Ralph de Diceto ruled that no dean should receive any portion of the offerings at obits, of the 'communia,' or of any pittances, except in so far as he was a prebendary or other dignitary of the cathedral.[263] A later declaration of the 'approved custom of the church,' by Simon Sudbury in 1368, asserts that a dean who was not a canon and prebendary could take no part in the business of the chapter beyond his duty of summoning and dismissing it.[264] It may be concluded that a non-resident dean was not a member of the ordinary chapter: and, therefore, that the existence of a dean who was not also a resident canon was a thing exceptional. A vacancy in the deanery was announced by the chapter to the bishop; but the canons, without episcopal licence, chose a candidate for the office, whom the bishop was obliged to confirm in the absence of canonical impediment.[265] The new dean swore that he would give canonical obedience to the bishop, and, further, took an oath of office which bound him to sit in his

place according to approved customs of the church, to guard the rights and liberties of the cathedral, to keep its possessions, and recover such of them as had been alienated. He received oaths of canonical obedience from major and minor canons in his own name and that of the chapter. In the presence of the resident brothers he installed the canons.[266] He nominated all who were to be ordained to benefices and dignities of the church, in the name of St. Paul he summoned the chancellor to his place.[267] He ruled over the souls of the ministers and beneficed clergy of the church; he alone could expel vicars from the choir, and might temporarily suspend the attendance of minor canons.[268] He presided over the chapter.[269] On lesser feasts he or his deputy said the office.[270]

There were thirty major canons in St. Paul's.[271] On their admission they swore to be faithful to the church, to render obedience to the dean and chapter, and, in so far as was legal, to guard the secrets of the chapter.[272] To each five psalms were allotted, which he must say every day in the church, and thus the whole psalter was daily recited. Every canon in succession served at the altar for one week, and then held the office of ebdomarius.[273] A prebend belonged to each, and, in addition, he received a daily allowance of bread and ale from the bakehouse and brewery of the cathedral, a pittance from the chamber,[274] and a proportion of the offerings at services. The thirty canons with the dean at their head formed the chapter.[275]

Such was evidently their theoretical position. But there came early into existence a regular body of non-resident canons who received the fruits of prebends almost as sinecurists. The practice was facilitated by the circumstance that each major canon had originally a vicar, who, in his absence, sat in his stall and took his part in the services of the church.[276] The cathedral endeavoured to enforce the performance of their duties on canons who were professedly resident, and to confine to them all participation in the offerings in the church. It became necessary to distinguish between resident and non-resident canons, and therefore to define the conditions of residence.

In the constitutions of Ralph de Diceto it is enacted that a canon who wishes to reside must

[256] *Reg. S. Pauli* (ed. W. S. Simpson), iii, 157.
[257] Ibid. 182.
[258] Ibid. 131.
[259] Lambeth MSS. 644, 57.
[260] *Reg. S. Pauli* (ed. W. S. Simpson), 11.
[261] Ibid. 13.
[262] *Hist. MSS. Com. Rep.* ix, App. i, 67.
[263] *Reg. S. Pauli* (ed. W. S. Simpson), 131.
[264] *Reg. S. Pauli* (ed. W. S. Simpson), 390.
[265] Ibid. 14.

[266] Ibid. 15.
[267] Ibid. 16.
[268] Ibid. 18, 19.
[269] Ibid. 16.
[270] Ibid. 17.
[271] Ibid. 23.
[272] Ibid. 26, 31.
[273] Ibid. 48, 24, 25.
[274] *Dom. Bk. of St. Paul's* (ed. W. Hale), 170.
[275] *Reg. S. Pauli* (ed. W. S. Simpson), 23.
[276] Ibid. 67.

profess such willingness before the dean and resident brothers in the quinzaine of certain feasts. With two clerks who are in holy orders, or about to enter them, and who have no other benefice, he must then take his place in the choir, and he must be present at canonical hours by day and by night. He may be absent for six days in the first quarter of the year, and, if he obtain the dean's leave, for three weeks and six days in the remaining three quarters. Longer absence disqualifies him for residence.[277] When William de St. Mere l'Eglise was bishop, it was further ordained that offerings made at processions should be distributed among brothers actually present at them,[278] and certain benefactors to the canons made a share in their favours conditional on personal attendance at services.[279]

An extensive and costly hospitality was incumbent on a canon in his first year of residence. He was obliged to entertain daily a number of the ministers and servants of the church; to make two great banquets to which he must invite the bishop, the major canons, the mayor, sheriffs, aldermen, and justices, and the great men of the court; and on the morrow of these to feast all the lesser clergy of the church.[280] Such hospitality was intended not only as a means of adding to the sustenance of the poorer servants of St. Paul's, and of preserving good feeling among the cathedral clergy, and between the cathedral, the City, and the court, but also for purposes of inspection.[281] The expense it involved came to be so disproportionate to the income of a major canon that its effect was to discourage residence.

A dwelling near the cathedral in which he was compelled to live was assigned to each resident canon.[282] Questions among them were decided by elected arbitrators.[283] There were statutes to regulate their conduct, their manners, their habit, and their tonsure.[284]

That the abuse of giving prebends to secular persons and children existed, is shown by an ordinance in the compilation of Baldock, that none shall for long be a canon, or have a voice in the elections, who is not in holy orders;[285] and by an appeal of Richard de Belmeis in 1136.[286] A canon did not invariably hold a prebend, for a regulation enjoins the dean or his deputy to assign to him a stall when he lacked such provision. In the further rule

that such canon has no part in the secret business of the chapter or in elections,[287] the ancient connexion between land ownership and political rights may probably be traced.

The other orders of clergy in St. Paul's were those of the minor canons, the vicars, and the chantry priests. The traditionary origin of the minor canons is prior to the Conquest.[288] They must be the subject of a reference, in 1162, to the 'prebendary clerks of the choir,' as distinct from the major canons.[289] In the time of Ralph de Diceto they were evidently an established institution.[290] The prebends of each consisted in a weekly allowance of 5d. from the chamberlain, with an additional 1d. on feast days, and certain other payments, notably from the manor of Sunbury; and in portions of bread and ale, called 'trencherbread' and 'welkyn.'[291] No record shows that the minor canons ever lived otherwise than in the separate lodgings near the cathedral, assigned to them by the dean and chapter. They were compelled to be in the church at canonical hours, by day and by night.[292] Every week two of them were deputed to help the ebdomarius.[293] They only could fill the offices of the cardinals.[294] Chantries, and such lesser dignities as those of the keeper of the Old or New Work, were frequently in their tenure.[295]

In the most ancient portion of the cathedral archives there is evidence of the existence of vicars. Each of them was appointed by the canon, who was his lord and to whose jurisdiction he was subject.[296] Yet they had some independence of status: they swore an oath of obedience and fealty to the dean and chapter;[297] in 1260 it was ruled that a vicar might not be removed from his place without cause, even at the death of his lord.[298]

The first chantry of St. Paul's was established by Dean Alard in the reign of Henry II;[299] the last by Robert Brokett in 1532.[300] In the intervening years constant foundations by gifts and bequests created a large body of clergy who formed an important class of the ministers of the cathedral. In a document among the cathedral archives it is stated that the

---

[277] Ibid. 125.
[278] Ibid. 183.
[279] Ibid. 35.
[280] Ibid. 125–9, 131.
[281] Ibid. 126.
[282] Ibid. 126, 128.
[283] Ibid. 31.
[284] Ibid. 28.
[285] Ibid. 19.
[286] R. de Diceto, *Hist.* (Rolls Ser.), i, 250.

[287] *Reg. S. Pauli* (ed. W. S. Simpson), 27.
[288] MSS. of D. & C. of St. Paul's, A. Box 73, 1908; Harl. MS. 980, fol. 179a.
[289] *Hist. MSS. Com. Rep.* ix, App. i, 12.
[290] *Reg. S. Pauli* (ed. W. S. Simpson), 127, 131, 133.
[291] Wilkins, *Concilia*, iii, 134; MSS. of D. & C. of St. Paul's, W. D. 2, fol. 91.
[292] *Reg. S. Pauli* (ed. W. S. Simpson), 102.
[293] Ibid. 11.
[294] Harl. MSS. 980, fol. 179a.
[295] *Hist. MSS. Com. Rep.* ix, App. i, 26; *Arch.* xliii, 199; MSS. of D. & C. of St. Paul's, A. Box 74, 1952; Box 75, 1959.
[296] *Reg. S. Pauli* (ed. W. S. Simpson), 18, 108.
[297] Ibid. 19.
[298] Ibid. 67.
[299] Dugdale, *Hist. of St. Paul's*, 24.
[300] Sharpe, *Cal. of Wills*, ii, 637.

rank of the chantry priests is more honourable than that of the vicars, and that, while they were not of the number which must chiefly be supported from the patrimony of St. Paul's, yet the church had in part taken them into her care, and therefore they must render help to her higher ministers.[301] Their duties, as determined by the terms on which their respective chantries had been founded, often included attendance at some rites of the cathedral; suit of the choir, or presence at certain hours.[302] They were in many cases explicitly subjected to the jurisdiction of the dean and chapter.[303] The property and advowsons of chantries were variously bestowed by the founders, frequently on the dean and chapter, and conditionally, in all cases, on the payment of chaplains or a chaplain,[304] who might have the custody of the endowment.[305] From one to four priests were as a rule assigned to a chantry.[306]

The chapter tended to be an exclusive body. The constitutions of Ralph de Diceto enact that a new resident may take no part in its business without a special summons from the dean;[307] both he and Henry de Cornhill state that the non-residents intervene only in arduous business.[308] Besides its functions of electing the bishop and the dean, the chapter represented the cathedral in all its external relations, and therefore held and administered property.[309] By approved custom and prerogative the dean and canons could not meet before the bishop except as the chapter, unless they had been summoned with such an intention.[310] Ordinances and declarations of practice were issued by the dean and chapter. They had the general supervision of the finance of the cathedral; and they examined and judged major canons before the dean could punish them.[311] All the ministers of the church attended the chapter held every[312] Saturday for the correction of offenders.

The great officers of St. Paul's were the archdeacon, the treasurer, the precentor, and the chancellor; and

were chosen from among the major canons.[313] Of these the most dignified were the four archdeacons of London, Essex, Middlesex, and Colchester, whose connexion with the cathedral can be traced from the beginning of the twelfth century,[314] and is probably more ancient. Their position shows the relation of St. Paul's to the see of London. Except as the most dignified of the canons after the dean,[315] they were officers not of the cathedral, but of the diocese.

The agent of the chapter, where money transactions with outside persons and communities were concerned, was the treasurer.[316] But the treasurer's financial function was not more important than his duty as the keeper of treasures, ornaments, service books, and vestments of the cathedral.[317] In this respect he had a deputy in the sacrist.[318] According to Dugdale and Le Neve the dignity of treasurer was founded in 1160 by Bishop Richard de Beames, who annexed to it the churches of Sudminster, Aldbury, Pelham Furneaux, and Pelham Sarners.[319] The cathedral had a sacrist in 1162.[320] Both officers were bound to the dean and chapter by oaths of faithful service.[321] The vergers, whose number appears to have varied from three to four, were paid by the treasurer, and presented to the dean and chapter by the sacrist, to whom they were subject.[322] In 1282 it was ordained that they should deliver their virges, their emblems of office, to the dean on every Michaelmas Day, and receive them back or not according to their deserts.[323]

In the department of internal finance, the chief officers were the chamberlain, the keepers of the bakehouse and the brewery, the keepers of the Old and New Work, and the almoner. Ralph de Diceto ordained that every month the chamber, the bakehouse, and the fabric of the cathedral should be inspected, and their accounts entered in the roll of the treasury, together with the rents from obits.[324]

The chamberlain received money payments from the farms and other sources; and paid stipends and pittances to the ministers of the church. He was responsible for the lights of the cathedral. Quarterly

---

[301] MSS. of D. & C. of St. Paul's, W. D. v, fol. 66.

[302] Ibid. A. Box 49 (209), Box 74 (1940), Box 75 (1969).

[303] Ibid. A. Box 74 (1941, 1920, 1952), Box 75 (1959, 1957); Lond. Epis. Reg. Stokesley, fol. 95 or 124.

[304] MSS. of D. & C. of St. Paul's, A. Box 74 (1920, 1952, 1917, 1928, 1933), Box 34 (169) (49).

[305] Ibid. A. Box 74 (1928), &c.

[306] Arch. lii, 148. There were seven priests in Holmes College (v. infra).

[307] Reg. S. Pauli (ed. W. S. Simpson), 129.

[308] Ibid. 130, 132.

[309] Ibid. 17, 18, 30.

[310] Ibid. 18.

[311] Ibid. 9, 65, 134, &c.; v. 19.

[312] The Saturday chapter was apparently still acknowledged as statutory in 1724, but may have been held irregularly, for at this date there was a proposition to discontinue it. In 1869 it was revived. Reg. S. Pauli (ed. W. S. Simpson), 206; Add. MS. 34263, fol. 31, Suppl. to Reg. S. Pauli, 14.

[313] Reg. S. Pauli (ed. W. S. Simpson), 26.

[314] Hist. MSS. Com. Rep, ix, App. i, 58. The archdeacon of St. Albans, whose office was founded in 1550, had no place in the chapter nor stall in the choir (G. C. Le Neve, Fasti (ed 1716), 198).

[315] Reg. S. Pauli (ed. W. S. Simpson), 20.

[316] Hist. MSS. Com. Rep. ix, App. i, 32, &c.

[317] Reg. S. Pauli (ed. W. S. Simpson), 21.

[318] Ibid. 21.

[319] Dugdale, Hist. of St. Paul's, 9; Le Neve, Fasti (ed. 1716), 201.

[320] Hist. MSS. Com. Rep. ix, App. i, 12.

[321] Reg. S. Pauli (ed. W. S. Simpson), 21, 124.

[322] Ibid. 72, 124.

[323] Ibid. 91.

[324] Ibid. 132.

accounts and immediate reports of any deficit in due payments were rendered by him to the dean and chapter. A resident canon was specially deputed for his supervision.[325]

The bakehouse and brewery were superintended by their keeper or keepers, who saw to it that rightful payments in kind were made by the farms, and who distributed portions of bread and ale to the ministers.[326] In disposing of surplus produce a preference was given to ecclesiastical over lay persons.[327]

The care of the building of St. Paul's belonged to the keepers of the Old and New Work who received and spent contributions to this end. The keeper of the New Work was bound to the dean and chapter by an oath of faithful service.[328]

The duties of the cathedral almoner fall into two divisions. He must distribute alms in the manner prescribed by those who conferred bequests and donations on the almonry, and bury poor men and beggars who died within the churchyard. Secondly, he superintended the education, general and specially connected with the ministry, of a number of boys, eventually eight, who were called the almoner's boys, and helped in the services of the choir and attended to the lights of the church.[329]

The office of almoner is first mentioned in the beginning of the twelfth century. Then Henry of Northampton granted to it the tithes of St. Pancras, which belonged to his prebend, and his house in Paternoster Row for a hospital for the poor.[330] The second function of the almoner probably originated in the will of Bishop Richard Newport, who left certain property to the almoner that he might, according to the judgement of the chapter, provide for the sustenance of one or two boys.[331] He was under an oath of obedience to the dean and chapter.[332]

The office of the precentor was next to that of the treasurer in dignity.[333] It existed in 1104, and probably in yet earlier times. But it was not endowed until the year 1204, when King John granted to it the church of Shoreditch. The precentor presided over the choir. From at least the thirteenth century he had a deputy in the succentor.[334] In Baldock's time another officer, the master of the school of song, was also subject to him.[335] The choir was further supervised by the junior and the senior cardinals whose offices are said to have originated at a remote date, and who received the profits of private funerals and anniversaries, and a portion of ale and bread double that which was allotted to other minor canons.[336]

The sphere of the chancellor, unlike those of the dean, the treasurer and the precentor, was not confined to the cathedral. In so far as his most ancient function was concerned, he was an officer of the City. At least in the reign of Henry I the master of the schools was a dignitary of St. Paul's;[337] between the years 1184 and 1214 he came to be called chancellor.[338] In the beginning of the fourteenth century the chancellor presided over all the teachers of grammar in London, and over all City scholars except those of St. Mary le Bow and St. Martin le Grand. He also presented the master of the cathedral school to the dean and chapter, and had charge of the school books and buildings.[339] He examined in the schools clerks of inferior degree who were candidates for ordination; and at his discretion presented them to the bishop. Within the cathedral he held a position in relation to the non-musical part of the service analogous to that of the precentor in the choir.[340] The lesser cathedral clergy were in his jurisdiction, and he could inflict on them punishments short of expulsion.[341] He was the chief secretary of the cathedral and the keeper of the chapter's seal.[342]

In the time of Ralph de Diceto there was a binder of books,[343] and in 1283 a writer of books[344] among the ministers of St. Paul's. By the beginning of the next century the two offices were combined in one person,[345] and thus they survived until the days of Colet.[346] A reference which seems to belong to the deanery of Baldock is to twelve scribes who were bound by an oath to be faithful to the cathedral, the

[325] Ibid. 74, 128, 30.

[326] Ibid. 75.

[327] In 1150 a major canon was keeper of the brewery (*Reg. S. Pauli* [ed. W. S. Simpson], 173); in the time of Baldock the chapter deputed certain residents to superintend the bakehouse successively (ibid. 30); in the sixteenth century it was unlawful for a resident canon to be keeper of the bakehouse, but a resident was set over the keeper (ibid. 245, 277). The name of this office may therefore have been variously applied to that of the chief baker and that of his supervisor.

[328] Ibid. 77, 100, 131.

[329] Harl. MS. 7041, fol. 22.

[330] *Reg. Eleemos. D. S. Pauli* (ed. M. Hackett), fol. 5.

[331] Ibid. fol. 38.

[332] *Reg. S. Pauli* (ed. W. S. Simpson), 76.

[333] Ibid. 13.

[334] *Reg. S. Pauli* (ed. W. S. Simpson), 50. The church of Shoreditch was eventually alienated from the precentor and conferred on the archdeacon of London (Newcourt, *Repert.* i, 96).

[335] *Reg. S. Pauli* (ed. W. S. Simpson), 22.

[336] Ibid. 326. Harl. MS. 890, fol. 179a.

[337] *Hist. MSS. Com. Rep.* ix, App. i, 29.

[338] Le Neve, *Fasti* (ed. 1716), 204.

[339] Newcourt, *Repert.* 108–10; *Reg. S. Pauli* (ed. W. S. Simpson), 226, 78.

[340] *Reg. S. Pauli* (ed. W. S. Simpson), 23, 49.

[341] Ibid. 18.

[342] Ibid. 326.

[343] Ibid. 133.

[344] Ibid. 173.

[345] Ibid. 13.

[346] Ibid. 227.

dean, and the chapter, and to write without fraud or malice.[347]

In a list of salaries which dates from the fourteenth century, there is an entry of the payment of twelve pence for the making of a chronicle; and the 'keeper of the clock' is mentioned as a servant of the church.[348]

The rites of the cathedral[349] and of churches dependent on it anciently followed a peculiar form known as the 'Usus Sancti Pauli.'[350] Services analogous to those held in chantries, and frequently instituted for the eternal welfare of the same persons, were the obits. There is a record of a bequest by Canon Ralph for the endowment of such a service in 1162;[351] in the reign of Richard II 116 obits were celebrated every year. The founders dictated the proportions of their bequests which should be spent on payments to a greater or less number of the clergy and servants of the cathedral; and, sometimes, on contribution to the lights of the church and its fabric.[352] Other services were maintained by gilds connected with St. Paul's. In 1197 Ralph de Diceto founded a Brotherhood of the Benefices of the Church of St. Paul. It included clerks not in priests' orders, and it met yearly to pray with all solemnity for dead brothers.[353] In that it afforded to the clergy connected with the cathedral a means of union and exclusiveness, it must have had importance. The gild of St. Anne, in the person of its twelve wardens, obtained from the dean and chapter, in 1271, free use and disposition of the chapel of St. Anne in the crypt.[354]

In the fourteenth and fifteenth centuries the church of St. Paul was frequently censured for the immorality, the avarice, and the negligence of ministers. In part this is due to the critical spirit of the age; in part, also, to the frequent papal provision of benefices, to the very prevalent custom of plurality, and to the abuse of nonresidence. Complaints of the lack of discipline, of the irreverence, and of the frequent absence from the choir of the greater and lesser clergy, provoked an exhortation from Bishop Gravesend. In a commission to Bishop Sudbury, Edward III declared St. Paul's to be destitute of all good rule.[355] The period of codification naturally preceded a period of needed reforms, which began in the end of the thirteenth century and lasted for several hundreds of years. An attempt to improve the intellectual state of the clergy is indicated by an appointment, made by the dean and chapter in 1281, of a certain 'proved theologian and gracious preacher' to rule over their school in theology for a year, and to preach at opportune times.[356] Bishop Gravesend made a more permanent provision; he ordained that the chancellor must sustain the charge of the lecture of theology, and must be a master or bachelor of this faculty before his first year of office had elapsed. At the same time the church of Ealing was appropriated to the chancellorship. In 1308 this ordinance was confirmed by Ralph Baldock.[357] The office of sub-dean was instituted by Ralph in 1295: it was tenable by a minor canon appointed by the dean, who was invested with the dean's authority in relation to the inferior clergy of the cathedral.[358] Between the years 1300 and 1450 three classes of measures deal with the question of residence: those which aimed at enforcing the performance of their duties on resident canons, those which were designed to increase the number of residents, and those which endeavoured to safeguard the participation of non-residents in the church property. The regulations of Diceto in this matter were more stringent than those of Baldock. The latter exacted a 'moderate assiduity of attendance in the church,' saving in the case of illness or urgent business. Further,

> if any be so wise that he is fitted for the great affairs of the church, let him hold himself in readiness, and he will be understood to serve the church, although he be not assiduous at hours.[359]

Such a privilege was liable to wide interpretation. In 1311 and 1312 the king intimated to the dean that certain canons who were absent beyond seas on business which touched the king, the kingdom and the church, should be considered as 'resident.'[360] The injunctions of Bishop Robert Braybrook, issued with the consent of Dean Thomas Evrere, repeated the regulations[361] of Ralph de Diceto. They resulted in a controversy between the dean and the residents; both parties submitted to the king's arbitration, and he commanded that, under

[347] Ibid. 78.

[348] MSS. of D. and C. of St. Paul's, D. 2, fol. 91.

[349] A curious service was held on Innocents' Day, when the office was conducted by a boy bishop and by boy ministrants, who corresponded to the dignitaries and clergy of the cathedral (Harl. MS. 7041, fol. 21). Another and stranger survived until the reign of Elizabeth. In 1302 Sir Walter le Band, in consideration of a grant of land in Leigh, made by the canons to his father, bound himself that he and his heirs should, at the hour of the procession, deliver to the canons in the cathedral a doe on the day of the Conversion of St. Paul, and a fat buck on the feast of St. Paul's Commemoration. The ceremony was duly performed with much solemnity (Dugdale, *Hist. of St. Paul's*, 16).

[350] Dugdale, *Hist. of St. Paul's*, 22.

[351] *Hist. MSS. Com. Rep.* ix, App. i, 12.

[352] *Doc. Illus. Hist. of St. Paul's* (ed. W. S. Simpson), 61–106.

[353] *Reg. S. Pauli* (ed. W. S. Simpson), 63.

[354] *Hist. MSS. Com. Rep.* ix, App. i, 27.

[355] *Reg. S. Pauli* (ed. W. S. Simpson), 105.

[356] Ibid. 88.

[357] Lond. Epis. Reg. Baldock and Gravesend, fol. 17, 19.

[358] *Reg. S. Pauli* (ed. W. S. Simpson), 94.

[359] Ibid. 34.

[360] *Cal. of Close*, 1307–13, pp. 357, 419.

[361] *Reg. S. Pauli* (ed. W. S. Simpson), 151.

penalty of £4,000, residence should be according to the form of the church of Salisbury.[362] But no settlement was reached, for in 1433 Bishop Robert Fitz Hugh, desiring 'to still all divisions and discords,' ordered that a resident canon should be present in the church at one canonical hour every day except during his legitimate period of absence, and on all great feasts.[363] Bishop Robert Gilbert, in 1442, defined such period as that between the feast of the Relics and the feast of the translation of St. Edward, king and confessor. He forbade resident canons to let their official houses to any lay persons without leave from the bishop, the dean and the chapter.[364]

A bull of Boniface IX in 1392 stated that hardly five canons resided in the church of St. Paul, and ascribed the circumstance to the extravagant hospitality incumbent on a canon in his first year of residence, which commonly cost from 700 to 1,000 marks sterling. The pope therefore ruled that a canon's oath to observe the customs of the church did not apply to his duties as a host, and that instead of discharging them he should pay 300 marks for the use of the church.[365] But the ancient practice continued, for it is a subject of complaint in a letter from the king to Robert Braybrook in 1399, in which it is asserted that the incomes of only two or three prebends sufficed for its observance.[366] The bishop thereupon ordered that the expenses of a canon's first year of residence should not exceed 300 marks.[367] In a bull of Martin V, in 1417, it is declared that this sum cannot be provided from the revenue of any prebend for ten or twelve years; the limit is reduced therefore to 100 marks; and the pope concedes, at the instance of the minor canons, that the money be shared, in part, by the lesser cathedral clergy, and in part spent on the fabric, the ornaments, and the books of the church.[368]

The non-resident canons were frequently the king's nominees. Edward III says of them that many are his 'familiar friends.'[369] Hence kings endeavoured to protect their interests. In the commission of 1370 Edward III complains that the resident canons have diverted the treasures of the cathedral to their private uses, and that they absorb the daily allowance of the non-resident canons and of the lesser ministers.[370] In like manner Richard II wrote to Bishop Braybrook that, in contradiction

to the pious intentions of founders, a few residents received all the emoluments of prebendaries, and the bread and ale intended for non-residents.[371] The case was tried at the bishop's court in the deanery of Reginald Kentwood, and judgement was given for the non residents on the score that they, as much as other canons, swore observance of the statutes of the cathedral.[372]

In the latter half of the fourteenth century the efforts for reform had a significant expression in the formation of various corporations in connexion with St. Paul's. The movement appears to have been due consciously to a literal faith in the virtue which emanated from a gathering of 'two or three.'[373] In 1352 a gild of St. Katherine was formed to keep one wax light burning in St. Katherine's Chapel. In 1362 the brothers and sisters agreed to maintain a chantry priest who should celebrate in the chapel for all faithful departed. This gild had, in 1389, two wardens who were citizens of London.[374] The brotherhood of All Souls was founded, in 1379, for the maintenance of the chapel over the charnel-house,[375] in which it had its centre, and the care of which had lately been urged in a sermon by the archbishop of Canterbury. It existed in 1389, but does not appear to have been careful of the charnel-house.[376]

But more important than these were the more or less developed corporations which were formed among the inferior clergy of the cathedral, and whose origin must in great part be ascribed to the influence of Robert Braybrook.

In 1353 Robert of Kingston, a minor canon, bequeathed his hall in Pardonchurchhaugh, with the adjoining houses, to his brothers, that they might have a common hall in which to take food together.[377] The minor canons seem to have been aroused at once to much activity of corporate existence. They obtained a charter from Dean Richard of Kilmington in 1356, which stated that they excelled all other chaplains in name and honour,

---

[362] *Cal. of Pat.* 1399–1401, p. 121.

[363] *Reg. S. Pauli* (ed. W. S. Simpson), 258.

[364] Lond. Epis. Reg. Kemp. pt. ii, fol. 24.

[365] *Reg. S. Pauli* (ed. W. S. Simpson), 197.

[366] Cott. MS. Julian, F. x, fol. 6.

[367] *Reg. S. Pauli* (ed. W. S. Simpson), 151.

[368] Ibid. 200.

[369] Ibid. 196.

[370] Ibid. 196.

[371] Cott. MS. Julian, F. x, fol. 6.

[372] MSS. of D. and C. of St. Paul's, D. 6, fol. 16.

[373] MSS. of D. and C. of St. Paul's, *passim*.

[374] Cert. of Gilds (P.R.O.), Chanc. No. 20.

[375] This chapel was dedicated to the Virgin, and stood over a vault in the churchyard in which many bones of the dead had been piled. It was rebuilt shortly before 1276, when Roger Beyvin and others founded in it a chantry of one priest. The revenue of the chapel was so diminished in 1430 that divine service was no longer held in it. It received a new endowment in this year from Jenkyn Carpenter, an executor of Richard Whittington, and a chantry of one priest was once more established in it, that there might be prayers for the souls of the departed, and especially for those of Roger Beyvin and Richard Whittington (Dugdale, *Hist. of St. Paul's*, 126, 274; *Cal. of Wills proved in Ct. of Hustings*, i, 29, 42).

[376] Cert. of Gilds (P.R.O.), Chanc. No. 209*b*; Seymour, *Surv. of Lond.* i, 650.

[377] *Reg. S. Pauli* (ed. W. S. Simpson), 322.

and that they were able to officiate in the place of major canons at the great altar and the choir.[378] It was confirmed by Bishop Simon Sudbury, and in 1373 by a bull of Urban VI.[379] Finally they acquired a charter of incorporation from Richard II in 1395–6, and in the same year they 'gathered together in the common hall of their college' and defined the rules and customs which bound them. By the king's charter they received the title of the College of the Twelve Minor Canons in the Church of St. Paul in London. It was ordained that one of them should be set over the others as warden, and that he, with the college, should constitute a legal person.[380] Bishop Braybrook ruled that henceforth the minor canons must take food in their new hall at due hours in common, 'for the increase of the fervour of their devotion and charity;' and imposed on them a penalty of £300 if they should fail to fulfil their promise of keeping the statutes and ordinances of their college. The bishop of London was constituted their visitor.[381]

Several colleges took form almost contemporaneously among the chantry priests. A dwelling for the chaplain or chaplains was often part of the endowment of a charity.[382] Before 1318 a piece of land in the churchyard was assigned to the chantry priests,[383] and lodgings situated on it and called 'chambers' might thenceforth be granted to the holders of chantries, by donors or legators, or by the dean and chapter.[384] Thus a number of chantry priests came to live in the building variously known as the 'Presteshouses' and St. Peter's College.[385] These chaplains were compelled personally to inhabit the separate chambers allotted to each; and always, or usually, to keep such in repair at their own cost.[386] In 1391 Bishop Robert Braybrook ordered that all chantry priests, who belonged to no other college of the cathedral and who were bound to give suit to the choir, should take their food in the hall of the 'Presteshous' and that the dean and chapter should allot chambers to as many of them as possible.[387] By this measure the corporate life of the chaplains must have been stimulated and defined. Their technical position, however, remained that of a congregation of individuals; in 1424 they had no common seal.[388] Their property was probably regarded as being vested

for their use in the dean and chapter. Yet individual priests paid rents to the body of the chaplains;[389] their college had statutes which they were bound to observe.[390] In a compilation by Colet it is stated that the chantry priests of the College of St. Peter's must obey their proctor. If this official was, as his name implies, representative, a considerable development of corporate life is indicated.

Of the 'other colleges,' to which Braybrook alludes, Holmes' College was the most considerable. Adam of Bury, once mayor of London, built a chapel of the Holy Ghost near the north door of St. Paul's, and by the terms of his will a chantry was founded there for three priests.[391] As a site for their residence the dean and chapter assigned land, in 1386, to Roger Holmes, an executor of Adam and a canon of the cathedral.[392] He had contributed to the cost of erecting the chapel, and by his testamentary dispositions the number of priests who celebrated in it was increased to seven.[393] These formed Holmes' College, the object of frequent bequests. Certain statutes, made by Roger with the consent of the bishop, the dean and the chapter, enacted that every member of the college must swear to be faithful to the community and to keep the secrets of its hall; that the seven priests should choose yearly one of their number to preside over the others; and that each should subscribe a fixed sum for the maintenance of their common meals.[394] Holmes' College does not appear ever to have received a charter of incorporation.

The triumph of the house of Lancaster was celebrated by the building of a chapel, by John of Gaunt's executors, at his tomb, and that of the Duchess Blanche in St. Paul's. In 1403 a chantry of priests was founded in the new chapel;[395] and Bishop Braybrook granted a piece of land which had belonged to his old palace for the provision of a dwelling for the chaplains. The dean and chapter were empowered to compel them to lodge and to partake of common meals in the house which came to be known as 'Lancaster College.'[396]

Within the cloister in Pardonchurchhaugh Gilbert Becket erected a chapel in which he was buried.[397] It was rebuilt by Thomas More, clerk, who received a licence to found in it a chantry of three priests.[398] More's intentions were, however, fulfilled only

[378] Ibid. 323.
[379] Wilkins, *Conc.* iii, 134.
[380] *Arch.* lxiii, 183 et seq.
[381] Lond. Epis. Reg. Braybrook, fol. 34.
[382] MSS. of D. and C. of St. Paul's, A. Box 74, 1934, &c.
[383] Ibid. A. Box 74, 1918.
[384] Ibid. A. Box 74, 1922, 1938, 1950; *Cal. of Wills proved in Ct. of Hustings*, i, 184, ii; 539, 637.
[385] MSS. of D. and C. of St. Paul's, A. Box 75, 1960.
[386] Ibid. A. Box 74, 1938, 1950.
[387] *Reg. S. Pauli* (ed. W. S. Simpson), 149.
[388] MSS. of D. and C. of St. Paul's, A. Box 75, 1960.

[389] Ibid. A. Box 74, 1950; Box 75, 1960.
[390] *Arch.* lii, 174.
[391] Sharpe, *Cal. of Wills*, ii, 254.
[392] *Hist. MSS. Com. Rep.* ix, App. i, 28.
[393] *Cal. of Wills proved in Ct. of Hustings*, ii, 254.
[394] MSS. of D. and C. A. Box 75, 1998.
[395] *Cal of Pat.* 1401–5, p. 214.
[396] MSS. of D. and C. of St. Paul's, A. Box 74, 1941.
[397] Dugdale, *Hist. of St. Paul's*, 181.
[398] *Cal. of Pat.* 1422–9, p. 179.

by his executors. They obtained both a similiar licence in 1424, and a grant that 'the chaplains of the chantry of St. Anne and St. Thomas the Martyr' should form a corporation and have a common seal. These chaplains were made capable of acquiring property, but only on condition that they rendered it to the dean and chapter, who must hold it on their behalf and pay a yearly rent to each.[399] The dean and chapter and the thirty-two chantry priests of the 'Presteshouses' assigned to the three chaplains a dwelling in the 'Presteshouses.'[400] In the year 1427 a bequest increased their number to four.[401]

The chantry priests of St. Paul's seem to have been remarkable, even in the most secular period of the church's history, for neglect of their obligations.[402] An early attempt to introduce discipline among them must have taken form in an effort to enforce their attendance on the choir; for, in 1325, Sir Henry of Bray formally protested that such suit on his part had been not the fulfilment of a duty but an act of grace.[403] The chantries of the cathedral provided an outlet for priests who sought to escape the duties of other benefices. Thus Chaucer says of his good parson, that

> He sette *not* his benefice to hire
> And lefte his shepe accombred in the mire,
> And ran to London, unto Seint Poules,
> To seken him a chaunterie for soules.[404]

But the fault lay in some degree with the slight, often diminished, endowments of many chantries, insufficient to provide a living for a man, while the duties attached to them were in many cases enough to occupy all a man's care.[405] In 1391, therefore, Bishop Braybrook united such a number of chantries as to reduce their whole number by thirty-two; and ordained that henceforth no beneficed clergy might hold chantries in St. Paul's.[406] He exhorted all chaplains to fulfil the ordinances by which their places had been founded, and framed new regulations for the priests of united chantries. In virtue of these they were, before the admission, examined as to their fitness for the choir, to which an oath bound them to give suit.[407] In 1408 Bishop Clifford united four chantries into one.[408]

The number of vicars tended to diminish; lay and unfit persons were admitted among them. A

regulation of the year 1290,[409] and others which occur in the compilations of Baldock and Lisieux,[410] order that they consist of deacons and sub-deacons in equal proportion, that their number be increased, that they be persons of moral life able to sing in the choir. In 1332 an injunction exhorted them to seemliness of conduct and habit.[411] They gained some additional independence in this period. In 1313 they were declared to be themselves responsible for their absences from the cathedral.[412] Dean Geoffrey de Lucy granted that each vicar should, while he was duly present at hours, receive from the church a penny a day;[413] and the sum was increased by Dean Henry Borham.[414] With the consent of the chapter Bishop Braybrook appropriated to them the church of Bunstead, and five marks from the revenues of the church of Finchingfield.[415] The vicars never formed a technical corporation: in later times they used the seal of the dean and chapter, or severally signed with their individual seals.[416] They had a common hall in which they were compelled to take their food, unless they were invited elsewhere.[417]

The tendency to uniformity brought a disposition to follow the Sarum Use in the churches of St. Paul's, an innovation which was jealously resisted by the dean and chapter. In 1375 the dean did his utmost that the ancient rite of his cathedral might be preserved in the church of St. Giles Cripplegate.[418] Yet by the beginning of the fifteenth century the more universal form was generally used in the chantries of St. Paul.[419] In 1414 Bishop Clifford ordered that the Use of Sarum should be followed in the choir.[420]

The movement towards reform from within continued in the fifteenth century. The practice of diverting the property of the cathedral to the private uses of the resident canons was well established, and hence there were remedial ordinances of Bishops Savage,[421] Warham,[422] and Fitz James.[423] Warham's statute, which Fitz James confirmed, annulled all allocations of land, rents, and profits, and instituted a new officer in the general receiver. Bishop Warham also ruled that four major canons must be present in

[399] MS. of D. and C. A. Box 74, 1933.
[400] Ibid. A. Box 75, 1960.
[401] Sharpe, *Cal. of Wills*, ii, 467.
[402] *Reg. S. Pauli* (ed. W. S. Simpson.) Bk. ii, 3, *Ann. Lond.* (Rolls Ser.) 224; MS. of D. and C. A. Box 75, 1969.
[403] MS. of D. and C. of St. Paul's, A. Box 74; A. Box 73, 1908.
[404] *Prologue*, lines 509–14.
[405] *Reg. S. Pauli* (ed. W. S. Simpson), 150.
[406] Cf. lists of chantries in fourteenth cent. and temp. Edw. VI, *Arch.* lii, 168 and 178.
[407] *Reg. S. Pauli* (ed. W. S. Simpson), 150.
[408] Lond. Epis. Reg. Walden, fol. 7.

[409] *Reg. S. Pauli* (ed. W. S. Simpson), 84.
[410] *Reg. S. Pauli* (ed. W. S. Simpson), 67, 84.
[411] Ibid. 103.
[412] Ibid. 67.
[413] Ibid. 186.
[414] MS. of D. and C. of St. Paul's, W. D. 2, fol. 91.
[415] Lond Epis. Reg. Braybrook, fol. 395.
[416] MS. of D. and C. of St. Paul's, A. Box 11, 1100.
[417] *Reg. S. Pauli* (ed. W. S. Simpson), 67.
[418] *Hist. MSS. Com. Rep.* ix, App. i, 52.
[419] *Cal. Pap. Let.* iv, 226.
[420] *Hist MSS. Com. Rep.* ix, App. i, 52.
[421] *Reg. S. Pauli* (ed. W. S. Simpson), 260.
[422] Ibid. 213.
[423] Ibid. 206.

the chapter[424] when arduous business was in treaty; that the bishop and any two major canons could settle disputes between the dean and the canons; that the dean must be a prebendary or dignitary of the cathedral,[425] who should begin his residence within a year of his appointment; that all resident and non-resident canons must be present in the cathedral on feast days.[426]

But the greatest reformer of St. Paul's was John Colet. After he had made an epitome[427] of the statutes of the cathedral,[428] he showed to Wolsey, in 1518, a series of regulations which were chiefly enlargements of Warham's statutes. These, in a further amplified form, were eventually enacted by Wolsey, as papal legate.[429] Such unusual procedure was due to the enmity which existed between Colet and Bishop Fitz James.[430] At the same time the dean was at contention with the residents, who had no sympathy with his frugal mode of life, and who accused him of a desire to treat them like monks.[431] His statutes seem to have arisen from his single initiative enforced by legatine authority, and it appears that neither they nor those of Warham were ever obeyed.[432]

In his lifetime, however, Colet must have wrought much improvement, for he was consistently supported by the king and by Archbishop Warham. A confirmation, obtained from Leo X, of the neglected bull, by which Martin V had limited the compulsory expenses of residence, may have secured a reform.[433] Colet made separate compilations of the statutes which bound the chantry priests; and possibly included new enactments among them. An oath of faithful service to the church, the dean, and the chapter, and of obedience to the ordinances by which their chantries had been founded, was henceforth compulsory for all chaplains, and they were forbidden to leave the City without leave from the dean and chapter.[434] In one respect the measures of Colet are particularly consonant with the spirit

of his age. He made a practice of preaching in the cathedral on every feast day, and his sermons were not dialectical exercises, but expositions of Scripture. His congregations were large, and included most leading men of the court and City.[435] The chancellor had for long neglected his duty of lecturing in theology; and here only Colet seems to have secured the cooperation of the bishop. An ordinance of Fitz James provides that, except during certain definite seasons, the chancellor shall read a lecture in the cathedral twice or three times a week, according to the amount of leisure allowed by feast days.[436]

A preacher of the reformed religion has alluded to the sloth and the irreligion by which Colet was met.

> In Paul's abbeys at their midnight prayers were none commonly but a few brawling priests, young quiristers and novices, who understand not what they said; the elder sort kept their bed or were worse occupied. … For their continual massing afore noon … these shorn shaveling priests would neither receive together one of them with another, nor yet the people have any part with them.[437]

Of the Protestant measures[438] of general application the dissolution of gilds[439] and chantries largely affected St. Paul's. Not only did it work a great change in the persons of the ministers and in the service, but further, the revenue of chantries had been, in spite of the poverty of chantry priests, a considerable source of wealth to the cathedral. In the fourteenth century the gross annual income

---

[424] In 1502 it was ruled that no man who was not of English birth on both sides and born in England might hold a prebend or dignity in St. Paul's, or treat of secret business in the chapter. Ibid. 210.

[425] The manor and rectory of Sutton and the advowson of Chiswick were at this time appropriated to the deanery. Ibid. 211.

[426] *Reg. S. Pauli* (ed. W. S. Simpson), 210–11.

[427] Colet's epitome differs from its predecessors in an assertion that the portion of the dean is double that of other residents.

[428] *Reg. S. Pauli* (ed. W. S. Simpson), 217.

[429] Ibid. 237.

[430] Erasmus, *Life of Colet* (transl. J. H. Lupton), 39.

[431] *Reg. S. Pauli* (ed. W. S. Simpson), 418–19; Erasmus, *Life of Colet* (transl. J. H. Lupton), 24 et seq.

[432] *Reg. S. Pauli* (ed. W. S. Simpson), 418–19.

[433] Ibid. 200.

[434] *Arch.* lii, 163–4.

[435] Erasmus, *Life of Colet* (transl. J. H. Lupton), 24 et seq.

[436] *Reg. S. Pauli* (ed. W. S. Simpson), 143.

[437] *Works of Pilkington* (ed. G. Scholefield), 481 et seq.

[438] In 1551 the communion table was removed to the south end of the church. In 1552 Cranmer forbade the organ to be played, and, on All Saints' Day, 'the book of the new service of bread and wine' was first used (*Chron. of Greyfriars* [Camden Soc.], 71–6).

[439] The mystery of the armourers of London formed a Gild of St. George; and the brothers and sisters maintained certain lights and divine services in a chapel of St. Paul's. They received a charter of incorporation in 1451–2, when Henry VI took the title of their founder (Pat. 31 Hen. VI, pt. 2, m. 12). The most important of the gilds which centred in the cathedral was the Brotherhood of Jesus, which met in Jesus Chapel in the crypt, and of which the dean was perpetual rector. It acquired a charter of incorporation in 1457–8. It had two secular wardens, sometimes persons of high rank, and was licensed to acquire lands to the yearly value of £40. It held services in the chapel at certain times for which the brothers and sisters made fixed payments to the ministers of the church. On the vigil of the feast of the Name of Jesus, they burnt a bonfire at the door of the crypt in the churchyard (*Reg. S. Pauli* [ed. W. S. Simpson], bk. v). The Gild of the King's Minstrels received a charter of incorporation in 1469, and was thereby bound to pray for the king and his consort, for his soul after death, and those of his ancestors, and for all faithful departed, in the Chapel of the Virgin of St. Paul's (Rymer, *Foed.* xi, 642).

of sixty-four chantries was £297 13s. 8d.; and the annual stipends of priests varied from 6s. to £6 13s. 4d.[440] In 1547 the annual value was £646 6s., of which £244 18s. 8d. was paid to the chaplains, each of whom received from twenty to eighty-five per cent. of the income of his chantry.[441] Another loss was suffered by the cessation of the practice of celebrating obits, which, however, had become less frequent than in the middle ages. Dean Colet recommended that these services should be held often, in order that the dead might be succoured by a multitude of suffrages; he ordered the chapter to examine what obits ought to be observed.[442] Yet in 1547 the number of those regularly kept had sunk to fifty-four. At the same time the annual income for the maintenance of obits had been reduced from £183 18s. 3½d. in the fourteenth century to £104 1s. 2d.[443]

During a period of some three hundred years from the middle of the sixteenth century, the only important innovations in the internal history of St. Paul's concerned the organization and endowment of preaching. The significance of a visitation by Grindal, in 1561, consists in a calendar which he made to indicate the order in which resident and non-resident canons were compelled to preach on feast days.[444] Alexander Ratcliff bequeathed £400 to the dean and chapter in 1615, half of which he destined for 'gentleman scholars' of Oxford and Cambridge who should preach at St. Paul's cross. This duty fell to prebendaries after the cross had been removed.[445] In 1623 Dr. Thomas White left an annual sum of £40 for the maintenance of three weekly lectures on divinity; and directed that a pulpit should be erected in the cathedral, to be used when the weather prevented resort to the churchyard.[446]

There occurred also some significant interpretations and illustrations of the constitution of the cathedral. Thus, before Cromwell's visitation of religious houses in the province of Canterbury, Cranmer suspended, temporarily, episcopal and all minor ecclesiastical jurisdictions; and in his mandate to the bishop of London he used the title 'legate of the apostolic see.'[447] which he had abandoned

in the convocation of 1533.[448] In consequence the bishop and chapter, at the visitation in St. Paul's, made a formal protest, which the archbishop's registrar refused to enter. It was sent to the king as an appeal, and appears to have received no notice.[449] The chapter was probably deterred from pleading in this instance the privilege of exemption from metropolitical visitation, because lately, by Act of Parliament, the king had been empowered to override such liberties,[450] and the visitation was by royal commission. A different course was taken when, in 1636, a visitation was proposed by Laud, as archbishop of Canterbury. The dean and chapter, in a petition to Charles I, then brought forward their ancient claim to exemption. In reply the king, after challenging them to prove not only that the coming visitation was without precedent, but further, that precedents existed against it, ordered them to submit.[451]

Bishop Bancroft made a visitation in 1598,[452] and a very disorderly state of affairs was disclosed among the minor canons, the only collegiate clergy left in the cathedral; who still 'kept commons together in their hall, dinners but not suppers, for their allowance would not maintain both.' It had been ordained by Act of Parliament that the college should bear the charge of all children born within its precincts; and to rule a number of households with means framed for the control of celibate priests was a difficult task. Between some families feuds existed so bitter and violent that the authority of the dean and chapter was openly flouted. Minor canons admitted strangers into the college as lodgers; all but three of them had let their official houses. Secularity seems, on the whole, to have increased among them with the Reformation, while their ancient vices, the consequences of ignorance, sloth, and self-indulgence, were at least as prevalent as ever.[453]

*H. Douglas-Irvine*

## Revised List of the Deans of St. Paul's

This list is taken from the following volumes: *John Le Neve, Fasti Ecclesiae Anglicanae, St. Paul's, London, 1066–1300*, comp. D. E. Greenway (London, 1968), pp. 4–8; *1300–1541*, comp. J. E. Horn (London, 1963), pp. 4–7.

Ulman (Wulman), occurs 1086–1107 (?Ranulph Flambard)

[440] *Arch.* lii, 158 et seq.
[441] Ibid. 172.
[442] *Reg. S. Pauli* (ed. W. S. Simpson), 236.
[443] For calendar of obits see *Doc. Illus. Hist. of St. Paul's* (ed. W. S. Simpson), 74–106.
[444] Add. MS. 34298, fol. 6. In 1882 by a minute of the chapter the order in which sermons were appointed to be preached on festivals and in Lent, by dignitaries and prebends, was set forth in an amended calendar. *Suppl. to Reg. S. Pauli* (ed. W. S. Simpson), 18 and 19.
[445] *Suppl. to Reg. S. Pauli* (ed. W. S. Simpson), 126.
[446] Ibid. 134.
[447] *L. and P. Hen. VIII*, vii, 1683.
[448] Wilkins, *Conc.* iii, 769.
[449] Strype, *Mem. of Cranmer*, i, 49.
[450] Stat. at Large, 25 Hen. VIII, cap. 21, sec. 20.
[451] Add. MS. 34268, fol. 18.
[452] *Reg. S. Pauli* (ed. W. S. Simpson), 272–80.
[453] MSS. of D. and C. of St. Paul's, A. Box 53, no. 17.

William [de Mareni], occurs 1111, 1138

Ralph of Langford, occurs 1142; died 1154 or later

Hugh de Marney (Mareni), appointed 1157/8; died 1179/80

Ralph de Diceto, elected 1180; died by May 1201

Alard de Burnham, occurs 1200/1; died 1216

Gervase de Houbrugge, occurs 1216, 1217

Robert of Watford, occurs 1217/18; died 1228

Martin de Patteshull, occurs 1228; died 1229

Geoffrey de St. Lucy, occurs 1231; died 1241

William de St. Marie Eglise, elected 1241; died 1243

Henry of Cornhill, occurs 1243; died 1254

Walter of London or de Salerne, elected 1254; resigned 1257

Robert de Bartone, occurs 1257; died 1261

Peter of Newport, occurs 1261/2

Richard Talbot, occurs 1262; died 1262

John de Ebulo, occurs 1264

Geoffrey de Feringes, elected 1262; died 1267

John de Chishull, occurs 1268; resigned 1273

Hervey de Borham, elected 1274; died 1276

Thomas of Ingaldesthorpe, elected 1276; resigned 1283

Roger de la Legh, elected 1283; died 1285

William de Mountfort, elected 1285; died 1294

Ralph Baldock, elected 1294; resigned 1304

Arnald Frangerius de Cantilupe, provided 1306; died 1313

John de Sandale, elected 1314; resigned 1316

Vitalis de Testa, provided 1314; resigned 1322

Richard Newport, elected 1316; resigned 1317

Roger de Northburgh, elected and resigned 1317

John of Everdon, exchanged 1322; died 1335

Gilbert Bruera, provided 1335; died 1354

Richard de Kilvington, provided 1354; vacated 1361

Thomas de Trillek, elected 1361; resigned 1364

John of Appleby, provided 1364; died 1389

Thomas de Eure, provided 1389; died 1400

Thomas Stowe, elected 1400; died 1405

Thomas More, elected 1406; died 1421

Reginald Kentwood, elected 1422; died 1441

Thomas Lisieux, elected 1441; died 1456

Laurence Booth, elected 1456; resigned 1457

William Say, elected 1457; died 1468

Roger Radclyffe, elected 1468; died 1471

Thomas Winterborne, elected 1471; died 1478

William Worsley, elected 1479; died 1499

Robert Sherborne, elected 1499; resigned 1505

John Colet, by 1505; died 1519

Richard Pace, elected 1519; died 1536

Richard Sampson, elected 1536; resigned 1540

John Incent, elected 1540; died 1545

## Appendix

The manors which belonged to the patrimony of St. Paul's were, in 1181, Caddington, Kensworth, Ardleigh, Sandon, Belchamp St. Paul, Wickham St. Paul, Heybridge, Tillingham, Barling, Runwell, Navestock, Chingford, Barnes, Drayton, Sutton, Luffenhall, 'Edulvesnesa,' Norton, and Abberton in Essex. Of these all but the last four are identical in name with the places in which the canons held churches, and which include also Walton-on-the-Naze, Kirby-le-Soken, Thorpe-le-Soken, Willesden, and Twyford.[454] The manors of Uplee in Willesden and of Chelmsford and Leigh or West Leigh in Essex, were held in 1283.[455] The church of St. Pancras was held in 1345.[456] Ralph de Diceto gave the church of Barnes to the hospital of the almonry.[457] That of Chingford was alienated before 1363[458] Bishop Richard de Beames granted the churches of Aldbury, Brent Pelham, and Furneaux Pelham, all in Hertfordshire.[459]

The rectory manor of Sunbury was acquired in 1230;[460] the church of Brightlingsea in 1237;[461] the church of Chiswick, probably as a result of the ancient rights over Sutton, and that of Leigh, were held in 1252;[462] in 1320 the dean and chapter impropriated the rectory of Hutton in Essex.[463] A rent was received from the church of Rickling in Essex in 1422.[464] London churches in the patronage of St. Paul's were, at a date between 1138 and 1250,[465] those of St. Thomas the Apostle, St. Benet Paul's Walk, St. Peter Paul's Wharf, St. Augustine Watling Street, St. Thomas Knightrider Street, St. John Walbrook, St. Giles without Cripplegate, St. Mary Aldermanbury, St. Helen Bishopsgate, St. Michael Queenhithe, St. Benet Gracechurch Street, St. Botolph Billingsgate, St. Martin Orgar St. Martin's Lane, St. Mary Magdalen Milk Street, St. John Zachary Maiden Lane, St. Mary Magdalen Old Fish Street, St. Antholin Watling Street, St. Olave Old Jewry, St. Stephen Coleman Street, St. Michael le Querne.[466] The last two of these did not continue in the possession of St. Paul's.[467] The church of St. Nicholas Olave was granted to the dean and chapter by Gilbert Foliot; that of St. Michael Bassishaw came into their possession shortly before 1373;[468] they

[454] *Dom. Bk. of St. Paul's* (ed. W. H. Hale), 110–21.

[455] *Dom. Bk. of St. Paul's* (ed. W. H. Hale), 160.

[456] *Hist. MSS. Com. Rep.* ix, App. i, 38.

[457] *Reg. Eleemos. D. S. Pauli* (ed. M. Hackett), fol. 6.

[458] Chan. Inq. p.m. 37 Edw. III, No. 63 (1st Nos.).

[459] *Reg. S. Pauli* (ed. W. S. Simpson), iv, 2, 3.

[460] Matt. Paris, *Chron. Maj.* (Rolls Ser.), iii, 75.

[461] *Hist. MSS. Com. Rep.* ix, App. 1, 40.

[462] *Visit. of Churches of St. Paul's* (Camd. Misc.) i, 33.

[463] *Cal. of Pat.* 1317–21, p. 421.

[464] *Feud. Aids,* ii, 197.

[465] Newcourt, *Repert.* i, 550, quoted from Register of D. and C. of St. Paul's.

[466] *Arch.* lv, 291.

[467] Pat. 19 Eliz. pt. 6; Dugdale, *Hist. of St. Paul's,* App. 33.

[468] Newcourt, *Repert.* i, 508.

held the churches of St. Faith in the Crypt,[469] and of St. Gregory by St. Paul's which was appropriated to the minor canons between 1445–8.[470]

The 'manor of Norton' appears to have evolved into that of Folliot Hall, in High Ongar and Norton Mandeville, which was held in 1535.[471] At this date no rights in Willesden not assigned to prebends were called temporal, and there is no mention of the chapter's possession of a manor in Luffenhall apart from that of Ardeley. Additional manors which now belonged to the chapter were those of Paulhouse and Bowhouse and of Harringay or Hornsey, in London and Middlesex; and those of Beldame or Kentish Town, which may have been attached to the church of St. Pancras, and of Barnes, next Hadleigh in Essex.[472]

The rectories outside London impropriated by the cathedral in 1535 were those of Sunbury, Willesden, Kentish Town, Rickling in Essex, Belchamp St. Paul, Walton, Kirby, Brightlingsea and Tillingham; and the vicarages of Kensworth, Caddington, Ardleigh, Sandon, St. Pancras, Drayton, and Chiswick. The churches of Thorpe-le-Soken, Navestock and Twyford appear to have been alienated.[473] The dean and chapter presented to Wickham St. Paul's in the seventeenth and to Heybridge and Barling in the eighteenth century.[474]

---

[469] Ibid. 349.
[470] Ibid. 359; *Cal. Rot. Cart. et Inq.a.q.d.* (Rec. Com.), 387.
[471] *Val. Eccl.* (Rec. Com.), i, 360.

[472] Ibid. 360–2, 437, 434, 437, 443.
[473] Inst. Books, P.R.O.
[474] Inst. Books, P.R.O.

# HOUSE OF BENEDICTINE MONKS

## 2. ST. PETER'S ABBEY, WESTMINSTER

### INTRODUCTION

The original account of Westminster Abbey is generally sound, but much of it must now be regarded as having been superseded by work published since 1909. These have covered an increasingly wide range of topics, from the fabric and local context of the abbey, to its music, political role and personnel. An essential guide to this literature is *A Bibliography of Westminster Abbey*, comp. Tony Trowles, Westminster Abbey Record Ser., 4 (Woodbridge, 2005), which lists almost 1,900 books, articles and pamphlets relating to the Abbey, published between 1571 and the end of 2000. These are organised by subject and period. An additional 1,500 items concern Westminster School, St. Margaret's, Westminster and sermons known to have been delivered in the abbey. What follows here comprises references to a few select works, principally for the pre-Reformation history of the abbey.

General accounts of the history of the abbey are numerous, and vary in terms of detail, coverage and accuracy. Still useful is *A House of Kings: The History of Westminster Abbey*, ed. E. F. Carpenter (London, 1966), but see also Richard Jenkyns, *Westminster Abbey* (London, 2004). For the findings of recent archaeological investigations in the vicinity of the abbey, see C. Thomas, R. Cowie, and J. Sidell, *The Royal Palace, Abbey and Town of Westminster on Thorney Island: Archaeological Excavations (1991–1998) for the London Underground Ltd Jubilee Line Extension Project*, MoLAS Monograph Series 22 (2005).

Particularly useful for the pre-Reformation history of the abbey and its personnel are E. Mason, *Westminster Abbey and its People, c.1050–c.1216* (Woodbridge, 1996); B. F. Harvey, *Westminster Abbey and its Estates in the Middle Ages* (Oxford, 1977); eadem, *Living and Dying in England 1100–1540: The Monastic Experience* (Oxford, 1993). The abbey's relationship to the medieval vill of Westminster is studied in G. Rosser, *Medieval Westminster 1200–1540* (1989). Published medieval records include *Westminster Abbey Charters 1066–c.1214*, ed. E. Mason, (London Record Society, 25, 1988); B. F. Harvey, *The Obedientiaries of Westminster Abbey and their Financial Records c.1275 to 1540*, Westminster Abbey record series, 3 (Woodbridge, 2002) and *The Westminster Chronicle 1381–94*, ed. B. F. Harvey and L. C. Hector (Oxford, 1982). Some records generated by the abbey, but held elsewhere, were located by the English Monastic Archives project and are listed on its web site along with an extensive list of the abbey's estates, URL: http://www.ucl.ac.uk/history/englishmonasticarchives/index.htm (accessed 28 February 2007).

A good starting point for the architectural history of the church is S. Bradley and N. Pevsner, *London, 6. Westminster* (The Buildings of England) updated edn. (London, 2003), while the most up to date work on Henry VII's Lady Chapel is *Westminster Abbey: the Lady Chapel of Henry VII*, ed. T. Tatton-Brown and R. Mortimer (Woodbridge, 2003). For extensive detail on the building and architecture of the Gothic church, see H. M. Colvin, 'Westminster Abbey' in *The History of the King's Works: The Middle Ages*, vol. I, ed. R. A. Brown, H. M. Colvin and A. J. Taylor (H.M.S.O., 1963), pp. 131–59; *idem* (ed.), *Building Accounts of King Henry III* (Oxford, 1971), pp. 190–439; P. Binski, *Westminster and the Plantagenets: Kingship and the Representation of Power 1200–1400* (New Haven, 1995). Also useful are D. A. Carpenter, 'Westminster Abbey: some characteristics of its sculpture, 1245–59',

*Journal of the British Archaeological Association*, 3rd ser., 35 (1972), pp. 1–14; and *idem*, 'Westminster Abbey in Politics, 1258–1269', in M. Prestwich, R. H. Britnell, and R. Frame (eds.), *Thirteenth Century England VIII* (Proceedings of the Durham Conference, 1999) (Woodbridge, 2001), pp. 49–58. For the 'Cosmati pavement', see L. Grant and R. Mortimer, *Westminster Abbey: The Cosmati Pavements* (Aldershot, 2002). For the library of the abbey, see R. Sharpe, J. P. Carley, R. M. Thomson, and A. G. Watson, *English Benedictine Libraries,* Corpus of British Medieval Libraries, 4 (1996), pp. 608–33.

For the period during, and immediately following, the Reformation the role of the abbey in the context of Westminster is discussed in J. Merritt, *The Social World of Early Modern Westminster: Abbey, Court, and Community 1525–1640* (Manchester, 2005). For the abbey, see in particular the essays in *Westminster Abbey Reformed 1540–1640*, ed. C. S. Knighton and R. Mortimer (Aldershot, 2003). Key published records for the history of the abbey in the sixteenth and seventeenth centuries are the *Acts of the Dean and Chapter of Westminster 1543–1642*, ed. C. S. Knighton, 3 vols., Westminster Abbey Record Ser. 1–2, 5 (Woodbridge, 1997–2006).

*Matthew Davies*

The real date of the foundation of Westminster Abbey must probably always remain uncertain. There is hardly a charter before the time of Edward the Confessor which is not open to suspicion, there is no mention of the monastery in Bede nor yet in the Anglo-Saxon Chronicle before the year 1040, and there can be no doubt that the more important the house became the greater was the temptation to rival in antiquity the foundation stories of such houses as St. Paul's and St. Alban's. The legend of the destruction of the temple of Apollo by King Lucius and the building of the Christian church of St. Peter on its site is hardly worthy of consideration,[1] but the story of the East Saxon foundation is so intimately bound up with Westminster traditions that no account of the abbey would be complete without it.

The founder, according to this story, was a certain high-born citizen of London – afterwards identified as Sebert,[2] king of the East Saxons and nephew of King Ethelbert, at whose instigation the work is supposed to have been undertaken. But more honourable even than this ancient and royal foundation was the apostolic consecration of the church. After the completion of the building, St. Peter, it is said, came by night to the banks of the Thames and was ferried over the broad marshes which surrounded the site of the abbey on the island of Thorney, by a wondering fisherman. Proceeding to the church he performed the rites of consecration amid the chanting of celestial choirs, and on his return bade the awestricken boatman go to Bishop Mellitus of London, tell him what he had seen, and forbid him to repeat the ceremony, which he was to have performed on the morrow. St. Peter also caused the fisherman to take an unprecedented draught of salmon, one of which he charged him to present to the bishop in token of the truth of his story.[3] When the next day broke Mellitus came to the abbey and found the holy water, oil and crosses, the halfburnt candles, and the Greek and Latin alphabets inscribed upon the walls. He therefore, says one writer, completed what remained to be done, and collecting the relics of apostolic consecration, placed them in a shrine, where they still remained in the fourteenth century.[4]

The first extant version of this story is to be found in a thirteenth-century transcript of a work purporting to be written by one Sulcardus, a monk of Westminster at the end of the eleventh century;[5] but Richard of Cirencester, a monk of the house in the fourteenth century, gives the tradition in substantially the same form, and even William of Malmesbury, one of the most trustworthy of early English historians, and with no occasion for bias in this case, repeats the story at the end of the eleventh

---

[1] *Flores Hist.* (Rolls Ser.), i, 146 et seq.; Widmore, *Enquiry into the First Foundation of Westm. Abbey*, 2. But for possible traces of Roman occupation of Westminster, see *V.C.H. London*, i.

[2] Said to have been buried in the abbey, and translated in 1308, when, on opening the coffin, the monks found his right hand and fore arm untouched by decay. *Chron. Edw. I and Edw. II* (Rolls Ser.), i, 266.

[3] This was the origin of the tithe of salmon paid annually to the abbey from the Thames fishermen between Staines and Gravesend.

[4] Richard of Cirencester, *Speculum Historiale* (Rolls Ser.), i, 92–3.

[5] Cott. MS. Titus, A. viii, fol. 2 et seq.

or the beginning of the twelfth century.[6] It is interesting also to note that Gervase of Canterbury and the annalists of Bermondsey and Waverley, as well as Matthew Paris and Ralph de Diceto, both members of houses of rival antiquity, without giving the legend of the miraculous consecration, refer the date of the foundation to the time of Ethelbert.[7]

According to Sulcard the church, which was but a little one, was much neglected after the death of Ethelbert until King Offa proposed to establish a monastic congregation, but was prevented by his pilgrimage to Rome. This story is suspicious, as there is evident confusion on the part of the writer between Offa of East Saxony (709) and Offa of Mercia (757–96) who is really the next reputed benefactor of the house.[8]

Offa's charter, however, which takes the form of a grant of 10 cassates of land at Aldenham to 'the needy people of God in Thorney, in the dreadful spot which is called aet Westminster' has been accepted by several historians of the abbey as genuine.[9] This would seem to point to the existence of a monastery here before the year 785 – the date of the charter – for the grant was paid for by the abbot, and the 'needy people of God' must certainly have been a monastic congregation. Accordingly Widmore considered that the house was probably founded between the years 730 and 740, about the time of the death of Bede, by whom, he argued, it must have been mentioned, had it existed earlier. He further supposed it to have been a small foundation for under twelve monks, not sufficiently important to have been of royal foundation.[10]

Tradition goes on to say that the house was subsequently laid waste by the Danes, but restored by Edgar on the advice of Dunstan, who being a great reader, had made himself acquainted with the early history of the place. Edgar gave Dunstan control over the restored foundation, and the bishop, pursuing his usual policy, immediately placed in it twelve Benedictine monks.[11] One of Edgar's charters has been accepted by Widmore as genuine, but it has far less appearance of authenticity than that of Offa. Not only is the date given as 951, whereas Edgar did not come to the throne until 958,

but also Bishop Wulfred is wrongly mentioned as a contemporary of Offa.[12]

At the same time it is highly probable that the monastery was restored by Edgar and Dunstan. It was certainly in existence before the refoundation by Edward the Confessor,[13] but it is hardly likely that it was founded in the stormy period between the death of Edgar and the accession of Edward, and if it was founded before that time it may be safely assumed, even apart from the authority of William of Malmesbury,[14] that the great bishop would not pass it over in his reforms.

After this Westminster is supposed to have again fallen a prey to the Danes, but it would seem that the house was not wholly destroyed, and if the monks fled they must have returned, for the contemporary biographer of Edward the Confessor speaks of the king having determined, because of his love of the prince of the apostles, to restore a monastery built in honour of St. Peter, which stood outside the walls of London, 'parvo quidem opere et numero paucioribus ibi congregatis monachis sub abbate in servitio Christi,' though even for these few the livelihood given by the faithful was barely sufficient. The place, however, was suitable, lying as it did near the City, in the midst of fertile meadows, and on the banks of the great water way which carried the world's merchandise to London.[15]

This is sober history: legend again intervening tells how Edward, having subdued his kingdom, vowed a pilgrimage to Rome to return thanks for his success, but was absolved by the pope at the instigation of the English nobles, who feared for the hard-won safety of the realm if the king were to go abroad. The condition of the absolution was that Edward should build or restore a monastery in honour of St. Peter, but before the bishops bearing the message had returned to England, a hermit, Wlsinus by name, sought the king, and told him that the prince of the apostles had appeared to him in a dream foretelling the return of the ambassadors and pointing out the ancient monastery of Thorney as the spot where he wished his church to stand.[16]

However this may be, Edward threw himself into the work with characteristic devotion. The new building grew apace, and the king is said to have

[6] Will. Malmesbury, *Gesta Pontificum* (Rolls Ser.), 141.

[7] This post-Conquest evidence cannot of course be taken as any guarantee of the authenticity of the story of the East Saxon foundation, but as an indication of its wide acceptance within a few years of the death of the Confessor and for many years later, it has a certain value of its own.

[8] Cott. MS. Claud. A. viii, fol. 3. Cf. Plummer, *Baedae Op. Hist.* i, 322.

[9] See Widmore, *Enquiry*, 7 (the charter is printed in the Appendix), and Loftie, *Westm. Abbey*, 10.

[10] Widmore, *Enquiry*, 7.

[11] Cott. MS. Titus, A. viii, fol. 4 seq. and Will. Malmesbury, *Gesta Pontificum* (Rolls Ser.), 178.

[12] See Widmore, *Enquiry*; Loftie, *Westm. Abbey*, and *Dep. Keeper's Rep.* xl, 546. The charter given in Cott. MS. Faust. A. iii, fol. 17 seq. is a manifest forgery.

[13] *Lives of Edw. Confessor* (Rolls Ser.), 417, and see charter of Ethelred dated 986 in *Hist. MSS. Com. Rep.* viii, App. ii, 28, and one of Leofwine dated 998 in Kemble, *Cod. Dipl.* mccxciii.

[14] See above, note 11. The statement that Dunstan actually ruled the monastery is of course absurd.

[15] *Lives of Edw. Confessor* (Rolls Ser.), 417.

[16] Ibid., lines 1739–1814 of the French Metrical Life, and Cott. MS. Titus, A. viii, fol. 4.

brought monks to Westminster from Exeter, when he erected the latter into an episcopal see.[17] Many a legend grew up around the king and his new foundation, and the story of his illness and death about the time of the consecration of the abbey put the crowning touch to its connexion with the life and death of the last king of the old English royal lineage.[18] It is therefore not surprising that the Conqueror, with his usual diplomacy, made a great display of devotion to the church. He boasted that on his first visit to the place he had offered 5 marks of silver and a precious pall on the altar of St. Peter, two not less precious ones at the shrine of St. Edward and 2 marks of gold and two palls on the high altar. This was the beginning of that intimate connexion between the abbey and its royal patrons which has made its history more political and national than that of any other religious foundation in England. Two interesting entries in the Customary of the abbey illustrate this connexion. One, that the brethren were allowed to eat with bishops or Benedictine abbots either in the abbey or in the royal palace, as also with kings, queens, or other magnates. The other that the sacrist, in pointing out any relic in the church to a stranger, must do so shortly unless the visitor were a king or queen or some earl of royal lineage.[19]

The effect of this connexion upon the character of the house as a religious community is not easy to estimate in the absence of full visitation records. The lack of historians, and the extraordinary number of forged documents in a monastery which should have been in a position to produce as great a school of chroniclers as Saint Albans, do not speak very well either for the critical and literary sense of the house or for its scrupulousness. The works of Richard of Cirencester and of Robert of Reading and the other continuators of the 'Flores' of the so-called Matthew of Westminster are the best known historical writings produced in the abbey. John Bever or 'of London' wrote a history from the time of Eneas to 1306, chiefly compiled from Geoffrey of Monmouth and other sources. Sulcard, Sporley, and Flete, all wrote short annals of the abbey, chiefly concerned, however, with the characters of the abbots. The atmosphere, moreover, seems to have engendered a keenness of political partizanship

hardly in accordance with the monastic ideal. This was pre-eminently the case in the reign of Henry III, and again under Edward II, when the writer of the 'Flores' was bitterly hostile to the king, and a dispute arose concerning the election of an abbot who was said to be favoured by Piers Gaveston.[20] At the same time the royal influence was more than once exercised in favour of discipline, and in early days at least, secured the appointment of abbots of administrative ability and high character.

Edwin, who was a great friend of the Confessor and had apparently been abbot of Westminster almost throughout his reign, must have died within a few years of the Conquest,[21] and if the fifteenth-century chronicler of the house is to be believed, his successor was deposed after exhortation from King William and Lanfranc at the end of four years' rule.[22] The next appointment was the work of the king and the archbishop. Vitalis had been abbot of Bernay (Evreux diocese) and had done much to improve that house; he was now forced, against his will, to accept promotion to Westminster.[23] Hardly any details are known of his rule here, however, and his very name has been almost eclipsed by that of his more famous successor, Gilbert Crispin.

Gilbert was a Norman by birth and educated from a very early age in the abbey of Bec Hellouin under Anselm. The biographer of his family states that he had all the liberal arts at his finger ends, and that his life was so perfect as well in the sphere of action as in that of contemplation that Lanfranc, who must have known him as a young man at Bec, called him to be abbot of Westminster.[24] There can be no doubt that Anselm thought most highly of the new abbot, for he wrote to him in the warmest terms of congratulation on his promotion, rejoicing that God had been pleased to make known to men his secret judgement of Gilbert, and that having brought him up in learning and wisdom, and nurtured him in holiness, he had now called him to be a shepherd of souls.[25]

Crispin seems to have been a man of manysided activity, for as well as his scholarly and literary tastes he apparently possessed administrative talents, and was also employed politically by the king.[26] His best-known writings are the 'Vita Herluini,' the principal authority for the early history of the abbey of Bec,

[17] Leland, *Coll.* (ed. Hearne), i, 81.

[18] Cf. in the inventory of the abbey furniture taken at the dissolution of the house 'An Awlter clothe . . . with the Birth of or Lord and Seynt Edwards storye.' *Trans. of Lond. and Midd. Arch. Soc.* iv, 325.

[19] *Customary of St. Augustine's, Canterbury, and St. Peter's, Westm.* (Hen. Bradshaw Soc.), ii, 52, 123. In this connexion also may be noticed the thirty-two 'Quysshyns for Estates' noted in the inventory printed in *Trans. of Lond. and Midd. Arch. Soc.* iv, 346.

[20] *Hist. MSS. Com. Rep.* i, App. 94.

[21] Cott. MS. Faust. A. iii, and see Widmore, *History*, 17.

[22] Cott. MS. Faust. A. iii.

[23] *Angl.-Sax. Chron.* (Rolls Ser.), i, 350, and see letter of William I to the abbot of Fécamp, printed in Widmore, *History*, App. No. II.

[24] 'De nobili genere Crispinorum' in Migne, *Patrologiae*, cl, 738.

[25] Ibid. clviii, Letter xvi.

[26] *Dict. Nat. Biog.* and Eadmer, *Historia* (Rolls Ser.), 189.

and the 'Disputatio Judaei cum Christiano,' which he submitted to Anselm for approval.[27] According to Pitts and others he also wrote homilies on the canticles, treatises on Isaiah and Jeremiah, and on the State of the Church, and several other works of a doctrinal or critical description.[28]

His administrative zeal is illustrated by the fact that he enlarged the *camera* of the monks so that clothing might be provided for as many as eighty brethren over and above the abbot, for whose wardrobe 10 marks a year was in future to be set aside, with the stipulation that he should receive nothing further from the chamberlain.[29] A papal bull of doubtful authenticity ascribes to his influence also a grant of immunity from episcopal jurisdiction, and although the details were in all probability invented to meet later troubles,[30] the connexion of his name with the tradition shows that he left a general impression of vigorous government. It would seem, moreover, that he was an eager exponent of Christianity to the Jews, and had one Jewish convert amongst his monks at Westminster.[31]

After the death of Gilbert in 1117 a vacancy of four years ensued,[32] during which the abbey seems to have suffered considerably from unauthorized alienations. The next abbot, Herbert, a monk of the house, was appointed in 1121,[33] and all his energies and all the influence of the king hardly availed to restore the house to prosperity.[34] The reign of Stephen, moreover, brought fresh misery; Gervase of Blois, Herbert's successor, was a natural son of the king, and a bad ruler.

Within very few months of his consecration the chapter sent Osbert, the prior of the house, to the pope to obtain the canonization of the Confessor, but Innocent II replied that so important a festival ought to be to the honour of the whole realm and therefore asked for by the whole people, consequently he postponed the ceremony until sufficient testimony to the popular desire should be produced – probably a euphemism for the restoration of the order and good fame of the monastery, for at the same time the monks were exhorted to observe the rule and set a good example. There had evidently also been complaints as to alienations of the possessions of the church, and their recovery was committed to the bishop of Winchester.[35]

It was probably at this time that Innocent wrote to Gervase exhorting him to still the murmurs in the house, and to administer its goods with the counsel of the brethren. He was to try to recover the churches and tithes which had been dispersed without the consent of the chapter,[36] to banish strangers from sharing his secrets, to put down gatherings of knights and laymen in the monastery, to remember that ecclesiastical matters are altogether exempt from the secular arm, to try to be worthy of his calling, and to love the life of Christ-like poverty. The regalia of the Confessor and the insignia were not to be sold without common consent, and the brethren were to show canonical obedience to the abbot and to be of good conversation.[37]

The continuator of Symeon of Durham's 'Historia Regum' seems to imply that Gervase was removed through the influence of Henry II.[38] The prestige of the house certainly recovered under his successor Laurence, a monk of St. Albans.[39] He was evidently a man of considerable administrative ability, for he rebuilt part of the monastery which had been destroyed by fire and recovered many of the alienated estates.[40] A further point in his favour is the fact that in his time the pope consented to the canonization of King Edward, and conceded to the abbot the use of the mitre and gloves.[41] His relations with Saint Albans were chequered, and at one time much strained by the beginning of a lengthy quarrel as to the manor of Aldenham,[42] but as Laurence was summoned to attend the deathbed of Abbot Gorham,[43] it would seem that the breach between the two houses was not permanent.

Laurence died on 11 April, 1175,[44] and according to Ralph de Diceto his successor was one of the

---

[27] Both printed by Migne.

[28] See *Dict. Nat. Biog.*

[29] *Customary* (Hen. Bradshaw Soc.), ii, 149–50.

[30] See *infra*.

[31] 'Disputatio Judaei' in Migne, *Patrologiae*, clix, 1005 seq.

[32] *Angl.-Sax. Chron.* (Rolls Ser.), i, 371; ii, 214.

[33] Eadmer, *Historia* (Rolls Ser.), 291.

[34] *Magnum Rot. Scac.* (Rec. Com.), 150, and Cott. MS. Faust. A. iii, fol. 75*d*.

[35] Wilkins, *Concilia*, i, 418–19.

[36] In a 14th-cent. list of farms granted by various abbots the leases of seven manors and a church are attributed to Gervase, one lease to Gilbert, two important ones to Herbert, and one to Laurence the successor of Gervase (D. & C. Westminster, Book No. 11, fol. 134). One at least of those granted by Gervase was in favour of his mother Dametta (ibid. fol. 147). At the same time, if the dates are to be even approximately relied on, the pope's warning occurs so soon after the promotion of Gervase as to point to a legacy of evil from the period of the vacancy with which Herbert had failed to cope.

[37] Cott. MS. Claud. A. viii, fol. 47 *d.*

[38] Symeon of Durham, *Opera* (Rolls Ser.), ii, 330.

[39] *Gesta Abbat.* (Rolls Ser.), i, 159; see *Dict. Nat. Biog.* for a short account and estimate of his life.

[40] Cott. MS. Claud. A. viii, fol. 48. According to one authority Gervase had hardly left substance enough for the food and clothing of the convent (*Gesta Abbat.* (Rolls Ser.), i, 133).

[41] Cott. MS. Claud A. viii, fol. 48.

[42] *V. C. H. Herts.* ii, 150.

[43] For his relations with St. Albans see *Gesta Abbat.* (Rolls Ser.), i, *passim.*

[44] A copy of his sermons is extant at Balliol College, Oxford (Hardy, *Catalogue* [Rolls Ser.], ii, 410), and it was to his influence that the compilation of Ailred of Rievaux's Life of St. Edward was due (Higden, *Polychron.* [Rolls Ser.], vii, 226–7, and cf. *Gesta Abbat.* [Rolls Ser.], i, 159).

ten abbots appointed arbitrarily by Henry II at Woodstock early in July. Walter had been prior of Winchester, and his election is said to have been procured by bribery on the part of the king, who feared lest, if the great abbeys were allowed to choose abbots from their own numbers, his royal authority might be undermined.[45] Nothing is known, however, of the history of the house at this time beyond the fact that the papal nuncio, being received at the abbey *minus reverenter*, suspended the abbot from the use of the newly-acquired mitre and gloves, and the prior from his place in choir.[46] His anti-papal attitude may well have been one of Walter's strongest recommendations in the eyes of the king, and account in part for his promotion.

A curious story is told concerning the part played by the abbey during the absence of Richard I from England. It is said that the king on leaving Sicily for the East in 1191 gave special injunctions that the appointment of a new abbot to the then vacant chair at Westminster was to be left entirely to the will of the chancellor. Longchamp accordingly, by force of exactions and importunity, gradually persuaded the convent to allow him to introduce into the abbey, with a view to his election as abbot, his brother, who had been bred a monk at Caen, and for the better security of his plan he had the agreement committed to writing and sealed with the conventual seal. Upon Longchamp's disgrace, however, the monks, 'qui ante dies istos tam magni cordis exstiterant ut pro more sua facta non infecerent,' seeing the times had changed, set aside their covenant and elected as abbot their own prior, William Postard.[47]

This exchange was probably an advantage to the abbey, for Postard's rule appears to have been frugal and wise;[48] little evidence as to the fortune of the monastery during the reign of John is, however, extant. A few scattered notices of Abbot Ralph Papillon or of Arundel occur. He is said, by Leland,[49] to have been a friend of Abbot Laurence, and by him appointed prior of Hurley. The latter statement is supported by Ralph de Diceto, who says that he was elected at Northampton 'ne monachi emendicatis aliunde suffragiis uterentur.'[50] But of

his rule at Westminster hardly anything is known. He is supposed to have held the saints in special reverence and to have added to the magnificence of certain festivals,[51] and he did his utmost to uphold the dignity of office upon one occasion when the prior, 'vir simplex et trepidus,' offered himself for correction in chapter with the other obedientiaries who had been reproved by the abbot.[52] His rule, however, ended in disaster, for he quarrelled with his brethren and was deposed by the bishop of Tusculum in 1214, when his seal was broken in chapter.

The exact grounds of Abbot Ralph's downfall are open to question. According to Wendover, who calls him William, the charges brought against him were dilapidation and incontinency.[53] Widmore, however, scouts the latter charge, and points out that he must already have been an old man at this date;[54] moreover, the statement receives no corroboration from the Westminster chronicles. Matthew Paris in one place repeats Wendover's story word for word, but later on he gives an account of the event in his own words, and seems to know nothing of the charge.[55]

The abbey bore its share in the disturbances of the next two years,[56] and appears to have adopted a prominently royalist attitude, for in 1216 the monks refused to admit Louis of France, whose soldiers promptly plundered the royal treasure in the abbey.[57] The coronation of the young King Henry in October had to be performed at Gloucester, for Westminster was still besieged by the barons' party, but on 17 May, 1220, a second coronation was performed in the abbey by the archbishop of Canterbury.[58]

The history of the next thirty years is chiefly a record of rapid development. Internally the constitution was completely remodelled under Abbot Berking, and the new Lady chapel was begun under the auspices of the king;[59] externally the abbey became of sufficient importance to make its friendship a thing to be desired, and its independence a factor in the economy of the Church which could not

---

[45] Ralph de Diceto, *Opera* (Rolls Ser.), i, 401–2.

[46] Ibid. 404.

[47] *Chron. of Reign of Ric. I*, &c. (Rolls Ser.), iii, 405, 410, and 420. On 12 Oct. the benediction of the new abbot was performed by the bishop of London, and on the following Thursday Longchamp, trying to escape disguised as a woman, was captured by boatmen (Ralph de Diceto, *Opera* [Rolls Ser.], ii, 101).

[48] Cott. MS. Claud. A. viii, fol. 51. The author, though not contemporary, probably represents Westminster tradition.

[49] *De Script. Brit.* 246. He identifies him with Ralph the Almoner, to whom he ascribes some literary fame.

[50] *Opera* (Rolls Ser.), ii, 172.

[51] Cott. MS. Claud. A. viii, fol. 51.

[52] *Customary*, ii, 187. The prior's open humiliation of himself evidently scandalized the convent. There seems to have been a strong tradition in the house against lowering the dignity of the regular life by public penances. Ibid. 117.

[53] *Flores Hist.* (Rolls Ser.), ii, 94.

[54] *History*, 35.

[55] *Chron. Majora* (Rolls Ser.), ii, 568 and 576.

[56] Though the abbot is not mentioned on either side in the struggle for the Charter.

[57] *Chron. of Reign of Stephen*, &c. (Rolls Ser.), ii, 523. This is said to have been at the instigation of the English and French barons.

[58] *Flores Hist.* (Rolls Ser.), ii, 162, and Matt. Paris, *Chron. Majora* (Rolls Ser.), iii, 58.

[59] John de Oxenedes, *Chron.* (Rolls Ser.), 145.

lightly be neglected. It was some time between the years 1215 and 1223 that the abbeys of Westminster and St. Edmunds entered into an agreement for mutual aid. In times of vacancy the surviving abbot was to visit the sister house, if desired, and to receive the profession of its novices. Monks of either house were to be entertained honourably at the other, except in the case of those banished for grave misdemeanours. Prayers were to be mutually offered for deceased abbots and brethren. A similar treaty was made with Worcester in 1227, and with Malmesbury before 1283, and there is a tradition of one with the house of St. Victor of Paris.[60]

In 1221 Bishop Eustace of London claimed jurisdiction in the abbey, and appeal was made to Rome.[61] It is difficult to determine what were the exact rights of the case, as the abbey based its claim to exemption on a papal bull of the date of the foundation.[62] A very untrustworthy charter of Dunstan in 959 renounces all rights of the bishop of London in Westminster,[63] and there occurs in the doubtful grant of exemption to Abbot Gilbert already mentioned[64] a tradition of a quarrel as to episcopal claims as early as the time of Abbot Wulnoth, who died in 1049.[65] Other ostensible papal bulls of the twelfth century follow the Dunstan tradition.[66] However this may be, the claim to exemption was probably prescriptive, and the archbishop of Canterbury and the other arbitrators of 1222 were justified in pronouncing in favour of the abbey.[67] There seem to have been revivals of the question, in part at least, in 1229–30, 1254, and 1268.[68]

Westminster was one of the exempt houses which appealed against the visitation of the abbots of Boxley and Beigham and the precentor of Christchurch, Canterbury, in 1232. The papal mandate for the visitation seems to have been issued in due form, and upon the plea that several of the great houses were 'in spiritualibus deformata et in temporalibus … graviter diminuta.' In the case of Westminster at

least the latter charge was probably true, for when the prior of Ely visited a little later he ordered that the conventual seal should be kept under three keys to prevent unlawful alienations,[69] and in 1232 and 1235 special appeal was made to the abbot's tenants to give him an aid on account of his debts.[70] At the same time there is no reason to suppose that the condition of the house at this time was otherwise unsatisfactory; Matthew Paris calls the abbot *vir religiosus*, and Prior Peter, who died a few years later, was noted for his great holiness.[71] The visitors, however, on coming to St. Augustine's, Canterbury, behaved with such violence that the monks of that house, together with those of St. Edmunds, St. Albans, and Westminster, refused to acknowledge their authority.[72] In spite, however, of an appeal to Rome, and the issue of a papal indult, the visitors published an inhibition that no one should pray in or make offerings at Westminster, whereupon the pope ordered that if they did not revoke everything which they had done to the prejudice of the abbey, the bishop and prior of Ely and the prior of Norwich should annul their proceedings.[73]

The chief offender in the matter was the Cistercian abbot of Boxley,[74] and the event seems to have caused a serious coolness between Westminster and the whole Cistercian order. The compiler of the Customary, at the end of the thirteenth century, remarks that at one time Cistercians used to come to the abbey in great numbers, being received in the refectory and sleeping in the dormitory 'as brethren of our order,' and that not infrequently as many as four or more Cistercian abbots had dined together at the high table, but he implies that this had become a thing of the past since the repulse of the visitors.[75]

Abbot Richard de Berking died at the close of the year 1246.[76] Matthew Paris calls him 'vir prudens literatus et religiosus,' and his acquisitions led the Westminster chronicler to wish that all abbots would follow his example. From the pope he obtained the right to give episcopal benediction and first tonsure, and from the king he received a grant of the amercements of the abbey tenants. He gave to the abbey a reredos depicting the history of our Saviour, and another of the life of King Edward, as well as certain vestments, and the chronicler records with pride that he was *molestus sive onerosus* to his

---

[60] *Mem. of St. Edmund's Abbey* (Rolls Ser.), iii, 251; *Ann. Mon.* (Rolls Ser.), iv, 423; *Customary of Westm.* (Hen. Bradshaw Soc.), 108, Cott. MS. Faust. A. iii, fol. 262 d.

[61] Matt. Paris, *Chron. Majora* (Rolls Ser.), iii, 66.

[62] Wilkins, *Concilia*, i, 598–9, without stating, however, which bull or which foundation.

[63] D. and C. Westm. Book No. 11, fol. 35.

[64] *Supra.*

[65] Cott. MS. Faust. A. iii, fol. 157.

[66] D. and C. Westm. Book No. 11, fol. 6, 10, &c.

[67] Wilkins, *Concilia*, loc. cit. The appropriation of the church of Staines to the infirmary and guesthouse of the abbey, which was also in dispute, was confirmed, but the convent surrendered the manor and church of Sunbury to the bishop. Widmore (*Hist.* 63) thinks it was at this date that the first archdeacon was appointed.

[68] D. and C. Westm. Book No. 11, fol. 667, and Cott. MS. Faust. A. iii, fol. 183, 189d.

[69] *Cal. of Papal Let.* i, 142.

[70] *Cal. of Pat.* 1225–32, p. 478, and 1232–47, p. 98.

[71] *Flores Hist.* (Rolls Ser.), ii, 321.

[72] Matt. Paris, *Chron. Majora* (Rolls Ser.), iii, 238–9, and *Ann. Mon.* (Rolls Ser.), i, 89.

[73] *Cal. of Papal Let.* i, 133.

[74] Matt. Paris, *Chron. Majora* (Rolls Ser.), iii, 239.

[75] *Customary* (Hen. Bradshaw Soc.), ii, 37 and 107.

[76] Matt. Paris, *Chron. Majora* (Rolls Ser.), iv, 586.

neighbours. But his best claim to an honourable place in the annals of Westminster should be based on his division of the estates and organization of the constitution of the monastery.[77]

His successor, a second Richard, was elected on account of his friendship with the king.[78] Perhaps in consequence of this election the relations between the abbey and the crown became closer than ever. In 1247 Henry presented, and carried personally to Westminster, a portion of the blood of our Lord which had been sent to him from the Holy Land. The procession from St. Paul's was attended by all the priests of London vested in copes and surplices, and the king himself on foot and with eyes cast down carried the relic 'through the uneven and muddy streets.' After being borne in this wise through the City, and round the church and palace, amid singing and exultation, it was finally offered by Henry to 'God and St. Peter, and his dear St. Edward.'[79]

Unfortunately Henry's piety was as injudicious as his administrative policy, and anyone to whom he showed favour could not fail, sooner or later, to become involved in the political strife of the day. As early as the year 1222 indications had not been wanting of the possibility of an outbreak between the abbey and the City. In a wrestling match between the tenants of Westminster and the citizens of London, the former had suddenly, either on impulse or of set purpose, flown to arms and driven the Londoners back to the City. Here the common bell was rung, and in spite of the pacific efforts of the mayor, a serious political riot developed; the leader, Constantine son of Arnulf, encouraged his followers with the seditious cry 'Montis Gaudium, Montis Gaudium, adjuvet Deus et dominus noster Ludovicus.' The maddened populace threatened the houses of the abbot with destruction, stole his horses, and ill-treated his men, while he himself barely escaped by taking refuge in the house of one of the king's officials. Ultimately the justiciar held an inquiry, hanged the ringleaders, and, since the people still murmured, took sixty hostages and banished them to various castles throughout England.[80]

The king, however, failed to take permanent warning by this outburst. In 1250 he demanded for the abbey certain privileges prejudicial to the charters of the City. The mayor offered some resistance, and finally appealed to the earl of Leicester, who,

with other barons, effectually complained to the king, and rebuked the abbot, who was regarded as the instigator to the aggression.[81] At the same time, and according to Matthew Paris in the same spirit, Henry, to the great indignation of St. Albans, confirmed the rights of Westminster in the manor of Aldenham – a step which at such a time was less judicious than just. In the meantime it became evident that the king's devotion to the abbey was even a stronger motive with him than his friendship for the abbot. About the year 1251 Richard attempted to repudiate his predecessor's division of the abbey revenues, and meeting with opposition from the convent set out for Rome. He appears to have been a man of prepossessing appearance and manners, and no little business capacity, and was accordingly received with favour by the pope who made him one of his chaplains, and sent him home after a prolonged stay in Rome, armed with powers to reduce his convent to submission. Both parties appealed to the king, the convent in a spirit of humility, and the abbot apparently with the utmost confidence, relying on the papal authority and his own friendship with Henry. He must accordingly have been somewhat surprised when his overtures were utterly rejected, and he was driven from the royal counsels and favour. Seeing that victory was not easily to be his, he submitted to the arbitration of Richard earl of Cornwall and John Mansel, provost of Beverley, but when they pronounced in favour of the convent he attempted a further appeal to Rome, which was only frustrated by the king's order forbidding anyone to lend him money or to accept his bonds.[82]

In August, 1252, an amicable settlement was reached with the convent, though Matthew Paris states that the abbot was never restored to Henry's favour; this statement, however, is open to doubt in view of the part Richard played in the crisis of 1258. The king, being determined not to confirm the charters, and unable to obtain financial aid from the constitutional party without so doing, appealed to the abbots of St. Albans, Reading, Waltham, and Westminster for help. Abbot Richard at once acceded to this request, but the other three houses were proof against his evil example, and probably saved the political situation. Henry was forced to summon the Mad Parliament, and the committee of twentyfour was chosen, the abbot of Westminster being one of the twelve appointed by the king.[83] He died near Winchester in July of the same year, according to some authorities, of poison

[77] Cott. MS. Claud. A. viii, fol. 56. For his constitutional work see *infra.*

[78] *Flores Hist.* (Rolls Ser.), ii, 320.

[79] Matt. Paris, *Chron. Majora* (Rolls Ser.), iv, 641–3.

[80] Roger of Wendover, *Flores Hist.* (Rolls Ser.), ii, 265; Matt. Paris, *Chron. Majora* (Rolls Ser.), iii, 72 and 73; *Ann. Mon.* (Rolls Ser.), iii, 78–9; Cott. MS. Claud. A. viii, fol. 53.

[81] Matt. Paris, *Chron. Majora* (Rolls Ser.), v, 127–8.

[82] Matt. Paris, *Chron. Majora* (Rolls Ser.), v, 230–1, 238, 303–5.

[83] Ibid. 682–5; *Ann. Mon.* (Rolls Ser.), i, 447.

administered by the Poitevins, though it would seem scarcely politic on their part to avenge themselves thus on one of the most loyal of the king's adherents.[84]

Richard of Ware, the new abbot, reaped the fruits of his predecessor's anti-popular attitude. In 1265 Henry attempted to restore to the monks the liberties which had been taken from them by the City;[85] but in May, 1267, he himself was forced to borrow all the jewels, pictures, and precious stones of the church as well as the gold from the shrine of St. Edward.[86] The following year the popular party became so much exasperated that they broke into the church in the king's absence and carried off the royal treasure deposited there. The chronicler remarks that 'by God's mercy the rebels spared the monks and their goods,'[87] but there was probably not very much worth pillaging at the time, as the monastic jewels were not restored until February, 1269.[88] Far, however, from grudging all the turmoil into which his friendship drew them, the abbot and convent seem to have remained enthusiastic adherents of Henry to the end, and on the occasion of his severe illness in 1270, all the brethren, 'fearing to lose so great a patron,' went in procession in the rain from the abbey to the New Temple and back. On their return they found the danger was over, and at the king's command they chanted *Gaudent in coelis* 'because he had recovered in answer to the prayers of the monks.'[89]

About this time the character of the house seems to have fallen into somewhat unmerited disrepute. In 1269 the archbishop of Canterbury and Gregory de Neapoli held a visitation as commissaries of Cardinal Ottobon. The commissioners' report was to the effect that the monastery was in a much better condition than many had 'believed and hoped,' and their injunctions point rather to some slight slackness of administration than to any graver disorders. It would therefore seem probable that the rumours had been set on foot by the popular party in London, or by rival houses which were jealous of Westminster on account of the extraordinary favours showered upon it by the king. The cardinal enjoined that in future the obedientiaries should not make alienations of their property without consultation with the abbot, and that they should render their accounts four times yearly; that the prior should have his room in a place accessible to the whole convent and not at a distance from the

cloister as hitherto;[90] that the infirmarer should provide better for the quiet and comfort of the sick; that alms should not be misappropriated; that in future, to prevent the violation of the rule of poverty, the brethren should receive from the chamberlain their clothing rather than purchasemoney, which they had too often appropriated to other uses; that monks who had been in office on their retirement should not retain their silver cups at the common table; and that claustral brethren should not go to manors outside the monastery without good reason.[91]

Of the history of the next ten years little is known; the abbot was apparently frequently absent, for he was the king's treasurer, and was employed for long periods on foreign embassies and judicial eyres,[92] In January, 1279, however, John Peckham was consecrated archbishop of Canterbury. Robert of Reading remarks that 'in his prosperity he despised many, especially the Benedictines.'[93] However this may be, he certainly made his authority felt at Westminster. In 1281 he complained that the tenants of the abbey were defrauding his men of Lambeth at the ferry,[94] and in the same year he excommunicated the abbot together with the heads of other exempt religious houses within his province for refusing to attend a council at Lambeth.[95] A few months later a long-standing dispute with the bishop of Worcester as to visitation and jurisdiction in the cell of Great Malvern reached its height, and the archbishop characteristically gave his support to the diocesan against the exempt abbey.[96] In each of these cases Peckham would seem to have combined a real zeal for abstract justice and morality with a

[90] To approach the monastic ideal it must have been most necessary for the prior to be in close touch with the brethren, for according to Westminster tradition 'He is bound to show to all an example of good works … He should restrain the restless, comfort the weak-hearted, relieve the sick, be patient towards all men; he should reproach no man with evil, but be long-suffering, that by his mercy he may turn away wrath… Constantly bearing in mind that he as well as the abbot will be called upon to give account for (the brethren) before God. In all that he does he should always remember the end, and that he cannot carelessly pass over anything without danger to his soul.' *Customary* (Hen. Bradshaw Soc.), ii, 9

[91] Cott. MS. Faust. A. iii, fol. 210 et seq.

[92] *Cal. of Pat.* 1281–92, p. 109; ibid. 1272–81 *passim*.

[93] *Flores Hist.* (Rolls Ser), iii, 82.

[94] *Registrum Epist. Joh. Peckham* (Rolls Ser.), i, 283–4.

[95] *Ann. Mon.* (Rolls Ser.), iii, 397, and D. and C. Westm. 'Jurisdictions,' parcel 36, Nos. 2 and 3.

[96] This very unedifying affair belongs rather to the history of Great Malvern than to that of Westminster. Its chief importance in the abbey history is that it illustrates the tenacity with which the monks clung to their privilege of exemption even at the cost of maintaining a prior of evil life in one of their cells. Legally there can be little doubt that the position of the abbey was tenable, but morality and humanity seem to have been on the side of the bishop. See *V.C.H. Worc.* ii, 138–41.

[84] *Ann. Mon.* (Rolls Ser.), i, 460, and iii, 211.

[85] Cott. MS. Faust. A. iii, fol. 50.

[86] *Syllabus of Rymer's Foedera*, i, 76; *Flores Hist.* (Rolls Ser.), iii, 15, which, however, gives the date as 1268.

[87] *Flores Hist.* (Rolls Ser.), iii, 16.

[88] *Hist. MSS. Com. Rep.* iv, App. i, 191.

[89] *Flores Hist.* (Rolls Ser.), iii, 22.

singular lack of tact and respect for valued privileges, and ill-feeling ultimately ran so high that when the archbishop came to Westminster in 1283 the sacrist lost his temper, and threw a great and hard roll in his face, aggravating the offence with many insults. The occasion of the archbishop's visit and of the sacrist's outbreak is not specified, but it would seem that the latter had some interest – probably as a papal commissary – in a case then pending between Peckham and Theodosius de Camilla, dean of the royal chapel of Wolverhampton, as to the church of Wingham (Kent).[97]

The parishioners of Wingham were inhibited by the sacrist from the payment of tithes, and the archbishop may have gone to Westminster in this connexion. Possibly he asked to inspect the papal mandate for the inhibition, and it was this that the sacrist threw at him.[98]

In 1290 a quarrel arose between Westminster and the English Franciscans, and it was probably again owing to the influence of Peckham, himself a friar and conservator of the order of the Brothers Minor in England, that the abbey nearly had to submit to the utmost humiliation. It appears that a certain Brother William, once a Benedictine monk of Pershore, and subsequently professed a Friar Minor, had become apostate from his order and fled to Westminster. According to the custom of the house truants seeking refuge in the abbey were to receive one day's victuals from the sub-almoner and go where they would,[99] but in this case the sympathies of the convent seem to have been enlisted in favour of the delinquent, and he had been received and harboured by the brethren.

On 30 July, 1290, Peckham ordered the official of the bishop of London to publish sentence of excommunication against the apostate and his accomplices. On 7 October following the monks appealed to the pope. Apparently, however, the appeal was in vain, and the abbot and convent remaining obdurate, were excommunicated. Subsequently the proctors of both parties appeared before Matthew, cardinal of St. Laurence, who gave judgement on 4 April, 1291. He ordered the abbot and convent to acknowledge that the apostate could not remain amongst them without the loss of his own soul, to purge themselves upon the most stringent conditions of having helped him to escape, and to undertake to aid the Franciscans in his recovery. The abbot was to come specially to the next provincial chapter of Franciscans in London to humble himself publicly and to be received back to charity. He, however, protested that he would not

submit to the pronouncement, and in December, 1291, the more onerous terms were commuted for a sum of 60 marks, the last instalment of which was duly paid on 21 December, 1294.[100]

There is reason to suppose that the convent was in anything but a satisfactory condition at this time. In 1303 occurred the famous robbery of the king's treasury in the abbey, the story of which has so frequently been told that it scarcely requires repetition in detail. The more salient facts of the case cannot be doubted, namely that the treasure was taken from the usual depository within the abbey precincts[101] by a carefully organized and long-thought-out plan, which could not have been put into execution without the knowledge of some of the monks, that the sacrist, the sub-prior, the cellarer, seven monks and certain servants of the sacrist were guilty at least of collusion, and that the cellarer and certain of the monks had been in the habit of consorting with one of the chief culprits and joining with him in eating and drinking with women of evil life.[102] That the abbot was unaware of what was taking place in the monastery seems clear, but this is a doubtful point in his favour. He must have been guilty of extraordinary negligence to retain such men as Adam de Warefeld, Alexander of Pershore, and Ralph Morton as sacrist, subprior and cellarer, and a somewhat significant light is thrown upon his character by an entry in the annals of Worcester under the year 1300. As president of the General Chapter of Benedictines held at Oxford, Abbot Walter decreed, says the annalist, that every prelate might give his monks dispensation to eat flesh as seemed expedient to him; he also provided for the omission of lengthy prayers between the hours, and, adds the chronicler, 'dubito quod futuris temporibus superfluum videbatur Pater Noster.'[103]

But by far the most prejudicial evidence against him was given in the case of Prior Reginald de Hadham, which was only finally decided in 1308, after Walter's death. It would seem by the notarial instruments[104] that at some date previous to July, 1307, the prior and certain monks petitioned the abbot to reform abuses and to observe the compositions as to the division

---

[97] *Reg. Epist. Joh. Peckham* (Rolls Ser.), i, 385–6; ii, 395–6.
[98] Ibid. ii, 588, 617–8.
[99] *Customary* (Hen. Bradshaw Soc.), ii, 86.

[100] *Mon. Fran.* (Rolls Ser.), ii, 31–62. The prior and convent had evidently been willing to submit to the hardest terms (*Hist. MSS. Com. Rep.* iv, App. 178).
[101] Mr. Harrod in *Arch.* xliv, 373 et seq. has argued with every appearance of probability that the treasure was stolen not, as was formerly supposed, from the treasury in the cloister, but from the chapter-house crypt. This would account for much that is otherwise inexplicable in the details of the robbery, without supposing that the entire convent knew of what was going on and was in the habit of admitting seculars to the interior of the monastery.
[102] *Anct. Kal. and Inventories of the Exch.* (Rec. Com.), i, 251–290; Mr. Burtt's article in *Gleanings*, 282–90.
[103] *Ann. Mon.* (Rolls Ser.), iv, 547.
[104] D. & C. Westm. 'Priors,' 56.

of the revenues of the house. Walter thereupon conceived a violent prejudice against the prior, and without legitimate warning suspended him from his office. Reginald appealed to Rome, and Brother Roger of Aldenham, who drew up the instrument of the appeal, was consequently banished to the cell of Hurley. At the beginning of September,[105] despite the fact that the appeal was still pending, the abbot summoned the discontented monks for correction in chapter, and brought certain charges against Reginald, stating that his election as prior had been uncanonical, that he had misappropriated the revenues of other offices which he had held, that he had encouraged Roger of Aldenham in disobedience and vagrancy, that he had continued to exercise his office after his suspension, that he had appealed to Canterbury against the liberties of the house, and that he had had the abbot falsely and maliciously accused in the matter of the robbery of the treasury; he further summoned Reginald to purge himself, but when he showed himself ready to do so refused to accept his compurgators, excommunicated, deprived and imprisoned him in defiance of his appeal, and proceeded to the election of a new prior.

During the remainder of the year no word appears to have come from Rome, and the abbot and his party remained supreme in the house until Walter's death on Christmas Day. The following spring, however, the case was heard by papal commissaries, and as no one appeared on behalf of the late abbot and the witnesses were unanimous in praise of Reginald, the sentences against him and against Roger of Aldenham were reversed, and he was restored to his office.

This, however, was not the end of the troubles at Westminster. A vacancy of two years and sixteen weeks followed,[106] and evidently the rivalry between the two parties in the house continued and caused great disorder.

On 14 July, 1308, the king wrote to the prior and convent complaining of dilapidations and appointing a commission of lawyers to inquire into the case.[107] Even this seems to have been without permanent effect, and in May, 1310, Edward wrote again to the prior complaining that the abbey was

> moult abessez et empoverez par la dissolucion des moignes … qui ont alez avant ces houres desordenement wakerantz hors de lour meson … et degastent les biens de la meson a grant ameneusement des … aumones.

He exhorted the prior to keep the monks to the observance of their profession, and not to allow

them to leave the close without permission. If visible reforms were not speedily made the king threatened so to lay hands upon the monks and their goods that all the other houses of the order 'se chastieront par ensample de vous.'[108]

In the meantime, however, the new abbot had been admitted and consecrated. His election, as might have been expected at a time of such great internal dissension, had not been unattended with difficulties. When the choice fell on Richard de Kydington several members of the house complained of his *infamia et insufficiencia* suggesting that he was supported by Piers Gaveston,[109] and the prior of Sudbury appealed to Rome on the ground that he had not been summoned to take part in the election.[110] The appeal dragged on for many months, and after the death of the prior Roger of Aldenham complained that the elect was 'not free from some faults.' Whether there was any truth in the accusations does not appear, but in May, 1310, the pope ordered the benediction of Richard,[111] his election having been confirmed without the usual burdensome visit to Rome.[112] Richard's rule was short and apparently uneventful.[113] On his death in 1315 he was succeeded by William de Curtlington, who appears to have been trusted both by the king and the pope, being appointed in 1320 to audit the accounts of the town of Abbeville,[114] and in 1322 to administer the monastery of Abingdon during the suspension of the abbot.[115] He was, however, subjected to a systematic persecution by the papal officials for a debt incurred by his predecessor and long since pardoned by Clement V. An attempt was made to sequester the abbot's manors in Worcestershire, and he himself was put under sentence of excommunication, which was only removed in 1320 after frequent remonstrances from the king.[116]

[108] Ibid. 36, 33, No. 29 (1). The document is dated from Kennington, 23 May in the third year of the king, and Widmore and others have attributed it to Edward I. The patent rolls of 23 May, 1275, however, are dated from Westminster, while those of the corresponding day 1310 are dated from Kennington.

[109] *Hist. MSS. Com. Rep*. i, App. 94.

[110] *Cal. Papal Letters*, ii, 65.

[111] Ibid. 71.

[112] This visit, exacted by the pope on account of the immediate subjection of the abbey to the Roman see, was abolished in 1478 at the request of Edward IV; D. & C. Westm. 'Abbots,' 28.

[113] He was clearly an admirer of Abbot Walter; 'in all his acts,' says the Westminster Chronicle, 'he showed forth the praise of his predecessor.' Cott. MS. Claud. A. viii, fol. 63; also *Flores Hist*. (Rolls Ser.), iii, 140, where almost the same words are used.

[114] *Cal. of Pat*. 1317–21, p. 505.

[115] *Cal. of Papal Letters*, ii, 218.

[116] *Foedera*, ii, 369; *Syllabus of Rymer's Foed*. 196, 199; *Arch. Journ*. xxix, 148; Widmore's MS. Cat. of Doc. at Westm. Abbey, 134*b*, 136; *Cal. Papal Letters*, i, 118, 209.

[105] Apparently the abbot's own party in the house induced him in August to confirm the compositions for his successors, while reserving his own right to disregard them. D. & C. Westm. 'Compositions,' 13, 2.

[106] Cott. MS. Claud. A. viii, fol. 62*d*.

[107] D. & C. Westm. 'Jurisdictions,' 36, 33, No. 29 (6).

A somewhat discreditable affray took place in the monastery at the end of August, 1324. A quarrel having arisen between one of the masons of the king's chapel and a serving man of Westminster, the monks flew to arms, and after wounding the masons were received back to the monastery by the prior. The abbot was absent at the time, but on his return took no steps to punish the culprits, who, when the case was summoned before the justices, were found to have escaped.[117] The abbot was subsequently pardoned, on condition that he should stand his trial should anyone proceed against him.[118] A few years before Abbot William's death a fire, which broke out in the royal palace, destroyed a considerable portion of the monastic buildings, and large sums of money were spent on rebuilding, towards which the abbot procured the appropriation of the churches of Langdon, Sawbridgeworth, and Kelvedon.[119]

The election of Abbot Thomas de Henley in 1333 was confirmed by the pope in spite of some irregularity,[120] and in 1335 the new abbot received leave of absence from the king for seven years, to stay 'in universities or places where learning thrives, as well in parts beyond the seas as on this side, so that he go not to Scotland nor to other parts at war with the king.'[121] Thomas certainly intended to set out for his university the following year, though whither he went and how long he stayed does not appear. In 1340 he was in England and presided at the General Benedictine Chapter at Northampton, and In 1341 he and a fellow-monk were summoned for deer-stealing in Windsor Forest, though possibly the abbot was only involved as representative of the convent in all legal proceedings.[122]

The most important event of his rule was the dispute which arose in 1342 as to the visitation of the hospital of St. James. The king claimed that the right was annexed to the treasurership, and had only been exercised by such abbots of Westminster as held that office; Thomas, on the other hand, asserted that the hospital lay within the bounds of the parish of St. Margaret, Westminster, and therefore within the jurisdiction of the abbey.[123] The jurors gave evidence in favour of the abbot to the great annoyance of the treasurer, who, says the Westminster chronicler, was so angry that he grievously vexed the church, and impleaded the abbot to the end of his life.[124]

The succeeding abbot, Simon de Bircheston, acquired a most unenviable notoriety. The circumstances of his election are unknown, but twenty years earlier he had been one of the monks involved in the attack on the king's stonemason,[125] and his character does not seem to have improved with advancing years, for a general tradition of misrule clings to his name. In 1345 he received licence for three years to study in the schools or stay elsewhere where he would within the realm, with entire exemption from personal attendance at any Councils or Parliaments, and two years later he obtained a similar exemption for two years.[126] In March, 1349, the plague broke out in Westminster, and shortly afterwards it attacked the abbey. Early in May Abbot Bircheston and twenty-seven of the monks were dead, and Simon Langham, who had been chosen prior barely a month before, was left to administer the house.[127] This can have been no light task, for not only had great distress been caused by the ravages of the plague, but also the monastery was impoverished by the extravagance of the late abbot, the frauds of his associates, and the wastefulness of his relatives.[128] The prior, however, evidently had the confidence of the house, for the monks in their necessity elected him abbot. Together with certain other brethren he sold jewels and ornaments of the church to the value of £315 13s. 8d.[129] for the relief of the more pressing needs, and for his own part he refused to receive the customary gifts on his accession, and presented the garden called the 'Burgoyne' to the convent. Details of his rule at Westminster are not known, but the chronicler speaks of his love and care for the house, and the zeal with which he extirpated certain 'insolences, abuses, singularities, superfluities, and malices' which had crept into the monastery;[130] while another writer states that he speedily paid off the debts of his predecessor and recalled the brethren to saner and more honourable counsels.[131] By the summer of 1354 the good fame of the abbey had so far recovered that a certain Austin canon from Waltham Holy Cross, who desired to lead a stricter life than he found possible in his own community, petitioned for admittance at Saint Peter's.[132]

[117] Coram Rege R. 261, Trin. 18 Edw. II.
[118] Cal. of Pat. 1324–7, p. 176.
[119] Cal. Papal Letters, ii, 350, 393–4.
[120] Ibid. 410; Cal. of Pat. 1330–4, p. 465.
[121] Cal. of Pat. 1334–8, p. 116.
[122] Ibid. 238; Cott. MS. Cleop. A. viii, fol. 65; Cal. of Pat. 1340–3, p. 292.
[123] Year Bks. of Edw. III (Rolls Ser.), App. 359; Cal. of Pat. 1340–3, pp. 456–7.
[124] Cott. MS. Claud. A. viii, vol. 65. See also account of St. James's Hospital below.

[125] Coram Rege R. 261. In 1345 he was impleaded for participation in an assault on the men and goods of the earl of Northampton at Uxbridge, but possibly his share was not personal; Cal. of Pat. 1343–5, p. 502.
[126] Cal. of Pat. 1343–5, p. 535. Ibid. 1345–8, p. 350.
[127] D. & C. Westm. 'Niger Quaternus,' fol. 80; Gasquet, The Great Pestilence, 97.
[128] Cott. MS. Cleop. A. xvi, fol. 16a.
[129] D. & C. Westm. 'Niger Quaternus,' fol. 80.
[130] Cott. MS. Claud. A. viii, fol. 67.
[131] Ibid. Cleop. A. xvi, fol. 16a.
[132] D. & C. Westm. Press 6, Box 4, parcel 33.

In 1362 Langham was promoted to the see of Ely, but throughout a somewhat stormy career he appears never to have lost his affection for Westminster.[133] The completion of the cloisters and the erection of various other conventual buildings were probably paid for out of the residuary estate which he left to the fabric of the monastery,[134] and he gave to the monks a library of nearly a hundred volumes, as well as vestments and church furniture.[135]

The new abbot, Nicholas Litlington, was undoubtedly a vigorous administrator; already as a simple monk he had three times secured to the prior and convent the guardianship of the abbot's temporalities during vacancies, he had considerably improved some of the abbey estates, and he had been associated with Langham in the oversight of the finances of the monastery at the death of Simon de Bircheston;[136] after his election he showed equal energy in carrying out the enlargements of the monastic buildings which Cardinal Langham's bequests had made possible, and in pleading the cause of the abbey before Parliament when the rights of sanctuary had been violated.[137]

But the period of his rule was a time of no little turmoil in the monastery. On 10 August, 1378, two gentlemen named Shackle and Hawley who had escaped from the Tower and taken sanctuary at Westminster were pursued thither by their enemies; one of the fugitives was captured, and the other escaped to the choir of the church, where he was overtaken and slain at the moment when the gospel was about to be read at high mass. The service ceased immediately, but the mischief was already done, and the abbey, which had never before been violated, was polluted with the blood of Hawley and of one of the servants of the church who had attempted to stop the fray.[138] Apparently the abbot did not bestir himself to procure the reconciliation of the church, for in December the king wrote to him remonstrating at the cessation of all services and distributions and the misapplication of alms, and urging him to remedy the matter.[139]

The privilege of sanctuary which had thus been infringed was one of the most valued rights of the abbey; in his defence of it Abbot Nicholas quoted charters of Edgar and Saint Edward, but its real origin is doubtful; it was probably prescriptive, and based on a common consent and necessity in days when justice was primitive and summary. In a Westminster manuscript of the fifteenth century occurs the oath taken by a fugitive on admission. In the first place he must say truthfully why he came, then he must swear to behave properly and faithfully while there, to submit to all corrections and judgements of the president, and to observe all contracts which he might make while in sanctuary; if he came there on account of debt, he was to satisfy his creditors at the earliest opportunity, and without garrulous or insolent words; he was to promise not to sell victuals in sanctuary without special leave of the archdeacon, not to receive any fugitive or suspect person at his table, not to carry defensive weapons nor go out of sanctuary without permission, not to defame any of his fellow fugitives in any way, nor, finally, to do or permit any violence within the privileged precincts.[140] Even at this date sanctuary was no doubt claimed from time to time legitimately enough, as in the case of Elizabeth, widow of Edward IV, and the two young princes, but very frequently in the later Middle Ages it became a real obstacle in the way of justice. As early as the time of Hawley's murder the custom was evidently unpopular, and when the archbishop of Canterbury, in the name of all the clergy of England, petitioned the king in Parliament against the late violation, the lords replied that they had no wish to encroach upon the liberties of the church, but that grave abuses were occasioned by people taking sanctuary for debts they were well able to pay, and other petitions were presented against the immense range of misdemeanour which the general terms of the charters were construed to cover. Abbot Nicholas made a vigorous defence, and Richard II, while he acknowledged the losses and inconveniences which had arisen, and pronounced that henceforth the immunity should not be construed to cover fraudulent debtors, still maintained all the privileges of the church touching cases of felony, and because of his great love for the abbey extended its protection to such debtors as had lost their wealth by fortune of the sea, robbery, or other mischief.[141]

---

[133] *Dict. Nat. Biog.*

[134] Sir G. G. Scott, *Gleanings*, 206 et seq.

[135] D. & C. Westm. 'Niger Quaternus,' fol. 146d. et seq. The most highly valued of the volumes were chiefly glossed copies of various canonical and apocryphal books of the Bible. There was also a volume of 'Pope Innocent on the Decretals,' St. Bernard's 'De Consideratione,' 'The Consolations of Philosophy,' the 'Sentences' of Peter Lombard, St. Augustine's 'De Civitate Dei,' the first part of the 'Speculum Historiale,' Bede's 'Gesta Anglorum,' and several volumes of St. Thomas Aquinas. All the volumes are valued in francs.

[136] Cott. MS. Claud. A. viii, fol. 69; cf. *Cal. of Pat.* 1334–8, p. 556; D. & C. Westm. 'Abbots' (Acct. R. of N. Litlington), and Anct. Correspondence (P.R.O.), lvi, 88.

[137] Cott. MS. Claud. A. viii, fol. 69.

[138] D. & C. Westm. 'Niger Quaternus,' fol. 88d.

[139] Rymer, *Foedera* (Rec. Com.), iv, 52.

[140] D. & C. Westm. 'Niger Quaternus,' fol. 139d.

[141] *Rolls of Parl.* (Rec. Com.), iii, 37a, 50b–51; also Walsingham, *Hist. Angl.* (Rolls Ser.), i, 391, where the author remarks that wealthy debtors had been received there 'ibidem laetos ducentes dies, in comessationibus et conviationibus,' while their goods were as safe as those of the lords of the liberty of Westminster.

The abuses seem to have increased as time went on, for in 1474 Edward IV wrote to the archdeacon of Westminster, saying that he had heard that great resort was made to the sanctuary, and grave crimes and abominable excesses committed there, and exhorting him to restrain and punish them;[142] and in the reign of Henry VIII an extraordinary collection of criminals and fugitives of every rank and description were congregated at Westminster.[143] Yet it would seem that the system was even yet not wholly without supporters, for when attempts were made to abolish it by Act of Parliament under the later Tudors the bills were always defeated.[144]

Though the abbey does not appear to have suffered much from the rising of 1381, there must have been consternation in the hearts of the monks when they heard that the rebels were attacking Lambeth Palace, and their fears were not allayed when the warden of the Marshalsea, flying before the insurgents, took refuge in the church on Saturday, 14 June. There he was found by the mob a few hours later clinging to the pillars of St. Edward's shrine, and thence he was borne away to be beheaded in mid Chepe.[145] In the afternoon, however, the young king, accompanied by a great train of nobles, knights, and citizens, came to the abbey, where he was met by a procession of monks. At the door of the monastery Richard sprang from his horse, and in tears upon his knees kissed the cross, which was borne before the convent; thence he proceeded to the shrine, where he knelt long in prayer before returning to meet the rebels at Smithfield.[146] In 1382 Abbot Nicholas was one of the commissioners of the peace appointed to arrest and punish the insurgents.[147]

Nicholas died at the close of the year 1386, leaving to the abbey a considerable quantity of plate 'because of the love which the prior and convent bear and have borne him.' The vessels were all marked with his initials, and he left money for repairing and replacing them.[148] A document among the Westminster archives,[149] which has been attributed to this period, raises an interesting point as to his character. It is an English letter to the king from 'the senior and more part of the convent' complaining of the 'gret waste and destruction' which 'dayly encreceth' through the 'misgovernaunce' of the abbot. If this really refers to Litlington, and may be taken in conjunction with another entry[150] which

complains of the dishonesty of the abbot in the matter of certain lead which he borrowed from the convent for roofing his new buildings, it throws a curious light on the protestation of affectionate loyalty between the abbot and his brethren, cited above, and on the ostentation with which Nicholas left his initials on his bequests of plate and on the buildings which he carried out with Abbot Langham's money. The ultimate impression left by these various indications of his character is that of a man of great vigour and business capacity, but at the same time worldly and vain-glorious. It is traditionally reported that in the last year of his life, when he was quite an old man, on the rumour of French invasion he bought armour and set out with two fellow monks to assist in the defence of the coast.[151] The story, if it is true, bespeaks enterprise and courage in a man of his age, but hardly that spiritual calm which would better befit the declining years of a venerable Benedictine abbot.

It was, however, to Litlington's lavishness and love of splendour that Westminster owed the famous missal known by his name, and left by him to the high altar of the abbey.[152] From this it would appear that the Westminster Use was closely allied to that of Sarum. There are, however, certain differences in the introits and grails, and the sequences of St. Thomas of Canterbury, St. Edward the Confessor, St. Peter ad Vincula, and the Common of the Apostles are peculiar to Westminster, as are also the distribution of lessons on Easter Eve and the collect before the first lesson on that day. The missal also contains a greater number of prayers for private use by the celebrant than any other English mass book.[153]

On hearing of Litlington's death the king sent John Lakyngheth, a candidate of his own, to Westminster;

---

[142] *Hist. MSS. Com. Rep.* iv, App. 191.

[143] *L. and P. Hen. VIII.* v. 1124.

[144] *Com. Journ.* i, 48–9, 73, 76, 79.

[145] Higden, *Polychron.* (Rolls Ser.), ix, 4.

[146] Ibid. 5.

[147] *Cal. of Pat.* 1381–5, p. 139.

[148] D. and C. Westm. 'Jewels,' 63.

[149] D. and C. Westm. 'Abbots,' 15.

[150] 'Niger Quaternus,' fol. 81.

[151] *Dict. Nat. Biog.*

[152] Cott. MS. Claud. A. viii, fol. 69.

[153] The Litlington Missal has been printed by the Henry Bradshaw Society with a liturgical introduction by Dr. Wickham Legg, from which the above notes are taken; *Missale ad Usum Westm.* pt. iii, introd. *passim.* The liturgical colours given in the Westminster Customary (60–1) are as follows:– The first Sunday in Advent and every Sunday to the feast of the Purification (or Septuagesima Sunday if it fell earlier than the Purification), white. The vigil and feast of the Nativity, the feast of the Circumcision, high mass on St. Edward's Day, the octave of St. Edward's Day, high mass on the feast of the Epiphany, and the octave of that feast, white. Ascension Day and its octave, the vigil and feast of the Nativity of St. John Baptist, the feasts of the Assumption and the Nativity of the Virgin and the feast of St. Michael, white. Septuagesima, Sexagesima, and Quinquagesima Sundays, dark red (*sub-rubeus*). The first Sunday in Lent and Passion Sunday, black. The octave of Whitsunday, embroidered, or either *scinlillata*, red, saffron (*croceus*), or grey (*glaucus*). Passion Sunday to Ascension Day and other Sundays throughout the year except the above, also the feasts of the Decollation of St. John Baptist, St. Edward, St. Thomas the Archbishop, and other martyrs, red.

but the convent, disregarding the royal wishes, elected their archdeacon, William of Colchester. Richard was greatly annoyed, and for some time refused to admit the new abbot; eventually, however, he was pacified, and wrote to Rome, *satis gratiose*, on William's behalf.[154] The century closed prosperously. A long-continued dispute with the canons of St. Stephen's, Westminster, was decided largely in favour of the abbey;[155] Christchurch, Canterbury, gave their share of the common Benedictine hall at Oxford to the monks of St. Peter's,[156] and the king was munificent in his benefactions and in the assistance he gave towards the completion of the new buildings.[157] In the tragedy with which the reign ended Abbot Colchester played a somewhat inexplicable part. He was with the king in Ireland at Whitsuntide, but the following autumn he was one of the commissioners sent to the Tower to receive Richard's abdication,[158] and was among those who recommended the king's entire isolation from any of his former companions;[159] at the same time he was appointed one of the executors of his will,[160] and was suspected of complicity in the conspiracy against Henry IV in 1400.[161]

Very few details of the history of Westminster in the fifteenth century survive. Beyond a statement by one of the chroniclers of the day to the effect that if the Lollards succeeded, one of their first enterprises would be the destruction of the abbey,[162] the monastery seems to slip out of the general current of national history, and the few notices that do occur are purely domestic. About the middle of the century a discontented monk accused the abbot of having recourse to a necromancer to discover the thief of certain plate from his chapel and wine-cellar;[163] this in itself, however, is insufficient evidence as to the character of the abbot or the state of the house – one malcontent among some forty or fifty monks would be scarcely surprising, though it may be noted that the abbot resigned in 1463.[164] A real instance of misgovernment arose, however, some few years later, when Abbot George Norwich was asked to retire to another house for a time on account of his maladministration and debts. The debt incurred amounted to at least 3,037 marks 6s. 8d., and the resources which should have met it had been reduced by alienations and grants in

fee. A certain Brother Thomas Ruston, evidently a partisan of the abbot, was holding four offices, and had brought them to decay by his neglect; he had burdened the house with his own debts, and was suspected of having embezzled six or seven copes at the time when he was keeper of the vestry. The memorial presented to the abbot was signed by thirteen monks, two of whom, Thomas Milling, the prior, and John Eastney, were afterwards themselves abbots.[165] The tone of the document reflects great credit on the spirit of the house at the time: it is at once businesslike, moderate, and respectful, and the abbot wisely acquiesced in the scheme set before him, and appointed Milling one of the five commissioners to administer the abbey during his retirement.

Milling was elected to succeed Norwich as abbot in 1469,[166] but his rule was short, for in 1474 he was consecrated bishop of Hereford. He was succeeded by John Eastney, who, like Norwich, was appointed by papal provision.[167] Several slight indications point to a decaying vigour in the monastery at this time. That the abbey should surrender its cherished privilege of free election to the pope twice within a period of twelve years was without precedent; in 1478 moreover, the king complained to Sixtus IV that the house was going to decay on account of the civil war and floods,[168] and though the expression was doubtless an exaggeration, yet the pope thought the situation sufficiently grave to warrant him in absolving future abbots from going to Rome for confirmation.[169] The numbers of the brethren, moreover, during the fifteenth and sixteenth centuries show a steady decline. In the eleventh century Abbot Gilbert had made provision for eighty monks,[170] and about the year 1260 there is said to have been an increase in the community;[171] at the election of Abbot Islip in 1500, however, there were but forty-six monks present, in 1528 there were forty-four, in 1534 there were forty-three, and the following year forty-one, while the deed of surrender was signed only by the abbot, prior, and twenty-three others.[172]

But if numbers were declining the old splendour of ceremonial was still maintained. The funeral of Abbot Islip in 1532 must have been one of the most impressive scenes ever witnessed at Westminster.

[154] Higden, *Polychron.* (Rolls Ser.), ix, 89.
[155] See account of St. Stephen's, *infra*.
[156] *Lit. Cant.* (Rolls Ser.), iii, 14.
[157] *Cal. of Pat.* 1391–6, *passim*.
[158] Trokelowe and Blandford, *Ann.* (Rolls Ser.), 248, 252.
[159] *Rolls of Parl.* (Rec. Com.), iii, 426*b*.
[160] Nicolas, *Test. Vet.* 33.
[161] Trokelowe and Blandford, *Ann.* (Rolls Ser.), 330.
[162] Walsingham, *Hist. Angl.* (Rolls Ser.), ii, 298.
[163] *Hist. MSS. Com. Rep.* viii, pt. i, 265.
[164] *Cal. of Pat.* 1461–7, p. 290.

[165] D. and C. Westm. 'Abbots' (22).
[166] *Cal. of Pat.* 1467–77, p. 179.
[167] *Cal. of Pat.* 1467–77, p. 472.
[168] D and C. Westm. 'Abbots' (28).
[169] Ibid. See above, note 112.
[170] See above, note 29.
[171] D. and C. Westm. Book No. 11, fol. 662*d*.
[172] D. and C. Westm. 'Abbots' (30) and 'Monks' (47); *Dep. Keeper's Rep.* viii, App. ii, 48. Probably some of the monks had died of the plague which was rife in the abbey in 1536; *L. and P. Hen. VIII*, xi, 501.

The abbot had been an energetic statesman, an able administrator, and a great builder,[173] and he was mourned with extraordinary pomp. The magnificent obituary roll which was circulated amongst the religious houses of England announcing his death has an interest apart from the beauty and skill of its workmanship, due to the fact that it commemorates the last Englishman who died as abbot of this most national of English monasteries, and perhaps it is not altogether without significance that while the four pictures of the roll are mediaeval in character the drawing of the initial letter of the brief shows signs of renaissance influence.[174]

Not very much is known of William Boston, the last abbot. He seems to have acquiesced without much question in the dealings of Henry VIII and of Cromwell, and to have felt that private judgement was no match for authority. At the examination of Sir Thomas More in 1534 he said that however the matter seemed to the prisoner he had reason to think he was wrong seeing that the Great Council had determined otherwise; More, he argued, ought to 'change his conscience.'[175] The following year he wrote to Cromwell asking him to secure him the free bestowal of his bailiwick of Westminster, and stating that he would be glad to appoint Cromwell himself to the office.[176] His compliance, however, did not save his house from a visit from Dr. Legh, which, to judge from Ap Rice's report to Cromwell, was by no means respectful.[177] This was in October, 1535; in July of the following year the king issued royal injunctions to Westminster; the abbot was to administer the monastery according to the rule of St. Benedict and the custom of the house, 'notwithstanding any injunctions' given by the vicar-general or his commissaries; the monks were to be allowed to leave the monastery, with permission, for honest recreation; they might occasionally entertain women of upright life at their table, and when they were sick they were to be kept by the infirmarer, with help, in cases of need, from the abbot himself. The injunctions stated that the abbot was to render an account to the vicar-general as often as it seemed good, but Boston erased the entry, adding at the side 'oute wt this elles he and hys deputys may call me weeklye to accopt.'[178]

By the beginning of the year 1540 Boston was anxiously pleading to 'be delivered from the governance of this house' and seeking to avoid the king's indignation. He seems to have been thoroughly afraid of incurring Henry's wrath, for he wrote to someone in authority – probably Cromwell – 'As for my pension, I pass not how little soever it be, so I may have the King's Highness my gracious lord.' Possibly this seeming pusillanimity was accounted for by the fact that he was suffering from a painful disease, and expected but 'a very short painful bodily life.'[179] However this may be he seems to have obtained favour, but not the retirement he coveted; his convent was dissolved on 16 January, 1540, pensions of from £10 to 56s. 8d. being granted to seven of the brethren,[180] but in the following December the new cathedral church was erected, Abbot Boston being appointed dean of the new foundation.[181] With this point the history of Westminster as a religious house practically ends.

There is no lack of information as to the administrative details and daily life of the abbey. At a very early date Abbot Gilbert had made provision for the clothing of eighty monks, and Abbot William endowed the kitchen with a revenue of £150 11s. 9d., including the manors of Ashwell (Herts.), Longdon (Worcs.), and Morden (Surrey),[182] but the turning-point in the constitutional history of Westminster was reached when Richard de Berking made his composition with the monastery in 1225.[183] He assigned to the convent the manors of Feering, Stevenage, Wheathampstead, Aldenham, Battersea, Wandsworth, and Knightsbridge, with the farms of Deene and Sudborough, Shepperton and Halliford (Halgeford), Kelvedon and Hendon, with reliefs and escheats and the 10 marks a year which his predecessors had received for their clothing and £8 from the tithes of Droitwich; for fuel he assigned the farms of Denham (£15), Holwell (£6), and Datchworth (60s.), and the brushwood from Pyrford; for wages for the convent he assigned £6 from the church of Oakham; and for repairs in the dormitory and elsewhere, 100s. from the manor of Islhampstead and the revenues of the mills of Westminster, saving to the abbot free multure. To the charges of hospitality he appropriated the church of Staines and half the church of Wheathampstead with a rent of £10 from 'Wokendune' (Essex) and £8 from Westminster, and half the herbage of Westminster.

The composition goes on to say that the abbot in chapter deputed one or two brethren for the keeping of hospitality, while for keeping the

[173] Dict. Nat. Biog.

[174] See Vetusta Monumenta, vii, pt. iv, 'The Obituary Roll of John Islip' (ed. W. H. St. John Hope). These notes also contain extracts from the contemporary account of Islip's funeral, for which cf. also Widmore, Hist. 206 et seq.

[175] L. and P. Hen. VIII, vii, 575.

[176] Ibid. ix, 237.

[177] Ibid. 622

[178] D. and C. Westm. 'Jurisdictions,' 36, 33, 29 (13).

[179] L. and P. Hen. VIII, xv, 70.

[180] Ibid. 69.

[181] Ibid. xvi, 333

[182] Cott. MS. Faust. A. iii, fol. 237. It does not appear whether this was Postard or Humez.

[183] Ibid. fol. 225–30.

manors assigned to the convent 'he made some of the brethren proctors and obedientiaries as many as the convent thought fit.' This is evidently not the first institution of obedientiaries at Westminster, but it may have been the occasion of an increase in their numbers[184] and the definition of their status, for the document further states that the abbot must remove them readily on complaint of the convent, but that he could not do so at his own pleasure without assigning good cause. With regard to the maintenance of hospitality, the convent was to undertake all entertainment except that of kings, legates, archbishops, and nuncios with twelve or more horsemen; for these the abbot was to provide, as also for all guests whom he had himself invited. The abbot retained the advowsons of all churches on the conventual manors, as well as the service and wardship of all who owed knight's service, and he received the homage of every free tenant of the abbey. In return he had to answer to the king for all scutages, and to defend the abbey and its property in all suits ecclesiastical and secular; he was also bound to provide fuel and a dish of meat for the 'misericorde' of the convent from the feast of the Epiphany to Septuagesima, and gruel in Lent, as well as bread and beer on the occasion of the ceremonial feetwashing of the poor on Maundy Thursday and wine for the wassails of the convent on the same day. He had to secure the convent against inundations of the Thames, and to repair the walls of the monastery.

The convent, on the other hand, undertook to pay any fines which might be exacted by the king's court from any of their manors, to answer for the hidage on their own lands, and not to waste or alienate their woods or emancipate their villeins without the consent of the abbot. No abbot or prior was to visit the conventual manors without the consent of the whole convent, lest by too frequent visits its share should be diminished. With regard to the abbot's maintenance, he might eat in the refectory with the convent when he liked, and might at any time bring as many as four people with him; and when resident within the monastery or at Eye he was to receive six loaves daily from the cellarer, but when

elsewhere he could not claim bread or any other food from the convent. He was responsible for certain anniversaries and the liveries (*liberationes*) of the servants on the principal feasts.

This arrangement, with certain modifications, remained in force throughout the Middle Ages, but it was not always acquiesced in without question. In 1227 the convent complained that their share was not sufficient, and the bishops of Bath, Salisbury, and Chichester were called upon to mediate; the manors of Ashford (Midd.) and Greenford were added and 60s. from the manor of 'Suberk,' on condition that nothing should be exacted from the abbot in the way of victuals, firewood, or contributions towards the debts of the prior and convent.[185]

After the great quarrel with Abbot Crokesle in 1252, the bishop of Bath and John Mansel, provost of Beverley, made certain provisions which seem to point to an attempt on the part of the convent to interpret the original composition wholly in their own interests. The abbot was to be allowed to remove the obedientiaries according to the rule of St. Benedict, and for reasonable cause; he was not to be bound to find flesh for the convent, and was to be admitted to visit the five principal manors assigned to the cellarer, one day in the year, for purposes of correction, with reasonable procuration. For the appointment of the cellarers the prior and convent were to nominate four brethren, from whom the abbot was to make choice of two, and the guest-masters were to be chosen in the same way; the *celararius extrinsecus* was to choose honest seculars to act under him, and to hear such causes as ought not to be entertained by monks. The common seal was to be kept under four keys, held respectively by a monk appointed by the abbot, the prior, the sub-prior, and a monk appointed by the convent. The obedientiaries were to show their accounts annually or oftener, and any surplus was to be spent on hospitality; the abbot was not to send the brethren from place to place unnecessarily or without consultation;[186] the church of Ashwell was assigned to the guest-master, and the church of Feering for the support of an increased number of monks and additional anniversaries.[187]

That further difficulties as to the compositions arose at the end of the century may be gathered from a decree passed by the prior and convent during the vacancy on the death of Abbot Richard de Ware in 1283. Some of the clauses are merely in confirmation of the original compositions, others

[184] The following is a list of the Westminster obedientiaries compiled from various sources, between the reign of Edward I and the dissolution of the monastery: – Prior, sub-prior, chamberlain, two cellarers, almoner, sub-almoner, guest-master, third and fourth priors, master of the novices, archdeacon, precentor, succentor, infirmarian, sacrist, refectorian, steward of the granary, treasurer, treasurer *intrinsecus*, keeper of St. Mary's Chapel, keeper of the shrine of St. Edward, warden of the new work, wardens of the manors of Queen Eleanor, of Richard II, of Henry V, and of Henry VII, keeper of the churches, *scrutator*, bailiff of the liberty of Westminster and bailiff *extrinsecus*; while the abbot had a treasurer, seneschal, and bailiff of his own.

[185] D. and C. Westm. Book No. 11, fol. 662.

[186] This probably refers to the practice of banishing unruly monks to the cells of the abbey, as in the case of Roger of Aldenham in 1307 (see *supra*).

[187] D. and C. Westm. Book No. 11, fol. 662d.

point to fresh difficulties; thus the new abbot was to provide a grange for the conventual tithes at Staines; he was not to remove the cellarer, almoner, or guest-master without consent; he was not to imprison the brethren except for open theft, or on conviction of enormous crime; he was not to hand over the care of the walls against the Thames to any obedientiary; he was to have the appointment of only seven of the servants; he was to furnish the king's clerks at the Exchequer with bread and beer; he was not to extort money from the officers of the monastery, nor gifts on feast days from the gardener, keeper of the granaries, or others; he was to demand nothing from the chamberlain beyond one light for his bedroom. It was also arranged that the gifts to the abbot from the obedientiaries on the ten principal feasts were not to exceed 4s. each[188] if he were at Westminster, or 12d. if he were elsewhere. The agreement was to be enrolled in the martyrology, and read in chapter once a year. This provision, however, was not sufficient to prevent Abbot Wenlac from once more attempting to override the constitution;[189] his quarrel with Prior Reginald appears to have turned chiefly upon this point, and during the vacancy of 1308 the whole convent once more swore to the articles, and undertook that whichever of them should be elected as abbot should not procure from the pope any letters prejudicial to the arrangement.[190]

Passing from the general outlines of the constitution to the details of the daily life, it is clear from the Customary that the abbot, no doubt owing to his political position, could not be relied upon for the oversight of the daily routine. This was accordingly committed to the prior and sub-prior, and to that one of the obedientiaries who, as keeper of the order of the day, presided at the high table at meals, and regulated the entertainment of guests. The standard of courtesy in the monastery was high; thus if anyone made a noise with the cover of his cup, or upset anything on the cloth during the reading at meals, immediate and public penance was exacted.[191] Any one who was obliged to leave the table during meat had to go through an elaborate ceremony of asking leave of the president. No brother was to gaze about him during dinner nor to throw things from table to table, nor yet to sit with his hand under his chin or over his face, 'eo quod sic sedere mesticiae et doloris aut studii

immoderate, seu agoniae indicium est.' Everyone was to keep his tongue from talking, and to hold his cup with both hands according to the good old English custom. It was the Normans, according to the compiler of the Customary, who introduced the slovenly habit of holding the cup in one hand.[192]

Discipline in the dormitory is discussed at length in the Customary. The brethren were to prepare for bed as secretly and simply as possible, they were not to keep riding apparel or dirty boots about their beds, but everyone might have one peg and no more on which to hang his clothes. There were strict rules against gaycoloured counterpanes, and the utmost silence was enjoined – snorers and those who talked in their sleep were to be banished to a separate room. Each brother was to have a separate bed, chiefly, says the compiler of the Customary, because secret prayer is best offered to God when there is no witness. No one was to give place to unholy thoughts before he slept, but to lie down contemplating God only, that he might have rest of body and peace of mind. When the bell rang for mattins all were to rise promptly, to sign themselves with the cross, and repeat privately certain prayers before they spoke.

But if life in the monastery was carefully regulated, it can hardly have been austere. The plain convent food was supplemented with a goodly number of pittances;[193] the gardener had to supply apples, cherries, plums, pears, and nuts; and cheese, which had once been supplied only rarely and 'by the grace of God,'[194] was by the middle of the thirteenth century a usual dish. The large staff of servants were bidden to serve the brethren *mansuete et honeste*. As regards clothing, each monk had a new frock and cowl annually, and underclothing whenever he needed it; no one was to wear underclothing which had been much mended. Though, according to the rule, no brother ought to have other than lamb's wool lining to his cloak, yet in cases of manifest necessity a more costly fur

---

[188] Later altered to 'one sextarius of wine or its value.' D. and C. Westm. Book No. 11, fol. 669. The manor of Amwell was to be assigned to the cellarer as soon as the new abbot returned from Rome.

[189] Ibid. fol. 668.

[190] Ibid. 669.

[191] Unless there were guests present, when the penance was not exacted until the convent was alone.

[192] *Customary*, 127.

[193] The pittancer had to supply pittances from the revenues of the church of Oakham every day in the year, except on the feasts of St. Peter and St. Paul, and St. Peter ad Vincula, certain of the greater anniversaries, and Good Friday. They were supplied to all the brethren within the cloister, and to any guests in the guest-house within the precincts. Pittances might consist of rice, oysters, eggs, or cheese, but more properly they were of fish of various kinds – one and a half plaice, or two soles, six eels, or other fish in numbers according to their size. The pittancer also had to provide beer and mead on certain feast days (*Customary*, 75 et seq.). Pittances were also supplied on certain occasions by the obedientiaries, and the pittancer himself had other resources from which to draw.

[194] The brethren had once been expected to rise when the cheese was carried through the refectory, but this primitive custom had now been dropped.

might be used, provided it were hidden at the collar and cuffs with a lamb's wool edging, lest the sight of such luxury should be an occasion of stumbling to any. Felt boots and woollen socks were supplied at the vigil of All Saints, and stockings again at the vigil of St. Thomas, while on the Saturday before Palm Sunday boots and socks were to be distributed to any Benedictine guests, as well as to the members of the house. Hospitality was always regarded as one of the most sacred duties of the abbey; great stress is laid upon its observance in all the compositions, and in the Customary the most minute regulations are given for the entertainment of various ranks of guests, from the great Benedictine abbot down to the humblest clerk or truant monk.

The actual wealth of the church of the abbey is too well known[195] to require discussion, but there are many points of interest with regard to the revenue of the monastery and its distribution amongst the obedientiaries.

From the Valor[196] it appears that the clear value of the abbey property in 1535 amounted to the enormous sum of £3,470 0s. 2¼d. The abbot's lands in Gloucestershire included the manors of Deerhurst, Hardwicke, Bourton cum Moreton, and Todenham, and rents in Sutton; in Worcestershire he held the manors of Longdon, Chaddesley, Pensham, Binholme, Pinvin, Wick, Pershore, and Birlingham; in Middlesex he held the manors of le Nete, Staines, Laleham and 'Billets,' and the rectory of Hendon; in Surrey, the manor of Pyrford, and the farms of 'Alferthyng' and Wandsworth; in Buckinghamshire, the manor of Denham; in Oxfordshire, the manor of Islip with Stokenchurch; in Berkshire, rents in Poughley; and in Suffolk, the priory of St. Bartholomew Sudbury. The foundation of Margaret, countess of Richmond, was worth £91 2s. net, and included the rectories of Cheshunt (Herts.) and Swineshead (Lincs.), but out of this 24s. 3d. was paid annually in rents, and £26 13s. 4d. to two readers in theology at Oxford and Cambridge, £10 to a certain preacher at Cambridge, and £10 to the poor. The foundation of Henry VII was worth £580 17s. 5½d. clear; it included the rectories of St. Bride London, Great Chesterford, Newport Pound, Witham, Cressing, Chrishall, Ketton or Kedington? ('Ketton and Cowpes') and Good Easter (Essex), Stanford (Berks.), Swaffham (Norfolk), and Bassingbourn (Camb.); four of the prebends of St. Martin le Grand, the free chapels of Playden (Sussex), Tickhill (Yorks.), and 'Uplambourne' (Wilts.), the manor of 'Oswardbesoken,' (? Osberton, Notts.), and the priory of Luffield (Bucks.). The treasurer's was always

by far the most richly endowed of the conventual offices; in the fourteenth and fifteenth centuries his revenues came principally from some twentyfour demesne manors, chiefly in Hertfordshire, Essex, and Middlesex. His total income for the year 1302–3 was £658 0s. 2¾d.; from Michaelmas, 1378–9, it was £564 15s. 7¼d.; and two years later, £527 19s. 7¾d. At the close of the following century (1499–1500) it had risen to £837 2s. 7½d., and in 1501–2 it was £888 3s. 7¼d. His expenses fell chiefly into nine groups – purchase of corn and malt, gifts, anniversaries, pittances, kitchen expenses, pensions, pleas, subsidies and other contributions, and gifts to the abbot. Of these the purchase of corn was the heaviest item, ranging from £141 15s. 10½d. in 1378–9 to £248 9s. 8½d. in 1501–2; pittances in 1378–9 amounted to £16 19s. 1d., and in 1380–1 £13 16s. 8d., while in the sixteenth century they cost about £28 or £29 a year. Kitchen expenses seem to have been met by a fixed sum, in the fourteenth century £182 10s., and in the sixteenth £184 2s.; gifts in the fourteenth century cost about £33, and in the sixteenth £9 or £10. The total outgoings of the year 1378–9 were £834 1s. 6¼d.; those of the years 1499–1500 £791 7s. 4d.[197]

Turning to the rolls of the sacrist, his income for the year 1338–9 was about £100, in 1379–80 it was £222 6s. 10d. and in 1483–4 £191 2s. 7½d. His outgoings were chiefly purchases of wax and oil, wine for pittances and for the sacrament, coal and tallow, purchases of church furniture and the maintenance of the fabric of the church, and the usual wages, gifts, pittances, subsidies, and procurations. The general purchases of 1338–9 amounted to about £23, those of 1379–80 to £36 10s. 0½d., and those of 1483–4 to £43 7s. 10¼d. On church furniture in 1379–80 the sacrist spent £10 3s., including 6s. 8d. for mats for the choir and chapter, 4s. 6d. for red, white, and green thread for the abbot's vestments, 21s. 4d. for incense, 7s. 6d. for a pall for the high altar, and 25s. for bread for the sacrament; and in 1483–4 similar items amounted to £6 15s. 5d. The maintenance of the fabric cost £33 3s. 11¾d. in 1338–9, £43 16s. 1d. in 1379–80, and £56 8s. in 1483–4.

Another interesting account of the fifteenth century shows how the convent contributed to provide 'seyng' books for their church. The total cost of two books was 100s, the largest items being 26s. 8d. each for the writing, and in one case 14s. 4d. 'for fflorishing of grete lettres and for the lynyng of grete letters and smale.' The abbot and forty-eight monks contributed, and one brother 'payeth for the peecyng of the book and fyndeth the writer his bedde.'[198]

[195] See for example the inventory printed by Mr. Walcott in *Lond. and Midd. Arch. Soc. Trans.* iv. 313.

[196] *Valor Eccl.* (Rec. Com.), i, 410 et seq.

[197] D. and C. Westm. Treas. Rolls.

[198] D. & C. Westm. 'Monks,' 47, 5.

The new community which entered upon this goodly heritage of wealth and many-sided activity was intended to consist of a bishop, dean, twelve prebendaries, ten readers at the two universities, scholars to be taught in grammar, twenty students of divinity at Oxford and Cambridge, twelve petty canons to sing in choir, twelve laymen to sing and serve in choir daily, ten choristers, a master of the children, a 'gospellor' and a 'pistoler,' two sextons and twelve poor men decayed in the king's service.[199] The old community had not so far dissociated itself from the royal plans as to be totally excluded from the new foundation, and the abbot, prior, and several of the monks found places in the cathedral church. But the foundation was short-lived, and has but little history. In 1550 the bishopric was dissolved, and on 21 November, 1556,[200] just sixteen years after the first foundation of Henry's collegiate church, Dr. Feckenham, late dean of St. Paul's, and fourteen monks were once more installed at Westminster. On the following day

> they went in procession after the old fashion, in their monk's dress and cowls of black say, with two vergers carrying two silver rods in their hands, and at evensong time the vergers went through the cloister to the abbot and so went to the altar, and there my lord knelt in the convent, and after his prayers was brought into the choir with the vergers and so into his place and at once he began evensong.[201]

For a few short years something or the old splendour seemed to be restored to this little community; on 29 November, Feckenham was consecrated and wore his mitre, and in the following April the duke of Muscovy dined at his table – an indication of his high political place.[202] But, as Fuller justly remarks, the new abbot 'like the *Axiltree* stood firme and fixed in his own judgement, whilst the times like the *wheels* turned backwards and forwards round about him.'[203] The same writer goes on to tell the story of how when Queen Elizabeth sent for Feckenham shortly after her accession, he was found setting elms in the orchard at Westminster, and characteristically would not follow the messenger until he had finished his task.[204] But neither his saintliness nor his known justice to Protestants during the previous reign[205] could save him from the results of his firmness of attitude nor his monastery from a second dissolution.

On 21 May, 1560, the queen once more constituted the abbey a collegiate body consisting of a dean and twelve prebendaries,[206] as in Henry VIII's foundation, though, according to Widmore, the choir was not so large a body as that established twenty years earlier.[207]

*Phyllis Wragge*

## Revised List of Abbots

The list of Abbots is taken from *Heads of Religious Houses*, vol. 1, pp. 76–7, vol. 2, pp. 78–9; and vol. 3 (forthcoming).

> St Wulfsige, 958; died 993/7
> Aelfwig, 997–*c*.1020?
> Wulfnoth, *c*.1020?–1049
> Eadwine, *c*.1049; died 1068/71
> Geoffrey, occurs 1072
> Vitalis, appointed 1076; died ?1085
> Gilbert Crispin, ?1085; died 1117/18
> Herbert, elected 1121; died 1146/8
> Gervase, appointed 1138; removed *c*.1157
> Master Laurence, *c*.1158; died 1173
> Walter, elected 1175; died 1190
> William Postard, elected 1190; died 1200
> Ralph Arundel, occurs 1200; died 1214
> William du Hommet, elected 1214; died 1222
> Richard of Barking, elected, 1222; died 1246
> Richard de Crokesley, elected 1246; died 1258
> Philip (de) Levesham, elected and died 1258
> Richard of Ware, elected 1258; died 1283
> Walter of Wenlock, elected 1283; died 1307
> Richard de Kedyngton alias de Sudburia, elected 1308; died 1315
> William de Curtlyngton, elected 1315; died 1333
> Thomas de Henle(e), elected 1333; died 1344
> Simon de Bercheston, elected 1344; died 1349
> Simon de Langham, elected 1349; resigned 1362
> Nicholas de Litlington, elected 1362; died 1386
> William of Colchester, 1387–1420
> Richard Harweden, 1420–1440
> Edmund Kirton, provided by the pope 1440, ceded 1463
> George Norwich, provided 1463; resigned 1469
> Thomas Milling, 1469–74
> John Eastney, provided 1474–98
> George Fascet, 1498–1500
> John Islip, 1500–1532
> William Boston or Benson, last abbot of the old foundation, 1533
> John Feckenham, 1556–60

---

[199] *L. and P. Hen. VIII*, xvi, 333.
[200] *Hist. MSS. Com. Rep.* i, App. 96.
[201] *Machyn's Diary* (Camd. Soc.), 118.
[202] Ibid. 119, 132.
[203] *Church Hist.* (ed. 1655), bk. ix, 178–9.
[204] Ibid.
[205] *Dict. Nat. Biog.* He saved twenty-eight people from the stake at one time in Mary's reign.

[206] Pat. 2 Eliz. pt. 11, m. 26.
[207] *Hist.* 139.

# HOUSE OF BENEDICTINE NUNS

## 3. ST. HELEN'S, BISHOPSGATE

### INTRODUCTION

This is a generally sound account of the house but it should now be supplemented by Paxton, 'Nunneries', where a detailed history of the house from *c.*1370 to the Dissolution is provided. Paxton includes a good deal of unpublished material and an account of the urban property of the house. The general history of female Benedictines in England is considered by Eileen Power, *Medieval English Nunneries* (Cambridge, 1922) and Sally Thompson, *Women Religious: The Founding of English Nunneries after the Norman Conquest* (Oxford, 1991). Kathleen Cooke includes a discussion of the house in 'English Nuns and the Dissolution', in J. Blair and B. Golding (eds.), *The Cloister and the World: Essays in Medieval History in Honour of Barbara Harvey* (Oxford, 1996), pp. 287–301.

The fabric of the church, with an account of lost monuments, is comprehensively described in J. Bird and P. Norman (eds.), *Survey of London: Vol. IX, The Parish of St. Helen, Bishopsgate, Part 1* (London County Council, 1924). The surviving fabric is also described in *The Royal Commission on Historical Monuments, London, Vol. IV, The City* (London, 1929), pp. 19–24. The site and the estates belonging to the house are described in Honeybourne, 'Property', pp. 125–39. There is a convenient summary of locations of, and sources for, the priory's London property in *Documentary Sources*, p. 54. The priory's London holdings are included in the 1392 record of ecclesiastical property in McHardy, *Church in London*, pp. 39–77.

Surviving records relating to the house are listed on the web site of the English Monastic Archives project, along with a list of estates, URL: http://www.ucl.ac.uk/history/englishmonasticarchives/index.htm (accessed 28 February 2007).

The prioress, eleven nuns, eight secular chaplains and one clerk paid the Poll Tax in 1379, McHardy, *Church in London*, p. 2. Two chantry chaplains remained after the dissolution of the House and the nascent parish community in 1548 was served by a parish priest, Kitching, *Chantry Certificate*, p. 49.

*D. Anne Welch*

The nunnery of St. Helen was founded in the early part of the thirteenth century[1] by William son of William the goldsmith, in the place where a church of St. Helen had already existed in the reign of Henry II. The church had been granted to the dean and canons of St. Paul's by a certain Ranulf and Robert his son, who with a third person to be named by them were to hold it for their lives.[2] After the dean and canons gained possession they gave the patronage to William son of William, and not only allowed him to found the nunnery, but also to bestow on it the advowson of the church on condition that the prioress after election by the nuns should be presented to the dean and chapter and swear fealty to them,[3] and should promise to pay a pension of ½ mark from the church, the obventions of which the convent might for the rest convert to their own use, and neither to alienate the right of patronage nor become subject to any other body.

Though there is evidence that the claim of the nuns to some land was disputed, and was renounced by them before 1216,[4] there is nothing to show

---

[1] Before 1216, as Alard, the dean of St. Paul's who gave permission for the foundation, died in that year. Newcourt, *Repert. Eccl. Lond.* i, 363.

[2] Dugdale, *Mon. Angl.* iv, 551.

[3] The dean and chapter were careful to guard their rights from any episcopal encroachment which might result from the bishop's receiving the profession of nuns there. Lond. Epis. Reg. Sudbury, fol. 139.

[4] Cott. Chart. v, 6 (2).

what the endowment of the nunnery was at its foundation. Among its earliest possessions, however, may be reckoned a quit-rent of 4s. in the parish of All Hallows Lombard Street, sold by the prioress probably before 1230,[5] a rent of 26s. 8d. from land in the parish of St. Mildred, Canterbury, alienated by the convent in 1247,[6] and 6½ acres of land which they held in Stepney in 1248.[7] The earliest notices of the house occur in the will of William Longespee, earl of Salisbury, who left five cows to the nuns in 1225,[8] and in the gift of two oaks made by Henry III in 1224 to the master of St. Helen's,[9] an officer of whom there is no other mention.

The nuns figure in the inquisition of 1274–5[10] as having about sixteen years before closed with an earthen wall a lane called St. Helen's Lane running from Bishopsgate Street to St. Mary Axe, down which men had been used to ride and take carts. This is probably the lane crossing their ground which Henry III in 1248 had licensed them to inclose.[11]

Edward I gave to the priory in 1285 a piece of the True Cross[12] which he had brought from Wales, and went on foot accompanied by earls, barons, and bishops to present the relic. The nuns about this time seem to have been in need of financial help. They petitioned the king to examine their charters and allow them to hold in frankalmoign henceforth,[13] and it was no doubt in consequence of the inquiry he had ordered that he gave them in 1306 the right to hold a market and fair at Brentford.[14] Archbishop Peckham, in May, 1290, gave the prioress and nuns leave to celebrate the Festival of the Invention of the Cross notwithstanding the interdict placed on the City by his authority.[15] In October of the same year the pope offered relaxation of penance for a year and forty days to penitents visiting the convent church on the festivals of St. Helen and of Holy Cross,[16] and an indulgence of forty days was given by Ralph, bishop of London, in 1306, to those visiting the church and making contributions to the fabric.[17] These grants were in all probability made in aid of the rebuilding of the church, the expense of which

had largely been defrayed by two brothers, Salomon and Thomas Basing, the latter bequeathing also to its maintenance by will enrolled in 1300[18] some rents in the parish of St. Bartholomew the Little and elsewhere. Several of the Basings became nuns of St. Helen's,[19] one indeed was elected prioress in 1269;[20] this may account in part for the benefactions of the family, which altogether must have been extensive: William, the sheriff of 1308, is said by Stow to have been reputed a founder,[21] and Henry de Gloucestre, grandson of Thomas, by will dated 1332[22] established there a chantry of two chaplains which he endowed with an income of 11 marks of silver.

During the next few years the endowments of the nunnery received further additions: in 1344 the prioress and convent undertook to found a chantry in their church and one in St. Mary le Bow for the soul of Walter Dieuboneye of Bletchingley, cheesemonger of London, in consideration of his gifts to them;[23] in 1346 John de Etton, rector of Great Massingham, left them his dwelling-house and fourteen adjacent shops near Cripplegate for the maintenance of chantries;[24] and for the same purpose Walter de Bilynham bequeathed to the priory in 1349 tenements in the parishes of St. Mary Magdalen Old Fish Street, and St. Mary Axe, at Holborn Cross and 'Cokkeslane';[25] the church of Eyworth, co. Bedford, was also appropriated to them in 1331 by the pope at the king's request.[26] The nunnery, either through misfortune or mismanagement, could not have been very prosperous for some years before the Black Death, or the church would not have been reported in 1350 as in danger of going to ruin, a state of things which the pope tried to remedy by the grant of another indulgence.[27] Its need at this time may give a clue to the date of the attempt to recover the market and fair of Brentford, rights which the nuns considered they had lost because, being an inclosed

[5] Guildhall MS. 122, fol. 263.

[6] Cal. of Chart. R. i, 318.

[7] Doc. of D. and C. of St. Paul's, Liber A. fol. 44.

[8] Rot. Lit. Claus. (Rec. Com.), ii, 71.

[9] Ibid. i, 601b, 618, 643.

[10] Hund. R. (Rec. Com.), i, 413, 409, 420.

[11] Cox, Ann. of St. Helen's, Bishopsgate, 11.

[12] Chron. of Reigns of Edw. I and Edw. II (Rolls Ser.), i, 93. The chronicler says the Holy Cross called 'Neit.'

[13] Parl. R. (Rec. Com.), i, 475. Annis incertis Edw. I and Edw. II. The petition must have been after Nov. 1290, as they ask the favour 'for the sake of the soul of the late Queen.'

[14] Chart. R. 35 Edw. I, m. 18, No. 49.

[15] Reg. Epist. Johan. Peckham (Rolls Ser.), iii, 970 and 971.

[16] Cal. Pap. Letters, i, 521.

[17] Lond. Epis. Reg. Baldock and Gravesend, fol. 7.

[18] Sharpe, Cal. of Wills, i, 147. He speaks of himself and his brother Salomon as erecting the church. In this will, however, no mention is made of William, said to be brother of Thomas. Cox, op. cit. 6.

[19] Dyonisia de Gloucestre, a nun of St. Helen's, received from her uncle, Thomas Basing, a quit-rent in the parish of St. Botolph Billingsgate, for life. Sharpe, Cal. of Wills, i, 147. Elizabeth, daughter of Henry de Gloucestre, was also a nun there. Cox, op. cit. 7.

[20] Doc. of D. and C. of St. Paul's, A. Box 77, No. 2039.

[21] Stow, Surv. of Lond. (ed. Strype), ii, 100.

[22] Cox, op. cit. 6 and 7.

[23] Harl. Chart. 44, F. 45; Sharpe, Cal. of Letter Bk. F. 115.

[24] Sharpe, Cal. of Wills, i, 687. He left bequests to two nuns of the house, one of whom was his sister.

[25] Ibid. i, 581.

[26] Cal. Pap. Letters, ii, 368.

[27] Cal. Pap. Pet. i, 198.

order, they were unable to follow them up.[28] In 1374 the priory received an important bequest of lands and tenements in the parishes of St. Martin Outwich, St. Helen, St. Ethelburga, and St. Peter Broad Street, from another London citizen, Adam Fraunceys, mercer, charged with the maintenance of two chantries in the chapels of St. Mary and of the Holy Ghost[29] in the church.

A curious case occurred in 1385. Joan Heyronne, one of the nuns, on the plea that she was so crippled with gout that she was unable to perform her canonical duties, secretly appealed to the pope, and obtained from him an order that an allowance of £10 a year should be paid to her from the goods of the monastery. Constance, the prioress, seems to have resented this action, and with the help of the sub prioress and one of the nuns kept Joan shut up in a room, it was alleged without food suitable to her state of health, until the dean and chapter of St. Paul's commanded that she should be set at liberty and permitted to go where she would in the priory.[30] On which side right lay is doubtful: the prioress may have been exasperated by intrigues against her authority, but she appears to have been unduly severe, and this view of her rule is perhaps confirmed by the flight and marriage of another of her nuns in 1388.[31]

Too much discipline was certainly not the characteristic of the house in the next century, judging from two sets of injunctions, one issued by Dean Kentwode in 1432,[32] and the other believed to be also of that period.[33]

From the latter[34] it appears that the nuns hurried through the services, for they were ordered to say them fully and distinctly and not so fast as they had been doing, and that they were addicted to vanity in dress,[35] perhaps a result of the entertainment of guests by the prioress, which was forbidden in future. The prioress seems not to have taken her position seriously enough: she was told to content herself with one or two dogs, and one of her maids was to be removed for certain causes moving the dean and chapter, 'et hoc propter majorem honestatem dicte priorisse.' The dean was probably not satisfied about the administration of the house, since he required the holder of a corrody to show the grant, that it might be known whether he had fulfilled the services due from him, and ordered an inquiry to be made of the prioress and each nun whether there were other burdens on the nunnery; the prioress was also to show who had the custody of the missals, books, and ornaments, and how they were kept; and the number of seals was to be reported.

Dean Kentwode in 1432, after providing that divine service should be performed night and day, that the rule of silence was to be duly observed, and full confessions made to the confessor appointed by him, proceeded to order that secular women were not to sleep in the dorter; nor were secular persons to be admitted after compline or locked within the bounds of the cloister; a discreet nun was to be appointed to lock the convent doors so that nobody could get in or out, that the place be not slandered in future, and the prioress herself was to keep the keys of the postern door between the cloister and churchyard, 'for there is much coming in and out at unlawful times'; the nuns were not to look out into the street, not to speak to secular persons, nor receive gifts or letters from them without leave of the prioress, and the letters were to be such as could cause no ill report; measures were to be taken that strangers should not see the nuns nor the nuns them at service in the church; sisters appointed to office must be of good character; a suitable sister was to be chosen to teach the rule to those who did not know it; a proper infirmary was to be established where the sisters could be tended in illness; no dancing or revelling except at Christmas and other suitable times, and then in absence of seculars, was to be allowed. As was not unnatural amid so much laxity the business of the house was mismanaged, and fees, liveries, and perpetual corrodies were given to various persons, officers of the house and others, 'to … the dilapidation of the house's goods.' The impression gathered from the injunctions is that the priory was regarded as a kind of boarding-house. It is not unlikely that the rich City families found it a convenient place in which they could dispose of their unmarried daughters with an allowance,[36] and did not much consider whether they had a religious vocation.

The convent in 1458 paid £76 16s. 8d. in part payment of a larger sum,[37] and this borrowing of money may be a sign that they had begun the

---

[28] *Parl. R.* (Rec. Com.), ii, 403, No. 138. Annis incertis Edw. III.

[29] Sharpe, *Cal. of Wills*, ii, 171.

[30] Doc. of D. and C. of St. Paul's, A. Box 25, No. 1112.

[31] Ibid. A. Box 25, No. 1110.

[32] Cott. Chart. v, 6, printed in Dugdale, op. cit. iv, 553.

[33] *Hist. MSS. Com. Rep.* ix, App. i, 57.

[34] Doc. of D. and C. of St. Paul's, A. Box 77, No. 2041.

[35] They were ordered to wear veils according to the rules of their order, not too sumptuous in character.

[36] Besides the provisions by legacies already mentioned there is a deed (B.M. Chart. Toph. 39, quoted in Dugdale, op. cit. iv, 552) where a sum of 100s. was to be paid annually to the convent during the life of one of the nuns, Joan de Bures. The fact that Richard II in 1377 exercised his coronation right and nominated a nun to the priory seems to imply that by that time admission was desirable but not easy. *Cal. of Pat.* 1377–81, p. 20.

[37] Doc. of D. and C. of St. Paul's, A. Box 77, No. 2046.

alterations to the church to which Sir John Crosby is said to have contributed 500 marks.[38] Crosby would have been interested as a parishioner of St. Helen's, for he built his magnificent house close to the priory upon land rented to him by the convent in 1466.[39]

The satisfactory state of the house in the early sixteenth century is shown by the bishop of London's choice of one of the sisters to be prioress of Holy Cross at Castle Hedingham;[40] but the spirit of unrest roused by the religious changes under Henry VIII seems soon to have affected the priory, since in 1532 some nuns ran away.[41] A proof of the importance of the house at this time is furnished by the intrigues over the election of the last prioress in 1529.[42] A certain Margaret Vernon, who was not a member of the convent, solicited the support of Wolsey and of Cromwell in turn. According to her, the king's saddler had offered 200 marks to secure the appointment of his sister, and Margaret herself owned that she had been willing to pay Wolsey £100 for the post, which she however never obtained, Mary Rollesley, a sister of the house,[43] being made prioress.

There is some excuse for the nuns in the grants of annuities made by them in 1534–8, although they were forbidden by the Kentwode Injunctions: one was to Cromwell,[44] and the others to various persons 'for good counsel,'[45] of which they certainly stood in need. But these were as useless in averting the fate of the house as was the denial by the nuns of the papal supremacy,[46] though they may have obtained better conditions for the inmates. The priory was surrendered 25 November, 1538,[47] but there are no signatures to the deed.

In January, 1539, the king granted to the prioress, Mary Rollesley, a life pension of £30; to Mary Shelton one of £4; to five other nuns pensions of £3 6s. 8d. each; and to the remaining eight pensions of

four marks each.[48] The number of nuns appears to have been about stationary since 1466, when eleven besides the prioress witness a deed.[49] The convent was probably much larger in the fourteenth century, for in 1372 seven nuns took the vows at one time.[50]

The only official mentioned besides the prioress is the sub-prioress. The business of the nunnery was managed by a steward,[51] who collected the rents of the lands owned by the priory, and had an annual salary of £12 with 20s. for his livery, eatables and drinkables, two cart-loads of fuel, 10 qrs. of charcoal, and the use of a chamber within the priory precinct.[52]

From a document apparently of the sixteenth century[53] the household expenses of the priory for a year were £134 1s. 6d.; of this the sum of £22 was spent on corn, £60 13s. 4d. on meat and other victuals, £10 on thirty pittances. The debts of the house at the same time amounted to £90 4s. 4d., and included £15 owing to Robert 'at ye Cokke,' brewer, £6 13s. 4d. to a 'cornman,' £4 to a fishmonger, and 56s. 2d. to another, £9 12s. 4d. to a butcher, £6 13s. 4d. to a draper, and 20s. to John, the servant of the prioress.

The income of the house amounted in 1535 to £376 6s. gross and £320 15s. 8½d. net,[54] and was chiefly derived from possessions in London,[55] where the nuns held nearly the whole of St. Helen's parish and lands and rent in sixteen other parishes.[56] The convent also owned at this time the manor of Bordeston or Burston in Brentford,[57] which they had held in 1290, and woods in Edmonton, co. Middlesex; rents in Eyworth, co. Bedford, where they had land in 1316;[58] land in East Barming, co. Kent;[59] the manor of Marks[60] and land at Walthamstow,[61] co. Essex; rents in Ware, co. Herts., where they had a holding in 1392;[62] the manor of Datchet,[63] co. Bucks.; since 1303 and earlier they had held the advowsons of St. Mary Axe, St. John

[38] Weever, *Ancient Fun. Monum.* 421.

[39] Add. MS. 15664, fol. 228–30.

[40] Lond. Epis. Reg. Fitz James, fol. 137B.

[41] *L. and P. Hen. VIII,* v, 982. Petition to the king of John Stanton, servant to Thomas Patmer, late merchant of London, now in the bishop of London's prison. On complaining to Parliament on behalf of his master he had been told by the Lord Chancellor that he was at the conveying of certain nuns from St. Helen's.

[42] Ibid. v, 19. Margaret Vernon's letters are placed under 1531, but the last prioress was elected in 1529.

[43] Madox, *Formul. Angl.* 440. Elizabeth Rollesley, by will dated 1513, left to her daughter Mary, a nun of St. Helen's, a legacy of £5.

[44] Cox, op. cit. 14.

[45] Cox, op. cit. 20. 21 Jan. 1538, a pension of 4 marks to John Lewstre. Ibid. 22. 26 June, 1538, to John Rollesley an annuity of 4 marks. Ibid. 23, 24 and 25.

[46] *L. and P. Hen. VIII,* vii, 1025 (2).

[47] Ibid. xiii (2), 908.

[48] Aug. Off. Misc. Bk. 233, fol. 101–3. Six nuns were alive in 1556, of whom one was allowed 66s. 8d. a year, the others 53s. 4d. each. Add. MS. 8102, fol. 3.

[49] Add. MS. 15664, fol. 230.

[50] Lond. Epis. Reg. Sudbury, fol. 139.

[51] Cox, op. cit. 15.

[52] Ibid.

[53] Doc. of D. and C. of St. Paul's. A. Box 77, No. 2042.

[54] *Valor Eccl.* (Rec. Com.), i, 393.

[55] These were worth £312 6s. 4d. a year. Ibid. i, 392.

[56] *L. and P. Hen. VIII,* xviii (1), 982, 346 (54), 981 (68); xix (1), 1035 (50, 55, 68, 135), etc.

[57] *Parl. R.* (Rec. Com.), i, 475.

[58] *Feud. Aids,* i, 19.

[59] Hasted, *Hist. of Kent,* ii, 151. 'St. Helen's is a deputed manor in Barming . . . it formerly belonged to the nunnery of St. Helen's, London, hence its name.'

[60] Morant, *Hist. of Essex,* i, 68.

[61] *L. and P. Hen. VIII,* xv, 557.

[62] *Cal. of Pat.* 1391–6, p. 156.

[63] *L. and P. Hen. VIII,* xv, 498 (35).

Walbrook, St. Mary Woolnoth and St. Ethelburga, with pensions of 4 marks and 2s. respectively from the last two;[64] to them also belonged the rectory of St. Helen's[65] and the church of Eyworth,[66] appropriated to them in 1331.[67] The prioress in 1346 held a fraction of a knight's fee in East Barming,[68] and in conjunction with Anna le Despenser half a knight's fee in Eyworth.[69]

*M. Reddan*

## Revised List of Prioresses of St. Helen's, Bishopsgate

This list is taken from *Heads of Religious Houses*, vol. 1, p. 215, vol. 2, pp. 584–5 and vol. 3 (forthcoming).

D. occurs 1212–1216

Matilda, occurs 1200–1225 so poss. prioress before D.

Helen (Ellen), occurs 1229; died by 1255

Scholastica, el. 1255; died by 1269

Felicia de Basinges, elected 1269; occurs 1285

Orabella, occurs 1295

Joan of Winchester, died by 1324

Beatrix de Boteler, died 1332

Eleanor of Winchester, elected 1332; occurs 1348

Margery de Honilane, occurs 1349–1368

Isabel de Gloucestre, mentioned 1374 as former prioress

Mary, occurs 1376

Constance Somersete, occurs 1382; died 1398

Joan Parles, occurs 1399–1405

Margaret Bunting, occurs 1411 12

Margaret Stokes, occurs 1426, ?1449

Alice Wodehouse, occurs 1458

Alice Ashfield, occurs 1466–1473

Alice Trewethall, occurs 1488–1498

Elizabeth Stamp, occurs 1512; resigned 1528

Mary Rollesley, elected 1529; surrendered 1538

[64] *Mun. Guildhall Lond.* ii (1), 236.

[65] Ibid.

[66] *Valor Eccl.* (Rec. Com.), iv, 196.

[67] *Cal. Pap. Letters*, ii, 368.

[68] *Feud. Aids*, iii, 45.

[69] Ibid. i, 22.

# HOUSE OF CISTERCIAN MONKS

## 4. EASTMINSTER, NEW ABBEY, OR THE ABBEY OF ST. MARY DE GRACIIS

### INTRODUCTION

The existing entry is a reliable account of the foundation and endowment of the abbey which includes the estates outside London. It indicates that the abbey enjoyed a degree of papal favour in the fourteenth century which may have been due to royal patronage.

Recent archaeological and documentary studies have added to our knowledge of the size and location of the abbey as well as its wealth. C. Thomas, *The Archaeology of Mediaeval London* (Stroud, 2002), pp. 144–66 has a detailed description of the buildings and their construction. Further detailed articles include D. Gaimster, R. Goffin and L. Blackmore, 'The Continental stove-tile fragments from St. Mary de Graces, London, in their British and European context', *Post Mediaeval Archaeology*, 24 (1990), pp. 1–49. Of particular significance will be C. Philpotts, *Excavations at the Abbey of St. Mary Graces, East Smithfield, London*, MoLAS Monograph Series (in preparation: forthcoming 2007/8). The location and boundaries of the precinct are precisely described in Honeybourne, 'Property', pp. 227–52.

For what is known of the library, see D. Bell ed., *The Libraries of the Cistercians, Gilbertines and Premonstratensians*, Corpus of British Medieval Libraries, 3 (London, 1992), pp. 32–4.

The abbey's properties are listed in *Documentary Sources*, p 55, and the London property in the late fourteenth century is also listed in McHardy, *Church in London*. Details of the surviving archives of St. Mary Graces, together with a list of estates held by the house, have been collated by the English Monastic Archives project and are available online, URL: http://www.ucl.ac.uk/history/englishmonasticarchives/index.htm (accessed 8 February 2007).

*Leah Rhys*

In 1350 King Edward III founded in the parish of St. Botolph without Aldgate a monastery to be called St. Mary of Graces in honour of the Virgin, to whose mediation he attributed his escape from many perils by land and sea.[1] The site was a place called the New Churchyard of Holy Trinity, because it had been acquired by a certain John Corey, clerk, from Holy Trinity Priory for a burial ground during the plague.[2] St. Mary's was made subject to Beaulieu Regis,[3] and from this abbey came the five Cistercian monks[4] who under Walter de Santa Cruce,[5] as president, formed the convent of the new foundation.

The original endowment consisted of some lands and tenements in East Smithfield and Tower Hill which, like the site, had been bought by the king of John Corey,[6] and a sum of 20 marks to be received annually from the tellers of London for their ferma-gilda.[7] In 1358, however, the income thus derived being found insufficient, the king ordered 40 marks a year to be paid to them out of the Exchequer until he should provide otherwise for them, but he stipulated at the same time that

---

[1] Add. Chart. 39405. An inspeximus in the reign of Henry VIII.

[2] Stow, *Surv. of Lond.* (ed. Strype), ii, 13.

[3] *Cal. of Pat.* 1422–9, p. 89. Inspex. of patent of 1351.

[4] Add. MS. 15664, fol. 138, a transcript of Rot. Pat. 32 Edw. III, pt. 1, m. 20. The king asked that some monks might be sent from Beaulieu in 1351. *Cal. of Pat.* 1422–9, p. 89.

[5] He had been abbot of Garendon and came to St. Mary Graces at the king's request in 1350. *Cal. of Pat.* 1348–50, p. 560.

[6] These were given by the king in August, 1353. Add. Chart. 39405.

[7] Ibid.

another monk should be added to their number.[8] He moreover granted to them in 1367,[9] together with some small rents in London, the advowsons of St. Bartholomew's the Little and of Allhallows Staining,[10] and two years later he gave them lands, tenements, and rents in London worth about 60 marks a year which had been forfeited to the crown under the Statute of Mortmain.[11] But the king must have felt that the income of the abbey fell far short of the thousand marks with which he had intended to endow it,[12] and towards the end of his reign he took steps to supply the deficiency.

Before his death[13] he granted to the abbey the reversion of the manors of Westmill, Little Hormead, and Meesden, co. Herts., with the advowsons of the churches; and he enfeoffed John, duke of Lancaster, and others trustees of the manors of Gravesend, Lenches, Leybourne, Wateringbury, Gore, Parrocks and Bicknor, co. Kent, the manor of Rotherhithe and the reversion of the manor of Gomshall, co. Surrey, and the advowsons of the churches of Gravesend, Leybourne, and Bicknor, so that they might ultimately convey them to the convent in frankalmoign.[14] The trustees gave the property to the abbey in 1382 for a term of forty years,[15] the convent then leased it to Sir Simon de Burley, on whose death for treason in 1388 it fell to the crown.[16] King Richard, however, had no wish to benefit at the expense of the monastery, and committed the manors to certain persons who were to pay the revenues arising from them to the monks. Finally, in 1398, he made them over to the convent in frankalmoign.[17] King Edward had also bequeathed to the abbey in a similar way the reversion of the manors of Bovey Tracey, 'Northlieu,'[18] Holsworthy, 'Longeacre,' co. Devon; Blagdon, Lydford,[19] Staunton, co. Somerset; and 'Takkebere' co. Cornwall, with the advowsons of Blagdon, Lydford, 'Northlieu,' and Holsworthy; but when Sir James d'Audele, the life-owner, died, Richard II gave them to his half-brother John Holland, earl of Huntingdon, granting to the abbey instead 110 marks to be received every year

from Scarborough church as long as the schism and the war with France lasted, and afterwards from the Exchequer.[20] John Holland was executed in 1400, and his estates forfeited, whereupon Henry IV revoked the letters patent of his predecessor and gave the manors in question to the abbey in frankalmoign.[21] It is difficult to say what occurred afterwards, for though the abbey had possession of at least one of the manors after the Hollands had been restored in blood,[22] it appears to have held none of them in the next century.

In the early days of the foundation the endowment was probably little more than sufficient for the maintenance of the monks, so that the construction of the necessary buildings did not proceed very rapidly. The abbey church dedicated to St. Anne was aided by a relaxation of penance offered by the pope in 1374 to those who on the principal feasts during a period of ten years visited it and gave alms.[23] But the cloisters and houses were possibly not begun in 1368,[24] and were certainly not completed in 1379, for the trustees then made the convent an annual grant of 100 marks from the manors in Kent[25] partly to meet this expense, and in 1391 the abbot and monks received a pardon from the king for selling wood belonging to the manor of Wateringbury to raise funds for their new building.[26]

The abbey before the end of the fourteenth century appears to have occupied a position of some importance, for when Pope Boniface IX issued letters[27] exempting the Cistercian Order in England, Wales, and Ireland from the jurisdiction of the abbot of Citeaux as an adherent of the anti-pope Clement VII, the abbot of St. Mary's was ordered, with those of Boxley and Stratford, to convoke the order, and the abbey was named as the meeting place of the chapter-general. The royal foundation and patronage of the abbey may partly account for this and other tokens of papal favour: between 1390

[8] Add. MS. 15664, fol. 138.

[9] Add. Chart. 39405.

[10] This church was appropriated to them by the bishop of London, February, 1368. Lond. Epis. Reg. Sudbury, fol. 105 and 106.

[11] Add. Chart. 39405.

[12] Cal. of Pat. 1388–92, p. 364.

[13] In the fiftieth year of his reign. Newcourt, *Repert. Eccl. Lond.* i, 837, 847; Chauncy, *Hist. of Herts.* 330.

[14] Pat. 22 Ric. II, pt. 1, m. 26, in Dugdale, *Mon. Angl.* v, 718.

[15] Exemplif. 6 Hen. IV of the indenture, L.P. Exch. (Ser. 1), bdle. 7.

[16] Dugdale, op. cit. v, 718.

[17] Pat. 22 Ric. II, pt. 1, m. 26, in Dugdale, *Mon. Angl.* v, 718.

[18] Northleigh (?)

[19] West Lydford.

[20] Henry IV granted the money from the Exchequer. Exch. Letters Pat. (Ser. 1), bdle. 7.

[21] *Cal. of Pat.* 1399–1401, p. 274.

[22] The heir of the Hollands held at his death in 1417 the manor of Holsworthy among others (*Cal. Inq. p.m.* (Rec. Com.), iv, 24), but the convent certainly possessed it in 1421 (B.M. Chart. L.F.C. xiv, 27).

[23] *Cal. Pap. Letters,* iv, 199.

[24] The bishop of London in 1368 said that the abbot and convent had petitioned him to appropriate Allhallows Staining to them because they were extremely poor; the church, cloister, and necessary houses were not yet built, and their house was founded in a barren and uncultivated spot, all of which he found to be true. Lond. Epis. Reg. Sudbury, fol. 105.

[25] Madox, *Formul. Angl.* 268. The grant was made for the sustenance of the abbot and monks and 'pur les edefices necessaires illoeqx afferes come leur Religion demande.'

[26] *Cal. of Pat.* 1388–92, p. 397.

[27] This was about 1396. Burton, *Chron. Mon. de Melsa* (Rolls Ser.), iii, 258. The letters were revoked in 1397. *Cal. Pap. Letters,* v, 9.

and 1400 the pope conferred on three of the convent the dignity of papal chaplain,[28] and in 1415 the use of the mitre, ring, and other pontifical insignia was granted to the abbot and his successors.[29]

A case which occurred about 1401 shows that unruly spirits were sometimes found even within the walls of a monastery. Ralph Bikere, a monk of St. Mary, Swineshead, had been sentenced to imprisonment for violence to his abbot and breach of the rule concerning private property. He fled to St. Mary Graces, made his profession and was allowed to remain.[30] Soon afterwards the abbot of Beaulieu, during a visitation of St. Mary Graces, found that he had turned William de Wardon, the abbot, out of the dormitory, laid violent hands on him, hindered him from disposing of the goods of the monastery, and applied many of these goods to his own purposes, that he had then apostatized, appealed to the secular tribunal, and caused the appeal to be notified to his abbot.[31] He was sentenced by the abbot of Beaulieu to be imprisoned, and the judgement against him was finally confirmed by the pope,[32] though at first he had obtained letters of rehabilitation.[33] The house in 1427 was so much impoverished owing to the mismanagement of Abbot Paschal, who seems to have obtained his position wrongfully[34] and to have taken advantage of it to plunder the abbey,[35] that it was committed by the advice of the council to Humphrey, duke of Gloucester, the bishop of Winchester, the abbot of Beaulieu, and others.[36] A question as to the custody of the temporalities arose in 1441, the abbey being called upon to answer for £566 18s. 10d. said to be due to the king from its lands in London and Middlesex during the vacancy on the death of the last abbot, John Pecche. The abbot and convent appealed to the king, who acknowledged that his predecessors had never had the custody at such times, and promised for himself and his heirs that the convent should in future be unmolested in this respect.[37]

The civil wars do not seem to have affected the position of the abbey at all; its charters were confirmed by both Edward IV[38] and Henry VII,[39] and the abbot served on the various commissions

for the administration of the district adjoining the abbey, both under Edward IV[40] and Henry VIII.[41] It was probably during the reign of Edward IV that the Lady Chapel was added at the expense of Sir Thomas Montgomery.[42] After the difficulties with Rome had arisen the king appointed Henry More the abbot of St. Mary's, among others,[43] to visit the houses of the Cistercian order in England, Ireland, and Wales, and More received the thanks of Margaret, marchioness of Dorset, in 1533 for the zeal he had shown in the reformation of the house of Tiltey.[44] Reform, however, was not what the king wanted, and the abbey of Coggeshall must have been given to More *in commendam* in 1536,[45] either because his precarious health made a speedy recurrence of first-fruits likely,[46] or more probably because he could be relied on to surrender when required. More indeed gave it up to the king in about eighteen months,[47] and made a good bargain, for he was reimbursed for all his expenses and received a pension of 100 marks for life from Sir Thomas Seymour who obtained the site and lands.[48] The surrender of St. Mary Graces seems to have taken place in September, 1538.[49] At that time there were ten monks including the abbot, only one more than there had been in 1376,[50] before the richest endowments had been made. They all received pensions for life: the abbot 100 marks, the sub-prior £6 13s. 4d., and the others £5 6s. 8d. each.[51] More was still living in 1544.[52]

From the time of Richard II[53] there was a prior as well as an abbot; afterwards there appears to have

[28] Ibid. v, 275, 292, 310.

[29] Ibid. vi, 465.

[30] Ibid. v, 346.

[31] *Cal. Pap. Letters*, v, 517. It appears rather extraordinary that he should commit the same faults twice.

[32] *Cal. Pap. Letters*, v, 602.

[33] Ibid. v, 517.

[34] Nicolas, *Proc. and Ordin. of the Privy Council*, iii, 269. His entrance to the office is spoken of as 'intrusio.'

[35] The jewels of the house had apparently been pawned. Ibid.

[36] *Cal. of Pat.* 1422–9, p. 394.

[37] Add. Chart. 39405.

[38] *Cal. of Pat.* 1461–7, p. 162; 1476–85, p. 4.

[39] Add. Chart. 39405.

[40] *Cal. of Pat.* 1476–85, pp. 215, 466.

[41] *L. and P. Hen. VIII*, i, 1972; ibid. v, 166 (8).

[42] His will is dated July, 1489, and directs that his body shall be buried in the Lady Chapel which he had lately made. Nicolas, *Testam. Vet.* 396.

[43] *L. and P. Hen. VIII*, v, 978 (6).

[44] Ibid. vi, 1304.

[45] Ibid. xi, 385 (37).

[46] Ibid. xi, 392. Anthony Knyvet, writing to Cromwell, says that it would profit the king to give Coggeshall to More, since he was likely to have the first-fruits and the monastery again in a few years, for More was once a year 'almost gone.'

[47] Ibid. xiii (1), 221.

[48] Ibid.

[49] The pensions granted to the abbot and monks in April, 1539, were to be enjoyed from the preceding Michaelmas (Aug. Off. Misc. Bk. 233, fol. 262–3). Many of the abbey lands were made over by the abbot and convent in December 1538 to Sir Thomas Audley to be held of the king (*L. and P. Hen. VIII*, xiii (2), 969). Wriothesley, however, in his *Chron.* (Rolls Ser.), i, 94, says the surrender took place 31 March, 1539.

[50] The original number of monks was five; the king had ordered one more to be added in 1358 (Add. MS. 15664, fol. 138); and two were to be added as a condition of the bequest of Nicholas de Loveyne, knt., in 1375 (Add. Chart. 39405).

[51] Aug. Off. Misc. Bk. 233, fol. 262–3.

[52] *L. and P. Hen. VIII*, xix (1), 368, fol. 19.

[53] Burton, *Chron. Mon. de Melsa* (Rolls Ser.), 277. William de Wendover, the prior, was made abbot of Meaux in 1399. There is mention of another prior in 1400. *Cal. of Pat.* 1399–1401, p. 397.

been also a sub-prior, as at the dissolution one of the monks is so called.[54]

The income of the abbey in 1535 amounted to £602 11s. 10½d. gross and £547 0s. 6½d. net,[55] of which more than £300 was derived from rents and ferms in London and the suburbs,[56] and the rectory and tithes of Allhallows Staining.[57]

The convent owned two water-mills called 'Crasshe Mills' in East Smithfield[58] by the bequest of Sir Nicholas de Loveyne in 1375,[59] and the manor of Poplar,[60] co. Middlesex; the manors of Westmill, Meesden, and Little Hormead,[61] co. Herts; the manor and castle of Leybourne,[62] the manors of Wateringbury,[63] Fowkes,[64] Gore, Bicknor, Gravesend, Parrocks, 'Herber,' and Lenches,[65] Swancourt,[66] Slayhills Marsh,[67] tenements in Woolwich,[68] and land in Cobham[69] and Rainham,[70] co. Kent; the manors of Gomshall, and Rotherhithe,[71] and land in Ewhurst,[72] co. Surrey. They also possessed the advowsons of

St. Bartholomew's by the Exchange,[73] Westmill,[74] Hormead, Meesden,[75] Ridley,[76] Gravesend, Leybourne, and Bicknor,[77] and received a yearly pension of 40s. from the church of Emley,[78] co. Kent. In 1428 the abbot held half a knight's fee in Meesden, and in conjunction with John Tewe two knights' fees in Westmill.[79]

*M. Reddan*

## Revised List of Abbots of St. Mary Graces

This list is taken from *Heads of Religious Houses*, vol. 2, pp. 290–1 and vol. 3 (forthcoming), except where otherwise indicated.

William of Holy Cross, occurs 1350
John of Gloucester, occurs 1354
William of Wardon (Wardone), ?elected 1360; occurs until 1412.
Roger Grenewey, occurs 1411, 1417
William, occurs 1423
Paschal Gylot, occurs 1421, 1428
John Pecche, occurs 1425, 1431
Robert Welles, occurs 1436
William, occurs 1437
Richard, occurs 1456
Thomas Bene (Ben, Been), occurs 1458, 1475
John, occurs 1475–6
Edmund, occurs 1478, 1482
John Langton alias Gerves, occurs 1483; died 1514
Robert Prehast, confirmed as abbot 1514; occurs 1515
Henry More, elected 1516; surrendered 1538 but occurs as abbot 1539

[54] *L. and P. Hen. VIII*, xiv (1), 688. The office of prior seems to have been vacant at this time.
[55] *Valor Eccl.* (Rec. Com.), i, 398, 399.
[56] Ibid. i, 398. Edward III had given the abbey tenements and rents in the parishes of St. Dunstan in the East, St. Martin Vintry, All Saints 'at Heywharf,' St. Michael Paternoster, St. Sepulchre, St. Andrew Holborn, St. Swithin, St. Mary Woolchurch St. Bride, St. Mary Billingsgate, &c. Add. Chart. 39405. Tenements were also left to the monks in the parishes of St. Michael Queenhithe, and Allhallows Thames Street. Sharpe, *Cal. of Wills*, ii, 564, 437.
[57] *Valor Eccl.* i, 398.
[58] *Valor Eccl.* i, 398.
[59] Add. Chart. 39405.
[60] *Valor Eccl.* i, 398.
[61] Ibid.
[62] Ibid.
[63] Ibid.
[64] Hasted, *Hist. of Kent*, ii, 270.
[65] *Valor Eccl.* i, 398.
[66] Hasted, op. cit. ii, 584.
[67] Ibid. ii, 544.
[68] *Cal. Inq. p.m.* (Rec. Com.), iii, 162.
[69] Hasted, op. cit. i, 501.
[70] *Cal. Inq. p.m. Hen. VII*, i, No. 506.
[71] *Valor Eccl.* (Rec. Com.), i, 398.
[72] *Cal. of Inq. p.m. Hen. VII*, No. 400.

[73] Add. Chart. 39405.
[74] Chauncy, *Hist. of Herts.* 230.
[75] Newcourt, *Repert. Eccl. Lond.* i, 837, 847.
[76] B.M. Chart. Toph. 2; Hasted, op. cit. i, 281.
[77] Ibid. i, 452; ii, 208, 517.
[78] Ibid. ii, 675.
[79] *Feud. Aids*, ii, 446, 451.

# HOUSES OF AUSTIN CANONS

## 5. THE PRIORY OF HOLY TRINITY OR CHRISTCHURCH, ALDGATE

### INTRODUCTION

Although still useful, the original account of the development of the house has been modified by more recent work. John Schofield and Richard Lea, using recent archaeological discoveries, as well as pictorial and documentary evidence, have reconstructed the history of the priory and its surrounding complex from its foundation, through to the dissolution, J. Schofield and R. Lea, *Holy Trinity Priory, Aldgate, City of London: An Archaeological Reconstruction and History*, MoLAS Monograph, 24 (2005). For a brief overview of the history of the priory, and a description of its role in the civic community at the time of the dissolution, see E. J. Davis, 'The Beginning of the Dissolution: Christchurch Aldgate, 1532', *Trans. R. Hist. Soc.* (1925), pp. 127–50 and M. C. Rosenfield, 'Holy Trinity, Aldgate, on the Eve of the Dissolution', *Guildhall Miscellany*, iii (3) (October, 1970), pp. 159–73.

D. S. Luscombe offers comments on the achievements of the first prior of Holy Trinity Aldgate: 'Aldgate Priory and the Regular Canons in XIIth Century England', in *La Vita Comune del Clero nei Secoli XI e XII, Miscellanea del Centro di Studi Medioevali III*, vol. 2, pp. 86–9.

Surviving records relating to the house are listed on the web site of the English Monastic Archives project, along with a list of estates, URL: http://www.ucl.ac.uk/history/englishmonasticarchives/index.htm (accessed 28 February 2007). For the London property, see especially *Documentary Sources*, pp. 52–3. For an early fifteenth-century cartulary of Holy Trinity Aldgate, now in the Hunterian Museum, see *The Cartulary of Holy Trinity Aldgate*, ed. G. A. J. Hodgett (London Record Society, 7, 1971). Many of the original deeds of the priory have also survived, and are held in the collection of The National Archives. The priory's deeds have not been separated into their own series, but are mixed with the other deeds held by T.N.A., see for example, *Catalogue of Ancient Deeds*, 6 vols (London, 1890), I, A.1619–A.1625.

*John McEwan*

The priory of Holy Trinity, Aldgate, was founded in 1107 or 1108[1] by Maud, queen of Henry I,[2] on a spot once occupied by a church in honour of Holy Cross and St. Mary Magdalene. The abbey of Waltham had some kind of right there, but relinquished it on compensation by the queen,[3] and the new priory was freed from all subjection save to the bishop of London.[4] Besides the site of the house the queen gave to the canons the gate of Aldgate, with the soke pertaining to it,[5] including the churches of St. Augustine Pappey, St. Edmund Lombard Street, and Allhallows on the Wall,[6] and two-thirds of the ferm of Exeter, which amounted to £25 12s. 6d.[7] It is said that by her will she made other grants to the priory, but that while the king allowed the canons to have the relics and ornaments, among which were a piece of the True Cross and a wonderful basket of gold,

---

[1] 1107 A.D. is the date given by Matt. Paris, *Chron. Maj.* (Rolls Ser.), ii, 134; Matt. of Westm. *Flores Hist.* (Rolls Ser.), ii, 40. In Lansd. MS. 448, fol. 6, the date of foundation is given as 1108.

[2] The foundation has also been ascribed to Richard de Belmeis, bishop of London, see Dugdale, *Mon. Angl.* vi, 152, and to Norman, the first prior, see Matt. Paris, *Chron. Maj.* (Rolls Ser.), ii, 134, but there can be little doubt that the queen was the founder.

[3] Cart. Antiq. R. N. 1.

[4] Ibid. N. 13.

[5] Lansd. MS. 448, fol. 3; and Cart. Antiq. R. N. 14.

[6] Stow, *Surv. of Lond.* (ed. Strype), ii, 5.

[7] Lansd. MS. 448, fol. 3; Cart. Antiq. R. N. 15. It was £25 'ad scalam,' Cott. Chart. vii, 2; see Madox, *Hist. of Exch.* i, 276, 277.

silver, and precious stones sent to King Henry by the Emperor of Constantinople, he refused to let them have the lands bequeathed to them, or to allow her to be buried in their church.[8] Whether this was so or not, Henry showed himself on other occasions well inclined to them, granting them sac and soc, toll and team,[9] &c., in their lands; acquittance of all gelds and scots, aids and customs,[10] wardpenny and forfeitures;[11] and the exclusive right of trying their own tenants in their court.[12] He had, moreover, by royal charter[13] permitted them to close with a wall the road between the church and the city wall.

The priory received enthusiastic support from the citizens, pious women supplying the canons with food[14] in the early days of the foundation. But the best evidence of the feeling with which it was regarded is the grant which connected the house henceforth in such a peculiarly intimate way with the City, the gift of the soke of the English cnihtengild[15] in 1125,[16] in virtue of which possession the prior became the alderman of Portsoken Ward. The success of the house must doubtless be attributed largely to the first prior, chosen by Anselm's advice.[17] Norman, an Englishman by birth, had studied under Anselm in Normandy, and is famous for introducing the rule of St. Augustine into England for the benefit of St. Botolph's, Colchester, of which he had been a canon.[18] He considered that a prior, except in his greater responsibility, ought to differ in no way from the canons, and made rules that his successors should live in common with the brothers, and sleep

in the dormitory;[19] provisions not always observed by them.[20]

Norman died in 1147, and was succeeded by Ralph who had been made sub-prior some time before to relieve Norman of the burden of administration. His management of the affairs of the house is said to have been exceedingly able,[21] and the task could have been no easy one, considering that the priory, which was almost entirely burnt down in 1132,[22] suffered great losses by fire again while under his rule. He appears to have secured powerful supporters for the house – King Stephen[23] and Queen Maud,[24] two of whose children were buried in the church,[25] and Henry II[26] – and it was to him that Pope Alexander III directed the bull of 1162, granting the prior power to correct excesses in his priory, and to recall fugitives *notwithstanding royal or other secular prohibition.*[27]

Ralph, who died in 1167, had been a friend of Becket,[28] a fact which was duly noted when all connexion with the martyr redounded to the glory of the house. At the time, however, when Gilbert Foliot was excommunicated by Becket, William, Ralph's successor, and the convent did not side with the archbishop, but joined their prayers to those of 'their mother, the church of London,' in interceding with the pope on behalf[29] of the bishop of London.

During the interdict of 1208 the canons were not deprived of the consolation of religion, for by the bull of Innocent III in 1207[30] they were permitted in such circumstances to celebrate the divine offices

---

[8] Guildhall MS. 122, fol. 16. This is a transcript of the register of Holy Trinity, now at Glasgow. Stevens's account of the priory in *Hist. of Abbeys*, ii, is taken from the register.

[9] Anct. D. (P.R.O.), A. 6242; *Plac. de Quo Warr.* (Rec. Com.), 460, 461.

[10] Anct. D. (P.R.O.), A. 6286; *Plac. de Quo Warr.* (Rec. Com.), 460, 471, 472.

[11] Cart. Antiq. R. N. 4.

[12] Anct. D. (P.R.O.), A. 6286 (A.D. 1108–28); *Plac. de Quo Warr.* (Rec. Com.), 460, 471, 472.

[13] Cart. Antiq. R. N. 2.

[14] Guildhall MS. 122, fol. 12; Stevens, op. cit. ii, 77.

[15] Cart. Antiq. R. N. 3. Confirmation of the grant by Henry I, *Cart. Mon. de Ramesaia* (Rolls Ser.), i, 133. Convention between Reginald abbot of Ramsey and Prior Norman, by which the abbot gave up the claim which he had over the land of the gild which had been given to Holy Trinity church in return for the relinquishing of Norman's claim over the chapel and garden of the abbot (1114–30).

[16] Guildhall MS. 122, fol. 639; Round, *Commune of Lond.* 98. Stow gives 1115 as the date, op. cit. ii, 3.

[17] Guildhall MS. 122, fol. 11; Stevens, op. cit. ii, 75.

[18] Stevens, op. cit. ii, 77. He was absolved from his obedience by Arnulph, prior of St. Botolph's, when he was appointed head of Holy Trinity. The priory of St. Botolph appears to have claimed some kind of right there, *c.* 1223, for the arbitrators appointed by Pope Honorius III referred the matter to the bishop of London who decided that as the convent of Holy Trinity was only subject to the bishop of London, it was free from all visitation, &c. *Hist. MSS. Com. Rep.* ix, App. i, 24.

[19] Guildhall MS. 122, fol. 18; Stevens, op. cit. ii, 79.

[20] Lond. Epis. Reg. Baldock and Gravesend, fol. 5.

[21] Stevens, op. cit. ii, 79. The author of the register says that the revenues increased to double their value through his wisdom.

[22] Ibid. 179. This date may be a mistake for 1135, when a fire occurred which spread from London Bridge to St. Clement Danes.

[23] Dugdale, *Mon. Angl.* vi, 153. Queen Matilda confirms Stephen's grant to Ralph the prior and the monks of Holy Trinity of 100s. land in Braughing in frankalmoign.

[24] Lansd. MS. 448, fol. 5. Queen Matilda grants the priory the church of Braughing.

[25] See charter of Eustace, count of Boulogne, Cart. Antiq. R. N. 8.

[26] Anct. D. (P.R.O.), A. 6242. Grant by King Henry to the canons of Christchurch, London, that they shall hold their tenements in peace with all the liberties which they had in the time of King Henry his grandfather (1155–62).

[27] Rymer, *Foedera* (Rec. Com.), i (1), 21.

[28] Stevens, op. cit. ii, 79. The statements have to be taken with caution. The author of the register says that the death of the archbishop was that night revealed to Ralph in a dream. Ralph, however, was certainly dead at the time of Becket's murder.

[29] Robertson, *Materials for the Hist. of Thomas Becket* (Rolls Ser.), vi, 632–3. A similar letter was sent to the pope by Stephen, the next prior. Ibid. vii, 490.

[30] Rymer, *Foedera* (Rec. Com.), i (1), 82.

with closed doors, without ringing of bells, and in a low voice. But their property must have suffered with that of all the clergy from the royal exactions, and it is the more surprising that they should have taken the king's side in his quarrel with the barons. They certainly seem at first to have refused, like the deans of St. Paul's and St. Martin's, to publish the sentence of excommunication and interdict against the City and the opponents of the king when they were ordered to do so by the abbot of Abingdon in pursuance of the papal mandate,[31] but they must have ultimately given way, since Gualo, the papal legate, allowed them in 1217 to appropriate the church of Braughing, co. Herts., 'for their devotion and obedience to Rome in the discord between the king and barons in which they have suffered not a little damage.'[32]

The priory about this time[33] was under the guidance of Peter de Cornwall who, according to the fifteenth-century author of the register, possibly a partial critic, was the first of all the learned men of England of his day, and is said by his arguments to have converted a Jew to Christianity.[34] He not only wrote much himself, but appears to have encouraged others to write, for it is believed that the Itinerarium Ricardi I was the work of one of the canons, Richard de Temple, who succeeded him as prior.[35] The Lady Chapel dedicated by Archbishop Stephen Langton[36] was added to the church by Prior Peter.

The priory found itself involved in several struggles for its rights with the foreigners who came into England after the king's marriage, and must have heartily echoed the sentiments entertained by the clergy for Archbishop Boniface and by the inhabitants of the City for Queen Eleanor. The canons of Holy Trinity took the same stand as those of St. Bartholomew and St. Paul's in opposing the attempted visitation by the archbishop in May, 1250, and were excommunicated by him in consequence.[37] The pope declared the sentence of excommunication null and void,[38] but after two years decided the point in dispute against the priory, and condemned the convent to receive the archbishop as metropolitan to visit their churches, and to pay procurations.[39] In the case of the church of Bexley, of which the archbishop had despoiled the priory without a shadow of justice,[40] the papal court after long litigation pronounced in favour of the priory in 1254.[41] The convent, however, though completely establishing its claim, was not wholly victorious, for when Master William, who had been put into the church by Boniface, was raised to a bishopric, it was conferred by papal licence on Ubaldino, nephew of the cardinal of Santa Maria in Via Lata; and the court of Rome decided, while annulling the grants to William and Ubaldino, that the prior and convent were to pay an annual pension of 25 marks to the latter until they had secured for him a benefice worth at least 60 marks per annum.[42]

While this case was proceeding, a difficulty had arisen in the internal affairs of the priory itself.[43] There had been some irregularity about the appointment of the prior, John de Toking, but his election had been in the end confirmed by the bishop. He had been in possession for over two years, when during his absence at Rome,[44] presumably over the Bexley affair, an inquiry was ordered by the bishop, and he was suspended for non-observance of his oath. But John had been of service to Albert of Parma,[45] the papal legate in England, and the pope in 1254, declaring the oath simoniacal in nature, dispensed him from any obligation to fulfil it, and gave him power to hold the priory. It would seem that in the defence of the material interests of the house the prior neglected a more important duty, for the discipline and supervision must have been lax if Matthew Paris' tale is true that in 1256 one canon killed another, and then wounded himself to prove provocation.[46]

The king up to this time had shown himself well disposed towards the priory: besides the confirmation of their charters in 1227, he had in 1253

[31] Roger of Wendover, *Chron.* (Rolls Ser.), ii, 174. It is not stated, however, that the convent sent to the abbot a distinct refusal to obey, as the deans did.

[32] Lansd. MS. 448, fol. 5; Cott. R. xiii, 18 (2).

[33] The author of the register makes him prior from 1197 to 1221 (Stevens, op. cit. ii, 80), but Newcourt (*Repert. Eccl. Lond.* i, 560) gives Gilbert, 1214, between two priors, either of whom might be Peter de Cornwall, as the initial letter of both names is P.

[34] Stevens, op. cit. ii, 80.

[35] Stubbs, *Introd. to Memorials of Ric. I* (Rolls Ser.), i, pp. lxvi, lxvii.

[36] Robert Grosteste, *Epistolae* (Rolls Ser.), 191.

[37] Matt. Paris, *Chron. Maj.* v, 124.

[38] *Cal. Pap. Letters*, i, 264.

[39] Ibid. 276.

[40] The church had been given to them by William Corbeuil, archbishop of Canterbury, the grant being afterwards confirmed by Archbishops Theobald and Thomas Becket, and by Popes Innocent II, Eugenius III, Innocent III. Lansd. MS. 448, fol. 9; Rymer, *Foedera* (Rec. Com.), i (1), 14, 15, 82.

[41] Harl. MS. 6839, No. 23. Pope Innocent IV died Dec. 1254, and Alexander IV, his successor, ordered the sentence to be carried out in 1255.

[42] Rymer, *Foedera* (Rec. Com.), i (1), 362.

[43] *Cal. Pap. Letters*, i, 299.

[44] The papal letter above merely says he was suspended in his absence, but the letter of the pope in 1254, printed in Rymer, *Foedera*, i (1), 306, makes it clear that he had been to Rome.

[45] Albert had been sent to England in 1252 to offer Sicily to the earl of Cornwall. Gasquet, *Hen. III and the Church*, 349.

[46] *Chron. Maj.* (Rolls Ser.), v, 571.

granted them free warren in their demesne lands in the counties of Hertford, Kent, and Middlesex, and had given them leave to hold a weekly market and an annual fair at their manor of Corney.[47] It is possible therefore that his severity in taking the priory into his hand in 1256 because a thief who had escaped from Newgate took refuge there,[48] may have been due to the queen's influence.

Eleanor was just then engaged in a contest with the convent over the custody of St. Katharine's Hospital, which she was determined to wrest from them, though they held it by the grant of the founder, Maud wife of King Stephen.[49] The civil courts in 1255 twice decided that the perpetual custody of the hospital belonged to the priory. She then declared to Fulk, bishop of London, that the priory had wasted the goods of the hospital and unjustly detained its charters and seals, and requested him to make an inquiry. From the inquisition taken on St. Giles's Day, 1257, it appears that the priory and convent had appointed one of their own canons to be master of the hospital, but with this exception they do not seem to have exceeded their rights. The bishop, however, deprived them of the custody, and made the brothers and sisters of St. Katharine renounce all obedience to them. In 1261 Bishop Henry de Wengham and others succeeded, by threatening the prior with the king's displeasure, in obtaining an oral surrender of the custody. The canons appealed to Rome, and obtained a decision in their favour from Pope Urban IV,[50] but to no purpose; they never regained the custody of the hospital.

Eustace, prior 1264 to 1280, took advantage of the disgrace into which the City fell after Evesham, to inclose within the priory bounds a piece of the high road running from Aldgate to Bishopsgate.[51] Certain ordinances for the prior of Holy Trinity, issued by 'John bishop of London,' are probably to be attributed to Bishop John Chishull during Eustace's time of office.[52] In these the bishop enjoins the prior to dwell at home more with the brethren, giving greater attention to his divine ministry, and resorting more frequently than he is wont to the observances of his profession in choir, chapter, and other places, that he may teach his brethren by the example of his life, and by the word of doctrine inspire them with zeal for religion, not annoying

them with bitter words, but reproving them, if they go astray, in all patience. He is also ordered not to concern himself with secular business beyond what necessity demands,[53] but to appoint a fitting person of the monastery to each office with the consent of the convent or the greater part of the same. These persons, and the bailiffs of the manors, are to render an account of receipts and expenses twice a year before the prior and six of the older and more discreet of the chapter, and the next day a brief summary is to be given in the chapter, that the state of the house may be clear to all. The prior, whom all the convent shall obey, is to see that he carries on the business of the house with the counsel of the convent or the greater and senior part of the same. None of the canons is to eat or sleep elsewhere but in the places assigned for those purposes. They are not to be permitted to go beyond the bounds of the house except for good reasons, and then are to be accompanied by one of the older monks. Other injunctions are concerned with attendance at mass, the care of the sick canons, and the observance of the rule of silence, and that forbidding private property.

In the summer of 1290 the prior, William Aygnel, came into collision with the royal authority. He had cited Edmund earl of Cornwall, in the hall of Westminster, to appear before the archbishop of Canterbury, and as the earl was there in obedience to the king's summons to Parliament, the prior's action was considered to be in contempt of the king.[54] He was sent to the Tower to remain there during the king's pleasure, and a fine of £100 was imposed. But a few months later the canons paid such honour to the body of the late queen, which rested at the priory after entering London on its way to Westminster,[55] that they reinstated themselves in the king's favour, and the fine was remitted.[56]

A view of the condition of the priory at the beginning of the fourteenth century is afforded by the ordinances made by Archbishop Robert (Winchelsey) after a visitation in 1303.[57] It will be noted that the points on which amendment was needed are much the same as thirty years before. The brethren were all to be present at divine service, and no one was to absent himself before the end without leave of the sub-prior; silence was to be kept better than it had been, and those who persisted in talking when they should not were to be punished; the prior was not lightly to grant leave to the canons,

[47] *Cal. of Chart. R.* i, 427; Guildhall MS. 122, fol. 790.

[48] Stow, *Surv. of Lond.* (ed. Strype), ii, 5.

[49] Guildhall MS. 122, fol. 750–4; Ducarel, 'Hist. of Hospital of St. Katharine,' in *Bibl. Topog. Brit.* ii, 3 et seq.

[50] Rymer, *Foedera* (Rec. Com.), i (1), 439.

[51] *Rot. Hund.* (Rec. Com.), i, 407, 412, 418.

[52] They are on a little membrane which is fastened into the Lond. Epis. Reg. Baldock and Gravesend, fol. 5, at the place where the ordinances of Archbishop Robert Winchelsey, 1303, are given. If they are by Chishull their date would be 1275 or 1276.

[53] It may have been owing to this injunction that Eustace refused to act in person as alderman of Portsoken Ward and appointed a deputy. Maitland, *Hist. of Lond.* 1011.

[54] *Parl. R.* (Rec. Com.), i, 17.

[55] It seems to have reached the priory on 13 Dec. 1290. *Chron. of Edw. I and Edw. II* (Rolls Ser.), i, 99.

[56] *Cal. of Pat.* 1281–92, p. 420.

[57] Lond. Epis. Reg. Baldock and Gravesend, fol. 5, 6.

especially to the younger ones, to go out, and those canons who had leave to go beyond the bounds of the monastery were to take a fitting companion with them and to return within the time assigned; the canons were not to receive money for clothes, but clothes of one value and quality, and shoes, were to be given out according to the means of the priory by an officer deputed for that purpose, and the old clothes and shoes were to be given up before fresh ones were supplied; the prior, sub-prior, and cellarer were to visit the sick every day and supply them with suitable food; two-thirds of the convent were to dine in the refectory every day and were all to have food and drink of the same quality and quantity, and the prior was to make choice of the third part as seemed expedient to him and have them to dinner in his room; secular persons, and particularly women, were to be excluded from the choir, cloister, and other inner places, and especially from the offices of the house, unless they were women of good same passing through on a pilgrimage and leaving when their devotions were over. Then follow the ordinances dealing with the administration of the house: all the officers of the priory were to give an account of receipts and expenses to the prior before the older and more discreet of the whole convent as often as they should be required, but the rendering of the account was not to be deferred beyond a year; the seal was to be kept under guard of three keys, so that no document should be sealed out of the chapter or in the absence of the greater part of the convent, and every letter before and after sealing was to be read aloud in the presence of the convent or the greater part of the same; the alienation or letting at farm of the house's possessions, and the selling of liveries or corrodies without cause approved by the diocesan, were strictly forbidden, since in these matters the monastery was found to be exceedingly burdened. The regulations as to conduct indicate a laxness in the fulfilment of religious duties and in some of the minor observances of the rule, but nothing worse. That the inquisitors sent by the pope to inquire into the charges against the Templars sat several times at the priory[58] is doubtless no proof of anything but its great standing and the size of its buildings; but after the dissolution of the Order of the Temple one of the knights would hardly have been sent there to live[59] if the character of the house had not been good.

The ordinances dealing with the financial affairs of the priory disclose difficulties, of which there is clear evidence two years later when an action for the recovery of a debt of £300 was brought against the prior.[60] This seems to be the first notice of the burden

of debt[61] which, in spite of the riches of the priory, oppressed it at intervals henceforward. What was the cause of the strain in this instance it is impossible to say, for the corrodies and liveries may have been not the reason but the result of the need of money and a way of raising it.[62] Circumstances seem to have been sometimes unpropitious, since in 1282 the prior and convent had found papal bulls necessary to force their tenants to pay the rents due to them,[63] and the bishop of London, in appropriating the church of Bromfield to their uses, spoke of the burdens due to their charitable works and difficulties caused by hostility in time of war.[64] In 1318 again they alleged the sudden spoliation of the greater part of their substance as a reason for refusing Pope John's request to admit a certain John de Cantia as a canon.[65] They were, doubtless, referring to the seizures of their manors of Braughing and Corney and various other lands of which they recovered seisin in 1318–19; but although they were awarded damages to the extent of £432 18s. 10d. against Masters Geoffrey and John de Hengham and others, they had not received the money in 1324.[66] The canons found it easier to resist the pope than the king, who, not content with a provision for one of his clerks on the election of a new prior,[67] attempted, and for a time successfully, to charge the priory with the maintenance of some of his old and infirm servants. This method of performing a duty was too convenient not to be abused, and if Edward I obtained an asylum there for one[68] or two servants, his son provided in this way for four.[69] At last the prior and convent had to protest, and Edward III, acknowledging in 1335

58 Wilkins, *Concilia*, ii, 334, 335, 337, 344.

59 Dugdale, *Mon. Angl.* vi, 848.

60 *Year Books, Mich. 33 Edw. I to Trin. 35 Edw. I* (Rolls Ser.), 84.

61 The priory seems to have needed help, however, in 1250, when a chantry was erected for Master Richard de Wendover in return for 30 marks given by him to amend the state of the house. Doc. of D. and C. of St. Paul's, A. Box 24, Nos. 1748 and 1750.

62 Eustace son of David de Staunford granted to the prior and convent in 1256 rents and land in London for an annuity of 6 marks. Guildhall MS. 122 fol. 827–8. In 1284 Michael of St. Albans and Gonilda his wife quitclaimed to the priory some land and houses, or rather the lease of them, and in return Michael could have board and lodging if he chose to live in the priory, or if he wished to live with his wife a certain allowance of money. Sharpe, *Cal. of Letter Bk. A*, 158.

63 Rymer, *Foed.* i (2), 609.

64 Cott. R. xiii, 18 (18).

65 Lond. Epis. Reg. Baldock and Gravesend, fol. 37.

66 *Abbrev. Plac.* (Rec. Com.), 344.

67 In 1316 the king sent to the convent requesting them to assign a suitable pension to his clerk John de Funtenay until they shall provide him with a suitable benefice. *Cal. of Close*, 1313–18, p. 424; ibid. 1323–7, p. 506; ibid. 1330–3, p. 332; ibid. 1339–41, p. 464, &c.

68 *Cal. of Close*, 1318–23, p. 694. Request to prior and convent to grant to William de Lughteburgh, the king's envoy, for life such maintenance as Simon le Kew, deceased, had in their house at request of the late king.

69 *Cal. of Close*, 1313–18 p. 69; ibid. 1318–23, p. 694; ibid. 1323–7, p. 345; ibid. 1331–3, p. 392.

that such charges were contrary to the charters of the priory, promised that the corrodies should cease with the lives of the holders,[70] and although he did not altogether keep his word,[71] the practice soon afterwards died out.

There are occasional hints of the great importance of the house. In 1294[72] and 1309[73] the prior acted as one of the collectors of the taxes on the clergy; in 1340 he was appointed with the bishop of London and the dean of St. Paul's to collect and value the tax of the ninth sheaf, lamb, and fleece in the City;[74] and in 1316 the Court Christian, before which John de Warenne brought a suit for divorce from his wife, the king's niece, was composed of two canons of St. Paul's and the prior of Holy Trinity.[75] Like most monasteries it was used as a place for the deposit of valuables: a certain Tigel' Arundel had chests there in 1275;[76] Bartholomew de Badlesmere, from the statement of his widow in 1327–8, evidently kept some of the charters of his estates in the priory;[77] and during the London riots of 1326 a raid was made on the house, and the treasure placed there by the earl of Arundel was carried off.[78] But it is in its relation to the City that it is most interesting. It was one of the three London churches which had schools 'by privilege and authority of antiquity,'[79] St. Paul's and St. Martin's being the others. In times of distress or of rejoicing the church of Holy Trinity was the goal of the solemn processions made through the City;[80] and it was in the priory that the mayor and the representatives of the wards assembled in time of war to consider the question of the City defences.[81] That the prior as alderman of Portsoken took an active part in City affairs is shown by his being engaged with Thomas Romayn the mayor and others in 1310 in choosing the London contingent of the army raised for the war with Scotland.[82]

The very list of the monastery's property is sufficient testimony of the light in which the house

was regarded by the citizens, for it had possessions in seventy-two London parishes in 1291.[83] Nor had it by that date exhausted its popularity, as is shown by the grants and bequests still made to it, though there were now many newer foundations. Ralph le Blund[84] in 1295 left to the priory rents in the parishes of St. Mary Woolchurch and All Hallows Bread Street, for the establishment of a chantry;[85] Thomas Romayn, alderman, in 1312 bequeathed to it 100 marks;[86] Walter Constantyn in 1349 left tenements and a brewery in the parish of Holy Trinity for the maintenance of its church and the establishment of a chantry in the church of St. Katharine Cree;[87] Thomas de Algate, rector of 'Sheering,' co. Essex, left to his brother Nicholas the prior, and to the convent of Holy Trinity, tenements and rents in the parishes of St. Katharine within Aldgate, St. Andrew Cornhill, and St. Botolph without Aldgate;[88] and John Malewayn, in 1361,[89] left the residue of his goods, after payment of certain bequests, to the maintenance of chantries there, besides a money legacy to the work of the church. These are, moreover, only examples of many other bequests.[90]

The convent certainly needed everything it could get. The rebuilding of the church had been begun about 1339,[91] and engrossed all its available funds, even before the Black Death diminished its revenues, and thereby increased the difficulty of repaying loans which had to be contracted if the work was to go on. The pope in 1352 offered a relaxation of penance to those who contributed to the restoration during a period of ten years.[92] But the house was still burdened with debt in 1368 when Master John Yong, official of the court of Canterbury, gave £100 to its relief,[93] and was rewarded by a daily mass being established in the church for his good estate in life, and for his soul after death. The same fact is also apparent in the grants of corrodies and pensions

[70] Cal. of Pat. 1334–8, p. 117.

[71] Cal. of Close, 1343–6, p. 565. In 1345 Walter de Stodleye was sent to the priory to receive such maintenance as Master John de Stretford, deceased, had there at the king's request.

[72] Ibid. 1288–96, p. 396.

[73] Ibid. 1307–13, p. 227.

[74] Cal. of Pat. 1340–3, p. 28.

[75] Ibid. 1313–17, p. 434.

[76] Cal. of Close, 1272–9, p. 233.

[77] Parl. R. (Rec. Com.), ii, 430a.

[78] Chron. of Edw. I and Edw. II (Rolls Ser.), i, 321.

[79] Liber Custum. in Mun. Gildhall Lond. (Rolls Ser.), ii (1), 5, 'privilegio et antiqua dignitate.'

[80] Chron. of Edw. I and Edw. II (Rolls Ser.), i, 278. 1315 was a year of great scarcity, and a solemn procession was ordained to go up to the church every Friday; ibid. i, 358, the procession of rejoicing for the taking of Berwick, 1333, went from St. Paul's to Holy Trinity.

[81] Mun. Gildhall Lond. (Rolls Ser.), ii (1), 149.

[82] Cal. of Close, 1307–13, p. 307.

[83] Harl. MS. 60, fol. 7, 8.

[84] Ralph le Blund was sheriff in 1291.

[85] Sharpe, Cal. of Wills, i, 126.

[86] Ibid. i, 238. Thomas Romayn was mayor in 1309.

[87] Ibid. 594.

[88] Ibid. ii, 10.

[89] Ibid. ii, 39.

[90] For other bequests to them see Sharpe, Cal. of Wills, i, 536, 537, 580, 597, 636; ii, 17, 67, 155, 163, 197, 333, &c.

[91] From 1339 to 1345 there are continual acknowledgements of debt by the prior: £55 in 1339, see Cal. of Close, 1339–41, pp. 239, 339; £10 and £106 13s. 4d. in 1340, ibid. pp. 477, 490; £100 in 1341, ibid. 1341–3, p. 271; in 1343, £80, £200, and two sums of £40, ibid. 1343–6, pp. 102, 229, 233, 241; £40 in 1344, ibid, p. 363; and £120 in 1345, ibid. p. 572.

[92] Cal. Pap. Letters, iii, 434.

[93] Cott. MS. Nero, C. iii, fol. 179, 180. The gift is said to be in relief of the debt by reason of erecting and rebuilding of the church.

which were evidently made to raise money.[94] There may have been other complications which prevented the priory's extricating itself from its difficulties, for in 1369[95] the convent had procured from the pope a bull similar to that of 1282 directed against those who occupied its property, and when the king took it into his hands in 1380 he attributed the loss of revenues and the decrease in divine services to its being harassed by rivals.[96]

After this the convent appears to have enjoyed for more than half a century a tranquillity interrupted only by the arrest and imprisonment of one of its members by the council in 1429, for some unexplained cause.[97] In 1438, however, the condition of the house called for serious attention. The archbishop of Canterbury, in a letter to the bishop of London,[98] said that he had heard that the prior at the bishop's last visitation was accused of dilapidation and consumption of the goods of the house and other wrongdoings, and that the bishop, although requested by many noble persons to proceed to correction and reformation in these matters, had neglected to do so. The bishop answered that he had found nothing proved against the prior, William Clerk, for which he could be justly removed, but as his administration of the temporalities of the priory had been foolish and imprudent, he had committed the management of these, with consent of the prior and convent, to one of the canons and some secular persons, and hoped that the heavy burden of debt might in a short time be lightened and the necessities of the fraternity relieved. This arrangement did not suffice to meet the case, and the next year the king, to raise the house from the deplorable state of want[99] and insecurity to which it had been reduced by its inefficient head, took it into his hand, and committed it to the care of the abbot of Leicester, and the priors of St. Mary Overy, of Newark, and of Stone.[100] If the loans

requested for the defence of Guienne can be taken as showing the relative wealth of the lenders,[101] the priory seems in 1453 to have scarcely regained its old position,[102] though it probably had before 1481, as Edward IV marked his sense of the standing of the house by petitioning the pope to allow Prior Thomas Pomery to use the crosier and mitre.[103] The bishop of London had been accused of laxness in the exercise of his powers over the priory in 1438, but the same failing could hardly be urged against Bishop Hill in 1493.[104] On a visitation of the priory he found that Thomas Percy, the prior, had not only wasted the goods of the house, but had given occasion for scandal by his relations with a married woman named Joan Hodgis. Hearing afterwards that Percy, to facilitate his intercourse with Joan, had given her the office of embroiderer by letters patent to which he had forced the canons to affix the common seal, the bishop extorted a resignation from him by threatening to depose him, and put Robert Charnock in possession. Percy turned Charnock out, and was in turn forcibly ejected by the bishop. The case, tried first in the court of Canterbury and then at Rome, was decided against the bishop on the ground that he had exceeded his rights by taking the law into his own hands,[105] but a sentence adverse to Percy must also have been delivered, for he was not prior in 1506[106] nor in 1509,[107] though he may have been reinstated before his death in 1512.[108] In the early years of Henry VIII the priory must have seemed as important as ever to the ordinary observer, who could judge only by the position it held in the City and at the court,[109] and by its lavish hospitality.[110] But it was keeping

---

[94] The indenture between the convent and Robert de Denton, *Cal. of Pat.* 1377–81, p. 194, states that the pension of 25 marks and the 100 faggots yearly, &c., are given to him for a sum of money paid by him to the convent, and though there is not the same evidence in the other cases (ibid. 72 and 74), it is plain that they are agreements of the same kind.

[95] Stevens, op. cit. App. 328.

[96] When he appointed the archbishop of Canterbury, the Chief Justice of the King's Bench, &c., to the custody and rule of the priory, 1 Jan. 1381. *Cal. of Pat.* 1379–81, p. 599.

[97] Devon, *Issues of the Exch.* (Pell Rec.). It is the more mysterious as this canon, John Asshewell, is called prior, and William Clerk, who was elected in 1420, was still prior in 1438. See Dugdale, *Mon. Angl.* vi, 151; Lond. Epis. Reg. Gilbert, fol. 84.

[98] Ibid.

[99] Pat. 17 Hen. VI, pt. 2, m. 31. The king states that it has come to such want that of the lands, tenements, &c., belonging to it, alms and other works of piety for the souls of his ancestors cannot be maintained.

[100] Pat. 17 Hen. VI, pt. 2, m. 31.

[101] A certain measure of favour may have been shown to religious houses.

[102] £20 was required from the prior, £100 from one of the aldermen, Nicholas Wyfold, and £40 from Thomas Tyrelle, knt. *Letters and Papers I llust. the Wars of English in France* (Rolls Ser.), ii (2), 489.

[103] Tanner, *Notit. Mon.* quotes MS. 170, C. C. Camb. fol. 197.

[104] *Hist. MSS. Com. Rep.* ix, App. i, 119. Fabyan says, 'in this year (1493) Dr. Hylle, bishop of London, grievously pursued Percy, then prior of Christchurch in London.' *Chronicle* (ed. Ellis), 685.

[105] *Hist. MSS. Com. Rep.* ix, App. i, 119. 'The bishop . . . by taking the law into his own hands had been guilty of contempt of the executive, and was condemned to make amends.'

[106] *L. and P. Hen. VIII*, xvi, 503 (15). A lease by Prior Thomas Newton, Feb. 1506.

[107] Anct. D. (P.R.O.), A. 1773.

[108] He died prior in 1512. Lond. Epis. Reg. Fitz James, fol. 84.

[109] In the cellarer's account, *L. and P. Hen. VIII*, ii (1), 115, there are notices of presents to the queen, to the king's footmen, the king's waits, the lord of misrule of the king's house.

[110] See the Liber Coquinae, Mich. 1513–Mich. 1514. Ibid. Brewer remarked that the provision made for the guests was more plentiful and varied than that for the convent. The weekly bill for the steward who arranged for the guests amounted to more than that for the convent. On Trinity Sunday they entertained thirteen persons, and the menu was a very long one.

up appearances when it should have been engaged on retrenchment and strict economy. If it had ever been on a sound financial footing since the middle of the fifteenth century, it was again involved in difficulties by the maladministration of Percy, and on the accession of Henry VIII it owed money to the crown,[111] which it never appears to have been able to pay.[112] It was exempted from the payment of the two-tenths to the king in 1517 from its lands in Braughing, Layston, and Edmonton, because of the debts with which the house had long been and still was burdened.[113] In 1526 Bishop Tunstall gave leave to the prior, Nicholas Hancocke, to withdraw from the monastery for three years, in order to relieve the debts of the house, which was to be entrusted to the charge of suitable and skilful persons chosen by the prior and convent.[114] Its condition was evidently rather hopeless, and the reason given by the prior and convent for their surrender of the house to the king in February, 1532,[115] viz., that it had so deteriorated in its fruits and rents, and was so heavily burdened with debt, that unless a remedy were quickly provided by the king it must become extinct, was much nearer the truth than the majority of such statements. Hancocke's friends, however, considered that he had betrayed his trust to secure an easier competency for himself.[116] In that case the desired object was not immediately attained, since he was afraid to stir out owing to an undischarged butcher's bill.[117] No one would lend to him, he complained, as he had given up his house, and if something were not done for him he would have to go into sanctuary, which would be a disgrace to Cromwell.[118] At last he received an annuity of 100 marks,[119] with which he professed himself well satisfied. The canons, who numbered eighteen at the time of the surrender, are said to have been sent to other houses,[120] but it is clear that provision was not made for all, since John Lichefeld, one of the latest admitted, wrote to Cromwell, saying that after his religious training he is an entire outcast, for no house will receive him.[121]

In the face of all this it is curious to read that Parliament in 1533–4 confirmed the gift of the monastery to the king 'because the Prior and Convent had departed from the monastery leaving it profaned and desolate for two years and more whereby the services, hospitality, etc. … remained undone.'[122] At first there was some idea of placing the friars of Greenwich in the vacant house,[123] but in 1534 the king granted the site and all the possessions of the late priory in the parish of St. Botolph without Aldgate to Lord Audley.[124] The City, in spite of the fact that the prior was an alderman, seems to have made no protest either about the surrender of the house or about the king's grant, yet it is evident that they afterwards felt uneasy, for before the election of the first lay alderman of Portsoken in January, 1538,[125] there appears to have been some idea of buying Lord Audley's lands.[126]

The possessions of the monastery in 1291 were reckoned in the *Taxatio* of Pope Nicholas as worth £235 10s. 6¾d. per annum,[127] probably too low an estimate.[128] No valor exists for the whole property[129] in the reign of Henry VIII, but what the house held in London, valued at £121 16s. 6½d. in 1291[130] and £105 17s. 3¼d. in 1425,[131] was said to be worth £355 13s. 6d. in 1537,[132] and consisted of tenements within the site of the priory and in sixty parishes besides,[133] a pension of £100 paid from the farm of the City since 1361 in return for tithes granted by the priory to St. Mary Graces;[134] the churches of St. Botolph without Aldgate and St. Katharine Cree-church appropriated to the priory before the end of the twelfth century and by order of Pope Innocent III[135] served by two of the canons, and

---

[111] *L. and P. Hen. VIII*, i, 1639 and 3497.

[112] The priory may have paid this debt, but if so, it contracted another before the surrender. Ibid. v, 823.

[113] Lond. Epis. Reg. Fitz James, fol. 121.

[114] Ibid. Tunstall, fol. 156.

[115] Lansd. MS. 968, fol. 50, 51.

[116] He says that all his friends turn from him and make slanderous reports of him, saying he reckoned on good profit and quietness in giving up his house. *L. and P. Hen. VIII*, v, 1735.

[117] Ibid. v, 1731.

[118] Ibid. v, 1732.

[119] Ibid. v, 1065 (34). 20 May, 24 Hen. VIII, 1532.

[120] 'Chron. of Grey Friars,' *Monum. Francisc.* (Rolls Ser.), ii, 194.

[121] *L. and P. Hen. VIII*, v, 1744.

[122] Parl. R. 25 Hen. VIII (10).

[123] *L. and P. Hen. VIII*, vi, 115.

[124] Lansd. MS. 968, fol. 52–4.

[125] Rec. of the Corp. of Lond. Repert, x, fol. 17b.

[126] Ibid. ix, fol. 262–3, 270.

[127] *Pope Nich. Tax.* (Rec. Com.), 9, 12b, 13b, 14b, 18, 21, 21b, 22, 22b, 26, 26b, 29b, 37, 51b, 52.

[128] From Harl. MS. 60, fols. 7, 8, 19, 25, 29, 39, 41, 54, 56, 57, 61, 62, 64, 70, 78, the total appears to be a little over £290.

[129] A marginal note in the Lond. Epis. Reg. Tunstall, fol. 51, gives it as £508 13s. 9d. Wolsey's procurations in 1524 were rated on a value of £333 6s. 8d. *L. and P. Hen. VIII*, iv (1), 964.

[130] *Pope Nich. Tax.* (Rec. Com.) According to Harl. MS. 60, fol. 7, 8, £129 3s. 2½d.

[131] Stevens, op. cit. ii, 83. This was the worth of the rental.

[132] *L. and P. Hen. VIII*, xii (2), 777.

[133] In 1291 the priory held tenements in 72 parishes (Harl. MS. 60, fol. 7, 8); and in 1354 in 71 parishes. Anct. D. (P.R.O.), A. 2529.

[134] Close, 34 Edw. III, m. 41 in Add. MS. 15664, fol. 142.

[135] This pope in his fourth year confirmed the annexation of the church of St. Botolph and the chapel of St. Katharine and St. Michael within the cemetery of the monastery made by apostolic authority. Cott. R. xiii, 18 (28); Stevens, op. cit. ii, 85.

the advowsons of St. Edmund Lombard Street, St. Augustine Pappey, Allhallows on the Wall, the gift of the founder, and of St. Gabriel Fenchurch Street. From St. Edmund's a pension of 13s. 4d. appears to have been paid before the close of the twelfth century,[136] and from the others small sums were due yearly in 1301.[137] About 1175 it was arranged that the canons of St. Mary's, Southwark, should pay 10s. per annum from the church of St. Mildred.[138] At the time of the surrender the priory also held in Middlesex a manor at Tottenham,[139] and the church the gift of Simon, earl of Northampton, to the priory early in Stephen's reign,[140] the tithes being added by David, brother of William the Lion, king of Scotland, before 1214; lands in Bromley[141] and Edmonton,[142] where grants had been made to the convent before 1227;[143] in co. Herts the church of Braughing given to them by Queen Maud[144] the wife of Stephen, and appropriated to them in 1217;[145] the manor of Braughing,[146] where grants had been made to them by the same king and queen and by Hubert the chamberlain;[147] the manors of 'Bysholt,' Milkley, and Corneybury, and the church of Layston[148] acquired from Hugh Tricket in Stephen's reign,[149] the church being appropriated

to them between 1189 and 1199;[150] the advowson of Astwick,[151] given by Richard son of William between 1162 and 1170;[152] lands in Throcking[153] in which place and Hodenhoe they held two carucates in 1227 granted to them by Roger son of Brian and Matilda his wife,[154] in Wyddial and Westmill,[155] where they held land at the earlier date;[156] the manor of Berksdon,[157] the gift of Richard de Anesty before 1227;[158] the hamlet of Wakeley,[159] and tithes in Bendish[160] which were given by Hubert the chamberlain in Stephen's reign;[161] in 1291 the prior received a pension from the church of Wyddial[162] and in 1428 one also from that of Westmill;[163] in Essex the convent held the manor of Cann Hall or Canon Hall[164] with appurtenances in Wanstead and West Ham, which they possessed before 1207;[165] the church of Walthamstow which, granted by Alice de Toeni[166] and confirmed to them by Pope Eugenius III in 1147,[167] had been appropriated to them by William de Sainte Mere l'Eglise,[168] bishop of London 1191–1222; the churches of Black Notley and Bromfield, the gift of Walter de Mandeville before 1147,[169] the former paying a pension of a mark, increased to two by Bishop William de Ste. Mére l'Eglise, the latter church appropriated to the priory in 1292;[170] to the priory in 1291 and 1428 were also due pensions from Lambourne,[171] Stapleford Abbots,[172] and West Ham;[173] land in Leyton given by Simon de Molins and his wife Adelina was one of the earliest grants made to the priory;[174] at the Dissolution the priory held in Kent the church

---

[136] There was a dispute about the church between the priory and the chapter of St. Paul's, which was settled by Gilbert Foliot when bishop of London (1163–1189). It was then decided that the priory should present after the death of the present holder and should give half its pension to St. Paul's. From a confirmation of the settlement in 1300 the pension was evidently 13s. 4d. Cott. R. xiii, 18 (23 & 24).

[137] Lib. Custum. in Mun. Gildhall. Lond. (Rolls Ser.), ii (1), 234.

[138] Cott. Chart. xi, 52. The church itself is said to have been given to them in the time of Prior Norman, but was granted away for a small pension. Guildhall MS. 122, fol. 566.

[139] L. and P. Hen. VIII, xix (1), 812 (32). The prior's manor of 'Tottenham' is mentioned in a deed of 1310 (Anct. D. [P.R.O.], A. 7312), but in 1348 and in 1375 the earl of Pembroke held the manor. Chan. Inq. p.m. 22 Edw. III (1st Nos.), 47, file 46; 49 Edw. III (1st Nos.), 70, file 83.

[140] Cott. MS. Nero, C. iii, fol. 187. The grant was confirmed to the canons by Pope Innocent II in 1137. Rymer, Foedera (Rec. Com.), i (1), 14; B.M. Chart. L.F.C. xxx, 3.

[141] L. and P. Hen. VIII, xvii, p. 696.

[142] Ibid. xiii (1), 646 (13).

[143] Charter of 11 Hen. III, Dugdale, Mon. Angl. vi, 154.

[144] Cott. R. xiii, 18 (1); Lansd. MS. 448, fol. 5.

[145] Cott. R. xiii, 18 (2).

[146] Lansd. MS. 960, fol. 54.

[147] The charter by which the queen confirms her husband's grant is given in Dugdale, op. cit. vi, 153. For Hubert's gift of 4 librates of land in 'Brackinges', see charter 11 Hen. III, ibid. The prior was holding the manor in 1274. Hund. R. (Rec. Com.), i, 191.

[148] Lansd. MS. 968, fol. 54.

[149] Eustace, count of Boulogne, confirmed to the canons the land of 'Cornea' which Hugh Tricket sold to them. Cart. Antiq. R. N. 8. In 1253 they are said to hold the manor. Cal. of Chart. R. i, 427. For Hugh's grant of the church then called Lefstanchirche, see Cott. R. xiii, 18 (5), and for both manor and church, Chauncy, Hist. of Herts. 128.

[150] Newcourt, op. cit. i, 843.

[151] Lansd. MS. 968, fol. 54.

[152] He made the grant in the presence of Thomas, archbishop of Canterbury. Cott. R. xiii, 18 (8).

[153] L. and P. Hen. VIII, xii (2), 1027.

[154] Charter of Confirmation 1227, Dugdale, op. cit. vi, 153.

[155] L. and P. Hen. VIII, xii (2), 1027.

[156] Charter of Confirmation 1227, Dugdale, op. cit. vi, 153.

[157] Chauncy, op. cit. 119.

[158] At this date the grant was confirmed to the prior. Dugdale, op. cit. vi, 153.

[159] Chauncy says this came into the possession of the priory at some time after 6 Ric. I, and the canons held it and the church until the surrender of the house. Op. cit. 120.

[160] L. and P. Hen. VIII, xiii (1), 1519 (69).

[161] Lansd. MS. 448, fol. 4.

[162] Harl. MS. 60, fol. 29; Feud. Aids, ii, 465.

[163] Feud. Aids, ii, 463.

[164] L. and P. Hen. VIII, vi, 94; Morant, Hist. of Essex, i, 31.

[165] Newcourt, Repert. Eccl. Lond. ii, 639.

[166] Cott. R. xiii, 18 (15).

[167] Rymer, Foedera (Rec. Com.), i (1), 15.

[168] Newcourt, op. cit. ii, 635.

[169] Rymer, Foedera (Rec. Com.), i (1), 15.

[170] Cott. R. xiii, 18 (14).

[171] Harl. MS. 60, fol. 56, and Feud. Aids, ii, 204.

[172] Harl. MS. 60, fol. 57; Feud. Aids, ii, 204.

[173] Harl. MS. 60, fol. 62; Feud. Aids, ii, 194.

[174] It was confirmed by Henry I. Cart. Antiq. R. N. 6. See also Charter, 11 Hen. III, Dugdale, Mon. Angl. vi, 153.

of Bexley,[175] which with its tithes had been given to the canons by William Corbeuil, archbishop of Canterbury, between 1123 and 1135,[176] and the appropriation of the church must have been of early date, for a controversy as to the vicar's portion was settled by Archbishop Stephen Langton, 1207–1228;[177] in the same county Richard de Lucy had given them in Stephen's reign land in Lesnes,[178] to which they afterwards added more,[179] and the church of Lesnes[180] where a vicarage was ordained before 1218;[181] in the thirteenth century the priory held land in 'Hamstead,' co. Surrey,[182] and in the reign of Henry VI a messuage in the parish of St. Peter's, Oxford.[183]

The priory held in 1428 a quarter of a knight's fee in Edmonton,[184] where in 1353 it had also had another quarter called Peverel's fee,[185] one knight's fee in Alswyk,[186] two half fees in Berksdon,[187] and in Corney a quarter fee[188] and a half,[189] which latter it had possessed at an early date.[190]

*M. Reddan*

[175] Hasted, *Hist. of Kent*, i, 166.
[176] Lansd. MS. 448, fol. 11.
[177] Ibid. fol. 12.
[178] Cart. Antiq. R. N. 20. Stephen confirmed the grant. B.M. Chart. L.F.C. xiv, 6. The priory still held land there (parish of Erith) in 1518. *L. and P. Hen. VIII*, ii (2), 4654.
[179] B.M. Chart. L.F.C. xiv, 14, 20, 23, and L.F.C. xxiii, 22, 23.
[180] Thorpe, *Reg. Roff.* 325.
[181] B.M. Chart. L.F.C. xiv, 22.
[182] Add. Chart. 8793 and 9000.
[183] *Cal. Chart. R. and Inq. a.q.d.* (Rec. Com.), 378.
[184] *Feud. Aids*, iii, 383.
[185] Ibid. iii, 376.
[186] Ibid. ii, 446.
[187] Ibid. ii, 446, 453.
[188] Ibid. ii, 446.
[189] Ibid. ii, 453.
[190] *Lib. Nig. Scacc.* (Hearne), i, 390.

## Revised List of Priors of Holy Trinity, Aldgate

This list is taken from *Heads of Religious Houses*, vol. 1, pp. 173–4, vol. 2, pp. 415–16, and vol. 3 (forthcoming).

Norman, appointed 1107/8; died 1147
Ralph, elected 1147; died 1167
William, occurs 1169
Stephen, elected 1170; deposed 1197
Peter de Cornwall, elected 1197; died 1221
Richard de Temple, elected 1222; died 1250
John de Toting, elected 1250; died 1261
Gilbert, occurs 1261; died ?1268
Eustace, elected 1269; died 1284
William Aiguel, elected 1285; died 1294
Stephen de Watton, elected 1294, resigned 1303
Ralph of Canterbury, elected 1303; died 1316
Richard de Wymbysshe, elected 1316; resigned 1325
Roger de Poleye, elected 1325; resigned, 1331
Thomas Heyron, elected 1331; died 1340
Nicholas of Aldgate alias of London, elected 1340; died 1377
William de Risyng, elected 1377; died 1391
Robert Excestre or Exeter, elected 1391; died 1407
William Harrington or Haradon, elected 1407; died 1420
William Clerk, elected 1420, resigned 1439
John Asshewell, occurs 1429
William Clerk, occurs 1432; resigned 1439
John Sevenok or Sevenot, S.T.B. elected 1439; resigned 1445
Thomas Pomery elected 1445; died 1481
Thomas Percy, elected 1481; deposed 1493
Richard Charnock, royal assent 1495; died bef. 1505
Thomas Newton, elected 1505; died 1506
Thomas Percy, died 1512
John Bradwell, elected 1512; occurs 1520–1523, 1524
Nicholas Hancoke, elected 1524; surrendered 1532

# 6. THE PRIORY OF ST. BARTHOLOMEW, SMITHFIELD

## INTRODUCTION

There is now a very full account of the priory's history available in E. A. Webb, *The Records of St. Bartholomew's Priory and of the Church and Parish of St. Bartholomew the Great West Smithfield*, 2 vols. (Oxford, 1921). This adds a great deal of detail to the good but inevitably sketchy account below, and includes, among other sources, a transcription of B.L. Cotton Vespasian B ix, the Middle English source for the accounts of the founding of the priory. An annotated edition of the text, first edited by Moore in 1888, appeared as *The Book of the Foundation of St. Bartholomew's Church in London: The Church Belonging to the Priory of the same in West Smithfield*, ed. N. Moore, Early Eng. Text Soc., Orig. Ser., 163 (1923). A modern English version was printed in E. A. Webb (ed.), *The Book of the Foundation of the Church of St. Bartholomew London Rendered into Modern English* (Oxford, 1923).

An account of the fabric of the church and what was known of the monastic buildings from standing building surveys, archaeological reports and documentary sources can be found in volume 2 of Webb, *Records*, pp. 3–195. More recent work on the remains of the cloisters, updating Webb's findings, is reported in M. Gormley, 'St. Bartholomew-the-Great: archaeology in the cloisters', *London Archaeologist*, 8 (1) (1966), pp. 18–24. The location and boundaries of the precinct are described in Honeybourne, 'Property', pp. 66–72.

There is a convenient summary of locations and sources of the priory's property in *Documentary Sources*, p. 53. The priory's London property is included in the 1392 record of ecclesiastical property in McHardy, *Church in London*, pp. 39–77. Details of the surviving archives of St. Bartholomew's priory, together with a list of estates held by the house, have been collated by the English Monastic Archives project and are available online, URL: http://www.ucl.ac.uk/history/englishmonasticarchives/index.htm (accessed 8 February 2007).

A list of canons ordained in the London diocese between 1361 and 1539 can be obtained from the CD Rom accompanying Davis, *Clergy of London*. The canons of the hospital assessed for the 1379 poll tax can be found in McHardy, *Church in London*, p. 1. Webb, *Records*, has an account of each of the priors and numerous references to canons.

*Ann Bowtell*

The honour of founding the priory of St. Bartholomew appears to belong jointly to a clerk named Rahere[1] and to King Henry I,[2] for though the means were supplied by the king, it is to the enthusiasm of the clerk that both the origin and success of the scheme must be ascribed. According to an account written by a canon of the priory, apparently within seventy years of the foundation of the house,[3] Rahere spent his early life more like a courtier than a priest in attendance on the great nobles of his day, but experienced a change of heart while at Rome on a pilgrimage. He then fell ill and vowed, if he recovered, to found a hospital. Afterwards he had a dream in which St. Bartholomew appeared to him and directed him to build a church in his honour at Smithfield.[4] On his recovery and return to England he obtained this land from the king,[5] through the good offices of Richard bishop of London, and on it he built a house and church for a community of regular canons of whom he became the first prior, and, in close proximity, a hospital for the poor.

[1] Cott. MS. Vesp. B. ix, fol. 41.
[2] Leland, *Coll.* i, 54.
[3] Moore, *The Book of the Foundation of St. Bartholomew's Church in London*, xli.
[4] Cott. MS. Vesp. B. ix, fol. 41–3.
[5] Ibid. fol. 45*b*.

The author already quoted says this event took place in 1123,[6] and there seems no reason to doubt his statement,[7] though he is clearly mistaken in assigning the consecration of the cemetery by Bishop Richard to the thirtieth year of Henry I, as the bishop died in 1128. Rahere's position was a very difficult one, for in addition to the ordinary anxieties attendant on the establishment of a new foundation he had to contend with intense enmity, on one occasion a plot being made against his life.[8] The hostility towards him seems to have come not entirely from one quarter, for he intended to go to Rome to secure the support of the pope,[9] although he had already found in the king a powerful protector.

Henry gave the canons the site in West Smithfield, and the churches of Guileston, St. Nicholas, Little Yarmouth, Lowestoft, and Belton,[10] and also granted to them in 1133 very ample charters[11] of privileges: he declared them free from all services and customs except the episcopal customs, viz. consecration of churches, baptism and rule of the clergy; in all their lands they were to have sac and soc, toll and team, infangenthef and outfangenthef; to the prior was granted the power to settle all disturbances of the peace, assaults, and forfeitures in his demesne; they were to be quit of shires and hundreds, danegeld and other gelds, building and repairing of castles, and of ferdwite, hegwite, wardpeni and averpeni; throughout all the king's dominions their goods and men were to be free from toll, passagium, pedagium, wharfage, lastage, and stallage; and the king granted his firm peace to those going to or returning from the fair held at the priory for three days from the eve of St. Bartholomew. The king provided at the same time that on Rahere's death the canons should choose one of themselves as prior, but if there should not be a suitable person there, they were free to choose one from a well-known place; and that gifts of lands were not to be alienated without the consent of the chapter.[12] The house indeed seems to have been regarded as a royal foundation, and as such protected and patronized. Henry II confirmed all the privileges

granted to the canons by his grandfather, and added another that they should not be impleaded save in the king's presence;[13] Richard I laid down more definite rules with regard to the fair, granting the canons all the profits, forbidding the exaction of customs or tolls from those coming to buy and sell there, and ordering that no one should sell on the canons' land without their permission;[14] John took the canons, their men and possessions into his protection, and forbade any interference with the church which he calls his demesne chapel;[15] and Henry III in 1227 confirmed their charters.[16] But as usual the latter acted with an entire absence of fairness when the canons came into collision with one of his foreign favourites. Boniface of Savoy, as archbishop of Canterbury, was determined to exercise visitatorial powers in London. After being repulsed at St. Paul's and at the priory of Holy Trinity, he came to St. Bartholomew's.[17] The canons, dressed in their most precious copes, received him with much honour, but on hearing that he had come on a visitation the sub-prior, the prior being absent, informed him that the bishop of London alone possessed this right, and they ought not to submit to its exercise by another. The archbishop, beside himself with rage, struck the old man again and again; the canons went to the rescue of the sub-prior, and tried to drag him away; then Boniface's Provençal followers rushed into the church, and a contest ensued in which the canons came off badly, as they were not, like the archbishop, equipped in armour beneath their vestments. By the advice of the bishop of London four of the canons went to the king to complain, but he refused to hear them, and fearing the temper of the Londoners, who were furious with the archbishop, he forbade anyone to interfere in the controversy on pain of life and limb. Boniface followed up his disgraceful conduct by excommunicating the convent officials, but this sentence was shortly afterwards annulled by the pope.[18] The canons, however, never received any compensation for their sufferings, for the archbishop managed partly by threats, partly by promises, to suppress their complaints,[19] and the question of archiepiscopal visitations was decided against them by the court of Rome in 1252.[20]

The disputes of the priory with the City, both of which arose over the fair, were not marked by any

[6] Ibid. fol. 46.

[7] Stow, *Surv. of Lond.* (ed. Strype), iii, 232, gives 1102 as the date, but if Bishop Richard played the part supposed, this must be much too early, since he did not obtain the see until 1108. Matt. of Westm. *Flor. Hist.* (Rolls Ser.), ii, says the house was founded in 1123.

[8] Cott. MS. Vesp. B. ix, fol. 48*b*.

[9] Mr. Moore, op. cit. lxi, sees in this projected visit to Rome a sign that the canons had difficulties with the clergy.

[10] The grant was confirmed Sept. 1229, *Cal. of Chart. R.* i, 98.

[11] There are two charters of this date, in one of which the king says that he will maintain and defend this church as he does his crown. Inspex. 2 Hen. VI, Add. MS. 34768, fol. 9*b*–11.

[12] Add. MS. 34768, fol. 16.

[13] Ibid. 20–8.

[14] Cart. Antiq. R. L. (4).

[15] Charter dated December, 1203. *Chart. R.* (Rec. Com.), i, 115.

[16] Cart. Antiq. R. L. (6).

[17] Matt. Paris, *Chron. Maj.* (Rolls Ser.), v, 121–3.

[18] *Cal. Pap. Letters*, i, 264.

[19] Matt. Paris, *Chron. Maj.* (Rolls Ser.), v, 178, 188.

[20] *Cal. Pap. Letters*, i, 276.

violence. The prior and canons, by the counsel of the king's treasurer, William de Haverille, and of their sokereeve John de Kondres, set up on the first day of their fair in 1246 a new 'tron,' with which all weighing had to be done.[21] The mayor and the chief men of the City went on the next day to the priory and demanded that the practice should be abandoned as it was in contravention of the customs of the City, and the canons appear to have yielded the point at once.

In 1292 an attempt was made by the warden of London to deprive the priory of half the profits of the fair,[22] but the prior must have given satisfactory proof of his right to the whole, for the City never made any further claim.

The priory during this time had been steadily growing in wealth and importance. At the death of Rahere the house depended largely on obventions and charity, but the great increase in temporalities noticed between 1144 and 1174[23] seems to have been well maintained. In London it had received the church of St. Sepulchre from Roger, bishop of Salisbury,[24] the church of St. Michael Bassishaw[25] from G. bishop of London[26] in the twelfth century, and St. Martin's, Ironmonger Lane, from Ralph Triket before 1253.[27] In Essex it possessed the manor of Shortgrove, which it held as early as the reign of Henry II;[28] half the church of Danbury,[29] the gift of Earl William de Mandeville before 1190;[30] the hamlet of Langley, granted by Robert Fitz Roger, to whom it had been given by Henry II;[31] and the church of Theydon Bois, given by William de Bosco in the latter half of the twelfth century.[32] In co. Herts. the canons held the church of Hemel Hempstead in 1201;[33] and in 1253 the king confirmed to them the manor of Little Stanmore, the gift of William de Ramis,[34] to whom they owed also the church of Bradfield, co. Essex; the church of St. Laurence Stanmore, which had been given to them by Roger de Ramis;[35] lands in Shenley, obtained from Adam

son of Elias de Somery, and Saer[36] son of Henry; and lands and rents in Tewin, given with land in Hertford, Amwell, and 'Lockeleigh' by Alexander de Swereforde, canon and treasurer of St. Paul's, to endow a chantry of four chaplains.[37] The king also confirmed to them in 1253 the church of Mentmore, co. Bucks, which had been given to the priory by Hugh Bussell and William son of Miles, and half the church of Wenhaston, co. Suffolk, granted by Geoffrey Fitz Ailwin.[38] Between 1323 and 1353 lands were added for the establishment of chantries and anniversaries in Theydon Bois,[39] co. Essex, and in London,[40] Acton,[41] Kentish Town, and Islington,[42] co. Middlesex, in which last place the priory had a holding in 1253.[43]

The priory must have been popular in the City: in 1291 it had holdings in forty-eight London parishes,[44] and it is reasonable to suppose that much of this property was derived from London citizens, seeing that in the fourteenth century bequests from them were so numerous.[45] The standing of the house is probably shown by the frequent choice of the prior as collector of the clerical tenth.[46]

The archbishop of Canterbury visited the priory in 1303, and made certain ordinances:[47] the rule of silence is to be better observed by the canons; money is not to be assigned them for their clothes, but garments are to be allotted as needed, and the officer charged with this duty is never to give them before the old ones are handed up to him; the canons who are ill in the infirmary are to be provided with suitable food according to the means of the monastery; the doors of the cloister and the houses in it are to be kept more strictly and closed at proper hours, so that the brothers may not be disturbed at service by the

[21] Riley, Chron. of Mayors and Sheriffs of Lond. 13.
[22] Sharpe, Cal. of Letter Bk. C. 9.
[23] Cott. MS. Vesp. B. ix, fol. 59.
[24] Cart. Antiq. R. L. 14.
[25] Ibid.
[26] Either Gilbert Universalis, bishop of London 1128–41, or Gilbert Foliot, who held the see 1163–89.
[27] Cart. Antiq. R. L. 14.
[28] Morant, Hist. of Essex, ii, 585.
[29] Cart. Antiq. R. L. 14.
[30] He died in the second year of Ric. I. Newcourt, Repert. Eccl. Lond. ii, 203.
[31] Morant, op. cit. ii, 614.
[32] William de Bosco held a knight's fee in Theydon Bois in 1166. Morant, op. cit. ii, 162.
[33] They paid 200 marks for John's confirmation. Hardy, Rot. de Oblat. et Fin. (Rec. Com.), 181.
[34] Cart. Antiq. R. L. 14; Plac. de Quo Warr. (Rec. Com.), 478.
[35] Cart. Antiq. R. L. 14.
[36] Ibid.
[37] He died in 1246. Ann. Mon. (Rolls Ser.), iii, 171.
[38] Cart. Antiq. R. L. 14.
[39] Cal. of Pat. 1348–50, p. 270.
[40] Sharpe, Cal. of Wills, i, 234, 278, 301, 451, 683.
[41] Cal. of Pat. 1327–30, p. 184.
[42] Ibid. 1334–8, p. 2.
[43] Cart. Antiq. R. L. 14.
[44] Harl. MS. 60, fol. 627.
[45] Sharpe, Cal. of Wills, i, 234, 245, 249, 278, 301, 329, 350, 427, 451, 494, 508, 531, 578, 683; ii, 166, 208, &c.
[46] He occurs in this capacity in 1328, Cal. of Close, 1327–30, p. 312; in 1337, ibid. 1337–9, p. 33; in 1339, ibid. 1339–41, p. 502; and in 1362, Epis. Reg. Sudbury, fol. 88. The prior was the collector of 5d. in the mark of ecclesiastical goods in 1322. Hist. MSS. Com. Rep. viii, App. i, 633. In 1341 he, with the other collectors of wool, was rebuked by the king for his negligence, and empowered to appoint a deputy if unable to act. B. M. Chart. L. F. C. xiv, 28. In 1331 and 1340 he was appointed collector of the taxes imposed on the order by the general chapter. Cott. MSS. Vesp. D. 1, fol. 44b, 47b. It may also be remarked that it was at this priory that the earls and barons assembled to hear the result of their negotiations with the citizens of London in 1321. Chron. of Edw. I and Edw. II (Rolls Ser.), 296.
[47] Lond. Epis. Reg. Baldock and Gravesend, fol. 6.

concourse of people. There was evidently little fault to be found with the monastery, and corroboration as to its satisfactory state is furnished by the fact that in 1306 the bishop of London, after deposing the prior of St. Mary's, Bishopsgate, put the sub-prior of St. Bartholomew's in his place,[48] and in 1308 sent to St. Bartholomew's a canon of St. Osyth's to be disciplined for his wrongdoing.[49] The injunction ordering that no liveries are to be sold without the permission of the bishop or archbishop, and that the powers granted are not to be exceeded,[50] seems to indicate that money was needed just then, possibly for building, as additions were certainly made to the church soon afterwards.[51]

It seems probable that disputes between the priory and the hospital arose at an early date, for King John in 1203[52] declared that the hospital was at the disposition of the prior and canons, and that whoever would separate it from that church should come into the royal right; and Eustace bishop of London made an arrangement between them a few years later.[53] At length serious discord between the two houses made a settlement imperative, and this was accomplished by Simon bishop of London in 1373.[54] The authority of the priory over the hospital was maintained in a general way, viz. the brothers had to ask leave of the prior to elect a master and obtain his confirmation of their choice, and new brothers and sisters had to swear fealty to the prior. If the prior was practically excluded from interference with the internal affairs of the hospital, he was freed from all responsibility for its maintenance.

The advantages of the arrangement doubtless became more apparent to the priory at the beginning of the next century, when it experienced great difficulty in raising sufficient money for its own needs. In 1409 the monastery was in debt through the rebuilding of the cloister, bell-tower, and chapter-house, and further necessary work was prevented by lack of funds. Meanwhile its income had fallen off: inroads of the sea had seriously affected its property in the neighbourhood of Yarmouth; tenements in London, from which ten

years ago an income of 100 marks had been derived, now did not yield half that sum; and through the malice of a powerful enemy the endowment of a chantry had been lost, while the obligation of maintaining two priests for celebrating masses still remained.[55] The prior John de Watford, who was present at the Council of Pisa,[56] made use of his opportunity to plead the cause of his house, and Pope Alexander, the day after his election to the papacy,[57] granted a special indulgence to penitents who during a period of ten years visited the priory on the three days before Easter and on the Festival of the Assumption, and gave alms; and he empowered the prior to choose six priests to hear confessions on these occasions.[58]

The priory however seems to have plunged deeper and deeper into debt. When the bishop of London visited the house in 1433,[59] he found its affairs seriously embarrassed through extravagance and bad management: its income was about £500, and it owed much more than this sum, annual pensions and corrodies alone amounting to £107. Decided measures were necessary if the priory was ever to be freed from its obligations, and the bishop, at the request of the convent, took the financial administration for the time being entirely out of the hands of the prior and convent, and appointed his commissary to receive all the revenues, rendering an account twice a year to the convent in the presence of Walter Shuryngton, chancellor of the duchy of Lancaster. To the prior was assigned a sum of £20 for his maintenance, to each canon 100s., and to each clerk 48s. 4d., while small amounts were also allotted for pittances and as provision in case of sickness. Beyond these expenses and an allowance of £40 for repairs to property, the whole income of the house was to be devoted to the payment of debts.

At the end of the fifteenth century there was some ill-feeling between the priory and the City, and in consequence the drapers and tailors of London determined not to take booths in the precinct at the time of the fair.[60]

William Bolton, who became prior about 1506, made extensive improvements to both priory and church.[61] He had evidently great talent as a builder, and was appointed master of the king's works by

---

[48] Ibid. fol. 6.

[49] Ibid. fol. 16.

[50] Ibid. fol. 6.

[51] A bequest for the maintenance of the work of the church is made in a will enrolled in 1314. Sharpe, *Cal. of Wills*, i, 249. In 1321 the king pardoned the alienation of land in the parish of St. Sepulchre to the prior and convent of St. Bartholomew for the building and maintenance of the said church. *Cal. of Pat.* 1317–21, p. 597. St. Mary's Chapel which is mentioned in 1322 (Sharpe, *Cal. of Wills*, i, 301) appears to have been recently built (ibid. i, 427).

[52] *Chart. R.* (Rec. Com.), i, 115.

[53] Lond. Epis. Reg. Braybrook, fol. 285. Eustace was bishop of London 1221–29.

[54] Ibid. fol. 285–7.

[55] *Cal. Pap. Letters*, vi, 151.

[56] Wylie, *Hist. of Engl. under Hen. IV*, iii, 369.

[57] Capgrave, *Chron. of Engl.* (Rolls Ser.), 297.

[58] *Cal. Pap. Letters*, vi, 151.

[59] Doc. of the D. and C. of St. Paul's, A. box 25, No. 645.

[60] Rec. of the Corp. of Lond. Repert. i, fol. 38.

[61] Stow, *Surv. of Lond.* (ed. Strype), iii, 225. In 1517 the priory was exempted from the payment of the two-tenths to the crown, owing to the great expense of rebuilding the conventual church. Lond. Epis. Reg. Fitz James, fol. 121.

Henry VIII.[62] At the chapter of the order in 1518 the excuse made and accepted for his absence was the royal business; the same reason might possibly have been offered for his neglect to fulfil the office of visitor in the diocese of London, but in this case he was fined £10.[63]

Apparently his capacity lay all in the one direction, as when Wolsey tried to secure the see of St. Asaph for him in 1518, the king refused on the ground that though masters of the works had been promoted before, it had been not for their skill in building, but for other qualifications, such as profound learning.[64] For some years before he died in 1532 he was very infirm,[65] and his death was expected in 1527 when the friends of William Fynch, the cellarer, offered to contribute £300 to Wolsey's college at Oxford if the cardinal would help Fynch to obtain the post.[66] It is evident that outside influence was of great importance in elections at this time, for in 1529 another candidate was soliciting Cromwell's support,[67] and Robert Fuller, abbot of Waltham, who finally obtained the priory *in commendam*,[68] promised Cromwell to recompense him largely for his favour.[69]

The orthodoxy and the conduct of the canons must have been considered unexceptionable, or otherwise the judges of John Tewkesbury, on condemning him for heresy in 1531, would not have sent him to this monastery to remain there until released by the bishop of London.[70] It is certain, however, that Prior Robert was always prepared to adapt his views to those of the king in religious matters, for the compliance of the prior and canons can be read in the terms they secured when the priory was surrendered in October, 1539:[71] Fuller received a life grant of most of the property of the priory;[72] to the sub-prior was assigned an annual pension of £15; to each of ten canons one of £6 13s. 4d.; and to two others one of £5 each.[73] The pensions also seem to have been paid with great regularity.[74]

The number of inmates shows a great decrease from that of earlier times: in 1174 there had been thirty-five canons in the priory,[75] and there were twenty in 1381,[76] thirty years after the depopulation caused by the Black Death. The officers of the house included sub-prior, cellarer, sacristan, infirmarer, refector, and chamberlain.[77]

The income of the house in 1291 appears to have been about £152,[78] of which more than half was derived from property in London.[79] At the Dissolution its revenues were reckoned at £773 0s. 1¾d. gross, and £693 0s. 10¼d. net,[80] rents and ferms in London and the suburbs alone amounting to £451 3s. 7d.[81] Its property at that time comprised the manors of Canonbury, Acton, Renters in Hendon, Great Stanmore, Canons in Little Stanmore, and lands in Portpool, Little Stanmore and 'Shardington,' perhaps Charlton, co. Middlesex;[82] the manors of Langley Hall in Clavering,[83] and Shortgrove,[84] and meadowland in Walthamstow,[85] co. Essex; the manors of Tewin,[86] Holmes in Shenley,[87] and Walhall,[88] co. Herts.; the church of St. Sepulchre, which had very early been appropriated to the priory,[89] the church of Theydon Bois, co. Essex, which the canons had received licence to appropriate in 1335;[90] the rectories of Bradfield, co. Essex, Gorleston, Lowestoft, co. Suffolk, and Mentmore,[91] co. Bucks., and the advowson of the church of Tewin;[92] the oblations of the chapel of St. Mary, Yarmouth,[93] and pensions from the churches of Wenhaston, co. Suffolk, and Danbury,[94] co. Essex. In 1291[95] and 1428[96] the priory had also received a portion of 2 marks from the church of Sunbury in Middlesex.

[62] He held the post in April, 1518, *L. and P. Hen. VIII*, ii, 4083; and payments to him occur from Feb. 1519, ibid. iii, p. 1534.

[63] Cott. MS. Vesp. D. i, fol. 68.

[64] *L. and P. Hen. VIII*, ii, 4083.

[65] Ibid. xiii (1), 260.

[66] Ibid. iv, 3334.

[67] Ibid. iv, 5410.

[68] Ibid. v, 1207 (24).

[69] Ibid. v, 1044.

[70] Ibid. v, 589.

[71] Ibid. xiv (2), 391.

[72] Ibid. xvi, p. 715. The manors in Essex, Hertfordshire, and Middlesex, the fair, and the buildings in London except the chief messuage of the priory, which was in the tenure of Sir Richard Riche.

[73] Ibid. xiv (2), 391 (2).

[74] Aug. Off. Misc. Bk. 249, fol. 16, 16b, 20, 20b, 23, 23b; ibid. 250, fol. 21b, 22, 23, 23b, 24, 24b, 28b, 31b, 32, 32b, 34b, 35b.

[75] Cott. MS. Vesp. B. ix, fol. 59b.

[76] Lond. Epis. Reg. Braybrook, fol. 264.

[77] *Cal. of Chart. and R. in. Bodl. Lib.* 163.

[78] The reckoning has been made from the *Taxatio* for the diocese of London in Harl. MS. 60, fol. 6, 17, 26, 28, 39, 42, 59, 67, 73, 78, 81, 82, 86, 87, with the addition of property in other dioceses given in *Pope Nich. Tax.* (Rec. Com.).

[79] Spiritualities, £8 8s. 8d. and temporalities, £70 10s. 8d.

[80] *Valor Eccl.* (Rec. Com.), i, 407, 408.

[81] Ibid. i, 407. Auditors of the accounts of the collectors of rent in the City and suburbs were appointed in 1533 at a salary of 40s. per annum, and 20s. a year for their clerk. Harl. Chart. 83, A. 43.

[82] Mins. Accts. 32 Hen. VIII, given in Dugdale, *Mon. Angl.* vi, 297.

[83] Morant, *Hist. of Essex*, ii, 614.

[84] Ibid. ii, 585.

[85] Dugdale, op. cit. vi, 297.

[86] Ibid.; *L. and P. Hen. VIII*, xvi, p. 715.

[87] Add. Chart. 1992.

[88] *L. and P. Hen. VIII*, xvi, p. 715.

[89] Newcourt, *Repert.* i, 530.

[90] *Cal. of Pat.* 1334–8, p. 173. They owned the rectory in 1526. Lond. Epis. Reg. Bonner, fol. 47b.

[91] Dugdale, *Mon. Angl.* vi, 297.

[92] Chauncy, *Hist. of Herts.* 274.

[93] *L. and P. Hen. VIII*, xvi, p. 716.

[94] Dugdale, op. cit. vi, 297. A pension of 20s. from Danbury church was being paid in 1428. *Feud. Aids*, ii, 207.

[95] Harl. MS. 60, fol. 26.

[96] *Feud. Aids*, iii, 378.

The prior held in 1303 a quarter of a knight's fee in Bradfield,[97] and a fraction of a fee in Tewin;[98] in 1316 he held a whole fee in Little Stanmore;[99] in 1346, a quarter of a fee in Bradfield;[100] in 1428 he still held this quarter fee in Bradfield,[101] and appears to have held moreover half a knight's fee in Acton and a quarter in Islington.[102]

The church was rich in plate, possessing at the suppression of the priory more than 500 oz. of gilt plate, 370 oz. of parcel gilt, and 311 oz. of white plate.[103]

*M. Reddan*

## Revised List of Priors

The list is taken from *Heads of Religious Houses,* vol. 1, p. 174, vol. 2, p. 417, and vol. 3 (forthcoming).

Rahere, 1123; died 1144[104]
Thomas, elected 1144; died 1174
Roger, occurs 1185, 1187
Alan,[105] occurs 1180, 1189
Richard, occurs 1196, 1206
G. canon of Oseney elected and resigned 1213

John, occurs 1226; resigned 1232
Gerard, elected 1232; occurs 1238
Peter, occurs 1246; resigned by 1255
Robert, elected 1255; dead by 1261
Gilbert of Waldon, elected 1261; dead by 1263
John Bacun, elected 1264; occurs 1265
Hugh, occurs 1273; died 1295
John of Kensington, occurs 1306; died 1316
John of Pegsdon, occurs 1321; died 1350
Edmund of Braughing, elected 1350; resigned by 1355
John of Carlton, elected 1355; died 1361
Thomas of Watford, elected 1361; died 1382
William Gedney, elected 1382; resigned 1391
John Eyton or Repyngdon,[106] elected 1391; died 1404
John de Watford, elected 1404, resigned 1414
William Coventree, elected 1414; resigned 1436
Reginald Colyer,[107] elected 1436; died 1471
Richard Pulter, elected 1471; died 1480
Robert Tollerton, elected 1480; died 1484
William Guy, elected 1484; died 1505
William Bolton, elected 1505; died 1532
Robert Fuller, elected 1532; surrendered 1539

[97] Ibid. ii, 129.
[98] Ibid. ii, 434.
[99] Ibid. iii, 373.
[100] Ibid. ii, 154.
[101] Ibid. ii, 218.
[102] Ibid. iii, 383.
[103] *Monastic Treas.* (Abbotsford Club), 26.
[104] Nellie Kerling gives the date of death as 1143, *Cartulary of St. Bartholomew's Hospital,* (London, 1973), p.4.
[105] Webb does not include Alan as prior, *Records,* p.100. He says there is confusion with Alan Presbyter who was master of St. Bartholomew's hospital 1182–c.98, because he styled himself on occasion 'prior and brother of the hospital', St. Paul's MSS A Box 71 1798 (*Hist. MSS. Com.* 9th I 50b).

[106] *V.C.H. London,* i. shows two priors called John Eyton separated by Simon Wynchcombe. But Webb points out, *Records,* p.182, that Simon was not prior but a London citizen, an armourer, and his will is in Sharpe *Cal. of Wills,* vol. 2 p. 340. The two quoted references to Simon as prior in *V.C.H. London,* i. are in connection with pardons related to debts owed to him as an executor, *Cal. of Pat. 1391–6,* pp. 252, 257. Webb says this is simply an error and records one John Eyton, prior from 1391 to 1404.
[107] *V.C.H. London,* i. had 'John' between 'Reginald' and 'Reginald Colyer'. Webb says the reference to 'prior John', Dugdale, *Mon. Angl.* vi, 291, is a confusion with John Wakeryng who was master of St. Bartholomew's hospital at the time, *Records,* p. 212.

# 7. THE PRIORY OF ST. MARY OVERY, SOUTHWARK

## INTRODUCTION

The most authoritative account of the history of the priory, together with discussions of the buildings and precinct is to be found in Martha Carlin, *Medieval Southwark* (London, 1996), pp. 67–75. For the pre-Conquest minster and its subsequent regularisation as a house of Austin canons, see John Blair, *Early Medieval Surrey: Landholding, Church and Settlement Before 1300* (Stroud, 1991), pp. 101–2.

For a description of the surviving buildings (now Southwark Cathedral), see M. Cherry and N. Pevsner, *The Buildings of England. London 2: South* (London, 1983), pp. 564–72. The findings of recent archaeological investigations will be reported in D. Divers, and C. Mayo, *Excavations at Southwark Cathedral* [working title], Pre-Construct Archaeology Monograph (forthcoming, 2008).

The London properties belonging to the house are listed in *Documentary Sources*, pp. 94–5. Surviving records relating to the house are listed on the web site of the English Monastic Archives project, along with a list of estates, URL: http://www.ucl.ac.uk/history/englishmonasticarchives/index.htm (accessed 28 February 2007).

*Martha Carlin*

The original name of this priory, St. Mary Overy, signified St. Mary over the river. Stow recites a tradition, which he had from the lips of Linsted, the last prior, that, long before the Conquest, there was at Southwark a house of sisters endowed with the profits of a ferry across the Thames; but that afterwards it was converted into a college of priests who, in the place of the ferry, built the first wooden bridge over the Thames and kept it in repair. This tradition, however, is not supported by any known authority. Whatever may have been the nature of any earlier foundation on the same site, it was in the year 1106 that the order of regular or Austin Canons was established at St. Mary's, Southwark.[1]

The founders or re-founders at this date were William Pont de l'Arche and William Dauncey, two Norman knights. It is said that Bishop Giffard lent them much assistance, and in 1107 built the nave of the church; hence he was sometimes termed the founder.

The principal grants that were made to the canons in the twelfth century were the church of St. Margaret, Southwark, by Henry I, lands at Banstead by Mansel de Mowbray; two weighs of cheese at 'Badleking' in the manor of Kingston Lisle in Berkshire; lands at 'Waleton' by Alexander Fitzgerald; 60 acres of land at 'Wadeland,' Foots Cray, by William de Warren; the tithe of his farm at Southwark, and confirmation of grant of a stone building which had belonged to William de Pont de l'Arche, by King Stephen; the church of All Saints, Graveney, confirmed to them by Archbishop Lanfranc; and five City churches and many other advowsons from divers donors.[2]

On 11 July, 1212, a terrible fire broke out on the Surrey side of the water, occasioning the loss of about 1,000 lives, in which the priory church, together with London Bridge with its houses and chapels, was consumed. The conventual buildings were also all destroyed save the frater.[3]

In 1215, when the prior and canons had moved into their new house, having temporarily occupied the hospital of St. Thomas, an important agreement was made between Prior Martin and the archdeacon of Surrey, warden of the hospital, which is cited in the subsequent account of the hospital. The rebuilding after the fire was materially helped by the munificence of Peter des Roches, bishop of Winchester, who also built a spacious chapel dedicated to St. Mary Magdalen, which afterwards became the parish church of that name, and the south aisle of the priory church.[4]

---

[1] *Ann. Mon.* (Rolls Ser.), iii, 430; iv, 374.

[2] These benefactions and several others are set forth in detail by Manning and Bray (*Hist. of Surr.* iii, 562–5): original transcripts or abstracts of most of these charters are to be found in Cott. MS. Faust. A. viii, or in Nero, C. iii, where there are various original early charters of Southwark Priory on fol. 188, 196, 197, and 201.

[3] Matt. Paris, *Chron. Maj.* (Rolls Ser.), ii, 536; *Ann. Mon.* ii, 82, 268. The date (1207) given for this in the Annals of Bermondsey is clearly a mistake.

[4] Manning and Bray, *Hist. of Surr.* iii, 560.

In 1244 Bishop William de Raleigh, having incurred the enmity of the king, dared not tarry in his episcopal house, which adjoined the priory, but took refuge with the canons, and thence escaped by boat down the Thames to France.[5]

On 15 February, 1260, there was a great gathering in the priory church of Southwark, when Henry de Wengham was consecrated bishop of London by the archbishop of Canterbury, in the presence of the bishops of Worcester, Chester and Salisbury, and Richard, king of the Romans.[6]

In the time of Prior Stephen the rebuilding of the priory church was taken in hand. A thirty days' indulgence was granted in 1273 to all penitents who contributed to the fabric.[7]

On 1284 John Peckham, archbishop of Canterbury, visited the monastery, where it appears there was some friction among the brethren. On 21 May in that year he issued injunctions to the prior for the better order of the house. He commanded that no canon should on any account enter the city of London or the town of Southwark without another canon or lay brother, or eat or drink there unless with peers or prelates; that silence should be maintained in the church, choir, cloister and frater; that the sub-prior should not only study the dignity of religion, but also the bonds of charity, and should correct the faults of the brethren with due gentleness, especially in the absence of the prior; that the money of the house should be placed in the hands of two of the brethren, who should account for it to the prior. The archbishop inveighed particularly against 'the detestable crime' of any of the brethren holding property, and put any so doing under excommunication. He at the same time removed Hugh de Chaucumbe, the cellarer; William de Cristeshall, almoner and infirmarer; and Stephen, the chamberlain and sacrist, injoining that one canon should not hold the offices of almoner and infirmarer.[8]

The taxation roll of 1291 shows that the income then accruing from temporalities was considerable, viz. in Winchester diocese, £27 1s. 3d., of which above £22 was for rents in Southwark; in Chichester diocese, £2 1s. 4d.; in Rochester diocese, £8; in Lincoln diocese, £3 15s.; and in London diocese, rents out of no fewer than forty-seven parishes, amounting to £70 3s. 5½d. The only spiritualities entered are a pension of 13s. 4d. for the prior out of the rectory of St. Mildred's Poultry, and 2s. for the canons out of the rectory of St. Bartholomew the Less.

From an ecclesiastical taxation of a later date, cited in the priory register,[9] it appears that the priory then held the rectories of Graveney, worth yearly 8 marks; Wendover, 42 marks; Stoke Poges, 18 marks; Reigate, 20 marks; Betchworth, 24 marks; Banstead, 20 marks; Mitcham, 20 marks; Addington, 12 marks; Newdigate, 12 marks; St. Margaret, 13 marks; St. Mary Magdalen, 6 marks; and Tooting, 40s. There were also pensions to the priory of 4s. from the church of St. Mary Magdalen, of 2s. from Newdigate, of 20s. from Woodmansterne, of 4s. from Tooting, of 5 marks from Swanscombe (Kent), and of 13s. 4d. from Leigh.

On the day of St. Philip and St. James, 1304, the following nineteen were the professed of the priory: William Whaleys, prior; Adam de London, fraterer; Henry de Kersalton, pittancer; Henry de Blockele; Peter de Cheynham, precentor; Ralph de London, cook; John de Gatton; Geoffrey de Wendover; John de Lech lade; Roger de Wynton, sub-prior; Roger de Reygate, cellarer (erased); Symon de Westminster; John de Cantuar; John de Northampton; John de Wynton, sub-cellarer; Robert de Kancia, cellarer; Robert de Wells; and John de Ardenere.[10]

In May, 1313, the prior and convent of Southwark obtained licence for the appropriation in mortmain of the church of Newdigate, which was of their advowson.[11]

Henry de Cobham, keeper of certain of the late Templars' lands in Kent, Surrey and Sussex, was ordered in October, 1313, to pay to the bishop of Winchester the wages of 4d. a day assigned by the late archbishop of Canterbury and the whole provincial council for the maintenance of Richard de Grafton, a Templar placed in the priory to do penance.[12] The priory had to maintain other pensioners: thus in April, 1315, Peter prior of Southwark and his chapter granted to Thomas de Evesham, clerk of the king's chancery, in consideration of his good service to them, a yearly pension of 100s. for life out of their manor of Tadworth;[13] and in October, 1319, Hugh de Windsor was sent to the priory for his maintenance, in consideration of his good service to Queen Isabel.[14] And again a grant was made by Edward III in February, 1344, at the request of Richard earl of Arundel, who would have to come to London very often to treat of various matters for the king, that he should lodge in the priory, and have the use of suitable houses (chambers)

[5] Matt. Paris, *Chron. Maj.* (Rolls Ser.), iv, 285–6; *Flor. Hist.* (Rolls Ser.), ii, 270.

[6] Ibid. ii, 443.

[7] Harl. MS. 5871, fol. 184.

[8] *Reg. Epist. J. Peckham* (Rolls Ser.), ii, 717–18.

[9] Cott. MS. Faust. A. viii, fol. 166b.

[10] Cott. MS. Faust. A. viii, 49b. Another list drawn up in 1298 gives a total of twenty-one, but several are erased; and another of 1302 (both on fol. 50b) gives nineteen.

[11] Pat. 6 Edw. II, pt. 2, m. 9.

[12] Close, 7 Edw. II, m. 23.

[13] Ibid. 8 Edw. II, m. 9d.

[14] Ibid. 13 Edw. II, m. 15 d.

there for him and his household during the king's pleasure.[15]

Pardon was granted to the priory and convent of Southwark in 1314 for having acquired in mortmain, without the late king's licence, various shops and messuages in Southwark, and lands in Mitcham, Chelsham, and Kidbrooke;[16] and in January, 1332, a like pardon was granted them for entering without licence from the king's progenitors into 6 marks of rent in London, bequeathed to them by Sabina, late the wife of Philip le Taillour, citizen of London, for daily celebration for the souls of Philip and Sabina.[17]

The bishops of Winchester not infrequently used the priory church. For instance Bishop Sendale held ordinations there in 1316, 1317, and 1318;[18] on 10 March, 1352, John Sheppey was consecrated bishop of Rochester in this church.[19]

The priory was again burnt or severely damaged by fire in the reign of Richard II. Considerable repairs and rebuilding were at once undertaken.[20] The work must have been accomplished by the beginning of the year 1390, for on 7 February Bishop Wykeham commissioned his suffragan, Simon bishop of Achonry, to reconcile the conventual church of St. Mary Overy and the annexed church of St. Mary Magdalen, and to dedicate the altars and graveyard.[21] To this work John Gower, the poet, is said to have been a liberal contributor. Bishop Wykeham again on 12 February, 1391, obtained the services of John bishop of Sodor to reconcile the church of St. Mary Overy, the adjoining parish church of St. Mary Magdalen, and St. Mary's chapel in the conventual farmery, and their respective graveyards, after pollution by bloodshed.[22] The nature of the affray or accident is not known.

The bishop gave notice on 7 January, 1395, of his intention to visit the priory on the Wednesday after the conversion of St. Paul,[23] and in June, 1397, he commissioned John Elmere the official, William Stude an advocate of the Court of Arches, and John de Ware, to visit it.[24] The result of this latter visitation was that the newly appointed prior, Kyngeston, was found to be suffering from so serious an infirmity as to be incapable of ruling his house, and that the discipline had in consequence become

very lax. The custody of the house was therefore committed to the sub-prior and John Stacy, another of the canons, with full power of punishing excesses and delinquencies. They were to call to their aid, if necessary, William Stude and John Ware, the bishop's visiting commissioners. No canon was to leave the house except for some grave cause and with a special letter from the two custodians, under pain of imprisonment. The sub-prior was enjoined to have an account of rents received during the last four years made up for audit, and the bishop also put forth several other practical injunctions for the due management of the temporalities.[25]

In March, 1398, Prior Weston was licensed by the bishop to let benefices appropriated to the priory, with a proviso that none of the buildings belonging to these rectories were to be used as taverns or for any illicit or dishonourable trades that might bring discredit on the church. In the following month the bishop visited the priory.[26] In February, 1399, Prior Weston was admonished by Bishop Wykeham not to alienate the endowments of the house.[27]

By his will dated 15 August, 1408, the poet Gower left his body to be buried in the priory church, 40s. to the prior, 13s. 4d. to each priest-canon, 6s. 8d. to each canon in his novitiate, to each valet within the gates 2s., and to each serving boy 12d. For the service of the altar of the chapel of St. John, where he was to be buried, he left two full sets of vestments, one of 'blew' baudkyn mixed with white colour, and the other of white silk; one large missal, and a new chalice.[28]

In 1406 the marriage of Edmund Holland earl of Kent, with Lucy, daughter of the duke of Milan, who brought her husband a dower of 100,000 ducats, was celebrated in the parish church. Stow records another wedding in this church of some importance in February, 1424, when James I, king of Scotland, after a captivity of eighteen years, was released and married Lady Joan Somerset, daughter of the duchess of Clarence by her first husband, John earl of Somerset.

In the ninth year of the rule of Henry Werkeworth, in the year 1424, there was hanging in the tower of the priory a ring of seven bells. The first, called Augustine, weighed 38 cwt. 7 lb.; the second, Mary, 27 cwt. 3 qr. 13 lb.; the third, Stephen, 19 cwt. 3 qr. 7 lb.; the fourth, Ave Maria, 15 cwt. 9 lb.; the fifth, Laurence, 13 cwt. 7 lb.; the sixth, Vincent, 7 cwt. 21 lb.; and the seventh, Nicholas, 5½ cwt. 9 lb. But in that year Prior Henry caused the bells to be increased in weight and number so as to

[15] Pat. 18 Edw. III, pt. 1, m. 48.
[16] Ibid. 7 Edw. II, pt. 2, m. 23.
[17] Ibid. 6 Edw. III, pt. 1, m. 27.
[18] *Sendale's Reg.* (Hants Rec. Soc.), *passim.*
[19] Stubbs, *Reg. Sacr. Angl.* 77.
[20] Stow, *Chron.* 542, 597.
[21] Winton Epis. Reg. Wykeham, iii, fol. 241*b.*
[22] Ibid. iii, fol. 249.
[23] Ibid. iii, fol. 279.
[24] Ibid. iii, fol. 293*b.*

[25] Ibid. iii, fol. 296–7.
[26] Ibid. iii, fol. 301*b.*
[27] Winton Epis. Reg. Wykeham, iii, fol. 309*b.*
[28] Taylor, *Annals of St. Mary Overy* (1833).

form a ring of eight bells, which were hung in the newly constructed tower of the priory church on the vigil of St. Bartholomew's Day, 1424. The first bell was called Trinity, the second, Mary; the third, Augustine; the fourth, Laurence; the fifth, Gabriel; the sixth, All Saints; the seventh, John the Evangelist; and the eighth, Christopher.[29]

On the death of Prior Henry Werkeworth in January, 1452, the usual brief was sent forth from the convent inviting the prayers of members of other religious houses for the rest of his soul. A copy of this document, wherein the highest praise is given to the late prior – *vir industrie laudabilis* – is extant among the Peck MSS.[30]

John Bottisham the prior, who resigned in 1462, was granted a pension of twenty marks, in addition to his maintenance at the prior's table: also board and cloth for a gown for his servant. The ex-prior was further assigned a suitable chamber in the priory with a fireplace and wood for 300 fires; also six quarters of charcoal, and nine dozen pounds of tallow candles.

In 1469 the middle roof of the nave fell in; it was repaired with woodwork, as also was the roof of the north transept.[31]

A grant was made by Edward IV to Southwark Priory in 1475 of the advowson and appropriation of the parish church of West Tilbury, Essex, on condition of the convent promising to celebrate daily within their church a mass of St. Erasmus the Martyr, in which the priest should pray for the soul of the king's father, Richard duke of York, and for the good estate of the king and his consort Elizabeth, and for Edward prince of Wales and the king's other children, and for their souls after death.[32]

Dr. Thomas Hede, commissary of the prior of Canterbury, visited the priory on 6 May, 1501, during the vacancy of the sees of Winchester and Canterbury. Prior Michell reported favourably of the spiritual condition of the house, but he stated that there was a debt of £190 when he entered on his office, and that the debt did not now exceed £100, and that there were no valuables pledged. The seal was kept in the sacristy under four keys, the respective custody of which was in the hands of the prior, subprior, sacrist, and precentor. He had not ordered a balance sheet for that year, but was prepared to do so when requested. Richard Hayward, sub-prior, testified that silence was duly observed at the proper times and places; and that the debt of the house was the fault of the predecessor of the then present prior. William Kemp, sacrist,

Richard Holand, precentor, canons John Hale, Thomas Archer, John Corcar, Richard London, William Godwyn, Thomas Eustache, Humphrey Furnor, and William Major, acolyte, were content to report *omne bene*. William Walter, acolyte, said that he had been professed for six years, and was two years ago ordained acolyte, but that he had not been presented for further orders. John Hall, acolyte, twenty-one years of age, said he had been professed for seven years, and was ordained acolyte four years ago.[33]

An important chapter of the canons regular of St. Austin was held in their chapter-house, Leicester, on Monday, 16 June, 1518, when one hundred and seventy joined in the procession, of whom thirty-six were *prelati* or heads of houses. As night came on they adjourned till Tuesday morning at seven, and when they again assembled, the prior of Southwark, with every outward demonstration of trouble and sorrow, appealed for a stricter and verbal observance of their rule. His manner and address excited much stir, but he was replied to by many, particularly by the prior of Merton. On the first day of this chapter a letter had been read from Cardinal Wolsey observing with regret that so few men of that religion applied themselves to study. On Wednesday, the concluding day of the chapter, Henry VIII and his then queen were received into the order.[34]

In 1535 the clear annual value of this priory was declared to be £624 6s. 6d. Their rents in Southwark alone realized £283 4s. 6d.

On November 11th of this year there was a great procession by command of the king, at which were present the canons of this church, with their crosses, candlesticks, and vergers before them, all singing the litany.[35]

Prior Bartholomew Linsted and the convent 'surrendered' on 27 October, 1539. The prior obtained a pension of £100, two of the monks £8 each, and nine monks £6 each. A note to the pension list, which was signed by Cromwell, stated that the prior was to have a house within the close where Dr. Michell was dwelling.[36]

*J. C. Cox*

## Revised List of Priors of Southwark

Unless otherwise noted, the following list of priors is taken from *Heads of Religious Houses*, vol. 1, pp. 183–4; vol. 2, pp. 460–1; and vol. 3 (forthcoming).

[29] Cott. MS. Faust. A. viii, fol. 79*b*.
[30] Add. MS. 4937, fol. 266.
[31] Taylor, *Annals*, 28.
[32] Pat. 15 Edw. IV, pt. 2, m. 10.

[33] Cant. Archiepis. Reg. Sede Vac.
[34] Cott. MS. Vesp. D. i, 63.
[35] Taylor, *Annals*, 28.
[36] *L. and P. Hen. VIII*, xiv (2), 40.

Algod, 1106–1130

Algar, 1130–1132

Warin, *c*.1132–1142

Gregory, 1142–1150

Ralph, 1150–1154

Richard, 1154

Waleran (Valerianus), *c*.1154/5–1190

William de Oxenford, 1190–1203

Richard de St. Mildred, 1203–1205

William son of Samarus, ?1205

Martin, occurs *c*.1205; died 1218

Robert of Osney, elected 1218; died 1223

[Alexander occurs Michaelmas 1225].[37]

Humphrey, succeeded 1223; ?died 1240

Eustace, ?1240 jointly with

Stephen, succeeded 1240; ?died 1252

Alan, 1252 – resigned 1283

William le Waleys, elected 1283; deposed 1305

Peter of Cheam, elected 1305, died by 1327

Thomas of Southwark, elected 1327; resigned 1331

Robert (de), appointed 1331; d. by 1349

John (de) Pecham, elected by June 1349; resigned 24/25 Aug. 1349

Richard de Stakes, provided 24/25 Aug. 1349; occurs 1351

John (de) Pecham, elected by 1355; resigned 1361[38]

Henry (de) Collingbourne, elected 1361; died 1395

John Kyngeston, elected 1395; incapacitated by grave illness 1397 (with custody granted to the sub-prior, John Stacy); died 1397

Robert Weston, elected 1398–1414; occurs 1415

Henry Werkworth, occurs 1416; died 1452

John Bottisham, elected 1452; resigned 1462

Henry de Burton, elected 1462; died 1486

Richard Brigges, collated 1486; died 1491

John Reculver, elected 1491; resigned by 1499

Robert Michell, elected 1499; resigned 1512

Bartholomew Linsted *alias* Fowle, elected 1513; surrendered 1539

---

[37] Possibly an error, or perhaps Prior Humphrey was temporarily suspended, or resigned and was subsequently reinstated; an unnamed prior died in 1225, according to the Annals of Dunstable.

[38] 15 March 1355 Brother Nicholas de Ravenstone was described as acting as 'superior and principal warden' of the priory, by commission of Prior John de Pekham, C.L.R.O., Bridge House deed G.11. On 25 June 1355 Ravenstone (described as Sub-Prior) again occurs as Pekham's *locum tenens*. On 18 Sept. 1357 Sub-Prior Henry de Colyngborne was similarly acting as *locum tenens* for Prior John de Pekham in the latter's absence. Pekham resigned on grounds of incapacity 16 March 1361, S. F. Hockey (ed.), *The Register of William Edington, Bishop of Winchester, 1346–1366*, part 1, Hampshire Rec. Ser., 7 (1986), nos. 661, 1036, 1120, 1245.

# HOUSES OF MILITARY ORDERS

## 8. THE TEMPLE

### INTRODUCTION

The original article provides the best short account of the founding of the Order of the Knights Templar in London and of their Masters and other officers. It gives details of their diplomatic and financial dealings until their suppression in 1312, and also an account of the property when it passed to the Knights Hospitallers. This can now be supplemented by J. Bruce Williamson, *The History of the Temple; London from the Institution of the Order of the Knights of the Temple to the Close of the Stuart Period* (London, 1925), chs. 1–4. Agnes Sandys discussed the relations of the house with the royal administration, and includes a list of Treasurers of the New Temple 1214–1308, in 'The Financial and Administrative Importance of the London Temple in the Thirteenth Century', in A. G. Little and F. M. Powicke (eds.), *Essays in Medieval History presented to Thomas Frederick Tout* (Manchester, 1925), pp. 147–62.

The broader history of the Templars in England has been the subject of a large number of publications, perhaps the most effective of which is Thomas W. Parker's *The Knights Templar in England* (Tucson, 1963). The survey of the lands held by the Templars in England in 1185 (T.N.A. E164/16) was published by Beatrice A. Lees in *Records of the Templars in England in the Twelfth Century: The Inquest of 1185 with Illustrative Charters and Documents* (British Academy, 1935). She includes an account of the London house, pp. lxxxiv–xcv. The London charters and documents appear on pp. 156–73. For the London property of the house, see especially *Documentary Sources*, p. 56.

The fabric of the New Temple was described in The Royal Commission on Historical Monuments of England, *An Inventory of the Historical Monuments of London. 4, The City* (London, 1929), pp. 137–43. Detailed accounts and interpretations of discoveries made by archaeologists during the restoration of the Temple Church following World War II damage can be found in W. H. Godfrey, 'Recent discoveries at the Temple, London and notes on the topography of the site', *Archaeologia*, 95 (1953), pp. 123–40; M. B. Honeybourne, 'The Temple Precinct in the days of the Knights Templars', *Ancient Monuments Soc. Trans* n.s. 16 (1968–69), pp. 33–6, and C. M. L. Gardam, 'Restorations of the Temple Church, London', in *Medieval Art, Architecture and Archaeology in London,* ed. L. M. Grant, British Archaeological Association Conference Transactions, 10 (1990), pp. 101–17. Recent discoveries relating to the church and cloisters were published in J. Butler, *Saxons, Templars and Lawyers in the Inner Temple, Archaeological Investigations in Church Court and Hare Court,* Pre-Construct Archaeology Monograph 4 (2005). Archaeological investigations have also shed new light on the circular 'Old Temple', located further to the north close to High Holborn: see A. Telfer, 'Locating the First Knights Templar Church', *London Archaeologist*, 10, pt. 1 (2002), pp. 3–6.

*D. Anne Welch*

The first mention of the Knights Templars in connexion with England is in 1128, when Hugh de Payens, the master of the order, visited this country,[1] and received aid both in men and money for the cause. The foundation of the house outside Holborn Bars probably dates from this time, for Hugh de Payens before he left appointed a prior to preside over the English branch of the order,[2] and since

---

[1] Hoveden, *Chronicle* (Rolls Ser.), i, 184.

[2] Addison, *The Knights Templars*, 82.

other settlements here were cells of the Temple at London it follows that this central house must have been established early.

Among the first patrons of the Templars in this country were Earl Robert de Ferrers,[3] Bernard de Balliol,[4] King Stephen and Queen Matilda,[5] but the earliest grant made to them in London of which there is evidence was Henry II's gift or confirmation[6] of the place on the Fleet by Castle Baynard, the watercourse for a mill, a messuage by Fleet Bridge,[7] and the advowson of St. Clement Danes.[8] Henry seems to have been a great benefactor of the knights, for he gave them lands in other parts of England.[9] It is probably to him that they owed the silver mark paid from the revenues of many of the English counties in 1155,[10] since it is called 'alms newly constituted.'

In Henry's reign there are indications that the Templars were already playing that part in diplomacy and finance which was so remarkable a feature of their career. Richard de Hastings, the master of the Temple, and two others were entrusted with the castles which were to be delivered to Henry II on the marriage of his son with Margaret of France, and found it expedient to leave France when Henry by a piece of sharp practice had the two children married and secured the castles.[11] Hastings' influence was also used to persuade Becket to accept the Constitutions of Clarendon.[12] That the Templars were at this time employed by the king in monetary affairs is shown by Walter of Coventry's story[13] of Gilbert de Ogrestan, the Knight Templar who, appointed collector of the tenth, was detected in embezzlement in 1188, and severely punished by the master.

The extent of the possessions acquired by the Templars in England during a period of scarcely sixty years can be seen in the return to an inquisition ordered by Geoffrey Fitz Stephen, the master of the Temple, in 1185.[14] The list includes land in London, and in every part of the country, Essex, Kent, Warwickshire, Worcestershire, Salop, Oxfordshire, Cornwall, Lincolnshire, Yorkshire, &c., and the

holdings were large in many cases. At this time their possessions were divided into districts, apparently for the purposes of revenue, and one of these is called the 'Baillia' of London.[15] The master, of course, had his head quarters here, but the ordinary administration of the house seems to have been carried on as elsewhere by a preceptor.[16] There was also a prior,[17] whose duties were presumably religious, for he was warden of the chapel.[18]

In 1184 the house was transferred to what was probably a more convenient situation in Fleet Street,[19] and was henceforth known as the New Temple. The church, round like the one in Holborn,[20] was dedicated the next year by Heraclius, patriarch of Jerusalem, to the honour of God and the Virgin.[21]

Richard I confirmed to the Templars all the previous donations made to them, granting them exemption from all pleas, suits, danegeld, and from murdrum and latrocinium,[22] but otherwise he appears to have come but little in contact with them,[23] a striking contrast to the relations of the Templars and the crown in the next two reigns. If the papal bull declaring the immunity of persons and goods within the houses of the order was issued, as seems most likely, by Innocent III in 1200,[24] it would largely account for the use of the New Temple as a place of deposit for royal treasure which could be drawn upon as necessary. The other function of a bank performed by the New Temple, the advance of money, was made possible by the accumulation there of the revenues of the order in England. John had continual transactions of this kind with the Temple:[25] in 1212 he had 10,000 marks from which he directed sums to be paid out,[26] in 1213 he deposited 20,000 marks there,[27] while in 1215 Aymeric, master of the

---

[3] Cott. MS. Nero, E. vi, fol. 92.

[4] Dugdale, *Mon. Angl.* vi, 819.

[5] Ibid. 820, 821, 843; Cott. MS. Nero, E. vi, fol. 289.

[6] In the inquisition made in 1185 by the master of the Temple Henry II is not mentioned in connexion with this property, but Gervase de Cornhill is said to have given one messuage and William Martell another. Dugdale, op. cit. vi, 821.

[7] The grant printed in Dugdale, *Mon. Angl.* vi, 818, must have been before 1162 as T. the chancellor is one of the witnesses.

[8] Ibid.

[9] Ibid. 821.

[10] Hunter, *Great Roll of the Pipe*, 1155–58, pp. 3, 6, 8, 9, 13, 14, 16, 19, 21, 24, 26, &c.

[11] Hoveden, *Chron.* (Rolls Ser.), i, 218.

[12] Ibid. 222.

[13] *Hist. Coll.* (Rolls Ser.), i, 360.

[14] K. R. Misc. Bks. No. 16, given in Dugdale, *Mon. Angl.* vi, 821–31.

[15] Ibid.

[16] Doc. of D. and C. of Westminster, London, B. Box 1. An early grant of land by Castle Baynard is witnessed by William preceptor of London.

[17] Wilkins, *Concilia*, 346.

[18] Ibid. 335.

[19] Stow, *Survey of London* (ed. Strype), iii, 270.

[20] *Lond. and Midd. Arch. Soc. Trans.* (New Ser.) i, 257.

[21] Stow, op. cit. iii, 270. An interesting point in connexion with the removal from Holborn is raised by the alleged burial of the earl of Essex in the cemetery of the New Temple in or about 1163. Round, *Geoffrey de Mandeville*, 237.

[22] Rymer, *Foedera* (Rec. Com.), i (1), 49.

[23] i.e. of course in England.

[24] Cott. MS. Nero, E. vi, fol. 57. It is in the third year of the pontificate of Pope Innocent. If this is Innocent III the date would be 1200; if Innocent IV 1245.

[25] The money due to Queen Berengaria was sent to the Temple and paid out to her envoys there. *Cal. of Pat.* 1216–25, P. 243. See also Hardy, *Rot. de Liberate* (Rec. Com.), 8, where money owing to Queen Eleanor is to be sent to Aymeric, master of the Temple, 2 Nov. 1200.

[26] *Rot. Lit. Claus.* (Rec. Com.), i, 124, 134.

[27] Rymer, *Foedera* (ed. 1737), i (1), 56.

Temple, lent him 1,100 marks to obtain troops from Poitou.[28] Nor did John's dealings with the Templars end here: he had as almoner a Templar, Roger,[29] who in 1215 had charge of business[30] not usually associated with his office; Aymeric, the master, was sent by him as his envoy to Normandy in 1204;[31] a Templar and a Hospitaller were employed in a similar capacity in 1205;[32] it was at the preceptory of Ewell that he made his submission to the pope,[33] on which occasion Aymeric supplied him with the gold mark for the offering[34]; and he was residing at the New Temple when the barons made their demands[35] which led to the granting of Magna Charta at Runnymede, where Aymeric again figures as one of the king's supporters.[36] Naturally, John made several gifts to the order which he found so useful. The confirmation of their privileges in the first year of his reign can hardly be reckoned in this category, seeing that they paid for it £1,000,[37] but apart from this he gave to the Templars the isle of Lundy,[38] land at Huntspill and Cameley before 1203,[39] Harewood,[40] 'Radenach,'[41] and some houses in Northampton in 1215.[42]

The relations of Henry III with the Templars are in a greater degree those of his father. Through the New Temple was paid in instalments the money due to Louis of France,[43] and there were deposited 500 marks for the expedition to Poitou[44] in 1221 and for 'the good men of Rupella'[45] in 1232, and sums for similar purposes in 1224[46] and 1225,[47] while the king obtained loans[48] from the Temple as occasion arose. The house acted indeed as the royal treasury,[49] the king's wardrobe being located there in 1225.[50] The master of the Temple,[51] Alan Marcell, was employed by the king in negotiations abroad in 1224, and Robert de Sanford, master in 1236, was

one of those sent by the king to escort Eleanor of Provence to England;[52] Thomas, a Templar,[53] was in charge of the king's great ship in 1225 and 1226, and another Templar was acting as the king's almoner in 1241.[54] Henry had such a high opinion of the order that at one time he intended to be buried in the New Temple,[55] where he established in 1231 a chantry of three chaplains with an income of £8 a year.[56] In the eleventh year of his reign he had confirmed all grants made to the Templars with sac and soc, tol and team, &c., exempting them from sheriffs' aids, hidage, carucage, danegeld, &c., waste, regard and view of foresters, from tolls in markets and fairs throughout his realm, and granting them the amercements of their men.[57] He gave to them also a wood in Carlton called Kingswood,[58] and the manor and advowson of 'Roel.'[59]

The king was present with a number of the chief persons of the kingdom when, in 1240, the new part of the Temple church was dedicated.[60] Relaxation of penance had before this time[61] been offered to those visiting the church, some of the indulgences being perhaps anterior to the foundation in Fleet Street,[62] but after 1240 several prelates, among whom were the bishops of Ely, Waterford, and Ossory,[63] tried in this way to attract the alms of the faithful, particularly for the maintenance of lights. It is uncertain whether the papal indult of forty days was granted by Innocent III or Innocent IV.[64] The tombs of some of those buried there, among them the Earls Marshal[65] and Hugh Bigod,[66] and the relics in which the church was very rich,[67] may have thus[68] proved a source of income. The

---

[28] Rot. Lit. Claus. (Rec. Com.), i, 415.

[29] Ibid. i, 230.

[30] It was chiefly to do with ships, see ibid. 231b, 233b, 234, 236b, &c.

[31] Hardy, Rot. de Liberate (Rec. Com.), 81.

[32] Rot. Lit. Claus. (Rec. Com.), i, 27b.

[33] Addison, op. cit. 152.

[34] Rot. Lit. Claus. (Rec. Com.), i, 148b.

[35] Matt. Paris, Chron. Maj. (Rolls Ser.), ii, 584.

[36] Ibid. ii, 589.

[37] Hardy, Rot. de Oblat. and Fin. (Rec. Com.), 13.

[38] Dugdale, Mon. Angl. vi, 842.

[39] Hardy, Rot. de Liberate (Rec. Com.), 66.

[40] Rot. Lit. Claus. (Rec. Com.), i, 227.

[41] Ibid. i, 183b.

[42] Ibid. i, 196.

[43] Ibid. i, 415, and Cal. of Pat. 1216–25, p. 284.

[44] Cal. of Pat. 1216–25, p. 303.

[45] Rot. Lit. Claus. (Rec. Com.), i, 471b.

[46] Cal. of Pat. 1216–25, p. 523.

[47] Ibid. 1225–32, p. 54.

[48] Ibid. 1216–25, pp. 537, 544, 546; Rot. Lit. Claus. (Rec. Com.), i, 479, 612.

[49] Cal. of Pat. 1225–32, p. 466.

[50] Ibid. 1216–25, p. 505.

[51] Rot. Lit. Claus. (Rec. Com.), i, 626.

[52] Matt. Paris, Chron. Maj. (Rolls Ser.), iii, 335.

[53] Rot. Lit. Claus. (Rec. Com.), ii, 33, 98, 112.

[54] Matt. Paris, Chron. Maj. iv, 88.

[55] Cal. of Chart. R. i, 135, 211. Eleanor of Provence expressed the same wish, see Dugdale, op. cit. vi, 818.

[56] Cal. of Chart. R. i, 135; Cal. of Pat. 1225–32, p. 439.

[57] Dugdale, op. cit. vi, 844.

[58] 20 March, 11 Hen. III, Cott. MS. Nero, C. ix, fol. 28.

[59] Cal. of Chart. R. i, 211.

[60] Matt. Paris, Chron. Maj. (Rolls Ser.), iv, 11.

[61] H., archbishop of Canterbury, who offered an indulgence of this kind, was probably Hubert, 1189–1207. That of Wm. bishop of London, is dated 1205. Cott. MS. Nero, E. vi, fol. 24b.

[62] T., archbishop of Canterbury, may, be Theobald, 1139–62, and Thomas, archbishop of Canterbury, may be Thomas À Becket, 1162–70. Ibid. fol. 24.

[63] Ibid. fol. 25.

[64] Ibid. fol. 24.

[65] Matt. Paris, Chron. Maj. iii, 43, 201; iv, 136.

[66] Cott. MS. Nero, E. vi, fol. 25b.

[67] These included the knife with which St. Thomas of Canterbury was killed; two crosses containing wood of the True Cross, and some of the Holy Blood; and there were six pyxes and coffers containing relics not named. L.T.R. Enr. Accts. 18, rot. 7. This inventory is given in full in Baylis, The Temple Church, 141–5.

[68] Cott. MS. Nero, E. vi, fol. 24b, 25b.

size and situation of the Temple, and the power of its occupants, recommended it as a place of residence to other persons besides John. As early as 1192 the archbishop of York had stayed there[69] on the memorable occasion when he set the rights of Canterbury at defiance by having his cross held erect at Westminster, and the Temple church was suspended by the bishop of London from celebrating divine service in consequence. The association of the Temple with the collection of papal grants[70] in this country may have been an additional inducement to Master Martin, the notorious papal agent, to take up his abode there, 1244–5.[71] The ambassadors of the king of Castille were also lodged there in 1255,[72] when the apartments of Sanchez, the bishop-elect of Toledo,[73] must have presented a curious contrast to those of the brethren.

The Templars under Edward I hardly appear to have maintained the dominating position they had held during the last two reigns in the affairs of the crown. Guy de Foresta, the master of the Temple, is certainly represented as going to Scotland on the king's business in 1273;[74] the New Temple is mentioned as a royal treasury in 1274 and 1276,[75] and the Temple treasurer as the receiver of the tallage of London in 1274;[76] Hugh, the visitor-general of the order, was moreover appointed by the king in 1299[77] to repay the Friscobaldi for a loan. But instances of this sort were now rare, where before they were frequent, the Italian merchants taking their place in the royal finance, and the mendicant orders in diplomacy and other business. Yet the king's robbery of part of the treasure there in 1283[78] shows that as a place of deposit for valuables its popularity was still unrivalled or it would not have been singled out for this distinction, though a severe shock must then have been given to the credit it had hitherto deservedly[79] enjoyed.

The decline of interest in crusades, the fall of Acre, and loss of the Holy Land in 1291, and the rise of new religious orders, would all tend to decrease the gifts made to the Templars, but these were numerous[80] enough during the last years of Edward I to prove that the knights were still regarded with favour by many. There were absolutely no signs of the storm which was so soon to overwhelm them.

On 13 October, 1307, the Templars in France were all arrested by King Philip.[81] Edward II, far from crediting the accusations made against them, at first expressed himself strongly in their favour.[82] But on the receipt of a letter from Pope Clement V in November,[83] he abandoned their cause, and on 8 January, the Templars in England were by his order suddenly seized and imprisoned.[84] The process before the papal inquisitors, Deodatus, abbot of Lagny, and Sicard de Vaur, canon of Narbonne, did not begin until 20 October, 1309.[85] The charges may be summed up as blasphemy, apostasy, idolatry, and heresy: they were said to deny Christ at their reception into the order, to trample the cross under foot and spit on the crucifix, to adore the image of a cat, to believe that the grand master and the preceptors, many of whom were laymen, could absolve them from their sins, to make sacrilegious mockery of absolution, and to be guilty of the vilest immorality.[86] Misconception of symbolic ceremonies may account for some of the accusations, most of which, however, cannot be explained in this way, and seem too improbable to be true,[87] since it is difficult to see how such acts imputed, not to a few individuals, but to the whole body, could have long remained undiscovered, especially when the hospitality exercised at the various houses is remembered. The examination lasted until 18 March, 1310,[88] but elicited nothing derogatory to the order. The king then, urged by the pope, ordered the constable of the Tower to deliver his prisoners to the sheriffs of London[89] to be disposed of by them in various places in the City so that the inquisitors might have easy access to them.[90] In spite of the tortures inflicted, only three, of whom

[69] Hoveden, *Chron.* (Rolls Ser.), iii, 187.

[70] Matt. Paris, *Chron. Maj.* (Rolls Ser.), iv, 557; *Cal. Pap. Letters*, i, 170.

[71] Matt. Paris, *Chron. Maj.* (Rolls Ser.), iv, 379, 420.

[72] Rymer, *Foedera* (Rec. Com.), i, 325.

[73] Matt. Paris, *Chron. Maj.* (Rolls Ser.), v, 509.

[74] *Cal. of Close*, 1272–9, p. 57.

[75] *Cal. of Pat.* 1272–81, pp. 52, 140.

[76] *Cal. of Close*, 1272–9, p. 63.

[77] *Cal. of Pat.* 1292–1301, p. 419.

[78] Stow, *Surv. of Lond.* iii, 271. The treasures of the Poitevins had been seized there in 1258 for the use of the kingdom (Matt. Paris, *Chron. Maj.* (Rolls Ser.), v, 704), but in a period of upheaval necessity overrides all other considerations.

[79] The Templars had steadfastly refused in 1232 to surrender to the king the treasure Hubert de Burgh had entrusted to them until ordered to do so by the owner. Matt. Paris, *Chron. Maj.* (Rolls Ser.), iii, 232.

[80] In 1298 Ralph de Algate granted them 4 marks annual quit-rent in Walbrook. Cott. MS. Nero, E. vi, fol. 27. Edmund, earl of Cornwall, the king's cousin, gave them common pasture in all his hundred of Isleworth. Ibid. fol. 78. See also for alienations to them, *Cal. of Pat.* 1292–1301, pp. 26, 542; ibid. 1301–7, pp. 134, 301, 322.

[81] Addison, op. cit. 202.

[82] Ibid. 205, 207.

[83] Addison, op. cit. 207. A translation of the papal bull is printed by Baylis, op. cit. 123–6.

[84] Ibid. 210.

[85] Wilkins, *Concilia*, ii, 329.

[86] Wilkins, *Concilia*, ii, 331–2. *Chronicles of Edw. I and Edw. II* (Rolls Ser.), i, 180–2.

[87] See, however, Hallam, *Middle Ages*, i, 138–42.

[88] Wilkins, *Concilia*, ii, 346.

[89] Addison, op. cit. 243.

[90] Sharpe, *Cal. of Letter Book D*, 248, 259.

one, John de Stoke,[91] appears to have been the treasurer of the New Temple, confessed the truth of the articles. Testimony obtained by torture is always doubtful, and that given voluntarily must on this occasion be regarded with suspicion, for it was supplied by secular priests, monks and friars,[92] the enemies and rivals of the accused,[93] and even then it was often mere hearsay. The majority of the Templars, among them those of the New Temple, acknowledged themselves guilty of heresy, especially as to the efficacy of the absolution given by the master, submitted, and were reconciled to the Church.[94] The master, William de la More, however, refused to confess crimes of which he was innocent,[95] and remained in the Tower until his death.[96]

The number of Templars belonging to the New Temple at the time of their arrest may have been thirteen,[97] excluding the master. Of these, three were serving brethren, two, brothers, John de Stoke was treasurer, Michael de Baskervile, preceptor, and Ralph de Barton, priest, prior and warden of the chapel.[98] Some of these probably survived the suppression of the order in 1312 to subsist as best they could, for the pensions of 4d. a day were not regularly paid,[99] until they were received into various monasteries.[100]

The Templars at the time of the suppression owned in London and the neighbourhood the manor of Cranford[101] which had been given to them by John de Cranford,[102] the manor of Lilestone or Lisson Green[103] granted by Otho son of William in 1237,[104] lands in Hampstead and Hendon belonging to that manor,[105] the manor of Hampton the gift of Lady Joan Grey,[106] and land in Hampton and 'Wyke' given by Cristiana Haiwode;[107] pastureland in Isleworth,[108] meadowland in Hackney, co. Middlesex,[109] a tenement at Charing,[110] which appears to have been granted by Gilbert Basset before 1185;[111] tenements in Southwark valued in 1308 at £6 9s. 8d. net per annum;[112] lands and rents in the parishes of St. Clement Danes,[113] St. Dunstan West,[114] where they had a holding in the 12th century;[115] St. Bride,[116] St. Mary Somerset,[117] St. Sepulchre,[118] a messuage in 'Godrunlane' in the parish of St. John Zachary, the bequest of John de Valescines in 1256,[119] and a tenement in Holborn,[120] and a quay and mills on the Fleet,[121] probably the most valuable of their property in London. They seem to have received a further grant of land here shortly after 1185, since the gift of Walter son of Robert of land under Castle Baynard is not mentioned in the return to the inquisition of Fitz Stephen.[122]

The rents from the property in the City and suburbs alone from 10 January to Michaelmas, 1308, amounted to over £50, although deductions were made for tenements unoccupied.[123] The principal possession of the order in London was of course the New Temple itself, which is constantly referred to as a manor,[124] and from the size of the buildings[125] and extent of the ground[126] well deserved the term. The church contained altars to St. Nicholas and St. John besides the high altar, and appears to have been well

---

[91] The John de Stoke who confessed evidently resided at one time at the New Temple, see Wilkins, *Concilia*, ii, 345, 387.

[92] Ibid. 359–63.

[93] The Templars had received many privileges that had made them unpopular with the clergy, and illfeeling can be traced as far back as 1228, see Rymer, *Foedera* (3rd ed. 1737), i (1), 103; i (2), 8, 9.

[94] Wilkins, *Concilia*, ii, 390.

[95] Ibid.

[96] Addison, op. cit. 276.

[97] The sheriffs of London account for wages to fourteen brothers besides six chaplains, four clerks and four servants, &c. L.T.R. Enr. Accts. 18, rot. 7. Himbert Blanke, one of these brothers, was, however, preceptor of Auvergne, and therefore did not really belong to the London House. From the list of the Templars sent to the Tower there would seem to have been only eight at the New Temple besides the master (Wilkins, *Concilia*, ii, 346), but two had certainly died before this time. L.T.R. Enr. Accts. 18, rot. 7.

[98] Wilkins, op. cit. ii, 346–7.

[99] Addison, op. cit. 286.

[100] Dugdale, *Mon. Angl.* vi, 848, Nos. liii, liv.

[101] L.T.R. Enr. Accts. 20.

[102] Dugdale, op. cit. vi, 832.

[103] L.T.R. Enr. Accts. 20.

[104] Dugdale, op. cit. vi, 832; Cott. MS. Nero, E. vi, fol. 73.

[105] L.T.R. Enr. Accts. 20.

[106] Dugdale, op. cit. vi, 832.

[107] Ibid.

[108] Cott. MS. Nero, E. vi, fol. 66.

[109] Ibid.

[110] L.T.R. Enr. Accts. 20.

[111] Dugdale, op. cit. vi, 821.

[112] Cott. MS, Nero, E, vi, fol. 59b.

[113] *Cal. of Close*, 1307–13, p. 468.

[114] Ibid. 532.

[115] Doc. of D. and C. of Westm. Lond. D.

[116] L.T.R. Enr. Accts. 18, rot. 7.

[117] Ibid.

[118] Doc. of D. and C. of St. Paul's, A. Box 23, No. 267.

[119] Anct. D. (P.R.O.), A. 2136.

[120] L.T.R. Enr. Accts. 18, rot. 7.

[121] A complaint was made in Parliament in 1306 about the diversion of the water for these mills. *Parl. R.* (Rec. Com.), i, 200.

[122] Doc. of D. and C. of Westm. Lond. B. Box 1.

[123] L.T.R. Enr. Accts. 18, rot. 7.

[124] *Cal. Rot. Pat.* (Rec. Com.), 68, 133b.

[125] A council of prelates and clergy was held there in 1269, and mandates for convocations to be held there were issued in 1273, 1282, 1298, 1299, and 1302. Wilkins, *Concilia*, ii, 19, 93, 239, 253, 272. For mandate of 1299 see also *Cal. of Pat.* 1292–1301, p. 450. One national council at least was held there. Riley, *Chron. of Old Lond.* 159.

[126] The sheriffs in 1308 account for 60s. from the fruit of the garden sold in gross. L.T.R. Enr. Accts. 18.

provided with books,[127] plate and ornaments[128] of silver, silver gilt, ivory and crystal, altar-cloths and frontals and vestments.

The Temple was granted by the king to Aymer de Valence, earl of Pembroke, but Thomas, earl of Lancaster, claiming it as his fee, Aymer de Valence surrendered it to him on 1 October, 1314.[129] On the execution of Lancaster the manor again fell to the crown, and was made over a second time to Aymer de Valence in 1322,[130] but when he died without issue in 1324 it lapsed to the king according to the terms of the grant. The bull of Pope Clement V granting the lands of the Templars to the Knights Hospitallers[131] had been unheeded in England, but after the statute to the same effect in 1324[132] the knights of St. John were put in possession of the Temple with a great deal of the other property of the late order. It seems probable that they already held the consecrated portions such as the church and cemetery, since the claim of the prior to some houses erected by him on a portion of this ground, which had been seized by the younger Despenser, and escheated to the crown after his forfeiture in 1326, was evidently quite distinct from his right to the other portion of the manor.[133] William de Langford, to whom the king had let the Temple, had part of his rent remitted for giving up these tenements,[134] and in June, 1338, Edward III made a grant of the whole manor to the Hospital in frankalmoign.[135] The history of the Temple as a religious house however had really ended with the fall of the original owners. The prior of Clerkenwell appointed one of his brothers to keep the church, and the allowance to him and the other chaplains figures in the expenses of the Knights of St. John in 1328.[136] The accounts of 1338 show that there were then eight chaplains besides the warden, and that these eight were not of the order of St. John, but seculars like the thirteen who served the church in the time of the Templars.[137]

In 1338 a definite sum was allotted to the warden, but the next year Ficketsfield and Cotells Garden

were assigned him by the prior for his maintenance, and that of the lights and services of the church.[138]

The priests needed only part of the Temple buildings, and the others were let to the lawyers by the priory, it is said, in 1347,[139] at any rate about the middle of the fourteenth century.

The prior of Clerkenwell occurs twice in an interesting connexion with the Temple: in 1373, when he was engaged in a dispute with the City over a right-of-way through the Temple Gate to the Temple Bridge;[140] and in 1381, when the rebels did a great deal of damage out of hatred to the same Prior Robert Hales, then the king's treasurer.[141]

At the suppression of the order of Knights Hospitallers in England by Henry VIII in 1540 the New Temple, which in 1535 had been valued at £162 11s.,[142] passed to the crown.[143]

The master of the Temple and chaplains were still, however, allowed their stipends, and retained their posts, and a lease made by the master in 1542 of a messuage, and the master's lodging adjoining the church, stipulated that the four priests of the Temple should have two chambers in the house.[144]

The re-establishment of the order by Mary seems to have made no change at the Temple, except that the rent of £10 due from the two societies of lawyers was again paid to the prior, for Ermested, who had been master in 1540, continued to hold office.[145] When Elizabeth succeeded provision was made for the payment of the master, four priests, and the clerk, as in the last year of Edward VI, but how long the staff of priests was maintained it is difficult to say. There are no further references to them, though they seem to have been there in Stow's time.[146]

*M. Reddan*

## Revised Lists of the Masters, Preceptors and Wardens of the Temple Church

These are revised and amended versions of the lists in the *V.C.H.*

### Masters of the Temple
Richard de Hastyngs, 1160[147]
Richard Mallebeench[148]

[127] Among them were five antiphonaries, nine psalters, two legends, eight processionals, a martilogium and an organ book. Ibid.

[128] In silver and silver-gilt there were four chalices, three censers, two basins, two lamps, a vase with sprinkler, a chest for relics – this last worth £10 – two silver cruets, &c., while there were several objects in ivory, among them three pyxes and two tables with ivory images. Ibid.

[129] *Cal. of Pat.* 1313–17, p. 184.

[130] Rymer, *Foed.* (Rec. Com.), ii (1), 480.

[131] Ibid. 167.

[132] *Stat. of the Realm* (Rec. Com.), i, 194, 195.

[133] *Cal. of Close*, 1337–9, P. 72.

[134] Ibid. 416.

[135] *Cal. Rot. Pat.* (Rec. Com.), 133b; Sharpe, *Cal. of Letter Bk. G.* 324.

[136] Larking, *The Knights Hospitallers in Engl.* (Camden Soc.), 218.

[137] Ibid. 202.

[138] Cott. MS. Nero, E. vi, fol. 26b.

[139] Inderwick, *Introd. of Cal. of Inner Temple Rec.* i, p. xi.

[140] Sharpe, *Cal. of Letter Bk. G.* 322.

[141] Walsingham, *Hist. Angl.* (Rolls Ser.), i, 457.

[142] *Valor Eccl.* (Rec. Com.), i, 403.

[143] Inderwick, op. cit. i, p. xliii.

[144] Ibid. i, p. xliv.

[145] Inderwick, op. cit. i, p. xlvi.

[146] Ibid. i, p. xlix; Stow, *Surv.* (ed. Strype), iii, 272.

[147] Addison, op. cit. 277.

[148] Ibid.

Geoffrey son of Stephen, occurs 1180,[149] 1185[150]

William de Newenham[151]

Thomas Berard, occurs 1200[152]

Aymeric de St. Maur, occurs 1200,[153] 1216.[154] He died abroad[155]

Alan Marcell, occurs 1220,[156] 1228[157]

Amberaldus, occurs 1229[158]

Robert Mounford, occurs 1234(?)[159]

Robert Saunforde, occurs 1231, 1247[160]

Rocelin de Fosse, occurs 1250–1,[161] 1253[162]

Amadeus de Morestello, occurs 1254,[163] 1258–9[164]

Imbert Peraut, occurs 1267,[165] 1269[166]

William de Beaulieu, occurs 1274[167]

Robert Turvile, occurs 1277,[168] 1289[169]

Guy de Foresta, occurs 1290,[170] 1294[171]

James de Molay, occurs 1297[172]

Brian le Jay, occurs 1298;[173] d. 1298[174]

William de la More, occurs 1298[175] and at the suppression

### Preceptors of London

William de Bernewode, occurs *temp.* Geoffrey Fitz Stephen[176]

Alan, occurs 1205,[177] 1221[178]

Ralph de Leukeworth, occurs 1232[179]

Ranulph de Bremesgrave, occurs 1272[180]

Richard de Herdewyk, occurs 1294[181]

John de Mohun, occurs *c.*1296[182]

Ralph de Barton, *c.*1300[183]

Michael de Baskervile, occurs 1303,[184] 1308[185]

### Wardens under the Knights Hospitallers

Hugh de Lichfield, occurs 1339[186]

John Almayn, occurs 1374[187]

John Bartylby, occurs 1378–9[188]

John Burford, occurs 1380–1[189]

William Ermested, occurs 1540, 1542; d. 1560[190]

[149] Cott. Nero, E. vi, fol. 466.

[150] Dugdale, *Mon. Angl.* vi, 821.

[151] Doc. of D. and C. of Westm. Lond. B. Box 1. This document, a grant of land by Castle Baynard to Ralph the goldsmith, is undated, but it seems probable that it is later than a grant made by Geoffrey Fitz Stephen (ibid. Lond. D.), where William de 'Niweham' occurs as a brother of the Temple.

[152] Cott. MS. Nero, E. vi, fol. 466.

[153] Hardy, *Rot. de Liberate* (Rec. Com.), 8.

[154] *Rot. Lit. Claus.* (Rec. Com.), i, 17*b*, 286.

[155] See letter of Andrew de Celer announcing his death to Hubert de Burgh, *Dep. Keeper's Rep.* iv, App. ii, 156.

[156] *Rot. Lit. Claus.* (Rec. Com.), i, 415.

[157] Cott. MS. Nero, E. vi, fol. 466.

[158] Ibid.

[159] Ibid. This date can hardly be correct, unless 'Mounford' is a mistake for 'Saunforde.'

[160] Cott. MS. Nero, E. vi, fol. 149*b*.

[161] Hardy and Page, op. cit. 34.

[162] Cott. MS. Nero, E. vi, fol. 152.

[163] Ibid. fol. 466.

[164] Hardy and Page, op. cit. 40.

[165] Wilkins, *Concilia*, ii, 339. The dates occur in the testimony given by brothers of the Temple at the time of the suppression, and as they depend on memory they are probably not quite exact.

[166] Cott. MS. Nero, E. vi, fol. 466.

[167] Rymer, *Foedera* (Rec. Com.), i (2), 514.

[168] *Cal. of Pat.* 1272–81, p. 208.

[169] Wilkins, op. cit. ii, 341.

[170] Ibid.

[171] Ibid. 75.

[172] He became grand master of the order in 1297. Addison, op. cit. 193.

[173] Wilkins, op. cit. ii, 373.

[174] Addison, op. cit. 197.

[175] *Cal. of Pat.* 1292–1301, p. 391.

[176] He is called procurator of the 'baillia' of London in a grant of land made by the master, Geoffrey Fitz Stephen. Doc. of D. and C. of Westm. Lond. D. A certain William was preceptor *temp.* William de Newenham. Guildhall MS. 122, fol. 614–15.

[177] *Rot. Lit. Claus.* (Rec. Com.), i, 55*b*; Hardy. *Rot. Oblat. et Fin.* (Rec. Com.), 309.

[178] *Cal. of Pat.* 1216–25, p. 303.

[179] Ibid. 1225–32, p. 490.

[180] *Cal. Inq. p.m.* (Rec. Com.), i, 79*b*. He also appears to have been preceptor both before and after this date, as he witnesses grants by Imbert de Peraut and Guy de Foresta, masters of the Temple. Cott. MS. Nero, E. vi, fol. 301.

[181] *Cal. of Pat.* 1292–1301, p. 88.

[182] *Dep. Keeper's Rep.* vii, App. ii, 252. Some time between 1292 and 1302.

[183] Wilkins, *Concilia*, ii, 337, 346. He was preceptor for two years between 1298 and 1303.

[184] Ibid. 346.

[185] L.T.R. Enr. Accts. 18, rot. 7.

[186] Cott. MS. Nero, E. vi, fol. 26*b*.

[187] Sharpe, *Cal. of Letter Bk. G.* 322.

[188] Inderwick, op. cit. i, p. xxi.

[189] Ibid.

[190] Ibid. i, pp. xliii, xliv, xlix.

# 9. THE HOSPITAL OF ST. THOMAS OF ACON [ACRE]

## INTRODUCTION

This is a good account of the house and made effective use of John Watney, *Some Account of the Hospital of St. Thomas of Acon ...* (London, 1892). But the history of the Order in general, and the Cheapside house in particular, has been considerably illuminated by the substantial article by A. J. Forey, 'The Military Order of St. Thomas of Acre', *Eng. Hist. Rev.*, 92 (1977), pp. 481–503. Forey places the foundation of the Order at the time of the Third Crusade, and the establishment of the London house in the 1220s. He demonstrates that the link with Becket's sister Agnes was based on an inaccurate fifteenth-century tradition. For the fifteenth-century development of the hospital, see Anne F. Sutton, 'The Hospital of St. Thomas of Acre of London: the search for patronage, liturgical improvement, and a school, under Master John Neel, 1420–1463', in *The Late Medieval English College and its Context*, ed. C. Burgess and M. Heale (Woodbridge, forthcoming).

The site of the church and the hospital buildings is discussed and described in Honeybourne, 'Property', pp. 94–104 and plates II and XXV. The development of the site is fully analysed by Derek Keene in J. Imray (ed.), *The Mercers' Hall* (London Topographical Society, 1991), pp. 1–20. The important link with the Mercers' Company, and the establishment of a school at the hospital, are further explored by Anne Sutton, *The Mercery of London: Trade, Goods and People, 1130–1578* (Aldershot, 2005), pp. 72–4, 169–71. The London property of the house is listed, with sources, in *Documentary Sources*, pp. 55–6.

In 1379 the house had a master, six brothers, seven chaplains and a clerk, McHardy, *Church in London*, p. 2.

*Caroline M. Barron*

The hospital of St. Thomas of Acon was founded in honour of St. Mary and St. Thomas of Canterbury for a master and brethren of the military order of St. Thomas the Martyr by Thomas Fitz Theobald de Helles, whose wife Agnes was sister of the murdered archbishop.[1] The earliest grants of which anything is known, beyond the founder's gift in frankalmoign of the birthplace of the saint in the parish of St. Mary Colechurch for their church,[2] were those of Geoffrey Fitz Peter, earl of Essex,[3] who gave them the custody of the hospitals of St. John the Baptist and of St. John the Evangelist at Berkhampstead early in the thirteenth century, and of Margaret de Tanton, who made over to them her manor in Coulsdon, co. Surrey, shortly before 1235.[4]

In 1239 they also obtained a rent from some houses in the parish of St. Mary Colechurch, and then or shortly afterwards they received from Robert Herlizun tenements in the parishes of St. Giles without Cripplegate, St. Michael Bassishaw, and St. Mary Aldermanbury.[5]

From Henry III they acquired a messuage between the church of St. Olave and their house in 1268,[6] and in 1269 they received some houses in Ironmonger Lane from Richard de Ewelle in exchange for two mills at Wapping[7] obtained by them from Terric de Algate early in the century.[8]

---

[1] Chart. of 14 Edw. III, confirming grants to the hospital, printed in Dugdale, *Mon. Angl.* vi, 646. The grant by Thomas Fitz Theobald in the cartulary of the hospital belonging to the Mercers' Company is witnessed by Eustace de Fauconberg, bishop of London, 1221–9 (Watney, *The Hospital of St. Thomas of Acon*, 237). But this must be a confirmation of the deed of foundation, which Stubbs seems to think was early, for he argues from it that the Order of St. Thomas must have arisen before the surrender of Acre, 1191. *Introd. to Mem. of Ric. I* (Rolls Ser.), i, p. cxii, n. 5.

[2] Pat. 18 Edw. II in Dugdale, op. cit. vi, 647.

[3] Ibid. 647.

[4] Cott. MS. Tib. C. v, fols. 235b, 236b. The grant was confirmed by Henry III in the nineteenth year of his reign. Ibid. fol. 236.

[5] a Watney, op. cit. 21. Mr. Watney's information was derived from a cartulary belonging to the Mercers' Company, extracts from which he has printed in an Appendix, pp. 237–97.

[6] *Cal. of Chart. R.* ii, 98; *Parl. R.* (Rec. Com.), vi, 74b.

[7] Cott. MS. Tib. C. v, fol. 161 b.

[8] Ibid. fol. 153. There is an inspeximus, fol. 153b, of the charter after Terric's death by Geoffrey de Lucy, who became dean of St. Paul's 1237.

Ewelle returned the mills to them five years later as the endowment of a chantry in their church[9]; and in 1282 the reversion of a house in the parish of St. Stephen Walbrook was left them by Richard de Walbrook to maintain another chantry.[10] The church of St. Mary Colechurch, the advowson of which had been bought by the master and convent in 1247–8,[11] appears to have been appropriated to the hospital by Pope Alexander IV in 1257.[12]

There is very little early information about the house beyond the history of these acquisitions. The conventual church was probably begun in 1248, when the brothers had leave from the pope to erect a chapel. The episcopal licence for the consecration of a cemetery dates from about the same time.[13] At this period the community cannot have been very large, for twenty years later there are said to have been only twelve brothers.[14]

The house in 1279 was engaged in a contest with Archbishop Peckham as to his right of visitation,[15] and while still in disgrace it incurred the archbishop's anger on a fresh score. One of the brothers, Robert Maupoudre, seems to have run away, for the archbishop in August ordered him to be restored to the hospital without delay.[16] As he did not return, the master, Robert de Covelee, took the law into his own hands, and seized him and another priest, Thomas Carpenter, as they were about to celebrate divine service in St. Clement Danes and kept them imprisoned. The archbishop, in October, directed the dean of Arches to command the master to set the prisoners at liberty within two days, and summon him and his accomplices.[17] What happened exactly it is difficult to say; all that is certain is that the brethren were absolved on 30 November from a sequestration following on their refusal of visitation,[18] nothing more being said about Maupoudre's case.

About the end of the thirteenth century the Templars claimed the custody of the hospital in virtue of an agreement with the chief master of the order of St. Thomas of Acon. The brethren had

no desire to become subject to another monastic body, and at their request Edward I interposed,[19] and as if the house were vacant[20] appointed a warden to take charge of it during his pleasure.[21] When this warden, Henry de Durham, died, the king in 1304 gave the post to his clerk, Edmund de London, for life.[22] Edward II, however, soon after his accession forced Edmund to resign and gave the custody to the rector and convent of Ashridge, co. Herts.[23] The brethren now found themselves in the very position they had tried to avoid, and laid their case before the pope[24] and also before the king's council, who decided in 1315[25] that if the rector were allowed to hold the hospital the wish of the founder would be rendered of no effect, and accordingly annulled the grant, and appointed Robert de Bardelby, king's clerk, to be warden until the return to England of Richard de Southampton, who had formerly been elected master. Independence was thus restored to the house, not, however, much to its benefit. Henry de Bedford,[26] who succeeded Richard[27] in 1318, was either careless or rapacious,[28] and under his rule not only were the chantries neglected, but the house was reduced to great poverty, so that in 1327 outside intervention was again necessary, and the custody of the house was entrusted to the mayor and commonalty[29] of the City, who were empowered to amend whatever they saw amiss in its state. A few months later the church was broken into, and robbed of silver plate, books and vestments, and at the manor of Coulsdon some cattle were taken away.[30]

---

[9] Ibid. 160b.

[10] Sharpe, *Cal. of Wills.* i, 60.

[11] Watney, op. cit. 22.

[12] Watney, op. cit. 240. The bishop of London's letters of appropriation were not, however, given until 1262. Ibid.

[13] Ibid. 23, 237–8.

[14] Ibid. 24.

[15] *Reg. Epist. Johan. Peckham* (Rolls Ser.), iii, 1020.

[16] Ibid. i, 44.

[17] *Reg. Epist. Johan. Peckham* (Rolls Ser.), i, 75.

[18] Ibid. iii, 1020. The point is rather obscure, for the author of 'Annales Londinenses,' *Chron. of Edw. I and Edw. II*, says that in 1280 John de Peckham, archbishop of Canterbury, visited London and excommunicated the brothers of St. Thomas of Acon for their disobedience, but he does not specify in what the disobedience consisted.

[19] He took the house into his hand. Add. MS. 4526, fol. 38. This king, according to Dugdale, *Mon. Angl.* vi, 667, made a grant to the brothers of the advowson of the church of 'Rothelegh' and the chapels annexed, but it appears rather to have been given to the Templars for their convent at Acre.

[20] *Abbrev. Plac.* (Rec. Com.), 131.

[21] *Parl. R.* (Rec. Com.), i, 287.

[22] *Cal. of Pat.* 1301–7, p. 208.

[23] *Parl. R.* (Rec. Com.), i, 287.

[24] *Cal. Pap. Letters*, ii, 73. The pope summoned the rector to appear before him within four months with all the papers touching the case.

[25] The case was being tried in April, 1315, *Cal. of Close*, 1313–18, p. 224, and Bardelby was appointed in June, *Cal. of Pat.* 1313–17, p. 293.

[26] He was master Sept. 1318. Ibid. 1317–21, p. 205.

[27] Richard occurs Oct. 1317. Cott. MS. Tib. C. v, fol. 249b. A brother of the same name was reported by Henry de Bedford as a vagabond, and a mandate was issued for his arrest in 1318. *Cal. of Pat.* 1317–21, p. 260.

[28] He was deprived for simony and dilapidation, and evidently resisted the attempt of Nicholas de Clifton, who had been appointed to his place, to take possession. *Cal. of Pap. Letters*, ii, 273.

[29] Cott. MS. Faust. B. i, fol. 216b and 217 *Cal. of Pat.* 1327–30, p. 58.

[30] *Cal. of Pat.* 1327–30, p. 280. Robbery in two places at the same time rather suggests spite on the part of the perpetrators.

This connexion with the City probably accounts for the marked interest taken in the house by London citizens, as shown by the many bequests to the place and the number of chantries established there. In 1339 tenements and rent in Shiteburnelane (Sherborne Lane) and Candelwyk Strete (Cannon Street) were left by Matilda, widow of William de Caxton, to found a chantry,[31] and an annual rent of 7 marks from a 'seld' in the parish of St. Mary le Bow was bequeathed by Walter de Salyngg[32] for the same purpose; John Godchep provided for the maintenance of two chantries by the bequest of a tenement in the parish of St. Mary le Bow;[33] and chantries were established under the wills of Thomas de Cavendych, mercer and draper, 1348,[34] and of Simon de Benyngton, 1368.[35] There were also numerous legacies to the fabric and the work of the church.[36] The hospital did not depend, however, entirely upon its fixed income. Like the Templars, the brothers of St. Thomas had papal indulgences to collect alms in churches once a year,[37] and this may have been a profitable source of revenue, especially after the suppression of the older and more popular order,[38] though it had the disadvantage that adventurers and cheats sometimes forestalled the collectors[39] and reaped the harvest. The relaxation of penance granted by the pope in 1365 to those who on the principal feasts of the year during the next ten years visited the chapel of Holy Cross in the church of St. Thomas,[40] was either intended to repair the losses of the house consequent on the Black Death or to raise money for the rebuilding of the church, which does not, however, seem to have been begun until 1383.[41] This must have been a long and costly undertaking, for it was a large and beautiful church with choir, nave and side aisles,[42] and several chapels.[43] The pope in 1400 came to their aid again, and offered the indulgence of the Portiuncula to penitents who, on the feast of St. Thomas the Martyr, visited and gave alms for the conservation of the church. Many must have been expected to take advantage of it, for the pope gave an indult to the master and six other confessors deputed by him to hear the confessions.[44] The rebuilding operations appear to coincide with the increased importance of the house in Cheapside, which from 1379 was the principal house of the order.[45]

In 1444 the brothers seem to have felt the necessity of putting the house on a more secure footing. What was the immediate cause of their uneasiness does not appear, for the destruction or loss of title deeds mentioned was evidently not of recent date. In answer, however, to their petition to the king in Parliament,[46] it was ordained that the house should be reckoned a corporate body with powers to implead and be impleaded and to purchase, and should have a common seal; that the brethren on a vacancy might elect a master without first asking leave of the king, and without any obligation to grant the king a pension or corrody out of the hospital, seeing that there never was one granted before.

In 1454 James, earl of Wiltshire and Ormond, made over to the hospital the manor and the advowson of the church of Hulcott and a croft called 'Lytull Milne Hamme,'[47] co. Bucks, to endow a chantry in the church where his mother was buried,[48] and the house must have derived great benefit from grants in London,[49] for it continued

---

[31] Sharpe, *Cal. of Wills*, i, 458.

[32] Ibid. i, 436. See also *Cal. of Pat.* 1334–8, p. 422.

[33] Sharpe, op. cit. i, 441.

[34] Ibid. i, 547.

[35] Ibid. ii, 121. This does not exhaust the list. See ibid. i, 355, 535, 624, 636.

[36] Ibid. i, 504, 571, 637, 648, 658, 662, 686, 688, 692, 696; ii, 139, 144, 220, 229, 302.

[37] *Cal. of Pat.* 1301–7, p. 340.

[38] Protection for various periods is given to the attorneys of the master and brethren collecting alms, in 1318, *Cal. of Pat.* 1317–21, pp. 256, 260; 1319, ibid. 344; 1327, ibid. 1327–30, p. 5; 1329, ibid. 364; 1330, ibid. 1330–4, p. 9; 1331, ibid. 64.

[39] The king's bailiffs are ordered to arrest unauthorized persons collecting alms in name of the brethren in 1321, 1323–4, 1346. See *Cal. of Pat.* 1321–4, pp. 25, 234, 358; 1324–7, p. 48; 1345–8, p. 206.

[40] *Cal. Pap. Letters*, iv, 48.

[41] Protection from arrest was given by the king in 1383 to two stonemasons hired by the master of St. Thomas of Acon for the work of rebuilding his church. *Cal. of Pat.* 1381–5, p. 310. Some additions appear to have been made many years before, for Matilda de Caxton left a bequest to the new work of the church in 1339. Watney, op. cit. 292.

[42] Newcourt, *Repert. Eccl. Lond.* i, 554.

[43] The chapels of Holy Cross (Sharpe, *Cal. of Wills*, ii, 506), Our Lady, Holy Trinity, Sts. Nicholas and Stephen (Watney, op. cit. 133–4). There are also several altars mentioned besides (ibid.), and the offerings at two of these, viz. the altar of St. Thomas and the high altar, were of sufficient importance to be noted as a separate item in the *Valor Eccl.* (Rec. Com.), i, 391.

[44] *Cal. Pap. Letters*, v, 376.

[45] Stubbs, *Introd. to Mem. of Ric. I* (Rolls Ser.), i, p. cxii, *n.* 5. Earlier the master of the order had resided in Cyprus.

[46] *Parl. R.* (Rec. Com.), v, 74*b*. See also Lond. Epis. Reg. Tunstall, fol. 120.

[47] *Parl. R.* (Rec. Com.), v, 257*b*.

[48] Joan, countess of Ormond, was buried in the chapel of Holy Cross 1430. See Sharpe, *Cal. of Wills*, ii, 506, and Wriothesley, *Chron.* (Camd. Soc.), 171.

[49] Rents and tenements for the maintenance of chantries and obits were left by Robert Guphey, mercer, in 1412, Thomas White 1419, William Oliver 1432, Henry Frowyk, mercer and alderman, and William West, 'marbeler,' 1453, Stephen Kalk 1493, William Martyn, alderman, and Nicholas Alwyn, alderman, 1505. Sharpe, *Cal. of Wills*, ii, 395, 417, 460, 542, 562, 617; Misc. of Exch. bdle. 24, No. 8, fol. 14*b*. and 23–5*b*. An idea of the proportion of gain in these cases can be gathered from the details given in Misc. of Exch. bdle. 24, No. 8, fol. 55, as to two houses belonging to the hospital which brought in £11 7*s*. 2*d*., out of which a salary of £4 had to be paid to a chantry priest, leaving a clear income of £7 7*s*. 2*d*.

to be a favourite with the citizens.[50] Yet when John Yong became master on the removal of Richard Adams in 1510, he found it burdened with a debt of over £718.[51] Yong seems to have had a gift for finance, as he not only paid this off, but within the eight years following met all but £80 of expenses, amounting to £1,431 1s. 8d., for repairs to houses, mills, and other buildings in ruins, for walls by the Thames,[52] and for new buildings[53] within and without London – no easy task considering that the annual expenditure of the house exceeded its revenues by £117 4s. 2d. Some of the credit of this fortunate result is undoubtedly due to the Mercers' Company, whose relations with the hospital had long been of the most cordial kind,[54] and became even closer in 1514, when the master and brethren accepted the company as their defenders and advocates.[55] Under this arrangement the master of St. Thomas had to give an account of his administration every year before the wardens and assistants of the society, and when the mastership was vacant the company chose two or three of the convent, from whom the brethren had to elect a master within eight days. Rights such as these doubtless implied responsibilities, and the Divine Providence to which the writer of the account attributes the payment of the debt[56] probably took the form of the Mercers' Company.

It is evident that the convent acquiesced quietly in the religious changes: they acknowledged the king's supremacy in 1534,[57] and though objection was taken to the windows of their church where the story of St. Thomas of Canterbury was displayed,[58] nothing

was said against the brothers. The difficulties of which the master, Laurence Copferler, complained to Cromwell[59] in 1535, seem to have been caused by some business quite unconnected with the house, apparently his employment on a commission 'de walliis et fossatis,' such as preceding masters had served on.[60]

The house was surrendered 20 October, 1538,[61] and Sir Richard Gresham's petition that the work done there in aid of the poor and sick might continue under the rule of the City Corporation was unheeded,[62] the place being let to Thomas Mildmay.[63] The brothers, who had numbered twelve in 1444,[64] and nine in 1463,[65] seem in 1534 to have been reduced to six.[66] The deed of surrender was signed by two only, both of whom received pensions, the master £66 13s. 4d.,[67] and Brother Thomas Lynne £6.[68]

The revenue, in 1291 estimated at £46 16s.,[69] was in 1535 reckoned to be £332 6s. gross, and £277 3s. 6d. net.[70] Of this the greater part was derived from lands and rents and the rectory of St. Mary Colechurch in London,[71] and the rest from the manor of Harrow-on-Hill, and lands in Stepney, Wapping, and Bromley, co. Middlesex, the manor of Hulcott, and tenements in Buckingham, co. Bucks, the manor of Plumstead in Kent, the manor of 'Tawnton' in Coulsdon, co. Surrey, lands in West Ham in Essex, and rent in Northampton.[72]

[50] It is noticeable that nearly all the persons of importance buried in the church were London citizens; among these were Stephen Cavendish, mayor 1362, Sir Edmund Shaa, mayor 1482 (he founded a chapel in the church, Sharpe, Cal. of Wills, ii, 612), William Browne, mayor 1513, and Sir William Butler, mayor 1515. Stow, Surv. of Lond. iii, 37, 38. For a list of people buried there, see Watney, op. cit. 173–5.

[51] Misc. of Exch. bdle. 24, No. 8, preface.

[52] To prevent inundations on their lands in Stepney and Wapping. Abbrev. Plac. (Rec. Com.), 352.

[53] They had lately added a fresh piece of land to the hospital, which they obtained leave to connect with the old buildings by a gallery across a street, April, 1518. Stow, Surv. of Lond. (ed. Strype), iii, 39; Rec. of Corp. of Lond. Repert. 3, fol. 205b.

[54] Since 1407 the company had had for their use a room in the hospital, and a chapel in the church (Watney, op. cit. 36), and from 1442 they had made yearly payments to the hospital for masses for deceased brothers and sisters (ibid. 43). The hospital received from the mercers £66 13s. 4d. in 1502, £100 in 1511, and loans of £40 and £100 in 1513 and 1514 (ibid. 66, 67).

[55] The bishop of London's confirmation is dated 1514, but the hospital had obtained the assent of Pope Leo X before. Lond. Epis. Reg. Fitz James, fol. 118.

[56] Misc. of Exch. bdle. 24, No. 8, preface.

[57] L. and P. Hen. VIII, vii, 921.

[58] Ibid. viii, 626. These were removed. Ibid. xiii (2), 523.

[59] Ibid. vii, 1636. He says that the people cessed for payment of the labourers will not pay, and that he goes in fear of his life from the unpaid men.

[60] Cal. of Pat. 1476–85, pp. 215, 466, and L. and P. Hen. VIII, i, 1972.

[61] Ibid. xiii (2), 648.

[62] Ibid. xiii (2), 492.

[63] Ibid. xv, 282 (36). The church, cloister, vestry, chapter-house, sexton's chamber, and churchyard were sold by the king to the Mercers' Company, April, 1542. Ibid. xvii, 283 (55).

[64] Parl. R. (Rec. Com.), v, 74b.

[65] At least nine were engaged in the election of a master at that date. Lond. Epis. Reg. Kemp, ii, fol. 1. In 1510 there were eight brothers exclusive of Adams, the deposed master. Ibid. Fitz James, fol. 18.

[66] The acknowledgement of the king's supremacy was signed by the master and six others. Dep. Keeper's Rep. vii, App. ii, 293.

[67] Aug. Off. Bk. 233, fol. 26b. He died in 1557. Watney, op. cit. 121.

[68] Aug. Off. Bk. 233, fol. 26b.

[69] Harl. MS. 60, fol. 9, 39, 78. Of this £31 7s. 8d. came from property in London.

[70] Valor Eccl. (Rec. Com.), i, 391, 392. The net income as declared by Copferler 23 Oct. 1538 was £275 7s. 5d. Watney, op. cit. 125.

[71] In the parishes of St. Thomas the Apostle and Allhallows the Less, L. and P. Hen. VIII, xiv (1), 1355; St. Pancras Westcheap, ibid. xiv (2), 113 (23); St. Stephen Walbrook, ibid. (2), 619 (47); St. John Walbrook, ibid. xv, 1032, p. 557; St. Olave Old Jewry, ibid. p. 561; St. Mary le Bow, ibid. p. 562; St. Martin Ludgate, ibid. xv, 942 (77); St. Martin Ironmonger Lane, ibid. xvi, p. 715; and St. Bride, ibid. xviii (2), 241 (32). See also Watney, op. cit. 122–3.

[72] Valor Eccl. (Rec. Com.), i, 391.

The hospital of St. Thomas also held a hospital at Berkhampstead.[73]

*M. Reddan*

## Revised List of Masters of St. Thomas of Acon

This list is a slightly amended version of that in *V.C.H. London*, i.

John[74]
Vincent, no date[75]
Henry de Neville, occurs 1243–4[76]
Ralph Waleys, occurs 1244–5, 1248[77]
Ralph, occurs 1249[78]
Adam, occurs 1253[79]
William de Huntyngfeud, occurs 1267,[80] 1269[81]
Robert de Covelee, occurs 1273–4,[82] 1279[83]
Richard, occurs 1285–6[84]
Roger de Baggishouse, occurs 1289[85]
Richard de Southampton, occurs 1317[86]
Henry de Bedford, occurs 1318;[87] deposed 1327[88]

Nicholas de Clifton, occurs 1327[89]
Ra'ph de Combe, occurs 1330,[90] 1332[91]
Bartholomew de Colecestre, occurs 1333,[92] 1344[93]
William Myle, occurs 1347[94]
Thomas de Sallowe, occurs 1365;[95] died 1371[96]
Richard Sewell, elected 1371[97]
Richard Alred, occurs 1379;[98] died 1400[99]
William Bonyngdon, elected 1400;[100] occurs 1419[101]
John Neel, occurs 1420;[102] died 1463[103]
John Parker, elected 1463[104]
John Hardyng, occurs 1478, 1492[105]
Richard Adams, occurs 1505;[106] removed 1510[107]
John Yong, S.T.P., elected 1510;[108] died 1527[109]
Lawrence Copferler, elected 1527;[110] surrendered the house 1538[111]

[73] Watney, op. cit. 124. It appears to have been the hospital of St. John Baptist. Ibid. 47–8.
[74] Cott. MS. Tib. C. v, fol. 270.
[75] Ibid. fol. 270*b*.
[76] Watney, op. cit. 276.
[77] Ibid. 275.
[78] Cott. MS. Tib. C. v, fol. 270*b*.
[79] *Abbrev. Plac.* (Rec. Com.), 130. He is called 'warden.'
[80] Stubbs, *Introd. to Mem. of Ric. I* (Rolls Ser.), i, p. cxii, *n.* 5.
[81] Cott. MS. Tib. C. v, fol. 161*b*.
[82] Hardy and Page, *Cal. of Lond. and Midd. Fines*, 51.
[83] *Reg. Epist. Johan. Peckham* (Rolls Ser.), i, 75.
[84] Hardy and Page, op. cit. 60.
[85] *Cal. of Close*, 1288–96, p. 49.
[86] Cott. MS. Tib. C. v, fol. 249*b*.
[87] *Cal. of Pat.* 1317–21, p. 205.
[88] *Cal. Pap. Letters*, ii, 273.

[89] Ibid.
[90] *Cal. of Pat.* 1327–30, p. 499.
[91] *Cal. of Close*, 1330–3, p. 555.
[92] *Cal. of Pat.* 1330–4, p. 472.
[93] Watney, op. cit. 291.
[94] Ibid. 261.
[95] Sharpe, *Cal. Letter Bk. G*, 202.
[96] Dugdale, *Mon. Angl.* vi, 646.
[97] Ibid.
[98] McHardy, *Church in London*, p. 2. He was later (1391) ratified in his position of master by the king. *Cal. of Pat.* 1388–92, p. 473.
[99] Lond. Epis. Reg. Braybrook, fol. 337.
[100] Ibid.
[101] Sharpe, *Cal. of Wills*, ii, 417; Watney, op. cit. 273.
[102] *Cal. of Pap. Letters*, vii, 342.
[103] Lond. Epis. Reg. Kemp, ii, fol. 1.
[104] Ibid.
[105] Dugdale, *Mon. Angl.* vi, 646.
[106] Sharpe, *Cal. of Wills*, ii, 611.
[107] Lond. Epis. Reg. Fitz James, fol. 18.
[108] Ibid.
[109] Ibid. Tunstall, fol. 120. He was bishop of Gallipoli; *L. and P. Hen. VIII*, i, 5427.
[110] Lond. Epis. Reg. Tunstall, fol. 120.
[111] *L. and P. Hen. VIII*, xiii (2), 648.

# 10. THE HOSPITAL OF ST. MARY OF BETHLEHEM

## INTRODUCTION

The original article is generally reliable, but needs to be used alongside later studies devoted to the hospital, starting with E. G. O'Donoghue, *The Story of Bethlehem Hospital from its Foundation in 1247* (London, 1914). O'Donoghue's work is useful, although rather wordy, but used together with this account it is a good starting point, in particular for references to source material. However, the hospital has recently received a comprehensive modern history: J. Andrews et al., *The History of Bethlem* (London, 1997) in which pp. 21–129 are devoted to the development of the priory and hospital in the medieval period and is the most up-to-date account available.

Other references to the hospital can be found in the many general works that have been published on hospitals since 1900, and the most relevant to St. Mary of Bethlehem is R. M. Clay, *The Medieval Hospitals of England* (London, 1909), which highlights the use of the hospital from its early days as a hospital for the insane, and of its rescue during the Dissolution when it was bought by the City of London. N. Orme and M. Webster, *The English Hospital, 1070–1570* (London, 1995) also puts the hospital into the wider context of London and the rest of England. C. Rawcliffe, 'The Hospitals of Later Medieval London', *Medical History*, 28 (1984), pp. 1–21, adds detail about the general running of the hospital, particularly its finances, and makes extensive use of T.N.A. C270/22, the visitation of the hospital of St. Mary of Bethlehem, London in 1403.

For details of the locations and sources of the property of St. Mary of Bethlehem, see *Documentary Sources*, pp. 62–3. Honeybourne, 'Property', pp. 175–90, provides a thorough study of the property of the hospital, highlighting its unusual loss, rather than gain, in property. An online draft account of the manors and estates of the hospital is available for consultation, and provides some more valuable information, see 'Hospital of St. Mary of Bethlehem, Bishopsgate (Bethlem Hospital)', *V.C.H. Middlesex*, xiii. Available from http://www.middlesexpast.net/ (accessed 10 January 2007).

*Jessica Lutkin*

In 1247 Simon Fitz Mary, one of the sheriffs of London, made over his land west of Bishopsgate Street, near the church of St. Botolph without Bishopsgate, to Godfrey, bishop of Bethlehem, to found there a priory of canons, brothers and sisters, of the order of St. Mary of Bethlehem,[1] whose duties were to be prayers for the souls of the founder, of Guy de Marlowe, John Durant, Ralph Ashwye, and others, and the reception of the bishop of Bethlehem, and the canons and messengers of that church when they came to London. The house was to be subject to the bishop of Bethlehem, who was to receive from it an annual pension of a mark, to be increased as its wealth grew, and who had the right of visitation and correction. Fitz Mary also provided that the members of the house should wear on their copes and mantles the distinguishing sign of the order, a star, according to Matthew Paris,[2] red with five rays inclosing a circle of blue.

The institution was perhaps never very large. It was certainly of much less importance than the other house outside Bishopsgate. The respective spheres of St. Mary Spital and the rector of St. Botolph's had had to be determined within a few years of the foundation of the priory,[3] but it was not until 1362 that the building of a chapel[4] in honour of the Virgin and the Nativity of Jesus by the house

---

[1] Harl. MS. 539, fol. 95; Stow, *Surv. of Lond.* (ed. Strype), ii, 94. It is spoken of as the knighthood of St. Mary of Bethlehem. *Cal. of Pat.* 1348–50, p. 181.

[2] Matt. Paris, *Chron. Maj.* (Rolls Ser.), v, 631. Their dress was otherwise like that of the Dominicans.
[3] Dugdale, *Mon. Angl.* vi, 625.
[4] Lond. Epis. Reg. Stokesley, fol. 87, 88.

of St. Mary of Bethlehem made an agreement between the rector and this hospital necessary. By the arrangement then made the master and brethren were permitted to complete the chapel, have bells rung there, celebrate divine service, and receive offerings; they might also bury any who wished to be buried in the chapel or precincts, and have the oblations or obventions, except in the case of parishioners of St. Botolph's, when half the offering was to go to the rector. Considering that at this time their fixed income was only 33s.[5] per annum, and that the proceeds of the collection, which by royal licence[6] they made throughout the kingdom, had probably fallen off after the plague of 1350,[7] this settlement was important, and in order to swell the flow of offerings they obtained from the pope in 1363 a special indulgence, extending over a period of ten years, to those who at Christmas, the Epiphany, and the five feasts of the Virgin Mary, with their vigils, visited and rendered material aid to the hospital.[8] In 1389 it benefited, presumably to the extent of £100,[9] by the will of Ralph Basset of Drayton[10] who erected two chantries there. It must also have reaped some advantage from a gild called the Fraternity of St. Mary of Bethlehem established in the church in 1370.[11]

The connexion of the house with the bishopric of Bethlehem doubtless came to an end in the latter part of the thirteenth century, when the Holy Land was lost to Christendom, but how or when the king obtained the patronage it is impossible to say. The corporation of London in 1346 took the hospital under its protection,[12] and had certainly some kind of right over the place in 1350, for on the death of the master, John de Nortone, the serjeant was ordered to take possession of the house in the name of the City,[13] though the order was afterwards rescinded because the hospital had been let to a certain Robert Aaunsard, fishmonger, for a term of years. In 1381, when the king appointed William Welles as master, the City disputed his right, asserting that the hospital was in their gift.[14] At first they were successful,[15] but in the end the

crown gained the day, and appointed[16] as in the case of a royal free chapel, which the hospital resembled also in another point, viz. its exemption from the jurisdiction of the ordinary.

Some very interesting facts about the house were disclosed during a visitation by two of the king's clerks in March, 1403.[17] It had already become an asylum principally, though not exclusively, for the insane, and at that time there were six lunatics and three sick persons there. These people, or their relatives, contributed something to their support, but the amount varied, the highest rate mentioned being 12d. a week paid by a merchant of Exeter, who was there for six weeks. The hospital had a little property,[18] but was chiefly maintained by voluntary contributions, and it was calculated that the collections throughout England brought in about 40 marks a year, the obventions in the great and small chapels 52s., those on the great feasts another 52s., the box at the door of the house and the two boxes carried about London and the suburbs similar amounts, and the offerings for the poor on the day of the Parascene 20s. A collection throughout the diocese of London for the sick poor amounted roughly to 4 marks annually, and gifts of meat, ale, fish, salt, and candles were also made.

The management of the hospital appears at this time to have belonged to the office of porter, and Peter Taverner, who had received the post for life, had abused his trust in every way. He had rendered no accounts of the money accruing from the various collections, in some cases for four years, in others for fourteen, nor of bequests and payments made for the inmates. He had not distributed the alms, but with the money had bought fuel and made the poor pay for it, while his wife had taken the best of the contributions in kind. Not content with this, he had disposed of the beds and other goods, causing a loss to the hospital of about £40, and through him robbers had caused even worse damage. In spite of the remonstrances of the master he persisted in playing at dice and draughts, and in selling ale at his house within the close. It is incredible that Taverner's conduct would have been so long unchecked if the master had been constantly resident or really interested in the place, and it may be noted that the statement of one of the inmates that divine service was sometimes withdrawn by the default of the master or his curate was found to be true, and that the chapel was but poorly provided

---

[5] *Cal. Pap. Petitions*, i, 423.

[6] *Cal. of Pat.* 1327–30, pp. 446 551; 1330–4, pp. 107, 179, 541; 1334–8, p. 344; 1340–3, p. 72.

[7] *Cal. Pap. Petitions*, i, 423. The statement is that they had lost many of their benefactors by the pestilence.

[8] Ibid.

[9] Dugdale, *Baronage*, i, 380. As he left £200 for the establishing of four chantries, it seems most probable that half went to the two in St. Mary Bethlehem.

[10] Nicolas, *Testamenta Vetusta*, 126.

[11] Gild Cert. No. 202.

[12] Sharpe, *Cal. of Letter Bk. F*, 154.

[13] Ibid. 163.

[14] *Parl. R.* (Rec. Com.), iii, 128b.

[15] John Gardyner was appointed by them in 1381, and still held the post in 1389. Sharpe, *Cal. of Letter Bk. H*, 165, 338.

[16] Lincoln, who followed Gardyner, was nominated by the king. *Cal. of Pat.* 1385–9, p. 526; Sharpe, *Cal. of Letter Bk. H*, 338. In 1423 the king again appointed. *Cal. of Pat.* 1422–9, p. 135.

[17] Chan. Misc. R. No. 276.

[18] Lands and houses in the precinct, Dugdale, *Mon. Angl.* vi, 622e; a house near Charing Cross, Chan. Misc. R. No. 276.

with books and plate,[19] while it was also said to be his fault that there were no brothers and sisters in the hospital.[20]

The distinctive dress of the order had been abandoned,[21] and with it seems to have vanished most of the character of the original foundation. Some kind of reconstitution must have been effected, since in 1424 brethren and sisters were associated with the master in sending a proctor or quaestor to seek alms in the archdeaconry of Oxford.[22] But it is evident that in one important respect the hospital developed in the direction it had already taken in the fourteenth century, the office of master tending more and more to become a sinecure. Proof of this may probably be found in the hospital being let to farm by its head in 1454,[23] but there can be no doubt of the significance of the appointment of George Boleyn, a layman, in 1529, and on his forfeiture of a gentleman of the privy chamber.

In 1523 Stephen Gennings, a merchant-tailor, gave £40 to the City Corporation towards the purchase of the patronage of the house,[24] which, however, was not effected until 1546.[25] As there is no *Valor* there are no means of ascertaining what property the hospital had at this date, but the income derived from it seems to have been less than £40,[26] and was

so inadequate to the demands upon it that recourse was had in 1551 to the old practice of soliciting alms of the charitable, in this instance within the counties of Lincoln and Cambridge, the isle of Ely, and the city of London.[27]

*M. Reddan*

## Revised List of Masters, Wardens or Keepers of St. Mary of Bethlehem

This list is taken from Andrews et al., *The History of Bethlem*, pp. 723–4, where further biographical details are provided.

Thomas de Doncastre, occurs 1292–3
William de Banham, occurs 1330
Philip Dene, occurs 1339
John Matheu de Norton, occurs 1346–8
John de Wilton, occurs 1348
Robert Mannyel, occurs 1364
William —, occurs 1367
William Tytte, occurs 1380
John Gardyner, chaplain, appointed 1423
Robert Lincoln, appointed 1388–9
Robert Dale, appointed 1423
Edward Atherton, appointed 1437; occurs 1454
Thomas Arundel, appointed 1457
Thomas Henry DD, appointed 1459
John Brown, appointed 1459
John Smeethe, clerk, appointed 1470
John Davyson, removed 1479
Walter Bate and William Hobbs, appointed 1479
Thomas Maudesley, appointed 1485
John Deinman, appointed 1494
John Cavalari, appointed 1512/13
George Bulleyn, appointed 1529
Peter Mewtys, occurs 1537–46

[19] There was only one silver cup for the high altar. There were two missals, said to be neither sufficient nor suitable, a gradual not suitable, a breviary, and no manual. The vestments and ornaments were, however, declared sufficient. Chan. Misc. R No. 276.

[20] Dugdale, *Mon. Angl.* vi, 623. According to the evidence of one of the inmates, however, there was, at any rate, one sister. Chan. Misc. R. No. 276.

[21] Dugdale, op. cit. vi, 623.

[22] *Hist. MSS. Com. Rep.* ix, App. i, 213.

[23] Harl. Chart. 56, F. 48.

[24] Stow, *Surv. of Lond.* ii, 95.

[25] Ibid. 94; *Memoranda and Documents relating to the Royal Hospitals of London*, App. iv.

[26] In 1524 the procurations due to Wolsey from St. Mary's of Bethlehem were based on a value of £50. *L. and P. Hen. VIII*, iv, 964. But its income in 1555 is said to have been only £34 13s. 4d. *Cal. of S.P. Dom.* 1631–3, p. 424.

[27] Stow, op. cit. ii, 95.

# FRIARIES

## 11. THE BLACK FRIARS

### INTRODUCTION

The original article is detailed and based on a thorough search of printed sources. One of its problems is a reliance on C. F. R. Palmer's articles which, though very informative, often lacked references to the sources he had undoubtedly seen. However, although there are some gaps and minor errors in the detail, the article gives a full account of the convent's history and is still a good starting point.

A number of important studies on the Order's English province were published after the *V.C.H.* article of 1909. Important are E. Barker, *The Dominican Order and Convocation* (Oxford, 1913); B. Jarrett, *The English Dominicans* (London, 1921); B. Formoy, *The Dominican Order in England Before the Reformation* (London, 1925); R. F. Bennett, *The Early Dominicans* (Cambridge, 1937). The most important of these studies was W. A. Hinnebusch, *The Early English Friars Preachers* (Rome, 1951), based on detailed knowledge of the sources from the Order's centre and English government records. The most recent study of the Order's structure and early development is: S. Tugwell, 'The Evolution of Dominican Structures of Government III: The Early Development of the Second Distinction of the Constitutions', *Archivum Fratrum Praedicatorum*, 71 (2001), pp. 5–182.

The *acta* of the Order's four general chapters held in London were published in *Monumenta Ordinis Fratrum Praedicatorum*, ed. B. M. Reichert, vols I–II, Monumenta Ordinis Praedicatorum Historica, 3, 4 (Rome 1898–99), I, pp. 49–55 (1250), 117–21 (1263); II, pp. 69–75 (1314), pp. 228–35 (1335). A document relating to events at the 1314 general chapter has been published by A. G. Little, 'A Record of the English Dominicans, 1314', *Eng. Hist. Rev.*, 5 (1890), pp. 107–12.

The first study of the London house following the 1909 *V.C.H.* article appears to have been W. Martin and S. Toy, 'The Black Friars of London: a chapter in national history', *T.L.M.A.S.*, n.s. 5 (1929), pp. 353–79. More recent research on the Dominican priory in Holborn and the early history of the convent near Ludgate is included in Hinnebusch, *Early English Friars Preachers*, ch. 2. The Dominicans in London are also discussed in J. Röhrkasten, 'Londoners and London Mendicants in the Late Middle Ages', *Jour. Eccl. Hist.*, 47 (1996), pp. 446–77; and idem, *The Mendicant Houses of Medieval London, 1221–1539*, Vita Regularis, 21 (Münster, 2004), where an attempt was made to reconstruct the lost Dominican archives with the help of information contained in wills and central government records. Sources relating to the London property held by the friary are listed in *Documentary Sources*, p. 59. For the catalogue of the library of the Dominicans, see *The Friars' Libraries*, ed. K. W. Humphreys, Corpus of British Medieval Library Catalogues, 1 (London, 1990), pp. 199–203.

Hinnebusch included a map showing the location of the two sites (p. 22), a plan of the Ludgate convent (p. 39), and a conjectural ground plan of the church (p. 42). These were based on A. W. Clapham, 'On the Topography of the Dominican Priory of London', *Archaeologia*, 63 (1912), pp. 57–84 and idem, 'The Friars as Builders – Blackfriars and Whitefriars', in A. W. Clapham and W. H. Godfrey, *Some Famous Buildings and their Story* (London, 1913). The impact of the Dominicans and the other mendicant Orders on the topography of London is discussed in J. Röhrkasten, 'The Origin and Early Development of the London Mendicant Houses', in *The Church in the Medieval Town*, ed. T. R. Slater and G. Rosser (Aldershot, 1998), pp. 76–99. The shape and architecture of the conventual buildings in the sixteenth century has also attracted attention of scholars interested in the Blackfriars playhouse, with early contributions from A. Feuillerat, *Blackfriars Records, c.1555–1609*, Malone Society Collections, 2 (Oxford, 1913; repr. 1985); and J. Q. Adams, 'The Conventual Buildings of Blackfriars, London, and the Playhouses Constructed Therein', *Studies in Philology*, 14 (1917), pp. 65–87.

*Jens Röhrkasten*

The first Dominicans to enter England arrived at Canterbury in 1221 in the train of Peter des Roches bishop of Winchester.[1] Three of these came to London in August of that year[2] and settled in Holborn near the Old Temple. Their chief benefactor appears to have been Hubert de Burgh,[3] who made them many gifts and bequeathed to them his mansion near Westminster. By 1250 they must have been established in buildings of considerable size, for at that date a general chapter was held there[4] at which 400 members of the order were present. Their resources were, however, unequal to the task of providing for such a number,[5] and food was supplied on this occasion by various persons dwelling in or near London, among them the king and queen, the bishop of London, and the abbot of Westminster.[6] Henry III evidently thought much of the Dominicans: in 1256 he chose the prior of Holborn, John de Darlington, as his confessor,[7] and found him so useful in political affairs that he asked the provincial in 1265[8] that he might be appointed to assist him again. The king's favour naturally extended to Darlington's house, which received from him at this time (1258–61) stone for its building operations, and lead for its aqueduct.[9] Perhaps because of this tie with the court, which appears to have continued unbroken until the reign of Henry IV,[10] the Black Friars were never as popular as the Franciscans with the City.[11] In 1255, indeed, the convent had aroused extreme resentment on the

part of the citizens[12] by interceding on behalf of the Jews imprisoned on suspicion of complicity in the death of Hugh of Lincoln.

It is possible that in witnessing the success of the Friars Minors the Black Friars may have felt that they were handicapped by their position outside the City. This disability was removed in 1276, when Robert Kilwardby, the Dominican archbishop of Canterbury, obtained from the mayor and commonalty a commanding site on the Thames within Ludgate[13] and close to Montfichet's Tower which was now pulled down and the material used to construct the new house of Black Friars.[14] Of this new foundation Edward I was the principal patron[15]: in 1278 he granted for its aid all deodands falling to him during the next three years, and besides other sums,[16] a gift of 200 marks in 1280[17] to the building of their church, begun in 1279,[18] and dedicated to the honour of St. Mary the Virgin and St. John the Evangelist.[19] The work must have extended over some years. The church was still unfinished in 1288[20]; the cloister was being made in 1292,[21] and in 1312[22] and

[1] Stow, *Surv. of Lond.* (ed. Strype), iv, 72.

[2] Rev. C. F. R. Palmer, 'Provincials of the Friars Preachers in England,' *Arch. Journ.* xxxv, 135.

[3] Stow, loc. cit.

[4] *Monum. Ordin. Frat. Praedicat.* iii, 48.

[5] Matt. Paris, *Chron. Maj.* (Rolls Ser.), v, 127.

[6] Stow, *Surv. of Lond.* iv, 72.

[7] Rev. C. F. R. Palmer, 'The King's Confessors,' *Antiq.* xxii, 115.

[8] *Deputy Keeper's Rep.* v, App. ii, 63.

[9] *Hist. MSS. Com. Rep.* i, App. i, 95.

[10] *Antiq. ut supra.* Rev. C. F. R. Palmer says that the king's confessor was always a Dominican until the fall of Richard II. As regards this point, and the friars' employment in the king's service, see *Cal. Pap. Letters*, i, 243, 423, 426, 427, 436, and 437; iii, 34, 620; iv, 96; *Cal. Pap. Petitions*, i, 2, 244, 279, 284.

[11] 'Annals of Burton' in *Ann. Mon.* (Rolls Ser.), i, 347.

[12] The list of celebrated persons buried in Black Friars Church shows the importance of the convent, see Stow, op. cit. iii, 180–1. They include Hubert de Burgh, Isabel wife of Roger Bigod earl marshal, Elizabeth countess of Northampton, the earls of March and Hereford, Elizabeth countess of Arundel, John of Eltham duke of Cornwall, Richard Lord St. Amand, the countess of Huntingdon, the duchess of Exeter, Lord Fanhope, Tiptoft earl of Worcester, Sir Thomas Brandon, &c.

[13] The house evidently adjoined the City wall, which appears to have been pulled down there and reconstructed soon afterwards. *Cal. of Pat.* 1307–13, p. 159; ibid. 1313–17, p. 270; *Liber Custum.* in *Mun. Gildhall* (Rolls Ser.), i (2), 455.

[14] Stow, *Surv. of Lond.* i, 62.

[15] Ibid. iii, 177.

[16] *Cal. of Pat.* 1272–81, p. 252; *Cal. of Close*, 1279–88, pp. 448, 508.

[17] *Cal. of Pat.* 1272–81, p. 376.

[18] *Chron. of Edw. I and Edw. II* (Rolls Ser.), i, 88. In 1278 leave was granted by the bishop of London and chapter of St. Paul's. Palgrave, *Ancient Kalendars and Invent. of Exch.* (Rec. Com.), 71.

[19] *Antiq.* xxvii, III, Art. by Rev. C. F. R. Palmer.

[20] *Cal. of Close*, 1279–88, p. 508. The king directs a fine of 50 marks to be given to the expedition of the works of the Friars Preachers, London.

[21] *Cal. of Pat.* 1281–92, p. 484.

[22] Ibid. 1307–13, p. 483.

1313[23] more land was needed to enlarge the convent quarters, for a house of seventy inmates[24] required some space. Unfortunately there is no record, such as exists for the Grey Friars, of the contributors to these buildings, the cost of which could not have been defrayed entirely by the king. The friars had certainly obtained 550 marks for their house in Holborn from Henry de Lacy, earl of Lincoln,[25] and they doubtless received many bequests similar to that of Richard de Stratford,[26] a novice of the house, who, in 1281, assigned the proceeds of the sale of his property in London towards the building of the chapter-house, and that of Elizabeth de Bohun, countess of Northampton,[27] who left to the church 100 marks and the cross made of wood of the Holy Cross, besides altar cloths, &c.

The Black Friars of London received an ample share of the favours shown to the whole order by Edward II,[28] and most probably laid then[29] the foundation of the peculiar franchises[30] of their precinct. The king appears to have sometimes resided at the house,[31] and the amount of state business transacted there[32] in this reign is sufficient indication of the importance of the convent. The presence of the prior at the examination of the Templars in 1309[33] is also of significance in this connexion. It is possible that power may have turned their heads,[34] and that they may have shown the lack of becoming humility of which they were afterwards accused.[35] But the affection of the king was in itself quite sufficient to account for the hatred with which they were regarded by the City, where they became so unpopular that when the king fell

they feared for their lives and fled.[36] If it is true that Friar Dunheved was a member of the London house,[37] the convent was closely connected with the movement for the rescue of Edward II in which the Dominicans generally were implicated.

The power of the London friary had received a check from which it took a few years to recover – at least that seems to be the explanation of the length of time their contest with Hyde Abbey[38] lasted. Both the abbey and the friary claimed a certain Arnold Lym as belonging to their community. The bishop of Winchester decided in favour of the friars, but the monks overrode his sentence with papal bulls, kept possession of Arnold for about ten years, and blocked all action on the part of the friars until in 1347 in answer to a petition in Parliament the king ordered right to be done.

By this time they were on good terms again with the City, since in 1350 the mayor and commonalty petitioned the pope[39] to empower brother John de Worthyn alone to grant absolution there, and in case of his death to allow the prior of London, with the counsel and consent of the mayor, to appoint a brother of the same order, and although they may have been induced to act thus from a mistaken idea of Worthyn's influence with the pope,[40] there can have been no motive of self-interest in their letters to the pope, 24 November, 1364, in favour of the English provincial, Robert Pynk.[41] The general esteem in which the friars were held is also shown by the number of citizens who, during the next two centuries, chose their church and churchyard as a place of burial.[42] One of the numerous fraternities founded in the fourteenth century, viz. the brotherhood of the Assumption of our Lady, was established at the Friars Preachers in 1375.[43] The journeymen cordwainers who in 1387 tried to constitute themselves a gild, held their meeting at the Black Friars, and William Barton, one of the convent, promised to get them papal sanction.[44] Probably the precinct was chosen by the cordwainers owing to its special immunity.

The Dominicans, as might be expected, played a prominent part in the discussion over the Wycliffite heresy, the London house especially, owing to the

---

[23] Ibid. 556.

[24] Devon, *Issues of the Exch.* 129. 5 Dec. 9 Edw. II. 35*s.* paid to John de Wrotham, prior of the Friars Preachers, London, for 6*d.* each to 70 brethren of the convent.

[25] *Cal. of Close*, 1279–88, p. 428.

[26] Sharpe, *Cal. of Wills enrolled in Court of Hustings, Lond.* i, 52. The will itself has no date. It was enrolled in 1281.

[27] Nicolas, *Testamenta Vetusta*, 60.

[28] Riley, *Memorials of Lond.* 111; see also note 2.

[29] In 1347 the inhabitants of London petition the king about a debtor who had taken refuge at the Friars Preachers. *Parl. R.* (Rec. Com.), ii, 187*b.*

[30] Lansd. MS. 155 gives the liberties claimed by the inhabitants of the late dissolved houses of the Black and White Friars. They claimed to be free from all City laws and jurisdiction, and from arrest within the precinct by the City officers.

[31] Sharpe, *Cal. of Letter Bk. D*, 17. Tuesday after the Assumption of the B. Mary, 1311, the said Richer was presented before the king lying at the Preaching Friars, &c.

[32] *Cal. of Close*, 1313–18, p. 216; 1318–23, p. 313; 1323–7, pp. 411, 564; and *Cal. of Letter Bk. E*, 211.

[33] Wilkins, *Concilia Mag. Brit.* ii, 335.

[34] Charges were brought against the order in the general chapter held at London, 1314, by friars who afterwards apostatized and spread abroad their accusations, see Mr. Little's article in *Engl. Hist. Rev.* v, 107, and the royal writ against them, *Cal. of Pat.* 1313–17, p. 176.

[35] Riley, *Chron. of Old Lond.* 264.

[36] Ibid.

[37] Rev. C. F. R. Palmer, 'Provincials of the Friars Preachers,' *Arch. Journ.* xxxv, 150. Stow, however, in his *Annals* (ed. 1615), 225, says nothing about Dunheved being of the London convent.

[38] *Parl. R.* (Rec. Com.), ii, 186.

[39] Riley, *Memorials of Lond.* 257.

[40] Sharpe, *Cal. of Letters from Mayor and Corporation*, i, 15.

[41] Ibid. i, 241.

[42] Rev. C. F. R. Palmer, 'Burials at the Priories of the Blackfriars,' *Antiq.* xxiii, 122, and xxiv, 28, 76, 117, 265.

[43] Gild Cert. No. 188.

[44] Riley, *Memorials of Lond.* 495.

school of early foundation there[45] and its important position. The council of 1382 was held at the Black Friars, London, and the prior, William Syward, and two others of the convent[46] were chosen to take part in the proceedings. The examination of Sir John Oldcastle for heresy in 1413 also took place there.[47] The champions of orthodoxy, however, with the other mendicant orders, laid themselves open to the charge of heresy in 1465, and the friar preacher who in his sermon had maintained the doctrines of the London Carmelite reflecting on the beneficed clergy was examined before the bishop of London and made to revoke them as publicly as he had preached them before.[48]

The convent had learned by experience the wisdom of abstaining from political affairs, and although Richard II had been their patron, granting them in 1394[49] perpetual exemption from all tenths, fifteenths, subsidies, and tallages, they did not involve themselves in the movements which followed his fall. Their prosperity accordingly remained unbroken by the rise of the Lancastrian dynasty, and when Henry IV before the end of his reign reverted to the fashion of his predecessors of choosing a Dominican as confessor he appointed to this office one of their number, Friar John Tylle or Tilley.[50] The ambassadors of the duke of Brittany in 1413[51] and the French ambassadors in 1445[52] stayed at the friary, and it was there that the Parliament of 1449 met.[53] Neither the size nor the convenient situation of their buildings would alone account for this use of them. Sir John Cornewaill, Lord Fanhope, who was connected with the Lancastrian family by marriage, established a chantry in 1436[54] in the chapel which he had built in honour of the Virgin in the churchyard of the Black Friars and endowed it with an annual income of 40 marks, for the payment of which the Fishmongers' Company was responsible. Yet the Friars Preachers of London

could not have been partisans, for John Tiptoft earl of Worcester,[55] or some members of his family,[56] founded the chapel in the nave of their church in which he was buried after his execution in 1470. Moreover the annual grant of £20 which the London convent, instead of the general chapter,[57] had received from the crown[58] since the beginning of the French wars of Edward III was continued both by Yorkist[59] and Tudor[60] kings, while the house continued to be a favourite spot for the transaction of state business.[61]

Outwardly then the Black Friars must have seemed much the same as ever during the reign of Henry VIII except that their numbers had probably decreased[62] considerably since the early fourteenth century. The church was still a centre of religious activity[63] and a favourite place of burial for all classes.[64] But it appears as if the intimate connexion of the friary with the court had stifled much of the spirit of the house, for the religious changes of the sixteenth century met with the same acquiescence as the dynastic changes of the fifteenth. It is, however, impossible to judge of the character and feeling of the house by those of its head. Considering that John Hilsey as provincial was resident[65] at the Black Friars and that he in conjunction with Browne, the Austin friar, had a commission from the king to visit the friaries throughout the kingdom, it is natural that no difficulty was made over the acknowledgement of the royal supremacy, which was signed by the prior, Robert Strowdyll,[66] S.T.P., on behalf of the convent, 17 April, 1534. This did not, however, secure Strowdyll in his post. Hilsey was entirely subservient to the king and Cromwell, and consequently a convenient head

[45] Rev. C. F. R. Palmer, 'Prelates of the Black Friars of England,' *Antiq.* xxvi. Fr. Thos. de Jartz (born *c.* 1230) taught in Paris, London, and Oxford. See too *Cal. Pap. Letters,* v, 323. Berengarius, mastergeneral, ordained in the chapter held at London, 1314, that the friars of Ireland should have two students at Oxford, two at London, &c.

[46] Wilkins, *Concil.* iii, 157.

[47] *Coll. of a Lond. Cit.* (Camd. Soc.), 107.

[48] Ibid. 230.

[49] *Cal. of Pat.* 1391–6, p. 379.

[50] Rev. C. F. R. Palmer, 'The King's Confessors,' *Antiq.* xxiii, 26; *Cal. of Pat.* 1422–9, p. 22, Inspex. and Confirm. of letters pat. 26 June, 1 Hen. V, inspecting and confirming letters pat. 4 Jan. 14 Hen. IV of 40 marks a year for life to John Tylle, friar preacher, the king's confessor.

[51] Devon, *Issues of the Exch.* 319.

[52] *L. and P. illustrating wars of Engl. in France* (Rolls Ser.), i, 128.

[53] *Parl. R.* (Rec. Com.), v, 171*a.*

[54] *Parl. R.* (Rec. Com.), iv, 497 *a*; Pat. 15 Hen. VI, m. 18; Pat. 16 Hen. VI, pt. 2, m. 28.

[55] Fabyan, *Chron.* (ed. Ellis), 659.

[56] *Dict. Nat. Biog.*

[57] *Cal. of Pat.* 1343–5, p. 464.

[58] Pat. 35 Hen. VI, pt. 1, m. 8, says that they had received £20 yearly from Hen. III, Edw. I, Edw. II, Edw. III, Ric. II, Hen. IV, and Hen. V.

[59] *Parl. R.* (Rec. Com.), v, 597*b*; vi, 90*a.*

[60] *L. and P. Hen. VIII,* i, 264; ii, 2736; iii, 999, &c.

[61] Ibid. i, 5351, for a record of the reign of Edw. IV. Parliaments were held at Blackfriars 1514 and 1523. Ibid. i, 4848; iii, 2956; iv, 6043; see Stow, *Surv. of Lond.* iii, 177.

[62] In 9 Edw. II there were seventy friars, at the Dissolution only sixteen or seventeen, though it seems probable that the difference in numbers would not have been as marked as this earlier in the reign.

[63] The Fraternity of St. Barbara in this church was confirmed by the bishop of London in 1511. Lond. Epis. Reg. Fitz James, fol. 27. The Fraternity of the Conception of the Virgin Mary obtained the king's licence 23 Hen. VIII. *L. and P. Hen. VIII,* v, 766 (7).

[64] Nicolas, *Testamenta Vetusta,* 490, 548, 588; Stow, *Surv. of Lond.* iii, 181; Rev. C. F. R. Palmer, 'Burials at the Priories of the Black Friars,' *Antiq.* xxiv, 28, 76, 117, 265.

[65] *L. and P. Hen. VIII,* xiv (2), 64.

[66] Ibid. vii, 665.

for the London priory, and the convent being in his debt was obliged to support his candidature.[67] The bishop of Rochester was accordingly made prior commendatory of the Black Friars of London, March, 1536,[68] and finding Strowdyll difficult to live with he sent him to Dartford to be president there, to the disgust of the prioress.[69] Under such a prior,[70] those who like Friar John Maydland were opposed to the New Learning and all its supporters[71] would find it expedient to leave the house or suppress their opinions. The policy of Hilsey's appointment from the king's point of view was soon apparent: in the space of about two years he had become so convinced that the whole institution was antichristian, that he wished the friars to change their habits, as he trusted those honest among them had changed their hearts.[72] The surrender of the house was made 12 November, 1538, by the prior and fifteen friars.[73] Hilsey received a pension of £60 for the term of his life and the prior's lodging in Blackfriars[74] as he held it at the Dissolution.

The income of the convent from rents of houses and shops within the precinct amounted to £104 15s. 4d.,[75] and seems to have been exclusive of the various chantries and obits established there. Among these was the Cornewaill chantry already mentioned, one of 4½ marks for the soul of Henry VII, and another of the same amount for Thomas Rogers. A sum of £13 6s. 8d. was also paid yearly by the Goldsmiths' Company partly for masses and partly for the maintenance of a schoolmaster.[76] The amount of plate contained in the church was not as large as that owned by the Grey Friars, but comprised 400 oz. of gilt, 400 oz. of parcel gilt, and 332 oz. of white.[77]

During the short revival under Queen Mary the Friars Preachers were established at Smithfield.[78] The only officer mentioned besides the prior is the sub-prior.[79]

*M. Reddan*

## Revised List of the Priors of the Black Friars

This is an updated version of the list in the *V.C.H.*

Walter, occurs 1244[80]
John of Darlington, occurs 1262–63[81]
John de Sevenehok, occurs 1283, 1294[82]
Nicholas, occurs 1285[83]
Robert de Novo Mercato, occurs 1288[84]
William de Pykeringg (Pikeryng), occurs 1307, 1321[85]
John de Wrotham, occurs 1309–10, 1320[86]
John de la More, occurs 1321–2[87]
Hildebrand Burdon, occurs 1327[88]
Johannes, occurs 1344[89]
William Syward, occurs 1377–82[90]
John Deping (Pingh, Pyng), occurs 1383–96[91]
John Nonnyngton, occurs 1394[92]
Thomas Palmer, occurs 1396–1407[93]
John Montagu, occurs as prior in 1407[94]
Dr John Tyll, occurs 1408[95]
William Criel, occurs 1411[96]
Thomas de Berkles, occurs c.1417[97]
Dr John Rokhile, occurs 1448[98]
John Mersh, occurs 1455[99]
John Rideshall, occurs 1456[100]

---

[67] Ibid. x, 597 (50).

[68] Ibid. xi, 1322, 1323.

[69] Ibid. xi, 1322.

[70] Sir Geoffrey Pole said the bishop of London had told him that Hilsey appointed heretics to preach at St. Paul's Cross (ibid. xiii (2), 695). His banishment was demanded by the Lincolnshire rebels of 1536, ibid. x, 585.

[71] Ibid. ix, 846. The saying of Mr. John Maydland to Jasper Tyrell, 18 Nov., 27 Hen. VIII. 'Friar Maydland said he would like to see the head of every maintainer of the New Learning upon a stake —that of his principal among them—and to see the king die a violent and shameful death and to see the queen burned . . .'

[72] Ibid. xiii (2), 225.

[73] *L. and P. Hen. VIII*, xiii (2), 809; *Dep. Keeper's Rep.* viii, App. ii, 28. J. Roffen occurs both at the beginning and end of the list. If one of the friars happened to be named Rochester there were seventeen inmates of the friary.

[74] Aug. Off. Bks. 233, fol. 146*b*.

[75] Dugdale, *Mon. Angl.* vi, 1487. The tenements which had belonged to them and were afterwards let or sold seem to have been either in the precinct or adjoining. *L. and P. Hen. VIII*, xiv (1), 651 (55); xv, p. 559; xix (1), 80 (3); xix (2), 527 (25).

[76] Ibid. xiii (2), 809.

[77] *Monastic Treasures* (Abbotsford Club), 19.

[78] Machyn, *Diary* (Camd. Soc.), 171, 204.

[79] *L. and P. Hen. VIII*, xiii (2), 219.

[80] *Cal. of Pat.* 1232–47, 439–41.

[81] T.N.A. DL25/137; DL25/139.

[82] *Monumenta Conventus*, ed Palmer, 303; T.N.A. E159/57 m 11d.

[83] T.N.A. DL27/62; C.L.R.O., HR 16(51).

[84] T.N.A. E159/62 m 15d, perhaps until 1295

[85] T.N.A. E403/136 m 4; E403/195 m 1; B.L. MS Add. 9951 fol. 50v.

[86] T.N.A. E403/146 m 8, E403/170 m 5; E101/376/14 fol. 6r.

[87] T.N.A. E403/196 m 6; B.L. MS Stowe 553 fol. 8r.

[88] *Cal. Plea and Memoranda R.*, 1323–64, 46.

[89] *Cal. Plea and Memoranda R.*, 1323–64, 209.

[90] Emden, *Survey*, 448; *B.R.U.O.*, III, 1704.

[91] T.N.A. C270/29/15; B.L. MS Add. 32446 no. 7b.

[92] G.L. MS 9171/1 fol. 303r.

[93] T.N.A. E403/564 m 8; *B.R.U.O.*, III, 1421.

[94] B.L. MS Harl. 431 fol. 108v–109v.

[95] T.N.A. E403/595 m 3; according to *B.R.U.O.*, III, 1876 prior 1402–8 but this conflict with Thomas Palmer and John Montagu.

[96] G.L. MS 9051/1 fol. 246v–247r.

[97] T.N.A. PROB11/2 fol. 300r–v.

[98] T.N.A. E403/773 m 7.

[99] According to *V.C.H. London*, i. 502.

[100] G.L. MS 9171/5 fol. 209v, 226r.

Johannes, occurs 1461[101]
Thomas London, 1463–1475[102]
— de Wunchelseye, occurs 1490[103]
John Morgan (Morgan Jones), occurs 1508[104]
John Howden, occurs 1518, 1522–3[105]
Robert Strowdyl (Stroddle), occurs 1526, 1534[106]
John Hilsey, before 1536 to 1538[107]

**Subpriors**

Thomas de Wetwang, occurs *c.*1300[108]
Robert Giffard, occurs 1313[109]
Philippe, occurs 1481[110]
William Welhedd, occurs 1533[111]
— Peerson, occurs 1538[112]

---

[101] *Cal. of Close.* 1461–68, 63.
[102] B.L. Add. MS 32446 no. 19e.
[103] According to *V.C.H. London*, i. 502.
[104] *Cal. of Close*, 1500–9, 347; Emden, *Survey*, 375.
[105] *L. and P. Hen. VIII*, XIII i, no. 1180; T.N.A. E315/97 fol. 44r–v; G.L., MS 9531/10 fol. 152r.
[106] G.L. MS 9531/10 fol. 158v; Emden, *Survey*, 458.
[107] *L. and P. Hen. VIII*, X, no. 597 (50); vol. XIII ii no. 809.

[108] B.L. MS Add. 7966A fol. 24v.
[109] T.N.A. E403/165 m 1.
[110] G.L. MS 9171/6 fol. 314v–315v.
[111] G.L. MS 9171/10 fol. 217r
[112] *L. and P. Hen. VIII*, XIII ii, no. 219.

# 12. THE GREY FRIARS

## INTRODUCTION

This account is still a good starting point, but in the years since its publication quite a lot of additional work has been done. Some of these more modern publications would now be considered as standard points of reference. In terms of original material, Thomas Eccleston's account of the arrival of the Franciscans in England is now available in a more accessible form in A. G. Little (ed.), *Fratris Thomae vulgo dicti de Eccleston Tractatus de Adventu Fratrum Minorum in Angliam* (Manchester, 1951). For a translation, see E. Gurney Salter, *The Coming of the Friars Minor to England and Germany: Being the Chronicles of Brother Thomas of Eccleston and Brother Jordan of Giano* (London, 1926). C. L. Kingsford's book, *The Greyfriars of London* (Aberdeen, 1915), contains a transcription of the so-called *Register of the Grey Friars of London*, which is the primary source for much of the information on the foundation and development of the house and its buildings. It also includes lists of tombs in the church. For the Greyfriars library, see K. W. Humphreys (ed.), *The Friars Libraries*, Corpus of British Medieval Library Catalogues, 1 (London, 1990), pp. 216–23.

Kingsford's introduction is a good starting point for a general history of the house, but for more detailed information, see Jens Röhrkasten, *The Mendicant Houses of Medieval London 1221–1539* (Munster, 2004). Dr. Röhrkasten covers the establishment of the house and provides a careful survey of the way in which it is understood to have developed. The book has an excellent bibliography. For the relationship with Londoners see Röhrkasten's earlier article, 'Mendicants in the Metropolis: the Londoners and the development of the London Friaries', in M. Prestwich, R. H. Britnell and R. Frame (eds), *Thirteenth Century England VI* (Woodbridge, 1997), pp. 61–75. Also see Frances A. Maggs, 'Londoners and the London House of the Greyfriars' (unpub. MA thesis, Royal Holloway, University of London, 1996). This too has a useful bibliography. C. H. Lawrence's book, *The Friars: The Impact of the Early Mendicant Movement on Western Society* (London, 1994) provides background information on the order in Europe.

Many of the studies already mentioned will cover the development of the church and other buildings in the precinct as these were funded by donations and bequests, often from Londoners. For studies of the relationship between the design and function of mendicant buildings, however, see A. W. Clapham and W. H. Godfrey, *Some Famous Buildings and their Story* (London, 1913). In spite of the unpromising title this provides useful material on mendicant houses and churches, including this one. Also see A. R. Martin, *Franciscan Architecture in England* (Manchester, 1937). For the site of the London house, M. Honeybourne's article, 'The Precinct of the Grey Friars', *London Topographical Record*, XVI (1932), pp. 9–51, is essential reading, as is her earlier thesis (see Honeybourne, 'Property', pp. 143–70). For the London property of the house, see *Documentary Sources*, p. 59.

Only a certain amount of archaeological investigation has been possible on the site. See for example P. Herbert, 'Excavations at Christchurch Greyfriars, 1976', *London Archaeologist*, 3 (1976–80), pp. 327–32, and A. Johnson, 'Excavations at Christ Church, Newgate Street, 1973', *T.L.M.A.S.*, 25 (1974), pp. 221–2. See in addition J. Lyon, *Within these Walls: Excavations at Newgate*, MoLAS Monograph (in preparation). Useful also is L. A. S. Butler, 'The Houses of the Mendicant Orders in Britain: recent archaeological work', in P. V. Addyman and V. E. Black (eds.) *Archaeological Papers from York Presented to W. M. Barley* (York, 1984), pp. 123–36, which presents a survey of current research on the material culture of the friaries.

*Frances Maggs*

Of the nine Franciscans who landed at Dover, September, 1224,[1] four – Richard Ingworth, a priest, and Richard of Devon, an acolyte, both Englishmen, Henry Detrenizo (or de Trevizo), a Lombard, and Monacatus,[2] the last two lay brothers – proceeded to London, where they stayed with the Friars Preachers at Holborn for fifteen days. They then hired a house in Cornhill of John Travers, sheriff of London, and made in it little cells.[3] Here they remained, with others who joined them, until the following summer, when, their number being too large for their quarters, John Iwyn,[4] citizen and mercer of London, made over to their use, as by their rule they could possess nothing, some land and houses close to Newgate,[5] in the parish of St. Nicholas in the Shambles. The spot accorded well with their profession, for it must have been one of the most unpleasant in the unsavoury mediaeval city: it bordered on and soon included part of a lane so filthy from the blood of slaughtered animals that it was called Stinking Lane.[6] Once established, they gradually added to their space,[7] an urgent necessity considering that in 1243 there were eighty friars in the convent.[8]

The close adherence of the friars to the rule of their order in the first years of their settlement in London – for they lived on the poorest of food[9] and in buildings[10] of the simplest description – explains the enthusiasm[11] they excited in that city, which is shown by the large proportion of London citizens among their early benefactors. William Joyner,[12] who built them a chapel at a cost of £200, was probably the mayor of 1239; Henry le Galeys, mayor 1274, built the nave of their first church; Walter Potter, alderman of London, and sheriff in 1269 and 1272, gave the chapter-house and all the brass vessels for the kitchen and infirmary; Gregory de Rokesley, mayor 1274–80, built the

dormitory and furnished it; while the Basings and the Frowyks,[13] who bore so much of the expense of the water supply of the friary, were members of well-known London families. Salomon, one of the first novices and the second warden of the house there, became general confessor of the citizens. It was from Salomon,[14] while warden, that Roger bishop of London demanded canonical obedience, but owing to his admiration for the order consented to an indefinite delay, and future demands were of course stopped by the entire exemption of the friars from episcopal jurisdiction.

The necessity for intellectual training was very soon grasped by the Franciscans in England, and in this respect the London convent was early provided for by Albert of Pisa (minister of England, 1239), who established a reader there.[15] Its schools may account in some measure for the influential position it held in the next century.

The rebuilding of the church in the fourteenth century gives perhaps a better idea of the extraordinary position to which the friars had attained than could be gathered in any other way. It seems indeed to mark a new era in their history, for the principal contributors are of a different class from the early benefactors, queens and nobles now playing the part formerly taken by London citizens.[16] The foundation stone was laid in 1306 by Sir William Walden in the name of Queen-Margaret, the second wife of Edward I,[17] who not only bought the land necessary[18] for the extension,[19] but gave 2,000 marks during her lifetime and bequeathed 100 marks to the building.[20] She died before the church was finished, and was buried in front of the high altar. John de Bretagne, earl of Richmond, gave £300, a gold chalice, vestments, and carpets; Mary, countess of Pembroke, £70 and many other goods; Gilbert de Clare, earl of Gloucester, twenty great beams from his forest of Tunbridge worth £20, and as much more in money; his sister Margaret, countess of Gloucester, £26 13s. 4d. for the construction of an

---

[1] *Monum. Francisc.* (Rolls Ser.), i, 493.

[2] Or Melioratus according to Thomas de Eccleston, op. cit. i, 7.

[3] Thomas de Eccleston, op. cit. i, 9. They appear to have divided off spaces with piles of hay.

[4] *Prima Fundatio Frat. Min. Lond.* op. cit. i, 494.

[5] *Hund. R.* (Rec. Com.), i, 432. They are accused of blocking the road round the City wall 3 Edw. I.

[6] Stow, *Surv. of Lond.* (ed. Strype), iii, 129.

[7] *Monum. Francisc.* i, 496–506.

[8] Little, *Grey Friars in Oxf.* 44, n. 1.

[9] Thomas de Eccleston (*Monum. Francisc.* i, 9) says that in the time when W. was minister and H. warden, he saw the friars there drink sour beer and eat the coarsest bread.

[10] Ibid. i, 34. 'Angnellus . . . similiter dormitorium Londoniae persistente tecto immobili muris lapideis amoto luto fecit stabiliri.' In 1340 the house was not even inclosed. Ibid. i, 35–44.

[11] Brewer points out in the introduction to the *Monum. Francisc.* that the number of small gifts to them shows how widespread was the feeling in their favour.

[12] Ibid. i, 508; Harl. MS. 544, fol. 43.

[13] The Henry Frowyk mentioned in this connexion (ibid. i, 509) may be the Henry Frowyk who was sheriff in 1274.

[14] Thomas de Eccleston in *Monum. Francisc.* (Rolls Ser.), i, 41.

[15] Ibid. i, 47. Albertus on his arrival made Brother Vincent de Coventry reader at London.

[16] They had in the first period been patronized by Henry III, see *Monum. Francisc.* ii, 279, for a grant of wood, 13 Hen. III, and Harl. MS. 544, fol. 44, for his help to the aqueduct; and in the grants to the building of the church London citizens again showed themselves generous. It is the proportion that seems reversed in the two cases.

[17] *Monum. Francisc.* (Rolls Ser.), i, 513.

[18] Shepherd, 'The Church of the Friars Minors in London,' in *Arch. Journ.* lix, 245; *Monum. Francisc.* i, 503, 504.

[19] Harl. MS. 544, fol. 43. Joyner's Chapel afterwards, that is when this church was built, became a great part of the choir.

[20] *Monum. Francisc.* (Rolls Ser.), i, 513.

altar, and another sister, Eleanor le Spencer, £15 for a similar purpose; while a third, Lady Elizabeth de Burgh, gave £15, partly in wood, partly in money;[21] Robert, Lord Lisle, who afterwards became a friar in the convent, contributed more than £300. Queen Isabella expended over £700 on the completion of the church, and Queen Philippa gave £48 13s. 4d. to the church and £13 6s. 8d. to the expense of roofing it.[22] The church appears to have been both large and handsome, for it measured 300 ft. in length and 89 ft. in breadth, and the columns and pavement were of marble.[23] Between the aisled nave and the choir stood the altars of St. Mary, of Holy Cross, and of Jesus and the common altar, and on each side of the choir were two chapels, those of St. Mary and All Hallows on the north, and those of St. Francis and the Apostles on the south.[24] The church was finished in 1327,[25] but a storm in 1341 did great damage,[26] and work was still going on in 1345, when the cloister was being built[27] and the houses repaired. It is possible that additions were made throughout the century: the glazing of the windows was done at the cost of various people who were not all contemporaries,[28] and the choir stalls were the gift of Margaret Segrave, countess of Norfolk, about 1380.[29] The convent buildings were enlarged a little after 1360, an alteration made necessary by the numbers that joined the order.[30] In 1315 and 1325 there were seventy-two inmates of the friary,[31] and in 1346 the king had to check the influx of foreign friars into the London house,[32] ostensibly in the interests of the English brothers, but possibly in the fear of spies. There is also proof that about a hundred friars died at the time of the Black Death, for recent excavations on the site of the old burialground led to the discovery of a pit evidently made at the time of an epidemic, and about a hundred bodies in this had upon them the leaden crosses used by the

Franciscans, but in this case not inscribed with the formula of absolution, and showing other signs of hasty construction.[33]

It would perhaps be difficult to overrate the influence of the Grey Friars, particularly in the fourteenth century. Queen Isabella chose as her confessor one of this convent, Roger Lamborne, a man of good family,[34] and as the gifts of Gilbert de Clare to the church are said to have been made at the prompting of his confessor, Geoffrey de Aylesham,[35] so the generosity of Margaret, countess of Norfolk, may have been partly due to Friar William de Woodford.[36] Roger Conway of the convent of Worcester received a papal licence in 1355 to reside in London, for the spiritual recreation of himself and of the many English nobles coming to the friary.[37] He is interesting not only as a spiritual adviser of the fashionable world, but as having answered the tract of the archbishop of Armagh against the mendicant orders.[38] The regard in which the house was held is also testified by the persons of high rank[39] and the prominent citizens[40] who chose the church as a place of burial.

The popularity of the Grey Friars with the rich and powerful was doubtless one of the reasons for the vehement attacks made on them, although the attitude towards them can be sufficiently accounted for when one remembers that they continued the practice of begging while they had given up a life of poverty, and any doubt on this last point vanishes after seeing the list of property stolen from John Welle,[41] a Minorite dwelling in London, 1378. Their shortcoming in this respect was the immediate cause of Wycliffe's hatred. No definite part in this

---

[21] Ibid. 514.

[22] Ibid. 515.

[23] Harl. MS. 544, fol. 49.

[24] Mr. Shepherd, in the article already referred to, has constructed a very clear plan of the church and its different parts from Cott. MS. Vitell. F. xii.

[25] In *Monum. Francisc.* i, 513, it is distinctly said that the church was begun in 1306, and (i, 515) that the work was finished in twenty-one years, but this latter passage continues, 'inceptum enim erat MCCCXXVII.' According to the monk of St. Albans it was not yet dedicated in 1357, when Queen Isabella was buried there. *Chron. Angl.* (Rolls Ser.), 38.

[26] Riley, *Chron. of Old Lond.* 286.

[27] *Cal. of Pat.* 1343–5, p. 476.

[28] See Mr. Shepherd's notes on the donors of windows, op. cit. 259–62. Sums were bequeathed to the fabric of the church in 1361 and 1436. Sharpe, *Cal. of Wills*, ii, 49, 481.

[29] Harl. MS. 544, fol. 48. She gave all the material, and the making cost her 350 marks besides.

[30] *Monum. Francisc.* (Rolls Ser.), i, 512.

[31] Little, op. cit. 441, n. 1.

[32] *Cal. of Close*, 1346–9, p. 150.

[33] *The Antiquary*, lii, 72.

[34] *Monum. Francisc.* (Rolls Ser.), i, 541. He was her confessor in 1327, and still held the office in 1343. Little, op. cit. 2, 37; *Cal. Pap. Letters*, iii, 88. Either before or after his time John Vye, also friar of this house, was her confessor. E. B. S. Shepherd, op. cit. 269.

[35] *Monum. Francisc.* (Rolls Ser.), i, 514.

[36] Her connexion with him is shown by a grant she made to the Minoresses for the term of the life of 'her well-beloved father in God William de Wydford.' *Cal. of Pat.* 1381–5, p. 452.

[37] Little, op. cit. 239.

[38] Wadding, *Ann. Minorum*, viii, 127.

[39] See list printed by Mr. Shepherd from the Cotton MS. in the article in *Arch. Journ.* lix, 266–85: Queen Margaret died 1318; Queen Isabella died 1357; Queen Joan of Scotland died 1362; the heart of Queen Eleanor of Provence; Beatrice, duchess of Brittany, daughter of Henry III; Isabella, countess of Bedford, daughter of Edward III; John de Hastings, earl of Pembroke, died 1389; Margaret de Redvers, countess of Devon, died 1292; John, duke of Bourbon, died 1433; James, Lord Saye and Sele, died 1450; Richard Hastings, Lord Willoughby and Wells, died 1503; Walter Blount, Lord Mountjoy, K.G., 1474, &c.

[40] Gregory de Rokesley, mayor, died 1291; John Philpot, mayor, died 1384; Nicholas Brembre, mayor, died 1399; Stephen Jennyns, mayor, died 1523. *Arch. Journ.* lix, 266–85.

[41] Little, op. cit. 78.

controversy can be ascribed to the London house, for it was only after 1390 that Friar Woodford, Wycliffe's opponent, lived there.[42]

During the reign of Henry IV the part played in political affairs by some of the English Franciscans[43] must have caused all of the order to be looked at askance by the court. Hence perhaps the reason why it was not to noble patrons such as those who built their church, but to a London citizen, the celebrated Richard Whittington,[44] that they owed the new library, begun in 1421 and completely finished in about four years. In like manner it was to the efforts of two inmates of the convent, William Russell[45] the warden and Thomas Winchelsey, that they were indebted for most of the improvements in the convent buildings.

The names of these two friars occur again in another very different connexion. On 15 May, 1425, Russell[46] appeared before the archbishop of Canterbury, presiding in his provincial council at St. Paul's, on a charge of preaching that personal tithes need not be paid to the parish priest, but might be devoted instead to charitable purposes. The opinion of the archbishop was against him, and Russell professed himself willing to submit, but as he did not appear[47] to make the public renunciation of this doctrine at St. Paul's Cross in accordance with the archbishop's order, he was declared excommunicate. He thereupon betook himself to Rome, where he was imprisoned by the pope for his erroneous opinions.

Winchelsey, who was considered the most famous doctor of the order, had also been summoned before the same convocation[48] on an apparently groundless charge of heresy. When Russell however managed to escape to England in January, 1426, he was sheltered for a night at his friary, when it is said that Winchelsey came from Shene expressly to see him. In consequence of this Winchelsey was accused and condemned by convocation in April following for favouring heresy. He submitted to the court, and on behalf of himself, the London convent and the whole order, read a declaration

at St. Paul's Cross repudiating Russell's opinions. Russell probably surrendered himself,[49] as he was not kept long in prison by the bishop of London after he had recanted at St. Paul's Cross in March, 1427.

The Grey Friars may have thought that they had re-established their reputation for orthodoxy by the part their provincial played against Pecocke,[50] bishop of Chichester. The remembrance of their former check did not at any rate deter them from joining the Carmelites in their attack on the beneficed clergy in 1465,[51] and their representative in the disputation at Whitefriars went so far that he was cited to appear before the archbishop at Lambeth for heresy. He pleaded exemption from all episcopal jurisdiction, but the privilege was judged not to hold in this case. Whether he withdrew or explained away everything obnoxious to the authorities or not does not appear, but it would seem he was acquitted, and he alone ventured to answer Dr. Ive[52] when he lectured at St. Paul's Schools on the opposite side.

The return of the Grey Friars in 1502 to their whitish-grey habits, which they had for some reason temporarily abandoned,[53] looked at in the light of subsequent events, appears a ludicrous attempt at outward profession when the spirit had completely departed: for the rest of their history may be summed up as a firm determination to stand well with the king at whatever cost of principle. Their relations with the court are shown in the next collision with the ecclesiastical authorities. Dr. Henry Standish, then resident in the London house, provincial[54] of the Grey Friars, and a popular court preacher, was accused of heresy[55] in the convocation of 1515. He may have thought with some reason that the real charge against him was the opinion he had expressed in favour of the Act of 4 Henry VIII, by which the benefit of clergy was curtailed. At all events the king took this view, and the members of Convocation[56] found themselves in their turn accused of an attack on the secular power, and had enough to do to excuse themselves without pursuing the case against Standish.

The close connexion of the Grey Friars and the City was illustrated more than once about this

---

[42] Ibid. 247. But Shirley, the editor of *Netter's Fasciculi Zizaniorum* (Rolls Ser.), thinks that Woodford may have delivered a course of theological lectures which touched on Wycliffe's opinions at the Grey Friars of London in 1381.

[43] Stow, *Annals* (ed. 1615), 327. Eight grey friars were hanged at London and two at Leicester, all of whom had published that King Richard was alive. According to the chronicler Richard II had as confessor a Franciscan named William Apledore. Ibid. 287.

[44] *Monum. Francisc.* i, 579. The total expense was £556 16s. 8d., of which Whittington contributed £400.

[45] Ibid. 520.

[46] Wilkins, *Concilia*, iii, 438.

[47] Ibid. 439.

[48] Ibid. 433.

[49] Little, op. cit. 258.

[50] *Chron. of the Grey Friars of Lond.* (Camd. Soc.), 20.

[51] *Coll. of a Lond. Citizen* (Camd. Soc.), 229.

[52] Ibid. 231. It seems from the chronicle that these lectures took place after the citation for heresy, but it is not at all clear.

[53] *Chron. of Grey Friars of Lond.* (Camd. Soc.), 27.

[54] Rec. of Corp. of Lond. Letter Bk. M. fol. 237.

[55] *L. and P. Hen. VIII*, ii (1), 1314.

[56] Their bitterness against Standish comes out in more than one passage:, see *L. and P. Hen. VIII*, ii (1), 1312, where Tayler the prolocutor says that the strife between Church and State over ecclesiastical liberties was fomented by Standish; see also ibid. ii (1), 1313 (4).

time: on the petition of the warden and friars it was decided in 1514[57] that the mayor and aldermen as founders should go in procession to the house every year on St. Francis' Day; and when the nave of the church was to be paved with marble London citizens contributed the money; and a further outlay being necessary in 1518 the provincial and the warden applied to the City, and at the request of the Court of Common Council the sum required, £16 16s. 8d., was raised by the companies.[58]

The feeling that as Friars Minors of London they must sympathize with the London poor undoubtedly caused John Lincoln's attempt[59] to use their influence to persuade the City authorities to take measures against the foreigners with whom the populace was so enraged. But Dr. Standish was not the man to run any risk, and saying that it was not a fit subject to touch on in a sermon, escaped any ill consequences of the evil May Day of 1517.

The attitude of the friars in the affair of the prisoner who escaped from Newgate and took refuge in their church may have offended the City,[60] but in 1529 the usual procession was not to take place 'in consequence of the unkindness and ingratitude of the friars.'[61] Standish seems to have been taken as an example by the wardens during the period of religious change. Cudner, on behalf of his convent, acknowledged the king as supreme head of the Church in 1534,[62] and it is unlikely that Friar Forest and others of the Observants would have been sent to this house if the king had not been certain of the opinions entertained there. Chapuys said that the Observants, while they refused to take the oath, were treated by the Conventuals worse than they would have been in ordinary prisons,[63] and the hostility shown to them by Thomas Chapman, the warden, when Forest again fell under suspicion is sufficient indication of the treatment meted out to them in London. In a letter to Cromwell Chapman says[64] that he has not forgotten the command to search out Forest's friends, but the time assigned had been too short. He has now learned more, and sends the names of those who had given Forest a

small sum of money, adding: 'I will be true to my Prince, and so will all my Brethren. I dare depose for them that were no Observants.' One friar was so eager to show his loyalty that he laid information against one of his fellow brethren, misrepresenting a conversation of which he had only heard part.[65] The accused managed to clear himself,[66] but such spying must have made life unendurable, and gone far to justify the warden in declaring that 'all the house would willingly change their coats provided they have a living,' and that 'they all longed to change their coats.'[67]

The house was surrendered on 12 November 1538, by Thomas Chapman, S.T.D., the warden, and 26 friars.[68] Chapman was granted a life pension of £13 6s. 8d.,[69] and payments, but apparently not pensions,[70] were made to twenty of the friars. The fixed income of the house derived from lands and houses in the immediate neighbourhood of the church and monastery[71] was only £32 19s.,[72] so that the friars must still have depended on alms for the greater part of their revenues.[73] The importance of the house may be gauged by the amount of plate in the church at the time of the Dissolution—1,520 oz. of gilt, 600 oz. of parcel gilt, and 770 oz. of white plate.[74]

*M. Reddan*

---

[57] 1508 is given as the date in *Chron. of the Grey Friars of Lond.* (Camd. Soc.), 29. From the wording of the entry in the City records, however, the procession seems not to have been undertaken before 1514. Rec. of Corp. of Lond. Letter Bk. M. fol. 224.

[58] Ibid. Repert. i, fol. 13, 14.

[59] Grafton, *Chron.* (ed. 1809), ii, 289. See, too, Brewer, *The Reign of Hen. VIII*, i, 245, 249.

[60] 'Chron. of Grey Friars' in *Monum. Francisc.* (Rolls Ser.), ii, 193.

[61] Rec. of the Corp. of Lond. Repert. viii, fol. 62b.

[62] *L. and P. Hen. VIII*, vii, 665.

[63] Ibid. xiii (1). Pref. p. xvi. They were certainly severely treated. See letter of one imprisoned at Stamford. Ibid. vii, 1307.

[64] Ibid. xiii (1), 880.

[65] *L. and P. Hen. VIII*, xiii (1), 658. The accused friar, Geoffrey Turner, had been talking in the buttery with some laymen, and the conversation had turned on King John. The friar had said that the monk reported to have poisoned the king was to be blamed for striking before God struck.

[66] Turner figures as one of the friars at the surrender. *Dep. Keeper's Rep.* viii, App. ii, 28.

[67] In a letter to Master Newell, steward of the archbishop of Canterbury. *L. and P. Hen. VIII*, xiii (2), 251.

[68] Ibid. xiii (2), 808.

[69] Aug. Off. Misc. Bks. 233, fol. 163. The last payment made to him was 35 Hen. VIII. *L. and P. Hen. VIII*, xix (1), 368.

[70] Ibid. xiv (2), 236. They do not appear in the Augmentation accounts after this time, 31 Hen. VIII.

[71] *L. and P. Hen. VIII*, xv, 1032; xvi, 1500; xvii, 1258; xix (1), 1035 (6, 55).

[72] Stow, *Surv. of Lond.* (Strype's ed.), iii, 130. Stow says the church was valued at this amount, but as the church must have been worth much more, I have presumed that he meant the income of the friary.

[73] They benefited considerably by bequests, for although the sums left to them were often small, the friars were remembered in the wills of most London citizens. Another important source of income was the establishment of chantries and obits: in 1458 William Cantelowe arranged that daily masses should be said for him and Thomas Gloucester, and gave to the friars £200 for the repair of their church. Anct. D. (P.R.O.), A. 11314.

[74] *Monastic Treasures* (Abbotsford Club), 19. There are unfortunately very few notices of bequests like that of Marie de St. Pol, countess of Pembroke, who left a gold chalice and an image of St. Louis of France to the high altar of the Friars Minors. Sharpe, *Cal. of Wills*, ii, 195.

## Revised List of Wardens of the Grey Friars

The list below, except where indicated, is taken from John R. H. Moorman, *Medieval Franciscan Houses*, Franciscan Institute Publications History Series No. 4 (New York, 1983), p. 272.

Henry de Treviso, 1224
Solomon, 1231–3
John de Kethene, ?1233[75]
Peter of Tewksbury, 1234–6
Hugh, *c*.1245
A., *c*.1250
Roger of Canterbury, 1257[76]
J., 1282
William de Ludgarshale, vicar 1291[77]
Nicolas, 1294
Henry de Suttone, 1302
Thomas de Whapelad, 1303
Henry de Sutton, 1303, 1307
Robert de Basingstoke, 1309
Thomas de S. Dunston, 1310
Walter de Warleberge, 1311
John de Donton, 1322
William de Querle, 1330
John Mablethorpe, 1368
Robert de Madyngton, 1370

William Newe, 1377
Robert Hyndon, *c*.1391–7[78]
John Lyes, 1396
John Bruyll, 1398
John Kingsham, 1402
Robert Chamberlayn, 1403
Thomas Winchelse, 1422
William Russell, 1425
Roger Juyll, 1437
John Kyrye, 1440; 1458
Richard Clyff, vicar, *c*.1450
William Roser, vicar, *c*.1460
James Walle, *c*.1470[79]
John Allen, *c*.1475[80]
William Goddard jnr., 1485
Richard Shrewsbury, 1486
Robert Ingolsly, vicar, 1494
Andrew Bavard, 1508[81]
Christopher Studley, 1508[82]
Henry Standish, 1514
John Cutler, occurs 1514, 1518
Thomas Cudner, occurs 1526,[83] 1534[84]
Thomas Chapman, surrendered the house in 1539[85]

---

[75] *V.C.H.* lists Peter of Tewksbury before John de Kethene, but the dating is not inconsistent with the order above: in *V.C.H.* John de Kethene is said to have been Warden before 1239, while reference to Peter of Tewkesbury is said to be found in 1234.

[76] Not in *V.C.H.*, where reference to 'A.' is said to have been found *c*.1252–8 (overlapping the date given for the reference to Roger of Canterbury).

[77] Not in *V.C.H.*, where the additional name of Salomon de Ingeham is given (occurs 1292 or 1293). Kingsford (*Grey Friars*, p 54, note 1) comments that de Ingeham was actually a Dominican and the name should therefore not have been in the *V.C.H.* list.

[78] Presumably the 'Robert' of the *V.C.H.* list as references to both occur in the 1390s.

[79] In *V.C.H.* Walle appears immediately after Goddard. Walle is placed much later in the chronological sequence in *V.C.H.* as the date given is that of his death in 1494.

[80] In *V.C.H.* it is suggested that John Allen might occur after William Russell (1425), but it is made clear that this is very uncertain.

[81] Perhaps the 'Andrew' in the *V.C.H.* list.

[82] Not in *V.C.H.* At this point *V.C.H.* includes the name 'Walter Goodfield, *c*.1511(?)'. Goodfield is also mentioned by Kingsford (*Grey Friars*, p. 61). It is not clear why his name is omitted from Moorman's list.

[83] *L. and P. Hen. VIII*, iv (3), 5870 (6).

[84] Ibid. vii, 665.

[85] Ibid. xiii (2), 808.

# 13. THE WHITE FRIARS

## INTRODUCTION

The original article is based on a good crop of printed sources and a few items of unpublished material. It gives a reasonable outline of the convent's history but there has been quite a lot of more recent research. The date of the foundation of the Carmelite priory in Fleet Street is less clear than the original article would suggest, see J. Röhrkasten, 'The Origin and Early Development of the London Mendicant Houses', in T. R. Slater and G. Rosser eds., *The Church in the Medieval Town* (Aldershot, 1998), pp. 76–99, esp. p. 77. The foundations for a new approach were laid by Richard Copsey, who prepared a collection of published as well as many unprinted sources, in *The Medieval Carmelite Priory at London. A Chronology* (Rome, 1995). Moreover the importance of the convent as a house of learning was greater than indicated in the original article: in fact the convent was one of the Order's centres of study where hundreds of friars – also from abroad – received their training, see F.-B. Lickteig, *The German Carmelites at the Medieval Universities* (Rome, 1981). The cultural importance of the London Whitefriars was underlined by the study of one of its liturgical manuscripts, M. Rickert, *The Reconstructed Carmelite Missal* (London 1952). For the library of the house, see K. W. Humphreys (ed.), *The Friars' Libraries*, Corpus of British Medieval Library Catalogues, 1 (London, 1990), pp. 178–88.

Much work has been done on the history of the medieval Carmelites in general and the English province in particular. Crucial is Keith Egan, 'The Establishment and Early Development of the Carmelite Order in England' (unpub. Univ. Cambridge Ph.D. thesis, 1965) which addresses the issue of identity creation by the Order itself and traces the early phases of its English province. Other useful recent writings on the Order in England are: R. Copsey, 'The Carmelites in England 1242–1539: surviving writings', *Carmelus* 44 (1997), pp. 188–202; *idem*, 'The Visit of the Prior General, Peter Terrasse, to England in 1504–1505', *Carmel in Britain*, I (1992), pp. 176–204; *idem*, 'The English Carmelites at the Dissolution', *Carmel in Britain*, III (2004), pp. 327–40.

For the layout and topography of the London convent, see A. W. Clapham, 'The Topography of the Carmelite Priory of London', *Journal of the British Archaeological Association*, n.s. 16 (1910), pp. 15–32. The priory's only surviving physical remains were described by S. Toy, 'The Crypt at Whitefriars, London', *Journal of the British Archaeological Association*, n.s. 38 (1932), pp. 334–9. The topography is also discussed in Jens Röhrkasten, *The Mendicant Houses of Medieval London 1221–1539* (Münster, 2004), pp. 51–4. For the property of the house, see *Documentary Sources*, p. 59.

The turmoil surrounding the poverty debate in the 1460s, has been analysed by F. R. H. Du Boulay, 'The Quarrel Between the Carmelite Friars and the Secular Clergy of London, 1464–68', *Journal of Ecclesiastical History*, 6 (1955), pp. 156–74.

*Jens Röhrkasten*

The house of the Carmelites or White Friars[1] in Fleet Street was founded by Sir Richard Gray, knt., in 1241,[2] and thirteen years afterwards was of such importance that a general chapter of the order was held there.[3] The site was good owing to its proximity to the City and to the river, the main road between London and Westminster. Like all urban or suburban situations in mediaeval times, however, it must have left much to be desired as regards healthiness,

[1] Pope Martin IV changed the cloak of the Carmelites, which before had been of various colours, to white. Walsingham, *Hist. Angl.* (Rolls Ser.), i, 20.
[2] Stow, *Surv. of Lond.* (Strype's ed.), iii, 267.

[3] Villiers de St. Etienne, *Bibl. Carmel.* i, 623.

considering that in 1290 many of the friars died owing to their unsanitary surroundings.[4] The neighbourhood, perhaps because of its being outside the City gates, soon had other drawbacks, and in 1345 the friars complained that they were impeded in the celebration of divine worship by the brawls of people of bad character in the adjoining lane.[5]

The temptations and risks to which religious houses were exposed from the deposit of treasure there are illustrated by the robbery at the White Friars in 1305.[6] The robbers came after the hoard of a certain knight, and were helped by one of the friars. The prior and brethren were bound, and the sum of £400 was carried off by the robbers and their accomplice, who was afterwards caught and hanged.

This incident argues that the house was already of some standing, but its importance increased greatly after the fall of the Templars, when, with the neighbouring priory of the Black Friars, it succeeded to the position hitherto held by the Temple as a centre for the transaction of affairs of state. The Chancery was established there for a time,[7] and, during the reigns of Edward II and Edward III especially, councils, both royal[8] and ecclesiastical,[9] were held at the White Friars.

That the house owed its position not merely to a convenient situation is shown by the employment of its members in political and diplomatic business. The convent seems to have gained its freedom from livery of the king's stewards and marshals through Friar Adam Brown who was a clerk of Edward II.[10] John de Reppes, prior in 1343, was engaged in important negotiations for both the king and the pope between 1344 and 1348.[11] He received in return many privileges from the pope, among them leave to retain his chamber in the London house for life,[12] and faculties similar to those of bishops to meet the requirements of the many noble personages who came to confess to him.[13] This seems to indicate that, like the Franciscans and Dominicans in the

fourteenth century, the White Friars were popular with the English nobility.[14] Their patrons, however, were not all of the one class. Thus, while the priory was rebuilt in 1350 by Hugh Courtenay, earl of Devon,[15] it was to the mayor and commonalty of the City that they owed the grant of Crockers Lane for the west end of their church;[16] and the frequent mention of the friars in the wills of London citizens[17] attests the general favour in which they were held. Moreover, the fraternity of the Conception of the Blessed Virgin Mary, established in the conventual church about 1364, was said to owe its foundation to certain 'poor men' of the City and suburb.[18] It may also be noticed, as bearing on this point, that when the rebels of 1381 were carrying on their work of destruction at the Temple and the Savoy they appear to have left the White Friars in peace, and although one Carmelite, Richard Lavingham, fell a victim to them, it was as a friend of Archbishop Sudbury that he suffered.[19]

Judging from the class of house in the close, the priory must have occupied a large area in 1385;[20] but in 1396 some ground along the river was acquired[21] for the extension of the friary, probably for the rebuilding of the church,[22] of which Sir Robert Knolles[23] bore the main expense. The choir, steeple, and other parts were added somewhat later by Robert Marshall, the Carmelite bishop of Hereford.[24]

Of the Carmelites summoned by the archbishop to the Council of 1382, one, at any rate, John Lovey or Loney,[25] was connected with the London house,[26] which had a not unworthy record in respect of learning. The increase in the library of the Carmelites, which dates from about this period, and was probably one of the fruits of the Wycliffite controversy, affords an example of this point in the

---

[4] *Parl. R.* (Rec. Com.), i, 61. In 1375, on complaint of the White Friars, the mayor and sheriffs were ordered to have a lane cleared of filth. Sharpe, *Cal. of Letter Bk. H*, 16.

[5] *Cal. of Close*, 1343–6, p. 544.

[6] *Flor. Hist.* (Rolls Ser.), iii, 128; *Chron. of Edw. I and Edw. II* (Rolls Ser.), 144.

[7] *Cal. of Close*, 1318–23, p. 313; 1330–3, p. 550; 1337–9, pp. 109, 146, 267, 284, &c.

[8] Ibid. 1307–13, p. 563; 1339–41, p. 339; Sharpe, *Cal. of Letter Bk. D*, 305.

[9] *Chron. of Edw. I and Edw. II* (Rolls Ser.), 286.

[10] *Cal. of Pat.* 1317–21, p. 61. He received the exemption for all houses built by him in the past and future within the precinct of Whitefriars, Fleet Street, and after his death the friary was to continue to enjoy the privilege.

[11] *Cal. Pap. Letters*, iii, 6, 8, 10, 11, 29, 33, 36.

[12] Ibid. 168.

[13] *Cal. Pap. Petitions*, i, 24. He was confessor to the earl of Derby.

[14] The list of persons buried in the church included Sir John Mowbray earl of Nottingham (*d.* 1398), Elizabeth countess of Athole, John Lord Gray, and Lord Vescey (1466). Stow, op. cit. iii, 268.

[15] Ibid. 267.

[16] Pat. 23 Edw. III, pt. 1, m. 7, quoted in Tanner, *Notit. Mon.*

[17] Sharpe, *Cal. of Wills*, i, 271, 404, 577, 620; ii, 107, 210, 232, 300, 375, &c.

[18] Gild Cert. No. 189.

[19] Villiers de St. Etienne, *Bibl. Carmel.* ii, 679.

[20] 26 Oct. 1385, Matilda de Well had licence to crenellate a dwelling in her lodging within the close of the Carmelite Friars. *Cal. of Pat.* 1385–9, p. 42.

[21] Ibid. 1391–6, p. 658.

[22] The church was either not finished or was being repaired in 1275, for the king gave them twelve oaks for the work. *Cal. of Close*, 1272–9, p. 261. The rebuilding probably extended over some time, for a bequest was left to the new work in 1386. Stow, *Surv.* iii, 268.

[23] Stow, op. cit. iii, 268; Fabyan, *Chron.* (ed. Ellis), 573.

[24] Stow, op. cit. iii, 268.

[25] Wilkins, *Concilia Mag. Brit.* iii, 158.

[26] Stevens, *Hist. of Abbeys*, ii, 167. He was buried in the church of the Carmelites, London. Weever, *Anct. Fun. Monuments*, 439.

persons of the two chief contributors, both at one time members of the White Friars, London: Robert Yvory,[27] provincial from 1379 to 1392; and Thomas Walden, confessor and privy counsellor of Henry V and English provincial.[28] But if the new ideas resulted in a multiplication of books to produce the learning to combat them, they also tended to affect the minds of the religious themselves in favour of change,[29] naturally enough if the tale told in 1391 by John Lethinard, an apostate Carmelite of London,[30] be true. There was something wrong when a child of twelve years of age could be persuaded to enter a convent, and when older forced to become professed by intimidation. The story is not improbable, for minors did enter the Mendicant orders,[31] and a Bill was introduced into Parliament in 1414 to forbid it.

In 1443 Pope Eugenius IV commissioned John, abbot of St. Benet of Holme, to try a similar case, that of John Hawteyn, *alias* Scharyngton, who had applied to Rome to be absolved from his vows on the ground that he had been forced against his will to enter the order of Carmelites in London[32] before he had completed his fourteenth year. A witness in his favour stated that Hawteyn at the age of eight had been placed in the London house by his parents, by whom he had afterwards been forced to make profession there, and the latter part of his testimony seems to receive support from the statement made by one of the friars that when Hawteyn ran away he was brought back by his mother. He was imprisoned at the White Friars by order of Thomas Walden, to whom his profession had been made,[33] and was afterwards kept under ward for a time at Oxford. Then, some years later, he tried again to leave the order. The Carmelites, in spite of their declaration that from fear of the statute they never received anyone under the age of fourteen, seem not to have felt very sure of their ground, since it was owing to them that the king stopped the proceedings, and when the royal prohibition was removed and the case resumed in 1446, they did not appear to plead, and the sentence, given March, 1447, was against them, declaring Hawteyn not bound to the observance of the rule.

The religious houses of London seem to be so completely disconnected with the history of the country in the fifteenth century that it is of some interest to find that a council between the two factions was held March, 1458, in the morning at the Black Friars, and in the afternoon at the Carmelites,[34] though it must be added that the two places were evidently chosen merely for their convenient situation.

The friars and the secular clergy had united for a short time in face of a common danger, but their interests were too much opposed to allow of a lasting peace between them. The Mendicants, who had been the party attacked in the fourteenth century,[35] in 1465 took the offensive. The incident seems to indicate that the popularity of the White Friars had somewhat waned, since Harry Parker, the Carmelite friar who preached the sermon at St. Paul's Cross[36] comparing the beneficed clergy to their disparagement with the friars as followers of Christ, owned afterwards that his sole object had been to draw attention to his convent for its pecuniary advantage. Attention was certainly attracted, but hardly with the result expected. William Ive, master of Whittington College, took up the gauntlet on behalf of the beneficed clergy, and disproved Parker's arguments, particularly the statement that Christ Himself was a beggar, the following Sunday. In the disputations that followed at the White Friars, the prior and provincial of the order, Dr. John Milverton, and Dr. Haldon, also a Carmelite of London, laid themselves open to a charge of heresy, and were cited to appear before the bishop of London. They pleaded privilege, but this did not avail in case of heresy, and on their failing to appear they were excommunicated, Ive pronouncing the sentence at St. Paul's Cross. Parker, the cause of all the commotion, was imprisoned by the bishop and abjured. Milverton, the provincial, had meanwhile gone to Rome to lay the matter before the pope, but he had no better fortune, being kept in the Castle of St. Angelo until he submitted. The king is said indeed to have asked the pope to punish the friars for creating the disturbance.

After this episode the White Friars seem to have been contented with obscurity. John Souley, one of the friars, formed a link between the traditions of his house and the new age as a man of learning and eloquence and a friend of Dean Colet.[37] Such notices of the house as occur indicate that it was still regarded with favour by the upper classes of the community: Lord Vescey was buried there according to his will of May 1466;[38] Sir John Paston in the Lady

---

27 Stevens, op. cit. ii, 167. Yvory was a Londoner of the rich merchant class. Villiers de St. Etienne, op. cit. ii, 693.

28 Stevens, op. cit. ii, 171.

29 The cases of apostasy from the various orders show this. For a Carmelite friar see *Cal. of Pat.* 1391–8, p. 357.

30 Lond. Epis. Reg. Braybrook, fol. 322–3.

31 Sharpe, *Cal. of Wills*, i, 382. In the will of John de Gloucestre, rector of Herdyngton, legacies were left to two friars of the Carmelite order for their clothing, and a guardian was appointed during their minority.

32 B. M. Chart. L. F. C. xx, 13.

33 He was called Walden's 'beaufitz,' and Walden, afraid that he might be suspected of favouring him on that account, insisted on his punishment.

34 Gairdner, *The Paston Letters*, i, 426.

35 By the archbishop of Armagh.

36 *Coll. of a Lond. Citizen* (Camd. Soc.), 228, &c.

37 Stevens, *Hist. of Abbeys*, ii, 175.

38 Nicolas, *Testamenta Vetusta*, 302.

Chapel of the church in 1479;[39] and the Marquis of Berkeley by his will of 5 February, 1491, arranged for the establishment of a perpetual chantry of two friars at the altar of St. Gascon;[40] moreover, when in 1527 the prior found himself unable to proceed with the rebuilding of a house in the precinct for lack of money, Margaret countess of Kent came to their aid with a loan of £60 that they might remember in their prayers her late husband who was buried in their church, and herself when she was dead.[41] Nor were signs of the king's goodwill altogether lacking.[42]

How far the prior, George Burnham, in acknowledging the king as supreme head of the church 17 April 1534,[43] represented the opinions of the friars it is impossible to tell.[44] Information was laid against one of them, Robert Austyn by name, for a sermon preached in St. Bride's June 1537 which showed that he preferred if possible to avoid the subject.[45] But actual opposition to the new doctrines was doubtless felt to be worse than useless when the provincial, a supporter of the royal policy,[46] had his head quarters there.[47] The priory was surrendered 10 November, 1538, the deed being signed by the prior John Gybbes and twelve friars.[48] Gybbes was in receipt of a pension of £10 until March 1544.[49] The possessions of the house, estimated as worth £26 7s. 3d. per annum by Stow[50] and £63 11s. 4d. by Dugdale,[51] included tenements in the parishes of St. Dunstan in the West[52] and St. Olave near the Tower,[53] but the most valuable part of the

property must have been the convent buildings and precinct which consisted of the church, chapter house, dormitory, fratry, kitchen, library, the cloister with its green, and several gardens, and which stretched from Fleet Street to the Thames and from Water Lane on the east to Serjeants' Inn and the Temple on the west.[54] The amount of plate belonging to the church, 114 oz. in gilt plate, 100 oz. parcel gilt, 244 oz. of white plate,[55] does not argue great riches or extravagant display.

*M. Reddan*

## Revised List of Priors

An amended version of the original list in *V.C.H. London* i

John Palgrave, named as prior without date[56]
John de Lacok, occurs 1309[57]
Edmund de Norwich, occurs 1323[58]
Osbert Pickingham, occurs 1330[59]
John Elin, occurs 1339[60]
John de Reppes, occurs 1343[61]
John Elm, occurs 1379[62]
Thomas Brome, occurs 1380[63]
John Loney, probably before 1393[64]
John French, occurs 1391[65]
Richard Lavenham, occurs 1399[66]
John Boteler, occurs 1406[67]
William Asshwell, occurs 1425[68]
Andrew Canterbury, occurs 1437[69]
Thomas Asshewell, occurs 1449, 1450, 1464[70]
John Milverton, occurs 1446[71]

[39] Gairdner, *The Paston Letters*, iii, 207, 262.

[40] Nicolas, op. cit. 408.

[41] Harl. Chart. 79, F. 32.

[42] Aug. 1509 Henry contributed £13 6s. 8d. to their general chapter on St. Laurence's Eve. *L. and P. Hen. VIII*, ii (2), p. 1457. A payment of £6 15s. to the prior and provincial of the White Friars is also noted 25 December 1530 among the King's Privy Purse Expenses. Ibid. v, p. 753.

[43] *L. and P. Hen. VIII*, vii, 665.

[44] In 1534 Cromwell evidently had his eye on the house, for among his remembrances is a list of books which the late prior had had of various printers. Ibid. vii, 923.

[45] Ibid. xii (2), 65. Two of the points against him were that he omitted the reverence due to his Prince and Supreme Head under God and that he did not preach against the usurped power of the bishop of Rome.

[46] John Bird, D.D., was appointed one of the preachers for Easter 1537. He was made bishop of Penrith 15 June, 1537, and afterwards bishop of Bangor and of Chester. *L. and P. Hen. VIII*, xii (1), 726, and note; xii (2), 191 (19).

[47] Ibid. xvi, 1500 (37b).

[48] Ibid. xiii (2), 788.

[49] Aug Off. Bk. 233, fol. 161b; *L. and P. Hen. VIII*, xix (1), 368, fol. 13. It was a life pension. The friars do not seem to have received pensions, at any rate none is recorded in the augmentation books.

[50] Stow, *Surv. of Lond.* (Strype's ed.), iii, 267. In the margin there is a note that the sum was given in the first edition as £62.

[51] Dugdale, *Mon. Angl.* vi, 1572.

[52] *L. and P. Hen. VIII*, xv, 210; xix (1), 1035 (15); see also *Cal. Inq. a.q.d.* (Rec. Com.), 363 and 382, for property here in reigns of Hen. IV and Hen. VI.

[53] *L. and P. Hen. VIII*, xix (2), 340 (34).

[54] Ibid. xv, 924 (105), xvi, 678 (24).

[55] *Monastic Treasures* (Abbotsford Club), 19.

[56] Weever, *Monuments*, 439.

[57] T.N.A. E403/143 m. 3.

[58] T.N.A. E403/202 m.6; E404/1/8 no. 67.

[59] Villiers de S. Etienne, *Bibl. Carm.* II, 521; B.L. MS Harl. 3838 fol.l 6r; *B.R.U.O.*, III, 1481.

[60] Stevens, *Hist. of Abbeys*, ii, 166.

[61] *Calendar of Papal Registers, Petitions, 1342–1419*, 24.

[62] T.N.A. E403/427 m 23; *B.R.U.C.*, 208

[63] T.N.A. C81/1793/19; *B.R.U.C.*, 95–6

[64] There are different dates of death: 1382 in B.L. MS Harl. 3838 fol. 80r–v and 1390 in *B.R.U.O.*, II, 1159; however, a London Carmelite of this name is still mentioned in the will of Thomas Vincent, mercer, in 1393, G.L. MS 9171/1 fol. 275r–276r.

[65] *Cal. Plea and Memoranda R.* (Lond.), 1381–1412, p. 179; he is perhaps identical with the prior John who requested the arrest of an apostate in 1393, T.N.A. C81/1793/27.

[66] G.L. MS 9171/3 fol. 53r; *B.R.U.O.*, II, 1109/10.

[67] *Cal. of Close* 1405–9, 149.

[68] G.L. MS 9171/3 fol. 131r–v.

[69] *Cal. Plea and Memoranda R.* (Lond.), 1413–37, p. 300.

[70] T.N.A. KB27/752 m 29d (*ex inf.* Dr. Susanne Jenks); *Cal of Close* 1461–68, 245; B.L. Lord Frederick Campbell Chs. xx.3.

[71] B.L. MS Harl. 1819 fols. 43v, 107r–v, 216v.

William Swafham, occurs 1465[72]
Andreas, occurs as 'nuper prior' 1483[73]
Thomas, occurs as former prior 1492[74]
William Bachelor, occurs 1507[75]
Master Thomas Lyell, occurs 1518[76]
John Whytynge, occurs as 1524[77]

Thomas Gaskyn, occurs 1527[78]
John Kele, occurs 1533[79]
George Burnham, occurs 1534[80]
John Gybbes (Cobbys), occurs 1538[81]

John Blysse, 1521 informator philosophie, magister novitiorum[82]

[72] Mentioned in the will of John Queldryk, G.L. MS 9171/5 fol. 193v–104r; not in office 1466 ('nuper prior', ibid. fol. 384r–385r); prior again in 1473 (G.L. MS 9171/6 fol. 132v–133r), *B.R.U.O.*, III, 1827.
[73] G.L. MS 9171/6 fol. 357v–358r.
[74] T.N.A. PROB11/9 fol. 88r–89r.
[75] T.N.A. E328/274.
[76] G.L. MS 9171/9 fol. 114v–115r.
[77] Copsey, *Carmelite Priory at London*, 49; *B.R.U.C.*, 638.

[78] B.L. Harl. Ch. 79 F. 32.
[79] *L. and P. Hen. VIII*, XVI, no. 1500 (22b).
[80] *L. and P. Hen. VIII*, VII, no. 665.
[81] T.N.A. E322/140; E314/77/5 fol. 9r.
[82] G.L. MS 9171/9 fol. 192v, 193v, 194v.

# 14. THE AUSTIN FRIARS

## INTRODUCTION

This article on the Austin Friars contains some useful material and the section on the convent's history in the sixteenth century is relatively detailed. Nevertheless it has clearly been overtaken by more recent research. It is, for example, no longer possible to deny the popular support for the house, see J. Röhrkasten, 'Londoners and London Mendicants in the Late Middle Ages', *Journal of Ecclesiastical History*, 47 (1996), pp. 446–77. For the library of the house, see K. W. Humphreys (ed.), *The Friars' Libraries*, Corpus of British Medieval Library Catalogues, 1 (London, 1990), pp. 7–9.

Significant progress has been made in the study of the Order as a whole as well as in the reconstruction of its English province. Important studies include: F. Mathes, 'The Poverty Movement and the Augustinian Hermits', *Analecta Augustiniana*, 31 (1968), pp. 5–154, 32 (1969), pp. 5–116; and A. Gwynn, *The English Austin Friars in the Time of Wyclif* (Oxford, 1940). F. Roth, *The English Austin Friars, 1249–1538*, 2 vols., Cassiciacum, 4 (New York, 1966) provides a history of the province with sections on the major convents, with a second volume consisting entirely of source translations. Other recent literature is discussed in F. Andrews, *The Other Friars. The Carmelite, Augustinian, Sack and Pied Friars* (Woodbridge 2006), pp. 69–171, 238–43.

There was considerable interest in the London convent in the early twentieth century: W. Cater, 'The Austin Friars, London', *Journal of the British Archaeological Association*, n.s. 18 (1912), pp. 25–44, 57–82; *idem*, 'Further Notes on the Austin Friars', *ibidem*, n.s. 21 (1915), pp. 205–30 and E. A. Foran, 'Historical Notes on Austin Friars, London', *The Irish Ecclesiastical Record*, 8 (1916), pp. 35–46; 9 (1917), pp. 130–53. Concerns about property holding by the London Austin Friars were included in a more general article by A. G. Little, 'A Royal Inquiry into Property Held by the Mendicant Friars in England in 1349 and 1350', in *Historical Essays in Honour of James Tait*, eds. J. G. Edwards, V. H. Galbraith and E. F. Jacob (Manchester, 1933), pp. 179–88. For the property of the houses, see *Documentary Sources*, p. 58

For a more recent attempt to set the history of the convent within the topographical and historical development of the city, see: J. Röhrkasten, 'The Origin and Early Development of the London Mendicant Houses', in *The Church in the Medieval Town*, eds. T. R. Slater and G. Rosser (Aldershot, 1998), pp. 76–99 and *idem*, *The Mendicant Houses of Medieval London 1221–1539*, Vita regularis, 21 (Münster, 2004) where the contribution of the convent to the religious life of the city is discussed.

*Jens Röhrkasten*

The earliest settlement of the Friars Hermits of the order of St. Augustine in these islands was made in Wales in 1252.[1] It was here probably that Humphrey de Bohun, earl of Hereford and Essex, and constable of England, came into contact with them on his return from the Crusade, since in 1253 he founded the house of that order near the church of St. Peter le Poor in Broad Street, London.[2]

The Austin Friars never seem to have aroused in the slightest degree the enthusiasm manifested by London citizens[3] for the Franciscans, neither did they show any of the abnegation and love of poverty which were the distinguishing features of the Grey Friars in the early days of the order. The site of the house, which was very different from that of Newgate, was not, of course, chosen by

---

[1] Stevens, *Hist. of Abbeys*, ii, 221.
[2] Stow, *Surv. of Lond.* (ed. Strype), 114.

[3] The bequests to them judged from Sharpe, *Cal. of Wills*, were inconsiderable.

them, but within thirty years of the foundation an incident occurred in which they display a distinctly grasping spirit. Sir Henry de Chikehull had given them a piece of land in Chichester subject to the condition that it was lawful for them to retain it. It was afterwards found that as the land was within a certain distance of the settlement of the Friars Minors of that city, it could not be possessed by any other order without infringing the privileges granted to the Franciscans by the pope. The Austin Friars were so reluctant to relinquish all claim to it that while they gave up the land they retained the title-deeds, until Chikehull at last, in 1382, invoked the aid of Archbishop Peckham.[4]

They were accused in 1321 of raising walls without any right in the parishes of Allhallows on the Wall and St. Peter's, Broad Street,[5] and it looks as if they had been taking advantage of the disturbances of the reign to encroach on the land on both sides. They may certainly have been tempted by their need of more space, for in 1334 they obtained some ground in order to extend their buildings,[6] and in 1345 Reginald de Cobham granted them three messuages for the same purpose,[7] while about this time other tenements were acquired from the priory of St. Mary without Bishopsgate.[8] The arrangement made with the rector of St. Peter's, Broad Street, as to tithes and oblations in 1349 points to recent acquisitions in the parish.[9] The rebuilding of their church in 1354 they owed to a descendant of their founder, another Humphrey de Bohun, earl of Hereford and Essex,[10] and the house doubtless benefited in 1361 under the will of the earl, who left 300 marks for masses to be sung by friars of the order.[11] Repairs were very soon necessary, for the tall and slender steeple was ruined by a storm in 1362.

The convent saw something of the horrors of 1381: thirteen Flemings who had taken refuge in the church were dragged out and killed by the mob,[12] but the animosity of the rioters does not seem to have extended to the friars.

In the contest of the Mendicants with the archbishop of Armagh no special share can be assigned to the Austin Friars of London; in the controversy with Wycliffe, however, they were well represented by Banchin, a friar of their house and afterwards prior, who took an active part in exposing the errors of his teaching in the council of 1382.[13] Five years later the convent came into contact with the Lollards in a more exciting way. A certain Peter Patteshull,[14] who had once been an Austin Friar and had become a Lollard, preached in the church of St. Christopher to a congregation imbued with the same views as himself, on the iniquities practised by the members of his old order.[15] Some of the convent, being informed, came to the church to hear him, and one openly protested. The Lollards set upon him, turned the friars out of the church, and roused by the charges made by Patteshull, determined to burn down the friary. They were checked by the prayers of two of the friars, and by that time one of the sheriffs arrived and persuaded them to disperse without doing any damage. How much foundation Patteshull had for his accusations – which were aimed at no particular friary, but at the order generally – it is impossible to say. Two friars had left the London house in 1364, taking with them books and other goods,[16] apparently owing to a disagreement with their superiors, and another had apostatized in 1387,[17] but neither case proves anything as to the state of the convent.

The formation of libraries seems to have been a feature of the age, and in this respect the Austin Friars were not behind the London friars of other orders, Prior John Low making great additions to the books of the house in the early fifteenth century.[18] Two members at least of the London convent besides Banchin and Low were renowned for their learning: Thomas Pemchet, D.D., who taught divinity at Pavia, became provincial of England, and died in London in 1487; and John Tonney, at one time also provincial, who died in 1490.[19]

The dynastic struggles which follow are not marked in any way in the history of the house except by the burial in their church of nobles who died on the scaffold or the battlefield,[20] for this church, like those of the other London friars, was a favourite

---

[4] *Reg. Epist. Johan. Peckham* (Rolls Ser.), i, 365.

[5] *Cal. of Close,* 1318–23, p. 314.

[6] *Cal. of Pat.* 1334–8, p. 31.

[7] Ibid. 1343–5, p. 458.

[8] *Lond. and Midd. Arch. Soc. Trans.* ii, 13.

[9] Doc. of D. and C. of St. Paul's, A. Box 22, No. 1654.

[10] *Fabyan Chron.* (ed. Ellis), 464; Stow, *Surv. of Lond.* (ed. Strype), ii, 114. The church was evidently large. It had two chapels, one dedicated to St. Thomas, the other to St. John, and altars to St. James and St. Mary in the east wing of the church. Harl. MS. 6033, fol. 31.

[11] Nichols, *Royal Wills,* 44.

[12] Stow, *Annals* (ed. 1615), 288.

[13] Stevens, *Hist. of Abbeys,* ii, 218; Wilkins, *Concilia,* iii, 158.

[14] He was a doctor of divinity of Oxford, and was celebrated for his learned sermons. Stevens, op. cit. ii, 218.

[15] Walsingham, *Hist. Angl.* (Rolls Ser.), 157, 158.

[16] *Cal. of Pap. Letters,* iv, 42, 43.

[17] *Cal. of Pat.* 1388–9, pp. 324, 386.

[18] Leland, *Coll.* iii, 54; Stevens, op. cit. ii, 219. Low, who was a noted persecutor of heretics, died 1436.

[19] Stevens, op. cit. ii, 220.

[20] Stow, *Surv. of Lond.* (ed. Strype), ii, 115. John de Vere, earl of Oxford, beheaded in 1463, and many of the barons slain at Barnet in 1471, were buried in this church.

place of sepulture with persons of high degree.[21] The friary probably profited considerably in this way: the Marquis of Berkeley gave the convent £100 for perpetual masses for the soul of his first wife Joan, who was buried there;[22] and Sir Thomas Brandon, who married the marquis's widow, bequeathed £60 in 1509 to establish a chantry for the marquis and this lady.[23]

In the reign of Henry VIII some light is thrown on the condition of the priory. In 1525 some of the friars were put in the Tower because a friar had died in their prison.[24] Whether anything was discovered detrimental to the priory or not, it was to this house that Dr. Barnes was sent in 1526 after he had done penance at St. Paul's for his heretical opinions.[25] Little restraint can have been put on him as the account of a heretic shows to whom he sold an English New Testament. Tyball went to the Austin Friars for the express purpose of getting the book and found Barnes in his rooms and several people with him, among them a merchant.[26] As Barnes was allowed to receive any visitors he chose he can have had little difficulty in obtaining these books, for the convent was surrounded by foreign merchants[27] who lived in houses within the close.[28] Apart, however, from the views of individual friars the priory's attitude with regard to the king's marriage and the questions arising from it is easily explicable. Cromwell lived near, and in 1532 began to build his huge house on land leased from the convent and adjoining their churchyard.[29] He therefore had exceptional opportunities for interference and influence,[30] of which he undoubtedly took advantage. He found a willing instrument in the prior, George Brown, who identified himself with the king's side,[31] and was duly rewarded afterwards by being chosen to be one

of the commissioners to visit all the houses of friars in England.[32] The principles of the rest of the house were not likely to prove an obstacle to Cromwell's wishes if some anonymous information[33] about 1534 against the friars be true. In this it is said that the services were scamped and neglected while the friars sat drinking in bad company; there was no common refectory, but they dined in sets in their rooms; no rules were kept, and the authority of the prior, who was incapable of maintaining discipline, was utterly disregarded. Although Brown does not seem to have been prior at this date[34] he must be held in some measure responsible for a state of things which could not have been of sudden development.[35] As is not unusual, the friars, while forgetting their duties had a keen idea of their rights, and in October, 1532, six of them had to do penance for a contest with the priest of St. Dunstan's in the East over the body of a stranger who had died in that parish.[36]

When in August, 1538, their church was used by the Lutheran preacher who came in the train of the Saxon and Hessian ambassadors[37] the end of the friary must have been felt to be near. In the following November the house was surrendered by the prior Thomas Hamond and twelve friars.[38]

The income of the convent, estimated at £57 0s. 4d.,[39] was derived from tenements in various London parishes, St. Benet Fink,[40] St. Andrew Eastcheap,[41] St. Lawrence,[42] Allhallows the Great, St. Martin (?) Queenhithe, and St. Christopher,[43] besides its principal holding in the parish of St. Peter le Poor, where one of its earliest possessions was the ground on which the church of St. Olave had stood.[44] A piece of their property can still be identified, for Cromwell's house after his attainder was sold to the Drapers' Company,[45] whose hall now occupies the

---

[21] Among those buried here were Humphrey de Bohun, earl of Essex, 1361, (Nicolas, *Test. Vet.* 66); Lucia, daughter of Bernaby Visconti, lord of Milan, and wife of the earl of Kent, died 1424; Richard, earl of Arundel, beheaded 1397; Aubrey de Vere, son and heir of the earl of Oxford; the marquis of Berkeley under his will of 1491; and Edward duke of Buckingham, beheaded in 1521 (Stow, op. cit. ii, 115, 116).

[22] Dugdale, *Baronage of Engl.* i, 365.

[23] Nicolas, *Test. Vet.* 497.

[24] *Monum. Francisc.* ii, 191.

[25] *Dict. Nat. Biog.* iii, 254.

[26] *L. and P. Hen. VIII,* iv (2), 4218.

[27] It had long been a foreign quarter. Chapuys lived close to the church. Ibid. x, 351. In 1535 the Spaniards wished to celebrate the emperor's victory in Africa in the church of the Austin Friars, but the provincial refused leave until he knew the king's pleasure. Ibid. ix, 330.

[28] Ibid. vii, 1670.

[29] Ibid. v, 1028.

[30] He appears to have had something to do with the election of Thomas Hamond as sub-prior. Ibid. vi, 1270.

[31] It was Brown who in his Easter sermon in 1533 recommended the people expressly to pray for Queen Anne, at which they left the church. Ibid. vi, 391.

[32] Ibid. vii, 233, sec. 18. He was then provincial.

[33] The jealousy of the alien friars which the writer displays, and his petition that the prior may be dismissed, show that the informer was one of the friars. Ibid. vii, 1670.

[34] There is no date to the document, which occurs among the papers of 1534. As Brown was provincial in April of that year, the prior referred to was probably Thomas Hamond.

[35] The house could hardly have become indebted to the extent of £300 in a few months. *L. and P. Hen. VIII,* vii, 676.

[36] Ibid. vi, 1270.

[37] Ibid. xiii (2), 232.

[38] Ibid. 806.

[39] Stow, *Surv. of Lond.* ii, 115. The plate amounted to 200 oz. in gilt and 176 oz. of silver gilt. *Monastic Treas.* 19 (Abbotsford Club). As the house was or had been in debt, some may have been sold.

[40] *L. and P. Hen. VIII,* xviii (1), 982.

[41] *L. and P. Hen. VIII,* xix (1), 1035 (6).

[42] Ibid. xix (2), 340 (34).

[43] Ibid. xix (2), 340 (51).

[44] Doc. D. and C. of St. Paul's, Liber A. fol. 64 b. Their agreement with the archdeacon of London about dues from this land is dated 1271.

[45] *L. and P. Hen. VIII,* xviii (2), 231 (12).

site. The friars seem also to have had possessions in the counties of Essex and Sussex.[46]

*M Reddan*

## Revised List of Priors of the Austin Friars

This is an amended version of the original list in the *V.C.H.*

William de Clare, occurs 1279[47]
Richard de Clare, occurs 1310[48]
Thomas de Dunolm, occurs 1322[49]
John, occurs 1349[50]
John de Ardern, occurs 1354–64[51]
William de Ainukelan, occurs 1364[52]
Robert Burton, occurs 1377[53]
Thomas Ashbourn, occurs 1383[54]
John Caustun, occurs 1386[55]
John Banchin (Bankyn, Bankynus), occurs 1387[56]
John Peter, occurs 1389[57]
John, occurs 1395[58]
John Brome, occurs early 15th century[59]

John Clerk, occurs 1419–22[60]
Master John Lowe, occurs 1428[61]
William Russell, occurs 1439[62]
Robert Giffharde, occurs 1463[63]
John Bury, occurs 1472[64]
Richard Blenet, occurs 1475[65]
James (perhaps Jacobus Hagis?), occurs 1490[66]
Nandinus de Belbe, occurs 1486–92[67]
John Bedford, occurs 1496[68]
Dr Yong, occurs 1508[69]
John Toneys, occurs 1513[70]
Gilbert Rose, occurs 1519[71]
Edmund Bellond, occurs 1520–1524[72]
Gilbert Rose, occurs 1525[73]
John Hendre, occurs 1531[74]
George Brown, occurs 1532–36[75]
Thomas Hamond, 1536–38[76]

### *Subpriors*

Thomas Letse, occurs 1364[77]
Roger Brerley, occurs 1499[78]

---

[46] The deed of surrender made mention of the house and all its possessions in counties Middlesex, Essex, Sussex, and elsewhere in England. Ibid. xiii (2), 806.

[47] Roth, *English Austin Friars*, ii, no. 220.

[48] T.N.A. E403/152 m 1.

[49] T.N.A. E403/200 m 2; B.L. MS Stowe 553 fol. 8r, 23r.

[50] *V.C.H. London*, i. 513.

[51] Perhaps Ainukelan's immediate predecessor: *Cal. of Close*, 1354–60, 59; Roth, *English Austin Friars* ii, nos. 409, 446, 483, 484; T.N.A. C81/1794/9).

[52] *Calendar of Papal Registers*, Letters, iv, 43.

[53] T.N.A. E403/461 m 20.

[54] G.L. MS 9171/1 fol. 108v–109v; *B.R.U.O.*, i, 54.

[55] Roth, *English Austin Friars*, II, no. 576.

[56] T.N.A. C81/1794/10; *Cal. of Pat.* 1385–89, 386; *B.R.U.O.*, i, 104.

[57] Roth, *English Austin Friars*, ii, no. 599.

[58] Roth, *English Austin Friars*, ii, no. 636.

[59] E.A. Foran, 'Historical Notes on Austin Friars, London', *Irish Ecclesiastical Record*, 5th ser. 8 (1916) pp. 35–46; 9 (1917) 130–53, p. 143.

[60] Roth, *English Austin Friars*, ii, nos. 607, 713.

[61] Gwynn, *English Austin Friars*, 281; *B.R.U.O.*, ii, 1168–9.

[62] C.L.R.O. HR164 (64); *B.R.U.O.*, iii, 1612.

[63] Roth, *English Austin Friars*, ii, nos. 871, 877.

[64] Ibid. no. 902; Emden, *B.R.U.O.*, I, 323.

[65] B.L. Harl. Ch. III C 23; Roth, *English Austin Friars*, ii, no. 911.

[66] T.N.A. LR14/87.

[67] Roth, *English Austin Friars*, ii, nos. 944, 946.

[68] Ibid. II, no. 971.

[69] Ibid. II, no. 992.

[70] Ibid. II, no. 1012; *B.R.U.C.*, 590/1.

[71] T.N.A. LR14/491; *B.R.U.C.*, 488–9.

[72] Roth, *English Austin Friars*, ii, nos. 1032, 1049; *B.R.U.C.*, 53.

[73] Roth, *English Austin Friars*, ii, no. 1064.

[74] T.N.A. LR14/90; *B.R.U.O.*, ii, 907.

[75] Roth, *English Austin Friars*, ii, nos. 1081, 1083, 1090, 1092, 1093, 1177; T.N.A. LR14/787.

[76] T.N.A. E322/131; LR14/86; LR14/708; Roth, *English Austin Friars*, ii, no. 1177

[77] Roth, *English Austin Friars*, ii, no. 484.

[78] T.N.A. PROB11/12 fol. 53v–54r.

# 15. THE FRIARS OF THE SACK OR OF THE PENANCE OF JESUS CHRIST

## INTRODUCTION

This account of the 'Fratres de Poenitentia Jesu Christi' does not really do justice to the subject. Although the Order was blocked from further development by a decision of the Second Council of Lyons in 1274 and it did not survive beyond the second decade of the fourteenth century, the Friars of the Sack formed a major religious organisation, comparable to that of the Carmelites, in their time.

This account should now be supplemented by reference to A. G. Little, 'The Friars of the Sack', *Eng. Hist. Rev.,* 9 (1894), pp. 121–7, which provides a brief introduction, since updated by general articles as well as those dealing specifically with the English province. Important articles are: R. W. Emery, 'The Friars of the Sack', *Speculum,* 18 (1943), pp. 323–34 and H. F. Chettle, 'The Friars of the Sack in England', *Downside Review* 63 (1945), pp. 239–51. The more recent literature is summarised in: R. I. Burns, 'Penitenza di Gesù Cristo, Frati della', in *Dizionario degli Istituti de Perfezione,* VI (Rome, 1980), col. 1393 and in F. Andrews, *The Other Friars. The Carmelite, Augustinian, Sack and Pied Friars* (Woodbridge 2006), pp. 175–223, 243–4.

The Order originated in Queen Eleanor's homeland of Provence and it is no coincidence that she was a major supporter of the friars in London. More recent work on the London convent can be found in: J. Röhrkasten, 'Mendicants in the Metropolis: the Londoners and the development of the London Friaries', in *Thirteenth Century England* VI, ed. M. Prestwich, R. H. Britnell and R. Frame, (Woodbridge, 1997), pp. 61–75; *idem,* 'The Origin and Early Development of the London Mendicant Houses' in, *The Church in the Medieval Town,* eds. T. R. Slater and G. Rosser (Aldershot, 1998), pp. 76–99 and *idem, The Mendicant Houses of Medieval London,* Vita regularis, 21 (Münster, 2004), pp. 57–60, 428–30.

*Jens Röhrkasten*

It was in 1257[1] that the friars of the Sack first appeared in London, where they were received and recommended by Peter of Tewkesbury in the chapter of the Franciscans.[2] They settled in a spot outside Aldersgate,[3] but afterwards removed to Coleman Street,[4] evidently close to a synagogue, for in 1271–2 they were said to be disturbed at their devotions by the howling of the Jews in their church. As a remedy Henry III gave the friars the synagogue to increase their house, and, while giving the despoiled Jews permission to build another, ordered them to be less noxious to the friars.[5]

At some date between 1265 and September 1271,[6] they bought from Queen Eleanor, then warden of London Bridge, for the sum of 60 marks and the maintenance of the chantry of Richard le Kew, certain tenements in Colechurch Street, in the parish of St. Olave Jewry, and of St. Margaret Lothbury. They also possessed houses in Candelwyk Street (Cannon Street), in the parish of St. Mary Abchurch,[7] bequeathed to them by Gilbert de Tanyngton as the endowment of a chantry. In spite of the suppression of the smaller orders of Mendicants by the Council of Lyons in 1274, the little community in London managed to maintain itself for some years longer. It figured in the wardrobe accounts of 28th year of Edward I,[8]

---

[1] *Engl. Hist. Review,* ix, article by Mr. Little, who refers to Matthew Paris, *Chron. Maj.* v, 612, 621.
[2] *Monumenta Francisc.* (Rolls Ser.), 72.
[3] Stow, *Surv. of Lond.* iii, 53.
[4] The hospital of St. Thomas of Acon held houses in 'Colchurche Strete,' opposite the church of the Friars of the Penance of Jesus Christ. See Cartulary printed in Watney, *Hospital of St. Thomas of Acon,* 256.
[5] Tovey, *Anglia Judaica,* 192. Tovey refers to Close, 56 Hen. III, m. 3.

[6] Sharpe, *Cal. of Letter Bk.* C, 61.
[7] Sharpe, *Cal. of Wills,* i, 14.
[8] *Liber Quotid. Contrarotul. Garderob.* 28 *Edw. I,* 31. 12 March, to the Friars of the Sack by Friar Edmund de Dover there, 19s.

and was still in existence in October, 1302.[9] But the condition of the friars must have been the reverse of flourishing, and in March, 1305,[10] the king granted them licence to make over their chapel to Robert Fitzwalter, who was to make himself responsible for a chantry of two chaplains for the souls of Eleanor the late queen, the king's ancestors, and others.

The house was presided over by priors, none of whose names survive.

*M. Reddan*

## Priors and Officers of the House

Since the appearance of the original *V.C.H.* article, some names have been discovered.

### *Prior*
Robert de Mapodre, 1274[11]

### *Subcustos*
Stephanus de Folburn[12]

---

[9] *Cal. of Pat.* 1301–7, p. 47.
[10] Ibid. 316. Robert Fitzwalter had petitioned the king for this licence in 1304. See *Parl. R.* (Rec. Com.), i, 162.

[11] C.L.R.O., HR6(32).
[12] C.L.R.O., Liber Horn fol. 285r.

# 16. THE CROSSED FRIARS

## INTRODUCTION

This article remains a generally sound account of the London house, although it is now clear that it was established before 1298: see Chester R.O. DCH/O/56. For a general history of the Order and for other events related to the London house, see Henry Chettle, 'The Friars of the Holy Cross in England', *History*, 34 (1949), pp. 204–220. For an understanding of the role played by the Crossed Friars, and the other mendicant houses in London, Jens Röhrkasten's *The Mendicant Houses of Medieval London 1221–1539* (Münster, 2004) is now indispensable. For England's interaction with the General Chapter in Brussels, as well as the development of the London house in the fifteenth century, see J. Michael Hayden, 'Religious Reform and Religious Orders in England, 1490–1540: the case of the Crutched Friars', *Catholic Hist. Rev.,* 86 (2000), pp. 420–38, esp. pp. 423–5, 429–36.

For descriptions, dimensions, names of previous owners and occupants of properties owned by the Friars, see Honeybourne, 'Property', pp. 215–37 and *Documentary Sources*, no. 93. For the taxation and properties of the Order in London in the late fourteenth century, see McHardy, *Church in London*, pp. 54, 56, 69, 76.

J. Michael Hayden, 'The Crutched Friars Revisited', *Clairlieu* (1995), pp. 64–85 has a list of nearly 200 clerics and lay brothers of the Crossed Friars in England, many from the London house, between 1234–1569.

*Jennifer Ledfors*

The Friars of the Holy Cross are said to have first come to England about 1244,[1] but it was not until 1298 that they obtained a footing in London. About that date, on land in Hart[2] Street, at first rented and afterwards bought from the prior of Christchurch, Aldgate, their house was founded by Ralph Hosier and William Sabernes, who afterwards themselves joined the order. During the following twenty years they were engaged in building the monastery and church,[3] to the great dissatisfaction of the rector of St. Olave's, who found himself thus deprived of a source of income. At length a settlement[4] was made by the dean of Arches and Stephen, bishop of London, which provided that all who so chose might be buried in the conventual church and cemetery, but the rector was to have the burial dues of those who belonged to or had died in his parish; the maintenance of a lamp in the church of St. Olave, and payment of an annual sum of 2½ marks, secured the priory from all other demands of the rector, who on his side was not to hinder the dedication of the monastery, church, and cemetery.

The material progress of the priory was not rapid, the acquisition of land and rent to the yearly value of 100s., for which they had received licence in 1331,[5] taking twelve years.[6] This property lay in Tooting,[7] Tooting-Graveney,[8] and 'Legham',[9] co. Surrey, and in the parishes of St. Olave, Hart Street, and St. Bartholomew without Bishopsgate (*sic*),[10] London. A chantry of two chaplains established there by Andrew de Bures[11] in 1331 was endowed with land in

---

[1] John de Oxenedes, *Chronica* (Rolls Ser.), 174.

[2] They were established there 28 Edw. I, for in that year a sum of 28s. to them figures in the king's Wardrobe Accts. *Lib. Quotid. Contrarotul. Garderob. 28 Edw. I,* 31. Prior Stephen granted to these two men three tenements for 13s. 8d. per annum. Stow, *Surv. of Lond.* (Strype's ed.), iii, 74. Later on it is said they founded their house on tenements purchased of Richard Wimbush, prior of Holy Trinity, 1319.

[3] In 1319 the church was built but not yet dedicated, and the cemetery was still unconsecrated. Guildhall MS. 122, fol. 126–7.

[4] Lond. Epis. Reg. Baldock and Gravesend, fol. 46, 47.

[5] *Cal. of Pat.* 1330–4, p. 41.

[6] Ibid. 1343–5, p. 115.

[7] Ibid. 1334–8, p. 222.

[8] Ibid. 1330–4, p. 223.

[9] Ibid. 416.

[10] Ibid. 1343–5, p. 115. Perhaps St. Botolph's without Bishopsgate.

[11] Ibid. 1330–4, p. 197. The land was alienated by Andrew to the prior and Crutched Friars of Welnetham to find two chaplains to celebrate in the London house. In 1350 the prior and convent of the Crossed Friars, London, granted to Sir Andrew de Bures and Alice his wife a room and stable in the priory whenever they came to London. Cart. Toph. 33.

'Aketons' and Waldingfield, Suffolk; another[12] for one chaplain by Dame Hewysia Gloucestre (1335) with a tenement in Seething Lane, and the house appears to have obtained one or two little pieces of land elsewhere,[13] but in 1341[14] the revenues of the priory were still so small that the convent was released from payment of the subsidy.

It would, however, perhaps be a mistake to imagine the house extremely poor. The fact that the friars were endeavouring in 1342 to provide accommodation at Oxford for thirteen of their number to study at the university[15] doubtless proves nothing but that they took the same interest in education as the friars of other orders; but it is difficult to believe that if they had been without financial support they would have begun a costly chapel in 1350.[16]

Moreover in 1359 three of the friars carried off goods estimated to be worth £87 13s. 4d.,[17] so that unless a large amount is to be deducted for the bulls and muniments stolen, the priory seems to have been fairly well furnished. This is not, by the way, the only robbery in which members of the house were concerned, since in 1391 John Bures, then prior, was pardoned for abetting a man who some years before had stolen property valued at 600 marks from the house of the bishop of Bath and Wells.[18]

Before the end of the century they had added considerably to their resources. John de Causton, alderman of London, in 1350 gave them a tenement with gardens and shops near the Tower, and a tenement called the Cardinalshat at 'Grascherche' as the endowment of the two chantries founded by him in the conventual church;[19] tenements near Dowgate, and in 'Syvedenlane' were bequeathed by another London citizen, Richard Rothyng, in 1379, also for the establishment of a chantry;[20] and in 1383 Sir Richard Abberbury, kt., granted to them lands and houses in Donington,[21] but these they seem afterwards to have lost, as in 1447 Richard's heir, Thomas de Abberbury, made them over to the duke of Suffolk.[22]

The priory must have been popular with the foreigners who lived round its precincts, for the Fraternity of the Holy Blood of Jesus, founded in the church in 1459, and the Brotherhood of St. Katharine, established there in 1495, were both of German origin.[23] It is evident too that the house was not viewed unfavourably by the citizens generally, since on the petition of the prior for aid in the rebuilding of the church in 1520[24] the City accepted the patronage of the foundation, pressed its claims upon the fellowships of London,[25] and in 1522[26] granted some common soil for its extension. It was probably to the good offices of their new patrons that the priory owed the bequest of £50 made to the new buildings in 1524 by Sir John Skevington, alderman,[27] and that of £6 13s. 4d. left in 1523 by Robert Collyns, haberdasher of London.[28]

Sir John Milbourne, who had been mayor in 1521, purchased some land of the friars in 1534 for his almshouses,[29] and had his obit celebrated in the conventual church.[30]

Such assistance as was procured was not, however, sufficient to rescue the house from its embarrassments. A woman named Margaret Johnson complained to Cromwell about 1534 that she and her husband had lent the convent large sums in 1512 and other amounts since, but had not for ten years received the annuity promised in return.[31] The priory in 1525 had borrowed money on security of a silver-gilt cross and some vestments, and in 1535 had not discharged the debt;[32] in 1527 it borrowed £27 10s. from George Tadlow, haberdasher of London;[33] and in 1538 it owed £40 to William Fernley, a mercer, and £100 to the executors of a certain Walter Marsshe.[34]

After 1530 monetary difficulties were not the only ones with which the convent had to contend. The religious changes did not meet with the approval of John Dryver, prior of the house in 1532, and of course spies were not lacking to report the imprudent expression of his opinions. He had said that if it were true that the king was determined to put down certain religious houses he should be called 'Destructor Fidei,' and in speaking of a fall the king's jester had had from his horse had

[12] Sharpe, *Cal. of Wills*, i, 406.
[13] *Cal. of Pat.* 1330–4, p. 49. Robert de Hegham had leave to alienate to them 15 acres of land and 8d. rent in Shudycampes and Nosterfeld.
[14] *Cal. of Close*, 1341–3, p. 175.
[15] *Cal. of Pat.* 1340–3, pp. 403, 498.
[16] Ibid. 1348–50, p. 445.
[17] Riley, *Mem. of Lond.* 303, 304.
[18] *Cal. of Pat.* 1388–92, p. 429.
[19] Doc. of D. and C. of Westminster, London, B. Box 1.
[20] Sharpe, *Cat. of Wills*, ii, 213.
[21] *Cal. Pap. Letters*, v, 12, 13.
[22] *Cal. Rot. Pat.* (Rec. Com.), 291.

[23] Stow, op. cit. ii, 75, 76; *Lond. and Midd. Arch. Soc. Trans.* iv, 44, 52.
[24] Rec. of Corp. of Lond. Repert. v, fol. 52. Just about this time, viz. in 1521, the bishop of London confirmed the Fraternity of the Visitation of the Virgin Mary in the church of the Crossed Friars, but the brotherhood of course may have been of earlier foundation. Lond. Epis. Reg. Fitz James, fol. 142.
[25] Stow, op. cit. ii, 74.
[26] Rec. of Corp. of Lond. Repert. iv, fol. 122b.
[27] *L. and P. Hen. VIII*, iv, 952.
[28] Ibid. iii, 3175.
[29] *Lond. and Midd. Arch. Soc. Trans.* iii, 138–42.
[30] Herbert, *Livery Companies of Lond.* i, 413.
[31] *L. and P. Hen. VIII*, viii, 161.
[32] Ibid. ix, 1168.
[33] Add. Chart. 24490.
[34] Aug. Off. Misc. Bks. 250, fol. 40, 41b.

remarked that 'the fool should say … that the king should have a fall shortly.'[35] It is unlikely that he would have been allowed to remain prior after this, and it was Edmund Stretam who as head of the house acknowledged the royal supremacy on 17 April, 1534.[36]

Robert Ball, the friar who was one of the witnesses against Dryver, was prior in 1535,[37] and was the subject of the well-known letter of John Bartelot to Cromwell.[38] Bartelot's story was that he and some others, having caught the prior in an act of gross immorality, had been bribed not to tell by a sum down and a promise of more. The prior not paying the second amount was arrested, but found a friend in the chancellor, who declared that it was a heinous robbery on Bartelot's part. As far as one can judge it appears to have been an attempt at intimidation and blackmail based on the fact that the court policy was known to have but the half-hearted adherence of the convent. It is not without significance that when the provincial of the Austin Friars in 1535 refused to let the Spaniards celebrate the emperor's victory in Africa in that church until he knew the king's pleasure, they went to the Crossed Friars for their service.[39] A priest there was reported to have tried to confirm a penitent in the old doctrines in February, 1535,[40] and in March, 1536,[41] a doctor and three or four others of the Crossed Friars were prohibited by Hilsey from hearing confessions. It is possible to see the reflection of these proceedings in the small number of names[42] appended to the deed of surrender, 12 November, 1538; for in December, 1350, before the priory had had time to recover from the ravages of the Great Pestilence, there had been eleven besides the prior and sub-prior,[43] but the convent at the Dissolution had dwindled to six. Raphael or Ralph Turner,[44] who heads the list, and was granted an annual pension of five marks for the term of his life,[45] was not the prior, so that the house appears to have been without a head at this time.

The possessions of the priory, valued at £52 13s. 4d.[46] per annum, included the chapel of 'Chockesmythes' with a messuage and garden adjoining and lands and wood in 'Wellutham' Magna, 'Wellutham'[47] Parva, and Bradfield Combusta, co. Suffolk,[48] the site of the late priory of Barham,[49] co. Camb., and tenements in St. Olave's Hart Street,[50] St. Dunstan's in the East,[51] Allhallows Dowgate, Allhallows Barking, and St. Botolph's without Aldgate.[52]

The plate of the house, forty-one ounces in parcel gilt,[53] seems a very small quantity, but that stolen[54] a few years before may never have been recovered, and some had certainly been pawned[55] or sold during the last period of the priory's existence.

*M. Reddan*

## Revised List of Priors of the Crossed Friars

The names of the Priors and Subpriors, where not otherwise indicated, come from J. Michael Haydon, 'The Crutched Friars Revisited', *Clairlieu* (1995), pp. 65–82.

Adam,[56] occurs 1319[57]
Thomas, occurs 1328[58]
Thomas Whatton, occurs 1343[59]
William de Charyngworth, occurs 1350,[60] 1356[61]
John Bures, occurs 1360,[62] 1379–80[63]
John Lynoth, occurs 1384[64]
John Quyntun, occurs 1390[65]
John Bures, occurs 1391, 1405[66]
Robert Stanlowe, 'late' prior, 1407[67]
John, occurs 1407[68]
Robert Trewemon, occurs 1411[69]

[35] *L. and P. Hen. VIII*, v, 1209.
[36] Ibid. vii, 665.
[37] Ibid. ix, 1168.
[38] Ibid. ix, 1092.
[39] Ibid. 330.
[40] Ibid. x, 346.
[41] Ibid. 462.
[42] *L. and P. Hen. VIII*, xiii (2), 807.
[43] Doc. of D. and C. of Westm. Lond. B. Box 1.
[44] *L. and P. Hen. VIII*, xiii (2), 807, and N.* In 1527 he was sacristan. Add. Chart. 24490.
[45] Aug. Off. Bks. 233, fol. 272b.
[46] Stow, op. cit. ii, 74.

[47] This may either be Welnetham or Waldingfield Magna and Parva.
[48] *L. and P. Hen. VIII*, xv, 436 (88).
[49] Ibid. xv, 942 (19). Babraham (?).
[50] Ibid. xvii, 1258.
[51] Ibid. xvii (1), 75.
[52] Ibid. xix (1), 1035 (6).
[53] *Monastic Treasures* (Abbotsford Club), 19.
[54] *L. and P. Hen. VIII*, vi, 578 (27).
[55] Ibid. ix, 1168.
[56] Stow, op. cit. ii, 74.
[57] Guildhall MS. 122, fol. 126; Cheshire R.O. DCH/O/56/2. Wrongly described as first prior, e.g. Maitland, *Hist. of London*, II, p. 782.
[58] Cheshire RO DCH/O/56/3.
[59] Helena M. Chew, *London Possessory Assizes: A Calendar* (London Record Society, 1, 1965), no. 223.
[60] Doc. of D. and C. of Westm. London, B. Box 1.
[61] Chew, *Possessory Assizes*, no. 223
[62] T.N.A. C81/1794/13.
[63] *Cal. Wills Husting*, ed. Sharpe, II, 213; Röhrkasten, *Mendicant Houses*, p. 199.
[64] Lond. Epis. Reg. Braybrook, fol. 390. He is probably identical with Bures.
[65] T.N.A. C81/1794/15.
[66] *Cal. of Pat.* 1388–92, p. 429; C.L.R.O., Hust. R. 136(11).
[67] Chew, *Possessory Assizes*, no. 223.
[68] Ibid.
[69] T.N.A. PROB 11/2, ff. 178v–179.

John Asshewelle, occurs 1428, 1432[70]

Peter Bishop, occurs 1436, 1440[71]

John Stancor, occurs 1455;[72] died 1467

William, died 1475

Thomas Whete, occurs 1484–91; died c.1512.[73]

Christianus Smalsman, occurs 1492;[74] died 1501

Sibertus Novimagii, 'late prior' 1527. Probably prior bef. Lucas.

— Lucas, before 1501[75]

William Bowry, occurs 1502;[76] died 1530[77]

William Crochum (Crochon, Crothyn etc), occurs 1531[78]

John Dryver, occurs 1533[79]

Edmund Stretam, occurs 1533, 1534[80]

Robert Ball, occurs 1535[81]

### Subpriors

Ralph de Coventre, occurs 1350[82]

John Leydamensis, occurs 1501[83]

John Bree, occurs 1508[84]

Gotfried Aquenis, occurs 1508–9

Hieronymus Leodiensis, occurs 1512[85]

Godfrid Botbren, occurs 1517[86]

Henricus —, occurs before 1518[87]

Egidius Endovia, occurs before 1530[88]

Sebastian Ruremundenam, occurs 1530–1[89]

Raphael Turner, occurs 1538[90]

[70] T.N.A. C81/1794/19; *Cal. of Close, 1429–35*, pp. 150, 193.

[71] *Cal. P. and M. London, 1458–82*, pp. 21–2; *Cal. of Close, 1435–41*, p. 371.

[72] G.L., MS 9171/5, f. 166v.

[73] Cheshire R.O., DCH/O/14; G.L. MS 15177; 9171/8, ff. 33v–34.

[74] *Definities der generale kapittels van de orde van het H. Kruis, 1410–1786*, ed. A. Van den Pasch (Brussels, 1969), p. 160.

[75] Ibid. no. 92.

[76] *L. and P. Hen. VIII*, viii, 161.

[77] *Definities*, ed. Van den Pasch, no. 121.

[78] *Cal. P. and M. London, 1458–82*, p. 22, n.1.

[79] *L. and P. Hen. VIII*, v, 1209.

[80] Ibid. vii, 665; Chesire R.O., DCH/O/31.

[81] *L. and P. Hen. VIII*, ix, 1092 and 1168.

[82] W.A.M. 13431.

[83] *Definities*, ed. Van den Pasch, no. 92.

[84] Ibid. nos. 99, 290.

[85] Ibid. no. 103.

[86] G.L., MS 9171/9 fol. 46r, 87r–88r, 94r–v, 113r–v, 126v.

[87] *Definities*, ed. van den Pasch, no. 110.

[88] Ibid. no. 121.

[89] Ibid. nos. 121–2.

[90] T.N.A. E314/77/5, fol. 1. *L. and P. Hen. VIII*, xiii (2), no. 807; xiv (1) no 1355.

# 17. THE PIED FRIARS OR FRIARS DE PICA
# (ALSO KNOWN AS FRIARS DE ARENO)

## INTRODUCTION

The original two articles on the Pied Friars and the Friars de Areno are very brief and do not provide a context for the religious house in question. The assumption that there were two religious Orders and two houses is not correct; there was in fact only one, which was known under different names.

The Order of the 'Fratres B. Mariae Matris Christi' probably originated in the diocese of Marseille in the mid-thirteenth century. Pope Alexander IV instructed the local bishop to give an approved rule to the 'prior et fratres beate Marie de Areno' in 1257, a reference to a church in a suburb of Marseille. The Order spread into different parts of Europe, with houses in France, Spain, Italy, the Low Countries and England, and was known under different names, 'Blancs-manteaux' in Paris, 'fratres de Pye' in Norwich (T.N.A. C47/4/2 fol. 25v) and 'beate Marie matris Christi', 'Ordo sancte Marie' or 'Ordo sancte Marie de Pica' near London (T.N.A. C47/4/1 fol. 20r, 44v, C47/4/4 fol. 38r), where they appeared after 1267, when Henry III gave them permission to reside in the kingdom. Shortly afterwards William de Plumpton, a royal official, handed over his property to the king for the friars' benefit. This area, situated not in London but in the parish of Holy Innocents on the road to Westminster, was further enlarged in 1270. Four years later the 'Friars of Areno' together with other smaller mendicant Orders were prohibited from accepting any new novices at the Second Council of Lyons. Despite this blow the community on the road between London and Westminster continued to exist and the friars were frequent recipients of royal alms. A regional chapter was still held here in 1304 and the last friar died in 1317.

For further information on the Order, see: R. W. Emery, 'The Friars of the Blessed Mary and the Pied Friars', *Speculum,* 24 (1949), pp. 228–38, and other titles in: K. Elm, 'Fratres B. Mariae Matris Christi', *Lexikon des Mittelalters* IV (Munich-Zurich, 1989), col. 851–2. J. Röhrkasten, *The Mendicant Houses of Medieval London 1221–1539* (Münster, 2004), pp. 61–2, 84 and F. Andrews, *The Other Friars. The Carmelite, Augustinian, Sack and Pied Friars* (Woodbridge 2006), pp. 224–30, 245.

*Jens Röhrkasten*

The London settlement of the Pied Friars is mentioned neither by Dugdale nor by Tanner, but that there was such a community seems certain, considering that it figures among other London houses receiving alms on the occasion of the second anniversary of Queen Eleanor of Castille,[1] and that the king's wardrobe accounts of 1300 record a gift to these friars of 8s.[2]

*M. Reddan*

[1] *Arch.* xxix, 179. She died 19 Edw. I.
[2] *Liber Quotid. Contrarotul. Garderob.* 28 *Edw. I.*

### List of Priors

Godefridus, 1287[3]

### *Recipients of royal alms for the convent*
William de Fakenham, 1297[4]
Walter de Eye, 1300[5]
Gilbert de London, 1303[6]
Hugo de Eboracum, c.1305,[7] 1310[8]

[3] T.N.A. C81/1794/24
[4] B.L. MS Add. 7965 fol. 9r
[5] Soc. Antiq. MS 119 fol. 17v; B.L. MS 35291 fol. 24v
[6] T.N.A. E101/363/18 fol. 2r
[7] T.N.A. E101/369/11 fol. 32v
[8] T.N.A. E101/374/7

# 18. THE FRIARS DE ARENO

## INTRODUCTION

See the account of the House of the Pied Friars (above no. 17).

*Jens Röhrkasten*

A priory for friars of the order of St. Mary de Areno was founded in Westminster in 1267 by William Arnand, a knight of Henry III. It lasted just fifty years, the community coming to an end with the death of the last brother, Hugh of York, in 1317.[1]

*M. Reddan*

[1] *Cal. of Close*, 1313–18, p. 503.

# 19. THE MINORESSES WITHOUT ALDGATE

## INTRODUCTION

The original article is generally reliable and provides much useful information. Since 1900 two studies have been devoted to the Minoresses. E. M. Tomlinson, *A History of the Minories, London* (London, 1907) expands on some of the documents used in the *V.C.H.* article, and usefully prints some of them in full. A. F. C. Bourdillon, *The Order of the Minoresses in England* (Manchester, 1926) provides greater detail on the Minoresses, and is particularly useful in establishing the relationship of the London Minoresses to other houses of Minoresses in England. This is the most useful work published, and provides further detail on the foundation of the London house, noble connections, links with the Friars Minor and the merchant community and discusses the range of bequests to the house. M. Carlin, *Historical Gazetteer of London before the Great Fire. St. Botolph Aldgate: Minories, East Side; The Abbey of St. Clare; Holy Trinity Minories* (typescript, London, 1987) provides information on the location and, most importantly, the plans of the church and precinct of the house of Minoresses. The relations of the house with London are discussed in Jens Röhrkasten, *The Mendicant Houses of Medieval London 1221–1539* (Münster, 2004), esp. pp. 64–6.

All other work on the London Minoresses appears in general studies of religious orders. Of these the most useful is Paxton, 'Nunneries', particularly in providing details about individual nuns and their connections with the nobility. The work also points to a useful published primary text: 'The Rewle of Sustris Menouresses Enclosid', in W. W. Seton (ed.), *A Fifteenth Century Courtesy Book and Two Franciscan Rules*, Early English Text Society, cxlviii, (1914), pp. 63–127. There is a discussion of the books and manuscripts belonging to the Minoresses to be found in Bell, *Nuns*, esp. pp. 149–52. There are some general observations on the Minoresses in E. Power, *Medieval English Nunneries* (Cambridge, 1922), which particularly draws attention to the women from the merchant class who took the veil at the Minories. For the property of the house in London, see *Documentary Sources*, p. 60. See K. Cook, 'The English Nuns and the Dissolution', in J. Blair and B. Golding (eds.), *The Cloister and the World* (Oxford, 1996), pp. 287–301, esp. p. 289 for a brief reference to the income of the house.

*Jessica Lutkin*

The house of the Grace of the Blessed Mary was founded outside Aldgate in the parish of St. Botolph in 1293[1] by the brother of Edward I, Edmund earl of Lancaster, for inclosed nuns of the order of St. Clare.[2] The first members of the convent were brought to England by the earl's wife Blanche, queen of Navarre, in all probability from France, since the rule prescribed for their observance by Pope Boniface VIII was that followed in the nunnery of the Humility of the Blessed Mary at Saint Cloud.[3] The original endowment consisted of lands and tenements in the suburbs of London and £30 rent in St. Lawrence Lane, Cordwainer Street, and Dowgate;[4] but in 1295 the earl made a further grant of land in the field of Hartington, co. Derby, and the advowson of the

---

[1] Or rather the foundation was then confirmed by the king, Pat. 21 Edw. I, m. 11, quoted in Dugdale, *Mon. Angl.* vi, 1553. It seems probable, however, that a slightly earlier date should be assigned, as the house is mentioned in the *Taxatio* of Pope Nicholas about 1291.

[2] As altered by Pope Urban IV. They were not Poor Clares, since they received endowments. Fly, 'Some account of an Abbey of Nuns,' *Arch*, xv, 93.

[3] Lond. Epis. Reg. Baldock and Gravesend, fol. 17. See also *Arch*. xv, 93, *n*. D.

[4] The £30 was allowed them out of the manor of 'Shapwyk,' co. Dorset (*Cal. of Pat.* 1292–1301, p. 87), until this grant was made in Nov. 1294. Dugdale, op. cit. vi, 1553.

church there,[5] and in the *Taxatio* of Pope Nicholas, Hartington and 'Northburgh' churches both are said to be appropriated to the nuns.[6] Some more property in London was soon acquired from Henry le Galeys, who endowed a chantry in the chapel of St. Mary built by him in the conventual church where he was buried.[7]

From the earliest foundation the house enjoyed important privileges. The king exempted them in 1294 from summonses before the justices in eyre for common pleas and pleas of the forest.[8] The pope, Boniface VIII, ordered that nothing should be exacted from them for the consecration of church and altars, or for sacred oil or sacraments, but that the bishop of the diocese should perform these offices free of charge; that in a general interdict they might celebrate service with closed doors; that sentences of excommunication and interdict promulgated against them by bishops or rectors should be of no effect,[9] and he declared them free from all jurisdiction of the archbishop of Canterbury and of the bishop of London,[10] and acquitted them of payment of tenths[11] to the pope.

The house indeed seems to have been at first richer in privileges than in revenue: in 1316 the nuns were exempted by the king from tallage on their land in London on account of their poverty;[12] in 1334 they petitioned the king that according to the papal bulls to them they might be quit of all papal impositions on the clergy or grants to the king, saying that otherwise they could not live;[13] and in 1338[14] and 1345[15] they were pardoned from contributing both to tenths and fifteenths out of pity for their straitened condition. At length in 1347[16] the king granted that they should henceforth be quit of all tallages, explaining in 1353[17] that the grant exempted them from payment of both lay and clerical subsidies.

It is possible that in these exemptions may be seen a sign not only of the nuns' poverty, but also of powerful influence exerted on their behalf, since the house always had a particular attraction for persons of rank.[18] Queen Isabella gave the nuns in 1346 the advowsons of the churches of Kessingland and Framsden, co. Suffolk, and Walton-on-Trent, co. Derby, with licence to appropriate them, so that they would pray for the soul of King Edward II,[19] and showed herself their friend in other ways.[20] She was not the only patron of the Grey Friars to extend her benefactions to the sisters of the order: Elizabeth de Burgh Lady Clare bequeathed in 1355 £20, ornaments, and furniture to the house, £20 to the abbess Katherine de Ingham, and 13s. 4d. to each of the sisters,[21] and Margaret countess of Norfolk granted to the convent in 1382 a rent of 20 marks from the Brokenwharf, London, for the term of the life of William de Wydford, a friar.[22] William Ferrers, lord of Groby, left to his daughter Elizabeth, a nun at the Minories, £20, and to the abbess and nuns 10 marks;[23] John of Gaunt in 1397 bequeathed £100 to be paid among the sisters;[24] and Joan Lady Clinton left to them by will in 1457 £45 to keep her anniversary.[25]

Margaret de Badlesmere, who was living in the nunnery in 1323,[26] was not the only widow of her position to find a retreat from the world there; for Margaret Beauchamp, after the death of her husband, the earl of Warwick, had an indult from the pope in 1398 to reside there with three matrons as long as she pleased,[27] and two of the abbesses had taken the veil after widowhood, Katherine wife of John de Ingham,[28] and Eleanor Lady Scrope, daughter of Ralph de Neville.[29] Henry earl of

---

[5] *Cal. of Pat.* 1292–1301, p. 170.

[6] *Pope Nich. Tax.* (Rec. Com.), 247.

[7] Sharpe, *Cal. of Wills*, ii, 96; *Chron. of Edw. I and Edw. II* (Rolls Ser.), i, 128. Galeys was mayor 1273 and 1281–3, and died 1302.

[8] *Cal. of Pat.* 1292–1301, p. 86; *Plac. de Quo Warr.* (Rec. Com.), 460.

[9] Lond. Epis. Reg. Baldock and Gravesend, fol. 17.

[10] Ibid. Bull of Aug. 1294.

[11] Ibid. Bull of June, 1295. They were exempted in 1319 from payments of tenths granted by Pope Clement V to the king on showing these letters of Boniface VIII. *Cal. of Close*, 1318–23, p. 166.

[12] *Cal. of Pat.* 1313–17, p. 449.

[13] *Parl. R.* (Rec. Com.), ii, 86a.

[14] *Cal. of Pat.* 1338–40, p. 86.

[15] Ibid. 1343–5, p. 434.

[16] Ibid. 1345–8, p. 410.

[17] Inspex. 1377, *Cal. of Pat.* 1377–81, p. 85.

[18] Those buried in the church included Elizabeth countess of Clare, d. 1360 (Nicolas, *Test. Vet.* 56); Agnes countess of Pembroke, under her will of 1367 (ibid. 72); Edmund de la Pole and Margaret his wife, and Elizabeth their daughter (Lansd. MS. 205, fol. 21); Elizabeth duchess of Norfolk, by her will of 1506 (Nicolas, op. cit. 483), and Anne her daughter (Lansd. MS. 205, fol. 21).

[19] *Cal. of Pat.* 1345–8, p. 125.

[20] It was at her request that Edw. III in 1340 gave them licence to acquire in mortmain property of the annual value of £30. Ibid. 467. In the last months of her life she gave alms to the nuns twice, the second donation being for pittances on the anniversaries of Edw. II and John of Eltham. Bond, 'Notice of the Last Days of Isabella, Queen of Edward II,' *Arch.* xxxv, 456, 464.

[21] Nichols, *Royal Wills*, 30. Among the articles bequeathed were a reliquary of crystal, a large chalice of silver-gilt, and two cruets 'costeles,' and two vestments, one of white the other of black cloth of gold.

[22] *Cal. of Pat.* 1381–5, p. 452.

[23] Nicolas, *Test. Vet.* 76.

[24] Nichols, *Royal Wills*, 153.

[25] Nicolas, *Test. Vet.* 284.

[26] *Cal. of Close*, 1323–7, pp. 46, 48.

[27] *Cal. Pap. Letters*, v, 177.

[28] *Cal. of Close*, 1339–41, p. 266; Lansd. MS. 205, fol. 21.

[29] Ibid. and *Arch.* xv, 104.

Lancaster in 1349,[30] and Matilda Lady de Lisle in 1353,[31] received leave from the pope to visit the convent with a limited number of attendants. The relations between the nunnery and the family of Thomas de Woodstock, duke of Gloucester, appear to have been of the closest kind. It was the duke who obtained for the nuns in 1394 the advowson of Potton church from the prior and convent of St. Andrew, Northampton, and arranged for its appropriation without expense to the abbey.[32] His house adjoined the conventual church, and the abbess and sisters allowed him to make a door between the two buildings so that he could enter the church as he pleased, a privilege they were not prepared to extend to the lady who took the house after the duke's death.[33] The duchess died in the nunnery,[34] and one of the daughters, Isabel, who had been placed in the nunnery at a very youthful age,[35] though she had permission from the pope to leave if she would, chose to remain,[36] and in the end became abbess.[37] All the nuns could not have been as contented with their lot, for in 1385 the king had ordered his serjeant-at-arms to arrest an apostate minoress, Mary de Felton, and deliver her to the abbess for punishment.[38]

This connexion with the Gloucester family would in itself be sufficient to account for the favour shown to the minoresses by Henry IV, who almost immediately after his accession gave them the custody of the alien priory or manor of Appuldurcomb during the war with France, with permission to acquire it in mortmain from the abbey of Montebourg in Normandy,[39] and in 1401, in a confirmation of privileges granted to them by his predecessors, added another, that no justice,

mayor, or other officer should have any jurisdiction within the precinct of the house except in the case of treason or felonies touching the crown.[40] The nuns did not succeed in purchasing Appuldurcomb,[41] and they had the custody[42] only until in 1461 Edward IV granted them the manor in mortmain.[43] He did so 'on account of their poverty,' though during the preceding century they must have acquired a good deal of property by bequests[44] and in other ways.[45] Either therefore the house must have had special difficulties at that time, or, as is more probable, its income was always rather small for the number it supported. In 1515 twenty-seven of the nuns died of some infectious complaint,[46] so that there could hardly have been less than thirty or thirty-five before the outbreak. The sum expended there on food[47] in 1532 was very little less than had been spent on the food of convent and guests at Holy Trinity Priory.

It must have been shortly after the outbreak of plague that the convent buildings were destroyed by fire. The mayor, aldermen, and citizens of London contributed 200 marks besides the benefactions of private persons, but at the special request of Cardinal Wolsey to the Court of Common Council, it was decided in 1520 to give 100 marks more to complete the building.[48]

The king also gave £200 at this time.[49]

The abbey was surrendered in March, 1539,[50] and the terms granted to the nuns were not disadvantageous when compared with those given to others. To the abbess, Elizabeth Salvage, was assigned a life pension of £40 a year, four nuns received life pensions of £3 3s. 8d. each, ten £2 13s. 4d., nine £2, and a novice £1 6s. 8d.;[51] no

---

[30] *Cal. Pap. Pet.* i, 166. He was allowed to enter with ten persons.

[31] *Cal. Pap. Letters,* iii, 488. She was allowed to enter once a year with two matrons.

[32] Add. Chart. 19951.

[33] *Cal. Pap. Letters,* v, 544.

[34] Trokelowe and Blaneforde, *Chron. et Ann.* (Rolls Ser.), 321. By will she left to the abbess and convent £6 13s. 4d. and a 'tonell' of good wine; to her daughter Isabel, minoress, then in her sixteenth year, various books, among them a French Bible in 2 vols. with gold clasps enamelled with the arms of France. Nicolas, *Test. Vet.* 147.

[35] The papal mandate says 'she was in infancy placed in the monastery and clad in the monastic habit.' *Cal. Pap. Letters,* v, 385.

[36] The pope's permission to depart was given in 1401. In 1403 the king pardoned one of the servants of the Minories at the supplication of the abbess and his kinswoman Isabel de Gloucestre. *Cal. of Pat.* 1401–5, p. 248.

[37] Fly, 'Some Account of an Abbey of Nuns,' *Arch.* xv, 105. Henry V in 1421 or 1422 authorized Henry archbishop of Canterbury and others to pay to the abbey of the Minories an annual rent of 26 marks from the manor of Wethersfield during the lifetime of the abbess, Isabella of Gloucester.

[38] *Cal. of Pat.* 1385–7, p. 86.

[39] Ibid. 1399–1401, p. 34.

[40] Ibid. 543.

[41] In 1429 they are said to be still negotiating for the purchase. *Cal. of Pat.* 1422–9, p. 504.

[42] The Act of Resumption in 1451 was not to be prejudicial to the nuns as regards this manor. *Parl. R.* (Rec. Com.), v, 224a.

[43] *Cal. of Pat.* 1461–7, p. 88.

[44] Sharpe, *Cal. of Wills,* ii, 119, 208, 225, 382, 388, 397, 452, 496. All these bequests were made between 1368 and 1441.

[45] *Cal. of Pat.* 1377–81, p. 432; ibid. 1382–92, p. 491; ibid. 1392–6, p. 530.

[46] *Chron. of the Grey Friars* (Camd. Soc.), 29. The chronicler simply says: 'This year was a great death at the Minories, that there died 27 of the nuns.' Stow, *Surv. of Lond.* (ed. Strype), ii, 14, says 27 of the nuns besides servants died of plague.

[47] *L. and P. Hen. VIII,* v, 1663. The year's account for victuals, 1532, was £64 9s. 11¼d. i.e. about 25s. a week. The weekly bills for guests and convent at Christchurch Priory in 1514 amounted to £1 6s. 5½d.

[48] Rec. of Corp. of Lond. Repert. v, fol. 15b, 80.

[49] *L. and P. Hen. VIII,* iii, 1536. Henry may have had a kindly feeling for the nuns with whom his mother had friendly relations. Nicolas, *Privy Purse Expenses of Eliz. of York,* 8 and 57.

[50] Wriothesley, *Chron.* (Camd. Soc.), i, 94.

[51] Aug. Off. Bk. 233, fol. 227–31.

provision appears to have been made for the six lay sisters.[52]

Stow estimated the house to be worth £418 8s. 5d. per annum,[53] but according to the *Valor* its income amounted to £342 5s. 10½d. gross, and £318 8s. 5d. net.[54] Its possessions included rents and ferms in London[55] parishes: St. Mary-le-Bow,[56] Allhallows Thames Street,[57] St. Michael Crooked Lane,[58] St. Botolph without Aldgate,[59] St. Magnus,[60] St. Martin Vintry,[61] St. Nicholas Shambles,[62] St. Andrew Undershaft;[63] messuages and shops in Whitechapel,[64] co. Middlesex; the manor of Appuldurcomb in the Isle of Wight; the manor of Woodley, co. Berks.;[65] lands called 'Brekenox' in Cheshunt, co. Herts.;[66] messuages in Ringwould, co. Kent, and Marchington, co. Stafford; the rectories and tithes of Hartington,[67] co. Derby, Potton, co. Beds.,[68] Kessingland and Framsden, co. Suffolk; tithes in Wrestlingworth, co. Beds., and 'Quenton,' co. Bucks.,[69] and a pension from the church of Leake, co. Notts.,[70] one of the earliest grants to the abbey,[71] as it is mentioned in the *Taxatio*.

M. Reddan

## Revised List of Abbesses of the Minories

The list comes from A. F. C. Bourdillon, *The Order of the Minoresses in England* (Manchester, 1926), p. 87 and M. Carlin, *Historical Gazetteer of London before the Great Fire. St. Botolph Aldgate: Minories, East Side; the Abbey of St. Clare; Holy Trinity Minories*, gen. ed. Derek Keene (typescript, London 1987), pp. 7–8, except where indicated.

Margaret, occurs 1294, 1295
Juliana, occurs 1301, 1303
Alice de Sherstede, occurs 1299, 1313
Margaret Fraunceys, occurs *c*.1317–19
Alice de Lacy, occurs 1322
Joan de Stokes, occurs before 1341
Katharine de Ingham, occurs 1349, 1371
Eleanor Neville/Scrope, occurs 1379; died 1398
Mary, occurs 1391
Isabella/Mary de Lisle, occurs 1397
Margaret Holmystede or Olmestede, occurs 1400, 1410
Isabella/Isabel of Gloucester, occurs 1413, 1424
Margaret Monyngton, occurs 1433, 1441
Christina Seint Nicholas, occurs 1444; died 1455
Katherine Willughby, occurs 1457
Elizabeth Horwode, occurs 1469
Joan/Johanna Barton, occurs 1479, 1481
Alice/Elizabeth Fitz Lewes, occurs 1493,[72] 1501
Elizabeth Boulman, occurs 1507
Dorothy Cumberford, occurs 1521;[73] died 1537
Elizabeth Salvage, elected 1537; died before 1555–6

[52] *L. and P. Hen. VIII*, xiv (1), 680.
[53] Stow, *Surv. of Lond.* (ed. Strype), ii, 14.
[54] *Valor Eccl.* (Rec. Com.), i, 398.
[55] In 1532 the steward of the Minories accounted for £148 4s. 11d. derived from rents in London. *L. and P. Hen. VIII*, v, 1663.
[56] Ibid. xv, 733 (33).
[57] Ibid. xvi, p. 727.
[58] Ibid. xviii (1), p. 554.
[59] Ibid. xviii (1), 346 (54).
[60] Ibid. xix (1), 1035 (6).
[61] Ibid. xix (2), 340 (39).
[62] Ibid. xix (2), 527 (6).
[63] Ibid. xix (2), 527 (25).
[64] Ibid. xv, p. 540. They were acquired by the nuns in 1480. *Cal. of Pat.* 1476–85, p. 65.
[65] *Valor Eccl.* (Rec. Com.), i, 397.
[66] *L. and P. Hen. VIII*, xv, 733 (64).
[67] This was let at ferm in 1526 to George earl of Shrewsbury for £26 13s. 4d. a year. B.M. Chart. Toph. 19.
[68] Given to them in 1394. Add. Chart. 19951.
[69] *Valor Eccl.* (Rec. Com.), i, 397. Quenton is probably Quainton.
[70] Ibid. v, 166.
[71] *Pope Nich. Tax.* (Rec. Com.), 311.
[72] Paxton, 'Nunneries', p. 25.
[73] Ibid., p. 61.

# HOSPITALS

## 20. THE HOSPITAL OF ST. BARTHOLOMEW, SMITHFIELD

### INTRODUCTION

This account still holds good but there is now much more information available. Norman Moore's massive work, *The History of St. Bartholomew's Hospital*, 2 vols. (London, 1918) concentrates on the medieval hospital and has transcriptions and translations of many documents from the hospital's archives and elsewhere. For a briefer account, see D'Arcy Power, *A Short History of St. Bartholomew's Hospital 1123–1923* (London, 1923). For a later history, though with much less than Moore on the medieval period, see V. C. Medvei and J. L. Thornton (eds.), *The Royal Hospital of St. Bartholomew 1123–1973* (London, 1974). E. A. Webb, *The Records of St. Bartholomew's Priory and of the Church and Parish of St. Bartholomew the Great West Smithfield* (Oxford, 1921) has a chapter on the relations between the hospital and the priory, pp. 76–92.

Nellie Kerling, *Cartulary of St. Bartholomew's Hospital* (London, 1973) calendars the fifteenth-century cartulary, mainly documenting the hospital's property but also containing early charters. The book has a useful introduction and includes a list of masters and a fifteenth-century rental. A modernised English version of B.L. Cotton Vespasian B ix, the Middle English source for accounts of the foundation of both the hospital and the priory, was published in E. A. Webb (ed.), *The Book of the Foundation of the Church of St. Bartholomew London rendered into modern English* (Oxford, 1923). An annotated edition of the Middle English text prepared by Moore in the 1880s appeared as *The Book of the Foundation of St. Bartholomew's Church in London: The Church Belonging to the Priory of the same in West Smithfield*, ed. N. Moore, Early Eng. Text Soc., Orig. Ser., 163, (1923).

For a summary of the sources and location of the hospital's London property, see *Documentary Sources,* pp. 61–2. The hospital's London property is included in the 1392 record of ecclesiastical property in McHardy, *Church in London*, pp. 39–77, which also has a valuation of the hospital for the 1379 poll tax (p. 2). The location and boundaries of the hospital's precinct are described in Honeybourne, 'Property', pp. 73–7. Moore has a substantial chapter on the hospital's property, *History*, 2, pp. 45–110.

A list of canons of the hospital ordained in the London diocese between 1361 and 1539 can be obtained from the CD Rom which accompanies Davis, *Clergy of London*. The staff of the hospital assessed for the 1379 poll tax are listed in McHardy, *Church in London*, p. 2.

*Ann Bowtell*

The hospital of St. Bartholomew was founded at the same time as the priory by Rahere in the reign of Henry I.[1] At first the priory and hospital seem to have been regarded as one institution, for the royal charter of 1133 was addressed to Rahere, the prior, the canons, and the poor of St. Bartholomew's Hospital;[2] but a separation between them must have occurred quite early, since the grants of Henry II[3] and Richard I[4] were made to the church and canons, that is to the priory, and there is evidence that by the beginning of the thirteenth century the hospital was a distinct

---

[1] Cott. MS. Vesp. B. ix, fol. 46.
[2] Cart. Antiq. R. L, 1.

[3] Ibid. 2, 8.
[4] Ibid. 9.

community[5] with possessions apart from those of the superior house.[6]

It is probable, therefore, that Alfune, the first proctor, was not concerned with the government of the hospital, but devoted himself entirely to finding the means of subsistence for the poor it sheltered, a sufficiently hard task, seeing that he begged food from door to door and in the markets of the city.[7] The later proctors, however, occupied the position and had the duties of masters,[8] and in the end took the name.

The rights of the priory over the hospital were the cause of much controversy, and the difficulty must have begun early, for the question was argued before Richard, bishop of London, about 1197.[9] It was then decided that the proctor of St. Bartholomew's should do solemn obedience to the prior and should swear to minister faithfully in the hospital and not to alienate the lands and rents of the house without the consent of the bishop, prior, and canons, nor to admit anyone to a perpetual allowance of food or clothing without the assent of the prior and canons; he must give an account twice a year of receipts and expenses in the presence of the bishop and the prior; the proctor was to be chosen by the canons and the brothers from the latter, or from another community if there were not a fit person in the hospital, but not from the priory; if unsuitable, he was to be removed by common counsel of the canons and brothers; chaplains were to be chosen by the prior and proctor, and to be removed by them if necessary; the brothers and sisters were to receive the habit from the prior in the chapter of canons and were to do obedience to the prior; all the brothers and sisters were bound to take part in the procession in the priory church on the Feast of the Purification of the Virgin, Palm Sunday, Easter Sunday, and Ascension Day. These ordinances apparently gave little satisfaction to the hospital, for the agitation to obtain more liberty led King John in 1204[10] to declare that he would treat attempts to free the hospital from its subjection to the priory as attacks on the crown, and in 1223 or 1224 Eustace, bishop of London, at the request of both priory and hospital, made other regulations,[11] which settled

the matter for a considerable period. They were as follows:– The prior was not to refuse his assent to the election of a master whom the brothers declared suitable; if he should consider the person elected unfit, the matter was to be referred to the chapter of St. Paul's; the prior was to give the master the habit in the chapter of the hospital; the brothers appear to have been excused from attendance at the priory church on the four festivals, but two were to go on St. Bartholomew's Day, with two candles of 4 lb. weight; the brothers were forbidden to erect an altar or image of St. Bartholomew in the hospital, and to have a bell tower or more than the two bells they then had, and on Easter Eve they were not to ring before the priory; they were refused the cemetery they had asked from Pope Benedict; the allowances of food and the share in the anniversaries of the canons were to be given as before by the priory to the members of the hospital.

Henry III, in the early part of his reign at any rate, appears to have taken an interest in the hospital: in 1223 he committed the custody of it to Maurice, a Templar,[12] until he could make further provision for it; in 1225 he gave the master four oaks for fuel,[13] and in 1229 six more;[14] and in 1230 excused the brothers from the payment of a tallage on their land in Hatfield.[15] Some idea of the hospital in 1316 can be gathered from the injunction of Gilbert Segrave, bishop of London,[16] who ordered that as the business of the house could not be carried on by fewer than seven brethren, of whom five were priests, there should in future be that number of brethren[17] and four sisters and not more; the difference in rank between the priests and laybrothers should be marked by their costume, the former wearing closed and round mantles, the latter short tunics; none should be allowed to buy their own clothing; the sisters should wear grey dresses which were not to fall below the ankles. Inferences may be drawn from certain of the ordinances: the sisters seem as usual to have been treated unfairly in the matter of food, since provision was made both as to quantity and quality; discipline was not perfect, or it would not have been necessary to order the brothers and sisters to obey the master, to forbid wordy warfare, and to provide for the punishment of manual violence; the care of the sick poor was perhaps somewhat neglected, since the bishop reminded the brothers and sisters that they

---

[5] Add. MS. 34768, fol. 37*b*, 38.

[6] A grant was made in the twelfth century by Stephen, the proctor, and the brethren with the consent of the prior. *Hist. MSS. Com. Rep*, ix, App. i, 22. In 1230 the hospital is mentioned as holding land in 'Hadfeld,' whereas the priory never seems to have possessed anything there. *Cal. of Close*, 1227–31, p. 301.

[7] Cott. MS. Vesp. B. ix, fol. 54–5.

[8] Settlement as to the institution of the procurator. Doc. of D. and C. of St. Paul's, A. Box 25, No. 643.

[9] Ibid.

[10] Add. MS. 34768, fol. 37*b*, 38.

[11] Doc. of D. and C. of St. Paul's, Lib. A, fol. 14.

[12] *Cal. of Pat.* 1216–25, p. 371.

[13] *Rot. Lit. Claus.* (Rec. Com.), ii, 39.

[14] *Cal. of Close*, 1227–31, p. 212.

[15] Ibid. p. 301.

[16] Lond. Epis. Reg. Baldock and Gravesend, fol. 39, 40.

[17] This injunction was observed for some time, for there were seven brothers present at the election of William Wakeryng as master in 1386. Lond. Epis. Reg. Braybrook, fol. 282, 287.

had entered the hospital to minister to their fellow creatures, and enjoined them to look after the sick in their turn as the master directed; he also ordered the master to visit the sick frequently and provide for their needs according to the power of the house; a difficulty which appears to have often arisen in the conduct of hospitals is shown by the injunction to the master to appoint a man of exemplary character to be doorkeeper, who would allow no one to enter the sisters' abode without leave of the master.

Two rolls were to be made of the income and all goods falling to the hospital, of which the master was to have one and the brethren the other, so that they might know how affairs were administered, and accounts were to be given every quarter by those who received and dispensed the revenues of the house.

Two years later, Bishop Gilbert's successor, Richard, visited the hospital,[18] and found that its resources had been much diminished through excessive granting of corrodies, and forbade such alienations in future except with the consent of the diocesan. He noticed on this occasion that immediate repairs were needed to the infirmary and other buildings.

The management of the finance of the hospital could have been no light task, for its endowments were not sufficient for its expenses and needed to be supplemented by an annual collection in churches,[19] a source of income abundant perhaps but inconstant because liable to be diverted.[20] The house was excused from payment of fifteenths and tenths by Edward I and Edward II because of its poverty,[21] and in 1341 the king ordered the subsidy not to be levied on its goods, on the ground that if it had to meet any further charges its alms must be diminished.[22] Another attempt to tax its possessions was, however, made about ten years later,[23] when it was probably less able to pay than ever, for in 1348 its debts amounted to £200[24] and the Black

Death must have seriously affected the value of its property both in London and in the country. The master, brethren, and sisters accordingly petitioned the king who, in 1352, declared them exempt from aids and ordered proceedings against them to be stopped.[25]

The foundation of chantries especially in the thirteenth century must have been of considerable benefit to the funds of the house: a chantry of two priests established by William de Arundell and Robert Newecomen in 1325[26] was endowed with 37 acres of land in the parishes of St. Giles and St. Botolph without Aldersgate; the celebrated John Pulteney gave the brethren in 1330 a messuage and four shops in the parish of St. Nicholas ad Macellas to maintain a chantry in the church of St. Thomas the Apostle and another in their own church;[27] and the hospital received in this way, among other property,[28] tenements in Holborn in 1339,[29] in the parish of St. Sepulchre in 1346,[30] and in Watling Street in 1379.[31]

The course of time had again made necessary a readjustment of the relations between the hospital and priory,[32] and Simon Sudbury, bishop of London, with the consent of both parties made a fresh arrangement on this subject in 1373.[33] He then ordained that the leave of the prior must be obtained by the brethren before they elected a master, that they should choose a suitable person, a priest, or such as could be speedily ordained, and that the prior was to present their choice to the bishop; the new master was to swear obedience to the prior and fealty to the prior and convent; brothers and sisters were to be admitted by the master on his own authority, but were to take an oath of fealty to the prior and convent within three days; the brethren and the canons were to ask alms in the name of their own house only, but if anything should be given to the brothers for the priory they were in duty bound to deliver it to the canons, who were to do the same as regards the hospital; the master was to correct the faults of the brethren and sisters if he could, but the prior was to help him if so requested; the master and brethren had full power to make any grants of their property without consulting the prior who in future was to have nothing to do with the hospital seal; the

[18] Lond. Epis. Reg. Baldock and Gravesend, fol. 39, 40.

[19] The master and brethren had received a papal indult for this. Cal. of Pat. 1324–7, p. 25.

[20] The king in 1324 and 1327 ordered his bailiffs to arrest persons pretending to be proctors of the brethren and collecting alms in their name. Ibid. 1324–7, p. 25; ibid. 1327–30, p. 18.

[21] Close, 26 Edw. III, m. 28, printed in Dugdale, Mon. Angl. vi, 296. An inquiry had been made as to whether the hospital had been exonerated from taxes by these kings, and it was found that payments had been made at certain dates, but that Edward II had exempted it from all tallages and taxes and that its tenements in London were all held in frankalmoign. Chan. Inq. p.m. 26 Edw. III (1st Nos.), 55.

[22] Cal. of Close, 1341–3, p. 114.

[23] A fifteenth and a tenth for three years were granted by the Commons in 1348 (Stubbs, Const. Hist. ii, 398). The petition of the brethren appears to have been made to the king in the Parliament of 1351.

[24] Cal. of Close, 1346–9, p. 542.

[25] Close, 26 Edw. III, m. 28, in Dugdale, op. cit. vi, 296.

[26] Cal. of Pat. 1324–7, p. 117.

[27] Ibid. 1330–4, p. 22.

[28] Remainder of tenements in Addlane. Sharpe, Cal. of Wills, i, 523. Remainder of rent in parish of St. Dunstan in the West. Ibid. ii, 44. Bequest by Thomas Morice for a chantry. Ibid. ii, 108.

[29] Ibid. i, 437.

[30] Cal. of Pat. 1340–3, p. 144.

[31] Sharpe, op. cit. ii, 212.

[32] Lond. Epis. Reg. Braybrook, fol. 285–7.

[33] Ibid.

ordinance of Bishop Eustace as to the offering in the priory church on St. Bartholomew's Day was to remain in force, and his prohibition to the brothers to erect an altar of St. Bartholomew within the hospital was repeated; but the hospital might now have a bell-tower and bells which could be rung on Easter eve at pleasure; permission was also given to consecrate a cemetery in which might be buried all dying within the bounds of the hospital as well as others, provided that such were not parishioners of St. Sepulchre's, or did not die within the limits of that parish or of the priory; the master and brethren were not henceforth to receive any allowance of food from the priory, and the master was to keep up the hospital of the sick. An appeal made in 1376 by three brothers and one of the sisters[34] shows how difficult it is to arrive at a just conclusion in these matters. If the ordinances did not exist the natural supposition would be that they had been, as they said, wrongfully deprived for three years of an allowance of food from the priory through the collusion of the master, whereas the allowance had been stopped by authority of the bishop.

It is unfair perhaps to pronounce judgement on the house from isolated cases relating to the conduct of individual inmates, such as that of Simon Dowel who had procured his election to the office of master by unlawful means, and was deposed by the bishop's commissaries in consequence in 1322,[35] or that of an apostate priest who at any rate repented and desired to return in 1355[36]; it is impossible, however, to avoid the feeling that the tone of a house must have been deplorable when, as in 1375, the master, Richard de Sutton, was publicly defamed for incontinence with one of the sisters and had to confess himself guilty.[37] Whether Sutton was afraid of the punishment that would be inflicted, or really had grievances against the bishop's commissaries, he appealed to the court of Canterbury and involved the bishop of London in a dispute with the archbishop over their respective jurisdictions. In the course of these proceedings he was excommunicated, but the punishment for his original offence is not recorded. He was not deposed, since he is mentioned eleven years later as resigning his post.[38]

The hospital was repaired by a bequest of Richard Whittington in 1423,[39] and before 1458 the church seems either to have been rebuilt or to have had a chapel added to it by Joan, Lady Clinton, for in her will of that date she speaks of 'my new church of the hospital of West Smithfield.'[40] The rebuilding of the chapel of St. Mary and St. Michael in the cemetery was due to one of the royal clerks, Richard Sturgeon,[41] who died in 1456.[42] Testimony to the good work done in the hospital is afforded by the king's pardon granted in 1464 to the master and brethren for all acquisitions in mortmain made by them without licence in consideration of the relief there given to poor pilgrims, soldiers, sailors, and others of all nations.[43]

There are indications that the brothers did not fall behind their age in attention to learning: John Mirfield used his experiences in the hospital to write a book 'Breviarium Bartholomei' at the end of the fourteenth century;[44] another brother received leave from the pope in 1404 to study theology for seven years at a university from which he was not to be recalled without reasonable cause,[45] while among the books presented by John Wakeryng, the master, to the library in 1463, was a beautiful copy of the Bible, the work of a member of the house named John Coke.[46]

Wolsey was empowered by the brothers in 1516[47] and 1524[48] to choose a master for them. In the first instance his choice fell upon one of themselves, Richard Smith, in the second upon Alexander Collins, prior of the Benedictine house of Daventry, whom he gave leave to change his order. When another vacancy seemed likely to occur in 1528 the king hoped that Wolsey would again secure the patronage[49] in which he expected to share, but this time the brothers asked the bishop of London to nominate, and Edward Staple was chosen.[50] This continual delegation of powers may have been a diplomatic move to secure powerful interest and protection. The pope in granting a dispensation in 1532 to John Brereton, one of the king's chaplains, to accept the hospital if it were offered to him, described the house as much in debt, its buildings greatly in need of repair, and its property deteriorated in value, and he suggested that Brereton as master might be able to relieve the hospital as he was already amply provided with benefices.[51] When Staple resigned his

---

[34] Doc. of D. and C. of St. Paul's, A. Box 25, No. 646.

[35] Lond. Epis. Reg. Baldock and Gravesend, fol. 49–50.

[36] *Cal. Pap. Letters*, v, 574.

[37] Doc. of D. and C. of St. Paul's, A. Box 54, No. 36.

[38] Lond. Epis. Reg. Braybrook, fol. 282.

[39] Stow, *Surv. of Lond.* (ed. Strype), iii, 232.

[40] Nicolas, *Test. Vet.* 284. Stow merely says she gave £10 to the poor of the house and was buried there, op. cit. iii, 233.

[41] Harl. MS. 433, fol. 296.

[42] Stow, op. cit. iii, 233.

[43] *Cal. of Pat.* 1461–7, p. 323.

[44] Moore, *A brief relation of the past and present state of St. Bartholomew's Hospital*, 21.

[45] *Cal. Pap. Letters*, v, 604.

[46] Stow says it was the fairest Bible he had seen, op. cit. iii, 232.

[47] Lond. Epis. Reg. Fitz James, fol. 66–70.

[48] Ibid. Tunstall, fol. 80–6.

[49] *L. and P. Hen. VIII*, iv (2), 4335.

[50] Lond. Epis. Reg. Tunstall, fol. 87–101.

[51] Ibid. Stokesley, fol. 91.

office it must have been a foregone conclusion that it would be given to Brereton, for he procured the king's ratification[52] of the papal bull about three weeks before he was appointed by Richard Gwent, to whom the brothers had committed the nomination.[53] In the circumstances it was hardly likely that any difficulty would be raised as to the acknowledgement of the royal supremacy, subscription to which was duly made in June 1534 by Brereton and three others.[54] Amid the general dissolution Sir Richard Gresham's appeal for the continuance of certain London hospitals[55] was successful as regards St. Bartholomew's, which was reconstituted in 1544.[56] The hospital, which in 1532 had consisted of a master and eight brethren,[57] was now to be composed of a master and four chaplains, namely, vice-master, curate, hospitaller, and visitor of the prisoners at Newgate,[58] and to these were added as before sisters to care for the sick. In 1547, however, another change took place: the king gave the hospital to the City, and it was then arranged that the vicar of the church and a hospitaller should minister to the spiritual needs of the sick inmates.[59]

Some of the property of the hospital was granted with it, but the house needed to be refurnished,[60] and to a large extent to be re-endowed, and the citizens made liberal donations to this work.[61] The business of the house was entrusted to twelve governors, of whom four were aldermen, who were chosen by the Lord Mayor and held office for two years, six retiring every year.[62] Sick and wounded soldiers and sailors found a refuge there both in 1627[63] and in 1644,[64] when in consideration of its services in this respect its lands were freed from assessment.[65] In the Dutch War of 1664[66] and during the war with France in 1705[67] the government again made use of the hospital.

An account of the City hospitals in 1667 estimates the number of persons relieved in that year at 1,383, and those then in the hospital at 196.[68] Much of its

income was derived from property in London, so that it naturally was much affected by the Fire,[69] and on this account the king gave permission to the governors for a time to turn the rooms in the Great Cloister into shops.[70]

Commissioners were appointed by William III in August 1691 to visit St. Bartholomew's among the royal foundations within the City,[71] but the result of the visitation has not been reported.

The religious side of the house, which still had some degree of prominence in 1544, seems to have become of less and less importance, and is not touched upon at all in a description of the hospital in 1800.[72]

In the *Valor* the revenues of the hospital are represented as £371 13s. 2d. gross and £305 6s. 5d. net.[73] Its possessions at that time comprised rents and farms in London valued at £292 4s. 6d. per annum; the manor of Ducketts in Tottenham and Harringay which had been made over to the house in 1460 by the feoffees of John Sturgeon to endow a chantry;[74] the manor or farm of Clitterhouse,[75] rents and ferms in 'Alrichesbiri,' where the masters and brothers had a holding in 1241;[76] Hackney Marsh, Cudfield Marsh, Willesden and 'Lyme hurst,' co. Middlesex; the manor of Fryern,[77] rents and ferms from Hatfield, 'Bradokes,' Rainham and Downham, which the master had held in 1326,[78] and from Burnham, Aveley, and 'Shernwood' Marsh, co. Essex; the ferm of Wollaston, co. Northants, where the hospital had property in 1275;[79] a rent in St. Albans, co. Herts., and a small holding in co. Bucks. St. Bartholomew's also owned the church of Little Wakering, co. Essex, which had long been appropriated to it;[80] the rectory of Hinton, co. Somerset, and the patronage of the church of Holy Cross,[81] an early foundation within

[52] *L. and P. Hen. VIII*, v, 1370 (13).

[53] Lond. Epis. Reg. Stokesley, fol. 91–2.

[54] *L. and P. Hen. VIII*, vii, 921.

[55] Ibid. xiii (2), 492.

[56] Ibid. xix (1), 812 (80).

[57] According to the bull of Pope Clement VII, Lond. Epis. Reg. Stokesley, fol. 91.

[58] *L. and P. Hen. VIII*, xix (1), 812 (80).

[59] *Memoranda and Documents relating to the Royal Hospitals*, App. iv, v.

[60] Moore, op. cit. 25. Rebuilding may have been necessary, too, for there is a note, Oct. 1546, in the Repertories of the Common Council, xi, fol. 288, of the Lord Mayor's engagement to finish the new hospital in Smithfield.

[61] Stow, op. cit. iii, 234.

[62] Moore, op. cit. 28–9.

[63] *Cal. of S.P. Dom.* 1627–8, p. 455.

[64] Ibid. 1628–49, pp. 668–9.

[65] *Hist. MSS. Com. Rep.* vi, App. i, 36.

[66] *Cal. of S.P. Dom.* 1664–5, p. 114; ibid. 1665–6, p. 6.

[67] *Cal. of Treas. Papers*, 365.

[68] *Cal. of S.P. Dom.* 1667, p. 21.

[69] Ibid.

[70] Ibid. Oct. 1668–9, p. 139.

[71] Ibid. 1690–1, pp. 473–4.

[72] Moore, op. cit. 27.

[73] *Valor Eccl.* (Rec. Com.), i, 388.

[74] Harl. MS. 433, fol. 296; Lysons, *Envir. of Lond.* iii, 50.

[75] It appears to have acquired this property in Hendon in 1446. Pat. 24 Hen. VI, pt. i, m. 5, quoted in Tanner, *Notit. Mon.*; Lysons, op. cit. iii, 6.

[76] Doc. of D. and C. of St. Paul's, A. Box 24, No. 608. A settlement was then made with the precentor of St. Paul's, who claimed it for his prebend of Portpool. Its property there was called a manor in 1326. *Cal. of Pat.* 1324–7, p. 270.

[77] Morant, *Hist. of Essex*, i, 221.

[78] *Cal. of Pat.* 1324–7, p. 270. Protection is granted to his servants carrying crops from his manors of Hatfield, Wakering, Rainham, and Downham. The hospital obtained some land in Downham and Ramsden Bellhouse in 1392. Ibid. 1391–6, p. 162.

[79] *Hund. R.* (Rec. Com.), ii, 10.

[80] Morant, op. cit. i, 307.

[81] *Mun. Gildhall, Lond.* ii (1), 238. It figures in the list of London churches in 1303 given in the *Liber Custum.*, but the entry is in a much later hand than the rest.

its precincts. Among the possessions of the hospital in 1535 there is no mention of the manor of 'Stretle,' co. Cambridge, which had been given to the master and brothers in 1370 to pray for the good estate of Sir Walter Manny, knt., and to keep his anniversary after death.[82]

*M. Reddan*

## Revised List of Masters of the Hospital of St. Bartholomew

From Rahere to John Needham, where the cartulary ends, the list is from Kerling, *Cartulary*, Appendix III, p. 177. This is her corrected list of masters. She comments on the dates in her introduction, pp. 4–8. From William Knyght onwards the names are an expanded and amended version of the list in the *V.C.H.*

The list in *V.C.H. London*, i, is headed 'Proctors and Masters' but Kerling just uses the term 'master'. She states that both terms are used in the cartulary for the same men, but the use of 'proctor' disappears by the end of the thirteenth century.

Rahere, 1123–43[83]
Hagno, 1137–47
Adam, 1147–75/6
Stephen, 1175/6–82
Hugh?
Alan Presbyter, 1182–c.98
Stephen, c.1198–1211
Hugh, 1212–23[84]
Maurice, 1223
William, 1224–46/7
Bartholomew, 1246/7–68/9
John Walton, 1269–80
John de Eylesbury, warden 1270–1
John de Camerwell, 1281
Geoffrey de Eystan, 1281–85
Thomas de Whitchester, 1285–99/1300

Hugh de Rothewell, 1300
Adam de Rothing, 1302/3–08
John Terefeld, 1309–10
William de Acton, 1312–22/3
Simon Dowell, 1321–22
William Rous, 1324–38
Thomas Willy, 1338–9
Thomas Litlington, 1339–41
Laurence Crandon, 1341/2–48
Walter de Basingbourne, 1348–54
Stephen de Maydenhethe, 1356–71
Richard Sutton, 1373–?86
William Wakeryng, 1388[85]–1404
Thomas Lakenham, 1406–12
Robert Newton, 1413–17[86]
John Bury, 1417[87]
John White, 1418–22/3
John Wakeryng, 1423–66
John Nedham, 1466–70
William Knyght, occurs 1471;[88] died 1473[89]
John Barton, occurs 1485[90]
Thomas Creveker, elected 1487;[91] died 1510[92]
Robert Beyley, elected 1510;[93] died 1516[94]
Richard Smith, LL.D., elected 1516;[95] died 1524[96]
Alexander Collins, elected 1524;[97] died 1528[98]
Edward Staple, elected 1528;[99] resigned 1532[100]
John Brereton, LL.D., elected 1532;[101] occurs 1534[102]
William Turges, S.T.B., appointed 1544[103]

---

[82] Chan. Inq. p.m. 43 Edw. III (2nd Nos.), 51.
[83] *V.C.H. London*, i has Alfune as first proctor, B.L. Cott. Vespasian B.ix, fol.54, but Kerling omits him from her list of masters. From the English version of Vespasian B ix printed in Webb, *Records*, Appendix I, pp. 401–2, it is clear that Alfhune assisted Rahere with the sick and Kerling presumably omits him because Rahere was in charge. *Heads of Religious Houses*, vol. I, p. 174 has 1144 as the date of Rahere's death.
[84] The reference in *V.C.H. London*, i, to a master called Hugh from the early thirteenth century seems likely to be to this man, *Hist. MSS. Com. Rep. ix*, App. i, *36*. The *V.C.H.* suggests that he is the same man as Hugh, a proctor, to whom there is as reference dated 1242/3, *Hist. MSS. Com. Rep. ix*, App. i *18*, but this seems unlikely given Kerling's evidence of a master of that name 1212–23. The later Hugh must have been working in a subordinate position to William the master at the time.

[85] *V.C.H.* has 1386 for the resignation of Sutton and the election of Wakeryng quoting Lond. Epis. Reg. Braybroke, fol. 282. Kerling says that 1386 'may be correct' for Sutton's resignation followed by Wakeryng's election in 1387/8, '*Cartulary*', p. 5.
[86] Kerling's date is 1415 which is the last mention of him in the cartulary but he appears in the pardon rolls in 1417, T.N.A. C67/36, m. 31.
[87] Kerling's dates are 1415–17 but she says that Bury is not mentioned in the cartulary and gives no reference. *V.C.H. London*, i, gives date of death 1417, Stow, *Survey*, iii. 233, from his monument in the hospital church. Given the later date for Newton, Bury's election and death in 1417 seem the most likely.
[88] T.N.A. C67/44/6.
[89] Weever, *Fun. Monum.* 435.
[90] Moore, *History*, vol. 2, pp. 113–14.
[91] Ibid. vol. 2, p. 114.
[92] Lond. Epis. Reg. Fitz James fol. 15.
[93] Lond. Epis.Reg.FitzJames, fol. 15.
[94] Lond. Epis. Reg. Fitz James, fol. 66.
[95] Lond. Epis. Reg. FitzJames, fol. 66–70.
[96] Lond. Epis. Reg. Tunstall, fol. 80.
[97] Lond. Epis. Reg. Tunstall, fol. 80–86.
[98] Lond. Epis. Reg. Tunstall, fol. 87.
[99] Lond. Epis. Reg. Tunstall, fol. 87–101. Staple was bishop of Meath and held the hospital in commendam, *L. and P. Hen. VIII*, v. 1370 (13).
[100] Lond. Epis. Reg. Stokesley, fol. 91.
[101] Lond. Epis. Reg. Stokesley, fol. 91–2.
[102] *L. and P. Hen. VIII, vii* 921. He was the last master of the original foundation *L and P. Hen. VIII, xix* (1), 812 (80).
[103] *L. and P. Hen. VIII, xix* (1) 812 (80).

View of an Archway of Blackfriars Monastery in Water Lane, Blackfriars, now part of a coffin maker's workshop. Anon artist, c.1830.

*(Guildhall Library, City of London)*

View of Austin Friars Church, 1815, by John Preston Neale (1780–1847), engr. W. Wallis.
*(Guildhall Library, City of London)*

Remains of the South and West walls of the House of St. Clare of the
Minoressess without Aldgate, 1812, by John Thomas Smith (1766–1833). Shows
damage after the fire of 1797, and demolition work in progress.
*(Guildhall Library, City of London)*

The remains of Kilburn Priory as it appeared in 1722. Anon artist, 1813.
*(Guildhall Library, City of London)*

THE CHAPEL OF

FOR LEPERS IN

SOUTHWARK,

*dedicated to S.* *Mary*

Founded prior to

**M B**

This Chapel Was Built
To the Honour of God and for the Use of
the Poor Infirm and Impotent People
Harbourd Within this Hospital

*May* *Mar.* *Bond Esq.* *Treasurer*
Annо 1636

THE HOSPITAL

KENT STREET,

CALLED LE LOCK,

*and S.* *Leonard.*

the XIV.th of Edw: II.

*Inscription over the Door*

The Lock Hospital Chapel, Southwark. Anon artist, pub. 1813. The hospital was originally built
for lepers in the twelfth century, closing in 1760. Kent Street is now known as Tabard Street.
*(Guildhall Library, City of London)*

View of St. Bartholomew's Chapel, Hackney. Anon, c.1830. The chapel was originally part of the hospital for lepers.
*(Guildhall Library, City of London)*

# 21. THE HOSPITAL OF ST. KATHERINE BY THE TOWER

## INTRODUCTION

The original *V.C.H.* article provides a good summary of the development of the hospital, but important new work was done by Catherine Jamison, *The History of the Royal Hospital of St. Katherine by the Tower of London* (Oxford, 1952). Christopher Kitching, 'The Decline of Hospitality in the Royal Hospital of St. Katherine by the Tower, 1660–98', *Guildhall Studs. in London Hist.* 1, (1973), pp. 7–12 is also useful on the decline in finances and the level of care and facilities offered to inmates. McHardy, *Church in London* has various references to the property and personnel of St. Katherine's. No new archaeological investigation or study of the fabric or material culture of the house has been carried out, but for the property held, see Honeybourne, 'Property', pp. 85–91, 197–9, and *Documentary Sources*, p. 62.

*Claire Martin*

The hospital of St. Katharine by the Tower was founded about 1148[1] by Matilda the wife of King Stephen for a master, brethren, sisters, and thirteen poor persons[2] on land in the parish of St. Botolph without Aldgate, bought for that purpose from the priory of Holy Trinity, Aldgate.[3] The queen gave to the hospital for its maintenance a mill near the Tower of London with the land belonging to it,[4] and confirmed the grant made by William de Yprès of an annual rent of £20 from 'Edredeshethe,'[5] afterwards Queenhithe. The perpetual custody of the hospital was conferred on the priory of Holy Trinity by Queen Matilda, who, however, reserved for herself and the queens, her successors, the choice of the master.[6]

Nothing further is heard of the house until 1255, when Queen Eleanor of Provence disputed the claim of the priory to its custody.[7] The condition of the hospital shortly before must have been most unsatisfactory, for the canons of Holy Trinity had appointed one of their own number master in order to reform the brothers who were always drinking and quarrelling,[8] and a suspicion arises that the priory may have been partly responsible for this by previously neglecting its

duty of supervision.[9] Whether the queen's action was determined by her desire to secure a better working of the hospital, or by her resentment at the encroachment on her right of presentation, it is impossible to say. The court of the Exchequer decided that the priory had established its claim to the custody, and an inquisition taken by the mayor and aldermen of London resulted in a similar verdict.[10] The queen then called to her aid the bishop of London, who, in 1257, visited the hospital, removed the master appointed by the canons, and without a shadow of right ordered the prior and canons to refrain henceforth from all interference with the hospital.[11] In 1261 Henry de Wengham, bishop of London, the bishops of Carlisle and Salisbury, with others of the king's council, prevailed on the prior to assent verbally to the renunciation of the convent's right, and then made a formal surrender of the hospital to the queen.[12]

Eleanor waited for some years and then dissolved the hospital, refounding it 5 July, 1273.[13] This new foundation she endowed with land in East Smithfield, and all her lands and rents in Rainham[14] and Hartlip, co. Kent, and in the vill of Reed,[15] co. Herts., for the support of a master and three brothers, priests, who were to say mass daily for the soul of

---

[1] Ducarel, in his 'Hist. of St. Kath. Hosp.' *Bibl. Topog. Brit.* ii, says it was founded in 1148. The charter by which Matilda made a grant to the priory of Holy Trinity in exchange for the land on which the hospital was founded must be either 1147 or 1148 in date, as it is witnessed by Hilary bishop of Chichester, 1147–74, and Robert bishop of Hereford, 1131–48.

[2] Ibid. ii, 1, 2, 100; Cott. Chart. xvi, 35.

[3] Dugdale, *Mon. Angl.* vi, p. 153, App. ix.

[4] Ducarel, op. cit. ii, 100.

[5] Ibid. 100, 101; Cott. Chart. xvi, 35.

[6] Guildhall MS. 122, fol. 750–4; Ducarel, op. cit. 2, 102.

[7] Ducarel, op. cit. 3.

[8] Ibid. 5.

[9] The letter of Pope Urban IV in 1264 shows that the prior and convent had had complete power there, instituting and depriving the brethren, who received from them the profession and habit, and took an oath to be subject to them in spiritual and temporal matters. Rymer, *Foedera* (Rec. Com.), i (1), 439.

[10] Ducarel, op. cit. 3, 4.

[11] Ibid. 4, 5, 6.

[12] Ibid. 6.

[13] Ibid. App. v.

[14] Hasted, *Hist. of Kent*, ii, 534. The manor of Queencourt, a farm called Berengrave, and a mill.

[15] Chauncy, *Hist. of Herts.* 93.

Henry III and the souls of past kings and queens of England,[16] some sisters and twenty-four poor persons,[17] of whom six were to be poor scholars. On the anniversary of the death of Henry III a thousand poor men were each to receive ½d. The right of appointing the master, of filling vacancies among the brethren and sisters, and of changing the articles of the charter was reserved by the queen for herself and her successors, queens of England.

In 1293 Thomas Leckelade who had been made master by Eleanor of Provence resigned, and the post was granted to Walter de Redinges for life.[18] His administration appears to have been the cause of the dilapidation and deterioration of which the brothers and sisters complained and which caused the king in April, 1300, to order a visitation of the hospital to be made by John de Lacy and Ralph de Sandwich.[19]

The hospital was harassed in 1310 by a demand of the Exchequer for a sum due from a former owner of the lands in Kent given to them by Queen Eleanor, but the king ordered the barons of the Exchequer to give the hospital a discharge.[20]

The right of the queen to make any change she thought fit in the hospital was called in question in 1333 and the point was decided completely in her favour. Richard de Lusteshull, who had been made master for life by Queen Isabella on 24 June, 1318,[21] was removed for wasting the goods of the hospital,[22] and his post given by Queen Philippa to Roger Bast. Lusteshull brought his case before the king and council in Parliament, and at first the king in 1333 ordered the justices to proceed to a trial and judgement even if Bast refused to appear.[23] Queen Philippa, however, showed that by the terms of the foundation charter the judges had no jurisdiction, and the king decided that the matter rested with the queen and her council.[24]

It is evident that Queen Philippa took a keen interest in the hospital. She tried on two occasions[25] to secure the appropriation to its use of the church of St. Peter, Northampton, with the chapels of Kingsthorpe and Upton, the patronage of which had been granted to the hospital in 1329 by the king.[26] In 1350 she founded a chantry in the hospital and provided for the maintenance of an additional chaplain by the gift of lands worth £10 a year.[27] At this time too she drew up a number of ordinances[28] to be observed by the inmates: the brothers and sisters were to have no private property except by the consent of the master; they were not to go out without his leave nor to stay out after curfew; the sisters were allowed 20s. a year for their clothing, the brothers 40s.; the costume was to be black with the sign of St. Katharine, and the wearing of green or entirely red clothes was prohibited; the brethren were to have no private conference with the sisters or any other women; negligence or disobedience on the part of the brethren and sisters was punishable by lessening their portion of food and drink but not by stripes; each sister was to receive in her room her daily allowance of a white and a brown loaf, two pieces of different kinds of meat value 1½d. or fish of the same value, and a pittance worth 1d.; the portion of both brothers and sisters was to be doubled on fifteen feast days; the master was to dine in the common hall with the brothers; the almswomen were to wear caps and cloaks of a grey colour; they were not to go out without leave of the master; if their conduct was bad they could be removed by the master with consent of the brethren and sisters. Other ordinances concern the care of the sick and the transaction of business relating to the property of the house.

The rebuilding of the church was begun by William de Kildesby the master, in 1343,[29] and Queen Philippa had directed that all surplus revenues of the hospital should be devoted to this work.[30] Judging, however, from the report following a visitation by the chancellor and others in 1377,[31] the master can have found it no easy matter to secure a surplus. Some time before it had been necessary to give up the distribution to the thousand poor persons on St. Edmund's Day in order to provide properly for the poor women and clerks; the income of the hospital was less than the expenditure by £14 14s. 6d. without reckoning provision for the master or for the repair of the church and its possessions, and although John de Hermesthorp, then master, had spent £2,000 on rebuilding[32] the nave of the church and other necessary work, much still remained to be done.

[16] Charter of foundation. Ducarel, op. cit. App. v.
[17] Ducarel, op. cit. 8, gives the number of sisters as three, and that of the poor women as ten, but in the charter of foundation the number of sisters is not specified, and there appear to have been eighteen bedeswomen.
[18] Cal. of Pat. 1292–1301, p. 33.
[19] Ibid. 548. The year before Walter had been ordered to appear before auditors with rolls and tallies and muniments to render accounts for the whole time of his custody.
[20] Cal. of Close, 1307–13, p. 285.
[21] Cal. of Pat. 1317–21, p. 164.
[22] A visitation of the hospital took place in 1327, and the visitors were empowered to remove the warden and any of the ministers, with the consent of Queen Isabella. Ibid. 1327–30, p. 60.
[23] Cal. of Close, 1333–7, pp. 47, 48, 63.
[24] Ibid. 171.
[25] In 1343, Cal. of Pap. Letters, iii, 88; and 1352, Cal. Pap. Pet. i, 236.
[26] Cal. of Pat. 1327–30, p. 420.
[27] Ducarel, op. cit. 11.
[28] Ibid. App. ix.
[29] Cal. of Pap. Letters, iii, 88.
[30] Ducarel, op. cit. App. ix.
[31] Cal. of Pat. 1377–81, p. 507.
[32] Bequests to the work of the church of St. Katharine in 1361, 1371, and 1375, are mentioned in Sharpe, Cal. of Wills, ii, 30, 143, and 189.

The petition of one of the ladies of the princess of Wales to have possession of a corrody granted her by the king was refused by the chancellor, who said that no corrody existed there and that the hospital was unable to support one.[33] It seems not unlikely that a reduction of the numbers on the foundation was gradually effected as a result of the report, for in 1412[34] there were ten poor women and not eighteen as before.

Meanwhile the hospital had been adding to its resources: Edward III in 1376 made a perpetual grant of £10 a year from the Hanaper for a chaplain to celebrate in the chantry founded by Queen Philippa,[35] and left in trust for the hospital the reversion of the manor of Rushindon in the Isle of Sheppey, and of a messuage, 60 acres of land, 200 acres of pasture, and 120 acres of salt marsh in the parish of Minster to provide another chaplain;[36] in 1378 Robert de Denton, who had intended to found a hospital for the insane in his messuages in the parish of Allhallows Barking, granted the property instead to St. Katharine's to establish a chantry;[37] John de Chichester, goldsmith of London, bequeathed to the hospital in 1380 lands and tenements in the parishes of St. Botolph Aldgate, St. Mary Abchurch, St. Edmund Lombard Street, and St. Nicholas Acon for a similar purpose;[38] in 1381 a messuage in Bow Lane was granted to St. Katharine's for daily celebrations for Thomas bishop of Durham;[39] and in 1380 Richard II allowed the hospital to acquire in mortmain from the alien abbey of Isle Dieu the manor of Carlton, co. Wilts., and the advowson of the church of Upchurch, in Kent,[40] in return for an annual payment of £40 during the war with France and for the maintenance of three additional chantry chaplains.

The hospital benefited considerably by the appointment of Thomas Beckington, the king's secretary, as master in 1440.[41] Henry VI not only gave to it in August of that year the manors of Chisenbury and Quarley, parcel of the alien priory of Ogbourne,[42] but on Beckington's representing that the revenues of the house were still insufficient,

he granted to it in 1441 an annual fair of twenty-one days from the feast of St. James, to be held on Tower Hill.[43] He, moreover, exempted the hospital and precinct from all jurisdiction save that of the Lord Chancellor and the master,[44] and acquitted it from payment of all aids, subsidies,[45] and clerical tenths;[46] no royal stewards, marshals, or other royal officers were to lodge in the hospital or its houses without the consent of the master,[47] and no royal purveyor was to take the goods and chattels of the hospital against the master's wish;[48] the master was to have court-leet and view of frankpledge within the bounds of the hospital;[49] and the master, brothers, and sisters were to have the chattels of felons, fugitives and suicides, waifs and strays, deodands and treasure trove,[50] assize of bread and ale, custody of weights and measures, the cognizance and punishment of all offences against the peace in the same place,[51] and the cognizance of all pleas and the fines and amercements of all persons residing in the precinct;[52] any writs they needed were to be given to them free of all payment;[53] they were not to be deprived of any of the above privileges because they neglected to use them.[54]

John Holland, duke of Exeter, who died in 1448, was buried in the church of St. Katharine, to which he made an important bequest of plate[55] and tapestry. He also directed that in the little chapel where his body rested a chantry of four priests should be erected, to be endowed with his manor of Great Gaddesden in Hertfordshire, though apparently some other endowment was arranged, for the manor figures in the possessions of his son Henry, on whose death it passed to the crown.[56]

The general pardon to the warden, brethren, and sisters on the accession of Henry VIII[57] must have been a matter of form, since it is evident that the hospital enjoyed the favour of both Henry VII and Henry VIII: at the funeral of the former the large

---

33 Queen Philippa had obtained a corrody for one of her ladies by special request, though she must have known the resources of the house. *Cal. of Pat.* 1377–81, p. 508.

34 John de Hermesthorp, the master, at that date left by will bequests to three brothers, three sisters, three secular chaplains, and ten poor women of St. Katharine's. Ducarel, op. cit. 13.

35 *Cal. of Pat.* 1377–81, p. 151; Anct. D. (P.R.O.), D. 973.

36 The reversion was made over to the hospital by the trustees in 1392. *Cal. of Pat.* 1391–6, p. 50.

37 *Cal. of Pat.* 1377–81, p. 266.

38 Sharpe, *Cal. of Wills*, ii, 219.

39 *Cal. of Pat.* 1377–81, p. 613.

40 Ibid. 559.

41 Ducarel, op. cit. 14.

42 The charter is given in App. xii, op. cit.

43 Inspex. of Queen Elizabeth given in App. viii, op. cit. 56.

44 Ibid. 56.

45 Ibid. 59.

46 Ibid.

47 Ibid.

48 Ibid. 60.

49 Ibid. 57.

50 Ibid.

51 Ibid. 58.

52 Ibid.

53 Ibid. 60.

54 Ibid. 61.

55 To the high altar a cup of beryl garnished with gold, pearls, and precious stones, a chalice of gold and all the furniture of his chapel except a chalice, eleven basins, eleven candlesticks of silver with eleven pairs of vestments, a mass-book, a 'paxbred,' and a couple of silver cruets which were to be given to the chapel in which he was buried. Ibid. 17–18.

56 Chauncy, *Hist. of Herts.* 559–60.

57 Ducarel, op. cit. 20.

sum of £40 was given to the sisters;[58] Henry VIII[59] and Queen Catherine established in the hospital church in 1578 a Gild of St. Barbara, to which belonged Cardinal Wolsey, the duke of Norfolk, the duke of Buckingham, and many other dis tinguished persons,[60] and amid the dissolution of so many monasteries and hospitals the king not only spared this house but in 1537 remitted the annual tenth, and the first fruits due from Gilbert Latham, who had been appointed master by Queen Jane Seymour.[61] The income of the house in 1535 was said to be £315 8s. 4d.,[62] and its expenses £284 8s. 4d., £186 15s. being paid to the inmates of the hospital, viz., to the three brothers, £24; three sisters, £24; three priests, £24; six clerks serving in the church, £40; ten bedeswomen, 10½d. a week each; the master of the children, £8; for the maintenance of the six children, £24; and £5 each to the steward, butler, cook, and undercook.[63]

The possessions of the hospital then included rents and ferms in the City and suburbs of London of an annual value of £211 19s. 6d.,[64] the manor of Queenscourt, with the farm of Berengrave,[65] land in the parish of Rainham,[66] Rushindon Manor, with the farm of Daudeley,[67] in co. Kent; the manor of Quarley,[68] co. Hants; the manors of Chisenbury Priors[69] and Carlton,[70] co. Wilts.; and the manor of Queenbury, co. Herts.[71]

In 1303 and 1428 the master held half a knight's fee in Reed, co. Herts.[72] The house also owned the advowsons of St. Peter, Northampton, with its chapels of Kingsthorpe and Upton,[73] of Queenbury,[74] and of Quarley.[75] The advowson of Frinsted, co. Kent, had been granted to St. Katharine's in 1329 by Sir John de Crombwell,[76]

who two years later obtained a papal mandate for its appropriation to the hospital.[77]

The religious changes must have greatly affected the house. The suppression of chantries under Edward VI not only deprived it of much of its property but of the principal reason of its existence. The new order of things was marked by the king's appointment of a layman as master in 1549,[78] and henceforth the post was regarded mainly as a reward for a servant of the crown. Fortunately most holders of the office held a more exalted view of their duty than Dr. Thomas Wilson, who used his position merely as an opportunity for plunder. He first attempted to sell the privileges of the liberty to the City Corporation, and when he was baulked in this by the action of the inhabitants, who appealed to Cecil in 1565,[79] he surrendered the charter of Henry VI to the queen and obtained a confirmation in 1566,[80] omitting the grant of the fair, which he sold to the City for £466 13s. 4d.[81]

The history of the house for more than a century was marked by no events of importance. In 1692 a certain Dr. Payne, in virtue of a patent he had obtained to visit exempt churches, attempted a visitation of St. Katharine's, but the brothers absolutely declined to acknowledge his jurisdiction,[82] and were successful in maintaining the privileges of their house. Complaints against the master, Sir James Butler, caused a visitation to be made in 1698 by Lord Chancellor Somers, who removed Butler and drew up some rules for the government of the hospital.[83] These order that the master shall be resident;[84] that provision shall be made for the performance of religious services by the brothers;[85] that chapters shall be held[86] at which all business is to be considered;[87] that the fines at the renewals of leases shall be divided into three parts, of which one is to be devoted to the repair of the church, another to be given to the master, and the third to the brothers and sisters;[88] any increase of the annual revenues shall be disposed of as follows: the allowance of the bedeswomen is to be doubled; the stipend of

---

[58] L. and P. Hen. VIII, i, 5735.

[59] If this had not been a favourite foundation of Henry VIII the bishop of Famagosta would not have sent certain relics to the king in 1512 out of respect for the hospital. Ibid. i, 3456.

[60] Stow, Surv. of Lond. (ed. Strype), ii, 627.

[61] L. and P. Hen. VIII, xii (1), 795 (45). The surplus of the house in 1535 was £31, which would not have sufficed for the tenth, amounting to £31 11s. 5d.

[62] Ibid. ix, App. 13. According to the Valor Eccl. (Rec. Com.) it was £338 3s. 4d. gross and £315 14s. 2d. net.

[63] L. and P. Hen. VIII, ix, App. 13.

[64] Valor Eccl. (Rec. Com.), i, 386.

[65] Hasted, Hist. of Kent, ii, 534.

[66] Cal. Inq. p.m. Hen. VII, i, 606.

[67] Valor Eccl. i, 386.

[68] Ibid.

[69] Ibid.; Hoare, Hist. of Wilts., Elstub and Everley, 17.

[70] Ducarel, op. cit. 120.

[71] Ibid.; Chauncy, Hist. of Herts. 93.

[72] Feud. Aids, ii, 433, 447.

[73] Bridges, Hist. of Northants, i, 445.

[74] Chauncy, Hist. of Herts. 93.

[75] The rectory of Quarley still belongs to the hospital. Lewis, Topog. Dict. of Engl.

[76] Cal. of Pat. 1327–30, p. 472.

[77] Cal. of Pap. Letters, ii, 353. Hasted, however (op. cit. ii, 514), says the advowson belonged to the owner of the manor, in which case St. Katharine's did not possess it.

[78] Lansd. MS. 171, fol. 236. Elizabeth appears to have gone a step further when she made the lieutenant of the Tower master in 1560. Cal. of S.P. Dom. 1547–80, p. 150.

[79] Ducarel, op. cit., 23–7.

[80] Ibid. 62–7.

[81] Ibid. 22. According to Ducarel the sale of the fair took place before the attempt on the privileges, but this can hardly be correct if, as he states, the appeal was made in 1565, for the confirmation of the charter is dated July 8 Eliz. i.e. 1566.

[82] Ibid. 32.

[83] Ibid.

[84] Stowe MS. 796, fol. 50.

[85] Ibid.

[86] Ibid.

[87] Ibid. fol. 52.

[88] Ibid. fol. 54.

£8 then given to each brother is to be increased until it reaches the sum of £40; the sisters' stipends are to be gradually raised to £20 each; the surplus is then to go to the master until his whole income amounts to £500; any further revenues shall be devoted to the maintenance of an additional brother, of another sister, of two more bedeswomen, and if more still remain, it shall be used to provide a school.[89] The income of the house seems to have benefited by Lord Somers' regulation, for a school was established there in 1705.[90] The church, which seems to have been repaired about 1640,[91] escaped damage from the fires which occurred in the precinct in 1672 and 1734, and from the Gordon Riots,[92] to be destroyed with the rest of the hospital buildings in 1825, when the site was needed for the St. Katharine's Docks.[93] A new church and hospital were then built in Regent's Park to continue Queen Eleanor's foundation, though numerous changes have made the house of the present day very unlike that of 1273.[94] However, there still are sisters, bedesmen, bedeswomen, brothers with religious duties to perform, and a master now also in holy orders, for Queen Victoria appointed clergymen in both the vacancies which occurred during her reign.[95]

*M. Reddan*

## Revised List of Masters of St. Katherine's Hospital

Unless otherwise indicated this list is derived from that in Jamison, *History*, pp. 189–91.

—, canon of Holy Trinity Priory, appointed *c.*1255; deprived 1257

Gilbert, appointed 1257

Walter de Runachmore, appointed 1263,[96] died or resigned before 30 October 1264

John de Sancta Maria, appointed 30 October 1268

Thomas de Chalke, occurs 1266

Stephen de Fulborne, occurs 1269

Thomas de Lechlade, appointed 1273; resigned 1293

Sir Ralph, occurs 1281–2

Simon de Stanbrigge, occurs 1288

Walter de Redinges, appointed 1293; occurs 1300

John Sandale, occurs 1315

Adam de Eglesfeld, appointed 1317, died between 10 February 1318/9 and 18 April 1319

Richard de Lusteshull, appointed 1318; deprived 2 April 1327

Roger de Bast or Basse, appointed 1327; resigned 22 September 1334

William de Culshoe or Culpho, appointed 23 September 1334; occurs 1336[97]

William de Kildesby, appointed 1339; died 1345–6

Walter de Wetewang, appointed 1347; resigned *c.*1348

William de Hogate, occurs 1348

Paul de Monte Florio or Monte Florum, occurs 1351

William de Walcote, occurs *c.*1358–60

John de Clisseby, occurs 1363–6

John de Hermesthorp, occurs 1368; died between 12 December 1411 and 5 February 1411/12

Richard Prentys, occurs 1411

John Everdon, occurs 1415–16

Robert Rolleston, appointed 1421; resigned before 18 June 1429

John Francke, appointed before 18 June 1429; died between 2 May and 14 Oct 1438

Thomas de Beckington, LL.D., appointed 1438; resigned ?1443

John Delabere, occurs 1446; resigned ?1447

William Cleve, occurs 1449/50

Henry Trevilian, occurs from 1461,[98] to 1469

Lionel de Wydeville, D.D., occurs 1475; left England 1483

William Wryxham or Wrexham, occurs 1484; re-appointed 29 November 1485

William Breton, appointed 10 October 1485

Richard Payne, appointed before 3 March 1496/7; occurs 1499[99]

John Preston, appointed 1508; occurs 1509[100]

George de Athequa, appointed before 8 October 1512. Hospital probably taken into king's hands *c.*1535 but Mastership held till February 1536/7

Gilbert Latham, M.A., appointed 1536/7; occurs 1545/6

---

[89] Stowe MS. fol. 54, 55.
[90] Ducarel, op. cit. 32.
[91] An action was brought at that time by the master, Henry Montagu, against the executor of the late master, Sir Robert Ayton, for dilapidations. *Cal. of S.P. Dom.* 1640, pp. 283, 295, 482.
[92] Ducarel, op. cit. 31, 33.
[93] Thornbury and Walford, *Old and New London*, v, 273.
[94] Ibid. v, 274. The master, sisters, bedesmen, and bedeswomen all seem to be non-resident.
[95] *St. Paul's Eccl. Soc. Trans.* v, xxxvi.
[96] Stow MS. 796, fol. 47.

[97] Ducarel, op. cit. 81.
[98] Stow MS. 796, fol. 47.
[99] Stow MS. 796, fol. 47.
[100] *L. and P. Hen. VIII*, i, 121.

# 22. THE HOSPITAL OF ST. MARY WITHOUT BISHOPSGATE [ST. MARY SPITAL]

## INTRODUCTION

The original account for St. Mary Spital is a thorough, but general, overview of the history of the Augustinian church and hospital from its foundation in the twelfth century to its dissolution in the sixteenth century. The best and most recent publication on the subject is C. Thomas, B. Sloane, and C. Phillpotts, *Excavations at the Priory and Hospital of St. Mary Spital, London*, MoLAS Monograph series, 1 (London, 1997). This not only deals with the fabric and material culture of the hospital, it also gives a thorough analysis of the history of the Augustinian church and hospital. The archaeology of the whole precinct and the cemetery of the hospital will be dealt with in R. Aitken, D. Bowsher, C. Harward, N. Holder, M. McKenzie, K. Pitt, and C. Thomas, *Medieval Spitalfields: The Priory and Hospital of St. Mary Spital and the Bishopsgate Suburb*, MoLAS Monograph Series (in preparation: forthcoming *c.*2009). A list of sources relating to property held by the hospital in London can be found in *Documentary Sources*, pp. 63–4.

*Christine Fox*

The priory or hospital of St. Mary without Bishopsgate was founded on the east side of Bishopsgate Street[1] by Walter Brown,[2] a London citizen, and Rose his wife, on ground demised to them for that purpose by Walter son of Eildred, an alderman. Brown endowed it with other land adjoining, which extended to the City boundary, and with 100*s.* rent from tenements in Blanchapelton, and in various London parishes, Allhallows Staining, St. Margaret Pattens, St. Peter the Little, St. Martin Ludgate, St. Sepulchre, and St. Martin Outwich. The foundation stone was laid by Walter, archdeacon of London, June, 1197, and the building was dedicated by William de Ste. Mère l'Eglise, bishop of London, 1199–1221, to the honour of God and the Blessed Virgin. The house consisted[3] of Austin canons, whose duties were religious, and lay brothers and sisters to whom the care of the sick poor was entrusted, all being under the charge of a prior. The prior and brothers acknowledged themselves subject to the bishop of London, and promised that they would not make alienations of land without his leave, which he could not, however, refuse unless it was clear that loss to the hospital would result. His permission had also to be asked in case of vacancy before the canons proceeded to elect.[4] The priory had only been in existence a short

time when for some reason it was refounded in 1235,[5] and the church was moved farther to the east.[6] The all-important question of the water supply was settled at the end of 1277[7] by the gift to them of a spring called 'Snekockeswelle' in Stepney by John, bishop of London, who gave them leave to inclose it and bring the water by underground pipes into the hospital precincts. The original endowment must by this time have been supplemented by numerous grants, but the income of the hospital up to 1280 evidently did not keep pace with the expenditure, since at that date the priory owed £63 8*s.*[8] for meat. Apparently all difficulty on this score had not vanished in 1303, for the archbishop of Canterbury, after a visitation, expressly stated that in his opinion the annual revenue of 300 marks[9] was sufficient to maintain the accustomed number of inmates, viz. twelve canons, five lay brothers, and seven sisters. Judging from these ordinances the administration of the priory had become rather lax. The ancient custom of allotting to the hospital a third of the convent flour supply, which the sisters afterwards distributed as needed, had been abandoned; bequests for special purposes had been diverted

---

[1] The high road is mentioned as the western boundary in Walter's charter, printed in Dugdale, *Mon. Angl.* vi, 623.
[2] Ibid.
[3] Lond. Epis. Reg. Baldock and Gravesend, fol. 5.
[4] Doc. of D. and C. of St. Paul's, Liber A. fol. 12.

[5] Dugdale, loc. cit.
[6] Ibid. from Leland, *Coll.*
[7] *Hist. MSS. Com. Rep.* ix, App. i, 29.
[8] Sharpe, *Cal. of Letter Bk. A*, 33. The prior was ordered to pay it within four years.
[9] Lond. Epis. Reg. Baldock and Gravesend, fol. 5.

to other uses,[10] and the lamps which at one time had been kept burning between the beds in the hospital had been taken away.[11] The sisters seem to have received neither their proper portions of food[12] nor their share of pittances, and no allowance was made to them for dress, which they appear to have provided for themselves out of the legacies[13] left by their charges to the priory. With regard to the canons the archbishop ordered that money was not to be given to them for clothing,[14] but that they should be provided with clothes uniform in colour and quality, and that on receiving the new they should give up the old; that those holding offices were to render full accounts before the whole convent,[15] and that the cloistral canons and other hospital officials were not to go beyond the boundaries of the house singly or together, nor were they to ask leave of the prior to do so except for the evident utility of the priory. Their conduct indeed had not been exemplary: disobedience was not uncommon,[16] and scandal and prejudice to the monastery had been caused by their frequenting the houses[17] of Alice la Faleyse and Matilda wife of Thomas, who apparently lived within the precinct. That the canons were themselves not anxious for reform is shown by the fact that in 1306 they elected as prior a certain Robert de Cerne,[18] a notoriously unfit person, and as such promptly deposed by Ralph, bishop of London. Ralph then exercised the right he had in such a case by appointing the sub-prior of St. Bartholomew's, Philip de London, whose probity he knew and who he hoped would improve both the tone of the house and the administration of its temporal affairs. Philip and the canons arranged[19] that the deposed prior should receive a double allowance of bread, ale, and other food, 40s. per annum for his other necessaries, and a room near the infirmary, and for his servant a black loaf, a gallon of small beer, and one dish from the kitchen every day, and 5s. annual wages, and that a companion should also be assigned to him.

The bishopric being vacant in 1316 commissaries of the dean and chapter of St. Paul's visited St. Mary's and issued some injunctions.[20] The canons at first declined to pay procurations, though it is difficult to see on what grounds, considering that when they needed to elect a prior in 1279[21] in similar circumstances they had tacitly acknowledged that the dean and chapter occupied the bishop's place. However, after a threat of excommunication[22] they owned themselves wrong and paid the sum demanded, and the chapter of St. Paul's returned it to them for the use of the sick of the house.

The better administration desired by the bishop appears to have been inaugurated by Prior Philip. The convent had been enriched to some extent between 1303 and 1331: in 1314 a chantry for four chaplains was erected by John Tany,[23] one for two in 1325 by Roger de la Bere;[24] in 1306 Edward I[25] had given to the priory some land in Shalford and the advowsons of the church of Shalford with Bromley Chapel annexed, of 'Woghenersh,'[26] Puttenham, and 'Duntesfeld,'[27] and leave to appropriate Shalford and Bromley and 'Woghenersh'; and in 1318 Edward II had granted the convent acquittance from all tallages,[28] aids, pontages, pavages, and other payments. When the king in 1341 ordered the exemption[29] of the priory from payment of the subsidy, he certainly said that its endowment was so slender as hardly to suffice for the maintenance of the convent and the poor in the hospital. This, however, may be another way of stating that the charity dispensed there was very great, as he had good reason to know, more than one of his old servants[30] finding an asylum there. The position occupied by the priory must have by this time attained some importance, for the prior was appointed one of the valuers[31] of the 9th fleece, sheaf, &c., in co. Middlesex in 1340.

The house was evidently the reverse of affluent towards the end of the fourteenth century. In

[10] The legacy of Ela, countess of Warwick, is to be expended as she directed under pain of greater excommunication and perpetual deposition from office, viz. 20s. per annum for pittance of canons, brothers, and sisters, 20s. to the poor for milk, 20s. to same for linen, and 20s. to them for wood. Lond. Epis. Reg. Baldock and Gravesend, fol. 5.

[11] Ibid. fol. 6.

[12] Ibid. fol. 5.

[13] Ibid. fol. 6. The sisters are to receive ½ mark annually for their clothes. Goods given or bequeathed by the sick lying in that house to the prior and convent shall be given up by the sisters, who are to take an oath so to do.

[14] Ibid. fol. 5.

[15] Ibid. fol. 6.

[16] Ibid. fol. 5.

[17] Ibid. fol. 6.

[18] Ibid. fol. 6.

[19] Ibid. fol. 9, 10.

[20] Doc. of D. and C. of St. Paul's, Liber A, fol. 73b.

[21] Doc. of D. and C. of St. Paul's, Liber A. fol. 11b.

[22] Ibid. Note in the cover of the book.

[23] Cal. of Pat. 1313–17, p. 92.

[24] Ibid. 1324–7, p. 98.

[25] Dugdale, Mon. Angl. vi, 625.

[26] This is probably Wonersh, co. Surrey.

[27] Duntesfeld appears to be Dunsfold, co. Surrey. March 28, 1342, the king granted licence to the prior and convent to appropriate 'Duntesfeld' and Puttenham. Cal. of Pat. 1340–3, p. 410.

[28] Plac. de Quo Warr. (Rec. Com.), 452; see, too, Cal. of Pat. 1340–3, p. 434, and Cal. of Close, 1339–41, p. 600.

[29] Ibid. 1339–41, p. 600.

[30] 17 Nov. 1309, Robert de la Naperie, who had been maimed in the king's service, was sent there to receive food and clothing and a chamber to dwell in. Cal. of Close, 1307–13, p. 236. When he died the king filled his place with Peter de Kenebell, 1330. Ibid. 1330–73, p. 159. Another such appointment was made 27 Oct. 1331. Ibid. 396.

[31] Cal. of Pat. 1338–40, p. 502.

1394 a sum of £86 10s. 6d. was owing to St. Paul's Cathedral for obits, chantries, and rents unpaid in some cases for many years;[32] in 1399 the prior had to pawn a silver gilt censer for £10;[33] and in 1400 it was arranged that in return for 300 marks granted to the prior and convent 'in their very great necessity for the relief of their house which was heavily burdened with debt,' they would give 12 marks annual quitrent from their possessions in certain London parishes to the chaplain of the chantry of St. John Baptist in St. James's Garlickhithe.[34]

The causes of its poverty can only be conjectured, but were probably the depreciation in the value of its lands owing to the Black Death, and repairs to the church and other buildings, since it is unlikely that they had escaped without much damage from the floods which in 1373 were said to occur there annually.[35] The pope in 1391 granted an indulgence to those who visited and gave alms to the church and its chapels and to the hospital at Christmas, Easter, and other great festivals,[36] and the benefit derived may have been considerable, for crowds of people flocked to the priory on the three days following Easter Sunday,[37] doubtless attracted by the sermons preached at the Cross in the churchyard.[38]

One of the canons in 1389 obtained a papal indult to hold a secular benefice,[39] and a similar grant was made to John Mildenhale, the prior, in 1401.[40]

The ordinances of William bishop of London, dated 20 June, 1431,[41] do not disclose anything very much amiss. They chiefly concern the sisters, who as usual had been deprived of their due both as regards food and clothing. Some scandal had apparently been caused by their access to the convent kitchen, and the bishop ordered that a straight and inclosed way (*via recta et clausa*) should be made at the expense of the priory from the door of the sisters' house to the kitchen window, from which the sisters could, without hindrance, carry away their own dishes and those for the sick. To provide against their frequent visits to the pantry their allowance of bread and ale was to be given out weekly, though the good this would do is not very obvious, as they still had to go for bread and ale for the sick and candles for watching as needed. Anyone desiring to become a sister was to be admitted at a year's

probation, and, if rejected, was to pay her own expenses, which otherwise were to be paid by the priory. At the admission and profession of a sister no exactions were to be made by the prior and convent; after profession the sisters were to be obedient to the prior, and were not to go beyond the bounds of the house except with the prior's leave and for the benefit of the house. The houses occupied by the sisters and by the sick were in need of repairs, which were to be done as quickly as the priory was able.

When Richard Cressall became prior, in 1484, he found that the property of the priory in London, the main source of the income of the house, had been allowed to fall into ruin,[42] and it was no doubt a strain to provide for the necessary repairs and at the same time to keep up the charitable work of the hospital. More revenue was needed, and in April, 1509, King Henry VII, for £400,[43] granted to the prior and convent in mortmain the priory of Bicknacre, where, at the death of the last prior, Edmund Godyng, only one canon was left.[44] Its possessions included the manor of Bicknacre and thirty-one messuages and land in Woodham Ferrers, Danbury, Norton, Steeple, Chelmsford, Mayland, Stow, East and West Hanningfield, Purleigh, Burnham, and Downham, and were estimated to be worth £40 10s. per annum.[45] Daily celebrations for the souls of the founder, benefactors, and King Henry VII were, by the bishop's orders, performed at Bicknacre by one of the canons of the New Hospital.[46] The house in 1514 further obtained licence to acquire in mortmain lands to the annual value of £100.[47]

There is no record of the light in which the religious changes of the time were regarded here, but the royal supremacy was acknowledged on 23 June, 1534, by the prior and eleven others,[48] and it is unlikely that the king had any difficulty with the house, judging from the pensions granted at its suppression in 1538. The prior, William Major, received £80 a year,[49] and payment seems to have been made with regularity[50]; the president, an official of whom there is no other mention,[51] had £8 per annum; three other priests, £6 13s. 4d. each; and two others £7 10s. and £4 respectively; the two

[32] Doc. of D. and C. of St. Paul's, A. Box 77, No. 2048.

[33] Ibid. A. Box 77, No. 2049.

[34] Harl. Chart. 44, F. 40.

[35] Through the stopping up of a water-course. Riley, *Mem. of Lond.* 375.

[36] *Cal. of Pap. Letters*, iv, 393.

[37] Ibid.

[38] Stow, *Surv. of Lond.* (ed. Strype), ii, 98. The sermons were established before 1398, and they took place on these days.

[39] *Cal. of Pap. Letters*, iv, 324.

[40] Ibid. v, 436.

[41] Lond. Epis. Reg. Gray, fol. 61.

[42] Lond. Epis. Reg. Fitz James, fol. 161–3.

[43] *Arch.* xi, 265.

[44] Lond. Epis. Reg. Fitz James, fol. 161–3.

[45] *Arch.* xi, 265.

[46] Lond. Epis. Reg. Fitz James, fol. 165. The bishop's confirmation was given 9 Nov. 1509.

[47] *L. and P. Hen. VIII*, i, 5534.

[48] Ibid. vii, 921.

[49] Ibid. xiv (2), 433.

[50] Aug. Off. Misc. Bk. 249, fols. 14b, 18b; Bk. 250, fols. 19, 24, 30b.

[51] It may be another name for the sub-prior who is not referred to on this occasion.

sisters 40s. each.[52] The small number of brothers and sisters, and the state of the church, the roof of which fell before the end of the year,[53] indicate either that the dissolution had been for some time foreseen[54] or that much of the spirit of monasticism had departed. Whatever view is taken of the prior and canons there can be no doubt that good work was done in a hospital of 180 well-furnished beds,[55] and Sir Richard Gresham, the mayor, in a letter to the king, begged that it might continue under the rule of the mayor and aldermen.[56] It would, indeed, have been no more than just, for the hospital had not only been founded, but to a great extent endowed, by London citizens.[57] The king, nevertheless, beyond allowing the sick already there to remain,[58] turned a deaf ear to Gresham's request, and in April, 1540, a grant was made to Richard Moryson[59] of the infirmary, the dormitory, the waste ground leading from the churchyard to the infirmary, the prior's garden and the convent garden within the inclosure, the stable in the prior's garden with some waste land adjoining, and the other tenements of the priory which extended into Shoreditch.

The income of the priory, estimated in 1318 at over 300 marks,[60] amounted in 1535 to £562 14s. 6½d. gross, and £504 12s. 11½d. net.[61] Of this the sum of £277 13s. 4d. was derived from tenements in London and the suburbs, where the house had holdings in 1318 in thirty-seven parishes.[62] It held, besides the property of Bicknacre Priory, in co. Middlesex the manor of Hickmans and lands and tenements called 'Burganes lands,'[63] probably those possessed in 1318 in Shoreditch, Hackney, and Stepney[64]; in co. Herts the manor of Beaumond Hall; in co. Essex the

manor of Chalvedon,[65] where land had been given by William Hobruge before 1318,[66] the manor of Sabur or Seborow Hall,[67] evidently the lands in Mocking, Orsett, and Chadwell, held by the priory in the fourteenth century,[68] the manor of Frerne or Fryern, which came into possession of the house about 1419,[69] and lands in West Tilbury and Mountnessing; in co. Surrey the manor of Long Ditton, which, with the advowson of the church, had been given to the canons by William earl of Essex,[70] the rectories and tithes of Shalford and Wonersh, and a pension from the church of Putney; in co. Cambridge lands and tenements in Whittlesea. A pension was also paid by the abbey of Bindon, co. Dorset.

In 1318 the prior had the homage and service of half a knight's fee in West Tilbury and East Tilbury.[71] The plate of the house at the Dissolution was of no great quantity:– 61 oz. of gilt, 106 oz. of white, and 19¼ oz. of parcel gilt.[72]

*M. Reddan*

## Revised List of the Priors of St. Mary without Bishopsgate

This list is taken from Thomas et al., *Excavations*, pp. 180–1.

Godfrey, occurs *c*.1210, *c*.1218
William, occurs *c*.1216, 1222
Geoffrey, occurs *c*.1231–2
Warin, occurs *c*.1232–3
William, *temp.* Henry III (or possibly earlier?)
Reginald, occurs *c*.1241–2
Robert Serve, occurs *c*.1243, 1248
Thomas, occurs *c*.1265–6
Roger, occurs *c*.1274–5; resigned 1279
William, occurs *c*.1289
Roger, occurs *c*.1296, 1298; no longer prior 1300
Robert de Cerne, deposed 1306
Philip de London, appointed 1306; occurs 1307
William Horton/de Heston, occurs *c*.1317, 1327
John de Aabyndon/Habitone, occurs *c*.1335, 1337
James, occurs *c*.1350
William Swyft, occurs *c*.1351–7
Thomas de Thorneston, occurs *c*.1367, 1373
John de Lyndeseye, occurs *c*.1378, 1379
William Helpaby/Helperby, occurs *c*.1382, 1383; resigned 1388

[52] *L. and P. Hen. VIII*, xiv (2), 433. In 1556 two sisters were receiving 40s. each and twelve men sums varying from 20s. to £6 13s. 4d. Add. MS. 8102, fol. 6.

[53] At the end of July, 1538. *L. and P. Hen. VIII*, xiii (2), 13.

[54] The members of the convent seem to have tried to propitiate those in power, as the pensions given by them show. Ibid. ix, 478; xvi, 745, fol. 3, 5, 6, 7, 9.

[55] Stow, op. cit. ii, 97.

[56] *L. and P. Hen. VIII*, xiii (2), 492.

[57] See patents of 11 Edw. II in Cott. MS. Nero C. iii, fol. 219–25; and Sharpe, *Cal. of Wills*, i, 4, 8, 47, 67, 141, 276, 342, 385, 568; ii, 313, 315.

[58] *L. and P. Hen. VIII*, xvi, 1500, p. 724. A lease was made in Dec. 1541 of the priory, except the buildings in which the infirm there lie for the term of their lives.

[59] Ibid. xv, 613 (3).

[60] It was reckoned at that amount in 1303 (Lond. Epis. Reg. Baldock and Gravesend, fol. 5), and between 1303 and 1318 one or two grants had been made.

[61] *Valor Eccl.* (Rec. Com.), i, 401–2. According to Stow, *Surv. of Lond.* ii, 99, its income was £478.

[62] Cott. MS. Nero C. iii. For the parishes where the tenements of the priory lay in 1535, see *L. and P. Hen. VIII*, xv, xvi, xvii, xviii, xix.

[63] *L. and P. Hen. VIII*, xix (2), 166 (38). Here these lands are described as in Hackney, Shoreditch, and Stepney.

[64] Cott. MS. Nero C. iii, fols. 220, 221, 225.

[65] Morant, *Hist. of Essex*, ii, 256.

[66] Cott. MS. Nero C. iii, fol. 225.

[67] Morant, op. cit. i, 224. The manor is said to be in the three parishes following.

[68] Cott. MS. Nero C. iii, fol. 225.

[69] Morant, op. cit. ii, 251.

[70] Cott. MS. Nero C. iii, fol. 225.

[71] Ibid.

[72] *Mon. Treas.* (Abbotsford Club), 26.

John Mildenhale, appointed 1388; occurs 1393–1403

Roger Pinchbek, occurs c.1407, 1414

Roger Jurdon, occurs c.1425, 1432

John Waleys, occurs c.1436, 1449

John, occurs c.1450

John Wallyngbury, occurs c.1451

William/John Torkesey/Turkey, occurs c.1454, 1458

Thomas Hadley, occurs c.1465–72; resigned 1472

William Sutton, elected 1472; resigned 1484

Richard Cressall, appointed 1484; occurs 1487–1515; canon in charge of Byknaker 1531

Thomas Bele/Bell (Episcopus Lydensis), occurs c.1524, 1529

William Major, occurs c.1531–9; received pension 1540–7

# 23. THE HOSPITAL OF ST. MARY WITHIN CRIPPLEGATE [ELSINGSPITAL]

## INTRODUCTION

This remains the best published account of the hospital. There is a later version of the founding charter printed (together with a copy of the hospital's dedication) in W. Reading, 'The History of the Ancient and Present State of Sion College and of the London Clergy's Library There', Annex to his *Bibliotheca Clerici Londoniensis in College Sion* (London, 1724). The principal difference in this version is that the founder has the nomination of the warden and all four priests. The differences are repeated in two different versions of the final version of the charter approved by the king so it is not clear which held good (T.N.A. C66/174/17 and G.L. MS 25121/1226). There is also a collection of the hospital's documents, not drawn on directly in the *V.C.H.* account, in The National Archives (mainly in class LR14), presumably deposited when the hospital was suppressed.

For a general account of the hospital, see Ann Bowtell, 'Elsingspital' (unpub. MA dissertation, Royal Holloway, University of London, 2001). A University of London PhD thesis by the same author is in preparation.

For the location of the hospital and the buildings, see Honeybourne, 'Property', pp. 238–45. A. W. Clapham, 'Three Medieval Hospitals of London', *Transactions of the St. Paul's Ecclesiological Society,* 7 (1911–1915), pp. 153–60, has a plan of the hospital church, which became the parish church of St. Alphage, before it was destroyed in 1777. He also has illustrations of the lower part of the tower which was incorporated into the new church, of which only that part now remains. There have been no excavations of the site of the hospital but a standing building survey was done of those remains, see G. Milne and N. Cohen, *Excavations at Medieval Cripplegate London* (Swindon, 2001), pp. 100–18.

Sources for the hospital's property in London are listed in *Documentary Sources,* p. 64. An assessment of the hospital's value for the 1379 poll tax and the sources of its property income in 1392 appear in McHardy, *Church in London,* pp. 2–3 and 39–77.

Virginia Davis has published a list of canons of the hospital ordained between 1362 and 1448 in 'Medieval English Ordination Lists: a London case study', *Local Population Studies,* 50 (1993), pp. 51–60. These names and the names of those ordained between 1489 and the hospital's suppression in 1536 can be obtained from the CD Rom accompanying Davis, *Clergy of London.* The names of those assessed for the 1379 poll tax are in McHardy, *Church in London,* pp. 2–3 and see D. S. Chambers (ed.), *Faculty Office Registers 1534–1549* (Oxford, 1966), pp. 36, 57 and 65 for those who secured dispensations at the suppression.

*Ann Bowtell*

The hospital of St. Mary within Cripplegate owed its origin to the compassion felt by William Elsing, mercer of London, for the blind beggars who wandered about the City without refuge of any sort. On some land belonging to him in the parishes of

St. Alphage and St. Mary[1] he established, in 1331,

[1] Cott. Chart. v, 2, printed in Dugdale, *Mon. Angl.* vi, 704, 706. See also Sharpe, *Cal. of Wills,* i, 562. Stow, *Surv. of Lond.* (ed. Strype), iii, 73, says that he founded the hospital in a place where there had been a nunnery.

a hospital that was intended to accommodate 100 persons of both sexes, but appears to have started with thirty-two inmates. By the founder's wish blind or paralysed priests were to be received in preference to any other people.[2] The government of the hospital and the performance of the religious duties for which the house was in part founded were entrusted to five secular priests, of whom one was to be the custos or warden. As the dean and chapter of St. Paul's had appropriated to the uses of the hospital the church of St. Mary Aldermanbury,[3] of which they were patrons, they were to have the nomination of the warden and two of the priests, the appointment of the other two resting with Elsing and his assigns. The warden was also to swear fealty to the dean and chapter and pay the pension of a mark due of old from the church of St. Mary Aldermanbury, and a second pension of half a mark in sign of the subjection of the hospital. Elsing laid down certain rules to be observed by the priests: they were not to hold any other preferment; the warden was to render an account of the revenues before two of his fellows every year; a complete suit of the same colour for all (including tunic, upper tunic, mantle, and hood), the price of which in the case of the warden was not to exceed 40s., and in that of the others 30s., was to be given to each every year, and a sum of money for other necessaries; there were also detailed regulations as to religious services in the chapel, and as to the visits to be paid to the sick in the hospital. The original endowment consisted of tenements in the parishes of St. Lawrence Jewry, St. Mary Aldermanbury, St. Alphage,[4] and St. Martin Ironmonger Lane, to which were soon added some in the parish of Allhallows Honey Lane.[5] Elsing, finding that the resources of the hospital were still too slender for its work – for shortly after the foundation there were sixty beds there – petitioned the king in council to be allowed to bestow upon it land or rent to the value of £40, and was permitted to purchase land worth £10.[6]

Within a few years of this foundation Elsing became doubtful as to the wisdom of his choice of secular canons. He may already have had proof that the hospital would suffer, as he said, through the seculars being permitted to wander about the City, and through their care for temporal things;

and in February, 1337–8, he petitioned the bishop of London that regulars might be put in their place.[7] The bishop, after consultation with the dean and chapter of St. Paul's, effected the change in 1340,[8] ordering that henceforth there should be there at least five Austin Canons, and that the number should be increased as the resources of the house grew. They were to be governed by a prior, who was elected by them with the assent of the dean and chapter of St. Paul's, and presented by the latter to the bishop for his confirmation. To the dean and chapter belonged the custody of the priory during a vacancy.[9]

The house received support from several other London citizens: in 1336 William de Gayton left a tenement in the parish of St. Botolph without Aldersgate[10] to provide a chantry; Robert Elsing, the son of the founder, endowed a chantry of three priests with £12 a year;[11] in 1377, by the will of Henry Frowyk, sen., a chantry was established and endowed with rents from tenements in the parishes of St. Lawrence Jewry, St. Martin Ludgate, and in the Old Change;[12] and John Northampton,[13] in 1397, left lands in the Ropery in the parish of Allhallows the Great to provide for the maintenance of a chantry priest.

It is evident that the state of the priory in 1431 must have been considered satisfactory by William Grey, bishop of London, for when he dissolved the college of secular priests at Thele (co. Herts., now Stanstead St. Margaret's) he transferred its possessions to Elsingspital,[14] charged with the maintenance of two regular canons at Thele and three at the priory in London to celebrate for the souls of the founders. The priory was in this way enriched by messuages, land, and £12 rent in Bowers Gifford, Chelmsford, Writtle, and Broomfield, co. Essex; land, rights of pasturage, and 100s. rent in Thele (now Stanstead St. Margaret's), Stanstead Abbots, Amwell, Broxbourne, and Hoddesdon, co. Herts.; and the advowsons of the churches of Thele and Aldenham, co. Herts., which were appropriated to the college.[15]

If the bishop by this measure had aimed not only at reforming the college of Thele but also at affording material aid to the finances of the hospital, the result was disappointing. In 1438 the house was indebted to the extent of £427 17s. 7¼d.,[16] and ten

---

[2] Dugdale, op. cit. vi, 706.

[3] In 1331. *Hist. MSS. Com. Rep.* ix, App. i, 17. Papal confirmation was given in 1397. *Cal. of Pap. Letters*, v, 10.

[4] Among these were tenements in Philip Lane bought by Elsing from Robert de Cherringe. Sharpe, *Cal. of Wills*, i, 362.

[5] *Cal. of Pat.* 1343–5, p. 113. These were confirmed by the king to the new foundation, 1343, but they were acquired while the hospital was still a college of secular priests.

[6] *Parl. R.* (Rec. Com.), ii, 401.

[7] Cott. Chart. xi, 33.

[8] Ibid. v, 10, printed in Dugdale, op. cit. vi, 707. The king's confirmation is dated April, 1342. *Cal. of Pat.* 1340–3, p. 415.

[9] See also Elsing's will in Sharpe, *Cal. of Wills*, i, 562.

[10] Ibid. i, 419.

[11] Stow, op. cit. iii, 73.

[12] Sharpe, *Cal. of Wills*, i, 201.

[13] Ibid. ii, 334. John Northampton had been mayor. Stow, op. cit. iii, 73.

[14] Lond. Epis. Reg. Gilbert, fol. 192.

[15] Ibid.

[16] Cott. Chart. xiii, 10.

years later it still owed over £200.[17] The cause of these difficulties can only be guessed at, but it may have been the building[18] or enlarging of the church, which must have been of considerable size, as after the Dissolution, when the principal aisle had been pulled down, the remaining part sufficed for a parish church.[19] An inventory in 1448[20] of the contents of the buttery, kitchen, great and little chambers, library,[21] treasury,[22] and church does not give an impression of poverty. The church[23] possessed one or two important relics,[24] and seems to have been well provided with furniture and ornaments,[25] and especially with vestments, of which it possessed six complete sets, white and red cloth of gold, green velvet, and fustian, besides innumerable copes and other vestments of all colours and materials, including one of blue velvet powdered with stars and crowns, the gift of John Hisbery.

It seemed impossible for the priory to free itself from debt: in 1454 it owed £110 7s. 9½d.,[26] and although most of this was paid off by Prior William Sayer, it was involved in 1461 to the extent of £78 18s., partly owing to faulty administration, which had allowed two canons to incur liabilities for which the house was ultimately responsible.[27]

By this date two more chantries had been established in the church: that of William Stokes, endowed with the reversion of tenements in the parishes of St. Michael Bassishaw, St. Sepulchre, and St. Botolph without Bishopsgate;[28] and that of William Flete, with an income of £30 a year.[29] The gross income of the house in 1461 amounted to £198 16s. 4d. From this deductions had to be made for payments of quit-rents, £30 6s. 8d.; for repairs and vacancies of tenements, £48; payments out of the William Flete Chantry, £12 13s. 4d.; anniversaries, £2; and payments to the poor in the hospital, £22 13s. 4d.; a total of £115 13s. 4d. The house appears in the end to have overcome its

difficulties, for there is no hint of anything of this kind later.

The royal supremacy was subscribed to 22 June, 1534, by the prior, Roger Poten, and ten canons;[30] it may therefore be presumed that the priory had numbered at least as many in the middle of the fifteenth century. The house was dissolved under the Act of March, 1536, as being of less yearly value than £200.[31] There is no account of what happened to the blind and sick poor in the hospital, but as the sisters[32] who had had the care of them had a house in the close[33] assigned to them, it is possible that they were not turned adrift.

Roger Poten was made king's chaplain, and in 1536 he was given the rectories of the parish churches of St. Mary Aldermanbury, London,[34] and of St. Margaret's, Stanstead Thele, for life.[35]

The gross income of the priory in 1535 was £239 13s. 11½d., net income £193 15s. 6½d.[36] The lands and tenements from which this was derived lay for the most part in London parishes, St. Mary Aldermanbury,[37] St. Alphage (Philip Lane),[38] St. Lawrence Old Jewry, St. Mary le Bow (Hosier Lane[39] and Bow Lane[40]), St. Martin Ironmonger Lane,[41] St. Michael Bassishaw, Allhallows the Great,[42] St. Vedast (Old Change),[43] St. Sepulchre,[44] St. Giles without Cripplegate, St. Michael Paternoster Royal, St. Botolph without Bishopsgate,[45] Allhallows Honey Lane,[46] St. Dunstan and Allhallows Barking;[47] to these must be added property in Hendon, co. Middlesex, the manor of Bury or Bowers Gifford and rent in Chelmsford, co. Essex, and rents in Thele, Amwell, Hoddesdon, and Stanstead Abbots, co. Herts. The

---

[17] Ibid.

[18] At Elsing's death the church seems to have been little more than begun, see *Cal. of Wills*, i, 562.

[19] Stow, op. cit. iii, 73.

[20] Cott. Chart. xiii, 10.

[21] There were about sixty books in the library.

[22] Among other articles in the treasury there were a horn with silver-gilt lid, three silver basins, a silver spice-plate, a silver salt-cellar with cover, a powderbox of silver, &c.

[23] Besides the high altar there were the altars of St. Mary, St. John the Baptist, St. Nicholas and Holy Cross. See also *Arch*. xliii, 244.

[24] Milk of the Blessed Virgin, a portion of the true Cross, and the head of one of the 11,000 virgins.

[25] There were five silver and silver-gilt chalices, a censer, and two pairs of bottles (*phialae*) of silver, three silver pyxes, and censers and candelabra, &c. of brass.

[26] Cott. Chart. xi, 68.

[27] Ibid.

[28] Sharpe, *Cal. of Wills*, &c. ii, 530.

[29] Pat. 33 Hen. VI, pt. 2, m. 4, quoted in Tanner, *Notit. Mon*.

[30] *Dep. Keeper's Rep*. vii, App. ii, 292.

[31] *L. and P. Hen. VIII*, x, 1238. In 'The Grey Friars' Chronicle' (*Monum. Francisc*. [Rolls Ser.], ii, 194) there is an entry that 11 May 22 Hen. VIII, i.e. 1530, 'the challons of Esyngspittylle was put owte,' but it is clearly a mistake, for according to the Valor the prior and convent were in possession in 1535.

[32] Sharpe, *Cal. of Wills*. The sisters are mentioned in a will of 1372.

[33] *L. and P. Hen. VIII*, xv, 612 (7).

[34] Ibid. xiii (1), 574.

[35] Aug. Off. Bk. 232, fol. 4b. The grant is not dated, but it appears to be 1537, as it follows one of that date. See also *L. and P. Hen. VIII*, xiv (1), 403 (70).

[36] *Valor Eccl*. (Rec. Com.), i, 389.

[37] *L. and P. Hen. VIII*, xii (2), 411 (1).

[38] Ibid. xv, 733 (42).

[39] Ibid. xii (2), 1311 (25).

[40] Ibid. xiv (1), 1355.

[41] Ibid. xvi, 715.

[42] Ibid. xviii (1), 623 (43).

[43] Ibid. xviii (2), 529 (10).

[44] Ibid. xix (1), 1035 (6).

[45] Ibid. xix (2), 340 (59).

[46] Ibid. xiii (1), p. 583.

[47] Dugdale, *Mon. Angl*. vi, 708, where an abstract of a roll 28 Hen. VIII in Augmentation Office is printed. Thomas Depden had bequeathed to the priory in 1440 a messuage called 'le Shippe on the hoop,' in the parish of Allhallows Barking. Sharpe, *Cal. of Wills*, &c. ii, 502.

priory held the churches already mentioned of St. Mary Aldermanbury[48] and Thele.[49]

*M. Reddan*

## Warden of the Hospital of St. Mary within Cripplegate

John de Cateloigne, 1331[50]

## Revised List of Priors of the Hospital of St. Mary

The list is an expanded and amended version of that in *V.C.H. London*, i.

?William Elsing, died 1349[51]
John de Wyndelsore, occurs 1351,[52] 1353[53]

John Gerard, before 1370[54]
Robert Draycote, occurs 1367;[55] died 1412[56]
John Dally, elected 1412;[57] resigned 1427[58]
Henry Hoddesdon, elected 1427;[59] resigned 1438[60]
John Bell, elected 1438;[61] occurs 1446[62]
John Thornburgh, occurs 1446 × 1451[63]
William Sayer, installed 1454;[64] occurs 1461[65]
Gilbert Sharpe, occurs 1462,[66] 1483[67]
William Bowland, occurs 1496[68]
John Wannel, occurs 1517;[69] resigned 1532[70]
Roger Poten or Pottyn, elected 1532[71] and was prior when the house was suppressed in 1536[72]

[48] *Valor Eccl.* (Rec. Com.), i, 389.
[49] *L. and P. Hen. VIII*, xiv (1), 403 (70).
[50] Cott. Chart. V,2, printed in Dugdale, *Mon. Angl.*, vi, 705. Also mentioned in the foundation charter 1330, T.N.A. C66/174/6, but it is not clear when he took up office. Probably resigned in 1335 if, as seems likely, he was the John de Cateloigne who was rector of the neighbouring church of St. Alphage, as he exchanged the benefice for one in Cambridgeshire in that year, G. Hennessy, *Novum Repertorium Ecclesiasticum Parochiale Londinense* (London, 1898) p. 60.
[51] Stow, *Surv. of Lond. iii 73*, says he was the first prior but there is no evidence that he was in orders and he was referred to as 'mercer' and 'founder' to the end of his life, for example in his will, TNA LR15/7/163. No prior or warden after John de Cateloinge is referred to by name until after William's death. William is sometimes described as 'custos' or warden, for example in Cott. Chart. XI. 33, where there is also a reference to a 'magister' in charge of the priests. The likelihood seems to be that William was in overall charge of the hospital himself.
[52] C.L.R.O. Husting Roll 79/81.
[53] Sharpe, *Cal. of Letter Bk. G,* 16.
[54] *Cal. of Close*, 1369–74, p. 295.
[55] C.L.R.O. Husting Roll, 95/74.
[56] G.L. MS 25513, f. 18v.
[57] G.L. MS 25513, ff. 19–19v.
[58] Lond. Epis. Braybrook, fol. 205.
[59] Lond. Epis. Braybrook, fol. 205.
[60] Lond. Epis. Reg. Gilbert fol. 111.
[61] Lond. Epis. Reg. Gilbert, fol. 111.
[62] T.N.A. C67/39, m. 37, *ex inf.* Jessica Freeman.
[63] G.L. MS 25121/552. The deed is undated but it must be after 1446 when Bell still prior and not later than 1451 when Nicholas Gervase, rector of St. Alphage and one of the parties to the deed, died, Hennessy, *Novum Repertorium,* p. 86 .
[64] Cott. Chart. xi, 68.
[65] Cott. Chart. xi, 68.
[66] T.N.A. C244/95/94.
[67] T.N.A. C67/51, m. 22, *ex inf.* Jessica Freeman.
[68] T.N.A. PROB 11/9 (will of William Puttenham); Stow, *Surv. of Lond.* iii 73.
[69] T.N.A. LR 14/1153, referred to only as 'John' the prior.
[70] Lond. Epis. Reg. Stokesley, fol. 57.
[71] Lond. Epis. Reg. Stolesley, fol. 57.
[72] *L. and P. Hen. VIII*, xiii (1), p. 574.

# 24. THE HOSPITAL OF ST. THOMAS, SOUTHWARK

## INTRODUCTION

There are modern accounts of the history of St. Thomas's Hospital, including its origins within the Priory of St. Mary Overy; its transfer to a new site and refoundation following a fire in the priory in 1212; the development of its precinct; and a list of its masters, in Martha Carlin, *Medieval Southwark* (London and Rio Grande, Ohio, 1996), pp. 22–3, 75–85, 96–7, and *passim* (see Index), Appendix V, 2 (pp. 286–7), and Figs. 1 (p. 20), 6–7 (pp. 34–5), 9 (p. 39), and 10 (p. 69). See also *eadem*, 'The Urban Development of Southwark, *c.*1200–1550' (unpub. Ph.D. diss., University of Toronto, 1983), pp. 236–48, 396–414, Figs. 5 (p. 617), 8 (p. 620) and 9 (p. 621), and Appendix II, ii (pp. 639–41). Also useful is Carlin, 'Medieval English Hospitals', in *The Hospital in History*, ed. L. Granshaw and R. Porter (London and New York, 1989), pp. 21–39 (especially pp. 3, 26, 28–33, 35); and *eadem*, 'The Medieval Hospital of St. Thomas the Martyr in Southwark', *Bulletin of the Society for the Social History of Medicine*, 37 (Dec. 1985), 19–23.

For a calendar of a cartulary from the end of the fifteenth century (B.L. Stowe MS 942), see Lucy Drucker (trans.) and F. G. Parsons (ed.), *The Chartulary of the Hospital of St. Thomas the Martyr, Southwark (1213 to 1525)* (privately published, 1932). Four surviving quires from an early fifteenth-century cartulary are in Bodleian Library, Oxford, MS Rawlinson D. 763, ff. 1–31. On fols. 2v–3r is a copy of the hospital's foundation charter, which was long believed lost; there is another copy in the episcopal register of John Stratford, Bishop of Winchester (1323–33), in Hampshire RO, Winchester, Reg. Stratford, f. 170r. On the general history of the hospital, see William Rendle, *Old Southwark and Its People* (Southwark, 1878), pp. 125–56; *idem*, 'St Thomas's Hospital, from its foundation to 1553', *Transactions of the Royal Society of Literature (of the United Kingdom)*, 2nd ser., 13 (1882), pp. 28–59; F. G. Parsons, *The History of St. Thomas's Hospital*, 3 vols. (London, 1932–6); and E. M. McInnes, *St. Thomas' Hospital* (London, 1963). For property in London held by the hospital, see *Documentary Sources*, pp. 95–6.

*Martha Carlin*

Within the precincts of the monastery of St. Mary Overy there was a building appropriated to the use of the sick and the poor, which maintained certain brethren and sisters.

This adjunct of the priory is said to have been founded by St. Thomas of Canterbury, and after his canonization was called by his name.[1] At the time of the disastrous fire of 1213 this building was much damaged; Amicius, who was archdeacon of Surrey from about 1189 to 1215, was then custos or warden of the hospital. The canons at once erected a temporary building for the reception of the poor at a little distance from the priory, and within its chapel they held their own services whilst the priory was being rebuilt.

Meanwhile Peter des Roches, bishop of Winchester, disliking the situation, added to the endowment of the hospital, and built a new house, which, though still in Southwark, was on a site where the water was purer and the air more healthy.[2] This new hospital, which was also dedicated to St. Thomas the Martyr, was completed by 1215.

In 1215 an indenture was made between Martin, prior of the church of St. Mary Southwark, and the canons of that place, and Amicius, archdeacon of Surrey, warden of the hospital of St. Thomas Southwark, and the brethren thereof, whereby the former granted that the brethren and sisters of the old hospital of St. Thomas might transfer themselves

[1] *Cal. Pap. Letters*, i, 304.

[2] *Ubi aqua est uberior et aer est sanior. Ann. Mon.* (Rolls Ser.), iii, 457. The date given for this translation of the hospital in these Annals is 1228, which is clearly wrong, as Amicius is mentioned as archdeacon of Surrey, a post he did not hold after 1215. There is also a mistake in the previous date of the fire, which is given as 1207 instead of 1213.

into the new hospital of the like dedication (which had been founded as the property of the church of Winchester, and was free from all subjection to the church of St. Mary), together with all their goods, rents and lands, saving the lands which the prior and canons had always retained to their own use, to wit, the whole land of Melewell or Milkwell in Camberwell and Lambeth, with the place of the old hospital and the whole of the garden in Trinity Lane, which Ralph Carbonel sold to the old hospital quit of all demand on the part of the warden and brethren against the said canons. In exchange for the land of Melewell, the canons gave the brethren 13s. rents in Southwark. The canons also granted that the market for corn and other goods, which used to be at the doors of the old hospital, should be transferred to the doors of the new hospital. They also provided that the old hospital (in ruins from the fire), on the withdrawal of the brethren and sisters, be shut up for ever, on condition that the canons might build whatever they liked on the plot, except a hospital, and they bound themselves that never hereafter should another hospital be built by them in the public street of Southwark. All writings that had been obtained from the pope or king *pendente lite* were to be surrendered, so that every occasion of litigation might be taken away.[3]

There is a large paper chartulary of this hospital, consisting of 321 folios, at the British Museum, which was drawn up about the year 1525.[4] It is not quite complete, and lacks unfortunately the first leaf. It begins at the top of the page, which is lettered *fundacione* with the end of an episcopal charter of confirmation of the grant of the tithe of hay in all his lordships made by Reginald de Brettyngherst to the brothers and sisters of the hospital. The first charter recited in full is a brief confirmation by Bishop Peter des Roches. This is followed by a grant of a cemetery and burial rights to the hospital by the prior and convent of St. Mary Southwark, under certain restrictions.

The hospital agreed not to have more than two bells weighing 100 lb. in their bell-tower (*campanario*), and to pay 6s. 8d. yearly to the priory and 12d. yearly at Easter to the vicar of St. Mary Magdalen. Burial was to be granted not only to all such as died within their own precincts, but also to all others who might desire it, and who were not parishioners of either St. Mary Magdalen's or St. Margaret's. This concession by the priory was obtained by the interference of Peter des Roches, who was bishop of Winchester from 1205 to 1238.[5]

A later instrument, however, given in the chartulary shows that the rector of St. Margaret's, as well as the vicar of St. Mary Magdalen's, secured 12d. a year by this agreement as to the cemetery, and the subsidy of the priory was reduced from 6s. 8d. to 2s.[6]

In 1238 the warden and brethren granted to Luke, archdeacon of Surrey, a hall in the chapel, stable and other appurtenances within the hospital precincts, for life, for his own occupation. He covenanted for himself and successors that they should not by virtue of this grant claim any authority, jurisdiction, property, or succession in the same to the damage of the warden and brethren. The archdeacon in 1249, under the title of Luke de Rupibus, papal sub-deacon, released to the hospital all his dwelling rights.[7]

All archidiaconal rights of visitation were ceded to the hospital, so that no archdeacon of Surrey nor his official could exercise any kind of jurisdiction over any persons, regular or secular, within the hospital in any causes, civil or criminal. The brethren or their commissary had sole cognizance of all such matters, and also had the proving of the wills of persons dying within their precincts. For these concessions the house paid an annual pension of 5s. 4d. to the archdeacons of Surrey at Easter. Nevertheless the hospital was not strictly a peculiar, for the bishop claimed and exercised powers of visitation.[8]

The following are the chief grants to the hospital in the earlier part of the thirteenth century cited in the chartulary: Alice de Chalvedon, widow, granted *circa* 1235 all her lands in Chaldon; in consideration whereof Adam de Merton and the brethren agreed to find her a suitable bed within the hospital for life, with all reasonable necessaries such as would suffice for two sisters of the house, and to her maid as to one of the maids of the house; she was also to have 5s. 6d. a year for her clothing and fuel, but to demand nothing else.[9] Everard de Caterham gave lands and 2s. rent at Caterham;[10] John de Marlow, clerk, gave mills and osier beds at Marlow, in Buckinghamshire,[11] and Richard de Clare earl of Hertford, and his son, Gilbert de Clare, lands worth £20 a year and quit-rents in the manor of Marlow.[12]

A commission was issued in November 1276 to inquire into the complaint of the brethren of the hospital, that Ralph le Aumoner and many others, claiming authority from Nicholas, bishop of Winchester, and asserting that the custody of the

---

[3] Pat. 33 Edw. I, pt. 1, m. 2. At that date there was an inspection and confirmation of a chirograph of 1215.

[4] Stowe MS. 942.

[5] Ibid. fol. 2.

[6] Ibid. fol. 4.

[7] Ibid. fol. 4, 4b.

[8] Stowe MS. 942, fol. 5, 6, 330.

[9] Ibid. fol. 292–3.

[10] Ibid. fol. 309.

[11] Ibid. fol. 313–14.

[12] Ibid. fol. 315 &c.

hospital belonged to the bishop, entered without leave of the brethren, and consumed and wasted the possessions, victuals, and other goods of the hospital.[13]

There was a considerable dispute at the time of the election of Richard de Hulmo as master in 1295, the bishop claiming the sole appointment, but eventually he compromised matters by nominating the choice of the brethren.[14]

In 1299 Isaac the Jew conveyed a house to the hospital, and that his grant might hold good, instead of a seal, he subscribed his name in Hebrew characters according to the Jewish custom.[15] On 18 April 1305 licence was granted to the master and brethren to acquire in mortmain 8 acres of land in Charlton by Greenwich from Robert de la Wyke; 4 acres of land in Combe and Greenwich from Ranulph, vicar of Greenwich; and 1½ acres of land in the latter places from John and William, sons of William le Flemyng, all for the maintenance of the poor and infirm within the house.[16]

Licence upon fine was obtained in June 1309 for the alienation in mortmain to the master and brethren of this hospital of yearly rents to the value of 28s. 2½d. in Beddington and Bandon, the gift of Walter de Dynesle, clerk, and of a messuage in Southwark, the gift of William de Hameldon, chaplain.[17]

In the following year there was a large bequest under similar licence, by Simon de Stowe, of a messuage and various plots of land in Beddington, Bandon, Mitcham, Southwark, and Newton for the sustenance of the poor in the hospital;[18] and again in 1311, by Walter de Huntingfield, of a mill, a messuage, 4 tofts, 63 acres of land, 3 acres of meadow, and 6s.[19] of rents. In 1313 there was further bequest by Dulcia le Drapere of a messuage and 8 acres of land in Beddington.[20]

Gilbert de Clare, earl of Gloucester and Hertford, granted in 1314 to the master and brethren of the hospital the advowson of the church of Blechingley, in exchange for all lands and tenements which they held in the town of Beddington, Bandon, Woodcote, Mitcham, and Croydon, and for the mills that they held in the parish of Marlow, Bucks. In the following year they obtained licence to appropriate the church of Blechingley.[21]

In June 1321 Stephen de Bykleswade, master, and the brethren and sisters, in consideration of the great benefits they had received from Henry de Bluntesdon, almoner to the late King Edward, ordered a daily mass at the Lady Altar for the said king and for Henry and his parents and benefactors.[22]

In February 1323 Bishop Asser, after visitation, gravely admonished the master of the hospital as to the irregular lives led by the brethren and sisters.[23] It was then ordered that they should all follow the rule of St. Augustine, and that the master should eat with the brethren.[24]

On 1 December, 1326, the bishop of Winchester granted to the master and brethren of this hospital, for the health of the souls of himself, his parents, Adam le Chaundeler and Joan his wife, and for the support of the sick poor resorting to the hospital, lands in Wimbledon, which he had acquired jointly with John de Windsor, his clerk, of the gift of Joan Chaundeler. This grant received royal confirmation in 1329.[25]

Stephen de Bykleswade's administration as master seems to have been careless, as he was several times suspended and the custody of the house assigned to others; but in February, 1330, he was formally reinstated by the bishop, and continued in office until March, 1338.[26]

This hospital, like almost every English religious house, suffered sadly at the time of the Black Death. In 1349 Walter de Marlowe, brother of the hospital, sought and obtained dispensation from illegitimacy at the hands of Pope Clement VI, in order that he might be appointed prior or master. The petition stated that the mortality amongst the brethren had left no one so fit to rule as the said Walter.[27] In 1350 a chantry was established in the Lady chapel for the soul of Ralph Nonley of Halstead.[28]

In 1357 the hospital presented an interesting petition to Pope Innocent VI, and obtained that which they sought. It was stated therein that the hospital of St. Thomas the Martyr, founded in Southwark by the saint himself, was resorted to by such numbers of the poor and sick that the master, brethren, and sisters of the rule of St. Augustine could not support their charges without alms; they therefore prayed for an indulgence of two years and eighty days to those who visited the hospital at Christmas, Easter, the feasts of the Blessed Virgin

[13] Pat. 4 Edw. I, m. 3 d. There is no entry pertaining to the hospital in the taxation rolls of 1291.

[14] Winton Epis. Reg. Pontoise, fol. 52; Stowe MS. 942, fol. 106.

[15] Stowe MS. 942, fol. 106.

[16] Pat. 33 Edw. I, pt. 1, m. 6.

[17] Ibid. 2 Edw. II, pt. 2, m. 3.

[18] Ibid. 4 Edw. II, pt. 1, m. 22.

[19] Ibid. 4 Edw. II, pt. 2, m. 18.

[20] Ibid. 6 Edw. II, pt. 2, m. 4

[21] Ibid. 8 Edw. II, pt. 2, m. 13.

[22] Winton Epis. Reg. Reynolds, fol. 352, m. 6b.

[23] Ibid. Asser, fol. 20b.

[24] Stowe MS. 942, fol. 330.

[25] Pat. 3 Edw. III, pt. 1, m. 32.

[26] Winton Epis. Reg. Stratford, fol. 9, 12, &c. Stowe MS. 942, fol. 280, 307.

[27] Cal. Pap. Petitions, i, 165; Cal. Pap. Letters, iii, 330.

[28] Stowe MS. 942, fol. 31–2, 324.

and St. Peter and St. Paul, and on Good Friday, and who lent a helping hand to the hospital.[29]

Henry Yakesley was appointed master by Bishop Edendon in 1361. The election devolved on the bishop owing to the death of all the brethren save one, but a special reservation of the future right of the brethren was entered.[30]

In January, 1372, the bishop deputed three commissioners to visit the hospital.[31]

Nicholas de Carrew paid the king 20s. in 1379 for licence to alienate to the master and brethren six messuages, three shops and one garden in Southwark; one messuage and 2 acres of land in Lambeth; five cottages and 1 acre of meadow in Bermondsey Street – in exchange for the manor called 'Freresmanoire,' a water-mill, and two gardens in Beddington, Croydon, Mitcham, and Carshalton.[32]

On the death of William de Welford in 1381 the bishop, as patron of the house, committed the custody to John Okeham and Robert Eton, the only two of the brethren then living.[33] During the vacancy on 9 December, 1381, the bishop sent a letter to the two custodians instructing them to admit Thomas Gouday, chaplain, to the fraternity.[34] On the same day Brothers Okeham and Eton invited the bishop to appoint to the mastership, whereupon the bishop delegated John de Bukyngham, canon of York, to admit Gouday as master, who took the oath of canonical obedience on 13 December.

Licence was granted to Edmund Halstede on 2 July, 1385, to have mass said in the chapel within the graveyard of the hospital until fifteen days after Michaelmas.[35]

The bishop gave notice of a personal visitation of the hospital on 28 June, 1387.

In 1388 Thomas, the master, and the brethren were charged with having appropriated to themselves a piece of ground outside their church, formerly common to the men of Southwark for selling and buying corn and other merchandise, and with stopping up a king's highway called 'Trynet Lane'; but it was found on inquisition that the hospital had enjoyed these premises since the time of King John, when the house was built.[36]

At the time of the death of Thomas Gouday on 17 December, 1392, there were four brethren of the house in addition to the master, namely, John Okeham, Thomas Sallow, Henry Grygge, and John Aylesbury. The bishop as patron and diocesan granted them on 18 December licence to elect; but the brethren on the following day devolved their right on the bishop and asked him to nominate. Wykeham's choice fell on Henry Grygge, and he was duly appointed on 15 January, 1393.[37]

It appears that Grygge sold some of the possessions of the house contrary to his oath to Bishop Wykeham,[38] and in 1399 he withdrew into foreign parts, when the custody of the hospital was committed to John Aylesbury, one of the brethren.[39] On 25 February, 1401, William Sharpe made his profession as a brother of the hospital. On the morrow the bishop renewed the custody to John Aylesbury, and issued a citation for Grygge to appear.[40] In December following Grygge received papal absolution.[41] Whether he ever returned to take up the duties of the office of master does not appear, but in July, 1414, John Reed, a brother of the house, was elected and confirmed as master.[42]

In 1436 the hospital of Sandon in this county, being greatly reduced in revenue, was united to this house.[43]

A letter from Sir Thomas More to Wolsey, dated 16 March, 1528, mentions the hospital of Southwark, and that the master was old, blind, and feeble. Though in the gift of the bishop of Winchester, the king was informed that Wolsey, as legate, might appoint a coadjutor, and he would like to have the same for his chaplain, Mr. Stanley. The king had two reasons for asking this: first, that Stanley was a gentleman born; and secondly, if he could get rid of him he would like to have a more learned man in his place.[44]

Very shortly after this, namely, on 20 May, 1528, aged Richard Richardson resigned his office, being allotted a pension of 40 marks.[45] Richard Mabbot was elected his successor on 22 May.

On 26 September, 1535, Richard Layton, the monastic visitor, wrote to Cromwell to the effect that he was going to visit the exempt monastery of Bermondsey, Southwark, and 'the bawdy hospital of St. Thomas' on his return out of Kent.[46] Layton's epithets and general language were usually coarse and often untrustworthy, but in this case his reference to the hospital seems justified, for master Mabbot was undoubtedly lax in discipline and bad in personal character.

[29] *Cal. Pap. Petitions,* i, 304.
[30] Stowe MS. 942, fol. 330.
[31] Winton Epis. Reg. Wykeham, iii, fol. 626.
[32] Pat. 2 Ric. II, pt. 2, m. 19.
[33] Winton Epis. Reg. Wykeham, 1, fol. 119.
[34] Ibid. i, 126.
[35] Ibid. iii, fol. 218.
[36] Stowe MS. 942, fol. 181.

[37] Winton Epis. Reg. Wykeham, i, fol. 224–5.
[38] *Cal. Pap. Letters,* v, 497.
[39] Winton Epis. Reg. Beaufort, iii, fol. 315.
[40] Ibid. iii, fol. 331.
[41] *Cal. Pap. Letters,* v, 497.
[42] Winton Epis. Reg. Beaufort, iii, 51–2; Stowe MS. 942, fol. 330.
[43] Winton Epis. Reg. Waynflete, ii, fol. 57.
[44] *L. and P. Hen. VIII,* iv, 4080.
[45] Winton Epis. Reg. Fox, v, fol. 156b.
[46] *L. and P. Hen. VIII,* ix (1), 44.

The *Valor Ecclesiasticus* of 1535 gave the clear annual value of the hospital at £309 1s. 11d., of which sum only £42 4s. was spent on the poor and infirm. There were at this time three laysisters – originally the sisters were also professed and of the Austin rule – and there were forty beds for the poor.

A complaint was addressed by certain parishioners of St. Thomas's Hospital to Sir Richard Longe and Robert Acton in July, 1536, against the master and brethren of the hospital, accusing them of maintaining improper characters within the precincts, refusing charitable relief to those in sickness, and even to those willing to pay – insomuch that a poor woman great with child was denied a lodging and died at the church door, while rich men's servants and lemans were readily taken in – refusing baptism of a child till the master had 3s. 4d., and other irregularities. The master was charged with often quarrelling with the brethren and sisters even in the quire of the church, of which strange instances were cited. As to the services in the church they complained that the usual three or four sermons in Lent had not been given, they had often scant two masses in a day, and they had been forced sometimes to seek a priest about the Borough to sing high mass. Moreover, the master had put down the free school formerly kept within the hospital, although there is £4 a year for its maintenance, was guilty of 'filthy and indecent' conduct, openly kept a concubine, claimed to be 'lord, king, and bishop' within his precincts, and sold the church plate, pretending it was stolen. The names of nine witnesses were appended to these grave allegations.[47]

On 4 July, 1538, Robert More, one of the priests of the hospital, confessed before Robert Acton, justice of the peace, that before the robbery of church plate the master sold two silver parcel-gilt basins, a silver holy-water stock and 'spryngyll,' a pair of parcel-gilt silver candlesticks, a parcel-gilt silver censer, and a pair of parcelgilt silver cruets. He delivered £5 to Robert as his portion. The master was robbed of as much plate as would go into a half-bushel basket. The master consulted the brethren about selling his house at Deptford Strand. More said if he did so he would sore offend his prince. The master bade them do as he commanded, and so they sold it deceitfully to John Asspele, proctor of the arches.[48]

An indenture was made in July, 1538, between the king and Richard Mabbot, the master, and the brethren, whereby the hospital exchanged their manor of Sandon by Esher with the parsonage of Esher, for the parsonages of Much Wakering, and of Helion Bumpstead, Essex.[49]

On 23 December, 1539, Thomas Thurleby, clerk, the last master, was presented to St. Thomas's Hospital, in the place of Richard Mabbot deceased. But this appointment could only have been made[50] with the idea of effecting a quiet surrender, for on 14 January, 1540, Thomas Thurleby, together with Thomas Ladde and Thomas Cowyke, surrendered the hospital and all its possessions to the king.[51]

*J. C. Cox*

## Revised List of the Masters of St. Thomas's Hospital (also called Wardens or Keepers, Rectors, Proctors, and Priors)

Unless otherwise noted, the following list is taken from Carlin, *Medieval Southwark*, Appendix V, 2 (pp. 286–7), which cites the sources for each entry. Cf. *V.C.H. Surrey*, ii. 124. The exact position of William de Creye in the sequence of the masters is uncertain.

Amicus (Amisius), occurs 1213; died by 26 Oct. 1216, and perhaps by Nov. 1215[52]

Robert 'the priest',[53] occurs 1217, 1219

Adam de Merton, occurs 1235

William de Creye, occurs *temp.* Hen. III

Thomas de Codeham, occurs 1248, and *ante* 1270[54]

Fulcher, occurs *post*-10 May 1258 and *temp.* Prior Alan of St. Mary Overy (1252–83)

Godard, chaplain of London Bridge, died 1271

Thomas de Lechelade, ?1271 – resigned *ante* 16 Dec. 1277

Richard de Bykleswade, ?Dec. 1277; resigned 19 Sept. 1283 but re-elected; died 1295

Richard de Hulmo, appointed 25 June 1295; occurs 1316[55]

[47] Ibid. xi, 168.

[48] *L. and P. Hen. VIII*, xiii (1), 1323.

[49] Ibid. xiii (1), 1348.

[50] Ibid. xiv (2), 780 (37).

[51] *Dep. Keeper's Rep.* viii, App. ii, 41.

[52] Diana E. Greenway, *Fasti Ecclesiae Anglicanae 1066–1300, vol. 2: Monastic Cathedrals (Northern and Southern Provinces)* (London, 1971), 'Archdeacons: Surrey', pp. 94–5 (available online at: http://www.british-history.ac.uk/report. asp?compid=33880; accessed 21 October 2005).

[53] Called Robert 'the priest', warden of the new hospital of St. Thomas the Martyr, Suthwark, in an undated charter in B.L. Stowe MS 942, f. 161v; Drucker (trans.) and Parsons (ed.), *Chartulary*, p. 93, no. 450.

[54] B.L. Stowe MS 942, fols. 141r, 144v, 254v; Drucker (trans.) and Parsons (ed.), *Chartulary*, p. 83, no. 401, p. 84, no. 411, and p. 149, no. 772.

[55] B.L. Stowe MS 942, fol. 64r–v; Drucker (trans.) and Parsons (ed.), *Chartulary*, p. 44, no. 208; see also Cecil Deedes (ed.), *Registrum Johannis de Pontissara Episcopi Wintoniensis A.D. MCCLXXI–MCCCIV*, I, Canterbury and York Society, 19 (1915), pp. 196–7, 200–1.

Stephen de Bykleswade, occurs 1321; 1328; reinstated 1331 and served until March 1338.[56] During Bykleswade's mastership, temporary custody of the hospital was granted to the following: Robert de Welles (10 April 1324); Thomas (8 June 1324); John de Wyndesore (29 Dec. 1326); and Brothers William de Stanton and Walter de Merelawe of St. Thomas's Hospital (jointly, 8 Aug. 1330; see both below).[57]

William de Stanton, occurs 1338,[58] 1348

Walter de Merlawe (see above), acting as Master 1349; died 1352[59]

John de Ivingho, appointed 18 Oct. 1352; died 1353

John de Bradewey, appointed 9 April 1353; resigned by Dec. 1353

John Bonenfaunt, appointed 13 Dec. 1353; resigned 25 July 1356[60]

John de Bradewey (Bradewyn), appointed 27 July 1356; dead or resigned by May 1361

Richard de Stokes, canon of St. Mary Overy, appointed 13 May 1361; dead or resigned by Dec. 1361

Henry de Yakesley (Yakeslee), appointed 10 Dec. 1361; died 1377

[According to an undocumented entry by Parsons, John de Haytefield was elected temporarily in 1377. However, the hospital cartulary reports that in 1377 Brother William de Wolford was elected after the death of Henry de Yakesley][61]

William Wylford (de Welford, de Wolford), appointed 11 April 1377; died by Aug. 1381

Thomas Goday (Godday, Gouday), 9 Dec. 1381–17 Dec. 1392

Henry Grygge, *alias* Brigge, *alias* Clerk, 15 Jan. 1393 – temporarily suspended *c.*1399–1401; occurs again 1402 and 1407

John Alesbury, 1400–1 (*loco* Grygge)

John Reede, 1414–died 1427[62]

Nicholas Bokland (Buckland), 1427 – resigned by April 1447[63]

William Crosse, occurs 1447; resigned 1477[64]

William Beele, 1477–1487

John Burnham, 1487–1501

Richard Richardson, 1501–1528

Richard Mabott, 1528 – died *ante* 23 Dec. 1539

Thomas Thurleby (Thirlby), presented 23 Dec. 1539 – surrendered hospital 14 Jan. 1540

---

[56] *V.C.H. Surrey*, ii. 122, 124; B.L. Stowe MS 942, fols. 58v–59r, 287v–288r; Drucker (trans.) and Parsons (ed.), *Chartulary*, p. 41, no. 195, and p. 169, no. 885; Winchester, Hampshire Record Office, Reg. Stratford, fol. 51r.

[57] Winchester, Hampshire Record Office, Reg. Stratford, fol. 3v, 9v–10r, 12v; 50v.

[58] B.L. Stowe MS 942, fol. 57r; Drucker (trans.) and Parsons (ed.), *Chartulary*, p. 40, no. 191.

[59] B.L. Stowe MS 942, fols. 29r, 30r; Drucker (trans.) and Parsons (ed.), *Chartulary*, p. 22, no. 94, and p. 23, no. 96; W. H. Bliss (ed.), *Calendar Papal Reg., vol. I, 1342–1419* (London, 1896), p. 165; Hockey (ed.), *Reg Edington*, I, nos. 645, 914.

[60] Hockey (ed.), *Reg Edington*, I, no. 1084.

[61] Parsons, *History of St. Thomas's Hospital*, I, p. 244; B.L. Stowe MS 942, fol. 310r; Drucker (trans.) and Parsons (ed.), *Chartulary*, p. 181, no. 943.

[62] B.L. Stowe MS 942, fol. 310v; Drucker (trans.) and Parsons (ed.), *Chartulary*, p. 182, nos. 946–7.

[63] B.L. Stowe MS 942, fol. 310v; Drucker (trans.) and Parsons (ed.), *Chartulary*, p. 182, no. 947.

[64] B.L. Stowe MS 942, fol. 310v; Drucker (trans.) and Parsons (ed.), *Chartulary*, p. 182, no. 948.

# 25. THE LEPER HOSPITAL OF SOUTHWARK [THE LOCK]

## INTRODUCTION

The most detailed account of this small leper hospital is now to be found in M. B. Honeybourne, 'The Leper Houses of the London Area', *T.L.M.A.S.*, 21 (i) (1963–7), pp. 10–54, esp. pp. 44–54. Although the Lock Hospital is first mentioned by name in 1315, Martha Carlin, *Medieval Southwark* (London, 1996), p. 24 points out that an undated Bridge House deed of perhaps the 1240s mentions the 'bridge called *la Loke*' and includes one Amisius de la Loke among its witnesses.

It is possible that the house was always too small and poor to have a resident warden, and was under the supervision of the City of London. In 1368 Richard de Rothingge, stockfishmonger, granted a parcel of land with a garden to 'the lepers of the hospital at *le Loke*, without Southwark' without mentioning a warden or other superior (C.L.R.O., Bridge House deed G.70). In 1375 two of the suburban leper hospitals, the Lock and Kingsland, near Hackney, each had its own 'foreman', both of whom had to swear an oath not to allow lepers into London, suggesting that the administration of these two hospitals was under the City's control. In 1389 the City appointed a pair of officers to supervise three of the suburban leper hospitals: the Lock, Kingsland, and St. Giles's, in Holborn (*Cal. Letter Bk. H*, pp. 9, 343; Riley (ed.), *Memorials of London*, pp. 384, 510–11). This arrangement evidently continued until at least 1447, when the masters who were to 'oversee and govern the poor lazars' of St. Giles, the *Look*, and *Kyngeslond* were required by the City to swear an oath (C.L.R.O., Journals, 4, f. 168r). By *c.*1500 a single officer was in charge of the Lock, but his appointment remained in the control of the City. In 1549 control of Kingsland and the Lock was transferred to the re-founded London hospital of St. Bartholomew. The last two lepers were sent there in 1557, and increasingly the inmates consisted instead of venereal patients (James Bettley, '*Post Voluptatem Misericordia*: The Rise and Fall of the London Lock Hospitals', *London Journal*, 10 (1984), p. 167).

*Martha Carlin*

On the outskirts of the Borough was a hospital for lepers under the joint dedication of St. Mary and St. Leonard. Stow speaks of it as the Loke or Lazar-house for leprous persons, which stood in Kent Street, without St. George's Bar, but he had failed to learn anything of its early foundation.[1]

It was probably of twelfth-century origin, like so many similar establishments outside English towns. The first notice that we have found of it occurs in the time of Edward II, when it had evidently been for some time endowed. The favours it obtained from Edward II and Edward III confirm the tradition that it was originally of royal foundation.

Protection was granted for one year on 4 June, 1315, for the master and brethren of the hospital, and their men and lands.[2] The like was repeated in June, 1316, for another year.[3] And again letters of protection were obtained from the same king on 10 April, 1320, to last for two years.[4] On 27 July of the same year these letters of protection were renewed for two years, and at the same time the brethren were authorized, in consequence' of the insufficiency of their income, to collect alms.[5]

Protection was again granted for two years, in September, 1328, wherein it was stated that the brethren had no sufficient livelihood unless they were succoured by the faithful.[6]

This was one of the four leper hospitals built for the reception of these sufferers outside London, for the injunctions against lepers entering the City were numerous and stringent. The other three named by Stow were those at Stratford le Bow, at

---

[1] Stow, *Surv*. (ed. Thomas), 156.
[2] Pat. 8 Edw. II, pt. 2, m. 9.

[3] Ibid. 9 Edw. II, pt. 2, m. 14.
[4] Ibid. 13 Edw. II, m. 11.
[5] Ibid. 14 Edw. II, pt. 1, m. 12.
[6] Ibid. 2 Edw. III, pt. 2, m. 21.

Knightsbridge, and between Shoreditch and Stoke Newington.[7]

John Pope, by his will of 1487, gave to this hospital 6s. 8d. towards its repair and maintenance. It was for a long time under the care of St. Bartholomew's Hospital.[8]

*J. C. Cox*

## Wardens appointed by the City of London for the Oversight of the Leper Hospitals

It is unclear if these included the Lock Hospital, or only concerned St. Giles, Holborn. Unless otherwise noted these lists are taken from Honeybourne, 'Leper Hospitals', pp. 10–13

Thomas de Haverill and William Hardell, 1191–1211

William Hardell and Thomas de Harvyle, 1218

William Hardell, Andrew de Uclose, and Andrew Bocherel, 1223

William Hardell and Thomas de Harvyle, 1230

Andrew Bocherel and Roger Duce, 1234–7

Sir Ralph Eswy, 1237–40

William Hardell, 1240–52

Adam de Basing and William FitzRichard, appointed 1246

Adam de Basing, 1252

Adam de Basing and Nicholas Bat, 1253

Adam de Basing and William FitzRichard, 1261–2

Walter Henry, 1270

Gregory de Rokesley, knight, 1280

Sir Ralph Eswy, 1283

Walter Henry, 1291

## Foremen, Wardens, Guardians, Surveyors, Masters, Guiders, or Governors of the Lock Hospital

William Cook ,occurs as foreman 24 Aug. 1375[9]

Robert Yvyngho and Gilbert Rothynge occur as wardens and surveyors of lepers at St. Giles' Hospital, 'les lokes', and at Hackney 13 Aug. 1389

Robert Mildenhale, pelter, and John Wassborn, mercer, occur as guardians and surveyors of lepers at St. Giles', 'les Lokes', and at Hackney 1 Sept. 1417

John Bacoun, grocer, and Peter Andrew, pelter, occur as wardens and surveyors of lepers at St. Giles' Hospital, 'les Lokes', and at Hackney 1 July 1432

John Bracy, tallowchandler, and Reginald Derlington, fishmonger, occur 1449[10]

— Whitehead surrendered the office of guider or governor of the Lock on account of his impotency and weakness, c.1500[11]

John Miller became guider or governor in place of Whitehead, c.1500[12]

## Wardens appointed by the City of London for the oversight of the leper hospitals (these evidently included the Lock Hospital)

William Brown, painter, and John Sendell, vintner, 1514

Thomas Barnwell, 1536

— Callard, 1542

Richard Holt and William Turke, 1543, 1547

Clement Cornwell, 1548–9

[7] Stow, *Surv.* (ed. Thomas), 184.
[8] Manning and Bray, *Hist. of Surr.* iii, 634.

[9] *Cal. Letter Bk. H*, p. 9; Riley (ed.), *Memorials of London*, p. 384.
[10] C.L.R.O., Journals, 5, f. 4v
[11] Honeybourne, 'Leper Hospitals of the London Area', pp. 46, 50.
[12] Ibid.

# 26. THE HOSPITAL OF ST. JAMES, WESTMINSTER

## INTRODUCTION

The account provides a good level of detail of the hospital, particularly of its early history and internal organisation, but has less information on the hospital's estates and its relationship to the neighbouring institution of Westminster Abbey. These aspects are discussed in Gervase Rosser, *Medieval Westminster 1200–1540* (Oxford, 1989), pp. 300–10. There is a brief mention of the hospital in M. B. Honeybourne, 'The Leper Hospitals of the London Area', *T.L.M.A.S.*, 21 (1963–7), pp. 3–61, in the context of other medieval London hospitals. There have been no archaeological excavations at the site and there is no printed source material. However, Eton College Archive, Windsor, Berkshire holds various fifteenth- and sixteenth-century account books for the hospital (ECR 61), from the period when it formed part of the College's endowment.

There is also a short (draft) history of the hospital online: 'Hospital of St. James', part of *V.C.H. Middlesex*, xiii, at http://www.middlesexpast.net/ (accessed 9 October 2006).

*David Lewis*

The hospital of St. James for leprous women, situated west of Charing, in the parish of St. Margaret's, Westminster, is said by Stow to have owed its origin to some London citizens who founded it at a period previous to the Conquest.[1] There is, however, no record of its existence until Henry II by a charter guaranteed the sisters in their possessions and encouraged people to give to them.[2] King John, in 1205, confirmed to them a hide of land in Hampstead, 40 acres of land in 'Northesel,' and a tenement in Cheap at the end of Bread Street, London, the gifts of Alexander Barentin, William son of the Lady and Stephen Blund, and granted that they should hold all their lands with sac and soc, tol and team, infangenthef, and with all liberties, free customs and acquittances.[3] To judge by the charter of Henry III in 1242, which is identical with that of John,[4] they can have made no further acquisitions of land for some time, though they may have received grants of money, such as thirty marks given to the hospital by Richard de Wendover in 1250 for the establishment of a chantry.[5] The house, however, does not seem to have been rich, and the

ordinance of the Legate Ottobon[6] about 1267, that the number of eight brothers and sixteen sisters was not to be exceeded must have been intended to benefit the hospital. In 1275 King Edward exempted it from payment of the twentieth,[7] and in 1290 he exacted no payment for the grant of an annual fair for which the brothers had petitioned.[8] They had asked at the same time that their charters might be confirmed without fees as they were poor.[9] The statutes of Legate Ottobon and Richard, abbot of Westminster,[10] to which reference has already been made, form the basis of all subsequent ordinances for the house. The rule of St. Augustine was to be read four times a year in English before the brothers and sisters; a chapter was to be held every Sunday, when faults were to be corrected; the brothers and sisters were to confess once a week and communicate four times a year; all were to be present at the services, and after there should be no drinking or meeting of the brothers for talking; obedience to the head was enjoined, and anyone found rebellious, drunken, or contentious, after a second offence was to be punished at the will of the abbot; no brother was to eat, drink, or sleep in the town or suburb, except in a religious house,

---

[1] Stow, *Surv. of Lond.* (ed Strype), vi, 4.

[2] John refers to this charter in his grant. *Rot. Chart. Johan.* (Rec. Com.), 117*b*.

[3] *Rot. Chart. Johan.* (Rec. Com.), 117*b*.

[4] *Cal. of Chart. R.* i, 269.

[5] Newcourt, *Repert. Eccl. Lond.* i, 662. Cardinal Ottobon speaks of the many masses the house was bound to celebrate. Cott. MS. Faust. A. iii, fol. 319*b*.

[6] Ibid. fol. 319*b*.

[7] *Cal. of Close*, 1272–9, p. 262.

[8] *Parl. R.* (Rec. Com.), i, 57*a*. They asked for a fair of four days, but the king gave them one of seven, beginning on the vigil of St. James. *Plac. de Quo Warr.* (Rec. Com.), 477.

[9] *Parl. R.* i, 57*a*.

[10] Cott. MS. Faust. A. iii, fol. 319*b*–21.

or in that of the king or of a bishop; silence must be observed at meals, of which there were to be only two a day; the brothers were to eat with the master, and food and drink should be the same for all; the sisters were to have a double allowance of bread and ale on St. James's Day; the clothes worn by brothers, chaplains, and sisters were to be of one colour, russet or black; sisters or brothers guilty of incontinency were to receive corporal punishment; the guardian of the spiritualities should have a companion in his work of keeping the ornaments and oblations; oblations were to be shared by all the members of the house.

The injunctions made after a visitation in 1277 by the sub-prior and two monks of St. Peter's[11] are almost identical, but there are one or two alterations and additions which are not without significance: if any brother be found contentious or drunken, correction shall be given on the following day, and not postponed until the next chapter; no brother shall eat or drink at any hour with the sisters, nor shall the brothers enter the sisters' house, or the sisters that of the brothers. In other ordinances, apparently about the same date,[12] it was enjoined that the vigil after the death of a brother or sister was to be kept without drinking or unseemly noise, that the sisters were not to bequeath goods without the prior's leave, while certain punishments were prescribed in the case of the brothers and sisters quarrelling and striking one another.

Conclusions might be drawn from these injunctions not very flattering to the house, and perhaps with justice, since there can be no doubt about the general laxness of administration and conduct prevailing there in the early fourteenth century.

At a visitation of the abbot of Westminster in 1317[13] it was found that the master had not held the Sunday chapter, and through his fault the sisters and lay-brothers had not communicated four times a year. He was also accused of having special beer made for himself and one of the brothers, John de Attueston, but he denied that this had been given to any but visitors. The charges against Attueston, who was then prior, were more serious: it was said, and evidently with truth, that he refused to give an account of the goods of the hospital received by him though he had sworn to do so, that he had divided the oblations offered on the feasts of St. James and St. Dunstan between himself and the master, and that he was in the habit of getting drunk and then of using abusive language to the

brothers and sisters, and of disclosing the secret business of the chapter.

In 1319 the abbot had to enjoin[14] the observance of the rule as to weekly chapters and the brothers and sisters receiving communion four times a year. He also ordered that the present number of three brothers and six sisters should be increased to that of eight brothers and thirteen sisters prescribed by the foundation charter, if the resources of the hospital allowed, and that four of the brothers should be priests in order to relieve the house of the cost of two secular chaplains; the master was not to dispose of important business without the consent of the brothers and sisters; the sisters were not to keep legacies except with the prior's leave; the brothers were forbidden to go to the sisters' rooms; men were to be appointed by the master to look after the brothers in case of illness so that women should henceforth be excluded from such work. The condition of the hospital was, however, worse than ever in 1320,[15] nor is it surprising considering that John de Attueston was then master. The property of the house was neglected so that rents had fallen off, and woods were cut down by the master as he pleased without the consent of the brothers and sisters. As to discipline there seems to have been absolutely none: one of the brothers, Richard de Thame, frequented a tavern and spent the money of the convent on his pleasures; another, John de Sydenham, used the rents which he collected to secure followers, for he aspired to the post of master; he also went to the sisters' rooms without the master's leave and ate and drank there in spite of the prohibition. It is clear that the sisters had no respect for the master or for the prior, spreading slanderous reports of the one and accusing the other of not knowing his office, and they did not deny that they were disobedient to both. Unfortunately they themselves were not examples of virtue: one of them, Margery Flyntard, had broken her vow of chastity; and the abbot declared that through their wandering about and the access of regular and secular persons to them not only scandal but crimes had resulted, and ordered that in future they were not to leave their rooms except for the cloister adjoining or to go to church.

---

[11] Ibid. fol. 316.

[12] Ibid. fol. 317.

[13] a Doc. of D. and C. of Westm., Westm. parc. 2, box 1.

[14] Ibid. Ord. of W. abbot of Westminster. These appear to be the same as those dated February, 1322, in Cott. MS. Faust. A. iii, fol. 321–3. In the latter, however, there is an interesting addition. The abbot has heard that the rule has been broken by which married persons cannot become professed without the consent of the husband or wife, and orders such people to be expelled, fol. 323.

[15] Visitation held before Master Richard de Gloucester and John de Buterle, vicar-general of the abbot of Westminster. Doc. of D. and C. of Westm., Westm. parc. 2, box 1.

Much the same disclosures were made when the abbot visited the hospital in 1334.[16] John de Sydenham, who had now realized his desire to be master,[17] was reported guilty of incontinence, and a similar allegation coupled the names of Brother John de Hoton and Sister Juliana. For the latter charge there may have been foundation since the abbot noted that some of the brothers visited the sisters' rooms, and ordered that the rule made in this respect should not be infringed in future.

The abbot's visitations and ordinances cannot be said to have been productive of reform, nor was such a result likely as long as bad conduct was no bar to promotion. It would be interesting to know at what date John de Hoton was accused of the murder of a woman in the hospital, as the case might have determined the king to put an end to the abbot's authority there. Hoton was master in 1337[18] and again in 1345,[19] but not in 1339,[20] for it was Henry de Purle who refused to obey the abbot's citation to appear before him, and was excommunicated in consequence.[21] As the abbot had been prohibited by the king from all interference with the hospital he was himself attached for contempt. The abbot contended that the hospital was held of him by fealty and suit at his court and by service of 20s. per annum and that the right of visitation had always belonged to the abbey except in case of a vacancy, when the king's treasurer had exercised it. It was, however, proved from the records that in 1252 the king had committed the custody of the hospital to the treasurer for the time being, and it was said that ever since he, as in right of the king, had given leave to the brothers and sisters to elect the master, had confirmed the elections, and exercised the right of visitation.[22] The inference was that the king must have possessed these powers in 1252 or he could not have given them to the treasurer, and according to the court the abbot himself had proved that the king was the patron by his admission that the treasurer visited the hospital when the abbey was vacant. Judgement was therefore given in favour of the king. The verdict certainly does not seem just. According to some constitutions of the time of Henry III[23] the abbot had had jurisdiction, for it was he who then appointed the prioress from among the sisters. The priests of St. James also

acknowledged the subjection of the hospital to the abbey by taking part in the procession at St. Peter's four times a year. If it be contended that these rules may have been earlier than 1252, yet it is an undoubted fact that the abbot had since that time repeatedly visited the hospital, and as abbot, not as treasurer.[24] Further inquiry was ordered by the king in 1342, but without any benefit to the abbey.[25]

The Black Death carried off the warden and all the brothers and sisters except William de Weston, who, in May, 1349, was made master, but in 1351 was deposed for wasting the goods of the hospital.[26] It is said that in 1353 the house was without inmates,[27] and the place appears to have been in much the same condition In 1384, when Thomas Orgrave, the master, with the consent of the treasurer, let to Elizabeth Lady le Despenser for her life, at a rent of 10 marks, practically the whole hospital, viz., the houses within the gate in front of the door of the principal hall, the hall with the upper and lower chambers at each end, the stone tower, the chamber over the entrance, the kitchen and bakery, the houses assigned to the master, and all the gardens and ground within the precincts.[28] It is possible that the hospital was in need of funds just then, since a papal relaxation granted in 1393[29] indicates that the chapel was being rebuilt, but money would hardly have been raised by a lease of the building of the hospital, if the inmates for whom the rooms were intended had been there to use them.

Whether the hospital had any ground for the claims it made to privilege of sanctuary in 1403 it is impossible to say. A horse-thief had taken refuge in the chapel and the coroner had set constables to watch him, but one of the chaplains told the men that no officers of the king ought to guard any felons there under penalty of excommunication, drove them away, locked the gates of the hospital and the church doors against them and allowed the felon to escape.[30]

Henry VI in 1449 granted to Eton College the perpetual custody of the hospital after the death of Thomas Kemp, then warden;[31] but Edward IV appears to have resumed possession of the house, for in 1467, when he made a regrant of the reversion

[16] Ibid.

[17] A roll of accounts by him begins in 1331. Ibid.

[18] *Cal. of Close*, 1337–9, p. 107.

[19] Ibid. 1343–6, p. 655.

[20] Ibid. 1339–41, p. 658.

[21] *Year Bks. of Edw. III, Mich. term year 13 to Hil. term year 14* (Rolls Ser.), 360.

[22] Ibid. 360, 361; Guildhall MS. iii, fol. 1207.

[23] Cott. MS. Faust. A. iii, fol. 314*b*–15.

[24] In 1317 the bishop of Ely was treasurer, *Cal. of Pat.* 1317–21, pp. 39, 164; in 1320 the bishop of Exeter, ibid. pp. 417, 438; in 1334 the bishop of Durham, *Cal. of Close*, 1333–7, p. 198.

[25] *Cal. of Pat.* 1340–3, p. 457.

[26] Gasquet, *The Great Pestilence*, 97.

[27] Gasquet, *The Great Pestilence*, 97.

[28] The royal confirmation of the indenture is given in *Cal. of Pat.* 1385–9, p. 215.

[29] *Cal. Pap. Letters*, iv, 466.

[30] *Cal. of Pat.* 1401–5, p. 328.

[31] Pat. 28 Hen. VI, pt. 1, m. 18, quoted by Tanner, *Notit. Mon.*

of the hospital to the college, one of his clerks was warden.[32] The college, however, certainly held St. James's from Michaelmas 1480[33] until the provost made it over to Henry VIII in October 1531.[34] The number of sisters during this period does not seem to have varied: in the time of Henry VII there were four, each of whom received £2 12s. and a quarter of a barrel of the best beer every year;[35] and at the dissolution of the hospital an annual pension of £6 13s. 4d. was assigned by the king to each of four sisters, three of whom were widows.[36] In the reign of Henry VII there were also two chaplains,[37] the stipend in this case being £6 13s. 4d.

In the early fourteenth century the average income of the house was probably about £35, although in 1335 it was double that amount.[38] At the Dissolution it was worth £100 a year according to Tanner. It had been rated at half this amount in 1524 for the procurations due to Wolsey,[39] but the religious houses on this occasion were for the most part estimated much below their real value. Its property then consisted of 160 acres bordering the high road from Charing Cross to Aye-hill, 18 acres in Knightsbridge, and some land in Chelsea and Fulham;[40] a tenement called the White Bear in the parishes of St. Mary Magdalen and All Saints, in Westcheap and Bread Street, London,[41] and lands called 'Chalcotes' and 'Wyldes' in the parishes of Hendon, Finchley, and Hampstead,[42] co. Middlesex. Much of this the hospital already owned in the fourteenth century, as the master's accounts of that period mention arable and meadow land round the house and the lands to the north of London.[43] It also owned until 1465 the advowson of St. Alban's, Wood Street, with an annual pension of a mark[44] of which it was possessed in 1303.[45]

*M. Reddan*

## Masters of St. James's Hospital, Westminster

Turold, c.1189–99[46]

Guncelinus, occurs 1218–19[47]

Roger, occurs 1242–3[48]

James, occurs 1245–6[49]

Godard, occurs 1252[50]

James, occurs 1252–3[51]

Walter, occurs 1256–9[52]

James, occurs 1259–73[53]

William, occurs 1278–9[54]

Godard, occurs 1286[55]

Walter de Sutton, appointed in 1312[56]

Nicholas de Oxonia, appointed in 1314[57]

William de Wolhampton, elected 1314;[58] occurs 1317[59]

John de Attueston, occurs in 1320[60]

Robert de Dunham, appointed in 1324[61]

Godfrey de Rudham, appointed in 1325[62]

Robert de Holden, appointed in 1326[63]

Philip de la Wyle, appointed in 1326[64]

John de Sydenham, occurs 1331–36[65]

John de Hoton, occurs 1337[66]

Henry de Purle, occurs 1339;[67] resigned in 1344[68]

John de Hoton, occurs 1345,[69] 1347[70]

---

[32] *Cal. of Pat.* 1467–77, p. 63.

[33] There are accounts of the receipts and expenses of the hospital from this date at Eton College. *Hist. MSS. Com. Rep.* ix, App. i, 353.

[34] *L. and P. Hen. VIII,* v, 606.

[35] *Hist. MSS. Com. Rep.* ix, App. i, 353.

[36] *L. and P. Hen. VIII.* x, 775 (1–4).

[37] *Hist. MSS. Com. Rep.* ix, App. i, 353.

[38] Acct. of John de Sydenham master of the hospital from Easter 1331 to Easter 1336, Doc. of D. and C. of Westm., Westm. parc. 2, box 1.

[39] *L. and P. H. Hen VIII,* iv, 964.

[40] Ibid. v, 406 (1).

[41] Ibid. v, 606. It may have held rents and tenements in other London parishes. Sharpe, *Cal. of Wills,* i, 16, 546, 601.

[42] *L. and P. Hen. VIII,* iv, 406 (4).

[43] Acct. of John de Sydenham.

[44] Newcourt, *Repert. Eccl. Lond.* i, 236.

[45] *Munim. Guildhall, Lond.* (Rolls Ser.), ii (1), 237.

[46] Doc. of D. and C. of Westm. Lond. M (2). He confirmed a grant made by the father of Richard bishop of London, and Richard Fitz Neal, who held the bishopric between 1189–99, appears to be the person meant, for Turold also occurs *temp.* Henry Fitz Ailwin, mayor, i.e. c.1189–1212, Anct. D. (P.R.O.), A. 7822.

[47] Hardy and Page, *Cal. of Lond. and Midd. Fines,* 13.

[48] Ibid. 27.

[49] Ibid. 30.

[50] *Year Book of Edw. III, Mich. year* 13 *to Hil. year* 14 (Rolls Ser.), 361.

[51] Hardy and Page, op. cit. 35.

[52] Ibid. 38, 39, 40.

[53] Ibid. 41, 42, 45; Anct. D. (P.R.O.), A. 1530; Hardy and Page, op. cit. 49.

[54] Hardy and Page, op. cit. 55.

[55] *Cal. of Close,* 1279–88, p. 422.

[56] *Cal. of Pat.* 1307–13, p. 414.

[57] Ibid. 1313–17, p. 156. He was to hold during the king's pleasure.

[58] *Year Book, supra,* 362.

[59] W. occurs in the visitation of the abbot in 1317, and it seems possible that he is the same as William de Wolhampton. Doc. of D. and C. of Westm., Westm. parc. 2, box 1.

[60] Visitation of 1320, ibid.

[61] During the king's pleasure. *Cal. of Pat.* 1324–7, p. 21.

[62] Ibid. 118.

[63] Ibid. 314.

[64] Ibid. p. 337.

[65] His accounts from 1331 to 1336 are among the Doc. of D. and C. of Westm., Westm. parc. 2, box 1; Visitation of 1334, ibid.

[66] *Cal. of Close,* 1337–9, p. 107.

[67] *Year Book of Edw. III, supra,* 359.

[68] *Cal. of Close,* 1343–6, p. 453.

[69] Ibid. 655.

[70] *Cal. of Pat.* 1345–8, p. 313.

William de Weston, appointed 1349;[71] deposed in 1351[72]

Thomas Orgrave or Bygrave, appointed 1375;[73] occurs 1386[74]

Richard Clifford, occurs 1387,[75] 1399[76]

Lewis Recouchez, occurs 1401[77]

Ludovic, occurs 1405[78]

William Kynwoldmersh, occurs 1415[79]

William Alnewyk, appointed 1422[80]

Thomas Kemp, occurs 1441–9[81]

Roger Malmesbury, occurs 1463–7[82]

Roger Lupton, occurs 1527[83]

[71] L.T.R. Mem. Roll, 25 Edw. III, m. 26, in Gasquet, *The Great Pestilence*, 97; Dugdale calls him Walter de Weston, *Mon. Angl.* vi, 638.

[72] Gasquet, op. cit. 97.

[73] Anct. D. (P.R.O.), A. 2334; Dugdale, op. cit. vi, 638, gives the name as Bygrave.

[74] *Cal. of Pat.* 1385–9, p. 215.

[75] Ibid. 376. He was then ratified in his estates as master.

[76] Ibid. 1399–1401, p. 3.

[77] Ibid. 1401–5, p. 9.

[78] T.N.A. KB 9/194, m.6.

[79] *Cal. of Pap. Letters*, vi, 360.

[80] *Cal. of Pat.* 1422–9, pp. 14, 17.

[81] Pat. 28 Hen. VI, pt. i, m. 18, quoted in Tanner, *Notit. Mon*; T.N.A. KB 27/722.

[82] W.A.M. 17782; *Cal. of Pat.* 1467–77, p. 63.

[83] Doc. of D. and C. of Westm., Westm. parc. 2, box 1.

# 27. THE HOSPITAL OF THE SAVOY

## INTRODUCTION

A much fuller account of the foundation, organisation and administration of the Savoy Hospital can now be found in R. Somerville, *The Savoy, Manor, Hospital, Chapel* (London, 1960), pp. 9–47. Somerville also provides a list of the surviving source material (pp. 230–1). A full account of the building of the hospital can be found in H. M. Colvin, D. R. Ransome and J. N. Summerson, *The History of the King's Works, vol. 3: 1485–1660*, pt 1 (London, 1975), pp. 196–206. An account of the London properties of the hospital in 1535 can be found in *Documentary Sources*, pp. 64–5.

Since Somerville wrote, a single roll of accounts for the hospital for the years 1525–6 has been identified and printed in translation: Molly Tatchell, 'Some Accounts of the Hospital of the Savoy for the year 17–18 Henry VIII', *T.L.M.A.S.*, 20 (1961), pp. 151–9.

*Caroline M. Barron*

The hospital of the Savoy, dedicated to the honour of the Blessed Jesus, the Virgin Mary, and St. John the Baptist, was founded by King Henry VII in 1505 on the south side of the Strand,[1] on the spot once occupied by the palace of Peter of Savoy, uncle of Eleanor of Provence.[2] The king seems to have died before the work was really begun, and the fulfilment of the scheme was left to his executors, who in 1512 obtained letters patent from Henry VIII empowering them to erect a perpetual hospital to consist of a master and four other chaplains who were to be a corporate body, with a common seal, and received licence to acquire in mortmain land to the annual value of 500 marks.[3] The buildings, for which Henry VII had bequeathed 10,000 marks,[4] and which were intended to accommodate 100 poor men[5] every night, must have taken some time to complete, and this is probably the reason why the first master, William Holgill, and the chaplains were not appointed before 1517.[6]

The statutes drawn up by the executors in 1523 give an interesting picture of the institution and its working.[7] The master was supposed to superintend the house generally, and had certain duties with regard to the management of its property;[8] the four chaplains exercised the functions of seneschal, sacristan, confessor, and hospitaller;[9] there were besides two priests, four altarists to assist in the services in the chapel, a clerk of the kitchen, a butler, a cook, an under cook, a door-keeper and an under doorkeeper, a gardener, a matron, and twelve other women.[10] The master received a stipend of £30 a year, each of the chaplains £4 and the priests £3 6s. 8d., and the others in proportion,[11] all except the master being fed at the expense of the hospital.[12] The uniform of all officials, male and female, was blue with a Tudor rose in red and gold embroidered on the breast.[13]

Every evening an hour before sunset, the hospitaller, the vice-matrons and others stood at the great door and received the poor, who, on being admitted, proceeded first to the chapel to pray for the founder, and then to the dormitory, where the matron and some of the women allotted the beds to them,[14] and four others prepared the baths and cleansed their clothing. The hospital only provided a lodging for the night except in the case of the sick, who were allowed to remain after the departure of the other men and were tended by the doctor and surgeon and the sisters.[15]

---

[1] In the parish of St. Clement Danes. Lond. Epis. Reg. Fitz James, fol. 118.

[2] Dugdale, *Mon. Angl.* vi, 726.

[3] Ibid.

[4] Stow, *Surv. of Lond.* (ed. Strype), i, 210.

[5] Cott. MS. Cleop. C. v, fol. 34b.

[6] Ibid. fol. 55b, 56b.

[7] Ibid. fol. 4b–54b.

[8] Ibid. fol. 37b, 38.

[9] Ibid. fol. 56b. Their duties are given fol. 7–10b and fol. 23.

[10] Ibid. fol. 15b–16.

[11] Cott. MS. Cleop. C. v, fol. 20b–22. Holgill was to have £40 a year on account of his many labours and continuous diligence in building the house, fol. 20b.

[12] Ibid. For the sums allowed for food see fol. 40b–41.

[13] Ibid. fol. 26b, 27.

[14] Each bed was well furnished with bed clothes, including counterpanes decorated with the red rose and three portcullises. Ibid. fol. 34b, 35.

[15] Ibid. fol. 24–25b.

The daily accounts of the clerk of the kitchen and the monthly accounts of the seneschal were to be made in the counting-house, but those of the master and all other officers in a room called the exchequer.[16] Two rooms in the tower opposite the great gate were appointed for a treasury, in which were to be kept the chests containing a reserve-fund of 500 marks, the yearly surplus, the money for the daily expenses, the legacies and gifts to the hospital, the jewels and ornaments not in every-day use, and charters and muniments.[17]

The visitation of the hospital was entrusted to the abbot of Westminster.[18]

William Holgill, the first master, seems to have been rather a privileged person: he received a larger salary than was to be given to any future master,[19] and in spite of the statute forbidding the master to accept any other office or administration,[20] he was allowed to act as surveyor to Wolsey,[21] and afterwards to hold the prebend of South Cave.[22] The income of the hospital, £567 16s. 3¾d. in 1535,[23] can have been barely sufficient to meet the necessary expenses, since when food rose in price Holgill had to draw on the reserve fund,[24] and the commissioners who under Sir Roger Cholmley, chief baron of the Exchequer, visited the hospital in 1551, found that the revenues fell short of expenditure by £205 4s. 2d.,[25] and they had evidently no fault to find with the way the establishment was conducted.[26]

The house was dissolved in 1553,[27] and its lands given by the king to Bridewell and St. Thomas's, Southwark,[28] but in 1556 it was refounded and endowed afresh by Queen Mary,[29] whose maids of honour provided the beds and other furniture.[30]

This new foundation had been in existence only a few years when it was almost ruined[31] by Thomas Thurland, the master, who was removed in 1570,

but not before he had burdened the hospital with his private debts by a misuse of the common seal, granted unprofitable leases, taken away the beds, and disposed of jewels and other treasures of the house.[32]

During the Civil War the place was used for the accommodation of sick and wounded soldiers,[33] and the master was superseded by a governor[34] or overseer.[35] At the accession of Charles II, the hospital was restored to its former state,[36] but some of the buildings were taken by the king in 1670 for the use of the men wounded in the Dutch war,[37] and the promise to give them back was not fulfilled either by him or his successors.[38]

It is probable that long before this time the office of master had practically become a sinecure. At any rate Dr. Walter Balconquall, who was master from 1621 to 1640, managed to combine his duties of master of the Savoy with those of dean of Rochester, and afterwards of Durham.[39] The report of a commission under William III shows that the hospital had outlived its usefulness, the relief of the poor being utterly neglected, and it was proposed to annex the mastership to the bishopric of Gloucester, and to pay pensions to twenty poor widows as well as the salaries to the four chaplains,[40] but nothing was done.

In 1702, however, Lord Keeper Wright visited the house and removed the chaplains because, in contravention of the statutes, they had omitted to subscribe to the oath on taking office and had not resided within the hospital.[41] As no master had been appointed since Dr. Killigrew's death in 1699,[42] the hospital was now without master and chaplains, and was declared by Wright to be dissolved.[43] Although it was exceedingly doubtful whether a visitor possessed such powers,[44] the Lord Keeper's

[16] Ibid. fol. 44.

[17] Ibid. fol. 45–46b.

[18] Ibid. fol. 30.

[19] Ibid. fol. 20b.

[20] Ibid. fol. 18.

[21] L. and P. Hen. VIII, iv, 4073, 5954.

[22] Ibid. ix, 661. In 1537 a certain John Parkyns begged Cromwell to give him the post of master of the Savoy, as Holgill had sufficient without it. Ibid. xii (1), 270.

[23] Valor Eccl. (Rec. Com.), i, 359.

[24] Lansd. MS. 20, No. 15.

[25] Ibid. No. 14.

[26] Ibid. No. 15. The behaviour of the officials was good, and the statutes had been kept since the death of the first master except in such respects as they were not in accordance with the law of the land.

[27] Cal. of S.P. Dom. 1547–80, p. 85.

[28] Stow, Surv. of Lond. iv, 106.

[29] Cal. of S.P. Dom. 1547–80, p. 85.

[30] Stow, op. cit. iv, 106.

[31] Cal. of S.P. Dom. 1547–80, p. 383. Archbishop Grindal and the other visitors writing to Cecil in 1570 said that if Thurland continues in office the house cannot long stand.

[32] Lansd. MS. 20, No. 21. He was also accused of not being resident, of going very seldom to church, and spending his time in playing bowls and gambling, of maintaining his relations at the expense of the hospital, etc. . . . He does not seem to have been able to deny the more serious charges, see Lansd. MS. 20, No. 19.

[33] Cal. of S.P. Dom. 1650, pp. 282, 366; Hist. MSS. Com. Rep. viii, App. i, 386.

[34] Hist. MSS. Com. Rep. x, App. iv, 510.

[35] Cal. of S.P. Dom. 1652–3, p. 224.

[36] Ibid. 1660–1, pp. 16, 107, 113, about the appointment of the master.

[37] Stowe MS. 865, fol. 2b.

[38] A regiment of foot was stationed there by Charles II; James II assigned places of residence there to Jesuits, and William III to French Protestants. Ibid.; Dugdale, Mon. Angl. vi, 726.

[39] Cal. of S.P. Dom. 1623–5, p. 492; ibid. 1639, p. 450.

[40] Add. MS. 11,599, fol. 3.

[41] Stowe MS. 865, fol. 3b–5.

[42] Ibid. fol. 8.

[43] Ibid. fol. 5b.

[44] The Lords judged that a visitor had power to reform but not to dissolve. Dugdale, Mon. Angl. vi, 726; see also Stowe MS. 865, fol. 6b–8.

action was effectual, and the hospital of the Savoy came thus to an end.

According to the statutes of 1523 the master was to be elected by the chaplains,[45] but from the time of Thurland the sovereign seems to have appointed[46] in reality, though the chaplains went through the form of election.[47]

The Savoy in 1535[48] held rents of assize in London, the manors of Shoreditch, 'Colkennington' (Kenton), and Goldbeaters, and some land in Shoreditch, co. Middlesex; the manors of Dengie, Helion Bumpstead, Aveley, Tailfeers, and Gerons,[49] co. Essex; the manors of Langley and land in Greenstreet, co. Herts; the manors of 'Denham-Duredent' and Marsworth, co. Bucks; the manors of 'Topcliffe,' 'Byrdlyns,' 'Nedehall in Hynton,' 'Alyn,' and land in Fulbourn, co. Camb.; the manors of Hastingleigh, 'Corston' (Cuxton?), Combe Grove, and 'Frannycombe,' co. Kent; the manors of Tibshelf, co. Derby, and of Bewick, co. York.[50] The advowson of Dengie church also belonged to the hospital.[51]

At the second dissolution of the house its possessions, which appear to have been worth £2,497 a year, with the exception of Dengie manor, seem to have been entirely different.[52] They comprised some land at Mile End, co. Middlesex, the manor of Dengie and rent of the manor of 'Sow,' co. Essex; rent out of Shabbington manor, co. Bucks; the manor of 'DentonGowerty,' co. Lincoln; Stanton under Bardon, co. Leicester; 'South Dowes' Hospital, Abington Mills, Harpale Mills, East Haddon, and lands in West Haddon, co. Northants; the manor of Garstang, rent out of the manor of 'Rannworth,' co. Lancaster, Howorth Grange, the manors of Acklam and Houghton, Sutton Grange, Woodhouse Grange, Cudworth, 'Kirkstall Inge,' 'Shelton-Coates,'[53] and Ryhill in co. York and the manor of 'Hallatreholm' in co. Durham.

*M. Reddan*

## Revised List of Masters of the Savoy Hospital to 1553

These names are taken from Somerville, *Savoy*, p. 236, where additional biographical material about the Masters is also provided.

William Holgill, appointed 1517; died 1548
John Ellis/Elys, elected 1548; died 1551
Sir Robert Bowes, appointed 1551; resigned 1552
John Gosnold, appointed 1552; resigned 1553

---

[45] Cott. MS. Cleop. C. v, fol. 18*b*. The statute which ordered the presentation to the abbot of Westminster never came into force as the abbey was dissolved before the first master died.

[46] Dugdale, *Mon. Angl.* vi, 726.

[47] Balconquall is said to be elected in 1621. *Cal. of S.P. Dom.* 1619–23, p. 239. It was probably managed as in the case of Dr. Killigrew, i.e. the king recommended him to the chaplains, who elected him. Ibid. 1663–4, pp. 198, 200.

[48] *Valor Eccl.* (Rec. Com.), i, 358–9.

[49] In 1553 Edward VI granted the manor of Gerons with appurtenances, messuages, and lands called le Newhouse and Tailfeers and Stewards in Great Parndon to the mayor and commonalty of London. Morant, *Hist. of Essex*, ii, 493.

[50] *Valor Eccl.* (Rec. Com.), i, 358 and 359.

[51] Newcourt, *Repert. Eccl. Lond.* ii, 211.

[52] Add. MS. 11599, fol. 4.

[53] Shawcot ?

# 28. WHITTINGTON'S HOSPITAL [ALMSHOUSES]

## INTRODUCTION

This account can now be supplemented with that to be found in Jean Imray, *The Charity of Richard Whittington: A History of the Trust administered by the Mercers' Company 1424–1966* (London, 1968), in which pp. 1–56 deal with the medieval history of the hospital and the related college. The ordinances for the almshouse (hospital) are printed as Appendix 1 (pp. 107–21) and the 1431 rental for the estate which supported both the almshouse and the college as Appendix 2 (pp. 122–7).

*Caroline M. Barron*

A hospital was founded in 1424 by the executors of Richard Whittington[1] for thirteen poor persons, who were to live in a house built for them to the east of the church of St. Michael Paternoster and next to the dwelling of the chaplains of Whittington College. The thirteen were to be citizens of London, preferably members of the Mercers' Company, or inferior ministers of Whittington College who could no longer fulfil their duties, and it was an essential condition to their election[2] and continuance as inmates[3] that they should have no other means of subsistence. They were to live in separate apartments within the house, but were to have their meals together. Their dress was to be of seemly form and dark in colour. One of their number called the tutor was to have the rule and administration of the house, and his superior position was marked by his receiving a weekly allowance of 16*d.*[4] instead of the 14*d.* allotted to each of the others, and by a relaxation in his case of the rule[5] prohibiting absence from the hospital. Certain religious duties were prescribed: the almsmen had all to be present at the daily services in St. Michael's Paternoster Royal, and had to pray for the souls of Whittington and Alice his wife, and after high mass they were to assemble round Whittington's tomb and recite the *De Profundis*; private devotions were also enjoined. The mayor of London was supervisor of the house, but it was with the wardens of the Mercers' Company that the care of the foundation mainly rested: out of every seven vacancies among the poor men they appointed six times, the master of Whittington College once, and they chose the tutor; an inventory of the movables of the house had to be made every year and shown to them, and the seal of the hospital could not be used without their leave.

The connexion between the hospital and the college must have been close from the first, and doubtless grew closer as in course of time former clerks of the college became pensioners in the hospital. Indeed, from a report made in 1538 about the feeling in the houses[6] it would be impossible to gather that they were two separate institutions, the tutor being mentioned as if like the choristers he belonged to the college. It is evident that this man, William Gibson, held strongly to the old opinions, for he said openly that 'the northern men rose in a good quarrel and that he trusted to see a new day.' Most of his fellows, however, were of the opposite party and 'were so weary of such communications that they were ready to go out of the house.'

This house of charity was not abolished at the Reformation, and in the eighteenth century still existed in the place where it had been founded, the men and women receiving then a pension of 3*s.* 10*d.* a week, and new clothes every three years.[7] In 1823 the Mercers' Company acquired some land in the parish of Islington and there built a chapel and thirty houses to accommodate a chaplain, a matron, and twenty-eight almswomen.[8]

*M. Reddan*

[1] Pat. 10 Hen. VI, pt. 2, m. 5, per Inspex. printed in Dugdale, *Mon. Angl.* vi, 744–6.

[2] No one of the livery of any company was to be admitted.

[3] If any of them inherited property worth 5 marks clear a year, he was not to remain in the hospital.

[4] The patent says 4*d.*, but as in another place the charter provides that if one of the members is attacked by leprosy he is to be removed to another place, but to receive 14*d.* a week, and his place in the hospital is not to be filled, this sum appears to have been the usual allowance. Dugdale, op. cit. vi, 746.

[5] He was not to be absent for twelve days without leave of the conservators, but the others could not be absent one whole day without his leave. Ibid.

[6] *L. and P. Hen. VIII*, xiii (2), 1202.

[7] Maitland, *Hist. of Lond.* 1325.

[8] *City of London Livery Companies' Com. Rep.* ii, 58; iv, 41.

### Tutors of Whittington's Hospital

This is based on the list in *V.C.H. London*, i, with corrections.

Robert (or John) Chesterton, appointed 1424[9]
William Gybson, appointed 1532;[10] occurs 1538[11]

---

[9] Dugdale, *Mon. Angl.* vi, 744; Imray, *Charity*, pp. 20, 111.
[10] Imray, *Charity*, 59.
[11] *L. and P. Hen. VIII*, xiii (2), 1202.

# 29. MILBOURNE'S ALMSHOUSES

## INTRODUCTION

The Milbourne Almshouses (also known as Melbourne Almshouses or the Drapers' Almshouses) were founded and endowed in 1535 by Sir John Milbourne, Draper, Lord Mayor in 1521–2. The almshouse supported fifteen poor and aged inmates from the Drapers' Company. This account of the Almshouses is still the most thorough overview of this institution. There has been no detailed study of the house but it has been mentioned in several more general works, in particular A. H. Johnson, *The History of the Worshipful Company of Drapers of London*, 5 vols. (Oxford, 1914–22) and John Schofield, *Medieval London Houses* (New Haven, 1994), pp. 60–2 and fig. 68.

There is no published list of the masters of the Almshouse.

*Christine Fox*

The foundation of Sir John Milbourne resembled Whittington's Hospital in some ways. The almshouses were built in 1535[1] on land bought by Milbourne of the Crossed Friars, and were intended for thirteen poor men and their wives, if they were married, members of the Drapers' Company, to whom the endowment, consisting of property in London, was entrusted. The poor men were to come every day to the conventual church, and to say the *De Profundis*, paternoster, ave, creed and collect for the benefit of the founder, his wife, children, and friends. The almshouses remained on the original site until 1862, when the Drapers' Company built new ones at Tottenham.[2]

*M. Reddan*

[1] Stow, *Surv. of Lond* (ed. Strype), ii, 78.

[2] *Lond. and Midd. Arch. Soc. Trans.* iii, 138–42.

# 30. THE HOSPITAL OF ST. AUGUSTINE PAPPEY

## INTRODUCTION

This is a sound account of the house, but should be supplemented by Thomas Hugo's article 'The Hospital of le Papey in the City of London', *T.L.M.A.S*, 5 (1881), pp. 183–221, which provides interesting and useful information not printed elsewhere, a transcription of the charter of the foundation and rules of the house and also a description of the exterior of the church, and its London site.

For a discussion of the extent of the hospital's site, see Honeybourne, 'Property', pp. 297–8, and see *Documentary Sources*, no. 99 for the London property held by the hospital.

*Jennifer Ledfors*

The miserable condition to which old and infirm priests were often reduced caused three chaplains of London, William Cleve, priest of a chantry in St. Mary Aldermary, William Barnaby, chantry priest in St. Paul's, and John Stafford, to found a Fraternity of Charity and St. John the Evangelist in their[1] aid in 1442.[2] For their purpose they obtained from Thomas Symmeson, the parson of Allhallows London Wall, the chapel of St. Augustine Pappey, once a parish church, but shortly before united to Allhallows',[3] the churchyard which had been bequeathed by William Cressewyk in 1405 to St. Augustine's,[4] and a house and garden adjoining. The fraternity as usual comprised both men and women,[5] but in this case the brothers were all to be priests;[6] it was a corporation, having perpetual succession and a common seal.[7] The government was in the hands of a master and two wardens elected every year by the brothers from their own numbers,[8] with the proviso that no member of the fraternity of sixty priests should be chosen for the posts.[9] These officers made ordinances for the regulation of the society,[10] received the money collected from the brothers and sisters,

and expended it as needed,[11] the brothers auditing once a year the accounts, which the wardens had to inscribe in a great register.[12]

The poor priests for whose benefit the gild had been established were given shelter, food and firing in the house close to the church,[13] and those who had been masters or wardens, and whose conduct during office had been exemplary, received in addition an allowance of 8*d*. or 6*d*. a week.[14]

The hospital came to an end with the suppression of the fraternities under Edward VI. Sir Robert Foxe, the master, and five other priests had pensions varying from 66*s*. 8*d*. to 40*s*. assigned to them,[15] and four of the number were still in receipt of these allowances in 1556.[16]

The property of the brotherhood, valued in 1548 at £24 11*s*. 8*d*. net per annum, consisted in part of the house where the priests lived, the farm of St. Augustine's and of the garden near, a tenement at Baynard Castle, and two messuages and six cottages in the parish of St. Michael-le-Querne.[17] The brothers may also have had a messuage in Paternoster Row which had been left to them in 1536,[18] but they had sold the cemetery of Pappey church in 1538.[19] A large part of their income had probably been derived from the contributions and fines of members of the

---

[1] Pat. 22 Hen. VI, pt. 3, m. 27.
[2] The date is given by Stow as 1430, but for the later date see Hugo, 'The hospital of the Papey', *T.L.M.A.S.* v, 196.
[3] The churches were united by William Grey, bishop of London, 1426–31. Newcourt, *Repert. Eccl. Lond.* i, 258.
[4] Pat. 22 Hen. VI, pt. 3, m. 27.
[5] Cott. MS. Vit. F. xvi, fol. 114*b*.
[6] Ibid. fol. 116*b*.
[7] Ibid. fol. 113*b*.
[8] Cott. MS. Vit. F. xvi, fol. 114*b*.
[9] Ibid. fol. 116*b*. If this brotherhood was first established in 1466 (*Cal. of Pat.* 1461–7, p. 516), the rules of the Pappey must have been made some years after the foundation.
[10] Cott. MS. Vit. F. xvi, fol. 114.

[11] Ibid. fol. 115.
[12] Ibid. fol. 115*b*.
[13] Pat. 22 Hen. VI, pt. 3, m. 27; Stow, *Surv. of Lond.* (ed. Strype), ii, 73.
[14] Cott. MS. Vit. F. xvi, fol. 116*b*.
[15] Chant. Cert. No. 88, m. 7; *T.L.M.A.S.* v, 204.
[16] Add. MS. 8102, fol. 4.
[17] *T.L.M.A.S.* v, 197–204.
[18] Sharpe, *Cal. of Wills*, ii, 642.
[19] Guildhall MS. 41, fol. 528.

society,[20] and bequests of money made to them[21] for their prayers.

*M. Reddan*

## Revised List of Masters of the Hospital of St. Augustine Pappey[22]

This list has been amended using Hugo, 'Hospital', pp. 198–202.

John Welles, occurs 1442, 1447
William Sayer, elected 1448
John Pynchebeke, elected 1449
William Leeke, elected 1459
John Colyn, elected 1459; occurs 1461
Robert Gretham, elected 1462
Ralph Kytson, elected 1463; occurs 1465
John Hede, elected 1466
John Bolte, elected 1479

Thomas Praty, elected 1480
John Bell, elected 1481
John Pyrules, elected 1482; occurs 1483
John Sclater, elected 1489
William Smythe
William Hulnesdale, elected 1491
Peter Corffe, elected 1492
Ralph Creke, elected 1493
Thomas Ashborne, elected 1504; occurs 1507
Thomas Daw, elected 1508
George Done[23]
William Robinson, elected 1519
Thomas Houghton, elected 1520; occurs 1521
William Hartopp, elected 1522
George Done, elected 1523
John More, elected 1524; occurs 1525
William Basse, elected 1526
George Dune, elected 1534; occurs 1535
Humphrey Town, elected 1536
George Dun, elected 1537
Robert Hanne, elected 1538; occurs 1539
Robert Fox, elected 1540
John —
John Benson
Robert Fox, elected 1547; occurs 1548[24]

---

[20] Brothers speaking ill of the master or wardens had to pay 12*d.* to the use of the poor priests. Cott. MS. Vit. F. xvi, fol. 117.

[21] Edmond Alynson in 1570 bequeathed 'to the common hutch of the broderhode off Pappe 10*s.*' Lond. Epis. Reg. Fitz James, pt. 2, fol. 5. The widow of Sir John Milbourne left them 10*s.* to come to her funeral and pray for her soul. Stow, op. cit. ii, 73. See also Lond. Epis. Reg. Bonner, fol. 181*b*, 191.

[22] Cott. MS. Vit. F. xvi, fol. 119*b*–23. The MS. is much injured, so that there are large gaps in the list.

[23] He held office for three years.

[24] Fox held the office two years in succession and was the last master.

# 31. JESUS COMMONS

## INTRODUCTION

The original, unsatisfactory, account of this college was updated by Catherine Jamison, as part of ongoing research commissioned by the V.C.H. This was published as 'Notes on Jesus Commons', *Notes and Queries*, 173 (1937), pp. 92–3. The brief article outlines the foundation of the 'commens of Jesus' by James Fynche, a London shearman, under the terms of his will of 1507. The college was located in property in Dowgate that was leased from the Minoresses without Aldgate. It was administered by the fraternity of the Shearmen, who later merged with the Fullers to form the Clothworkers' Company.

*Matthew Davies*

Stow speaks of a number of priests who lived together in Dowgate Ward in a house which had been left to them for that purpose, and which was well provided both with furniture and books. They were known as Jesus Commons, and were apparently a corporate body, filling up gaps in their ranks as they occurred through death or otherwise.[1] It is not impossible that the college was connected with a fraternity of priests to whom John Kyrketon, stockfishmonger, left a bequest at the end of the fourteenth century.[2]

Mention of it occurs in 1539, a priest reporting there words spoken by the parson of St. Mary Aldermary,[3] and again in 1543 when the parson of St. Ethelburga made to it a bequest of 7s. 6d.[4] It seems to have survived the changes under Edward VI, and to have become extinct through lack of members in the reign of Elizabeth.[5]

*M. Reddan*

[1] Stow, *Surv. of Lond.* (ed. Strype), ii, 201.
[2] Sharpe, *Cal. of Wills*, ii, 269.

[3] *L. and P. Hen. VIII*, xiv (2), 41 (3).
[4] Lond. Epis. Reg. Bonner, fol. 193*b*.
[5] Stow, op. cit. ii, 201.

# 32. DOMUS CONVERSORUM

## INTRODUCTION

This account of the Domus Conversorum is a solid and accurate one, which provides an excellent overview of the history of the house's administration and finance. More in-depth research into the Jewish converts themselves is included in Michael Adler's chapters on the Domus Conversorum in *The Jews of Medieval England* (London, 1939). A highly detailed study not only of the house's financial and administrative histories, but also of the converts and the position of the house within the overall conversion policy of thirteenth-century Europe is provided in Lauren Fogle, 'The Conversion of Jews in Medieval London' (unpub. Univ. London PhD thesis, 2005).

An overview of the house and particularly the Rolls Chapel, including some information on building works, can be found in T. Hardy, 'The Rolls House and Chapel', *Middx. and Herts. Notes and Queries*, 2 (1896). This work predates the *V.C.H.* entry, but is helpful nonetheless. The most extensive work on the physical structure of the house is in Fogle, 'Conversion of Jews', ch. 7.

Property holdings for the house are recorded in McHardy, *Church in London*, pp. 64–5, and (for London) in *Documentary* Sources, p. 60. An extensive analysis of all property holdings of the Domus Conversorum is included in Fogle, 'Conversion of Jews', chs. 4–5.

*Lauren Fogle*

In 1232 King Henry III founded in New Street, the present Chancery Lane, a hospital for Jews who had been converted to Christianity,[1] promising for their maintenance and that of the two chaplains who were to celebrate divine service in the chapel there,[2] a yearly sum of 700 marks from the Exchequer, until he or his heirs provided for them otherwise.[3] The king in giving to the converts in 1235 some lands and houses in London which had been John Herlicun's, granted them all escheats falling to him in London,[4] and they undoubtedly acquired some property in this way, as, for instance, the lands of Constantine son of Aluf in 1248;[5] he gave them, moreover, certain lands in Oxford in 1245.[6] The legacy of £100 left to the hospital by Peter des Roches, bishop of Winchester, was also devoted to the endowment of the house.[7]

Whatever income, however, they ultimately derived from such sources, it was never large enough to enable them to dispense with an annual grant which neither Henry III nor Edward I seems to have found easy to raise. In 1245, indeed, the king, unable to give them adequate help, tried to induce some religious houses[8] to maintain one or two converts for two years. If the number of robes given to the converts by the king corresponds in some measure to the number of persons belonging to the house, the hospital soon became large; 150 robes were given to the converts at Christmas, 1255–6, 171 the following Easter, and 164 at Whitsuntide;[9] so that at this time there must have been considerably more than a hundred people who received allowances, though all may not have been resident.[10] Naturally the first accommodation provided soon proved insufficient, and in 1265–6 the master was engaged in enlarging the place or in building new houses, and in 1275 the chapel was lengthened.[11] The

---

[1] Cart. 16 Hen. III, m. 18, printed in Dugdale, *Mon. Angl.* vi, 683.

[2] *Cal. of Close*, 1231–4, p. 37. The chapel and the buildings adjacent are said by Matthew Paris to have been built in 1233, *Chron. Maj.* (Rolls Ser.), iii, 262.

[3] Dugdale, op. cit. vi, 683.

[4] *Cal. of Chart. R.* i, 199.

[5] Ibid. i, 336. In other cases the property seems to have been granted to private individuals who paid a rent to them. Ibid. i, 307, 309, 322, 327.

[6] Ibid. i, 283.

[7] The king's writ orders that the money shall be used to buy lands for the maintenance of the Conversi. Close, 27 Hen. III, m. 9, quoted by Tovey, *Anglia Judaica*, 115.

[8] He sent one to Walsingham priory and a man and his wife to Abingdon Abbey. Tovey, op. cit. 228, 229.

[9] W. J. Hardy, 'The Rolls House and Chapel,' *Midd. and Herts. N. and Q.* ii, 51.

[10] Two converts in 1238 received them at the Tower, where they were employed. Ibid. 50.

[11] Ibid. 52.

chaplains also were increased to three in 1267.[12] Sums amounting altogether to £100 were allotted to them from the ferms of the counties in 1275,[13] but five years later the king made them a grant for seven years of deodands, the poll-tax of the Jews, the goods of Jews forfeited for any cause, and half the property of any Jews converted during that period.[14] At the same time he ordered that a school should be kept, and that converts able to learn a handicraft were to be taught one, and to be maintained only until they could support themselves, while the portions of clerical scholars who obtained ecclesiastical benefices were similarly to be withdrawn.[15] There is, unfortunately, no evidence whether these measures were carried out, but when an inquiry was made in 1308 as to the inmates who had died since 1290 and as to those still surviving, no information was forthcoming about certain men and women,[16] a fact which might be accounted for on the supposition[17] that they were gaining a livelihood elsewhere. The king also directed that the two priests and the clerk who served in the chapel were to be resident and were to collect the rents of the house and distribute them to the inmates as the warden advised.[18] The king's intention was evidently to reform the administration, a change in which had been much needed in 1272. The inmates of the hospital were then said to be begging from door to door, and to be almost perishing of hunger, because rich converts, who had other means of support, and who did not live in the house, received the revenues which ought to have been assigned only to the poor converts dwelling there.[19] Considering that this house was largely dependent on the royal bounty and that the management of its income was not always exemplary, it is curious that the warden was not bound to render an account to the Exchequer.[20] The result of the king's grants in aid of their finance was disappointing, and in 1281

he ordered that beside the poll-tax the converts should have 80 marks from the issues of the Jewry during his pleasure.[21] Funds were specially needed during this period to complete[22] the extensive alterations to the chapel begun in 1275.[23]

The converts in 1290 petitioned that the king would provide for them by giving them churches and escheats, as the grants from the Exchequer were paid very irregularly, but he did not assent to their request:[24] the expulsion of the Jews from England which occurred in that year may have been already under consideration, and it would certainly have been useless to endow permanently an institution which would soon come to an end. In February, 1292, he granted to the members of the house £202 0s. 4d. a year, this sum including the wages of the chaplains, and the portions of the converts, 10½d. a week in the case of a man, 8d. for a woman; as each inmate died the amount was to be proportionately diminished.[25] Of the ninety-seven who were there in 1292 about fifty-two survived in 1308, and the sum due from the king was accordingly reduced to £123 10s. 6d.[26]

A complaint, ostensibly by the converts, was made to the king in 1315 that the warden, Adam de Osgodeby, kept them out of their houses, and let them to strangers for the term of three lives to the king's prejudice.[27]

On inquiry by the chancellor, however, the affair resolved itself into an attempt by William de Crekelade, one of the chaplains, to regain a footing in the house from which he had been expelled by the former warden for defamation of the rest of the community. The converts, far from taking his side, declared him unfit to live in the house, and said that the warden paid him his wages against their will. They also showed that the tenements had been leased for the profit of the house with the consent of all, William included, and he was accordingly remitted to the warden for punishment.[28]

As the time approached when the extinction of the house might be reasonably expected, Edward III gave it fresh life by placing there the children of some converts[29] and certain converted Jews from

---

[12] Ibid. There were, however, only two priests and a clerk in 1280. *Cal. of Pat.* 1272–81, p. 371.

[13] *Cal. of Close*, 1272–9, p. 207.

[14] *Cal. of Pat.* 1272–81, pp. 371, 372. The property of converted Jews belonged to the king, but Edward on this occasion permitted them to retain half for themselves.

[15] *Cal. of Pat.* 1272–81, p. 376.

[16] Rymer, *Foedera* (Rec. Com.), ii (1), 62.

[17] This supposition is, however, doubtful, for one of the women, about whom *nothing was known*, was only prevented from appearing before the commissioners by illness, and petitioned for her allowance in 1315. *Cal. of Close*, 1313–18, p. 184.

[18] *Cal. of Pat.* 1272–81, p. 371.

[19] Pat. 56 Hen. III, pt. 1, m. 10, quoted by Tovey, op. cit. 194, 195.

[20] In 1286 John de St. Denis, keeper of the *Domus Conversorum*, was exonerated from rendering an account to the Exchequer as his predecessors never did so. *Cal. of Pat.* 1281–92, p. 228.

[21] *Cal. of Close*, 1279–88, p. 99.

[22] In 1281 the justices in Eyre were ordered to pay deodands to the warden of the House of Converts to complete the fabric of the chapel. Ibid. 107.

[23] Ibid. 1272–9, p. 207.

[24] *Parl. R.* (Rec. Com.), i, 49.

[25] Rymer, *Foedera* (Rec. Com.), ii (1), 62.

[26] Ibid.

[27] *Cal. of Close*, 1313–18, p. 228.

[28] Ibid.

[29] Two children of a conversa in 1336. *Cal. of Pat.* 1334–8, p. 259. Two sons of a conversus in 1337. Ibid. p. 494. The son of a conversa in 1344. Ibid. 1343–5, p. 213. See also case of Agnes, daughter of a convert in 1349. Ibid. 1348–50, p. 363.

foreign countries.[30] Still the inmates must have been few in number from 1344, when they seem to have been only eight.[31] In 1350 they had dwindled to four, and in 1371 there were only two.[32] The small amount allotted to the hospital may be the reason why the buildings and chapels were left unrepaired until their restoration by the warden, William Burstall, at his own cost,[33] since it was to provide for their future maintenance that at his request the house was annexed for ever to the Mastership of the Rolls in 1377.[34]

The accounts of the wardens[35] and the grants occasionally made to converts[36] show that the house was used for its original purpose for more than two centuries longer. The number of inmates was, however, always very small: in the second year of Henry V[37] there were eight converts, but often there were not more than two.

In 1534 three converts were in receipt of the usual portions of 10½d. a week,[38] and the hospital did not cease at the Reformation, for though there was no one there in 1552, two or three converts were certainly in residence from 1578 until 1608.

The accounts then cease, so that it is impossible to discover whether the hospital lasted until the Revolution. If it did, it probably did not survive it,[39] though it is said that a grant was made to two Jews in the reign of James II.[40]

The building itself was destroyed in 1717 to make room for the new house of the Master of the Rolls, who yet continued to be styled officially Keeper of the House of Converts, until 1873.[41]

Among the earliest possessions of the house in London were a capital messuage in Friday Street,[42] a 'seld' with shops in 'the Chepe,'[43] and rents in the parishes of St. Nicholas Acon[44] and St. Mary Colechurch.[45] In 1237 Henry III gave them also the church of St. Dunstan in the West,[46] of which they received all the issues until the bishop of London ordained in 1317 that a rector should in future be instituted there, and that he should pay to the converts the sum of £4 a year.[47] Their rents of assize in London and Oxford in 1279–80 amounted to £32 3s. 10d.[48] No specimen or description of the seal of this house appears to have survived.

*M. Reddan*

## Revised List of Wardens of the House of Converts

This is a corrected version of the *V.C.H.* list.

Walter Muclerk, Bishop of Carlisle, appointed 1232; died 1248[49]

Walter 'the Priest', occurs from 1234[50]

Robert, vicar of St. Werburga Friday Street, occurs from 1242[51]

William de Haverhill, occurs 1244[52]

The Dean of the Arches, occurs 1249[53]

Henry, vicar of St. Margaret's Friday Street, appointed 1250[54]

Adam de Chesterton, appointed 1265; died 1268[55]

Thomas de la Leye, appointed 1268; died 1270[56]

John de Sancto Dionisio, appointed 1270; died 1289[57]

---

[30] Edward of Brussels was sent there in 1339. Ibid. 1348–50, p. 400. Janethus of Spain was to receive the same allowance as the others of the house in 1344. Ibid. 1343–5, p. 190. A similar grant was made to Theobald of Turkey in 1348. Ibid. 1348–50, p. 87. The king ordered Henry de Ingleby, the warden, in 1356 to let John de Chastell, a convert, who had lately come to England, have the usual maintenance in the hospital. Close, 30 Edw. III, m. 13, quoted by Tovey, op. cit. 223.

[31] *Cal. of Close*, 1343–6, p. 313. It seems doubtful, however, whether the new inmates were included in this account.

[32] W. J. Hardy, 'The Rolls House and Chapel,' *Midd. and Herts. N. and Q.* ii, 57.

[33] Tovey, op. cit. 225.

[34] Ibid. The patent of Edward III was confirmed by Parliament in the first year of Richard II. *Parl. R.* (Rec. Com.), iii, 31a. Mr. Hardy shows (op. cit. 56), that most of the wardens from 1307 had been Masters of the Rolls.

[35] Hardy, op. cit. 60–5.

[36] *Cal. of Pat.* 1385–9, p. 397; ibid. 1401–5, p. 216.

[37] Hardy, op. cit. 60.

[38] *L. and P. Hen. VIII*, xi, 66.

[39] Hardy, op. cit. 66.

[40] Tovey, op. cit. 227.

[41] The custody of the hospital for his habitation was granted to him on his appointment to the Mastership of the Rolls. *Dep. Keeper's Rep.* lvii, App. 28.

[42] *Cal. of Chart. R.* i, 290.

[43] Ibid. 292.

[44] Ibid. 309.

[45] Ibid. 351.

[46] *Cal. of Pat.* 1232–47, p. 178.

[47] Lond. Epis. Reg. Baldock and Gravesend, fol. 37.

[48] Hardy, op. cit 54. For their property in Oxford see also *Hund. R.* (Rec. Com.), ii, 791, 798.

[49] The *V.C.H.* cited Hardy for Muclerk's wardenship, but the actual evidence is in *Cal. of Close* 1231–4, pp. 37, 77. See also Nicholas Vincent, 'Mauclerk, Walter (d. 1248),' *ODNB* (Oxford, 2004) [http://www. oxforddnb.com/view/ article/18355, accessed 15 October 2006].

[50] *Cal. of Close* 1231–4, pp. 415, 503; Devon, *Issues of Exch.*, p. 15.

[51] *Cal. of Pat.* 1232–47, p. 453. The *V.C.H.* noted he was the rector of the church of Hoo, but he was also vicar of St. Werburga Friday Street. See *Cal. of Chart R.* 1226–57, p. 290.

[52] The *V.C.H.* did not include Haverhill, but was called 'the custodian of the house of converts', in 1244. See *Cal. of Close* 1242–7, p. 165.

[53] The *V.C.H.* did not include the dean in their list, but the evidence is in *Cal. of Close* 1247–51, p. 238. Actual name not recorded.

[54] Hennessey, *Novum Repert. Eccl. Lond.* 378.

[55] Ibid.

[56] Ibid.

[57] *Cal. of Close*, 1272–9, p. 159; *Cal. of Pat.* 1272–81, p. 376.

Robert de Scardeburgh, appointed 1287[58]

Richard de Clippinges, appointed 1289[59]

Walter de Aymondesham, appointed 1290[60]

Henry de Bluntesdon, appointed 1297[61]

Adam de Osgodby, appointed 1307; died 1316[62]

William de Ayremynne, appointed 1316; resigned 1325; died 1336.[63]

Robert de Holden, appointed 1325; resigned 1327[64]

Richard de Ayremynne, appointed 1327; resigned 1339[65]

John de Sancto Paulo, appointed 1339[66]

Henry de Ingleby, appointed 1350; resigned 1371[67]

William de Burstall, appointed 1371; resigned 1381[68]

John de Waltham, appointed 1381; resigned 1386[69]

John de Burton, appointed 1386; died 1394[70]

John de Scarle, appointed 1394[71]

Thomas Stanley, appointed 1397; resigned 1402; died 1409[72]

Nicholas Bubwith, appointed 1402; resigned 1405; died 1424[73]

John Wakeryng, appointed 1405; resigned 1415; died 1425[74]

Simon Gaunstede, appointed 1415; died 1493[75]

John Frank(s), appointed 1423; resigned 1438[76]

John Stopyndon, appointed 1438[77]

Thomas Kirkby, appointed 1447; resigned 1455[78]

John Keilpenny, appointed 1455[79]

Robert Kirkham, appointed 1461[80]

John Morland, appointed 1471[81]

John Alcock, appointed 1471; resigned 1471[82]

John Morton, appointed 1472; resigned 1478[83]

Robert Morton, appointed 1478; resigned 1483; died 1497[84]

Thomas Barowe, appointed 1483; resigned 1485; died 1499[85]

William Elliot, appointed 1485[86]

David William, appointed 1487[87]

John Blith, appointed 1492[88]

William Warham, appointed 1494[89]

William Barons, appointed 1502[90]

Christopher Bainbrigg, appointed 1504[91]

John Young, appointed 1508[92]

Cuthbert Turnstall, appointed 1516[93]

John Clerk, appointed 1522[94]

Thomas Hannibal, appointed 1523[95]

John Taylor, appointed 1527[96]

Thomas Cromwell, appointed 1534; resigned 1536[97]

Christopher Hales, appointed 1536[98]

Sir Robert Southwell, appointed 1541[99]

[58] D'Blossiers Tovey, *Anglia Judaica* (London, 1990), p. 221. Unlikely that Scardeburgh was ever an active warden, since Sancto Dionisio did not die until 1289, though Scardeburgh may have assisted him. Scardeburgh was also chaplain to Edward I and Dean of York Minster, 1279–90.

[59] *Cal. of Pat.* 1281–92, p. 335.

[60] Ibid., p. 392. He was also Chancellor of Scotland.

[61] He was the king's chaplain and almoner. Ibid., 1292–1301, p. 341; *Cal. of Close* 1313–18, pp. 228–9.

[62] *Cal. of Pat.* 1307–13, p. 15; *Cal. of Close*, 1313–18, p. 374.

[63] *Cal. of Pat.* 1313–17, p. 534; Resigned when he was made Bishop of Norwich in 1325.

[64] *Cal. of Pat.* 1324–7, p. 179. Resigned to become warden of the hospital of St. James without Westminster. See *Cal. of Pat.* 1324–27, p. 314.

[65] *Cal. of Pat.* 1327–33, p. 42 and 1338–40, p. 256.

[66] *Cal. of Pat.* 1338–40, p. 256, and 1341–3, p. 236. Sancto Paulo was keeper of the Great Seal in 1334 and 1338–40. He was deprived of all offices (except the wardenship of the Domus Conversorum) in 1341. See Philomena Connolly, 'St. Paul, John (d. 1362),' in ODNB, [http://www.oxforddnb.com/view/article/24522 (accessed 17 Mar. 2007)]. Hennessey has included Michael de Worth as preceding Sancto Paulo as warden and John Thorsby as succeeding him, though neither were actually warden, but Master of the Rolls, to which the wardenship of the house of converts was formally attached in 1377.

[67] *Cal. of Pat.* 1348–50, p. 475; Hennessey, op. cit. 378.

[68] Hennessey, op. cit. 378. Burstall was the first Master of the Rolls to automatically be appointed warden of the house of converts.

[69] Newcourt, op. cit. i, 340.

[70] *Cal. of Pat.* 1385–9, p. 230, and 1391–6, p. 468.

[71] Ibid. Possibly resigned in 1397. He was Lord Chancellor in 1399 and died in 1403.

[72] Newcourt, op. cit. i, 340.

[73] *Cal. of Pat.* 1401–4, p. 120. Was Bishop of London, 1406; Bishop of Salisbury, 1406–7; Bishop of Bath and Wells, 1407–24.

[74] *Cal. of Pat.* 1401–5, p. 483; *List of Foreign Accts.* 53. Was Bishop of Norwich 1416–25.

[75] Newcourt, op. cit. i, 340; Hennessy, op. cit. 379.

[76] *Cal. of Pat* 1422–9, p. 139; *List of Foreign Accts.* 53. Resigned to become Master of St. Katherine's Hospital.

[77] Ibid. 53.

[78] Ibid. 53.

[79] Hennessy, op. cit. 379. Thomas Kirkby, however, accounted every year from 27 to 38 Hen. VI. List of Foreign Accts. 54.

[80] *Cal. of Pat.* 1461–7, p. 147.

[81] *Cal. Pat.* 1467–77, p. 245. Hennessey called him William Morland and also inserted a James Goldwell as his successor, but there is no mention of Goldwell in other sources.

[82] Ibid., p. 259. He resigned to become Bishop of Rochester. Founded Jesus College, Cambridge. According to Hennessey, he had been appointed before in 1462, but the appointment is not mentioned in the *Calendar of Patent Rolls*.

[83] Ibid., p. 334; *List of Foreign Accts.* 4. Resigned to become Bishop of Ely. Archbishop of Canterbury, 1486–1500.

[84] Ibid.; *Cal. of Pat.* 1476–85, p. 285. He had been granted the reversion of the office in 1477.

[85] Ibid., p. 462.

[86] Newcourt, op. cit., i, 340.

[87] Ibid.

[88] Hennessy, op. cit. 379.

[89] Ibid.

[90] Ibid.

[91] Ibid.

[92] Ibid.

[93] Ibid.

[94] Ibid.

[95] Ibid.

[96] Ibid.

[97] Ibid. and *L. and P. Hen. VIII*, xi, 202 (17).

[98] Ibid.

[99] Hennessy, op. cit. 379.

John Beaumont, appointed 1550[100]
Robert Bows, appointed 1552[101]
Nicolas Hare, appointed 1553[102]
William Cordell, appointed 1557[103]

Gilbert Gerard, appointed 1589[104]
John Egerton, appointed 1594[105]
Edward Lord Bruce, appointed 1603[106]
Edward Philips, appointed 1608[107]

[100] Newcourt, op. cit. i. 341.
[101] Ibid.
[102] Ibid.
[103] Ibid.

[104] Ibid.
[105] Ibid.
[106] Ibid.
[107] Ibid.

# COLLEGES

## 33. THE COLLEGIATE CHURCH OF ST. MARTIN LE GRAND

### INTRODUCTION

Since the publication of the original *V.C.H.* account, the history of St. Martin Le Grand, particularly the period from its foundation to the end of the twelfth century, has received considerable attention from historians. Pamela Taylor provides useful insights into the foundation of St. Martin Le Grand, as well as references to recent scholarship in 'Ingelric, Count Eustace and the foundation of St. Martin-Le-Grand', *Anglo-Norman Studies*, 24 (2001), pp. 215–37. For discussion of the events of the twelfth century, and corrections to the list of deans, see R. H. C. Davis, 'The College of St. Martin-Le-Grand and the Anarchy 1135–54', *London Topographical Record*, 23 (1974), pp. 9–26, esp. pp. 21–4.

Another area of debate is the role of the house as a sanctuary within the city of London, and its relationship with the civic community in the fifteenth century, for which see I. D. Thornley, 'Sanctuary in Medieval London', *Jour. Brit. Arch. Assoc.*, 2nd ser. 38 (1932), pp. 293–315 and C. M. Barron, *London in the Later Middle Ages* (Oxford, 2004), pp. 35–6. A list of sources relating to the London property held by the college can be found in *Documentary Sources*, pp. 54–5. On the precinct of the house, see M. B. Honeybourne, 'The Sanctuary Boundaries and Environs of Westminster Abbey and the College of St. Martin-le-Grand', *Jour. Brit. Arch. Assoc.* 2nd ser. 38 (1932), pp. 316–33. G. H. Cook, *English Collegiate Churches of the Middle Ages* (London, 1959), pp. 56–9, provides some brief commentary on the fabric of St. Martin Le Grand.

*John McEwan*

The dedication in honour of St. Martin, a favourite saint of Christian Britain, and architectural remains found in the nineteenth century, point to the early existence of a church in this place,[1] but nothing certain is known except that in 1068 William the Conqueror confirmed a grant of lands made a few months before by a certain Ingelric to the church of St. Martin in London, which he and his brother Girard had built at their own cost as a foundation of secular canons.[2] Ingelric, who was a priest, most probably of foreign origin, appears to have held an official position under both Edward the Confessor and William,[3] and in consequence the college was from the first not only well endowed but highly privileged. To the lands given by Ingelric, viz. Easter,

Mashbury, Norton, Stanford, Fobbing, 'Benedist' Chrishall, Tolleshunt, Rivenhall, and Ongar, a hide in Benfleet, a hide in Hoddesdon, and 2 hides with the church in Maldon, William added some land and moor outside Cripplegate; he made the college free from all episcopal and archidiaconal exactions and from services due to the crown, and granted them sac and soc, tol and team, infangenthef, blodwyte, burghbrice, miskenning, &c.[4]

The king directed the canons to choose of their number a suitable guardian of their goods who should keep them faithfully and distribute to each his share without deceit, so that the rest, freed from care, might devote themselves to prayer.[5] This appears to have been the origin of the deanery. Ingelric became the first dean,[6] but, like a number of his successors, seems still to have remained a royal official,[7] and so far detached from the college that the possessions of the deanery could be regarded as

---

[1] Kempe, *The Ch. of St. Martin le Grand*, 5, 6. The foundation of the church has been variously ascribed to Cadwallein, to his followers in his memory, and to Wythred king of Kent. Tanner, *Notit. Mon.*; Harl. MS. 261, fol. 107.

[2] Doc. of D. and C. of Westm. Reg. St. Martin le Grand, fol. 1; Lansd. MS. 170 (a transcript of the register), fol. 52; Dugdale, *Mon. Angl.* vi, 1324.

[3] Round, *The Commune of London*, 28, 36.

[4] Dugdale, *Mon. Angl.* vi, 1324.

[5] Ibid.

[6] Kempe, op. cit. 10; Round, *The Commune of London*, 28.

[7] Round, op. cit.

his private property.[8] The confusion caused by this dual capacity may be responsible for the grant made by the Conqueror on Ingelric's death of the church of St. Martin and all its property to Eustace count of Boulogne.[9]

If a charter in which the king refers to St. Martin's as his royal free chapel is rightly attributed to Henry I – though on this point there is room for doubt[10] – it is difficult to say what relations were established by this grant between the church and the count. Otherwise it would seem that Eustace thus became patron, for William Rufus, after a quarrel with the count, seized the land outside Cripplegate belonging to the church;[11] Queen Matilda, the heiress of Boulogne, speaks of 'my canons of St. Martin's,'[12] and William count of Boulogne was styled 'advocatus' of St. Martin's in 1158.[13] There is also no evidence of the appointment of a dean by the king, as such, before the death of Count William in 1160; as the Boulogne inheritance then passed to a woman,[14] it is possible that Henry II took the opportunity to make fresh arrangements with regard to the lands and rights of the honour.

The tie between St. Martin's and the Boulogne family being of this nature, the college might reasonably expect its fortune to rise when the heiress of Boulogne became queen; and it is perhaps worth notice that of the two churches added to St. Martin's in the reign of Henry I, St. Botolph's Aldersgate was given by Thurstan, a priest,[15] and St. Mary's Newport, through Roger[16] bishop of Salisbury, the dean, probably by him; while in Stephen's reign it was Queen Matilda herself who granted as provision for another canon the churches of Chrishall and Witham, with the chapel

of Cressing.[17] King Stephen, moreover, gave to the canons free warren on their lands of Easter, Norton, Maldon, and Tolleshunt.[18] The position of the church, however, at this time, was most unenviable, and nothing gives a better idea of the utter anarchy then prevailing than the history of St. Martin's. Although the college could depend on the favour of both parties in the Civil War, for when the empress was in power[19] it was secure through its dean, Henry de Blois bishop of Winchester, her supporter, yet its property was seized again and again by various persons under cover of the general disorder. Their land at Aldersgate,[20] Cripplegate,[21] Maldon,[22] and elsewhere[23] was all taken from the canons at different times, and Geoffrey de Mandeville not only deprived them of the church of Newport[24] and its appurtenances, but committed depredations on other possessions of theirs in Essex.[25] It may have been before the beginning of the war that the rebuilding of St. Martin's or some extensive addition to the church was undertaken, since Nigel bishop of Ely offered an indulgence of forty days to those of his diocese who contributed,[26] and he was more likely to be interested in St. Martin's while his uncle, Roger of Salisbury, was dean. If so, the work probably extended over some years, for the begging letter sent out by the college speaks of the troubles of the kingdom as having affected the church.[27] The canons, to induce liberality, promised to receive all who helped this cause into the fraternity of their

---

[8] Charter of Count Eustace, Reg. of St. Martin le Grand, fol. 10*b*; Lansd. MS. 170, fol. 61; Kempe, op. cit. 34.

[9] Reg. of St. Martin le Grand, fol. 10*b*.

[10] It is dated 39th year, so that unless the scribe made a mistake in transcription the charter cannot have been by Henry I. Reg. fol. 7; Lansd. MS. 170, fol. 57; Kempe, op. cit. 39.

[11] Reg. of St. Martin's, fol. 11; Lansd. MS. 170, fol. 62; Kempe, op. cit. 34. In a writ of King Stephen to Richard de Lucy and the sheriff of Essex, the phrase occurs 'as Roger bishop of Salisbury best held in the time of Count Eustace of Boulogne, and henceforth up to the death of King Henry,' Reg. fol. 21.

[12] Doc. of D. and C. of Westm. St. Martin le Grand, parcel 2, Cartul. of St. Martin, item 116.

[13] Ibid. St. Martin le Grand, parcel 4, No. 13247.

[14] Mary, William's sister, who was at that time abbess of Romsey, but received a papal dispensation to marry the count of Flanders. *Dict. Nat. Biog.* xxxvii, 54.

[15] Doc. of D. and C. of Westm. Cartul. of St. Martin le Grand, item 120.

[16] Doc. of D. and C. of Westm. St. Martin le Grand, parcel 1, an exemplification in 1440 of an inspeximus of Edward III. Henry I, at the petition of Roger bishop of Salisbury, grants to the church of St. Martin the church of Newport, which the canons after the death of Bishop Roger shall hold free and quit for ever.

[17] Doc. of D. and C. of Westm. Cartul. of St. Martin le Grand, item 124; also St. Martin le Grand, parcel 1, Exemplif. of 1440.

[18] Reg. of St. Martin le Grand, fol. 10; Lansd. MS. 170, fol. 61; Kempe, op. cit. 55.

[19] The empress ordered Osbert Octodeniers to seise Henry bishop of Winchester of certain lands in London, which belonged to the deanery of St. Martin, and of which he and his church had been disseised, as Dean Roger and Fulcher had held them. Reg. of St. Martin's, fol. 12; Lansd. MS. 170, fol. 63; Kempe, op. cit. 51.

[20] See Stephen to Osbert Octodeniers and all the barons of London, Reg. fol. 11*b*; Kempe, op. cit. 44.

[21] Henry bishop of Winchester to the justices and sheriffs of London. He speaks of the canons having long sustained unjust spoliation within and without the City, and requests that they may restore their property without Cripplegate. Reg. fol. 11*b*; Kempe, op. cit. 63.

[22] Letters of Stephen and the bishop of Winchester as to the land at Maldon. Reg. fol. 12*b*; Kempe, op. cit. 45.

[23] It is evident from a letter of Queen Matilda to Baldwin de Witsand that they were not allowed peaceful possession of their land at Good Easter. Cartul. item 139; Reg. fol. 21; Kempe, op. cit. 58.

[24] Ibid.

[25] Geoffrey's letter ordering that the canons' corn at Good Easter shall be restored to them. Doc. of D. and C. of Westm. Cartul. of St. Martin, item 133; Kempe, op. cit. 61.

[26] Doc. of D. and C. of Westm. Cartul. of St. Martin, item 129.

[27] Ibid. item 109. The letter was taken round by Thomas, chaplain of St. Martin's.

church, and set forth the various remissions of penance offered to the charitable: forty days by the bishop of Winchester to those of his diocese who gave alms; fifteen days by Alberic, bishop of Ostia and papal legate, to all benefactors of St. Martin's; and forty days every year to those who on 4 July, the anniversary of the dedication, visited the church and made an offering. W. bishop of Norwich, besides aiding the canons in this way, gave them leave to preach in the cause of their church throughout his diocese.[28] The gift of a piece of the cloth in which the body of St. Cuthbert had been wrapped,[29] made to St. Martin's by Hugh bishop of Durham at some time between 1171 and 1189, may have had some connexion with these building operations, for such a relic, even without the bishop of London's indulgence,[30] must have been a great financial benefit; it is more probably, however, a sign of the important position already held by St. Martin's.

The year 1158 marks the constitution of the prebends of St. Martin's.[31] William I had ordered the 'Custos' of the property of the college to assign a proper portion to each canon, but the arrangement cannot have been wholly satisfactory, since it was at the request of the canons that the share of each was fixed. The dean was to have the church of Newport and land to the value of 20s. in Tolleshunt, the prebend being called Newport;[32] Maldon provided for two canons, one of whom was called prebendary of Keton;[33] out of Good Easter were formed four prebends, known afterwards as Imbers, Fawkeners, Paslowes, and Burghs or Bowers;[34] the church and land of Chrishall, 10s. in Tolleshunt and 10s. in Hoddesdon made an estate for another canon,[35] and land worth 100s. within and without London for the eighth; the land assigned for the support of the ninth lay in Norton and 'Selga,' and appears to have been the prebend called Norton-Newerks.[36] The rest of their lands in and without London, the church of Witham,

the chapel of Bonhunt,[37] the tithes of Tolleshunt, and anything in future accruing, were settled on the community of canons residing in the church.

The canons resident might be absent on their business four times a year, if they were not away more than fifteen days. If they should be absent constantly, clerks must be appointed as substitutes. The canons, moreover, who did not frequent the church had to find suitable vicars, paying to them 2 marks a year, to the community of canons a mark, or half a mark if their absence were for study, and to the work of the church half a mark.

The issues of the church of Maldon were to be devoted to the lights of St. Martin's, and the tithe of Good Easter to the work of that church.

A further readjustment was found necessary a few years later, and in the time of Godfrey de Lucy[38] some land which had belonged to the prebend of the dean and that of Master Ivo de Cornwall was assigned to the holder of the London prebend, the dean receiving in exchange the chapel of Bonhunt and land in London valued at 15s., and Master Ivo land there worth 12s. 6d.

The thirteenth century is an important period in the history of St. Martin's; it is a time of disputes and settlements of titles to possessions, of internal development, and of the establishment of its rights and immunities as a royal free chapel. Up to about 1250 there is a continual succession of agreements and suits: Innocent III in 1203 confirmed a composition made between St. Martin's and the House of the Holy Spirit at Writtle over tithes;[39] in 1235 Roger bishop of London, by command of the pope, settled a dispute between the dean and chapter of St. Martin's and the chaplain of St. Nicholas Shambles, about a pension;[40] the vicar of St. Botolph's Aldersgate seems to have refused to pay the pension owing from his church at intervals between 1225 and 1349, and as a result there were constant legal proceedings against him;[41] in 1236 the college was engaged in a suit against the priory of Brissant;[42] an agreement was made at the same date by Herbert, canon of St. Martin's, and the rector

[28] Doc. of D. and C. of Westm. St. Martin le Grand, parcel 2. W. was bishop of Norwich 1146–75.

[29] Ibid. The event occurred when G. de Luci held the deanery.

[30] Gilbert bishop of London offered twenty days' relaxation of penance to the parishioners of St. Paul's who visited St. Martin's within twenty days of the anniversary of the reception of the relic. Cartul. item 144.

[31] Doc. of D. and C. of Westm. St. Martin le Grand, parcel 4, No. 13247; ibid. Reg. of St. Martin, fol. 10b; Lansd. MS. 170, fol. 61b; Kempe, op. cit. 65, 66.

[32] It is called by that name in a document of 1391. Doc. of D. and C. of Westm. No. 13311.

[33] Ibid. St. Martin le Grand, parcel 3, No. 13215. The other is probably that known as Cowpes.

[34] Ibid. No. 13268, No. 1002; Morant, *Hist. of Essex*, ii, 458.

[35] A prebend called Chrishall figures in a list *temp.* Hen. VII. Doc. of D. and C. of Westm. No. 13324.

[36] Ibid. No. 13314.

[37] Wicken Bonhunt.

[38] Henry bishop of Winchester claimed the chapel of 'Bonant' as belonging to his church of Newport. Cartul. of St. Martin's, item 118. The dispute of the canons with the bishop over this chapel may have occasioned the letter of Thomas archbishop of Canterbury to them. In this he stated that he had received the mandate of the pope to protect anything belonging to the jurisdiction of the bishop, and commanded the canons to obey him as their dean. Reg. fol. 17; Kempe, op. cit. 68.

[39] Doc. of D. and C. of Westm. St. Martin le Grand, parcel 2.

[40] Ibid. Lond. C.

[41] Ibid. Lond. B. box 2 (1); ibid. Lond. B. box 3.

[42] Ibid. St. Martin le Grand, parcel 4, No. 13245.

of Old Ongar about some property;[43] in 1238 Pope Gregory XI ordered an inquiry into the complaints of the dean and chapter against the abbot and convent of Walden, the master of the Temple, and other persons for injuries done to them in the matter of tithes, possessions, and legacies;[44] and in 1253 a case was begun between St. Martin's and St. John's, Colchester.[45]

The most striking change, perhaps, in the college itself, was the foundation, about 1240, of a new prebend[46] for two additional canons.[47] It was called Newland, and was formed out of property in Good Easter,[48] acquired for this purpose by Herbert, the canon mentioned above, who was chamberlain of St. Martin's,[49] and altogether an important member of that church.[50] It may be inferred that perpetual vicars were established in 1158 by the article ordaining that every nonresident canon was to appoint a vicar. They undoubtedly formed part of the college in 1228, for canon Richard de Elmham left by will in 1228 to each vicar 12d., and to their refectory a cloth and a towel.[51] As in 1304 there were only two resident canons[52] there should then have been eight perpetual vicars, or ten if the prebend of Newland be considered. Some statutes that date from the late fifteenth century, but are probably a recapitulation of earlier rules,[53] declare that each prebend shall find a vicar priest for service in the church except the prebend of Maldon, which ought to have a vicar deacon, and the prebend of Norton which finds the vicar sub-deacon. In 1503 there were eight perpetual vicars who were priests,[54] so that it would seem that at one time there must have been in all ten vicars.

There were seven vicars in 1235, for they witness a document,[55] but whether there were more at that date it is impossible to say.

In 1254 two chantries for the souls of Thomas Mauger and William de Winton, to be served by two perpetual vicars, were established in St. Martin's,[56] and the terms of foundation leave it at least uncertain whether two new vicarages were not then created.[57] If, however, the number of vicars was complete in 1254, these chantries may be regarded as a first attempt to supplement the original provision for the vicarages. That something needed to be done in this direction was probably even then evident, but no general measures were taken until Dean Louis of Savoy ordained[58] in 1279 that as the vicars could not live on what they received, each was to have 12d. a week, and that the canons should have of the gift of Adam de Fyleby, chamberlain of the church, in compensation for the diminution of their commons, the manor of Parva Benfleet, 7 acres of land in Good Easter, and houses and rents in London.

St. Martin's was one of the three churches in which the abbot of Abingdon ordered the sentence of excommunication and interdict against the baronial party and the city of London to be published,[59] and the dean, Geoffrey de Boclande, and the chapter were excommunicated with the canons of Holy Trinity and of St. Paul's for their refusal to obey. These three churches were no doubt selected for this work as the most important in London, but if a further reason for the choice is sought it may perhaps be found in the intimate connexion of the cathedral and priory with the City, and the peculiar position of St. Martin's, especially in relation to the crown.

The possession of the honour of Boulogne and the kingdom of England for a time by one person would undoubtedly foster the idea that St. Martin's was a royal chapel, and facilitate its becoming one in fact on the death of Count William. It is just after this event that the king first appears incontestably as patron,[60] though the candidate

[43] Ibid. parcel 4, No. 13253.

[44] Ibid. parcel 2.

[45] Ibid. parcel 2 and parcel 4, No. 13246.

[46] The dean and chapter in that year leased to Herbert for his life a tenement in Newland which they had of his gift. Ibid. parcel 4, No. 13269.

[47] There is in the Cartulary of St. Martin's a bull of Pope Innocent confirming the grant of the prebend to two canons. It was also held by two canons at the time of the appropriation of St. Martin's to Westminster Abbey. Ibid. parcel 4, No. 13301.

[48] Ibid. parcel 3, No. 13215.

[49] Ibid.

[50] There are many notices of him scattered among the documents relating to St. Martin's, especially in the Cartulary and in No. 13215. He was acting as procurator of the college in 1238. *Cal. of Pat.* 1232–47, p. 218.

[51] Doc. of D. and C. of Westm. St. Martin le Grand, parcel 4, No. 13262.

[52] Ibid. parcel 4, No. 13272.

[53] Ibid. parcel 2. Statutes of the college of St. Martin's and oaths to be taken by the vicars perpetual and canons resident. The rule that a canon might bequeath a year's fruits of his prebend by will is older than the time of Geoffrey de Boclande, who allowed a canon to do the same when he left to join a stricter community. Ibid. parcel 2.

[54] Doc. of D. and C. of Wesm. parcel 3, No. 13215.

[55] The settlement by Roger, bishop of London, about the church of St. Nicholas Shambles. Ibid. London, C.

[56] Ibid. London, O-V. See also Inspeximus of John de Heselarton. Ibid. St. Martin le Grand, parcel 2.

[57] 'Idem presbiteri nomina perpetuorum vicariorum fortiantur cum aliis vicariis ecclesie in mensa et dormitorio moraturi.' Ibid. London O–V.

[58] Ibid. St. Martin le Grand, parcel 2, Inspeximus of Dean John de Heselarton; ibid. parcel 3, No. 13215.

[59] Roger of Wendover, *Chron.* (Rolls Ser.), ii, 174.

[60] When the king made William son of Count Theobald dean subject to the consent of the bishop of Winchester (Cartulary, item 149). There is also no reason to doubt that the King Henry who gave a charter of protection to his free chapel of St. Martin's was Hen. II as supposed. Reg. fol. 7; Lansd. MS. 170, fol. 57.

for the post of dean had thought it expedient to use the influence of the abbess of Romsey, the representative of the Boulogne family.[61] Richard[62] and John[63] subsequently appointed the dean as if by undoubted right. It was, however, some time before the point was reached when the king regarded an infringement of its privileges as an attack on his royal prerogative.

When in the reign of Henry II an attempt was made by the archdeacon of Essex to exact dues from the church of Maldon, which was exempt as belonging to St. Martin's, it was the archbishop who intervened at the request of the canons.[64]

In 1225 a similar case occurred, but it was treated in very different fashion. The archdeacon of Colchester tried to exact procurations from the church of Newport, and on the dean's refusal to pay impleaded him in virtue of papal letters before the archdeacon, chancellor, and dean of Oxford. The king, after ordering the archdeacon of Colchester in vain to desist from his suit, forbade the judges to proceed in the matter, as it might be prejudicial to his royal dignity.[65]

On another occasion, when Henry, rector of St. Leonard's, brought a cause in Court Christian in 1238 against Herbert, canon and procurator of St. Martin's,[66] about certain things touching the state and liberties of that church, the king directed that the case should be stopped until he had appealed to the pope. Again in 1250 Henry summoned Fulk, bishop of London, to answer for exacting jurisdiction in the churches of Newport and Chrishall which as prebendal churches of St. Martin's were not subject to the ordinary.[67] The struggle thus begun continued for a century, and Henry's successors showed themselves equally determined in their maintenance of the exemptions of their chapel.

Archbishop Peckham involved himself in a difficulty with Edward I for excommunicating the dean who had opposed the exercise of any jurisdiction but his own in Newport,[68] and the same king utterly forbade procurations to be exacted from St. Martin's on behalf of two cardinals in 1295.[69] The procurations demanded by the papal nuncio in 1309,[70] and by the collectors of the cardinal of Sts. Marcellinus and Peter, and the cardinal of St. Mary

in Via Lata in 1317[71] were likewise prohibited by the king who in 1313 ordered the bishop of London to refrain from his attempt to exercise authority in St. Martin's and the churches annexed.[72]

Although the king in pursuance of his policy with regard to the royal chapels had refused to allow papal provisions to prebends,[73] he yet received the support of the pope.

Clement V in 1306 forbade delegates or subdelegates of the pope to promulgate sentences of excommunication, suspension or interdict against the king or his chapels without special licence of the apostolic see,[74] and in 1317 John XXII inhibited any ordinary, delegate, or sub-delegate to publish sentences, or do anything contrary to the exemptions of the king's free chapels.[75]

This freedom from all authority except that of the king, while it secured for the college a powerful position against the outside world, had drawbacks both material and spiritual. From the first the deanery was held by a royal official, and in many cases it can only have been bestowed for services to the king without any regard to the recipient's fitness for such a post. Dean Guy de Rossilian was freed in 1248 by papal indulgence from the obligation to take holy orders,[76] and William de Marchia, the treasurer, dean in 1291, was only a sub-deacon.[77] It must be remembered, too, that the canons, who were appointed by the dean,[78] were of the same class as himself, clerks attached to the households of royal or noble personages,[79] and holding many benefices besides their prebends.[80] This does not imply a slur on their conduct, but it would give a reason why the discipline, always less in a college of secular priests than in a body belonging to an order, may have been still further relaxed in this instance. In fact St. Martin's can always be better imagined as a corporation of officials than as a religious house. It seems indeed as if the spiritual side of the place

[61] William son of Count Theobald says the king gave him the deanery 'for love of my father, and at the prayer of the abbess of Romsey.' Cartulary, item 149.

[62] Cart. Antiq. R., RR. (16).

[63] Cart. Antiq. R., H. (1).

[64] Reg. fol. 17; Lansd. MS. 170, fol. 68b; Kempe, op. cit. 68.

[65] Rot. Lit. Claus. (Rec. Com.), ii, 80.

[66] Cal. of Pat. 1232–47, p. 218.

[67] Reg. fol. 18; Lansd. MS. 170, fol. 70.

[68] Reg. Epist. John Peckham (Rolls Ser.), i, 184.

[69] Cal. of Close, 1288–96, p. 423.

[70] Ibid. 1307–13, p. 236.

[71] Ibid. 1313–18, p. 596.

[72] Ibid. 84.

[73] Hen. III in 1238 opposed the attempt of the legate to give a prebend in St. Martin's to a clerk in virtue of papal letters. Cal. of Pat. 1232–47, p. 227. In 1303 Edw. I ordered the dean and chapter to ignore the papal provisions made to Henry nato Braunche de Sarracenis. Reg. fol. 20. Lansd. 170, fol. 71b.

[74] Rymer, Foedera (Rec. Com.), i (4), 45; Kempe, op. cit. 89.

[75] Cal. of Pap. Letters, ii, 433.

[76] Ibid. i, 242.

[77] Ibid. i, 530.

[78] The right was granted by John to Richard Briger with the deanery in 1199 (Cart. Antiq. H (1), and Harl. 6748, fol. 18), and was given to the dean for ever by the charter of Hen. III to Walter de Kirkeham. Cott. MS. Claud. D, ii, fol. 129b.

[79] Cal. of Pap. Letters, ii, 39, 233, 286, 294, 323, 395; Cal. of Pap. Petitions, i, 49, 73, 381, 589.

[80] The Calendar of Papal Letters is full of dispensations to them to hold several benefices, see, i, 577; ii, 4, 19, 39, 53, 72, 121, 205, &c.

was felt to be somewhat lacking as early as the beginning of the thirteenth century, or there would have been no need for Geoffrey de Boclande to make provision for the canons who left the college for a stricter rule.[81]

Since many of the deans may be said to have owed their appointment to their administrative ability, it might be presumed that the college suffered from maladministration less than other religious bodies. On the other hand it is quite as likely to have been neglected while the dean occupied himself with the king's business or pursued his own interests, and in support of this theory it may be remarked that Peter of Savoy while dean seems to have spent almost all his time abroad,[82] and could have felt little pride in his church or he would not have violated its customs by committing the task of hearing the accounts of its chamberlains and other ministers to persons who did not belong to St. Martin's, and who appointed places outside for this business.[83] It is, too, at least doubtful whether most of the deans who received higher preferment[84] were not promoted for services to the king rather than to St. Martin's.

The state of the college in 1323 therefore hardly causes surprise. It was found then that books and ornaments were lacking; that the officers and other ministers left undone the duties for which they received their stipends, and raised quarrels and scandals among themselves, while some led dissolute lives elsewhere, and that the sums which should have been devoted to the repair of the church, the payment of commons, and to salaries were applied to other uses.[85] The commissioners appointed by the king to make the visitation attributed the blame largely to the dean, Richard de Ellesfield,[86] and he was removed. Twenty years afterwards, in 1343, another inquiry was necessary owing to the waste and dilapidation of the church and its possessions through the negligence of its deans,[87] and in 1344 a lawsuit had arisen because Dean John de Heselarton, after declining to take

the part he should have in the election of the master of the hospital of St. Leonard Newport, which was subject to St. Martin's, had refused to admit the priest elected, and had committed the custody of the house to another.[88] On the occasion of the visitation of 1343 the two canons resident had a grievance against Heselarton about the portion assigned to them from the commons of the church on account of residence, and it was ordained by the Lord Chancellor in 1345 that they and future canons resident were to receive £20 a year between them besides pittances and obits.[89]

An extensive improvement to the church appears to have taken place between 1258 and 1261 when Henry III gave the canons marble columns and stone for the construction of a pulpit, some sculptured figures of kings for decoration and 200 freestones for the chapel of St. Blaise.[90] It is not unlikely that the bishops of Coventry, Durham and Laodicea in offering relaxation of penance in 1260 to those who visited and prayed at the tomb of Matilda de la Fauconere de la Wade in St. Martin's[91] may have intended to help the church as well as benefit Matilda's soul. The dean and chapter certainly secured a great benefit for themselves by obtaining permission in 1286 to close the road running from Foster Lane to St. Nicholas Shambles,[92] as the canons had found the public road between their houses and the church so inconvenient that in the reign of Henry III they had spanned it with causeways.[93] Although the outside world was thus shut out it could still make itself painfully evident to the ministers of St. Martin's, for dung-heaps were raised by the neighbours so near the wall of the close that, as the dean and chapter complained in 1331, the air in their church and dwellings was corrupted.[94] Unless the buildings of St. Martin's had been greatly neglected it is hardly conceivable that the wind could have played such havoc with the church, bell-towers and cloisters that the canons despaired of repairing them and in 1360 thought of abandoning the place.[95] The state of affairs disclosed in 1343 could not have been remedied at once, and a bequest of Dean Useflete shows that the cloister at least needed some repairs in 1348,[96] the eve of the

[81] Doc. of D. and C. of Westm. St. Martin le Grand, parcel 2.

[82] In April, 1298, he went to Rome. *Cal. of Pat.* 1292–1301, p. 337. The next year he was still abroad. Ibid. 404. Royal letters of protection issued in 1302, 1304, and 1305 show that he was not in England then. Ibid. 1301–7, pp. 28, 234, 316.

[83] Appeal of Giles de Audenardo, chamberlain of St. Martin's, on behalf of his fellow canons against the dean in 1301. Doc. of D. and C. of Westm. St. Martin le Grand, parcel 4, No. 13268.

[84] The number is considerable. Godfrey de Lucy became bishop of Winchester in 1189, William de Ste. Mère Eglise, bishop of London in 1199, Luke was promoted to the see of Dublin in 1229, Henry de Wengham to the see of London in 1260, William de Champvent to Lausanne, 1274, William of Louth to Ely in 1290, Peter of Savoy to Lyons in 1308.

[85] *Cal. of Pat.* 1321–4, pp. 355 and 385.

[86] *Cal. of Close,* 1323–7, p. 303.

[87] *Cal. of Pat.* 1343–5, p. 99, 185.

[88] Ibid. pp. 329, 346.

[89] Doc. of D. and C. of Westm. Cartulary *dorso.* A claim was made under this settlement in the sixteenth century. Ibid. No. 13215.

[90] *Hist. MSS. Com. Rep.* i, App. i, 95.

[91] Doc. of D. and C. of Westm. St. Martin le Grand, parcel 2.

[92] Ibid. parcel 1.

[93] Ibid. Henry III gave them leave to do so in 1257.

[94] Ibid. parcel 2, Cartulary *dorso.*

[95] Dr. Hutton's excerpt from Pat. Rolls, Harl. 6960, given in Dugdale, *Mon. Angl.* vi, 1323.

[96] He left for this purpose twenty-four cows and a bull to the college. Sharpe, *Cal. of Wills,* ii, 2.

Black Death. This terrible epidemic by carrying off the cultivators left the lands of the college waste and desolate, and its income consequently inadequate even to the ordinary expenditure.[97] The situation was saved in 1360 by the munificence of the dean, William de Wykeham, who at his own expense not only restored but beautified the church and cloister, and built a chapter-house adorned with a worked stone ceiling.[98] This new chapel was consecrated and dedicated[99] to the Holy Trinity[100] in 1378. It is evident that the resources of St. Martin's had received from the Plague a blow from which they took long to recover: in 1372 the pope granted a special indulgence to those visiting the church on certain feast-days during the next twenty years;[101] in 1381 the king exempted the canons from payments of tenths and subsidies during the life of Walter Skirlawe, then dean,[102] a term extended to thirty years in 1384,[103] and in 1385 gave them the advowson of the church of Bassingbourn with licence to appropriate.[104]

The income of the church or its ministers[105] was augmented during this period by the endowment of a chantry by Joan Hemenhale in 1361,[106] of others by John Band, canon resident, in 1370[107] and Thomas Stodelee in 1395,[108] and the appropriation to St. Martin's in 1399 of St. Botolph's without Aldersgate.[109]

It is clear that in the fourteenth century the position of St. Martin's as a royal free chapel was secure, for its ecclesiastical immunities rather increased than diminished. A suit in 1354 over the tithes and oblations of St. Alphage's Cripplegate was brought by the former parson of that church against the priest who then held it, and because the advowson belonged to St. Martin's, though the church was not appropriated, it was held that the Court of Canterbury had no jurisdiction.[110] Again in 1381 the king claimed that the dean of St. Martin's had from time immemorial exercised all ordinary jurisdiction within the Tower of London, a right not based on any existing charter, and that the bishop of London had exceeded his powers in placing the Tower chapel under an interdict.[111]

In the fifteenth century St. Martin's had, however, to meet a formidable attack from another quarter on different grounds. The City beyond trying once or twice to make the college pay part of a tallage,[112] had hitherto scarcely questioned its special privileges.[113] While, however, it was becoming even more conscious of itself as a corporate body and more jealous and resentful of exemptions from its dominion within its bounds, the evils caused by the privileges of St. Martin's did not grow less. As the elements of disorder increased during the reign of Richard II, the precinct of the church owing to its right of sanctuary became a nest of corruption.

In 1402 the Commons complained to the king in Parliament[114] that apprentices and servants carried off their master's goods to St. Martin's and lived there on the proceeds of the sale, that forgers took up their abode and carried on their nefarious work there, that the inhabitants of the place bought in the City things for which no payment could be obtained, and that robbers and murderers used the place as a convenient refuge from which they issued to commit fresh crimes. The king ordered that the privileges should be shown before the council, and that there should be reasonable remedy, but evidently nothing was done.

In 1430 the mayor and sheriffs took the law in their own hands and forcibly removed from the sanctuary a certain canon of Waltham,[115] but they had to put him back. Undaunted by this check the sheriffs in 1440 took away from St. Martin's a soldier and the men who had rescued him as he was being taken from the prison of Newgate to the Guildhall. The dean and chapter appealed to the king, and in spite of the resistance of the City they won the day.[116]

One of the sheriffs and some of the goldsmiths of London in 1448 visited the shops of their craft in the precinct. The dean did not oppose their examination but prevented its being used as a precedent against the immunities of the place by himself ordering anything condemned by them to be destroyed and the offenders to be committed to prison.[117]

[97] *Cal. of Pap. Letters*, vi, 208.

[98] Dugdale, op. cit. vi, 1323.

[99] Doc. of D. and C. of Westm. Cartulary *dorso*.

[100] Ibid. St. Martin le Grand, parcel 3, No. 13215.

[101] *Cal. of Pap. Letters*, iv, 177.

[102] *Cal. of Pat.* 1377–81, p. 619.

[103] Ibid. 1381–5, p. 375.

[104] Ibid. p. 552

[105] The chantries of Hemenhale and Band were each served by a perpetual vicar. Doc. of D. and C. of Westm. No. 13215.

[106] Sharpe, *Cal. of Wills*, ii, 46.

[107] Doc. of D. and C. of Westm. London L. 1, 2.

[108] *Cal. of Pat.* 1391–6, p. 639.

[109] Lond. Epis. Reg. Braybook, fol. 176.

[110] Doc. of D. and C. of Westm. Cartulary *dorso*.

[111] Ibid.

[112] There is a writ of King Edward to the mayor and sheriffs of London, and another to the treasurer and barons of the exchequer about the exemption of St. Martin's from tallage. Reg. fol. 9 and 9*b*; Lansd. MS. 170, fol. 59 and 59*b*. Kempe says the attempt was made in 1314, op. cit. 103.

[113] King Edward, but which one is not clear, in a letter to the mayor and sheriffs speaks of their having taken away transgressors found within the close, and says that such an act is 'in contempt of us and our crown.' Reg. fol. 9; Lansd. MS. 170, fol. 59*b*.

[114] *Parl. R.* (Rec. Com.), iii, 504*a*.

[115] Reg. of St. Martin le Grand, fol. 27*b*, 28*b*; Kempe, op. cit. 113.

[116] Ibid. fol. 33–48; Kempe, op. cit. 117–32.

[117] Reg. fol. 58; Kempe, op. cit. 133.

Although the privileges of St. Martin's were found to hold good even against the king himself as the cases of William Caym[118] and Sir William Oldhall[119] in 1451 sufficiently proved, the abuses of the right of sanctuary were too notorious to be ignored any longer, and the council in 1457 ordained[120] that persons taking refuge there should be registered by the dean; that they should not retain their weapons; that control should be kept over notorious criminals; that stolen goods should be restored to their owners if they claimed them; that makers of counterfeit plate and jewels should not be allowed in the sanctuary; that men exercising their trades there should observe the rules of the city in this respect; and that vice should not be countenanced. The exemptions of St. Martin's outlived the church itself, though the right of sanctuary was curtailed under Henry VIII.

Considering the relations that had always existed between the dean and the sovereign, it would not have been easy for him to remain neutral amid the dynastic changes which now took place. Dean Stillington did not make the attempt, but threw in his lot with the Yorkists, and was employed by Richard III in the negotiations with the duke of Brittany for the surrender of the duke of Richmond.[121] As a natural consequence he was removed when Richmond became king, James Stanley being put in his place.[122]

In 1503 St. Martin's le Grand entered on a new phase, for it was appropriated with all its possessions except the prebend of Newland to the use of Westminster Abbey as part of the endowment of the chapel founded there by Henry VII.[123] Stanley became bishop of Ely in 1506,[124] and must have given up his deanery then if he had not done so before;[125] the prebends of Keton,[126] Cowpes,[127] Chrishall,[128] Imbers,[129] Paslowes,[130] Knight's Tolleshunt,[131] and Good Easter[132] were resigned

by their holders between February, 1503, and May, 1504; those of Fawkeners and Burghs appear to have been vacant.[133]

The abbey gained the issues of these estates, and the chapel services possibly lost little. There were still two canons resident and there seem not to have been more for two centuries,[134] in 1391, indeed, there was only one.[135] On the other hand the number of vicars may have been reduced: the accounts of 1391 mention eighteen vicars, a sacrist, and a clerk; those of 1385, seventeen vicars, a sacrist, and a clerk,[136] while after the appropriation there were eight vicars, three clerks, a sacrist, the keeper of the 'vestiarium,'[137] and the clerk of the church. There were four choir boys in 1503 as in 1304.[138]

No great changes can have been introduced until 1508 for the protest of John Fisher, one of the prebendaries of Newland, was made in November of that year.[139] Fisher complained that the abbot, with the bishops of London and Winchester, had visited the chapel, had abolished the ancient statutes and customs of the place without the consent of the canons and vicars perpetual, had taken away the common seal, and deprived the canons and vicars of their fruits and obventions, and Fisher himself of the emoluments of his prebend. The arbitrators decided in November, 1509, in favour of Fisher and his fellow canon:[140] they were to have the arrears of their prebend, but were to expend almost the whole sum on the chapel; they were to receive 5 marks a year each; compensation was to be given them for their loss of the profits of the convent seal;[141] they were to enjoy the statutes and old constitution and were to have the presentation of four vicars' stalls. The statutes made by Abbot Islip for the college[142] will enable some idea to be formed not only of the daily life of the members, but also of their standard of conduct. Two of the most discreet of the chaplains were to be named every year, and to govern the others as the abbot's procurators; each chaplain was to take his turn to act as seneschal for a fortnight and superintend the

---

[118] Caym, one of the followers of Jack Cade, took refuge there, and the dean kept him in his prison, but would not give him up. Reg. fol. 58; Kempe, op. cit. 136–7.

[119] The king, suspecting him of treason, set persons to watch him while in sanctuary. The dean however insisted that they should be withdrawn. Reg fol. 60*b*; Kempe, op. cit. 140–4; Devon, *Issues of the Exch.* 476.

[120] Stow, *Surv. of Lond.* (ed. Strype), iii, 103 and 104.

[121] *Dict. Nat. Biog.* liv, 378.

[122] *Parl. R.* (Rec. Com.), vi, 292*a*.

[123] Harl. MS. 1498; Kempe, op. cit. 158.

[124] *Dict. Nat. Biog.* liv, 71.

[125] The fact that things were not much changed until 1508 seems to prove that Stanley held the deanery until 1506.

[126] Doc. of D. and C. of Westm. St. Martin le Grand, parcel 3, No. 13202.

[127] Ibid. No. 13208.

[128] Ibid. No. 13203.

[129] Ibid. No. 13205.

[130] Ibid. No. 13232.

[131] Ibid. No. 13233.

[132] Doc. of D. and C. of Westm. No. 13199.

[133] In a document which seems to be a statement of what the ministers were receiving at the time of the appropriation these prebends are recorded as in the hands of the lord, one through the promotion of the last holder, the other through death. Ibid. No. 13215.

[134] Ibid. A bequest was made in a will of 1304 to the two canons then resident. Ibid. No. 13272.

[135] Ibid. No. 13311.

[136] Ibid. No. 13310.

[137] Ibid. No. 13215.

[138] Ibid. No. 13272.

[139] Ibid. No. 13300.

[140] Ibid. No. 13302.

[141] They were before paid 3*s.* 4*d.* for affixing their seal to leases of property belonging to the commons. Ibid. No. 13215. Each was now to have 3*s.* 4*d.* a year. Ibid. No. 13277.

[142] Ibid. St. Martin le Grand, parcel 2.

expenses of the house; no one was habitually to absent himself from the services, and there was to be no talking in the choir or presbytery before and after, but especially at the time of service, except of matters pertaining to the divine office, and that in a low voice; the priests were all to sleep in the dormitory unless they had good reason for their absence; at table one of the priests was to read the Bible or some homily aloud that vain conversation might be avoided, and no one was to withdraw before grace had been said, except by leave of the procurator or seneschal; no one was to write with his knife on the vessels, candlesticks or tables of the hall or rooms, nor wilfully tear the cloth or towel; the priests were commanded under certain penalties not to cause quarrels or discords among themselves or reveal the secrets of the house, not to use angry words to each other or hit each other with swords or sticks within the hall or close; the priests were to have tonsures and not to wear rings; they were forbidden to use bad language; they were not to engage in trade; they were ordered not to bring any woman suspected or defamed by day or night within the close to their rooms.

The college was suppressed in 1542, and all the members were pensioned, the one prebendary of Newland receiving £20 a year, three vicars £4 each, another £6, the fifth £6 13s. 4d., the sixth, who was to serve the cure, £10 16s. 6d., three clerks, 40s. each and two others, 53s. 4d. each.[143]

The plate possessed by the church at the time of the Dissolution was considerable in weight at least, 194 oz. gilt, 182 oz. parcel gilt, and 144 oz. white.[144] The vestments both in quantity and quality appear to have been worthy of the place:[145] there were forty-six copes alone, some of them costly and beautiful, among which may be noted four of cloth of gold, the gift of Dean Cawdray; another of the same material, the gift of Sir William Oldhall;[146] one of red bawdekyn, with stars of gold and orphreys of white bawdekyn; two of white damask with arms of silver; one of crimson velvet powdered with flowers and orphreys of green velvet; a green one barred with gold, the orphreys of red velvet with stars and crowns of gold; others decorated with birds and harts of gold, peacocks, eagles and dragons; one of blue satin 'oysters fedders and roses,' and orphreys of 'red saten fyne gold'; and several with needlework orphreys.

The income of the chapel in 1291 amounted roughly to £209.[147] In 1535 the annual value of its property then in the hands of the abbot of Westminster was worth about £356 1s 9½d.,[148] but to this must be added the issues of the prebend of Newland and of eight chantries, equal to £90 18s. 9d.[149] Among the possessions of St. Martin's were the prebends or manors of Imbers, Fawkeners, Paston, and Burghs,[150] and other property in Good Easter, possibly the manor of Newerks,[151] and the manor of Mashbury, mentioned in 1273 as held by the college;[152] lands in Knight's Tolleshunt, Norton,[153] Maldon,[154] and North Benfleet,[155] co. Essex, and Hoddesdon, co. Herts; the rectory of St. Andrews, Good Easter, from early times a prebendal church;[156] the church of Newport Pound, of old appurtenant to the deanery;[157] the church of Witham, where a vicarage was ordained in 1222;[158] the chapel of Cressing, which belonged to Witham;[159] the prebendal church of Crishall,[160] the rectory of St. Mary of Maldon, or the prebends of Cowpes and Keton,[161] co. Essex, and the rectory of Bassingbourn, co. Cambridge. A fair in Good Easter had been granted by the king in 1309,[162] and a portion of 5s. from the chapel of Bonhunt, co. Essex, had been paid in 1291.[163] St. Martin's in 1215 held one knight's fee in Mashbury.[164]

The tenements in London where the college had had holdings in eleven parishes in 1291[165] amounted

[143] L. and P. Hen. VIII, xvii, 74.

[144] Aug. Accts. ibid. xvii, 258.

[145] Doc. of D. and C. of Westm. Misc. parcel 63, No. 25. A large number was of course necessary, for the church had at any rate six chapels. Ibid. St. Martin le Grand, parcel 4, No. 13310 and parcel 3, No. 13215.

[146] Probably a thank offering after living in sanctuary at St. Martin's.

[147] Harl. MS. 60, fol. 9, 9b, 44, 58, 59, 62, 65, 73, 76, 86.

[148] Valor Eccl. (Rec. Com.), i, 411, 412.

[149] Ibid. i, 385.

[150] Morant, Hist. of Essex, ii, 458. Ct. R. of 'Passelewes Manor in Good Easter,' Doc. of D. and C. of Westm. No. 1002; Ct. R. of Imbers, No. 13268.

[151] Acct. of Collector of Rents, 1385. Doc. of D. and C. of Westm. No. 13310. In 1506 there was a prebend of Newerks in Good Easter. Ibid. No. 13314.

[152] The land at Mashbury, with the mill, was let to Canon Herbert in 1239. Ibid. No. 13274. The manor was let with the tithes of Good Easter and Newland in 1273. Ibid. No. 1130.

[153] The land in these two places formed two prebends.

[154] L. and P. Hen. VIII, xvii, 714 (5).

[155] Property here belonged to the deans in 1291 (Harl. 60, fol. 59 and 76), and the dean or the college in the time of Hen. VII. Doc. of D. and C. of Westm. No. 13324.

[156] Ibid. No. 971.

[157] Cal. of Inq. p.m. i, 808.

[158] Newcourt, Repert. Eccl. Lond. ii, 675.

[159] Ibid. ii, 197.; Doc. of D. and C. of Westm. No. 13287.

[160] Valor Eccl. i, 412.

[161] In 1428 there were two prebends of St. Martin's in the church of St. Mary of Maldon. Feud. Aids, ii, 187. The Valor says nothing about Maldon, but mentions the prebendal churches of Cowpes and Keton, the latter of which was certainly in Maldon, Doc. of D. and C. of Westm. No. 13310.

[162] Exemplification of 1440. Ibid. St. Martin le Grand, parcel 1.

[163] Harl. MS. 60, fol. 65. For the agreement under which this sum was due, see Cartul. of St. Martin's.

[164] Pipe R. 17 John, m. 1.

[165] Harl. MS. 60, fol. 9b.

in 1535 to about half the entire revenues.[166] St. Martin's also held the appropriated church of St. Botolph without Aldersgate,[167] and a pension of 6s. 8d. from St. Katharine Coleman, 20s. from St. Nicholas Cole Abbey, and 60s. from St. Nicholas Shambles, which had been paid in 1291,[168] in some cases much earlier.[169] In 1291, and presumably in 1535, the college possessed, besides the advowsons of the above churches,[170] those of the following:– St. Agnes, granted to St. Martin's between 1140 and 1160 by Abbot Gervase and the convent of Westminster;[171] St. Leonard Foster Lane, built within the precinct early in the thirteenth century;[172] St. Alphage, which had been connected with St. Martin's since the time of Roger, bishop of Salisbury,[173] and in 1291[174] and 1526[175] paid a pension of 33s. 4d.

*M. Reddan*

## Deans of St. Martin Le Grand

The chronology of the first five deans is from Davis, 'St. Martin Le Grand', p. 23. The remainder of the list is from *V.C.H. London,* i.

Ingelric, alive in 1068 but dead by 1086
Fulcher
Roger of Salisbury, died 1139
Henry of Blois, 1139–?1171
Godfrey de Lucy, 1171?–1189
William de Ste. Mère l'Eglise, appointed 1189;[176] promoted 1199[177]
Richard Briger, appointed 1199[178]
Geoffrey de Boclande, occurs 1211,[179] 1225[180]

Luke, appointed 1225,[181] promoted 1229[182]
Walter de Kirkeham, appointed 1229;[183] occurs 1236[184]
Guy de Rossilian, appointed 1244;[185] occurs 1254[186]
Hugh, appointed c.1253?[187]
Henry de Wengham, appointed 1254;[188] promoted 1260[189]
William de Champvent, appointed 1262;[190] promoted c.1274[191]
Louis of Savoy, appointed 1274;[192] resigned c.1279[193]
Geoffrey de Neubaud, appointed 1279;[194] occurs 1280[195]
William of Louth, appointed 1283;[196] resigned 1290[197]
William de Marchia, appointed 1290;[198] occurs 1292[199]
Peter de Savoy, occurs 1294;[200] 1308[201]
William de Melton, appointed 1308;[202] occurs 1314[203]
Richard de Ellesfield, appointed 1317;[204] removed 1325[205]
Richard de Tysshbury appointed 1325;[206] removed 1326[207]
John le Smale, appointed 1326[208]
John de Wodeford, appointed 1328;[209] resigned 1343[210]

[166] *Valor Eccl.* (Rec. Com.), 1, 411 and 385. The chantries were endowed almost, if not entirely, with property in London.
[167] Accts. of John Islyppe, abbot of Westm. for St. Martin le Grand, Mich. 1526 to Mich. 1527. Doc. of D. and C. of Westm. No. 13319.
[168] Harl. MS. 60, fol. 9.
[169] In the time of Dean Godfrey de Lucy the church of St. Nicholas Cole Abbey was granted by the chapter to one of the canons for his life. Doc. of D. and C. of Westm. Cartul. The pension from St. Nicholas Shambles was paid before 1235, for a difficulty about it was settled then by the bishop of London. Ibid. London, C.
[170] *Mun. Gildhall. Lond.* (Rolls Ser.), ii, (1), 235.
[171] Doc. of D. and C. of Westm., Cartul. of St. Martin le Grand, item 101.
[172] Newcourt, op. cit. i, 392.
[173] Cartul. of St. Martin, item 138.
[174] Harl. MS. 60, fol. 9.
[175] Doc. of D. and C. of Westm. No. 13319.
[176] Cart. Antiq. R. R. R. (16). Dugdale gives the date of the appointment as 1177, but this seems to be a mistake.
[177] To the see of Lond. Stubbs, *Reg. Sacr. Angl.*
[178] Cart. Antiq. H (1).
[179] A fine between him and the prior of Holy Trinity Aldgate. Doc. of D. and C. of Westm. Lond. O–V.
[180] *Rot. Lit. Claus.* (Rec. Com.), ii, 80.

[181] *Cal. of Pat.* 1216–25, p. 550.
[182] To the see of Dublin. Ibid. 1225–32, p. 236.
[183] Ibid. 274.
[184] Ibid. 1232–47, p. 146.
[185] Ibid. 423.
[186] Ordin. by him for chantries of Thomas Maugre to William de Wynton. Doc. of D. and C. of Westm. Lond. Box O–V.
[187] Kempe, op. cit. 89. The date must be wrong, see preceding note.
[188] Newcourt, *Repert. Eccl. Lond.* i, 426.
[189] To the see of Lond. Stubbs, op. cit.
[190] Newcourt, op. cit. i, 426.
[191] To the see of Lausanne. *Cal. of Pat.* 1272–81, p. 49.
[192] Ibid.
[193] Ibid. 360.
[194] Ibid.
[195] Doc. of D. and C. of Westm. Lond. D.
[196] *Cal. of Pat.* 1281–92, p. 54.
[197] He was then bishop-elect of Ely. *Cal. of Pat.* 1281–92, p. 354.
[198] He was the king's treasurer. Ibid. 375.
[199] *Cal. Letter Bk. C,* 9.
[200] Ibid. 77.
[201] *Cal. of Pat.* 1307–13, p. 65.
[202] Ibid. p. 92. That was in August, yet in October the king ordered the church to be taken into his hand on account of the promotion of Peter of Savoy to the archbishopric of Lyons. Ibid. 141.
[203] Ibid. 1313–17, p. 119; *Cal. Letter Bk. C,* 315.
[204] *Cal. of Pat.* 1317–21, p. 40.
[205] *Cal. of Close,* 1323–7, p. 303.
[206] *Cal. of Pat.* 1324–7, p. 128.
[207] The appointment was revoked. Ibid. 246.
[208] *Cal. of Pat.* 1324–7, p. 246.
[209] Ibid. 1327–30, p. 262.
[210] On an exchange of benefices with John de Heselarton. Ibid. 1343–5, p. 14.

John de Heselarton, appointed 1343;[211] occurs 1344[212]

Thomas de Useflete, appointed 1345;[213] occurs 1347[214]

William de Cusancia, appointed 1349;[215] and 1355[216]

William de Wykeham, appointed 1360[217]

Simon de Northwode, occurs 1363,[218] 1364[219]

William de Mulsho, appointed 1364;[220] occurs 1370[221]

Walter Skirlawe, appointed 1377;[222] resigned 1383[223]

John Bacun, appointed 1383[224]

Richard Mitford, appointed 1385;[225] resigned 1389[226]

Roger Walden, appointed 1390[227]

William de Pakyngton, appointed 1390[228]

William de Assheton, appointed 1390;[229] occurs 1396[230]

Thomas de Langley, appointed ?1395[231]

Thomas de Stanley, occurs 1399;[232] resigned 1402[233]

Thomas Tuttebury, appointed 1402[234]

Richard Dereham, S.T.P., appointed 1403;[235] occurs 1414[236]

John Stena, or Stone, occurs 1416[237]

William Kynwolmersh, appointed 1420–1;[238] occurs 1422[239]

John Stafford, appointed 1422;[240] occurs 1425[241]

William Alnwick, resigned 1426[242]

John Estcourt, appointed 1426;[243] occurs 1427[244]

Thomas Bourchier, appointed 1427;[245] occurs 1434[246]

Richard Cawdray, appointed 1435;[247] occurs 1455[248]

Robert Stillington, appointed 1458;[249] removed 1485[250]

James Stanley, appointed 1485;[251] occurs 1499[252]

[211] *Cal. of Pat.* 1343–5, pp. 14, 21.

[212] Doc. of D. and C. of Westm. parcel 2, Cartul. of St. Martin le Grand, *dorso.*

[213] *Cal. of Pat.* 1343–5, p. 548.

[214] Doc. of D. and C. of Westm. Lond. E–K. The oath taken by him to pay a pension from St. Catherine Coleman; Sharpe, *Cal. of Letter Bk. F,* 164.

[215] *Cal. of Pat.* 1348–50, p. 305.

[216] Sharpe, op. cit. G, 42.

[217] Newcourt, *Repert. Eccl. Lond.* i, 427.

[218] Ibid.

[219] Doc. of D. and C. of Westm. parcel 2, Cartul. of St. Martin le Grand, *dorso.*

[220] Newcourt, op. cit. i, 427.

[221] Doc. of D. and C. of Westm. Lond. L. (2), royal confirmation of Ordin. for chantry of John Bande.

[222] Dugdale, op. cit. vi, 323.

[223] On an exchange of benefices with John Bacun. *Cal. of Pat.* 1381–5, p. 281.

[224] Ibid. 281, 345.

[225] Ibid. 1385–9, p. 67.

[226] On his promotion to the see of Chichester. Ibid. 228.

[227] Ibid. 167. This could not have taken effect, for three months later, when Pakyngton was appointed, the deanery was said to be void by the consecration of Mitford as bishop of Chichester. Ibid. 234.

[228] Ibid.

[229] Ibid, 295.

[230] Lease by him of tenements to Walter Fairford and another, 10 August, 20 Ric. II. Doc. of D. and C. of Westm. Lond. B, Box 1.

[231] Dugdale, op. cit. vi, 1324. The date is difficult to understand, considering the above, *n.* 248.

[232] *Cal. of Pat.* 1399–1401, p. 5.

[233] Ibid. 1401–5, p. 185.

[234] Ibid. p. 185.

[235] Ibid. p. 207.

[236] Doc. of D. and C. of Westm. Lond. A, Box 3. Indenture about the house called 'Le Piry.'

[237] Dugdale, *Mon. Angl.* vi, 1324; Doc. of D. and C. of Westm. No. 986.

[238] Dugdale, op. cit. vi, 1324.

[239] *Cal. of Pat.* 1422–9, p. 1.

[240] He was keeper of the king's privy seal. Ibid. 15.

[241] Lease of church of St. Botolph Aldersgate. Doc. of D. and C. of Westm. Lond. B. Box 2 (1).

[242] On his promotion to the see of Norwich. *Cal. of Pat.* 1422–9, p. 348.

[243] Ibid.

[244] Newcourt, *Repert. Eccl. Lond.* i, 428.

[245] *Cal. of Pat.* 1422–9, p. 452.

[246] Lease of church of St. Botolph Aldersgate. Ibid. Lond. B. Box 2 (1).

[247] Dugdale, op. cit. vi, 1324.

[248] Lease of tenements in parish of St. Michael ad Bladum. Ibid. Lond. M.

[249] Dugdale, op. cit. vi, 1324.

[250] *Parl. R.* (Rec. Com.),. vi, 292a.

[251] Ibid.

[252] Lease of tenements in parish of St. Michael le Querne. Doc. of D. and C. of Westm. Lond. M.

# 34. THE ROYAL FREE CHAPEL OF
# ST. STEPHEN, WESTMINSTER

## INTRODUCTION

The original *V.C.H.* account remains a generally sound guide to the foundation and history of St. Stephen's Chapel in the Palace of Westminster. The lack of discussion of the fabric is perhaps understandable given the destruction of the chapel in the 1834, the difficulty of interpreting the surviving masonry, and the variable reliability of the drawings published subsequently. Nevertheless, important strides have been made in understanding the physical appearance and development of the chapel, and of particular significance is the account of the building and later refurbishments of the chapel contained in R. A. Brown, H. M. Colvin and A. J. Taylor, *The History of the King's Works 1–2: The Middle Ages*, (London, 1963), esp. vol. 1, pp. 510–27. A brief but useful assessment of the surviving medieval fabric can be found in S. Bradley and N. Pevsner, *London, 6. Westminster*, updated edn. (London and New Haven, 2003), pp. 228–9.

These and other more recent publications have underlined the importance of the chapel in terms of architectural style and cultural expression, particularly the development of decorated Gothic architecture, the perpendicular style, and wall painting. The lack of physical evidence means that there is some debate over the exact place of the chapel, and its known architects, in the origins of perpendicular architecture. The chief accounts remain J. H. Harvey, 'St. Stephen's Chapel and the Origin of the Perpendicular Style', *Burlington Magazine*, 88 (1946), pp. 192–9; and M. J. Hastings, *St. Stephen's Chapel and its Place in the Development of the Perpendicular Style in England* (Cambridge, 1955); but see also C. Wilson, *The Gothic Cathedral: The Architecture of the Great Church, 1130–1530* (London, 1990), p. 204.

Also of interest for the fabric and decoration of the chapel are A. Martindale, 'St. Stephen's Chapel, Westminster, and the Italian Experience', in *Studies in Medieval Art and Architecture*, ed. D. Buckton and T. A. Heslop (Stroud, 1994), pp. 102–12; J. Cherry and N. Stratford, *Westminster Kings and the Medieval Palace of Westminster*, British Museum, occasional paper, 115 (London, 1995), pp. 28–49; and E. Howe, 'Divine Kingship and Dynastic Display: the altar wall murals of St. Stephen's Chapel, Westminster', *Antiquaries Journal*, 81 (2001), pp. 259–303.

For the subsequent use of the chapel as a meeting place for the Commons in Parliament, see A. Hawkyard, 'From Painted Chamber to St. Stephen's Chapel: the meeting places for the House of Commons at Westminster until 1603', *Parliamentary History*, 21 (2002), pp. 62–84.

*Matthew Davies*

The chapel of St. Stephen in the palace of Westminster was, according to Stow, founded by King Stephen.[1] There is no doubt that it existed in the time of King John for the names of two of the chaplains are recorded: Gervase who became vicar of St. Mary's, Cambridge, in 1205,[2] and his successor in office, Baldwin of London, clerk of the exchequer.[3]

Henry III appears to have taken a great interest in the chapel which he provided with vestments,[4] altar-frontals,[5] images[6] and tapestry[7] and beautified

[1] Stow, *Surv. of Lond.* (ed. Strype), vi, 54.
[2] *Rot. Chart. Johan.* (Rec. Com.), 145.
[3] Ibid. 161; Cart. Antiq. R. A.A. 40.

[4] *Rot. Lit. Claus.* (Rec. Com.), ii, 117. Order to the treasurer to pay William de Castellis five marks for amending vestments and a chalice for the chapel of St. Stephen, Westminster, 1226. *Cal. of Close*, 1231, p. 10. The king orders a cope of red samite for the chapel in 1231.
[5] *Cal. of Close* 1231–4, p. 9.
[6] Ibid. 207.
[7] Devon, *Issues of the Exch.* (Pell Records), 13.

in various ways.[8] It was rebuilt in 1292 by Edward I[9] who was assisted by the papal indulgence offered to those visiting the chapel on certain festivals,[10] but in 1298 it was burned down[11] about four years after its completion.[12]

In 1330 a new chapel was begun,[13] apparently on a more ambitious scale for masons were still at work on it in 1337,[14] and it could not have been finished very long before workmen were again being employed in large numbers,[15] probably to make its appearance correspond to the important change in its position recently made by the king. There had been four chaplains in the reign of Henry III[16] but they seem to have been afterwards reduced to one[17] whose office was regarded as of no great value,[18] when in 1348 Edward III ordained that there should henceforth be a college there consisting of a dean, twelve secular canons, thirteen vicars, four clerks and six choristers to whom he assured an income of £500,[19] the difference between this sum and their revenues being paid to them from the exchequer.[20] The pope, in answer to the king's petition in 1349, gave to the dean power to correct the canons and exempted them from the jurisdiction of the ordinary, stipulating, however, that the dean should receive cure of souls from the bishop and be subject to him in all things relating to it.[21] He also empowered the dean to enjoy the fruits of his benefices while residing in the deanery. The king in 1354 exempted them from the aids for knighting the king's eldest son and marrying his eldest daughter, and from all other contributions, tallages, fifteenths and clerical tenths,[22] from payments for munitions of war[23] and liveries of seneschals and marshals;[24] he forbade the seizure of their goods and those of their

men by his provisors[25] and excused them from paying any pension or corrody to the king or his heir against their will;[26] he acquitted them and their tenants of toll, pannage, pontage, kaiage, lestage &c., scots and gelds, hidage and scutage, shire courts, hundred courts, view of frankpledge and murdrum.[27] He ordered moreover that the dean and canons should have the amercements, fines and forfeitures incurred by their men and tenants;[28] that they should have wreckage and waifs and strays on their lands,[29] sac and soc, infangenthef, and outfangenthef, view of frankpledge, pillory, tumbrel and gallows;[30] and granted them free warren in all their demesne lands,[31] acquittance of pleas of the forest and freedom from all charges that the foresters could make.[32] They were to have the return of all briefs and attachments of pleas of the crown in all their lands and fees;[33] the cognition and correction of small breaches of the peace committed by the vicars or servants within the college, and the cognition in their courts of all pleas of those living on their lands.[34]

To provide accommodation for the members of the college, the king gave them in 1354 a chamber in the gate of the palace and a hospice and other buildings within the precinct, with a piece of ground bounded by the chapel, the receipt of the exchequer, Westminster Hall and the Thames for a close.[35] The endowment of the college, however, to the extent designed by the king, could not be accomplished very quickly. By the foundation charter the college received a large hospice in Lombard Street, and the advowsons of the churches of Dewsbury and Wakefield, co. York, with licence to appropriate.[36] To these the king added three more churches, Sandal[37] and Burton,[38] co. York, and Bledlow,[39] co. Bucks, between 1351 and 1360; the sum of £35 14s. 7d. from the ferm of the city of York in 1351;[40] 'Sewtestower' in Bucklersbury in 1358;[41] rents amounting to £66 13s. 4d. from houses in the Staple

[8] In 1234 the king ordered it to be wainscoted. *Cal. of Close* 1231–4, p. 378. In 1240 a payment of £50 was made for the works done there. Devon, *Issues of the Exch.* 13.

[9] Dugdale, *Mon. Angl.* vi, 1348.

[10] *Cal. Pap. Letters*, i, 537. This was dated 1291.

[11] Dugdale, op. cit.

[12] In 1294 timber was being supplied from the royal forest of Pembere for the work. *Cal. of Close*, 1288–96, p. 350.

[13] Dugdale, *Mon. Angl.* vi, 1348.

[14] *Cal. of Close* 1337–9, p. 41.

[15] Rymer, *Foedera* (Rec. Com.), iii, (1), 193; 18 March, 1350, warrant to Hugh de St. Albans, master of the painters in the chapel at Westminster, to take painters and other workmen in the counties of Kent, Middlesex, Essex, Surrey and Sussex.

[16] Devon, *Issues of the Exch.* 34. Payment of 180s. was made for their stipends from Easter to Michaelmas, 1257.

[17] *Cal. of Pat.* 1334–8, p. 316.

[18] *Cal. Pap. Letters*, ii, 280.

[19] Harl. MS. 410, fol. 14, 15. In 1361 this was increased to £505. For the number of clerks and choristers, see *Issue Roll of Thomas de Brantingham* (Pell Rec.), 466.

[20] This was at any rate done in 1360, Harl. MS. 410, fol. 20.

[21] *Cal. Pap. Petitions*, i, 187.

[22] Harl. MS. 410, fol. 3

[23] Ibid. fol. 4.

[24] Ibid. fol. 4b.

[25] Ibid. fol. 7, 8.

[26] Ibid. fol. 9.

[27] Ibid. fol. 5, 5b.

[28] Ibid. fol. 6.

[29] Ibid. fol. 7.

[30] Ibid. fol. 9.

[31] Ibid.

[32] Ibid. fol. 10.

[33] Ibid. fol. 11.

[34] Harl. MS. 410, fol. 11.

[35] Ibid. fol. 2.

[36] Ibid. fol. 14b, 15.

[37] Ibid. fol. 16, in 1351.

[38] Ibid. fol. 17b. This church must have been appropriated immediately, for it was granted in May, 1356, and is mentioned as appropriated in July, when the king allowed the canons to re-unite a portion of tithes to the church. Pat. 30 Edw. III, pt. 2, m. 5, in Add. MS. 15664, fol. 141.

[39] Harl. MS. 410, fol. 21.

[40] Ibid. fol. 17.

[41] Ibid. fol. 18.

of Westminster before 1360;[42] and a hospice called 'La Reole' in London in 1369.[43] Before his death the king also enfeoffed John of Gaunt and others in trust for the college, of the manors of Ashford, Barton, Buckwell, Eastling, Mere, and Langley by Leeds, with the advowsons of the churches, a parcel of meadow in Eynsford, and the reversion of the manors of Elham and Colbridge, co. Kent,[44] and of Winchfield, co. Southants.[45] These the feoffees let to the dean and canons for forty years in 1382, but before the grant in mortmain which they intended could be effected, the lands were seized by Sir Simon de Burley, who held them by letters patent of King Richard. Burley was attainted in 1388, and the lands came in consequence into the king's hands. The canons then put in their claim, and Richard at first granted them the profits arising from the lands for a term of years, but finally in 1398 carried out King Edward's wish and gave them the lands themselves.[46]

The interest of Edward III in his foundation was constant. It was at his request that the pope offered an indulgence in 1349[47] and again in 1354[48] and 1361[49] to those who helped the chapel by gifts or bequests or who visited it on the feasts of the Assumption, of St. Stephen, St. George, and St. Edward. It was to him, too, that the canons owed their bell-tower with its three large bells.[50] He also purchased a great missal and an antiphon for the chapel[51] in 1362 at a cost of £33. But perhaps there is nothing that better illustrates the king's relations with the college than his grant of £34 to the vicars, clerks, and choristers in 1370 'in relief of their charges because of the dearness of provisions.'[52] The college probably owed something of the king's generosity to their position. It was impossible for him to forget men who were actually living in the palace, many of the canons being moreover his clerks. But it was also a situation which involved obligations, and if the college had a large income,[53] they certainly needed it, for they seem to have been expected to keep open house for the nobles coming to the court.[54]

A quarrel which was to last for years began in 1375[55] between the college and the abbey because the dean had proved the will and administered the estates of two inmates of Westminster Palace.[56] The abbot and convent claimed that as the church of St. Margaret and all the chapels in the parish were appropriated to them, St. Stephen's, which lay in the parish, belonged to them, and the dean and canons had no right to receive parochial tithes and oblations or exercise jurisdiction in the parish or chapel.[57] They therefore obtained letters from Pope Gregory XI, and the dean was cited to appear before papal delegates at St. Frideswide's, Oxford.[58] But the matter now touched the crown, and in February, 1377, Edward III interposed,[59] and after a declaration that his free chapels were exempt from all jurisdiction, ordinary and delegate, except that of his chancellor, forbade archbishops, bishops, or others to hold any pleas concerning them to his prejudice or to molest the dean.[60] The prohibition was renewed by Richard II in December,[61] but in July, 1378, the dean and chapter were excommunicated and suspended.[62] The king then sent ambassadors to Pope Urban VI asking that the case might be submitted to the chancellor, and his request was granted on condition that an agreement was made between the parties within a year. No settlement being arrived at in that time, the matter was referred to Parliament in 1380, but with no result. A further appeal was then made to Rome,[63] and sentence was given against the college in 1382;[64] the dean and chapter nevertheless refused to pay the fine and costs[65] to which they were condemned, and although they were excommunicated for contumacy[66] they did not yield until 1393.[67] The next year[68] an agreement was at length made with the abbot and convent as follows:[69] The chapel of St.

[42] Ibid. fol. 20.

[43] Ibid. fol. 22b.

[44] Hasted, *Hist. of Kent*, iii, 192.

[45] Harl. MS. 410, fol. 24.

[46] Ibid. fol. 25.

[47] *Cal. Pap. Petitions*, i, 188.

[48] *Cal. Pap. Letters*, iii, 538.

[49] *Cal. Pap. Petitions*, i, 372.

[50] Stow, *Surv. of Lond.* (ed. Strype), vi, 54.

[51] Devon, *Issues of the Exch.* 177.

[52] *Issue Roll of Thomas de Brantingham*, 466.

[53] It seems doubtful whether it was really large. The stipends must have absorbed most of it.

[54] The king petitioned the pope in 1349 to allow benefices to the value of £200 to be appropriated to the dean and canons because their expenses in entertaining were so great. *Cal. Pap. Petitions*, i, 186.

[55] Pope Gregory's letters are of that date. Doc. of D. and C. of Westm. Westm. parcel 23, pt. 3 continued, No. 18514A.

[56] Ibid. pt. 2 continued, No. 18482.

[57] *Cal. Pap. Letters*, iv, 328, 462.

[58] Doc. of D. and C. of Westm. Westm. parcel 23, pt. 3 continued, No. 18524A.

[59] Ibid. pt. 2 continued, No. 18490.

[60] Mandate of Richard II, *Cal. of Pat.* 1377–81, p. 95.

[61] Ibid.

[62] Doc. of D. and C. of Westm. Westm. parcel 23, pt. 2 continued, No. 18477.

[63] Ibid.

[64] Points were being raised in January, 1383, in consequence of the judgement. Ibid. No. 18492.

[65] The abbot and convent estimated their expenses at 500 marks. Ibid.

[66] Ralph de Kesteven was absolved in 1390 from the excommunication he had incurred as a member of the college. *Cal. Pap. Letters*, iv, 328.

[67] Ibid. iv, 462.

[68] In August, 1394, the agreement is stated to have been lately made.

[69] Cott. MS. Faust. A. iii, fol. 293–314; Doc. of D. and C. of Westm. Westm. parcel 23, pt. 2 continued, No. 18470.

Stephen's with the chapterhouse and the chapels of St. Mary in the Vault and St. Mary of Pewe, as well as the cloister and the houses within the precinct[70] inhabited by the thirty-eight persons serving in the chapel, the new kitchen of the vicars, and a room beneath the star chamber, were to be exempt from the jurisdiction of the abbot and convent; all other chapels and places within the palace as well as the houses of the thirty-eight if not inhabited by them were to remain subject to the abbot and convent; the dean and college were not to be exempt for faults committed without the precincts and in the parish of St. Margaret. The abbot and convent were to have probate of wills of all persons within or without the precinct except of the thirty-eight persons, the probate of whose wills belonged to the dean; the members of the households of the thirty-eight were to be considered parishioners of St. Margaret's; the dean and college should have free burial in their chapel and cloister as far as the thirty-eight were concerned, but in the case of others half of all oblations should go to the abbey unless bequests were made to a member of the college separately, when the monks were not to participate; with these exceptions all oblations and obventions made in St. Stephen's were to go to the dean and college, but those offered in the chapel of St. John the Evangelist and all other oratories within and without the precinct were to belong to the abbot and convent; the dean and college might have a baptismal font for baptizing the children of kings and magnates, but they were to administer no other sacraments to any without the authority of the abbot and convent especially granted; the dean and college were bound to give the greater tithes from their precinct to the abbey but not the lesser; the dean was to receive investiture from the abbot, and at his installation was to take an oath to observe the agreement; as an indemnity to the abbey the college promised to pay an annual pension of 5 marks.

The interests of the crown were so bound up with those of the royal chapel in the above controversy that during the period of its duration some special sign of the king's favour might almost be expected to occur, and it was in 1384, after the judgement pronounced against the chapel at Rome and while the dean and chapter still refused to submit, that the king was arranging to build a cloister for the college across the close and a house for the vicars.[71]

The firm establishment of the college as a whole had hitherto been the main concern. When this was secured, attention could be given to details. Thus

the position of the vicars and clerks seems to have received too little consideration,[72] until in 1396 King Richard ordained, on condition that they observed the obit of the late Queen Anne, that the vicars, clerks, and choristers should henceforth form a corporate body which should have a common seal and power to acquire land,[73] and of which one of the vicars, elected by themselves without any necessity to ask the king's leave or assent, should be warden.[74] This ordinance, however, was not to affect the power of the dean and canons to appoint the vicars and to exercise authority over them. The king granted to them in frankalmoign the houses which he had built for them, and also a piece of land between the palace and the river where they were making a garden at their own cost.

The numerous grants made to St. Stephen's during the next century for the maintenance of anniversaries and chantries must have amounted in the end to a considerable sum. Among other gifts the college received £50 in 1399 for the anniversary of Dean Sleford;[75] in 1410 a rent from a messuage in Bishopsgate Street for that of Canon Fulmere;[76] and £20 bequeathed to them for the same purpose by Canon Adam de Chesterfield, who also left them a large missal worth £11 6s. 8d., a great gradual worth £7 13s. 4d., and a new ordinal worth £5;[77] £50 in 1425 for the annual obit of Canon Orgrave;[78] £40 in 1427 for the anniversary of Canon Merston;[79] 100 marks in 1471 for Dean Kirkham's anniversary;[80] £82 in 1478 for the anniversaries of two canons,[81] and tenements in Warwick Lane in 1498 for the anniversary of another canon.[82] Six houses in the staple of Westminster were made over to the college in 1442 as the endowment of a chantry for the soul of William Prestwyk, one of the masters in chancery, either in the oratory of St. Mary of Pewe or in St. Stephen's.[83] A chantry of two priests was founded there in 1455 for the soul of William Lindwood, bishop of St. Davids,[84] who had been buried in the

[70] This was very carefully defined, and was not to be extended. Cott. MS. Faust. A. iii, fol. 295–99, 310.
[71] Cal. of Pat. 1381–5, p. 365. Edw. III had built cloisters for them. Smith, Antiq. of Westm. 222.
[72] See supra the grant made to them on account of dearness of provisions in 1370. Rich. II in his grant speaks of their indigence.
[73] They could thus have property quite apart from that of the college, and in 1469 the dean and canons made over to them a yearly pension of 7 marks from their messuages in Westminster. Cal. of Pat. 1467–77, p. 150.
[74] Ibid. 1391, p. 669.
[75] Cott. MS. Faust. B. viii, fol. 16b.
[76] Ibid. fol. 21.
[77] Ibid. fol. 9b.
[78] Ibid. fol. 8.
[79] Ibid. fol. 18.
[80] Ibid. fol. 36.
[81] Ibid. fol. 41b, 47.
[82] Ibid. fol. 49.
[83] Ibid. fol. 28–32b.
[84] Doc. of D. and C. of St. Paul's, A. Box 76, No. 2001.

lower chapel in 1446,[85] and who bequeathed to the college 600 marks of the money owing to him by the crown for the completion of the cloister and bell-tower.[86] A sum of £100 was paid in 1471 for an obit and a daily remembrance of Canon John Crecy and Thomas Lord Stanley,[87] and in 1480 Richard Green gave to the college 200 marks to provide perpetual masses for his soul.[88] Among the benefactors of the college were numbered also Walter Hungerford, knt., lord of Haytesbury and Homet, treasurer of England, and Ralph, Lord Cromwell, for whose anniversaries agreements were made in 1428 and 1437.[89]

The chapel had perhaps more need of these gifts and bequests than might be imagined. Its income of £500 was certainly large for those days, but it could never have allowed much margin over the expenditure,[90] since Edward III in 1360 gave the chapel £5 a year more because the charges exceeded its revenues by that amount.

In 1437, indeed, the dean declared that they needed at least £100 a year more to discharge their obligations.[91] The rents derived from the houses in the Staple were no longer paid,[92] and the money due from the exchequer was not obtained without a great deal of trouble. Henry VI, therefore, in place of these two sums, which amounted to £110 7s. 11d., and for the observance of the anniversaries of his father and mother, granted to them the alien priory or manor of Frampton, co. Dorset, estimated at £166 13s. 4d. per annum.

Considering the close relations between the sovereign and a free chapel and the particular proof which the king had just given of interest in St. Stephen's, it is strange to find one of the canons, Thomas Southwell, accused in 1441 of aiding Roger Bolingbroke in his attempt to kill the king by necromancy at the instigation of Eleanor Cobham.[93]

The king's favour to the rest of the college was, however, unaffected by this incident. He granted to the dean and canons in 1445 two fairs in Frampton.[94] In 1453 he gave them the custody of the clock-tower in his palace with wages of 6d. a day, and the houses within the precinct of the palace once occupied by

Dean Sleford.[95] Two years later they were deprived of the wages by an Act of Resumption, but they received them again in 1461 from Edward IV, who besides confirming the grants made to them by his predecessors added to their possessions in 1469 the alien priory or manor of Wells and the rectory of Gayton, co. Norfolk,[96] and in 1466 gave them power to appoint constables, reeves, and bailiffs in their manors and fees, and exempted their men and tenants from being elected as constables or other officers of the king.[97]

The dean and canons followed the example of the vicars and clerks in 1479, and obtained permission from the king to form themselves into a corporate body with a common seal and power to acquire lands and to implead and be impleaded. They also received licence to acquire in mortmain lands, rents, knights' fees, and advowsons to the value of £100 yearly, and were acquitted of the payment of fees or fines for royal letters or charters.[98]

The dean must have been in a special degree the confidential servant of the king. It was emphatically the case with the last two holders of the office, Wolsey,[99] and his successor, John Chamber, who was chaplain and physician to the king.[100] Chamber seems to have been wealthy as he spent 11,000 marks on building a cloister at St. Stephen's,[101] and he sent twenty soldiers to the army against France in 1544, as many as the archbishop of Canterbury.[102]

This last expense certainly may have been defrayed by the college, which could have well afforded it, for its financial difficulties must have vanished long before it was dissolved by Edward VI in 1547.[103]

The pensions allotted were as follows:– To the dean £52 10s., to each of the eleven canons £18 7s. 4d., to each of the eleven vicars £6 13s. 4d., to four chantry priests £6 each, to one of the clerks £6 13s. 4d. and to the other three £6 each, and to every chorister, of whom there were seven, 53s. 4d.[104] In Mary's reign six prebendaries and four choristers were still receiving pensions.[105]

Its revenues amounted in 1535 to £1,085 10s. 5d. gross, and £458 4s. 10¾d. net, £565 being paid yearly to the dean, canons, and vicars.[106] Its possessions

[85] L. and P. illus. the Wars of Engl. in France (Rolls Ser.), ii (2), 764.
[86] Arch. xxxiv, 415.
[87] Cott. MS. Faust. B. viii, fol. 37.
[88] Ibid. fol. 43–45b.
[89] Ibid. fol. 11, 12, 26b.
[90] Harl. 410, fol. 21.
[91] Harl. R. N. 19.
[92] It was found in 1379 that they had in this way lost £59 14s. 3½d. a year for the last three years, and they were paid from the exchequer. Smith, Antiq. of Westm. 95.
[93] Stow, Annals (ed. 1615), 381.
[94] Hutchins, Hist. of Dorset, ii, 297.

[95] From the confirmation of various grants made by Edw. IV in 1461. Cal. of Pat. 1461–7, p. 163.
[96] Ibid. 1467–77, p. 163; ibid. 172.
[97] Cal. of Pat. 1461–7, p. 487.
[98] Ibid. 1476–85, p. 172.
[99] L. and P. Hen. VIII, i, 5607.
[100] Ibid. He continued to be the king's physician; ibid. xv, 861, and xvi, 380, fol. 109.
[101] Dugdale, Mon. Angl. vi, 1349.
[102] L. and P. Hen. VIII, xix (1), 274.
[103] Dugdale, Mon. Angl. vi, 1349.
[104] Chant. Cert. no. 88 dorso.
[105] Add. MS. 8102, fol. 6b.
[106] Valor Eccl. (Rec. Com.), i, 428.

comprised tenements in London and Westminster, and a small payment from the ferm of the City;[107] rent of assize in Lambeth, co. Surrey;[108] the manors of Wells and Gayton,[109] and lands in South Lynn[110] and Wiggenhall St. Mary's,[111] co. Norfolk; the manor of Winchfield, co. Southants;[112] a payment of £35 14s. 7d. from the ferm of York; the ferm of some mills there;[113] the manors of Frampton and Burton and rents of assize in Winterborne Came, co. Dorset;[114] land in Bledlow, co. Bucks;[115] the manors of Elham, Ashford, Queencourt, Eastling or Northcourt, Bredhurst, Merecourt, Wichling, Langley,[116] Colbridge,[117] Plumford and Painters,[118] and land in Eynsford,[119] Iwade,[120] and Harty Isle,[121] co. Kent; the manor of 'Codyngton,'[122] co. Sussex; the rectory of Fen Stanton,[123] co. Huntingdon, which had been given to them in 1394 by Thomas earl of Nottingham;[124] the appropriated churches of Wakefield with the chapel of St. Leonard, of Dewsbury, Sandal, Penistone,[125] and Burton, co. York; the rectory of Frampton and the chapel of St. Lawrence in Burton, co. Dorset;[126] and of Gayton in Norfolk.[127] In 1431 the dean held the manor of Overland in Loningborough Hundred, co. Kent, by the service of a knight's fee in Elham.[128]

St. Stephen's, as the chapel in the king's palace at Westminster, was of course particularly rich in vestments and plate. In the long inventory of vestments, the total value of which was estimated at £336 19s. 6d.,[129] there were mentioned children's copes and albs, evidently those worn by the boy-bishop and his attendants in the festivities of St. Nicholas's Day, which seems always to have been observed there.[130] At the beginning of the fourteenth century the chapel possessed many ornaments of gold or silver-gilt adorned with precious stones and enamels,[131] and at the Dissolution it had at least 2,250 oz. of silver gilt and 436 oz. of silver parcel gilt besides the jewels in the various articles and a cross and chalice of gold.[132]

*M. Reddan*

## Revised List of the Deans of St. Stephen's College, Westminster

Thomas Cross, appointed 1348; died 1349[133]

Michael de Northburgh, D.C.L., occurs 1349[134]

Thomas de Keynes, appointed 1355[135]

Thomas Rous, appointed 1367[136]

William de Sleford, appointed 1369;[137] occurs 1395[138]

Nicholas Slake,[139] appointed 1396;[140] occurs 1411[141]

John Prentys, occurs 1425[142] and 1437[143]

William Walesby, occurs 1453[144] and 1455[145]

Robert Kirkham, occurs 1459;[146] died 1471[147]

John Alcok, appointed 1471;[148] died 1472[149]

Peter Courtenay, appointed 1472;[150] resigned 1478[151]

Henry Sharpe, occurs 1478,[152] 1480[153]

William Smyth, occurs 1491[154]

[107] Ibid.

[108] Ibid. Some tenements in Lambeth were bequeathed to the college about the middle of the fifteenth century by Margaret wife of Henry Wroughton. Cotton. MS. Faust. B. viii, fol. 34b–36.

[109] *Valor Eccl.* i, 428.

[110] Blomfield, *Hist. of Norf.* iv, 628.

[111] Ibid. 767.

[112] *Valor Eccl.* i, 428.

[113] *Valor. Eccl.* (Rec. Com.), i, 428.

[114] Ibid.

[115] *Cal. of Inq. p.m. Hen. VII,* i, No. 106.

[116] *Valor Eccl.* i, 428.

[117] Hasted, *Hist. of Kent,* ii, 433.

[118] Ibid. ii, 793.

[119] Ibid. i, 309.

[120] Ibid. ii, 641.

[121] Ibid. ii, 677.

[122] *Valor Eccl.* i, 428.

[123] Ibid.

[124] *Cal. of Pat.* 1391–6, p. 518.

[125] The church of Penistone had been appropriated to them in 1412. Pat. 14 Hen. IV, m. 6, see Tanner, *Notit. Mon.*

[126] *Valor Eccl.* i, 428.

[127] Blomfield, *Hist. of Norf.* iv, 767.

[128] *Feud. Aids,* iii, 69.

[129] *Lond. and Midd. Arch. Soc. Trans.* iv, 365, &c.

[130] In 1382 the king paid £1 to the boy-bishop there. Devon, *Issues of the Exch.* 222. Henry VIII in 1576 gave to the boy-bishop 20s. during pleasure. *L. and P. Henry VIII,* ii, p. 876. A similar payment was made in 1526. Ibid. iv, p. 869.

[131] Smith, op. cit. 164–70.

[132] *Lond. and Midd. Arch. Soc. Trans.* iv, 366, &c.

[133] Newcourt, *Repert. Eccl. Lond.* i, 746.

[134] *Cal. Pap. Letters,* iii, 398.

[135] Newcourt, op. cit. i, 746.

[136] Ibid. i, 747.

[137] Ibid.

[138] Ibid. 1391–6, p. 553.

[139] In 1391 Nicholas Slake, king's clerk, was made archdeacon of Wells (ibid. 1388–92, p. 478); in 1394 he held a prebend of St. George's Windsor which he exchanged for one in the chapel of Bridgnorth (ibid. 1391–6, p. 485); in 1395 he became prebendary of Tamworth, and warden of the free chapel of Sherborne. Ibid. 621.

[140] *Cal. of Pat.* 1391–6, p. 684.

[141] Cott. MS. Faust. B. viii, fol. 19b, 21.

[142] Cott. MS. Faust. B. viii, fol. 9.

[143] Ibid. fol. 26b, 28.

[144] *Cal. of Pat.* 1461–7, p. 163.

[145] Doc. of D. and C. of St. Paul's, A. Box 76, No. 2001.

[146] Doc. of D. and C. of Westm., Westm. parcel 23, pt. 2, No. 18440.

[147] Ibid. 259.

[148] Ibid.

[149] Ibid. 332.

[150] Ibid.

[151] Doc. of D. and C. of Westm., Westm. parcel 23, pt. 3, No. 18509.

[152] Cott. MS. Faust. B. viii, fol. 41b.

[153] *Cal. of Pat.* 1476–85, p. 215.

[154] Rymer, *Foedera* (ed. 3), v (4), 29.

Edmund Martyn, occurs 1498[155]

Thomas Hobbis, S.T.P., occurs 1507[156]

William Atwater, occurs 1509[157]

John Forster, occurs 1509[158]

Thomas Wolsey, occurs 1514[159]

John Chamber, appointed 1514,[160] was the last dean[161]

[155] Smith, op. cit. 133.

[156] Doc. of D. and C. of Westm., Westm. parcel 23, pt. 2, No. 18448.

[157] Smith, op. cit. 133. Dean of king's chapel (?).

[158] Cott. MS. Faust. B. viii, fol. 53.

[159] *L. and P. Hen. VIII*, i, 5607.

[160] Ibid. Smith, op. cit. 134, says Dr. Vecy occurs 1515, but probably refers to king's chapel.

[161] Dugdale, *Mon. Angl.* vi, 1349. He occurs 1542. *L. and P. Hen. VIII*, xvii, 714 (5).

# 35. THE CHAPEL OF ST. PETER AD VINCULA IN THE TOWER OF LONDON

## INTRODUCTION

The entry for the Chapel of St. Peter ad Vincula in the Tower of London remains the most complete history of the chapel published to date.

A survey of the fabric of the church can be found in Royal Commission on Historical Monuments (England), *An Inventory of the Historical Monuments in London 5, East London* (London, 1930), pp. 92–3. This provides further detail on the architectural development of the chapel and also the fixtures and fittings contained therein including the bell, monuments, organ, piscina and plate. In addition to this work, see also S. Bradley and N. Pevsner, *London 1: The City of London* (London, 1997), pp. 369–70. Since the excavations carried out during the 1870s there have been no further archaeological studies published of the chapel.

*Christian Steer*

When and by whom the chapel of St. Peter ad Vincula in the Tower was founded is uncertain, though it must have been in existence long before 1241[1] when Henry III directed various repairs to be made in the chancels of St. Mary and St. Peter, and the images to be repainted.[2] Edward I, in 1272, appointed a chaplain to pray for his father's soul at a salary of 50s. a year,[3] but whether this was in addition to the chaplain who had before officiated in the chapel at the same salary[4] is not clear.[5] In the reign of Edward III, however, the only chaplain mentioned was one who was called the rector, and who received 60s. a year from a tenement in 'Candelwykstrete,'[6] until the king, in 1354, made the chapel practically collegiate by the addition of three chaplains,[7] enlarging the foundation by two more in 1356.[8] To provide for their maintenance he granted to them a rent of 31s. 8d. from tenements on Tower Hill and Petty Wales, 5s. from a tenement near St. Katharine's, customs due to the Constable of the Tower for stal-boats and weirs on the Thames, 10 marks a year from the Exchequer, and annual sums to be paid by the master and workmen of the Mint.[9] At the king's request, moreover, the pope gave permission for the appropriation to them of the church of Allhallows Barking.[10] The faculty, however, cannot have been used, for Allhallows was not appropriated until the time of Richard II,[11] and then for the benefit of the abbey of Barking, to which the patronage of the church belonged,[12] and when Henry IV, in 1402, gave the church and chapel of Allhallows as an appendage of St. Peter's to Thomas Haliwell,[13] the abbess claimed them as her property and was successful in proving her ownership.[14] Edward III seems only to have set up a series of chantries in the chapel, and Stow is doubtless correct in designating the priest who in 1429 killed a friar imprisoned in the Tower as the parson of St. Peter ad Vincula.[15]

Edward IV intended to erect a college in the strict sense of the word, and in February, 1483, issued letters patent[16] establishing a corporation of a dean, sub-dean, treasurer, and precentor, who were to be known as the dean and canons of the royal free chapel of the household; they were to be governed by ordinances made by the king, and as endowment were to hold the chapel, its oblations, tithes, and profits, and had leave to acquire lands to the value of £100 a year. The king's death, however, before the fulfilment of his purpose, put an end to

---

[1] Hennessy, *Novum Repert. Eccl. Lond.* 372, says it was founded probably by Henry I.

[2] Stow, *Surv. of Lond.* (ed. Strype), i, 68.

[3] Bayley, *Hist. of the Tower of Lond.* 115.

[4] Devon, *Issues of the Exch.* 26.

[5] If there was only one there when three were added in 1354, the papal grant of 1355 should have been made to four chaplains, not five as it was. *Cal. Pap. Letters*, iii, 562.

[6] Bayley, op. cit. 123.

[7] Ibid.

[8] Stow, op. cit. i, 68.

[9] Bayley, op. cit. 123.

[10] *Cal. Pap. Letters*, iii, 562.

[11] Newcourt, *Repert. Eccl. Lond.* i, 237. Licence granted, 1385. *Cal. of Pat.* 1385–9, p. 43.

[12] Edward III had held it by grant of the abbess and convent, but Richard II gave the advowson back to the abbey. *Cal. of Pat.* 1385–9, p. 43.

[13] Ibid. 1401–5, p. 124.

[14] Ibid. 490.

[15] Stow, *Ann. of Engl.* (ed. 1615), 358.

[16] *Cal. of Pat.* 1476–85, p. 341.

the scheme.[17] Presumably, therefore, the institution continued on the lines laid down by Edward III until the suppression of chantries and colleges[18] left the rector the sole incumbent of the chapel. In 1551 the chapel was deprived of the exemption it had hitherto enjoyed from episcopal authority and was made subject to the bishop of London.[19]

*M. Reddan*

## Rectors of the Collegiate Chapel of St. Peter in the Tower

This list is unchanged from that in *V.C.H. London*, i.

Thomas, occurs 1393[20]

Thomas Haliwell, appointed 1402;[21] resigned 1405[22]

Geoffrey Wyke, appointed 1405[23]

Robert de Morley, appointed 1413[24]

John Dabrichecourt, appointed 1413[25]

John Salmonby, appointed 1416; vacated 1421[26]

Edmund Warcop, occurs 1440[27]

John Forster, died 1445[28]

John Palmer, appointed 1445; vacated 1446[29]

John Clampayne, appointed 1446–7; vacated 1448–9[30]

Thomas Carr, appointed 1449;[31] vacated 1457–8[32]

Edmund Russell, appointed 1457–8[33]

Richard Martyn, appointed 1476;[34] resigned 1482[35]

William Fitz Herbert, appointed 1482[36]

John Gunthorpe, appointed 1483[37]

Richard Surland, appointed 1486; died 1509[38]

Roger Norton, appointed 1509[39]

Nicholas Willen, occurs 1535[40]

Richard Layton, LL.D., resigned 1535[41]

John Ogden, appointed 1535;[42] died 1537[43]

John Button, appointed 1537[44]

Richard Taylor, 1545–6[45]

---

[17] Dugdale, *Mon. Angl.* vi, 1458.

[18] The chapel could have been classed under either head, for the chaplainships were called chantries in a grant of 1362. Stow, *Surv. of Lond.* i, 68.

[19] Newcourt, *Repert. Eccl. Lond.* i, 530.

[20] *Cal. of Pat.* 1391–6, p. 265.

[21] Ibid. 1401–5, p. 124.

[22] Ibid. 500.

[23] Ibid.

[24] Hennessy, *Novum Repert.* 373.

[25] Ibid.

[26] Ibid.

[27] Ibid.

[28] Dugdale, op. cit. vi, 1458. Dr. Hutton's excerpts from the patent rolls.

[29] Hennessy, *Novum Repert.* 373.

[30] Ibid.

[31] Dugdale, op. cit. vi, 1458.

[32] Hennessy, op. cit. 373.

[33] Ibid.

[34] *Cal. of Pat.* 1467–77, p. 563.

[35] Ibid. 1476–85, p. 256.

[36] Ibid.

[37] That is he was created dean of the new college by Edward IV. Ibid. 341.

[38] Hennessy, op. cit. 372.

[39] Ibid.

[40] Ibid.

[41] *L. and P. Hen. VIII*, viii, 291 (11).

[42] Ibid.

[43] Ibid. xii (1), 539 (46).

[44] Ibid.

[45] Hennessy, op. cit. 373.

# 36. THE CHAPEL OF ST. THOMAS ON LONDON BRIDGE

## INTRODUCTION

For a recent assessment of the significance of the bridge to the city, see D. Keene, 'London Bridge and the Identity of the Medieval City', *T.L.M.A.S.*, 51 (2000), pp. 143–56, esp. 146. A recent volume devoted to the archaeology of London Bridge includes extensive commentary on the history of the bridge chapel: B. Watson, T. Brigham and A. Dyson, *London Bridge: 2000 Years of a River Crossing* (London, 2001), esp. pp. 109–114, 212–14. For a biography of the first recorded bridge chaplain, see D. Keene, 'Colechurch, Peter of (d. 1205)', *Oxford Dictionary of National Biography* (Oxford, 2004), http://www.oxforddnb.com/view/article/5868 (accessed 29 Jan. 2007). The role of the bridge chaplains in the administration of the bridge and its endowment has proved controversial. In the late twelfth and early thirteenth centuries, a number of bridge chaplains played a prominent role in raising money for the bridge and administering the endowment, J. McEwan, 'Medieval London: the development of a civic political community, c.1100–1300' (unpub. Univ. London Ph.D. thesis, 2007), ch. 2. By the end of the thirteenth century, however, the bridge's endowment had been brought firmly under the control of the civic authorities, who thereafter provided for the needs of the chapel, the chaplains and the bridge clerks: V. Harding and L. Wright, *London Bridge: Selected Accounts and Rentals, 1381–1538* (London Record Society, 31, 1995), pp. xvi–xvii. See also, R. Lloyd, 'Pre-Reformation Music in the Chapel of St. Thomas the Martyr, London Bridge' (unpub. Univ. London M.Mus. thesis, 1995).

*John McEwan*

The chapel on London Bridge was founded before 1205, in honour of St. Thomas à Becket, by Peter de Colechurch,[1] the chaplain who supervised the building of the bridge[2] begun in 1176.[3] The original structure was of very short duration, for it was burned down in 1212,[4] but it was rebuilt when the bridge was restored. From the first there are said to have been there two priests and four clerks,[5] who may probably be identified with the preachers licensed by King John in 1207 to preach in aid of the bridge.[6] A grant of a corrody in 1277 shows that there were then two or more chaplains, and that they and other persons called brothers of the Bridge lived together,[7] though where the house was situated is not indicated.[8] The Bridge-house, however, was referred to in a will of 1272,[9] and between 1265 and 1271 the brothers of the Bridge-house assented to the alienation of certain tenements which had been left to them by Richard le Keu on condition that they maintained a chantry.[10] Three other chantries were established in the chapel in 1334, 1349, and 1363,[11] yet it is not certain that the number of chaplains increased correspondingly, since in 1350 there were four, and in 1381 five chaplains and a clerk.[12] More priests, however, must have been needed than before, and this may have been the cause of the building of a new chapel between 1384 and 1397.[13] There is an

---

[1] Stow, *Surv. of Lond.* (ed. Strype), i, 54. Colechurch died four years before the bridge was completed in 1209, and was buried in the chapel, which must, therefore, have been finished, or nearly so, at that date. Newcourt, *Repert. Eccl. Lond.* i, 395. Peter, who was a priest of St. Mary Colechurch, the church in which St. Thomas had been baptized, built the chapel at his own cost. Welch, *Hist. of the Tower Bridge*, 29.

[2] *Rot. Lit. Pat.* (Rec. Com.), i, 58.

[3] Welch, op. cit. 29.

[4] Matt. Paris, *Chron. Maj.* (Rolls Ser.), ii, 536.

[5] Stow, op. cit. i, 54.

[6] *Rot. Lit. Pat.* (Rec. Com.), i, 58. Wace, the king's almoner, was one of them. He had been made warden of the bridge in 1205. *Rot. Lit. Claus.* (Rec. Com.), i, 49.

[7] *Liber Albus in Mun. Gildhall. Lond.* (Rolls Ser.), iii, 449–52.

[8] Dr. Sharpe thinks they lived in a house attached to the chapel. *Cal. of Letter Bk. B.* 216, n. 2. The Bridge-house in Southwark does not seem to be mentioned until the 15th century.

[9] Welch, op. cit. 90.

[10] Sharpe, *Cal. of Letter Bk. C.* 61. Queen Eleanor of Provence, as warden of London Bridge, made the tenements over to the Friars of the Sack subject to the same condition.

[11] Welch, op. cit. 73.

[12] Ibid. 257.

[13] Ibid. 71. Mr. Welch thinks that only the lower chapel had existed before.

interesting account of the contents of the chapel in 1350:[14] the books comprised three portifories, three Legends of Saints, four psalters, three graduals, a Tropary, two antiphonars,[15] a quire, an Ordinal with a Martyrology of the Saints, an 'Epistolar,' and three missals, one having large gilt letters; among the vestments were four sets for weekdays, one for Sundays, and one for festivals; the plate was of no great quantity, but the relics included a portion of the True Cross, and some inclosed in a purse which was kept on the altar for the pilgrims who visited the chapel.

The history of the chapel in the 15th century was marked by more than one contest. The priests were suspended in 1419–20 for some reason which is not disclosed, but which to the wardens appeared unjust, the difficulty, however, could not have been very serious, as absolution was obtained from the bishop of London for half a mark.[16]

The oblations of the chapel, and the administration of the sacraments by the chaplains were the subject of a dispute in 1433 between the rector of St. Magnus on one side and the mayor and commonalty of the City and the wardens of the bridge on the other, the former declaring that the chapel was within the parish and that the oblations belonged to him, the others maintaining that it had always been free from payments to the rector.[17] The bishop of London decided that the chaplains should have the oblations for the use and work of the chapel and the bridge, paying to the rector 20*d*. every year in lieu of all claims, and that they might freely administer the sacraments in the chapel as had ever been the custom.[18]

A few years later a controversy arose between the bishop of London and the bridgemasters over the suspension of the priests of the chapel;[19] and a papal bull confirming the privileges of the chaplains appears to have been necessary in 1465–6.[20]

At this date the pope granted an indulgence of forty days to those who visited the chapel on the Feast of St. Thomas of Canterbury, and on the day of his Translation, and contributed to the repairs of the chapel; and in the same year he increased the indulgence offered to 100 days and extended its benefits to those also who visited the chapel on Good Friday and the Feast of the Assumption of B. V. Mary.[21]

Money may then have been needed for repairs or improvements, and the offerings of the many were the best means of raising it. Only a few persons could make such gifts as Anneys Breteyn, who in 1489 gave £40, in part payment of £60, towards some work within the building.[22]

The cost of the chapel for the year ending at Michaelmas, 1484, was £33 5*s*. 3*d*,[23] almost exactly the same sum as in 1381–2,[24] so that there may have been five chaplains in 1484 as in 1381, yet the number evidently varied, wages being paid in 1444–5[25] to four chaplains and in 1494 to two chaplains and four clerks.[26]

It was decided by the City in October, 1538,[27] that from henceforth there should be only two priests and a 'conduct' in the Bridge-chapel, the others being dismissed with a quarter's wages. In 1541–2 there was only one priest, with a clerk as assistant,[28] and in 1548 he was ordered to deliver the goods and ornaments to the bridge-master and shut up the chapel,[29] which was subsequently defaced and turned into a dwelling-house.[30]

*M. Reddan*

[14] It is an indenture between the outgoing wardens of the bridge and the new wardens. Riley, *Mem. of Lond.* 263.

[15] Two new antiphonars and two calendars were added in 1397. Welch, op. cit. 76.

[16] Ibid. 73.

[17] Lond. Epis. Reg. Gilbert, fol. 201–2.

[18] Ibid.

[19] Rec. of Corp. of Lond. Index to Journals.

[20] Welch, op. cit. 73.

[21] Ibid 71.

[22] Ibid. 72.

[23] Arnold, *Chron.* (ed. 1811), 271 and 272.

[24] Welch, op. cit. 257. The chaplains were paid 11*s*. 5½*d*. a week and the clerk 1*s*. 3*d*.

[25] Stow, op. cit. i, 54.

[26] Welch, op. cit. 72.

[27] Rec. of the Corp. of Lond. Repert. x, fol. 48*b*.

[28] Welch, op. cit. 77.

[29] Rec. of Corp. of Lond. Repert. xi, fol. 412*b*.

[30] Ibid. Repert. xii, No. 1, fol. 35.

# 37. THE COLLEGE OF ST. LAURENCE POUNTNEY

## INTRODUCTION

Little work has been done on this college since the original *V.C.H.* article appeared, and it remains the best account available. For a biography of the founder, see Roger L. Axworthy, 'Pulteney, Sir John (*d.* 1349)', *Oxford Dictionary of National Biography* (Oxford, 2004), http://www.oxforddnb.com/view/article/22887 (accessed 29 Jan 2007).

A list of the masters and the chaplains attached to the college taxed in 1379–81 is given in McHardy, *Church in London*, p. 4. The income at the suppression of the college in 1548 is given in Kitching, *Chantry Certificate*, p. 38.

*Robert A. Wood*

John Poultney, mayor of London, added to the church of St. Lawrence, 'Candelwyk Street,'[1] a beautiful chapel in honour of Corpus Christi and St. John Baptist, and in it established a chantry of a master and six other secular priests,[2] apparently in augmentation of an earlier foundation of two chaplains[3] by Thomas Cole. This must have occurred at the beginning of the reign of Edward III, since from the terms of the king's petition to the pope on Poultney's behalf in July 1332, it is evident that the chantry was then in existence.[4] As endowment Poultney gave the rectory of St. Laurence, the advowson of which he obtained from Westminster Abbey in 1334;[5] a messuage in that parish in 1336;[6] messuages and rents in the parishes of St. Martin Orgar, St. Bride, St. Margaret Bridge Street, and in seven other London parishes,[7] and the manor of Catford[8] in Kent in 1338; the advowsons of the churches of West Tilbury, co. Essex, Speldhurst, co. Kent, Cheveley, co. Cambridge, Shenley, co. Herts, and Napton, co. Warwick, in 1345;[9] and the manor of Speldhurst in 1346.[10] Poultney's care for his foundation was unremitting: he used the king's interest with the pope on more than one occasion,[11] and the result may be seen in the many papal concessions he received, among them

being a relaxation of penance granted in 1337[12] and 1345[13] to those who assisted the chapel with their alms. The scheme appears to have been of gradual development, for the college did not take its final form until 1344, when the number of chaplains was increased from seven to thirteen,[14] and the statutes were not drawn up before 1347.[15] These provided[16] that on the death of the first master the chaplains should choose another from among themselves and present him to the bishop of London; a sub-master,[17] appointed and removable by the master, was to have the custody of the books and ornaments and oversight of divine service, and also administration of the college during a vacancy; he was to receive 53*s.* 4*d.* a year, the other chaplains 40*s.* each, and out of these salaries they were to find their clothes, which were to be of the same kind; the chaplains and the four choristers were to reside in the house provided for this purpose near the church, to have their meals in the common refectory, and to sleep in the dormitory; the chaplains were to be always resident; they were never to enter a tavern, they were not to go out without leave of the master nor to walk about the City without a companion assigned by him, and they were to be within the gates before nightfall. As regards services, they were to observe the use of Sarum;[18] each priest was to have cure of souls among members of the college

---

[1] The chantry is said to be founded near the church of St. Laurence. Rymer, *Foed.* (Rec. Com.), ii (2), 841.

[2] Ibid. Seven priests, ii, 536. A royal grant of Jan. 1334 mentions the master and chaplains. *Cal. of Pat.* 1334–8, p. 60.

[3] Stow, *Surv. of Lond.* (ed. Strype), ii, 189.

[4] Rymer, *Foed.* ii (2), 841.

[5] Doc. of D. and C. of Westm., Lond. L. (1).

[6] *Cal. of Pat.* 1334–8, p. 262.

[7] Ibid. 1338–40, p. 1.

[8] Ibid. pp. 104, 203.

[9] He had obtained the royal licence for the appropriation of these churches to the college. Ibid. 1343–5, p. 489.

[10] Ibid. 1345–8, p. 64; Hasted, *Hist. of Kent*, i, 428

[11] *Cal. of Pap. Letters*, ii, 383, 542.

[12] Ibid. ii, 536.

[13] Ibid. iii, 175.

[14] *Cal. of Pap. Petitions*, i, 37.

[15] They are undated, but John de Stratford, who died in 1346, is called the late archbishop of Canterbury. Wilson, *Hist. of Parish of St. Laurence Pountney*, 53.

[16] Ibid. 53–7.

[17] A bequest of a chalice and paten was made to Sir John Norwiche, sub-master, by Idonia Salesbury in 1386. Sharpe, *Cal. of Wills*, ii, 274.

[18] For this they had special leave from the pope. *Cal. Pap. Petitions*, i, 39.

and parishioners for a week in turn; all the priests were required to be present at mattins, vespers, and compline and to remain in the choir until the service was ended.

A few rules were made concerning the college property: a tripartite inventory of goods was to be made every year, the three parts being kept by the master, the sub-master, and the chaplains, and shown to the bishop of London at least once a year; the master was to apply any surplus income to the benefit of the college, and he was forbidden, even with the consent of the chaplains, to grant a corrody or pension out of the revenues; there was never to be a common seal. The endowment of the college at that time may be presumed to have been ample, and to this must be added the property bequeathed to it for the maintenance of chantries in the church during the next half-century;[19] yet for some unexplained reason its income seems to have dwindled until in 1420 it is said to have been only £12. Poverty, therefore, may have been one of the causes of the neglect of obligations which was the subject of complaints against the master in Parliament on two occasions, though it must be admitted that no excuse of this kind was offered on his behalf. John Carpenter, in 1430, petitioned the king in Parliament[20] to ordain that the master should carry out the terms of Poultney's will and distribute every year 4 marks to the prisoners of Newgate, as he had done before the gaol had been taken down and rebuilt. In 1439 the dean and chapter of St. Paul's stated that the sums for Poultney's obit and for the maintenance of three chantry priests in the cathedral had not been paid for two years, and they requested that they might have power to distrain on the possessions of the college in such circumstances.[21] The college would probably have rejoiced as much as the king if the investigations of Henry Sharp, the master, in 1457 for the discovery of the philosopher's stone[22] had been successful.

According to a patent of 1525 the patronage of the college had been granted to the duke of Buckingham by Henry VII,[23] though there is no evidence as to how it had come into the king's hands. On the

duke's attainder Henry VIII gave it to the marquis of Exeter, but as the patent to the marquis was void on some technical ground,[24] and appears not to have been renewed, the king henceforth nominated the masters.

No opposition was raised to the dissolution of the college under the Act of 1547.[25] The master, William Latimer, had adopted the new doctrines, and with them the ways of his party, and was merely interested in securing for himself a share of the plunder.[26] Pensions were assigned to Latimer and the three other chaplains of the college and to four 'conducts.'[27]

The clear income of the college at the time of its surrender was estimated at £79 17s. 10d,[28] Its possessions included rents of assize and ferms in London amounting to £25 16s. 8d.; the manors of Catford and Speldhurst,[29] in Kent; the rectory of St. Laurence Pountney; the rectory of Allhallows the Less, the gift of Adam, bishop of Winchester, in 1336;[30] a pension of £2 from the church of St. Mary Abchurch, which with the advowson had been obtained by an exchange made with the marquis of Suffolk in 1447;[31] the advowson of Eastling[32] in Kent, given to Poultney for that of Napton, co. Warwick, by the archbishop of Canterbury in 1348;[33] the rectory of Napton, received in exchange for 'Pulteney's Inn' from the earl of Arundel in 1385.[34] The college had held the rectory of Speldhurst from 1347 to 1448, but had then given up all but its patronage of the church.[35]

*M. Reddan*

### Revised List of Masters of the College

William de Chetewode, occurs 1338,[36] 1348[37]

Robert Witherdeley or Wyteley, presented 1363;[38] occurs 1391[39]

[19] Idonia, formerly wife of Robert Salesbury, left for this purpose lands and tenements in the parishes of Allhallows the Less, St. Michael Crooked Lane, and St. Olave Hart Street. Sharpe, *Cal. of Wills*, ii, 274. Edelena Atte Legh ordered the sale of lands for the endowment of a chantry. Ibid. ii, 179. Gilbert Marion in 1391 left to the master and parishioners his tenement at the corner of the churchyard. Ibid. ii, 290. Margaret, widow of William Wotton, left to the master and wardens in 1404 part of a tenement in the parish of St. Magnus. Ibid. ii, 361.

[20] *Parl. R.* (Rec. Com.), iv, 370*b*.

[21] Ibid. v, 9.

[22] Wilson, op. cit. 58, 59 *n*. a.

[23] *L. and P. Hen. VIII*, iv, 1610 (5).

[24] Ibid. iv, 2576.

[25] Wilson, op. cit. 67–8.

[26] Ibid. 69.

[27] Chant. Cert. No. 88, m. 7. Five pensions varying from 20s. to £6 were still paid in Mary's reign. Add. MS. 8102, fol. 4.

[28] *Valor Eccl.* (Rec. Com.), i, 387.

[29] *Cat. of Chart. &c. in Bodl. Lib.* 101. In 1539 the master and brothers let the manors of Speldhurst and 'Harwarton' in Kent for sixty years at 56s. 8d. per annum. Add. Chart. 211.

[30] *Cal. of Pat.* 1334–8, p. 308. Poultney gave to the bishop and his successors in return the right of appointing one of the chaplains. Ibid. 319. See Wilson, op. cit. 36.

[31] Pat. 26 Hen. VI, pt. 1, m. 11, in Tanner, *Notit. Mon.*

[32] Hasted, *Hist. of Kent*, ii, 758.

[33] *Cal. of Pat.* 1348–50, pp. 130, 132.

[34] Ibid. 1381–5, p. 527; Dugdale, *Hist. of Warw.* 337.

[35] Hasted, op. cit. i, 435–6.

[36] *Cal. of Pat.* 1338–40, p. 104.

[37] In Poultney's will. Wilson, op. cit. 58.

[38] Newcourt, *Repert. Eccl. Lond.* I, 389.

[39] Sharpe, *Cal. of Wills*, ii, 330.

Nicholas Mocking, presented 1399;[40] occurs 1411[41]

William Thorp, occurs 1426; resigned 1433[42]

John Pye, instituted 1433[43]

John Thurston, occurs 1447,[44] 1448[45]

Henry Sharpe, LL.D, occurs 1457;[46] resigned 1481[47]

Richard Hethcoat, instituted 1481;[48] resigned 1488[49]

Richard Ruston or Smith instituted 1488;[50] resigned 1525[51]

John Stevyns, M.A., presented 1525;[52] resigned 1532[53]

John Blackden, presented 1532;[54] died 1536[55]

Thomas Starkey, presented 1536;[56] died 1538[57]

William Latimer, presented 1538;[58] and was master at the surrender 1547[59]

[40] *Cal. of Pat.* 1399–1401, p. 175. He appears to have been presented by the king.

[41] *Cal. Pap. Letters,* vi, 292. He was then sub-dean of Wells, and held prebends in St. David's, Hoo in Hastings, and other places.

[42] Wilson, op. cit. 58, says he was master for more than seven years, and then exchanged his office for the rectory of St. Mary Abchurch.

[43] Newcourt, op. cit. i, 389.

[44] *Hist. MSS. Com. Rep.*ix, App. i, 28; Wilson, op. cit. 58.

[45] *Hist. MSS. Com. Rep.*ix, App. i, 16.

[46] Wilson, op. cit. 58.

[47] Newcourt, op. cit. i, 389.

[48] Ibid, I, 389.

[49] Ibid.

[50] Ibid.

[51] Ibid.

[52] Newcourt, op. cit. i, 389. He was presented by the king, as were his successors. Wilson, op. cit. 60.

[53] Newcourt, op. cit. i, 389.

[54] Ibid.

[55] *L. and P. Hen. VIII,* xi, 1417 (29).

[56] Ibid.

[57] Ibid. xiii (2), 491 (14).

[58] Ibid.

[59] Wilson, op. cit. 60.

# 38. THE COLLEGE IN THE GUILDHALL CHAPEL

## INTRODUCTION

This good account of the chapel and college at Guildhall can now be supplemented by Caroline M. Barron, *The Medieval Guildhall of London* (London, 1974), pp. 23–4 and 33–41.

The site of the chapel and the adjacent college was extensively excavated in the 1990s, see D. Bowsher, T. Dyson, N. Holder and I. Howell, *Excavations at London's Guildhall: Medieval Origins and Development*, MoLAS Monograph series (forthcoming, 2007/8).

At the dissolution of the Chantries in 1548 the lands and tenements which supported the warden and three priests of the college, who also served the Guildhall chapel, were valued at £51 8s. 4d. (Kitching, *Chantry Certificate*, p. 45).

*Caroline M. Barron*

The new chapel of the Guildhall must at least have been begun in 1299, for Henry le Galeys then gave to the Fraternity of Pui 5 marks annual quit-rent to maintain a chaplain there.[1] Either the building operations extended over a long period or extensive repairs[2] were soon needed, since in 1326 Thomas de Wake, lord of Lidel, and John de Stratford, bishop of Winchester, promised to supply the timber and lead to complete the church.[3]

In this chapel – dedicated to the honour of God, St. Mary, St. Mary Magdalen, and All Saints – Peter Fanelore, Adam Fraunceys, and Henry Frowyk proposed in 1356 to found a chantry of five chaplains at the altar of St. Mary.[4] Their intention, however, does not seem to have been carried out until 1368, when Fanelore was dead.[5] Of the college of five chaplains one was to be warden with a salary of 13 marks a year, the others receiving 10 marks each from the revenues of the endowment, viz., two tenements in the parish of St. Vedast and one in the parish of St. Giles without Cripplegate. The clerk who aided the priests in the mass was to have 6 marks a year. The warden was to collect the rents and pay his fellow priests, and accounts were to be given

before the two founders during their lifetime, and after their death before the mayor and chamberlain, any surplus over expenses being kept in a chest with three keys held by the mayor and chamberlain, the warden, and the four chaplains respectively. When the post of warden was vacant it was to be filled by Fraunceys and Frowyk while they lived, but when they were dead, the priests, after asking leave of the mayor, were to elect one of themselves. The advowsons of the other chaplaincies, after the death of the founders, lay with the mayor and chamberlain.

The Corporation seems to have had the supervision of the chantry, judging from its order to the chamberlain in 1417 to seize the lands of the chapel because the chaplains wandered about and neglected their duties.[6]

The chapel was so ruinous in 1430 that it was decided to rebuild it, and in order to get more space for the new building the chaplains' house was taken down and another on the north side of the Guildhall assigned to them instead.[7] The work proceeded somewhat slowly: overseers were appointed in 1439,[8] and it was not until October, 1444, that the chapel was at last dedicated.[9] In December of that year the warden and priests were commanded to perform choral service there daily.[10] The chapel was

---

[1] Sharpe, *Cal. of Letter Bk. E*, 1. This fraternity interested itself in the support of the chapel. *Liber Custum. in Mun. Guildhall. Lond.* (Rolls Ser.), ii (1), 227.

[2] Price, *A Descriptive Account of the Guildhall of the City of Lond.* 111.

[3] Sharpe, *Cal. of Letter Bk. E*, 215. On a visit to the Guildhall they asked why the works had stopped, and were told by the mayor that with their assistance and that of other great men the chapel would soon be finished. Their handsome contribution was the result of the hint.

[4] Riley, *Mems. of Lond.* 288. A chantry of some kind appears to have been already established there, but the college, though then projected, was not constituted until later.

[5] Harl. Chart. 79 G. 38.

[6] Rec. of Corp. of Lond. Journ. i, fol. 24; Price, op. cit. 119.

[7] Newcourt, *Repert. Eccl. Lond.* i, 361. They evidently lived and dined together, for Edmund Alynson in 1510 bequeathed to the commons of Guildhall College '5 sawssers, a olde plater, a wyne quartte pott and 2 belle candelstykks,' and 4d. every Friday for a year to pray for his soul at grace. Lond. Epis. Reg. Fitz James, ii, fol. 5.

[8] Rec. of Corp. of Lond. Journ. iii, fol. 39.

[9] Ibid. iv, fol. 48b.

[10] 'Cum Nota,' ibid. fol. 55b.

still unfinished, the City companies being asked in 1446 to contribute to the expense of roofing it.[11]

A chantry was founded there in 1435[12] by Henry Barton, who bequeathed also some ornaments to the chapel;[13] chantries were also erected by Roger Depham and Sir William Langford,[14] while the gild of St. Nicholas, founded by the parish clerks of London, added in 1449–50 two more chaplains to those then celebrating in the chapel, but in 1475 took away one for lack of funds.[15]

Stow says that the college consisted of a warden, seven chaplains, three clerks, and four choristers,[16] but from the ordinances of Bishop Bonner in 1542,[17] the number of priests seems not to have been more than seven, the custos and three chaplains established by the original foundation and the three annexed to the same.

The bishop's attention must have been drawn to the college by the unruliness of the priests, as he observes that the founders had made no ordinances, and in consequence the chaplains recognized no spiritual person in the college as their governor and refused to obey the custos. The bishop accordingly ordered that in future they should be obedient to the custos as their head, and that the highest seat in chapel and college should be assigned to him. Small misdemeanours were to be judged by the custos and two chaplains, but serious offences were to be dealt with by the bishop. Culprits not submitting to punishment were to be reported to the bishop, and in case of contumacy to be expelled. The bishop made arrangements for the daily celebration of masses in the chapel, and then proceeded to lay down rules for the life and conduct of members of the college: every year two of the chaplains, viz., one of each of the two sets, were to be appointed to provide the food, drink, and fuel; every week one of the commoners was to be steward, and prepare and see the food served at table; dinner was to be at 11 a.m., and supper at 5 or 5.30 p.m., according to the season; persons arriving after grace at the end of the meal must pay extra for bread and drink; anyone wanting more delicate fare than that provided must pay for it himself; anyone having fault to find with the meals was to tell the custos, steward, or bursars quietly; the four children, evidently the choristers, were to serve at all meals, and to take turns to say

grace and read a portion of the Bible in the middle of dinner; no one except the bursars was to breakfast in the buttery or kitchen; none was to soil the table with liquor or wipe his knife upon it; the chaplains must not haunt taverns or alehouses; no weapons were to be worn within the precinct; the slander of a fellow-commoner was punishable by a fine of 4d. to the commons; in case of a blow the fine was to be 6s. 8d.; none without special leave of the custos was to have a layman, a stranger, lodging in his chamber within the precinct; chaplains or priests having rooms in the college were not to sleep away from the same; no woman was to go alone into any of the rooms in the precinct except to attend to cases of severe illness, and then with leave of the custos; the college gates were to be shut every night at a certain hour, and those coming in later were to be fined.

The college was suppressed with other chantries and colleges by Edward VI.[18] Pensions were paid to three chaplains of the college and to another chantry priest.[19]

The income of the college was estimated by the Valor at £37 7s. 4d. gross and £33 16s. 8d. net;[20] its property lay in the London parishes of St. Leonard Foster Lane, St. Giles without Cripplegate, and St. Andrew Hubbard, in which last Stephen Spilman had granted a messuage and garden in 1397–8 for the better maintenance of the warden and chaplains.[21]

The chapel was purchased from the king in 1550 by the Corporation of London.[22]

*M. Reddan*

## Wardens of Guildhall College

This is a corrected version of the list to be found in the *V.C.H.*

William de Bramptone, appointed 1356[23]
Edmund Noreys, occurs 1389[24]
John Bernard, occurs 1430[25]
Thomas Francis, appointed 1448; died 1488[26]
Robert Sandewiche, occurs 1548[27]

---

[11] Price, op. cit. 125.
[12] Ibid. 121.
[13] After a long contention with the wardens of St. John's Walbrook, an arrangement was effected in 1448, and a silver cross enamelled and gilt, and a suit of vestments of white cloth of gold, were handed over to the chapel. Ibid. 122.
[14] Stow, *Surv. of Lond.* (ed. Strype), iii, 42.
[15] Christie, *Parish Clerks*, 27–8.
[16] Stow, op. cit. iii, 42. It is strange that no reference is ever made to the chantry of two chaplains founded by Gilbert de Bruera, dean of St. Paul's in 1348. Doc. of D. and C. of St. Paul's, A. Box 76, Nos. 2005–6.
[17] Lond. Epis. Reg. Bonner, fol. 14–17.
[18] The lands were in the king's hands in June, 1548. Rec. of the Corp. of Lond. Journ. xv, fol. 370.
[19] Chant. Cert. No. 88, m. 5. Three were receiving pensions in Mary's reign. Add. MS. 8102, fol. 4.
[20] *Valor Eccl.* (Rec. Com.), i, 385. From this must be deducted three stipends of 10 marks each.
[21] Stow, op. cit, iii, 42.
[22] Newcourt, op. cit. i, 362. 17 April, 4 Edw. VI, the king's letters patent of Guildhall Chapel or College made to the mayor and corporation of London Rec. of Corp. of Lond. Repert. xii, fol. 1–221b.
[23] Riley, *Mem. of London*, 288.
[24] Sharpe, *Cal. of Letter Bk. H*, 339.
[25] *Cal. of Pat.* 1429–1436, 57–8.
[26] Weever, *Anct. Fun. Mon.* 399.
[27] Kitching, *Chantry Certificate*, p. 45 n. 2.

# 39. WALWORTH'S COLLEGE IN ST. MICHAEL CROOKED LANE

## INTRODUCTION

Since the original account appeared, nothing further has been written about this foundation so this account remains the best available. For up to date biographies of Lovekyn and Walworth, see Charles Welch, 'Lovekyn, John (*d.* 1368)', rev. Roger L. Axworthy, and Pamela Nightingale, 'Walworth, Sir William (*d.* 1386?)', both in *Oxford Dictionary of National Biography* (Oxford, 2004), http://www.oxforddnb. com/view/article/17051 and 28660 (accessed 29 Jan 2007).

The names of the chaplains attached to the college in 1379–81 are recorded in McHardy, *Church in London*, p. 28, and additional details of the rents received by the college are to be found in *ibid*, p. 42. The close connection between the church of St. Michael, Walworth's College and the Stockfichmongers' Company is discussed by Nicholas Rogers in 'Hic Iacet…The Location of Monuments in Late Medieval Parish Churches', in *The Parish in Late Medieval England*, ed. C. Burgess and E. Duffy (Donington, 2006), pp. 261–81, esp. pp. 269 and 278–81.

At the suppression of colleges and chantries in 1548 there were five chaplains who continued to pray for William Walworth and whose stipends were met from the lands and tenements given by him, see Kitching, *Chantry Certificate*, p. 22.

*Robert A. Wood*

The church of St. Michael Crooked Lane owed much to two prominent London citizens, John Lovekyn, who was four times mayor, and his sometime apprentice, William Walworth, of Wat Tyler fame: Lovekyn rebuilding the church and Walworth adding the choir and side chapels.[1] In 1381, moreover, Walworth obtained permission from the king to suppress certain chantries established in the church by Pentecosten Russel and John Harewe, William Burgh, Henry Gubbe, William Jordain, Walter Mordon, and Thomas atte Leye, the endowment of which had in course of time become insufficient, and to found in their place a college of a master and nine chaplains to celebrate for the founders of the chantries, for Walworth and his wife Margaret, and for John Lovekyn.[2] The property which had belonged to the chantries in Crooked Lane, Bridge Street, Thames Street and elsewhere was settled on the college,[3] and further provision for its maintenance must have been made by Walworth on a very ample scale,[4]

since the royal licence given to the college in 1381 to acquire in mortmain lands and tenements to the annual value of £40 could only have been granted with a view to his benefactions.[5] At the time of the foundation Walworth had assigned to the priests a house near the church for a dwelling-place.[6] Important, however, as the college was in size, it remained only a chantry and never absorbed into itself the organization of the parish church[7] as did Poultney's College and Whittington's.

It lasted until the general suppression of colleges and chantries in the reign of Edward VI.[8] Pensions of £5 a year were then paid to seven priests and one 'conduct.'[9]

*M. Reddan*

---

[1] Stow, *Surv. of Lond.* (ed. Strype), ii, 185.

[2] Pat. 4 Ric. II, pt. 2, m. 12, printed in Dugdale, *Mon. Angl.* vi, 1380.

[3] Ibid.

[4] Either by grants during his lifetime or by bequest. He seems to have arranged by his will in 1385 that his wife should assign the revenues of certain property in the City to the college, and that after her death some tenements and rents should be entrusted to the rector and churchwardens of St. Michael's for that purpose. Sharpe, *Cal. of Wills*, ii, 251.

[5] *Cal. of Pat.* 1377–81, p. 612.

[6] Ibid. 609.

[7] The rector of the church continued as before and seems not to have been connected in any way with the college. Sharpe, *Cal. of Wills*, ii, 251; *Valor Eccl.* (Rec. Com.), i, 371; *L. and P. Hen. VIII*, v, 1693 (7).

[8] Tanner, *Notitia Mon.*

[9] Chant. Cert. No. 88, m. 5. By 1556 the eight were reduced to five. Add. MS. 8102, fol. 4.

# 40. THE FRATERNITY OF THE HOLY TRINITY AND OF THE SIXTY PRIESTS IN LEADENHALL CHAPEL

## INTRODUCTION

No further work specifically on this fraternity has been done since the *V.C.H.* article was published. However, Honeybourne, 'Property', pp. 299, 566, describes the property held by the house, and this is also listed in *Documentary Sources*, p. 143. Some of the properties and obligations of the Fraternity are set out in Kitching, *Chantry Certificate*, pp. 35, 39, while G. Milne (ed.), *From Roman Basilica to Medieval Market* (London, 1992), pp. 39–50, 126–33 has details of the development of the Leadenhall. For Eyre, see Caroline M. Barron, 'Eyre, Simon (*c.*1395–1458)', *Oxford Dictionary of National Biography*, Oxford University Press, 2004, http://www. oxforddnb.com /view/article/52246 (accessed 29 Jan 2007).

*Claire Martin*

Simon Eyre, who built a granary for the City in Leadenhall, left by his will in 1459 3,000 marks to the Drapers' Company to establish within a year of his decease in the Leadenhall Chapel a college of a master, five secular priests, six clerks, and two choristers, and to found a school for teaching grammar, writing, and singing.[1] For some reason unknown the terms of the will were not carried out either by the Drapers' Company or by the prior and convent of Holy Trinity, who became legatees on the same conditions on the default of the company.[2] In 1466, however, Edward IV, at the request of Queen Elizabeth, granted licence to William Rous, chaplain, and John Reseby and Thomas Asheby, priests, to found in the Leadenhall Chapel a fraternity to be called the Fraternity of the Holy Trinity and the Sixty Priests of London.[3] If the rules of the Pappey were drawn up[4] at the time of that hospital's foundation in 1442 the brotherhood

of the sixty priests must have been in existence before it was connected with Leadenhall, as it is there mentioned.

The City in 1512 seems to have attempted to carry out Eyre's wishes to some extent by granting to these priests the use of the chapel on condition that they prayed for the souls of Simon Eyre and his wife.[5]

There is no account of any endowment except the small bequests often made to them by will; such as the legacy of 20*s.* left to them in 1507 by John Overton, priest of St. Thomas of Acon,[6] 20*s.* to their common box by a chantry priest of St. Mary-at-Hill in 1509;[7] 10*s.* for a trental of masses in 1510 by the priest of St. Peter's Cornhill.[8]

The fraternity was suppressed at the general dissolution of chantries and gilds in the reign of Edward VI.

*M. Reddan*

---

[1] Stow, *Surv. of Lond.* ii, 84 (ed. Strype).
[2] Ibid.
[3] *Cal. of Pat.* 1461–7, p. 516.
[4] Cott. MS. Vit. F. xvi, fol. 116*b*.

[5] Rec. of the Corp. of Lond. Repert. 2, fol. 140.
[6] Lond. Epis. Reg. Fitz James, pt. 2, fol. 2.
[7] Ibid. fol. 1.
[8] Ibid. fol. 5.

# 41. WHITTINGTON'S COLLEGE

## INTRODUCTION

This remains an excellent account of Whittington College. Jean Imray has drawn attention to the maladministration of the college during the mastership of Edward Underwood, who was largely absent, neglected divine services and allowed the buildings to become dilapidated until the Mercers' Company intervened: see *The Charity of Richard Whittington: A History of the Trust administered by the Mercers' Company 1424–1966* (London, 1968), ch. 3.

The documents relating to the dissolution of the college in 1546–1548 have been printed (Kitching, *Chantry Certificate*, p. 47).

The academic calibre of the masters of the college is attested by the fact that almost all of them were graduates, as were several of the fellows. For a study of the last master, see J. Andreas Lowe, 'Richard Smyth: Stations in a Life of Opposition' (unpub. Univ. Cambridge PhD thesis, 2001).

*Caroline M. Barron*

The church of St. Michael Paternoster Royal was the parish church of the wealthy Richard Whittington, and therefore had a special claim on him. At the beginning of the fifteenth century it needed enlarging, and was also in a ruinous state, so that he determined to rebuild it entirely, and in 1411 began the work by adding a piece of ground to the site.[1] His idea was to make the new church collegiate, but before he could complete his project he died early in 1423. His executors, however, with the consent of the king[2] and the archbishop of Canterbury, erected there in 1424[3] in honour of the Holy Ghost and St. Mary a perpetual college of five secular priests, of whom one was to be master, two clerks and four choristers. William Brooke, the rector of St. Michael's, was made master, and it was ordained that henceforth the office of master should be held to include that of rector.[4] When a vacancy occurred one of their number was to be chosen by the chaplains and presented by the wardens of the Mercers' Company to the prior and chapter of Christchurch, Canterbury, who as patrons of the rectory[5] were to present him to the bishop for institution; vacancies among the chaplains[6] were

to be filled by the master and senior chaplains; the clerks and choristers were to be appointed and were removable by the master and chaplains, and when past work were to be supported in the Whittington Almshouse; all the members of the college were to live in a house built by Whittington at the east end of the church; the master was to have a salary of 10 marks besides the oblations of the church, each chaplain 11 marks, the first clerk 8 marks, the second 100*s.*, the choristers 5 marks each, and out of this they were to provide their food and clothing, but the cook was paid out of the college funds; the dress of the chaplains was to be of one style and colour; residence was obligatory, no chaplain being permitted to be absent for more than twenty days in the year, and then for good cause; the college was to have a common seal which was to be kept with the charters in the common chest; the goods of the college were not to be alienated by the master and chaplains except for urgent necessity; an inquiry into debts was to be made at the general chapter held annually; the supervision of the college was vested, after the decease of the executors, in the mayor of London and the wardens of the Mercers' Company.

The property of the church then became that of the college,[7] but more was needed, and the executors in February, 1425, granted to the master and chaplains £63 a year from Whittington's possessions until lands and rents equal in value should be given.[8] This

---

[1] Letter Bk. I, fol. 86, quoted by Riley in *Mem. of Lond.* 578.
[2] *Cal. of Pat.* 1422–9, p. 259.
[3] Pat. 10 Hen. VI, pt. 2, m. 7, inspecting and confirming the foundation, is given in Dugdale, *Mon. Angl.* vi, 739–43.
[4] For the arrangement with the priory of Christchurch see *Cal. of Pat.* 1422–9, p. 274.
[5] They were compensated for the loss of the advowson by an annual payment of 13*s.* 4*d.* Sharpe, *Cal. of Wills*, ii, 458.
[6] Choice was to be made of men who had not other benefices nor possessions.

[7] Presumably this is the endowment which is spoken of as insufficient. Pat. 10 Hen. VI, pt. 2, m. 6, per inspect. Dugdale, *Mon. Angl.* vi, 743.
[8] Ibid.

sum was derived from property in the parishes of St. Michael Paternoster Royal, St. Lawrence Jewry and St. Mary Magdalen Milk Street, and was settled permanently on the college by the will of George Gerveys in 1432.[9] Land for enlarging the college and for making a new burial ground was also acquired at that time.[10]

The charter of foundation provided that the chaplains chosen should be versed in letters,[11] and the observance of this rule is proved by the history of the college. One of the masters, William Ive, played a leading and successful part as the champion of the beneficed clergy in the controversy raised by the mendicant orders in 1465,[12] and his statement of the case was sent to the pope with that of the bishop of London and the archbishop of Canterbury.[13] He was at that time keeper of the St. Paul's School.[14] In 1490 the members of the college under the presidency of Edward Underwood, the master, founded the Fraternity of St. Sophia for the reading of a divinity lecture.[15] The reputation of the college was maintained till the end, for the last master, appointed in 1537, was Richard Smith, the first regius professor of divinity at Oxford.[16] Opinion was divided in the college on the religious question at this time, but the supporters of the royal policy were in the majority,[17] and must then have reckoned the master among their number. There was a point, however, beyond which Smith was not prepared to go, and under Edward VI he was deprived of his offices and fled to Louvain.[18] The college was dissolved in 1547, and pensions

were paid to six priests, two 'conducts,' and four choristers.[19] It was revived under Mary, and Smith again became master,[20] but on the accession of Elizabeth it was finally dissolved. The annual income was estimated by Dugdale at £20 1s. 8d.,[21] but for Wolsey's procurations in 1524, the rating of which was generally very low, it was reckoned at £36.[22]

*M. Reddan*

## Revised List of Masters of Whittington's College

This is a corrected version of the list in the *V.C.H.*, using George Hennessy, *Novum Repertorium Ecclesiasticum Parochiale Londonense* (London, 1898), pp. 333–4, except where otherwise indicated.

William Brooke, appointed 1424

John Clench, D.Th., appointed 1424

Richard Purlingland, D.Th., appointed 1427

Reginald Pecocke, D.Th., appointed 1431; resigned 1444

John Eyburhall, S.T.P., appointed 1444; resigned 1464

William Ive D.Th., appointed 1464; resigned 1470

John Collys D.Th., appointed 1470; resigned 1479

Nicholas Good, D.Th., appointed 1479; died 1479

Edward Lupton, MA., appointed 1479; died 1482

John Green, S.T.B., appointed 1482

Robert Smith, D.Th., occurs, 1484;[23] resigned 1488

Thomas Lynley, D.Th., appointed 1488; died 1492[24]

Edward Underwood, D.Th., occurs 1490; resigned 1495[25]

Stephen Douce, S.T.B., appointed 1496; resigned 1509

Humphrey Wistowe, D.Th., appointed 1509; died 1514

John Walgrave, B.Th., appointed 1514; resigned 1520

Edward Felde, D.Th., appointed 1520; died 1537

Richard Smith, D.Th., appointed 1537; deprived 1549; restored 1555; deprived 1559[26]

[9] Sharpe, *Cal. of Wills*, ii, 457. The ordinances and endowment of the college were at the request of John Carpenter confirmed in 1432 by the king in Parliament. *Parl. R.* (Rec. Com.), iv, 392b.

[10] Sharpe, op. cit. ii, 457. It is evident that these bequests were not fresh grants, but were all in pursuance of Whittington's intentions, as his executor, John Carpenter, is mentioned in connexion with every one of them. The making of a new churchyard had been part of Whittington's plan in 1411. See Riley, op. cit. 578.

[11] Dugdale, op. cit. vi, 739.

[12] *Collections of a London Citizen* (Camd. Soc.), 228.

[13] Ibid. 231.

[14] Ibid. 230.

[15] Newcourt, *Repert. Eccl. Lond.* i, 492. For the sermons to be preached by the chaplains under the terms of Gilbert Heydok's will by an ordinance of Archbishop Warham in 1509, see ibid.

[16] *Dict. Nat. Biog.* liii, 101.

[17] William Gibson, the tutor, had said that the Northern men rose in a good quarrel, but many were so weary of such communications that they were ready to go out of the house. Both Gibson and one of the choristers said that Friar Forest died in a right quarrel. *L. and P. Hen. VIII*, xiii (2), 1202.

[18] *Dict. Nat. Biog.* liii, 101.

[19] Chant. Cert. No. 88, m. 4, *dors*. In Mary's reign pensions were paid to eleven persons. Add. MS. 8102, fol. 5.

[20] Newcourt, op. cit. i, 494.

[21] Newcourt, op. cit. 492.

[22] *L. and P. Hen. VIII*, iv, 964.

[23] *B.R.U.O.*, p. 1719.

[24] *B.R.U.O.*, p. 1194.

[25] *B.R.U.O.*, p. 1931.

[26] *B.R.U.O. 1501–1540*, p. 525.

# 42. THE COLLEGE IN ALL HALLOWS BARKING

## INTRODUCTION

The original *V.C.H.* account remains the most up to date survey of the college. A near-contemporary description of the college can be found in Stow, *Survey of London*, ed. Kingsford, I, pp. 130–1. For mention of an obit maintained by the masters, wardens and bedesmen of the college, see Kitching, *Chantry Certificate*, pp. 29–30.

*Jennifer Ledfors*

The chapel of St. Mary in the church of Allhallows Barking was founded by Richard I, but although it may have had from early times a reputation for special sanctity, it does not seem to have acquired its great attraction as a place of pilgrimage until the reign of Edward I, who in consequence of a vision placed an image of the Virgin there, and obtained a special indulgence from the bishop of London for those who visited the chapel, and contributed to its repair.[1]

In 1442 John Somerset, chancellor of the Exchequer, and Henry Frowik and John Olney, aldermen of London, established a gild of St. Mary, to which Henry VI granted the custody of the chapel, reserving, however, the right of the parish church to oblations.[2] Edward IV in 1465 granted to the master of the gild, the notorious John Tiptoft, earl of Worcester, and to the wardens the manor of Tooting Bec and the advowson of Streatham, county Surrey, part of the alien priory of Ogbourne, for the maintenance of a chantry of two chaplains to pray for the good estate of himself and his family in life, and for their souls after death.[3] The rules for the chantry made by the master and wardens[4] ordered that the chaplains should not have other benefices, nor a temporal patrimony exceeding five marks; vacancies were to be filled by the master and wardens within six months; each chaplain was to receive, if a graduate, £10 a year, if not £8, but the king in limiting the liability of the gild as regards the chantry in 1470 fixed the salary of the first chaplain definitely at £10, and that of the second at £8[5]; they were to have a month's holiday every year

on obtaining leave of the master and wardens, but were not both to be absent at the time of the chief festivals, and penalties were to be imposed in case due leave of absence was exceeded; an arrangement was to be made with the vicar so that the services in the chapel on Sundays and festivals did not interrupt those in the church.

The chaplains were exempted by the king in 1470 from payments of all tenths, fifteenths, tallages, and subsidies.[6]

Richard III is said to have rebuilt the chapel, and to have erected there a college of a dean and six canons,[7] but there is no account of the further endowment which would have been necessary, and no mention ever occurs of a royal foundation there other than the chantry of Edward IV. The chantries afterwards established by Sir John Rysley and Sir Robert Tate[8] added five persons to those ministering in the chapel,[9] and Chicheley's chantry provided for a priest and a 'conduct,'[10] so that at the Dissolution there were altogether five priests and five 'conducts,' all of whom seem to have received pensions.[11]

*M. Reddan*

### Dean or Master of the Chapel of St. Mary, in Allhallows Barking

Edmund Chadertone (?)[12]

---

[1] Lond. Epis. Reg. Gilbert, fol. 194; Newcourt, *Repert. Eccl. Lond.* i, 238.
[2] *L. and P. Hen. VIII*, i, 5242 (1).
[3] *Cal. of Pat.* 1461–7, p. 428; *Parl. R.* (Rec. Com.), vi, 94*a* and 343*b*.
[4] Exch. T.R. Misc. Bk. 110.
[5] *Cal. of Pat.* 1467–77, p. 192.
[6] Ibid.
[7] Stow, *Surv. of Lond.* (ed. Strype), ii, 32; Harl. MS. 433, fol. 105. Yet there seems to be no trace of the college in the calendar of patent rolls.
[8] Maskell, *Hist. of Allhallows Barking*, 16.
[9] Chant. Cert. No. 88, m. 4 *d.*
[10] Ibid.
[11] Ibid.
[12] He is called the first dean. Stow, op. cit. ii, 32; Harl. 433, fol. 102.

# ALIEN HOUSES

## 43. THE HOSPITAL OF ST. ANTHONY [OF VIENNE]

### INTRODUCTION

The original *V.C.H.* entry gives a balanced account of this relatively prosperous hospital, concentrating on the period after the Alien Priories Act of 1414. A more detailed account is provided in David. K. Maxfield, 'St. Anthony's Hospital, London: a Pardoner-Supported Alien Priory, 1219–1461', in *The Age of Richard II*, ed. J. L. Gillespie (Stroud, 1997), pp. 225–47. For a particular incident, see *idem*, 'A Fifteenth Century Lawsuit: the case of St. Anthony's Hospital', *Journal of Ecclesiastical History*, 44 (1993), pp. 199–223.

Some early charters (*c.*1295) of the hospital are at St. George's College Archive, Windsor Castle, but most relate to the period 1430–1700: see J. N. Dalton (ed.) *The Manuscripts of St. George's Chapel, Windsor Castle*, Historical Monographs relating to St. George's Chapel, Windsor Castle, 11 (Windsor, 1957), pp. 275–93. This material was used by Roderic Morgan for 'The Hospital of St. Anthony of Vienne in Threadneedle Street *c.*1450–1550' (unpub. Univ. London MA thesis, 1987). A list of sources relating to the hospital's estates can be found in *Documentary Sources*, pp. 60–1.

No archaeological research has been carried out at the site of the hospital and there is no printed source material, other than brief extracts in Dalton's catalogue of St. George's College archive. A map of the site is provided in G. Rose, 'A plan of the site and buildings of St. Anthony's hospital, Threadneedle Street, *c.*1530', *London Topographical Record*, 16 (1932), pp. 1–8.

*David Lewis*

The brothers of St. Anthony of Vienne established a cell before 1254 on some land given to them by Henry III, in a place previously occupied by a synagogue.[1] In the bull of Pope Alexander V confirming the grant the place is not further described. The hospital of St. Anthony when mentioned later was certainly in the parish of St. Benet Fink, but this seems too far removed from the Jewry to contain a synagogue. Either the brothers changed their quarters afterwards or at one time the Jews spread beyond the Jewry, and it is possible to give this interpretation to an order of Henry III, 1252–3, that there should be no synagogues except where they existed in the reign of John.[2] The house was founded for a master, two priests, a schoolmaster, and twelve poor men,[3] but there appears to have been no endowment,

for in 1291 their whole property[4] which lay in the parish of St. Benet Fink was not worth more than 8*s.* a year,[5] so that they must have depended entirely on alms. Of the income derived in this way one source was sufficiently curious. Any pig that was considered by the supervisor of the London market unfit to be killed for food had a bell attached to it by a proctor of St. Anthony's, and was then free of the street to pick up what it could. As it was a merit to feed these animals, they often throve, and were then taken by the house.[6] The privilege seems to have been abused, for in 1311 Roger de Wynchester, the renter of the house, promised the City authorities that he would not claim pigs found wandering about the City, nor put bells on any swine but those given in charity to the house.[7]

---

[1] The bull of Pope Alexander V referring to the grant belongs to that year. Doc. of D. and C. of St. George's, Windsor, Reg. Denton, fol. 267. For the information contained in the documents at Windsor I am indebted to Mr. Leach, who kindly placed his notes at my disposal.

[2] Close, 37 Hen. III, m. 18, given in Tovey, *Anglia Judaica*, 146.

[3] Harl. MS. 544, fol. 72.

[4] In Blomefield, *Hist. of Norf.* viii, 118, there is mention of a grant of 40 acres of land and 10*s.* rent in Felbrigge to the Hospital of St. Anthony of Vienne, in 1273–4, but in the Taxatio of Pope Nicholas nothing is said of a holding there.

[5] Harl. MS. 60, fol. 16.

[6] Stow, *Surv. of Lond.* (ed. Strype), ii, 120.

[7] Sharpe, *Cal. of Letter Bk. D*, 251.

It is not improbable that the brothers were in greater need of money than usual, as they were building their chapel in 1310.[8] Over the erection of this oratory they had involved themselves in a quarrel with the bishop of London, whose rights they had disregarded in neglecting to ask his leave to build. The case came before the court of Arches, and the brothers not appearing, judgement was given in August, 1311, that the chapel was to the prejudice of the bishop and of the parish church of St. Benet Fink, and was to be reduced to the form of a private house within eight days on pain of greater excommunication. The brothers now found it expedient to give way, and the proctor submitted to the will and ordinance of the bishop.

During the wars with France and the schism the hospital was cut off from intercourse with the parent house. The warden, Geoffrey de Lymonia, was excused by Clement VII, the antipope, in 1380, from the contributions due to Vienne, which he had been unable to pay for three years because he could get nothing from his preceptory,[9] so that either Geoffrey had never obtained actual possession or the house had been taken for a time into the king's hands.[10] In 1385 it was paying a yearly fine of twenty marks.[11]

It is clear that when the preceptorship became vacant the king would not allow Clement's candidate to take possession,[12] and in 1389 he put in as warden one of his clerks, John Macclesfield.[13] Boniface IX agreed to confirm him in the office if he took the habit within three months, but on his failing to do so gave the hospital to one of the canons.[14] However, at the king's request, the pope afterwards allowed Macclesfield to hold the house for ten years *in commendam*, enjoying all its privileges and exemptions.[15]

The hospital was now practically a royal free chapel and this may account for the benefits conferred on it by Pope Boniface IX. In 1392 he granted 100 days' remission of penance to those who during seven years visited the house of St. Anthony on the chief festivals connected with our Lord, the Virgin Mary, and St. Anthony, and gave alms to the fabric of the

chapel and the maintenance of the sick and poor.[16] In the same year he gave to the hospital the issues of the church of All Saints, Hereford, and the annexed chapel of St. Martin, which had been given to the house at Vienne in 1249 by Henry III.[17]

The pope in 1400 at Macclesfield's request appropriated to St. Anthony's the church of St. Benet Fink,[18] the advowson of which had been given shortly before by John Sauvage and Thomas Walington.[19] This grant, however, can have been of no effect, for in 1417 a dispute of long standing between the hospital and the rectors of the church, touching the oblations claimed by the latter from the chapel of St. Anthony, was settled by the brethren agreeing to give the rector and his successors a pension of six marks.[20] It was not until 1440 that St. Benet's was appropriated to the hospital by the bishop of London for the maintenance of the grammar school.[21] The pope had, also owing to Macclesfield's representations, in 1397 issued a mandate to the bishops of England and Ireland, ordering them to recommend to the people of their dioceses those seeking alms for the hospital, and not to extort anything from them or hinder them in any other way.[22] The importance of these collections will be seen when it is remembered that they were by far the largest means of support possessed by the house. In 1391 the hospital had been excused from a liability incurred by a former warden 'in consideration of its having no possession temporal or spiritual of much value, nor anything but the alms of the people for the maintenance of divine service, the support of the sick and the repair of the house.'[23]

From his dealings with the pope Macclesfield might be judged a zealous advocate of the cause of his preceptory. It is evident, however, that his motives were not disinterested, since Adam de Olton, presumably his successor, informed Pope Martin V that he had alienated much of the property of the house and granted pensions to his children, and other persons, and in 1424 the pope ordered the bishop of Winchester to annul such alienations as should be found unlawful.[24]

It may be presumed that any damage done to the finances was set right, for five years later the master acquired a messuage and garden and some land adjoining from the abbot of St. Albans to enlarge

[8] Doc. of D. and C. of St. Paul's, Liber A. fol. 94 and 94*b*.

[9] *Cal. Pap. Letters*, iv, 240.

[10] Tanner, *Notit. Mon.* says that it was often seized during the wars with France.

[11] *Cal. of Pat.* 1381–5, p. 553.

[12] In 1386 Clement VII speaks of Avallonus Richardi who had been appointed by him to the preceptory of London vacant by the death of Geoffrey de Lymonia as being unable to get possession. *Cal. Pap. Letters*, iv, 254. Richard Brighous was master in 1385. *Cal. of Pat.* 1381–5, p. 553.

[13] *Cal. of Pat.* 1388–92, p. 124.

[14] *Cal. Pap. Letters*, iv, 419.

[15] Ibid. iv, 430. As he still held the house, however, in 1417 the time must have been extended. *Cal. of Pat.* 1422–9, p. 156.

[16] Denton Reg. fol. 289.

[17] Ibid. fol. 290.

[18] *Cal. Pap. Letters*, v, 311.

[19] *Cal. Rot. Chart. and Inq. a.q.d.* (Rec. Com.), 354.

[20] *Cal. of Pat.* 1422–9, p. 156.

[21] Lond. Epis. Reg. Gilbert, fol. 183.

[22] *Cal. Pap. Letters*, v, 18.

[23] *Cal. of Pat.* 1388–92, p. 389.

[24] Denton Reg. fol. 303; *Cal. Pap. Letters*, vii, 373.

the buildings of the house and make a garden and cemetery.[25] There were then fourteen priests and clerks there, and many poor and sick who had to be lodged elsewhere.

A bull of Pope Eugenius IV in December, 1441, exempting the brothers from eating in the refectory and sleeping in the dormitory, shows that the new buildings for the convent were not yet finished.[26] Henry VI, in June of that year, describes the house as wretched and almost desolate, reduced to the very verge of poverty, although it was under the rule of his vigilant and prudent chaplain, John Carpenter.[27] The brothers doubtless found it none too easy to meet their extraordinary as well as ordinary expenses, yet it seems strange if the house were so very poor that it is never the first consideration in the grants made to it.

It was for the maintenance of the school that St. Benet Fink was appropriated, and in 1442 the king granted to the brethren the manor of Pennington with pensions in Milburn, Tunworth, Charlton, and Up-Wimborne, co. Southants, to maintain at Oxford University five scholars, who were to be first instructed in the rudiments of grammar at Eton College.[28] The bequest of William Wyse in 1449 of his brewery, 'Le Coupe super le hoop,' in the parish of Allhallows London Wall, was also charged with the maintenance of a clerk to instruct the children of St. Anthony's in singing to music and plain singing, besides the usual celebrations for the testator's soul.[29] It would be interesting to know whether there is a connexion between the teaching of music at St. Anthony's and the establishment by the king's minstrels there of a fraternity in 1469.[30]

The hospital had come into the king's possession[31] under the Alien Priories Act of 1414, and was treated henceforth as a royal free chapel: Henry VI appointed the wardens,[32] and Edward IV on two occasions[33] gave the right to present on the next vacancy of the house. The connexion with the house at Vienne probably ceased after the fourteenth century. The employment of the use of Sarum had been authorized in 1397, as the brothers were unable to obtain the books necessary for the celebration of service according to the rule of their order,[34] and in 1424 the pope ordered them to celebrate service after the use of London as long as the wars lasted, because few or no canons having come for many years from Vienne, the custom of the order could not be easily observed.[35] The popes evidently acquiesced in the change in the position of the hospital, for Pope Eugenius IV, at the request of Henry VI, gave leave in 1446 to the bishops of Worcester and Norwich, the provost of Eton and William Say, the warden, to make statutes for St. Anthony's, London,[36] and Pope Nicholas V in 1447 exempted the hospital from all spiritual and temporal jurisdiction, especially from that of the monastery of St. Anthony, Vienne.[37]

The independent existence of the hospital was not of long duration, as it was annexed and appropriated to the college of St. George, Windsor, in 1475.[38] It must have been quite prosperous at that time, since the sum total of its receipts in 1478–9, viz. £539 19s., exceeded its expenses by £96 4s. 10d.[39] From the accounts it may be gathered that the surplus was not obtained by stinting the inmates of food.[40]

The church was rebuilt in 1499 on the old site, to which other ground had been added,[41] and rededicated in July, 1502.[42] To this work the principal contributor was Sir John Tate, a London alderman, who gave both land and money.[43]

It is interesting to compare the list of wages paid in 1522[44] with that in 1545: the first shows that there were then in the house besides the master, four priests, a steward, the curate of St. Anthony's, a schoolmaster, a master of the song-school and seven other clerks, an usher of the school, and a butler; in 1545, those receiving stipends were two priests,

[25] *Cal. of Pat.* 1422–9, p. 517.
[26] Denton Reg. fol. 314.
[27] *Corres. of Bekynton* (Rolls Ser.), i, 235.
[28] Stow, *Surv. of Lond.* (ed. Strype), ii, 120.
[29] Sharpe, *Cal. of Wills*, ii, 524.
[30] *Cal. of Pat.* 1467–77, p. 153.
[31] In 1409 Pope Alexander V had attempted to put in as master a canon of Vienne, but John Macclesfield still held the post in 1414. *Cal. Pap. Letters*, vi, 162; *Cal. of Pat.* 1422–9, p. 109.
[32] See letters patent in Harl. MS. 6963, fol. 24, 68, 116.
[33] *Parl. R.* (Rec. Com.), v, 526b.
[34] *Cal. Pap. Letters*, v, 4.

[35] *Cal. of Pap. Letters*, vii, 373. Adam de Olton, then master, was styled, however, canon of the monastery of St. Anthony, Vienne. *Cal. of Pat.* 1422–9, p. 108.
[36] Reg. Denton, fol. 317.
[37] Ibid. fol. 318.
[38] *Cal. of Pat.* 1467–77, p. 115. After this the post of master was given to one of the canons of Windsor.
[39] Doc. of D. and C. of St. George's, Windsor, St. Anthony's Hospital Accts. xv, bdle. 37, No. 15.
[40] The accounts for 7 Oct. 1494, were as follows:— In herbs, ½d.; in veal to stew at dinner, 10d.; in ribs of beef to roast at dinner, 21d.; in 3 qrs. of mutton for all the house at supper, 20d. On Easter Day, 1495, the sum of 17s. 8d. was expended in four lambs for all, seven capons for the hall, 100 eggs, two green geese for the master at dinner, eighteen chickens, six rabbits for the master at supper, half a 'veal' for the poor men and children at dinner and supper, and 3 gallons of red wine and claret. Ibid. xv, bdle 37, No. 21. 29 Sept. 1501, the meat for broth cost 4d.; twentyfour geese for the hall at dinner, 13d.; lamb for the poor and children, 7d.; 'fyschmen' in the hall for all the day, 7d.; four rabbits for the hall at supper, 8d.; mutton for the poor, 6d. Ibid. xv, bdle. 37, No. 25.
[41] Stow, op. cit. ii, 120.
[42] Doc. of D. and C. of St. George's, Windsor, St. Anthony's Hospital Accts. xv, bdle. 37, No. 25.
[43] Stow, op. cit. ii, 220.
[44] Doc. of D. and C. of St. George's, Windsor, Accts. of St. Anthony's Hospital, xv, bdle. 37, No. 33.

the steward, the schoolmaster, a clerk for the mass of Our Lady, the curate of St. Benet Fink, and the sexton.[45] Provision was still made at the latter date for the twelve poor men, but evidently it was no longer a place where the sick were cared for: probably this work was given up when the best part of the hospital's income was cut off,[46] for although an agent of St. Anthony's was raising money as late as 1537 by collecting offerings and selling hallowed bells for cattle,[47] such efforts must soon have been abandoned. St. Anthony's pigs still existed in 1525,[48] but by this time they too may have disappeared.

The income was then only £55 6s. 3d., and fell short of the expenditure by £40 11s. 11d.[49]

The hospital was despoiled, not by the crown, but by a prebendary of Windsor named Johnson, who gave the almsmen a weekly pension of 1s. each, and turned them out of their houses:[50] as the accounts of 1565 make no mention of commons, it is evident that this event had already taken place.[51] The church was let in Elizabeth's reign to French Protestants.[52]

The property of the hospital in 1565[53] comprised the manors of 'Esehall,'[54] 'Walens,' and 'Fryslyng,' which figure in the hospital accounts at a much earlier date as 'Esthall,' 'Valance,' and 'Thyrstelyng,'[55] and land called 'Jurdens land' in co. Essex; the rectories of All Saints and St. Martin in the city of Hereford, in the possession of the house since 1392;[56] a tenement in Winchester, another in Portsmouth, tenements in London, among them being three tenements near the school, and the capital messuage, called 'Lady Tate's House,' then in the tenure of Sir Henry Sydney and the rectory of St. Benet Fink.

*M. Reddan*

## Masters or Wardens of the Hospital of St. Anthony

This is a revised version of the list in *V.C.H. London,* i.

Reymond de Basterneys, ?1287[57]
John, 1311[58]
Geoffrey de Lymonia, 1380[59]
John Savage, 1382[60]
Richard Brighous, 1385 and 1389[61]
John Macclesfield, appointed 1389; occurs 1417[62]
Adam de Olton, appointed 1423; occurs 1424[63]
John Snell, appointed 1431; occurs 1432[64]
John Carpenter, S.T.P., occurs 1434, 1440; resigned 1444[65]
Walter Lyert, appointed 1444[66]
William Say S.T.P., occurs 1446–63, 1454[67]
Peter Courtenay S.T.P., appointed 1470[68]
Richard Surlond, occurs 1499[69]
Roger Lupton, occurs 1509–10[70]
John Chambre, occurs 1521–2[71]
Anthony Baker, occurs 1545[72]

[45] Harl. MS. 544, fol. 72.

[46] It seems probable, however, that the work had ceased before, for in the hospital accounts from 1494 onward there appears to be no mention of sick persons, while the entries about the poor men are frequent.

[47] *L. and P. Hen. VIII*, xii (1), 934. Letter of Charles Wynfelde to Cromwell, saying that the vicar of Kimbolton had managed almost to suppress the old opinions in his parish, when Harry Cleipulle brought letters under the king's broad seal to collect for St. Anthony's, and the people thinking it was according to the king's wish, offered to the cross and bought the bells Cleipulle had for sale. For the dean of St. George's letter of attorney to Cleipulle, see Anct. D. (P.R.O.), A. 12452.

[48] Rec. of Corp. of Lond. Repert. vi, fol. 101b. The steward of St. Anthony's was to be warned to appear before the next Court of Common Council and show the agreement made between the City and the house concerning St. Anthony's pigs.

[49] Harl. MS. 544, fol. 72.

[50] Stow, op. cit. ii, 120.

[51] Doc. of D. and C. of St. Paul's, A. Box 77, No. 2057.

[52] Stow, op. cit. ii, 120. The rent was £4 a year in 1584. Doc. of D. and C. of St. George's, Windsor, Accts. of St. Anthony's Hospital, xv, bdle. 37, No. 76.

[53] Doc. of D. and C. of St. Paul's A. Box 77, No. 2057.

[54] There is a manor of Easthall in the parish of Bradwell. Morant, *Hist. of Essex*, i, 377.

[55] Doc. of D. and C. of St. George's, Windsor, St. Anthony's Hospital Accts. xv, bdle. 37, No. 4. The document is not dated, but some of the proctors occur in the accounts of 1478–9. Ibid. xv, bdle. 37, No. 15. Valance in this is said to be in the parish of Dagenham. There is a place called Frestling in the parish of Butsbury, see Morant, op. cit. ii, 49.

[56] See note 16.

[57] *Cal. Letter Book A*, 105, n. 1, Dr Sharpe says he may have been the master of St. Anthony's priory, Cornwall.

[58] Doc. of D. and C. of St. Pauls, Liber A, fol. 94b.

[59] *Cal. of Pap. Letters*, iv, 240.

[60] Harl. Chart. 50 D. 59. He is called Procurator.

[61] *Cal. of Pat.* 1381–5, p. 553; Memoranda K. R. Hil. 12 Ric. II.

[62] *Cal. of Pat.* 1388–92, p. 124. John, commander, master, and governor, makes a grant at this date, see Inspeximus, 1423, *Cal. of Pat.* 1422–9, p. 156.

[63] Ibid. p. 108; *Cal. of Pap. Letters*, vii, 373.

[64] Harl. MS. 6963, fol. 24; Sharpe, *Cal. of Wills*, ii, 475.

[65] Doc. of D. and C. of St. George's, Windsor, Denton Reg. fol. 306; Lond. Epis. Reg. Gilbert, fol. 183; Harl. MS. 6963, fol. 68.

[66] Ibid.

[67] Doc. of D. and C. of St. George's, Windsor, Denton Reg. fol. 317; Sharpe, *Cal of Wills*, ii, 524. He was confirmed in his office in 1461 by Edw. IV. *Cal. of Pat.* 1461–7, p. 11; *Parl. R.* (Rec. Com.), v, 520b.

[68] Pat. 49 Hen.VI in Harl. MS. 6963, fol. 116.

[69] Doc. of D. and C. of St. George's, Windsor, St. Anthony's Hospital Accts. XV, bdle. 7, No. 23. (Denton Reg. fol. 306); Ibid. No. 35.

[70] Ibid. No. 27.

[71] Ibid. No. 33.

[72] Harl. MS. 544, fol. 72.

# 44. THE HOSPITAL OF ST. MARY ROUNCIVALL

## INTRODUCTION

The substantial facts in the narrative appear to be correct, although brief. A more complete history is given by David K. Maxfield, 'St. Mary Rouncivale, Charing Cross: the hospital of Chaucer's Pardoner', *Chaucer Review*, 28 (1993), pp. 148–63; and Gervase Rosser, *Medieval Westminster 1200–1540* (Oxford, 1989), pp. 310–21. The hospital is also briefly mentioned in Honeybourne, 'Property' pp. 206–7, in the context of other medieval London hospitals.

A short (draft) history is also provided at: 'Hospital of St. Mary Rouncevall', part of *V.C.H. Middlesex*, xiii: http://www.middlesexpast.net (accessed 10 October 2006).

There have been no archaeological excavations at the site of the hospital and there is no printed source material.

*David Lewis*

This hospital was founded near Charing Cross by William Marshal, earl of Pembroke, in the reign of Henry III, and therefore before 1231, when William the second earl marshal died, and was endowed by him with 100*s.* rent at Southampton, land worth £13 in 'Netherwynter,' and a carucate of land in Ashingdon.[1] It was the chief cell in England of the Priory of St. Mary at Rouncivall in Navarre.[2] The brothers are mentioned between 1244 and 1260 as the patrons of a church in London called St. Mary 'Aylward,'[3] and by the middle of the next century the house had acquired a little more property, but its income must have been derived principally from alms which persons were sent from the hospital to collect.[4] Richard II, on a vacancy of the house about 1382, granted the custody to his clerk Nicholas Slake. On this occasion the prior of Rouncivall protested, and his claim to the ownership of the hospital seems to have been successful;[5] in 1393, however, the king again appointed a warden of the hospital,[6] which probably passed entirely out of the control of the priory at Rouncivall before it came into the possession of the crown under the Act of 1414.[7]

About 1421 the vicar of St. Martin's in the Fields complained to the pope that the master and brothers under pretext of letters of Boniface IX detained tithes and other parochial rights due to him. The genuineness of these and other letters produced by them had appeared so doubtful to the archbishop of Canterbury that he had detained them, and in 1422 he was ordered by the pope to send them to the papal chancery to be examined.[8] The archbishop's suspicions were found to be justified, the letters of Boniface IX, Urban VI, Clement VI, and Urban V were declared forgeries, and the pope commanded that they should be publicly denounced as such and burned, and that those who had forged them and those who knowing them to be false had made use of them were to be punished.[9] The tithes, of course, were restored to the vicar. Poverty probably was the cause of this reprehensible attempt to replenish the convent's funds, for just before this sentence the pope had granted a special indulgence to persons visiting and giving alms for 'the sustentation and repair of the chapel of the poor hospital of St. Mary Rouncevall whose buildings are in need of no small repair.'[10]

Nothing further is heard of the house until 1478, when Edward IV granted it with all its property in frankalmoign to a fraternity or gild consisting of a master, wardens, brethren, and sisters, founded in the chapel there in 1474, for the maintenance of three chaplains and of the poor coming to the hospital.[11] There had been a brotherhood established in St. Mary's in 1385, especially to celebrate the Feast of the Nativity of the Virgin,[12] but whether this had any connexion with the gild of 1474 does not appear.

---

[1] Plac. Cor. Reg. apud Westm. de term Mich. 7 Rich. II, Rot. 21 Midd. printed in Dugdale, *Mon. Angl.* vi, 677.
[2] Dugdale, loc. cit.
[3] Reg. of Fulk Bassett, bishop of Lond. Doc. of D. and C. of St. Paul's, W.D. 9, fol. 51.
[4] *Cal. of Pat.* 1345–8, p. 196.; ibid. 1381–5, p. 117.
[5] *Supra, n.* 1.
[6] *Cal. of Pat.* 1391–6, p. 311.
[7] Stow, *Surv. of Lond.* (ed. Strype), i, 124.

[8] *Cal. of Pap. Letters*, vii, 238.
[9] Ibid. 282–3.
[10] *Cal. of Pap. Letters*, vii, 251.
[11] *Cal. of Pat.* 1476–85, p. 114.
[12] Guildhall MS. 142, fol. 112.

The story of the hospital ends with the dissolution of the fraternity in November, 1544.[13]

At the time of the surrender the hospital possessed a messuage and field in the parish of St. Clement Danes, which it had received from the king in 1542 in exchange for some tenements and a wharf in the parish of St. Margaret Westminster.[14] About 1291 it held some land in Hawkwell and Ashingdon, co. Essex,[15] and in the fourteenth century a rent of 2s. in Norwich[16] and 10 acres of land in Kensington.[17]

The head of the house was styled prior during the thirteenth century,[18] but afterwards master or warden.

*M. Reddan*

## Revised List of Masters or Wardens

This is a revised version of the list in *V.C.H. Middlesex*, i.

Nicholas Slake, occurs 1382[19]
Garcias Martyn,[20] occurs 1389[21]
John Gedeneye, appointed 1393[22]
Nicholas Cook, 1397[23]
John Newerk, occurs 1399[24]
Richard Bromefeld, died 1526[25]
Roger Elys, appointed 1526[26]
William Jenyns, occurs 1542[27]

[13] *L. and P. Hen. VIII*, xix (2), 590.
[14] Ibid. xvii, 283 (54).
[15] Harl. MS. 60, fol. 71.
[16] *Cal. of Pat.* 1307–13, p. 222.
[17] *Cal. of Close*, 1333–7, p. 423.
[18] *Cal. of Pat.* 1272–91, p. 283; 1281–92, p. 476; 1292–1301, p. 14.

[19] *Cal. of Pat.* 1381–5, p. 117.
[20] Surname given in G.L. MS 34004, f. 19.
[21] Ibid. 1388–92, p. 152.
[22] Ibid. 1391–6, p. 311.
[23] T.N.A. KB 9/175 m. 25.
[24] *Cal. of Pat.* 1399–1401, p. 25.
[25] *L. and P. Hen. VIII*, iv, 2002 (27).
[26] Ibid.
[27] Ibid. xvii, 283 (54).

# 45. THE HOSPITAL OF ST. GILES WITHOUT CRIPPLEGATE

## INTRODUCTION

Stow in his account of this hospital may have conflated two distinct institutions. It seems that after 1272 a cell, dependent on Cluny abbey in France was established in the parish of St. Giles, which may have incorporated a hospital or almshouse. It is probable that this house was among the alien priories suppressed *c*.1414: see *Med. Rel. Houses* (1971 edn.), pp. 327, 374). Stow claimed that Henry V rebuilt the house, at the corner of Whitecross and Fore Streets and founded a brotherhood there dedicated to St. Giles. In fact this brotherhood had been founded by a London citizen, Guy Clerk, in 1284–5 in association with the building of a chapel dedicated to the Virgin on the south side of the church of St. Giles. By 1388 the fraternity supported a chaplain and sustained poor members of the brotherhood with weekly payments, see T.N.A. C47/42/205. The fraternity secured licences to hold lands in mortmain in 1392 and 1443 (*Cal. of Pat.* 1391–6, pp. 170, 178 and ibid. 1441–6, pp. 140–1, 207) and this may have enabled it to take over the Cluniac hospital building in the fifteenth century. By 1548 there is no reference to an almshouse, but the fraternity paid alms of nearly £20 every year to sixteen poor householders from rents received from lands which they claimed to have held for a long time (Kitching, *Chantry Certificate*, p. 10).

For the substantial property held by the fraternity, including a Common Hall, see McHardy, *Church in London*, pp. 72–3; Janet Loengard (ed.), *London Viewers and their Certificates* (London Record Society, 26, 1989), nos. 26, 93, 112, 192, 291; *Cal. of Pat.* 1547–8, pp. 294–5; 1548–9, p. 398; 1549–51, pp. 382, 391; 1549–50, pp. 422–3.

*Jessica Freeman*

All that is known about this hospital is the statement of Stow,[1] that there had been such a house in Whitecross Street in the time of Edward I, and that it was suppressed by Henry V, who founded in its place a brotherhood for the relief of the poor.

[1] Stow, *Surv. of Lond.* (ed. Strype), iii, 88.

*M. Reddan*

# 46. THE HERMITS AND ANCHORITES OF LONDON

## INTRODUCTION

The *V.C.H.* entry still provides a useful starting point for information about London solitaries, but several valuable books and articles have been published since it was compiled.

See Rotha Mary Clay, *The Hermits and Anchorites of England* (London, 1914) for a general introduction to the subject of the eremitic life, plus tabulated list of cells and occupants, including London. Dr Eddie Jones at the School of English, Exeter University, is currently updating this work. See also R. M. Clay, 'Further studies on medieval recluses', *Journal of the British Archaeological* Association, 3rd ser. 16 (1953), pp. 74–86 for further primary sources and a discussion of William Lucas and Simon Appulby, ankers at London Wall.

Other useful works include Jennifer Mary Collis, *The Anchorites of London in the Late Middle Ages* (unpub. MA thesis, Royal Holloway and Bedford New College, University of London, 1992); Mary C. Erler, 'A London Anchorite, Simon Appulby: His Fruyte of Redempcyon and its Milieu', *Viator*, 29 (1998), pp. 227–39; Ann K. Warren, *Anchorites and their Patrons in Medieval England* (Berkeley, 1985) and Ann Warren's article 'The Nun as Anchoress: England 1100–1500', in *Medieval Religious Women. Vol. 1: Distant Echoes*, ed. John A. Nichols and Lillian Thomas Shank, Cistercian Studies Ser., 71 (Kalamazoo, MI, 1984), pp. 197–212. Gervase Rosser includes a brief discussion of the house of the anchoress adjacent to St. Margaret's church in *Medieval Westminster 1200–1540* (Oxford, 1989), p. 201, n. 144. Although published much earlier than the *V.C.H.* a useful sketch of architectural details of the chapel of St. James (part of Cripplegate hermitage) was reproduced in A. J. Kempe, '*Capella Sancti Jacobi De Inclusario*, Hermitage on the Wall, or Lambe's Chapel', *Gentleman's Magazine*, n.s., 95 (1825), pp. 401–2.

*Amanda Moss*

Hermits are so different from anchorites, the first being free to wander as they would and the others being actually inclosed in the cell,[1] that at first it seems impossible that any difficulty could arise in distinguishing the two kinds of devotees. Yet it is not always easy to make the distinction, for the word hermitage is constantly used with the meaning of anker-hold,[2] and a recluse is sometimes styled hermit.[3] There is no doubt, however, that both were to be found in London during the middle ages, for bequests to 'every hermit and recluse in London and the suburbs'[4]

were by no means rare, and Edward III in 1370 gave of his alms 13s. 4d. each to three hermits and eight anchorites in London and the suburbs.[5]

There were at least two places in or near the City wall where hermits at one time lived. A cell at Bishopsgate was certainly first occupied by hermits although afterwards by anchorites. The king in 1346 granted to Robert, the hermit of Bishopsgate, his protection for a year while collecting alms in divers parts of England.[6] The same hermitage had been given by the king to a hermit named John de Warwyk four years previously,[7] and a hermit in 1361 seems still to have been the occupant.[8] In 1370, however, a bequest was made to the anchorite of Bishopsgate,[9] and in 1426 mention occurs of a

---

[1] *Arch. Journ.* xxiv, 342.

[2] Fosbroke, *British Monachism*, 494. The hermitage behind the Tower in which a recluse lived is an example of this use. Bayley, *Hist. of Tower of London*, 125.

[3] Friar John Ingram who is designated hermit in a will of 1371, Sharpe, *Cal. of Wills*, ii, 147, is spoken of as a recluse in another of 1376, ibid. ii, 189. There is said at one time to have been an anchorite called the hermit of New Brigge living near the Black Friars. Steele, *Anchoresses of the West*, 100.

[4] Sharpe, *Cal. of Wills*, i, 654; ii, 107, 145, 147, 220, 234, 237; Nichols, *Royal Wills*, 153.

[5] Devon, *Issue Roll of Thomas de Brantingham*, 395.

[6] *Cal. of Pat.* 1345–8, p. 194.

[7] Ibid. 1340–3, p. 501.

[8] Sharpe, *Cal. of Wills*, ii, 107.

[9] Ibid. ii, 146.

woman recluse there.[10] An anchoress of that place is said by Stow to have received 40s. a year from the sheriffs of London.[11]

The hermitage of Cripplegate appears to have been an earlier and more important foundation. It was in existence in the reign of John, who ordered an inquiry about a house which had belonged to Warin the hermit of Cripplegate.[12] The advowson in the thirteenth century belonged to the king,[13] so that the hermitage may have been founded by the crown, but if this is not the case, at any rate it owed much to royal grants and protection. A lane and an area near the City wall had been given by the king at some time previous to 1272 for the enlargement of the chapel of St. James[14] which formed part of the hermitage, and Edward I on several occasions appointed wardens to keep the goods of this chapel from spoliation on the death of the hermit.[15] In 1300 the king granted the custody to William de Rogate, one of Prince Edward's clerks,[16] on condition that he found a chaplain to celebrate in the chapel for the king, and that he increased the income of the place by two marks a year. Possibly the resources of the chapel were not very large even then, for a certain Thomas de Wyreford, the chaplain of a hermitage by Cripplegate, was accused, and found guilty before the bishop of London in 1311, of encroaching on the rights of St. Olave's Silver Street: he had heard confessions and administered sacraments without sufficient authority, and had proclaimed an indulgence to those visiting his hermitage.[17]

The practice of casting the responsibility of the chapel on a keeper was continued by Edward II,[18] apparently with unsatisfactory results, since in 1330 it was said that through the negligence of these keepers the chapel with its ornaments and the houses belonging to the hermitage had not been properly maintained,[19] and at last the king in 1341 made over his rights to the abbot of Garendon.[20] A second chaplain was added in 1347 when Mary de St. Pol, countess of Pembroke, founded in St. James' a chantry for the soul of her late husband,

Aymer de Valence, endowing it with a tenement in Fleet Street and another in Sherbourne Lane.[21]

The history of the chapel from the time it became a cell of Garendon is uneventful.

On the suppression of the abbey in 1536 it came into the king's hands again[22] and was sold by him in 1543 to William Lambe,[23] who left it in 1580 to the Clothworkers' Company with sufficient property to pay a minister to officiate there.[24]

## Revised List of Hermits of Cripplegate

Warin, died 1205[25]
Jordan de Eston[26]
Robert de St. Laurence, appointed by Henry III, occurs 1275;[27] died 1291[28]
William de Wynterburn, appointed 1291;[29] resigned 1296[30]
John de Bello, appointed 1296[31]
Thomas de Wyreford, occurs 1311[32]
Alan Chauns, appointed ?1332[33]
John de Flytewyk, appointed and resigned 1341[34]
John, bishop of Ayobenensis, occurs 1380[35]

A certain William 'le Ermite' or 'le Heremite' disposed of property in the parish of St. Clement Danes in 1265–6[36] and 1268–9,[37] but his hermitage, of course, was not necessarily in that neighbourhood.

[10] Nicholas, op. cit. 250.
[11] Stow, Surv. of Lond. (ed. Strype), ii, 90.
[12] Rot. Lit. Claus. (Rec. Com.), i, 60.
[13] Cal. of Pat. 1274–81, p. 99.
[14] Edward I in 1290 speaks of the grant as made by his predecessors. Ibid. 1281–92, p. 401.
[15] The mayor of London was made keeper in 1275, ibid. 1272–81, p. 99, the constables of the Tower in 1281, ibid. 450, and the treasurer and the custos of London in 1286, ibid. 1281–92, p. 226.
[16] Cal. of Pat. 1292–1301, p. 532.
[17] Lond. Epis. Reg. Baldock and Gravesend, fol. 29.
[18] Grants of the custody were made in 1326 and 1330. Cal. of Pat. 1324–7, p. 251 and 1330–4, p. 14.
[19] Ibid. 1330–4, p. 59.
[20] Ibid. 1340–3, p. 145.
[21] Sharpe, Cal. of Letter Bk. F, 180. The foundation may have been earlier, for the abbey had had licence to acquire two messuages in the City and suburbs from the countess in 1343. Cal. of Pat. 1343–5, p. 133.
[22] Henry appointed two persons to serve the chapel in January 1537 (L. and P. Hen. VIII, xii (1), 311 (28)), at least this is presumably what is meant by the grant of the chapel to William Melton, chaplain, and William Draper, 'literatus,' since it was granted to them again for life in 1548 five months after the sale to Lambe. Ibid. xviii (1), p. 547.
[23] Ibid. xviii (1), 346 (66). Stow in his Survey, iii, 128, says that Lambe obtained it from Edward VI, a mistake noticed by Newcourt, Repert. Eccl. Lond. i, 369.
[24] Newcourt, op. cit. i, 369.
[25] Rot. Lit. Claus. (Rec. Com.), i, 60.
[26] Cal. of Pat. 1258–66, p. 29
[27] Cal. of Pat. 1272–81, p. 99.
[28] Cal. of Pat. 1281–92, p. 464.
[29] Ibid.
[30] Ibid. 1292–1301, p. 185.
[31] Ibid.
[32] Lond. Epis. Reg. Baldock and Gravesend, fol. 29.
[33] Cal. of Pat. 1330–4, p. 233. He is one of four to whom the custody of the chapel was granted, but as he is designated 'heremyt' it seems probable that he would serve the place.
[34] Cal. of Pap. Letters, ii, 554. He had been a Benedictine and had left the order and been sent by the abbot of Garendon to the hermitage. He appears to have soon tired of this and returned to the Benedictines.
[35] A. Gwynn, 'The date of the B-text of Piers Plowman', Review of English Studies, 19 (1943), p. 8.
[36] Hardy and Page, Cal. of Lond. and Midd. Fines, 43. The messuage is described as in 'Denschemanparosch' which sounds like 'Danish men's parish.'
[37] Ibid. 45.

A hermit is mentioned twice in the fourteenth century as living near the church of St. Lawrence Jewry, in 1361,[38] and in 1371 when a bequest was made to Richard de Swepeston by name and to Geoffrey his companion.[39]

There was also in 1361 a hermit at Charing Cross, whose cell must have been the hermitage known in the fifteenth century as the chapel of St. Katharine.[40]

The profession of hermit lent itself easily to fraud, and the impostor who in 1412 was sentenced to the pillory for pretending to be a hermit[41] was probably not the only one of his kind. He is described as going about 'barefooted and with long hair, under the guise of sanctity … saying that he had made pilgrimage to Jerusalem, Rome, Venice and the city of Seville in Spain; and under colour of such falsehood he had and received many good things from divers persons, to the defrauding and in manifest deceit of all the people.' No such inducement to deceive offered itself in the case of the anchorites, who had to obtain the licence of the bishop to become recluses and whose cells were generally attached either to a parish church or to a religious house[42] in order to ensure them the means of subsistence, for in an unfrequented place they might have starved.

Katharine wife of William Hardel constructed for herself in 1227 an anker-hold by the chapel of St. Bartholomew's Hospital,[43] and mention is made in 1228 of an anchorite by the church of 'All Saints Colman,'[44] and in 1255 of an 'inclusa' of St. Margaret Pattens.[45]

Behind the chapel of St. Peter at the Tower of London there was an anker-hold known as the hermitage of St. Eustace, mentioned as early as 1236, when the king ordered a penny to be paid every day to the recluse of this place, of which he was patron.[46] On one occasion it was granted by Henry III to a woman, Idonia de Boclaund,[47] but in 1371 it was held by a man.[48]

At the latter date there was another cell in the immediate neighbourhood, for the Swansnest, the abode of John Ingram, an anchorite[49] in 1371 and 1380,[50] was close to St. Katharine's Hospital.

A cell was built in the turret of the wall near Aldgate by a recluse named John[51] who was living there in 1257–8,[52] but in 1325 the place seems to have survived in name only.[53] It is true Simon Appulby, priest, made his profession as an anchorite in 1513 before the bishop of London in the priory of Holy Trinity,[54] which must have been quite close to the spot, and this would argue that the cell had not disappeared; it is however more likely that Appulby lived in the monastery.

The ankerhold attached to the abbey of Westminster[55] may possibly be traced back to the thirteenth century, since Nicholas the hermit of Westminster occurs in the Pipe Rolls from 1242 to 1245.[56] But the notices are more frequent later. To the anchorite monk in the church of Westminster, John Bares, citizen of London, left 20s. by will in 1384.[57] It is reported that the monk recluse there used his influence to secure adherents to the party of the lords appellant against Richard II.[58] Henry V after his father's death confessed to Humphrey of Lambeth, the anchorite of Westminster.[59] Sir John London, recluse in the church of St. Peter, who figures in the list of benefactors of Syon Monastery,[60] received a bequest of £10 in 1426 from the duke of Exeter.[61] The cell was sometimes occupied by a woman: Henry VI in 1443 gave an annuity of 6 marks to the anchoress there,[62] and forty years afterwards a similar annuity was granted also to a female recluse by Richard III.[63]

The licence of the bishop of London to Beatrice de Meaus in 1307 to live as an anchoress near the church of St. Peter Cornhill in a place where anchorites used to live before[64] proves that the cell

[38] Sharpe, *Cal. of Wills*, ii, 107.

[39] Ibid. ii, 147. In *Anchoresses of the West*, 240, these are said to be recluses, but authority for the statement is not given.

[40] The chapel was granted to the king's servitor, Edmund Tankard, in 1462. *Cal. of Pat.* 1461–7, p. 214. The hermitage is mentioned in a lease by the abbot of Westminster, 1519. Doc. of D. and C. of Westm. Westm. parcel 3, pt. 4.

[41] Letter Bk. I, fol 113, cited by Riley, *Memorials of Lond.* 584.

[42] Fosbroke, op. cit. 492, 494. The author of *Piers the Plowman* knew London well, and while referring to wandering hermits in disparaging terms he evidently approved of anchorites. *Piers the Plowman* (ed. Skeat), i, 2, 3.

[43] *Rot. Lit. Claus.* (Rec. Com.), ii, 181b.

[44] In the will of Richard de Elmham, canon of St. Martin's, *Arch. Journ.* xxiv, 343.

[45] Guildhall MS. iii, fol. 1260.

[46] Bayley, *Hist. of the Tower of Lond.* 125.

[47] Ibid.

[48] Sharpe, op. cit. ii, 147.

[49] He is called a recluse in a will of 1376. Ibid. ii, 189.

[50] Ibid. ii, 147, 228.

[51] *Hund. R.* (Rec. Com.) i, 413, 420. He is here described as a hermit, but it is evident from a fine of 1257–8 that he was a recluse.

[52] Hardy and Page, op. cit. 39.

[53] The garden on the south side of Aldgate called 'The Hermitage' was then leased for 10s. a year to Peter de Staundone. Sharpe, *Cal. of Letter Bk. E*, 193.

[54] Lond. Epis. Reg. Fitz James, fol. 41.

[55] It was on the south of the chancel of St. Margaret's. See Lease of 1730 among Doc. of D. and C. of Westm. Westm. *Extra.* No. 14.

[56] Guildhall MS. iii, fol. 956, 988, 1004.

[57] Lond. Epis. Reg. Braybrook, fol. 389–90.

[58] Stow, *Ann.* (ed. 1615), 318.

[59] Steele, op. cit. 240.

[60] Add. MS. 22285, fol. 70.

[61] Nichols, *Royal Wills*, 250.

[62] Harris Nicholas, *Proc. and Ord. of the Privy Council*, v, 282.

[63] Steele, op. cit. 240.

[64] Lond. Epis. Reg. Baldock and Gravesend, fol. 9.

THE RELIGIOUS HOUSES OF LONDON AND MIDDLESEX

was not then a new foundation.[65] It was inhabited by Beatrice or by another woman in 1324,[66] but in 1345 and 1348 a male recluse was in possession.[67]

Mention is made in 1345 of an anchorite, and in 1361 of an anchoress at St. Benet Fink.[68]

A recluse called Lady Joan lived in St. Clement Danes in 1426.[69]

The anchoress at Allhallows London Wall, for whom the sum of 4 marks was received by the wardens of the church from the bishop of London in 1459,[70] was succeeded in a year or two by an anchorite, William Lucas, who died about 1486. The accounts of this church contain some interesting details concerning recluses of this kind. In these they figure not only as the recipients of charity but as contributors to the church. Among other sums given by Lucas are 3s. 4d. to church work, 2s. 8d. to 'ye makyng of ye new bolles of laton of ye beme,' and 3s. 4d. for painting the church. Simon, to whom the cell was granted after Lucas'

death, gave to the church on one occasion a stand of ale, on another 32s. towards the new aisle, and in 1500–1 he presented a chalice weighing 8 oz. An anchorite's servant probably had to be useful in many ways, for a payment is recorded to Simon's servant for plastering the church wall. Simon the Anker was the author of a treatise called *The Fruit of Redemption*, printed by Wynkyn de Worde in 1514. Since in 1532 a grant of the next presentation was made by the Court of Common Council to an alderman, it must be concluded that the advowson of the cell then belonged to the City.[71] It appears to have been suppressed in 1538, the anker-house being given to the City swordbearer.[72]

There was also a cell attached to the Blackfriars, and here Katharine Foster lived with her maid from 1471 to 1479.[73] It is believed that this house is identical with that inhabited before by an anchorite known as the hermit of New Brigge. The place must have been occupied until the Dissolution, for in 1548 Katharine Man, former recluse of the Blackfriars, relinquished her right to the anchoress-house to the commonalty and received a pension of 20s.[74]

*M. Reddan*

[65] This might otherwise have been inferred from an inquisition of 1324, where the jurati state that the house in which an anchoress lives was built eight years ago by the parishioners of St. Peter's Cornhill on the king's soil. Of course this would not make the date of foundation 1307, but there was often great vagueness as to time. *Parl. R.* (Rec. Com.), i, 419.
[66] Ibid.
[67] Sharpe, *Cal. of Wills*, i, 483, 638.
[68] Ibid. i, 483; ii, 107.
[69] Nichols, *Royal Wills*, 250.
[70] Churchwardens' Accts. of Allhallows, London Wall.

[71] Rec. of Corp. of Lond. Repert. viii, fol. 214b.
[72] Ibid. Repert. x, fol. 36b–37b.
[73] Steele, op. cit. 100.
[74] Ibid.

# PART II

# MIDDLESEX HOUSES

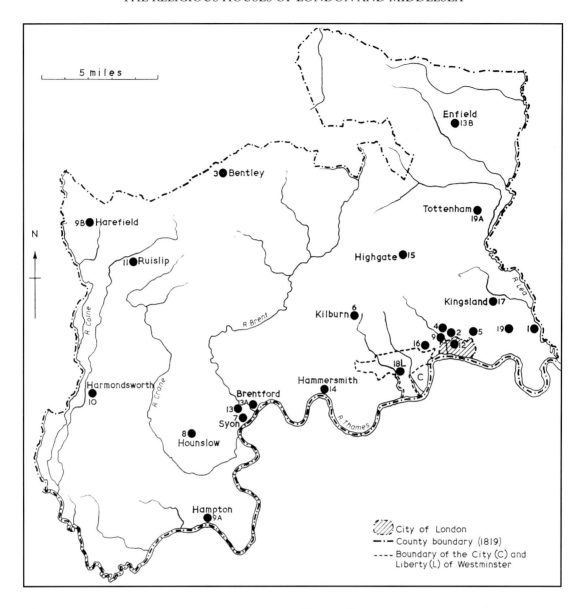

KEY:

BENEDICTINE NUNS
  1. Stratford at Bow Priory

CARTHUSIAN MONKS
  2. Charterhouse

AUGUSTINIAN CANONS
  3. Bentley Priory

AUGUSTINIAN CANONESSES
  4. Clerkenwell, St. Mary's Priory
  5. Haliwell Priory
  6. Kilburn Priory

BRIDGETTINES
  7. Syon Abbey

TRINITARIAN FRIARS
  8. Hounslow Priory

KNIGHTS HOSPITALLERS
  9. Clerkenwell, St. John's Priory
    9A. Hampton *camera*
    9B. Harefield commandery, later *camera*

ALIEN HOUSES
  10. Harmondsworth Priory
  11. Ruislip Priory

HOSPITALS
  12. Aldersgate (in London)
  13. Brentford, All Angels
    13A. Brentford, St. Mary, St. Anne, and St. Louis
    13B. Enfield, St. Leonard
  14. Hammersmith
  15. Highgate, St. Anthony
  16. Holborn, St. Giles-in-the-Fields
  17. Kingsland
  18. Knightsbridge, St. Leonard
  19. Mile End, St. Mary Magdalen
    19A. Tottenham, St. Loy

**SKETCH MAP OF THE RELIGIOUS HOUSES OF MIDDLESEX**
*(Reproduced from V.C.H. Middlesex, i, p. 152)*

# NOTE ON THE MIDDLESEX LEPER HOSPITALS

The *V.C.H. Middlesex* accounts of the leper hospitals or lazar houses around London were written by Marjorie Honeybourne from her article 'The Leper Hospitals of the London Area', *T.L.M.A.S.*, 21(1), 1963, pp. 1–54. Relatively little research specifically on English leper hospitals has been published since, although see C. Rawcliffe, *Leprosy in Medieval England* (Woodbridge, 2006) for an accessible broader study. Though not published, a good overview of the foundation of leper houses of medieval England in general can be found in M. Satchell, 'The Emergence of Leper-Houses in Medieval England, 1100–1250' (unpub. University of Oxford D.Phil. thesis, 1998). This includes a useful Gazetteer of English leper houses, focussing particularly on their dates of foundation and geographical locations (with grid references where known). The entries relating to the London and Middlesex houses do not, however, add a great deal to the *V.C.H.*

Though the original accounts, supplemented by Honeybourne's article, are still very useful, especially for the mid-sixteenth century onwards, recent research by the V.C.H. shows that they are incorrect in assuming that four of the six secular lazar houses were founded by the City of London in the fourteenth century, an assumption made initially by John Stow (Stow, *Survey of London*, ed. C. L. Kingsford (1927), ii. 146), and that the remaining two, Highgate and Hammersmith, were 'taken over' by the City later. Honeybourne's references actually show that only two of the hospitals, Kingsland (Hackney) and the Lock (in Surrey), were founded by the City of London, who paid sums for their maintenance and repair. Of the other two claimed to be City foundations, Knightsbridge was founded by private individuals, and Mile End is likely to have been similarly founded: whereas Kingsland and the Lock received many bequests from London citizens, Mile End and Knightsbridge were almost entirely supported by local bequests and Hammersmith from bequests from nearby parishes (*ex inf.* Jessica Freeman).

The idea that all the leper hospitals were placed strategically around London by authority in an organised way (Honeybourne, p. 5) is therefore wide of the mark, and though the City made some early provision, the majority of the lazar houses were the result of later private enterprise, often by lepers themselves. Knightsbridge and Highgate were founded in the 1470s and the first reference to Mile End is also in that decade; the first known reference to Hammersmith is in 1500. The coincidence of dates suggests they were all founded in response to the royal ordinance of 1472, which threatened penalties if lepers were not sequestered from the community.

In 1549 the six leper hospitals were under the joint governance of two aldermen of London and two commoners of St. Bartholomew's, but the absence of records for St. Bartholomew's before 1549 makes it uncertain how the various lazar houses came to be associated with that hospital; it is probable the connection grew up on an *ad hoc* basis as St. Bartholomew's sought accommodation for its sick poor. The City's involvement with the four private houses was the result of this association, as the City had received St. Bartholomew's as a hospital for the poor from the Crown in 1546, and is the reason why the City had supervision without actually owning them all.

*Patricia Croot*

# HOUSE OF BENEDICTINE NUNS

## 1. THE PRIORY OF STRATFORD AT BOW[1]

### INTRODUCTION

The original *V.C.H.* article provides a good narrative of the priory. In the mid-twelfth century, Mary, daughter of king Stephen, a nun at St. Sulpice des Bois in the French diocese of Rennes, together with several companions, was settled at Stratford after her father became king of England. However, when discord arose with the existing nuns, a new house was founded for the princess at Lillechurch in Kent (see Thompson, *Women Religious*, pp. 131, 166). The role of the prioress of Stratford is discussed in Carol M. Meale, 'Women's Piety and Women's Power: Chaucer's prioress reconsidered', in A. J. Minnis, C. C. Morse, and T. Turville-Petre (eds.), *Essays on Ricardian Literature in Honour of J. A. Burrow* (Oxford, 1997), pp. 39–60 and in Valerie G. Spear, *Leadership in Medieval English Nunneries* (Woodbridge, 2005).

Additional information on the identities of the nuns themselves and also of their staff, tenants, recipients of ecclesiastical patronage and others, as well as on the spiritual services the nunnery provided, may be found in Paxton, 'Nunneries', *passim*, and esp. pp. 312–23. The Appendices list chaplains, lay officials, graduate presentees in the London diocese and recipients of annuities and corrodies.

There is more material on the Priory's property in London in McHardy, *Church in London*, and G. A. J. Hodgett (ed.), *Cartulary of Holy Trinity, Aldgate* (London Record Society, 7, 1971) and in *Documentary Sources*, p. 96.

*Jessica Freeman*

The priory of St. Leonard, Stratford at Bow, first mentioned in 1122,[2] was a house of Benedictine nuns.[3] In the 16th century the nuns accepted a tradition[4] that the house had been founded by a Bishop of London, who was, according to Leland, William, Bishop of London 1051–75.[5] Leland also suggests that William Roscelin granted an estate in Bromley to the nuns,[6] in which case Roscelin may be regarded as co-founder of the house. It would appear more probable that the founder of the priory was Maurice, Bishop of London 1086–1107, or Richard de Belmeis I (1108–27). No manor attributable to this house occurs in Domesday, but a 5-hide manor of Bromley is mentioned in the Middlesex Hidage *post* 1096.[7] Since the foundation almost certainly included land nearby and since this Bromley manor is not attributed specifically to any other holder, it is a fair inference that it was the nuns' manor. Comparison with the Domesday Survey suggests that this manor included 2 hides which in 1086 belonged to the Bishop of London's manor of Stepney and three hides which were held by Robert, son of Roscelin.

The priory stood near the banks of the Lea. The chapel of St. Mary in the priory church served as the parish church for the parish of St. Leonard, Bromley, and its site is indicated today by a small park lying about 200 yards south of Bow Bridge. The priory lay to the south of the church.[8]

In 1535 the priory was worth £121 a year and had possessions in Middlesex, London, Surrey, Cambridgeshire, Essex, Kent, and Hertfordshire.[9] In Middlesex the nuns had the manor of Bromley, to which part of East Smithfield belonged. This property included at least two water-mills on the Lea.[10] From the end of the 12th century the nuns held the advowson of Islington church.[11] In

---

[1] It is variously called St. Leonard Bromley and St. Leonard Stratford; the latter is the style in the earliest reference to the house (1122) and in Dugdale and the *Valor*.

[2] *Rouleaux des Morts*, ed. L. Delisle, 341; *Med. Rel. Houses*, 219.

[3] Guildhall MS. 9531/3, f. 346v.

[4] Ibid. ff. 157, 159v; 9531/10, f. 117v.

[5] Leland, *Collectanea*, i. 55.

[6] Ibid.

[7] See p. 137.

[8] L.C.C. *Survey of Lond.* i. 15–16.

[9] Dugdale, *Mon.* iv. 120–3.

[10] Ibid. 122; *Valor Eccl.* (Rec. Com.), i. 409.

[11] St. Paul's MS. W.D. 9, f. 148v; B.M. Add. MS. 35824, f. 10v.

London the priory held various tenements, devised by citizens, in Ivy Lane,[12] Candlewick Street,[13] the parish of St. Antholin,[14] and the parish of St. Benet Sherehog.[15] In Surrey the nuns held houses, shops, and tenements in Southwark, devised in 1350 by a royal clerk to support a chaplain in the chapel of St. Mary in the priory church,[16] and a number of other small properties and rents.[17] In Cambridgeshire they held the manor of Haslingfield, given to them by Christine de Sumeri and her sons, and confirmed by King Stephen.[18] It was held in free alms.[19] Property in Cambridge itself, which had been acquired by St. Leonard's in the 14th century,[20] had been alienated before the Dissolution. In Essex the priory had lands and rents in Great Oakley, Lambourne, Corringham, Ilford,[21] and West Ham (acquired in the 13th century),[22] a portion of the tithes of Wethersfield,[23] and the rectories of Buttsbury, Berners Roding, and Norton Mandeville,[24] the last by the gift, made before 1188, of Galiena Dammartin and her son Bartholomew.[25] In Kent the nuns had the tithes of the manor of Fawnes,[26] probably in Crundale parish. In Hertfordshire the priory was said in 1535 to receive revenues from East Reed and Braughing, but there is no other record of possessions in these places.[27]

Apart from the two manors of Bromley and Haslingfield the nuns' most valuable properties were their four appropriated churches.[28] Between 1163 and 1183 they were involved in a controversy with the Canons of St. Paul's about Islington church. The matter was finally settled and in the presence of Bishop Gilbert Foliot it was agreed that the nuns were to hold the church from the canons for the annual payment of a mark, and were to find a suitable clerk to serve it.[29] No vicarage was established in any of the Essex churches as long as the priory held them,[30] but one was established in Islington at some time between 1259 and 1347.[31]

An undated charter of Stephen, first recorded in an *inspeximus* of 1366, is the earliest statement of liberties enjoyed by the priory. It is, however, a statement in general terms, for it merely confirmed the priory's tenure in Haslingfield of all the liberties which Christine de Sumeri had there, whatever they may have been.[32] Liberties confirmed to the priory by Henry II included quittance of the shire, the hundred, and assizes, as well as the amercements of its own men in whatever court they were imposed and their chattels if they suffered as felons; the confirmation was produced in an *inspeximus* of 1318.[33] The last was successfully maintained in 1229 when the chattels of one of the priory's Bromley men were delivered to the prioress in virtue of the charters of Henry II and Richard I.[34] All these liberties were confirmed in 1189, 1198, 1247, 1318, 1366, 1390, 1408, and 1414.[35]

In 1293–4 *quo warranto* proceedings were taken to determine the priory's right to conduct its own assizes of bread and ale and its own view of frankpledge and its right to a pillory in Bromley. The prioress denied that the priory had a pillory but defended its other privileges by producing charters granted by Richard I and Henry III.[36] Five years later *quo warranto* proceedings were taken to test the priory's right to sac and soc, tol and team, infangentheof, and similar conventional privileges, together with view of frankpledge and to the chattels of felons and amercements of its own men. The evidence showed that all these liberties, except view of frankpledge, had been confirmed by Henry III, and a local jury swore that the priory had enjoyed view of frankpledge from time immemorial.[37] In 1347 the priory was able to prove that the manor of Haslingfield was held in free alms, and therefore was exempt from the aid levied in that year.[38]

The dowries of the nuns who entered it and gifts from the citizens of London also increased the wealth of the convent. In 1282 Archbishop Pecham, who was trying to secure the admission of a particular postulant, promised that the convent would acquire numerous friends and rich benefactors through her.[39] There is, however, no specific information about the dowries of Stratford nuns. The priory occurs frequently in the wills of the citizens of London[40] and in those of local people.[41] Some of the bequests

---

[12] *Cal. of Wills in Court of Husting*, ed. R. R. Sharpe, ii (1), 120.

[13] Ibid. ii (2), 446.

[14] Ibid. 490–1.

[15] Ibid. 522–3.

[16] *Cal. Pat.* 1348–50, 463.

[17] Dugdale, *Mon.* iv. 122; *Valor Eccl.* (Rec. Com.), i. 409.

[18] Dugdale, *Mon.* iv. 120.

[19] *Cal. Close,* 1346–9, 185.

[20] B.M. Add. MS. 5843, p. 357.

[21] *Valor Eccl.* (Rec. Com.), i. 409; Dugdale, *Mon.* iv. 122.

[22] *Cal. Pat.* 1338–40, 261–3.

[23] Dugdale, *Mon.* iv. 123.

[24] Ibid. 122.

[25] Guildhall MS. 9531/6, ff. 173v–4.

[26] *Valor Eccl.* (Rec. Com.), i. 409.

[27] Ibid.; Dugdale, *Mon.* iv. 123; *V.C.H. Herts.* iii. 251 306–15.

[28] Dugdale, *Mon.* iv. 122.

[29] St. Paul's MS. W.D. 9, f. 148v.

[30] Ibid. ff. 56, 58v, 87v; Newcourt, *Repertorium*, ii. 118, 439–40, 503.

[31] St. Paul's MS. W.D. 9, f. 48v; Newcourt, *Repertorium*, i. 677.

[32] *Cal. Chart. R.* v. 194.

[33] Ibid. iii. 383–4.

[34] *Close R.* 1227–31, 213.

[35] Ibid.; *Cal. Chart. R.* i. 323–4; iii. 384; v. 194–5, 325, 441, 469.

[36] Dugdale, *Mon.* iv. 121.

[37] Ibid.

[38] *Cal. Close,* 1346–9, 185.

[39] *Reg. Epist. Joh. Pecham* (Rolls Ser.), i. 356.

[40] *Cal. Wills in Court of Husting,* i. 84; ii (1), 8, 37, 114, 119, 177, 185, 206, 212, 220, 224, 234, 300, 341, 349.

[41] Guildhall MS. 9171/1–10, *passim.*

were made with a request that prayers be said for the donor or his family.[42] Sometimes the bequests were made not to the convent but to individual nuns;[43] in 1433 Alice Seyntpoull left a gift to Idonea Appelby, a nun there,[44] and in 1477 John Gayton, 'Steward of the House and Church of Saint Leonard called the Nunnery', left a small pension to his daughter Elizabeth,[45] who later became the prioress. In 1392 the widow of a draper left 20 marks to a relative – possibly a daughter – living at St. Leonard's, on condition that she became a nun.[46] London priests also remembered the convent in their wills.[47] It was probably by means of such bequests that some city properties were burdened with rents to the nuns such as those reserved for them in 1273, when some tenements in the parish of St. Stephen, Walbrook changed hands.[48]

The priory received occasional gifts from the king. Small money grants from Henry II are recorded in the pipe rolls.[49] In the 13th century the nuns had gifts of wood from the forest in Essex;[50] a grant of this kind, made in 1267, gave timber for use in the building operations on the priory church.[51]

The nuns had to make a number of annual payments out of these endowments. The annual mark for Islington church continued to be paid to St. Paul's until the Dissolution, and the canons also received a number of other payments. Synodals and procurations had to be paid annually for the churches held by the nuns, and there were small payments to other religious houses.[52] In 1371 the nuns acquired the farm of two parts of the tithes of Buttsbury from the priory of Tutbury (Staffs.). They were to pay 13s. 4d. every year at Easter, and 40s., as well as all the arrears, in case of default.[53] One payment expected from St. Leonard's was felt to be exceptionally heavy. In 1339 the prioress complained that she was forced to pay a disproportionate sum for the upkeep of a wall along the Thames known as 'le priouressewal' in respect of some land she held in West Ham Marsh. This land, acquired in the 13th century, had been under water for several years, yet the prioress had often been

distrained to pay whilst other landowners, whose holdings in the area were more profitable, were not assessed. The prioress brought her grievances before the commissioners of walls and ditches, who decided that all who held land in the marsh should share the burdens and that St. Leonard's should not be taxed disproportionately.[54]

So small a religious house was not likely to play an important part in the political or ecclesiastical history of the kingdom. In the 14th century, however, Stratford for a time became fashionable. The convent appears to have been the residence of Elizabeth of Hainault, and at her death in 1375 she seems to have been on terms of intimacy with the Stratford nuns.[55] She directed that she should be buried in the chapel of St. Mary in the priory church and it has been concluded that she lived in the convent.[56] It was presumably to visit her aunt that Elizabeth of Ulster, wife of Prince Lionel, went to Stratford in 1356; her infant daughter Philippa seems to have stayed at the nunnery.[57] Elizabeth of Hainault made bequests to a nun called Argentyn[58] who was also mentioned as one of the nuns in 1380–1;[59] she occurs twice in Elizabeth's will. If, as has been suggested,[60] Argentyn was the model in part for 'madame Eglentyne' in the Canterbury Tales,[61] she must have been a woman of a certain gentility and fashion.

Although in the 14th century the priory acquired prestige from the visits of members of the royal family,[62] this must have been a severe strain on a house that was far from wealthy. In 1282 the prioress called attention to the poverty of the convent.[63] As a house which claimed to be small and poor, Stratford was often exempted from taxation. In 1235 and again in 1237 part of the money owed by the nuns for the tax on movables was remitted.[64] When a second tax was raised in 1237, the commissioners were ordered, pending investigations, to take nothing from Stratford;[65] later, all that was owed by the priory on that occasion was remitted.[66] In 1359 the nuns were excused payments for their lands in Bromley which had been flooded by the Lea.[67] This seems to have been regarded as an important

42 Cal. Wills in Court of Husting, ii (2), 446, 490–1; Cal. Plea and Memoranda R. (Lond.), 1458–82, 102.
43 Cal. Close, 1354–60, 517–18; Cal. Wills in Court of Husting, i. 34, 110; ii (1), 120; Guildhall MS. 9171/5, f. 123.
44 Ibid. 9171/3, f. 350v.
45 Ibid. 9171/6, ff. 234v–6v; p. 177.
46 Cal. Wills in Court of Husting, ii (1), 303.
47 Reg. Abp. Langham (Cant. and York Soc.), 356; W.A.M., Cart. of St. Martins-le-Grand, f. 94v.
48 B.M. Harl. Chart. 47. I. 44.
49 Pipe R. 1183 (P.R.S. xxxii), 75; 1188 (P.R.S. xxxviii), 30, 31.
50 Close R. 1231–4, 24; 1234–7, 50; 1247–51, 211, 422; 1251–3, 58; Cal. Pat. 1232–47, 493.
51 Close R. 1264–8, 309.
52 Dugdale, Mon. iv. 122–3.
53 Cartulary of Tutbury Priory, ed. A. Saltman (Staffs. Rec. Soc. 4th ser. iv), 98–99, 252.

54 Cal. Pat. 1338–40, 261.
55 Guildhall MS. 9171/1, f. 16v.
56 J. M. Manly, Some New Light on Chaucer, 202–20.
57 B.M. Add. MS. 18632, f. 101v; E. A. Bond, 'New Facts in the Life of Geoffrey Chaucer', Fortnightly Review, 15 Aug. 1866.
58 Guildhall MS. 9171/1, f. 16v.
59 E 179/44/347.
60 Manly, New Light on Chaucer, 202–20.
61 Chaucer, Canterbury Tales: Prologue, l. 121.
62 See above.
63 Reg. Epist. Joh. Pecham (Rolls Ser.), i. 366.
64 Close R. 1234–7, 55, 424.
65 Ibid. 1237–42, 11.
66 Ibid. 29.
67 Cal. Pat. 1358–61, 175.

precedent, since the pardon was exemplified by Richard II in 1380.[68] In 1409 it was conceded that the nuns should be excused all payments for their lands in Bromley for the fifteenth and all payments for a fifteenth less than £28.[69] In 1354 an indulgence was granted to those who visited the priory[70] and in 1411 another was granted to all who visited it and gave alms for the fabric and for the support of the community.[71]

In 1282 the prioress had a dispute with Archbishop Pecham. The archbishop ordered her to admit as a nun the daughter of one of the citizens of London. The prioress refused, saying that the girl was too young and that the convent had its full complement of nuns and could not afford any more. Pecham dismissed these excuses as frivolous, reminded the prioress that she owed him obedience as her metropolitan, and threatened to excommunicate her.[72] She then turned for help to the Bishop of London, stating, in addition to her other objections, that the girl was deformed. Replying to a letter on the subject from the bishop, Pecham alleged that the greater part of the convent was on his side, and that only the prioress was making difficulties. He added that he wished that not only the Stratford nuns, about whom there were so many scandals, but all other worldly nuns were deformed, so that they might lead no one into sin.[73]

Although the Bishop of London was the diocesan as well as the patron of the nunnery,[74] little is known of its relations with him. Bishop Gilbert Foliot presided when the nuns made their agreement with the Canons of St. Paul's about Islington church.[75] In 1282, as has been seen, Bishop Richard Gravesend interceded on their behalf with the Archbishop of Canterbury. The only occasion recorded of the bishop being present at the clothing and profession of new nuns was in 1397, when Bishop Braybrooke celebrated High Mass in the priory church and received the profession of six novices.[76] Only in the 16th century is there any information about the bishop's part in the election of prioresses. The bishop's vicar presided at the election in 1520 and the bishop subsequently confirmed the new prioress.[77] In 1528 Prioress Eleanor Sterkey resigned her office into the hands of Bishop Tunstal. The nuns, perhaps under pressure, decided to settle

the election of the new prioress by way of simple compromise, and to this end submitted their rights to the bishop, who appointed Sybil Kirke, formerly Prioress of Kilburn.[78] It is possible that this action and appointment was connected with some attempt to reform the nunnery, for a party gathered round Eleanor Sterkey, who was still living in the convent after her resignation. A petition to the king was followed in 1533 by a second petition, this time to Cromwell, asking for the removal of the 'supposed prioress' and claiming that Sybil Kirke made up the shortness of meat and drink with a fresh supply of threatening words; the old lady 'who is the rightful prioress' was like to die for want of sustenance.[79] It is possible that this was a somewhat exaggerated picture of an attempt by the new prioress to enforce the Rule. The new prioress was supported by Bishop Stokesley, whose chancellor confirmed her in office and encouraged her to be firm.[80] The outcome of these disturbances is not known, but for some years after the Dissolution Sybil Kirke continued to receive the pension due to the head of the house.[81]

In 1354 there were 30 nuns in the priory[82] but the poll tax of 1380–1 gives the names of only 14 nuns, including the prioress and sub-prioress.[83] There were eight professed nuns and one novice at the election of the prioress in 1520,[84] and ten professed nuns at the election in 1528.[85]

As a small house, with an income of less than £200, St. Leonard's was among those foundations suppressed in 1536. In 1537, after the dispersal of the nuns, the site of the priory was granted to William Rolte, together with most of its property except some of the London city tenements, which were granted to Sir Ralph Sadler.[86] Rolte did not hold the lands for long, and by 1540 the whole property had passed to Sadler.[87] In 1541 his tenure was confirmed by the king, and the original grant to William Rolte was cancelled.[88]

There are no means of determining the plan of the convent. The royal grant of 1537 mentions the house and site of the priory, and the church, 'steeple', and churchyard.[89] The 'steeple' disappeared, but the eastern limb of the church continued to be used for worship. The description

[68] Ibid. 1377–81, 534.
[69] *Cal. Chart. R. 1341–1417*, 441, 469.
[70] *Cal. Papal Regs.* iii. 523.
[71] Ibid. vi. 228.
[72] *Reg. Epist. Joh. Pecham* (Rolls Ser.), i. 356.
[73] Ibid. 366.
[74] See p. 156.
[75] Ibid.
[76] Guildhall MS. 9531/3, f. 346v.
[77] Ibid. 9531/9, ff. 157–9.

[78] Ibid. 9531/10, ff. 117–19v.
[79] *L. and P. Hen. VIII*, vi, p. 677.
[80] Ibid.
[81] Ibid. xiii (I), p. 574; xvi, pp. 354, 356.
[82] *Cal. Papal Regs.* iii. 523.
[83] E 179/44/347.
[84] Guildhall MS. 9531/9, f. 157.
[85] Ibid. 9531/10, f. 117v.
[86] *L. and P. Hen. VIII*, xiv (1), p. 161.
[87] B.M. Add. MS. 35824.
[88] *L. and P. Hen. VIII*, xvi, p. 383.
[89] Ibid. xiv (1), p. 161.

by Lysons[90] and prints of the early 19th century[91] give little idea of the appearance of this part of the church in the Middle Ages. In 1805 the church was a small rectangular building, lighted by an haphazard collection of windows of indeterminate dates; the medieval floor appears to have been considerably lower than the ground level of 1805,[92] and the east window had been replaced *c.* 1700 by a primitive apse for the communion table. Inside there were signs that there had been a south aisle, but the most striking feature was the Norman choir arch, with dog-tooth ornament, at the west end. The arch had been blocked up and everything to the west of it had disappeared by 1805. The building as Lysons saw it survived until 1842, although in a dilapidated condition. In 1842–3 a new church in the neo-Norman style was erected on the site.[93] This was destroyed in the Second World War.

*H. P. F. King*

[90] Lysons, *Environs of Lond.* ii. 62.
[91] Guildhall Libr. interleaved copy of Lysons, *Environs of Lond.*
[92] J. Dunstan, *Hist. of Par. of Bromley*, 72.
[93] Ibid. 70; E. Sinker, *The Church in Bromley for a Thousand Years*, 30–34.

## Revised List of the Prioresses of Stratford

This list is taken from *Heads of Religious Houses*, vol. 2, p. 612, and vol. 3 (forthcoming).

Lettice, occurs 1203
Alice, occurs 1226/7
Katherine, occurs 1245; *c.*1250
Lucy, occurs between 1264 and 1284
Letitia de Markam, occurs 1321
Isabel la Blunt (Blounde), occurs 1341, 1344
Maud (Matilda), occurs 1368, 1371
Mary Suharde, occurs 1375, 1397
Alice Burford or Burwood, occurs 1412 and before 1425
Elizabeth Frunceys, occurs 1420
Amy or Anne Gracious or Graciane, occurs before 1436; died 1436
Margaret Holbeche, occurs 1436
Katherine Washburne, occurs 1477
Elizabeth Gayton, occurs 1505; died 1520
Helen Hyllard, elected 1520; died 1522[94]
Eleanor Sterkey, elected 1522; resigned 1528
Sybil Kirke, elected 1528; surrendered 1536–7

[94] Guildhall MS. 9531/9, ff. 158–58v; *L. and P. Hen. VIII,* iii (2), p. 986.

# HOUSE OF CARTHUSIAN MONKS

## 2. THE LONDON CHARTERHOUSE

### INTRODUCTION

The original account by Knowles remains an excellent guide to the history and development of the Carthusian house, from its foundation in 1371 to the Dissolution. It drew on the author's own published work and the earlier history by W. H. St. J. Hope.

For a more recent overview of the Carthusian Order in England, see G. Coppack and M. Aston, *Christ's Poor Men: The Carthusians in England* (Stroud, 2003); J. A. Gribbin, *Aspects of Carthusian Liturgical Practice in Later Medieval England*, Analecta Cartusiana, 99:33 (Salzburg, 1995).

Perhaps the most significant recent work on the history of the London Charterhouse since 1963 has been by Andrew Wines, whose unpublished Cambridge doctoral thesis, 'The London Charterhouse in the Later Middle Ages: an institutional history', was completed in 1998. In print by the same author is 'The University of Life and the London Charterhouse: practical experience versus scholarly attainment within the Carthusian leadership', in *The Church and Learning in Later Medieval Society: Essays in Honour of R. B. Dobson*, ed. C. M. Barron and J. Stratford (Donington, 2002), pp. 100–9. The Library of the Charterhouse is discussed by A. I. Doyle, 'Libraries of the Carthusians', in Vincent Gillespie (ed.), *Syon Abbey, with the Libraries of the Carthusians*, Corpus of British Medieval Library Catalogues, 9 (2001), pp. 614–29.

Of particular importance has been recent work on the archaeology and material culture of the Charterhouse, described fully in B. Barber and C. Thomas, *The London Charterhouse*, MoLAS Monograph Series, 10 (London, 2002). Related articles include M. Barratt and C. Thomas, 'The London Charterhouse', *London Archaeologist*, 6 (1991), pp. 283–91 and C. Bowlt, 'The great conduit and the London Charterhouse', *London Archaeologist*, 10 (2003), pp. 121–3. The Survey of London's volume on the London Charterhouse is currently in preparation, and will deal primarily with the post-Dissolution structures.

For the London property of the House, see *Documentary Sources*, pp. 56–7. For details of the surviving archives of the London Charterhouse, together with a list of estates held by the house, see the English Monastic Archives project web site, URL: http://www.ucl.ac.uk/history/englishmonasticarchives/index.htm (accessed 28 February 2007).

Additional information on the property and personnel of the house can be found in Wines, 'London Charterhouse'.

*Matthew Davies*

The London Charterhouse,[1] known as the House of the Salutation of the Mother of God, was founded at Smithfield, a little to the north-west of the city wall, by Sir Walter Manny and Bishop Michael Northburgh of London in 1371, but the foundation was only the final event in a prolonged series of negotiations and changes of plan.[2] The

---

[1] The story of the London Charterhouse has often been told. See in particular L. Hendriks, *The London Charterhouse*, a careful account, with appendix, by a modern Carthusian; W. H. St. J. Hope, *Hist. of the London Charterhouse*, a posthumous publication of material assembled by a distinguished antiquary, with many original documents printed; E. M. Thompson, *English Carthusians*, a careful, scholarly account using all the known material and printing a number of documents; and D. Knowles and W. F. Grimes, *Charterhouse*, an account of the post-Second World War excavations and discoveries, with plans and diagrams of the monastic buildings.

[2] The principal authority for the early history is a register or cartulary now at the P.R.O. (L.R. 2/61); the narrative portions of this are printed all but entirely (although not consecutively) in Hope, *Charterhouse*, 28–36, 47–52, 77–88, which also contains many of the relative charters. The register was compiled shortly before 1500 by an anonymous monk.

Black Death had reached England in the summer of 1348, and was at its height in London in the early months of the following year. When the capacity of the city graveyards proved inadequate, Manny, as a work of charity, rented from the Master and Brethren of St. Bartholomew's Hospital for an annual sum of twelve marks a close of some 13 acres known as Spital Croft, with the understanding that he should be granted full possession when he could provide the hospital with property of equal value in exchange.[3] The graveyard was dedicated on the feast of the Annunciation 1349 by Ralph Stratford, Bishop of London, who preached on the word 'Hail' of the angel Gabriel. This circumstance, itself possibly a consequence of Manny's devotion to this particular incident in the gospel, gave the name that the future monastery was to bear, the House of the Salutation of the Mother of God.

On the same day the foundations were laid of a chapel wherein masses were to be celebrated for those buried in the graveyard, for Manny intended to establish a college of twelve secular priests with a provost, of the type that was becoming common. This project was never executed, although papal permission for it was obtained.[4] Instead, a hermitage for two inmates was erected, in which continual prayers were to be offered for the dead.[5]

So matters stood for a number of years. The first suggestion of a Charterhouse seems to have come from Michael Northburgh, Bishop of London 1355–61, who on his journeys to and from the papal court had visited and admired the Charterhouse at Paris. He approached Manny with the suggestion that they should co-operate in the foundation of a monastery in Spital Croft.[6] The suggestion was in harmony with a recent change in the policy of the Carthusian Order. The Grande Chartreuse and all early Charterhouses had been founded of set purpose in desert places, and even the *conversi* or lay brethren had been accommodated in buildings at a considerable distance from those of the monks. Hitherto the English foundations at Witham and Hinton (Som.) and at Beauvale (Notts.) had conformed to this pattern. More recently, however,

continental houses had been founded on urban sites, as at Paris, Bruges, Cologne, and Liège, where the strict and secluded community had served as a living contrast to the worldliness and vice of a great city. Northburgh hoped with reason for a similar result in London. Manny was agreeable to the proposal,[7] and the bishop approached the priors of Witham and Hinton.[8] The Carthusians, at least in the early centuries of their Order's existence, rarely made foundations spontaneously as a 'swarm', like the Cistercians, but responded to an invitation from a founder who was expected to provide the buildings and endowment. In this case the priors accepted the invitation; both died shortly afterwards, and it was left to a subsequent Prior of Hinton, John Luscote, to raise the matter again with Manny when on a visit to London.[9] Manny was still willing to act, and after some delay the general chapter in 1370 accepted the new foundation and appointed Luscote, relieved of his charge at Hinton, as its administrator.[10] When, however, he arrived in London with a companion, a deacon *redditus*[11] named John Gryseley, he found that no building had been started. Manny had offered the Hospital of St. Bartholomew the manor of Streetly (Cambs.) in exchange for their lands; the manor, however, owed service to the Bishop of Ely, who was supported by his chapter in maintaining that he could not alienate the rights of his see without papal permission.[12] This was obtained with the assistance of Simon Sudbury, Bishop of London, whose aid Luscote had solicited, and who offered the Bishop of Ely sufficient compensation for the loss of service. The requisite papal permission was given by Urban V in May 1370, when he committed to Archbishop Whittlesey the decision as to the sufficiency of Sudbury's proposed compensation, and Whittlesey's licence was duly issued in June.[13] These and other delays, caused partly by the chapter of St. Paul's and partly by an anchoress who lived alongside the graveyard chapel, had held up all building operations. Even now events moved slowly. It was not until December that the inquisition *ad quod damnum* returned a verdict that the king

---

[3] L.R. 2/61, ff. 10–10v; Hope, *Charterhouse*, 29–30; transactions also recorded in Stow, *Survey*, ii. 81, 82, and *Chron. Galfridi le Baker*, ed. E. M. Thompson, 99.

[4] Bull of Clement VI cited in that of Urban VI printed in Hendriks, *Charterhouse*, 360–2, and Hope, *Charterhouse*, 27–28.

[5] Two hermits in 1354, Thomas Stapelow and Walter of Dorset, obtained an indulgence of 40 days for all contributors and bedesmen (E 135/15/1). This document, dated from Avignon, specifically gives the dedication of the church as 'the Assumption' not 'the Annunciation', and the Assumption is one of the days when the indulgence may be gained, but all this may be the error of a foreign scribe.

[6] L.R. 2/61, ff. 30–31.

[7] Ibid. ff. 31–32; cf. charter cited ibid. ff. 21–22 (*Cat. Anct. D.* ii. B 2315), and also bull of Urban VI, n. 12 above.

[8] L.R. 2/61, f. 32 cites letter.

[9] Ibid. f. 33.

[10] C. le Couteulx, *Annales Ordinis Carthusiensis, s.a.* 1370, 1398.

[11] A *redditus* was a vowed inmate of a Charterhouse, of status immediately below the monks and above the *oblates* and *conversi*; a clerk *redditus* was at this time always a deacon; cf. Thompson, *Carthusians*, 123–4, 172, n. 2, correcting Hope, *Charterhouse*, 13–14.

[12] L.R. 2/61, ff. 34–35.

[13] Ibid. f. 34; Lambeth MSS., Reg. Whittlesey, f. 28v; royal permission to alienate Streetly given 7 May 1370; cf. *Cal. Pat. 1367–70*, 415.

would suffer no loss by the foundation, and two more months passed before the royal licence was issued.[14] At last, on 28 March 1371, came Sir Walter Manny's foundation charter,[15] and about the feast of the Ascension (15 May) the founder and the prior made an agreement with Henry Yevele, the celebrated master mason, for building the first cell and beginning the great cloister.[16] Seven months later, on 15 January 1372, Manny died, and was buried before the high altar[17] in the chapel of the graveyard, now to be the monastic church.

Meanwhile Prior Luscote, as 'visitor' of the province, had been authorized to summon monks from each of the existing houses to become founding members of the new community: a monk and a lay brother from Hinton, two priests from Witham in addition to John Gryseley, and two from Beauvale.[18] With them he lived in makeshift buildings for many years; indeed, Prior Luscote died in 1398 before the communal rooms and the great wall of the enclosure had been completed.

In contrast to the slow progress with the buildings, the nucleus of property owned by the Charterhouse was complete within twenty years.[19] Spital Croft or, as it was re-named, New Church Haw, was conveyed to Manny and others by St. Bartholomew's Hospital in 1370, and at the same time the Hospital conveyed to them about 3 acres of land north of the main block;[20] the Hospitallers of St. John in Clerkenwell had conveyed another piece of 3 acres northwest of the Pardon churchyard to Manny,[21] but for some reason it did not pass to the monks either by Manny's foundation charter or at his death. It was therefore bought on behalf

of the monks and subsequently released, along with all the other properties, to King Edward III and by him granted to the Charterhouse in 1376.[22] Shortly afterwards, in 1377, the builders were faced with a problem. The great cloister was planned on the ample scale of 300 by 340 feet; as projected its eastern alley and cells would lie outside the parish boundary, which was also the eastern boundary of New Church Haw, and the construction was in consequence halted. The land, however, belonged to St. Bartholomew's, who once more came to the rescue and made over 4 acres to the monks.[23] This transfer completed the site of the monastery with its offices, gardens, and orchards, today bounded on the east by Goswell Road, on the north by Clerkenwell Road, and on the west by the gardens at the rear of houses in St. John's Street. Two more grants of land, the one by the Hospitallers of St. John in 1384, the other by Westminster Abbey in 1391, gave the Charterhouse fields to the north and north-west of their existing property.[24] All these parcels of land combined to give the monks a compact area of some 30 acres, forming a parallelogram almost 300 by 600 yards in extent, and giving space not only for an orchard surrounding three sides of the cloister, but also for a vegetable garden, hayfield, and wilderness to the north – the last-named harbouring at least the smaller species of game.[25] This area remained without addition or diminution until the suppression of the house.

The original endowment of the Charterhouse consisted of £2,000 from Michael Northburgh, together with some articles of plate, and the manors of Ockholt in Romney Marsh (Kent) and Knebworth (Herts.) from Sir Walter Manny, together with a claim to debts and arrears amounting to £4,000, due to Manny from the king and the Black Prince.[26] In the event the monks had little profit from Manny's legacies, as Ockholt was partially submerged by the tides, Knebworth taken from them unjustly, and the royal debts permanently dishonoured.[27] As a consequence the Charterhouse depended for the major part of its income on the gifts, large and small, in cash and in real estate, occasional

[14] Hope, *Charterhouse*, 24–25 (from P. Bearcroft, *Hist. Account of T. Sutton*, 174–5); *Cal. Pat.* 1370–4, 44.

[15] L.R. 2/61, f. 21; *Cal. Pat.* 1370–4, 44. Charter preserved at Charterhouse.

[16] 'Henrico Revell' in L.R. 2/61, f. 35, but it is clear that Yevele is indicated: he appears later among benefactors: *Cal. Pat.* 1391–6, 160.

[17] L.R. 2/61, f. 12; Hope, *Charterhouse*, 35: '*Sepultusque … in ecclesia predicta … ante gradum majoris altaris*'.

[18] L.R. 2/61, f. 11v; Hope, *Charterhouse*, 35 (names given).

[19] Map of this property, in parcels as acquired, in Knowles and Grimes, *Charterhouse*, 19; this assumes, as did the present writer in 1952, the inclusion of Pardon churchyard (see n. 28).

[20] Deed in L.R. 2/61, f. 15. G. S. Davies, *Charterhouse in Lond.* 4–6, and Hope, *Charterhouse*, 18, assert the identification of this land with Pardon churchyard. Thompson, *Carthusians*, 168, denies this, stating that Stow is the sole authority for the bishop's connexion with Pardon churchyard. This seems to overlook the reference in Hope, op. cit. 5 to the medieval chronicler Geoffrey le Baker (see n. 11 above): '*episcopus Londiniensis emit illam croftam Nomenneslond vocatam*', but even so the grant by Sir Thomas Docwra in 1514 of 'a chapell called the Pardon chapel … and … the chapellyard', printed in Malcolm, *Londinium Redivivum*, i. 382, seems to prove that St. John's still held the area at that date.

[21] L.R. 2/61, f. 19; Hope, *Charterhouse*, 22–23.

[22] E 303/Lond./34 (cf. also / 149); *Cal. Pat.* 1374–7, 380–6. The manor of Huntingfield (Kent) was granted 6 Mar. 1377: *Cal. Pat.* 1374–7, 434.

[23] Hope, *Charterhouse*, 26; *Cal. Pat.* 1377–81, 238 (18 May 1377).

[24] Hope, *Charterhouse*, 26.

[25] Clerkenwell Rd. was formerly known as 'Wilderness Street'. In 1473 a general chapter prohibited hunting by secular persons on the Charterhouse property (Bodl. MS. Rawlinson D 318, f. 153v).

[26] L.R. 2/61, ff. 13v–14; Hope, *Charterhouse*, 77–78. Manny's will, dated St. Andrew's day 1371, is in Lambeth MSS., Reg. Whittlesey, f. 120v.

[27] L.R. 2/61, ff. 78–79.

or substantial, from personal friends and humbler donors, mainly Londoners. The founders of cells are enumerated below; in addition, the 'Register' and the evidence of wills show a constant stream of gifts and legacies of property, money, and valuables from the foundation to the early 16th century. As might be expected, the greater part of the property so devised lay in or near London, and consisted of tenements in the City and suburbs, and pastures and gardens on the outskirts, but there were a few manors and some house property at a distance, and the rectories of at least five churches. The monks seem to have found difficulty with distant property, no doubt because it was impossible for one of their own body to visit or supervise it; some of the original property was very soon lost, and there is also mention of two manors in Kent, Plumstead and Hintingford, and a church in Somerset, Norton Veal (now Norton St. Philip),[28] lost, so it was alleged, through the sharp practice of enemies. The house was in financial difficulties as early as 1393, and early in the reign of Henry IV the monks were reduced to such straits by losses and obligations that they were forced to appeal to the king, who in 1403 took the Charterhouse into his hands for a time and administered its affairs.[29] Forty years later Henry VI acknowledged further losses by a licence to acquire in mortmain property of £40 annual rent, and added a second tun of wine yearly to that given by Edward III.[30] The only major benefaction of land in the later 15th century was the gift by Edward IV, 'through the persuasion and advice of Thomas Colt', of the alien priory of Ogbourne (Wilts.), with a manor and other property in Great Ogbourne (Ogbourne St. George) and Little Ogbourne (Ogbourne St. Andrew).[31] Hitherto King's College, Cambridge, had had a title to Ogbourne, and it was some years before the Charterhouse was able to realize the gift. They were helped by Bishops Alcock of Ely (1486–1500) and Russell of Lincoln (1480–94) and the final arrangement was in force from about 1500. By that time the College was in possession, farming the property, and paying a yearly rent of £33 6s. 8d., about half of the rent they received, to the Charterhouse.[32]

The bulk of the land at a distance was, so far as can be seen, farmed out for a lump annual sum, but the monks appear to have kept in hand the demesne at Bloomsbury, where they employed a bailiff, to provide dairy produce for the house. Their own gardens and orchards adjoining the monastery would have sufficed for vegetables and fresh fruit. So far as can be seen from the procurator's accounts over a run of nine years (1492–1500)[33] receipts of all kinds fluctuated greatly according as gifts and legacies were forthcoming or not, or as house property fell into disrepair or was lost for one reason or another. Moreover, a well-connected and energetic procurator, such as Philip Underwood, with wealthy relatives in the City, could manage, by calling in debts, soliciting gifts, and making the most of rents, to swell the annual receipts considerably. Underwood's predecessor in 1492–3 could only realize £589 in receipts; Underwood raised this to £1,067 in his first year, and in his last account of 1500 this had risen to £2,012. There is some evidence that Underwood cared more for administration and money-winning than for the Carthusian life; he was removed from office after eight years and in 1514 by special dispensation transferred himself from the Charterhouse to the Knights of St. John at the nearby Clerkenwell Priory.[34] Thirty years after Underwood had ceased to be procurator his successor of the day returned to the commissioners of the tenth in 1536 a gross income of £736.[35]

The fabric of the London Charterhouse was constructed over a long period of years. The two founders had provided land and a sum of money, but both they and the monks seem to have relied on private benefactors to come forward and finance the building. Thus the great cloister was constructed cell by cell as funds permitted, and since the names of the donors have been preserved, it is possible to date the progress within fairly narrow limits. The London monastery was from the first intended to be a 'double' house, that is, one for twenty-four monks and a prior. The cells were built round the cloister in a clockwise direction beginning at the south-western angle, where the doorway led to the outer world, and they were distinguished by the letters of the alphabet which, with one letter doing duty for I and J, V representing also U and W, and three bearing the letter S, gave a total of twenty-five cells. The donors[36] and the approximate date of the cells were as follows:

| | |
|---|---|
| A. | Sir Walter Manny and Sir William Walworth (1371) |
| B. | Sir William Walworth (1371) |
| C. | Adam Fraunceys (after 1374) |
| D. | Walworth, applying bequest of John Lovekyn (after 1374–5) |

[28] Ibid. f. 79.

[29] Cal. Pat. 1401–5, 174 (8 Nov.).

[30] Ibid. 1441–6, 104 (30 June 1442).

[31] Ibid. 1461–7, 141, 176 (23 Feb.); cf. Cal. Papal Regs. xii. 308–9 (13 Jan. 1469); V.C.H. Wilts. iii 394–6.

[32] Cf. L. and P. Hen. VIII, i (1), p. 319; xiv (2), pp. 99, 347; King's Coll. Camb., Ledger Bk. i, ff. 172v–3v; Mundum Bk. for 1502–3. The writer owes these references to Mr. J. Saltmarsh.

[33] S.C. 12/25/55.

[34] Hendriks, Charterhouse, 73.

[35] Valor Eccl. (Rec. Com.), i. 430–1.

[36] L.R. 2/61, ff. 12–12v, 14–14v; Hope, Charterhouse, 49, 80. Dates discussed in detail in Hope, op. cit. 68–73, and in Knowles and Grimes, Charterhouse, 25–26 (notes).

| | |
|---|---|
| E. and F. | Adam Fraunceys (after 1374) |
| G., H., and J. | Walworth and Lovekyn (after 1374–5) |
| K. | Mary of St. Pol, Countess of Pembroke (after 1376) |
| L. and M. | Adam Fraunceys (after 1374) |
| N. | Felice Aubrey (after 1378) |
| O. | Margaret Tilney (after 1393) |
| P. | Sir Robert Knolles and Constance his wife (after 1389) |
| Q. | John Buckingham, Bishop of Lincoln (probably after 1398) |
| R. and S. | Thomas Hatfield, Bishop of Durham (probably after 1381) |
| T. | William Ufford, Earl of Suffolk (after 1381–2) |
| V | Richard Clyderhow (after 1419) |
| X. | John Clyderhow (c.1436) |
| Z. | Joan Brenckley (after 1406) |
| S. | Margery Nerford and Christine Upstones (probably before 1394) |
| S. | Robert Manfield, Provost of Beverley (probably after 1419) |

This list of donors of cells shows very clearly how wide was the appeal of the Charterhouse. We can divide the twenty-odd benefactors into at least five distinct classes – the nobility, the hierarchy, the soldiers of fortune, the office-holding, administrative class, and the prosperous citizens and their wives. It may be noted that the last two cells on the south side near the church (Z and S) may well have been completed before those in the east alley of the cloister, as also the sacrist's cell, below the treasury near the church. Altogether the completion of the full tale of cells took some sixty years. We are told that in 1412 nineteen had been completed.[37]

The other buildings were even longer in achieving completion. The chapel, originally built for the graveyard by Manny, was used as the conventual church. The Carthusians, differing from every other order of monks and canons in this, gave no architectural prominence to their churches. The only one to remain in a fair state of preservation, that of Mount Grace (Yorks. N.R.), is even smaller and meaner in exterior appearance than that of the London Charterhouse must have been. The original building was a simple rectangle of 94 by 38 feet, divided internally into presbytery, choir, and a small (25 by 35 ft.) 'body of the church' at the western end, divided from the choir by a wooden screen with two altars against its western face. Into this space the public, including even women, asserted their right of entry, and it was only in 1405 that an extension to the west, 30 feet in length, was provided in response to urgent commands of Visitors to exclude women

from the monastic church.[38] This ante-chapel was separated from the original church by a second screen, and called the chapel of St. Anne. In the year of its consecration, however, the two regular visiting superiors from abroad forbade women to visit the church at all. Nevertheless, the original 'body of the church', augmented now by the 'chapel' of St. Anne, remained accessible to men, and benefactors continued to found chapels and to erect tombs. Some of these chapels are specifically mentioned in the records of the monastery,[39] others have been identified after excavation, and yet others are only known to have existed through mention in a post-Dissolution survey. Those whose sites are known with certainty were as follows:[40] due south of the high altar the small (12 by 15 ft.), almost square chapel of St. John the Evangelist was built out of a legacy by Robert Boteler, and consecrated in 1437. South of the original 'body of the church' was a somewhat larger chapel (19 by 22 ft.) dedicated to St. Michael and St. John the Baptist, and adjoining this to the east a smaller one (12 by 16 ft.) of St. Jerome and St. Bernard. Both were built and endowed by Sir John Popham (d. 1463–4), whose tomb was in the larger of the two, and were consecrated in 1453. On the north side lay two chapels: that to the west, corresponding to Popham's chapel of St. Michael, was the chapel (18 by 20 ft.) of Sir Robert Rede (d. 1519), dedicated to St. Catherine; adjoining it to the east was that of St. Agnes, founded by William Freeman and consecrated in 1453. The exact position and dimensions of this last chapel are unknown, as its site is covered by existing buildings. Adjoining the presbytery to the north, beneath the existing 'tower', was the vestibule to the chapter-house, and in it were two altars dedicated to St. John the Baptist and St. Hugh of Lincoln. Finally, there is documentary record of two small chapels to the east of the high altar, but it is not clear whether they were on ground level or were on the first floor and connected with the prior's 'new cell' which lay behind the church.[41] The chapter-house, an essential requirement for the regular life, had not been begun at the death of Prior Luscote, and the altar in the room, dedicated to St. Michael, was not consecrated until 1414.[42]

---

[38] L.R. 2/61, ff. 12v–13; Hope, *Charterhouse*, 49–50.

[39] L.R. 2/61, ff. 16–17; Hope, *Charterhouse*, 84–88.

[40] Fuller account and plan in Knowles and Grimes, *Charterhouse*, 51–63.

[41] Cf. S.C. 12/36/26, and extracts in Knowles and Grimes, *Charterhouse*, 84–86.

[42] Chronicler states that the chapter-house had not been begun at Luscote's death: L.R. 2/61, f. 12v; Hope, *Charterhouse*, 49; but a will of 10 Feb. 1394 shows money left 'ad faciendum opus cementarium cujusdam novae domus capitularis': *Cal. Wills proved in Court of Husting*, ed. R. R. Sharpe, ii. 309; Hope, *Charterhouse*, 91. For consecration see L.R. 2/61, f. 13; Hope, *Charterhouse*, 51.

---

[37] L.R. 2/61, f. 12v; Hope, *Charterhouse*, 49; cf. L.R. 2/61, f. 14, and Hope, op. cit. 79.

A Carthusian church, by primitive tradition and decrees of general chapter, was simple, austere, and without elaborate ornament, but here, as in some other respects, the monks of London had to pay a price for the support and endowment they received from the city at their gate. Rich well-wishers not only gave them ornaments and built and furnished chapels, but demanded that their bodies should rest in the church under tombs of their own specification.[43] From the instructions of testators[44] and the inventory of the commissioners of suppression[45] we can gain an impression of the appointments of these chapels, with their screens and retables. Woodwork, alabaster carvings, paintings, and silverwork were set off by the damask and brocades of the curtains, frontals, and vestments.

In a Charterhouse, in contrast to other monastic houses, the community rooms were very small and few in number. Dormitory and warming-house, infirmary, noviciate, and abbot's lodging formed no part of the complex, and the refectory or frater was used only on Sundays and feast-days, and had to accommodate only a small community. At the London Charterhouse the frater lay between cell A (the prior's) and cell B, and was presumably built in conjunction with those cells about 1371. Accommodation for the lay-brothers, stores, and guests lay outside the great cloister to the south-west of the south-west angle, where the exit lay to the outside world. Here there were ultimately two courts. One, immediately to the west of the church, formed the so-called Little Cloister (41 by 35½ ft.), the Master's Court of the modern establishment. It was constructed in 1436[46] and its western range of buildings held the guest rooms, needed in any case for visiting monks, and occupied also in London in the early 16th century by a few privileged laymen. Beyond this again to the west lay the slightly larger court (the modern Wash-House Court) round the three outer sides of which lay the quarters of the laybrothers, kitchens, brewhouse, and cellars. The laundry apparently lay outside the cloister east of the chapter-house. Of these buildings, the Little Cloister was constructed in 1436 from a legacy of John Clyderhow. For the lay-brothers' quarters no documentary evidence is available, but the existing buildings are clearly of the early Tudor period (1490–1535), and it is possible that the letters I.H., which are picked out in darker brick on an external wall of the court, are those of Prior Houghton.

Finally in the last decades of the House's existence, a new cell was built for the prior and three little cells to accommodate the influx of postulants under Tynbygh or Houghton. These were situated at the south-east corner of the precinct, east of the church, and approached from the cloister by a door or passage west of cell Z.[47]

One more feature of the monastery remains to be noted: the piped water-system.[48] Originally the monks no doubt depended upon wells, but a Carthusian monastery, with its numerous individual cells, felt the need for a distributed supply, and in 1430 we find John Ferriby and Margery his wife enfeoffing the prior and convent with a spring in their meadow called Overmede at Islington, and with a strip of land for laying the pipes of a conduit.[49] This spring was a mile north of the Charterhouse, and the monks secured permission from the owners of the intervening land, the Hospitallers of St. John of Jerusalem at Clerkenwell and the nuns of St. Mary's Priory, Clerkenwell, to lay lead pipes under their pastures.[50] Later both those houses drew water from the Islington springs by similar conduits. The cost of this installation was met by gifts from William Symmes and Anne Tatersale, and in the latter half of 1431 the water was brought into the great cloister. Medieval water engineers, like their modern counterparts in the public utility services, often drew plans of the piping to assist future maintenance workers. This was done at the Charterhouse, and an elaborate plan exists,[51] giving not only the location of the pipes, buildings, and taps, but showing also in elevation the church and other features of the southern range, together with the *age*[52] or conduit-house in the middle of the great cloister, which resembles the fountain in the Great Court at Trinity College, Cambridge. It was an elaborate erection containing the cistern into which the main discharged, and whence the water was drawn off by pipes to the cells and offices of the house. Several copies of this plan exist; the oldest and most elaborate, covered with descriptive annotations, may date from soon after the installation and is certainly earlier than about 1500, although it bears later notes dated 1512. Fifteen years after the water had been laid on, three brewers endeavoured to assert the right of those living near the Charterhouse to

[43] Hope, *Charterhouse*, 100–4, has list of burials, partly from Coll. of Arms MS. A. 17.

[44] Hope, *Charterhouse*, 89–99.

[45] L.R. 54/11.

[46] L.R. 2/61, f. 13; Hope, *Charterhouse*, 52.

[47] Cf. Knowles and Grimes, *Charterhouse*, 74–82.

[48] Hope, *Charterhouse*, 107–44.

[49] Ibid. 133–4; L.R. 2/61, f. 98v.

[50] L.R. 2/61, f. 13; Hope, *Charterhouse*, 51.

[51] Original roll preserved at Charterhouse and reproduced in Hope, *Charterhouse*, 107; several later copies exist. Cf. Knowles and Grimes, *Charterhouse*, 35, and account in Hope, *Charterhouse*, 107–33, based on same writer's article in *Archaeologia*, lviii. 293–312.

[52] For the term '*age*', see Hope, *Charterhouse*, 141–2, with citations from Ducange.

the regular overflow, and filed a bill in Chancery that the executors of William Symmes should be summoned to support their claim. The executors, however, gave testimony in favour of the monks; they were left by their benefactor entirely free to do what they willed with their surplus water, and judgement was given accordingly in 1451.[53] Six years later the original spring in Overmede showed signs of failing. Margery, the widow of the original donor, was still alive and was now married to Lord Berners; she and her husband therefore gave permission for the monks to use other springs in the same field.[54]

The site of the Charterhouse, alongside a public graveyard on the outskirts of the city, rendered its inmates liable to disturbances and visits of all kinds, especially in the early years before the cloister and enclosure wall were completed. The two last decades of the 14th century were a time of general unrest. The Peasants' Revolt of 1381 had met with some support in the City and the Archbishop of Canterbury had been murdered by the mob, while almost at the same time the Lollards and their supporters were responsible for anti-clerical and anti-monastic agitation. These currents of feeling may have helped to excite irresponsible citizens who already had a grudge against the nuns of Clerkenwell and the Carthusians for occupying what was claimed as a public space hitherto used by the citizens for games and recreation. On three or four occasions crowds surrounded the house, destroying buildings and moving boundary walls.[55] Less violent, but felt as a more constant burden, was the practice of citizens in regarding the church as a public one in which women as well as men could worship. Fear of violence and sense of obligation for benefactions combined to make the monks chary of enforcing their rights,[56] and privacy was not finally secured until 1405, when the regular Visitors from abroad ordained that a strong wall should be built south of the church, and that women should not be allowed within it.[57]

The London Charterhouse came into being when the Carthusian Order was about to undergo a period of stress. The hermits of the Grande Chartreuse, originally a group who had every expectation of remaining remote and alone, had gradually developed into an order with a constitution modelled in part on that of the Cistercians. The governing body was

the General Chapter, meeting yearly at the Grande Chartreuse on the fourth Sunday after Easter, and consisting of the community there and the priors of all other Charterhouses, under the presidency of the Prior of the Grande Chartreuse. This chapter passed legislation, settled appeals, ratified elections, and appointed Visitors. As the Order spread it was divided into provinces for the purpose of visitation and supervision; provincial Visitors were appointed, usually from among the priors, although General Chapter could always depute Visitors from outside for a particular purpose. As the Order for a long time had only two small houses in England (Witham, 1178, and Hinton, 1227), no province had been erected and Visitors had been appointed from France, but in 1343 a third house had been founded at Beauvale (Notts.), and it may be that the experience of thirty years of war between England and France, together with the prospect of an important foundation in London, led the chapter in 1370 to institute an English province. John Luscote was appointed 'rector' of the new venture and provincial prior over the other houses.[58] Henceforth the London Charterhouse came to have a kind of unofficial precedence, and the disciplinary missives or, as they were called, 'charters', of the General Chapter to the various houses all passed through the hands of its prior.

The English province and the London Charterhouse had been in existence for less than ten years when the Great Schism began in 1378. The Carthusians, like the other international orders, were divided regionally in their allegiance. The English province followed the nation into the camp of the Roman Pope Urban VI in 1380, and in 1385 the general chapter of this section of the Order was transferred to Seitz in Austria. English priors were excused from the long and circuitous journey, but English affairs were discussed at Seitz and decisions communicated to England until the Order was reunited in 1411.

Decisions of General Chapter from time to time directly affected the London Charterhouse. Thus in 1405 the chapter at Seitz sent two Visitors from Holland who made rigorous decrees on enclosure;[59] in 1490 the chapter allowed the Bishop of Lincoln, John Russell, at the time 'conservator' of the rights and privileges of the Carthusians, to build a house within the precincts.[60] Shortly after this, a more important question arose. One of the Visitors, Prior John Ingleby of Sheen, took exception to the frequent acceptance of gifts and benefactions made to individual religious. The community of London

---

[53] Ibid. 129–32.

[54] Ibid. 142–3.

[55] Hope, *Charterhouse*, 49–50, 58; L.R. 2/61, ff. 12v–13, 14. These riots have left traces in the records: *Cal. Close*, 1389–92, 77 (23 Oct. 1389); 1402–5, 516 (6 May 1405).

[56] *Cal. Papal Regs.* v. 256 (17 Mar. 1399): women gaining Porziuncola indulgence may enter church, choir, and cloister.

[57] L.R. 2/61, ff. 50–51; Hope, *Charterhouse*, 43–44.

[58] Le Couteulx, *Annales, s.a.* 1370, 1398.

[59] L.R. 2/61, ff. 50–51; Hope, *Charterhouse*, 43–44.

[60] Bodl. MS. Rawlinson D 318, f. 156v.

took this ill, and in 1494 brought up at General Chapter a series of questions on the subject. Might a prior allow a donor to give a sum of money to be spent for the benefit of a particular monk? Might small objects such as books be given to individuals for life? Might a gift, made without conditions to an individual, be kept by the prior for that individual's use? Might the sick and aged be allowed to retain a few pence for medicine? Might lands or rents be accepted on condition that the income should be divided between the monks or priests for their use? All these questions reflected common problems in the London Charterhouse. Those who had received advice or edification, or who wished to secure prayers, naturally wished to show their gratitude or gain their end by means of gifts to an individual. Every one of the above questions had been answered implicitly in the affirmative by the contemporary black monks, and it is therefore significant that the chapter returned a firm negative to all. This produced division in the London convent, since certain legacies had been accepted, one of which allotted a yearly half-mark to the prior and procurator, in return for prayers, and the other an annual 20s. to be divided among all the priests celebrating an anniversary. Prior Ingleby, the Visitor, was called in as arbitrator, and used his powers to suspend several of the capitular decisions, but the stricter party appealed to the General Chapter of 1496, and the fathers there upheld the firm answers of their predecessors.[61]

Few details of the lives of individual monks have been preserved. The elderly monk who compiled the 'Register', apparently between 1488 and 1500, had, when a young monk, known three elders, John Nevyll, Thomas Gorwey, and William Hatherley, sometime Prior of Hinton, who had themselves known John Homersley, who had entered the house in 1393. Gorwey in particular, one of Homersley's novices, had often told the chronicler of his way of life. 'Homersley', he recorded, 'was a man of great simplicity and gentleness, who walked without blame in the way of the commandments of God and the observances of the Carthusian Order. He loved his cell and its solitude, and he shut his mouth against evil, lest he should transgress in his speech. He spoke rarely and in few words of things of good repute, but he justified the word of God by his works.' He never ceased from copying books for the church, frater, and cells, and when written he took them to the prior's cell; 'he took no steps to see that they were given to anyone in particular, or put in any special place, but leaving them with the prior he went back in silence to his cell'. If he was ever

pressed to receive gifts or money from a benefactor, 'he took it straightway to the prior's cell and left it with him. If he failed to find the prior there he left the money on the ground by his door, laying a tile on it if it was windy, and thought no more about it'. The chronicler goes on to relate various visions and trials of Homersley, who died shortly after 1440.[62]

After the account of Homersley in the 'Register', and the notes of various gifts, we have no personal details of individuals before the priorate of William Tynbygh, which began in 1500. Thenceforward until the end, the principal authority for the domestic life of the house is the 'history' of Maurice Chauncy, who was a young monk there in the last half-dozen years of its existence. The son of John Chauncy, a landowner of Sawbridgeworth (Herts.), he was born in 1509 and became in due course a student of the law at Gray's Inn. He took the habit at the Charterhouse at about the time of Prior Houghton's election. Although, as we shall see, he failed to stand firm to the end in opposition to the Royal Supremacy, he retained his sense of vocation, crossed to Flanders in 1546, and became a professed monk of the Charterhouse of Bruges, whence he returned in 1555 as leader of the group that refounded Sheen in Mary's reign. His chronicle of the last days of the London priory, *Historia aliquot Martyrum*, has a complicated literary history, still to be fully elucidated, and exists in at least five versions. The work is in aim a piece of hagiography or propaganda; Chauncy was neither a critical historian nor a writer of genius; he was frankly a panegyrist, and had a love of the marvellous which impairs his credit even when he is writing of what he knows well. He often digresses from his narrative and expatiates in scriptural quotations and parallels. Nevertheless, his basic sincerity and trustworthiness are unquestionable, and he was an eyewitness of much of what he describes.[63]

He begins with a short notice of Prior Tynbygh. Here he was writing, long after the event, of what he had only hearsay information. He tells us that Tynbygh, a native of Ireland, although not necessarily an Irishman by race, joined the community in 1470 after a conversion of which the details give every sign of being mythical. William Tynbygh was indeed almost certainly the son of Nicholas Tynbygh, gentleman, a member of a

[61] Ibid. ff. 158 sqq; Thompson, *Carthusians*, 273–5. Some of this material also in Jesus Coll. Camb., MS. Q.A. 12.

[62] L.R. 2/61, ff. 14v–15v; Hope, *Charterhouse*, 80–84.

[63] Thompson, *Carthusians*, 343–53, discusses the literary history of *Historia Martyrum* (to 1932), and it is again discussed in M. Chauncy, *Passion and Martyrdom of Holy Eng. Carthusian Fathers*, ed. G. W. S. Curtis, 28–33. A briefer bibliographical note, which takes account of the rediscovery of the original version in Guildhall MS. 1231, is in D. Knowles, *Rel. Orders in Eng.* iii. 222–3. In the text above the edn. cited is that of V. M. Doreau (Montreuil-sur-Mer).

well-known Dublin family whose fortunes can be traced in the records of the city of Dublin from 1332 onwards.[64] He became in turn sacristan and vicar (or second-incommand), and was elected prior in 1500, remaining in office for nearly thirty years; he resigned in 1529 and died less than two years later. Whatever discount we allow for Chauncy's enthusiasm, there can be no question of Prior Tynbygh's holiness of life, and he duly received from the General Chapter of 1531 the single word of the traditional laconic panegyric: '*qui sexaginta annis laudabiliter vixit in ordine*'.[65] To him, more than to any other, must be attributed the high standard of discipline and observance that distinguished the House of the Salutation even among its sister houses in the reign of Henry VIII.[66] He is recorded as having solemnly warned his brethren that their strength and security lay in unity; in later years these words were taken as evidence of a spirit of prophecy. It was he who received to the habit John Houghton, Sebastian Newdigate, and others who were to show themselves true Carthusians in the hour of trial.

Tynbygh was succeeded by John Batmanson, around whose name some confusion has occurred.[67] There were in fact two men of that name. The elder, a civilian and judge of some eminence, who appears in the records shortly before and after 1500, disappears from sight about 1516, and the opinion has become current that he joined the Carthusians and became prior. Recently, however, it has been shown that the Carthusian Batmanson was ordained deacon in 1510; this clearly distinguishes him from his namesake, and other evidence makes it possible, if not probable, that the two were father and son. The younger Batmanson became in due course Prior of Hinton 1523–9 and was called thence to hold office at London. He was a scholar of some note, although without university training, and wrote against Luther. He was even considered sufficiently qualified to be asked by Edward Lee, later Archbishop of York, to criticize Erasmus's *New Testament* when it appeared in 1516. This drew upon him not only some caustic comments from the sensitive humanist, but a long letter from Sir Thomas More in which More, who had known the Carthusian when he was a student of the law, attacked Erasmus's opponent with considerable

asperity.[68] Although by no means an old man when he was elected prior, Batmanson died after two years in office, and was succeeded by John Houghton.

Houghton, who was born in 1485–6, came of gentle family in Essex.[69] He had taken a degree in laws at Cambridge from God's House, later Christ's College, and had then studied in private for the priesthood and lived at his father's home as a secular priest before taking the monastic habit in 1515. Seven years later he became sacrist and after five more years procurator. In 1530–1 he was elected Prior of Beauvale, but in six months' time the unanimous vote of the London community recalled him to be prior of the house of his profession. Under his rule the good observance was raised to a still higher level by the personality and example of a prior who combined holiness of life with a genius for leadership and inspiring guidance. Maurice Chauncy's glowing pages describing the Charterhouse as he knew it in the years 1531–5 may reflect both the youthful hero-worship and the later sorrowful nostalgia of the writer, but in their main lines they carry conviction, and we may well believe his statement that Houghton would have deserved canonization as a monk, even had he not died as a martyr.

The reputation of the Charterhouse had stood very high for at least fifty years. At the end of the previous century the young Thomas More had spent four years as an inmate of the house in his early days at the law, attending the offices and following much of the monastic routine before deciding that his call lay elsewhere. Twenty years later Chauncy, also a law student, was familiar with the remark that those who wished to hear the divine service worthily performed should go to the Charterhouse.[70] In Houghton's day we are told that Sir John Gage, vice-chamberlain of the court, thought of becoming a monk there when he could no longer serve the king. Not only the quality, but the number also of recruits was remarkable, and it is probable that here, as at contemporary Mount Grace,[71] there was a 'waiting-list' of postulants, and that it was this that made necessary the addition of a group of 'little' cells at one corner of the cloister.

There were in Prior Houghton's day thirty choir monks and eighteen lay brethren, and of the monks some twenty were under the age of thirty-eight when he took office.[72] Of several of these we have

---

[64] For this identification, first made by Prof. Aubrey Gwynn, S.J., see the Dublin periodical *Studies*, xlix. 328.

[65] *Charta capituli generalis* 1531, cited by Hendriks, *Charterhouse*, 74; Chauncy, *Historia aliquot Martyrum*, 74. Notices of Tynbygh, Batmanson, and Houghton in *D.N.B.*, but all require considerable revision.

[66] Some accounts, etc., surviving from Tynbygh's priorate are summarized in *L. and P. Hen. VIII*, viii, p. 232.

[67] In this matter the author is indebted to Dom Andrew Gray for information. Refs. in Knowles, *Rel. Orders*, iii, App. I.

[68] *Corresp. of Sir Thomas More*, ed. E. F. Rogers, 165– 206; cf. Knowles, *Rel. Orders*, iii, App. I, and P. S. Allen, *Desiderii Erasmi Opus Epistolarum*, iv. 259. More was in the Charterhouse 1499–1503.

[69] Chauncy, *Historia*, ch. iv, *De sancto et discreto regimine Prioris*.

[70] Chauncy, *Historia*, 69.

[71] Cf. Knowles, *Rel. Orders*, iii. 239, n. 6.

[72] Chauncy, *Historia*, 58, 65.

information from Chauncy or elsewhere. After the prior, the two personalities most clearly visible are those of William Exmew and Sebastian Newdigate.[73] Exmew, born *c.* 1506, was of good family and had received a humanist's education at Christ's College, Cambridge; his knowledge of Greek in particular is noted. Under Prior Houghton he served first as vicar and then as procurator, a very common sequence of offices. Newdigate came of a landowning family of Harefield (Mdx.), later of Arbury (Warws.). He had many connexions with families in other counties: his mother was a Nevill of Lincolnshire and two of his sisters were to become ancestresses of the Dormers and Stonors, two well-known recusant families of the Elizabethan age. Two other sisters were nuns, of Haliwell and Syon, and two brothers, knights of Malta. He himself had been a page at court and later a gentleman of the privy chamber; he had left the royal service for the Charterhouse when the matter of the divorce was mooted. Other members of the community were Humphrey Middlemore, another man of good family[74] and procurator in 1535; Richard Bere, nephew of the great Abbot of Glastonbury, John Rochester, brother of Sir John Rochester, comptroller of the household under Mary; and James Walworth, perhaps a son of the City family that had been among the first benefactors of the house. Of the others, Everard Digby, Oliver Batmanson, and John Boleyn bore well-known names. Equally well-known to history, although for other reasons, was Andrew Boorde or Bord,[75] a medical student of some note. Boorde had always been something of a misfit, and in 1535 had already received some kind of dispensation from the full observance.[76] He was later, after the first executions, but before the end of the house, to depart altogether for the career of a secular priest. Boorde was not the only difficult character with whom Houghton had to deal. There were George Norton, who fell into melancholy, threatened suicide, and was dispensed, later becoming a canon in the West Country; Nicholas Rawlings, sometime secular priest, who had been professed when ill before his full noviciate was up, and had ever since cherished a grievance; John Darley, who left during the troubles to take a 'service' as a secular priest at Salisbury; and Thomas Salter, who spoke ill of his brethren and superiors to their enemies.[77]

The Carthusians, along with all other subjects of the king, were required in the spring of 1534 to swear to the first Act of Succession, and thus to accept the annulment of Henry's first marriage by Cranmer and the legitimacy of Anne Boleyn's offspring.[78] Their sympathies had unquestionably lain with Queen Katherine, whose marriage they considered valid, and they had shown interest in Elizabeth Barton, although they were not so far committed with her as their brethren at Sheen. When the commissioners arrived on 4 May to tender the oath Houghton replied in the name of all that Carthusians did not meddle with the king's affairs; they asked only to be left in peace. He added that he could not see how a marriage of such long standing could be declared invalid. He was therefore conveyed to the Tower along with his procurator, Humphrey Middlemore. After deliberation there they agreed to take the oath, so far as was lawful, and were sent home, where they found the community still unwilling to swear. The commissioners, Bishop Roland Lee and Thomas Bedyll, were unsuccessful at their first visit, and at their second, on 29 May, they obtained the adhesion only of Houghton, Middlemore, and six others. Finally, Lee and Sir Thomas Kytson, one of the sheriffs of London, who brought a band of men-at-arms, were successful in extracting an oath from all.[79] So far as can be seen from Chauncy's narrative, the opposition of the monks was based on a disapproval of the Boleyn marriage rather than on a realization, such as influenced More and Fisher, that papal supremacy was at stake, for when in June 1534 commissioners endeavoured to extract an acceptance of the royal supremacy, at least nine of the community refused to take the oath, when such a refusal was not as yet criminal.[80]

Houghton knew well that further demands would come, and urged his monks to spend their time in prayer and preparation for their trial. Less than a year in fact elapsed before the Act of Supremacy (November 1534), followed by the Treasons Act, laid anyone who denied that the king was supreme head on earth of the Church of England under liability to a charge of high treason. In the spring of 1535 commissioners were appointed to secure general acknowledgement of the royal supremacy; this was usually obtained by administering an oath upon the gospels in terms of acceptance. The preparations made at the Charterhouse for the day of ordeal, and the scenes in chapter-house and church described by Chauncy, are a familiar page of

---

[73] Knowles, *Rel. Orders*, iii. 226–7.

[74] Middlemore's kin held lands at Edgbaston and Studley (Warws.): cf. *V.C.H. Warws.* iii. 181.

[75] *D.N.B.*

[76] Letter in B.M. Cott. MS. Cleop. E. IV, f. 70, printed in Thompson, *Carthusians*, 413–14.

[77] See Chauncy, *Historia*, ch. viii, *De fratribus reprobis*, and Thompson, *Carthusians*, 387–92.

[78] For what follows the authority is mainly Chauncy, *Historia*.

[79] Certificates printed in Rymer, *Foedera*, xiv. 492, and Hendriks, *Charterhouse*, 368–70; cf. *L. and P. Hen. VIII*, vii, p. 283.

[80] B.M. Cott. MS. Cleop. E. VI, f. 209.

Tudor history made immortal by Froude.[81] While awaiting the summons, Houghton was visited by the Priors of Beauvale and Axholme. The former, Robert Laurence, was a professed monk of London who had succeeded Houghton on the latter's recall. After a series of interviews and examinations before Cromwell,[82] the three priors were lodged in the Tower; they were tried on 28–29 April and condemned to death for refusal to accept the royal supremacy.[83] They were executed at Tyburn on 4 May.[84] When Houghton had been imprisoned Humphrey Middlemore, now vicar, was in charge, and had as his principal counsellors William Exmew, the procurator, and Sebastian Newdigate; when they resisted all persuasions to take the oath[85] they also were removed to Newgate, where they remained for a fortnight chained by neck and legs to posts. Finally, on 11 June, they were tried[86] and condemned, and on 19 June executed. After their departure the monks of the orphaned community were subjected to every kind of persuasion and petty persecution, deprived of their books, harassed by visitors, vexed by the continual presence in the cloister of Cromwell's men,[87] and urged by the Bridgettines of Syon to submit;[88] some months later (perhaps in April 1536) they were given as superior William Trafford, sometime procurator of Beauvale, who had at first made a brave show of refusing the oath to the royal supremacy,[89] but had subsequently capitulated and become entirely subservient to Cromwell. A little later a further expedient was tried. Four of the most stubborn were exiled; Chauncy and John Foxe were sent in May 1536 to Beauvale, Rochester and Walworth to Hull;[90] a little later eight more were sent to Syon,[91] and between 1535 and 1538 half-a-dozen monks from other houses were imported to London. At last in May 1537, when the Council threatened to suppress the house out of hand if the oath were refused, a division was created, some agreeing to swear in order to save their way of life; among these was the chronicler Chauncy.[92] Ten, however, still refused to swear; three priests, a deacon, and six lay brothers.[93] On 18 May these were lodged in Newgate and chained to posts, where all save one died of starvation or disease during the summer. The one survivor, William Horne, was kept a prisoner and executed at Tyburn on 4 August 1540.[94] Meanwhile the two at Hull had been executed at York by the Duke of Norfolk in May 1537, on the same charge as their brethren in London.[95] In all, eighteen Carthusians were executed, seventeen of them professed monks of the London Charterhouse. Within a few weeks of the removal of the recalcitrants in May, the rump of the community was induced to surrender the house (10 June),[96] but it was not until 15 November 1538 that the House of the Salutation was actually disbanded.[97] When that was done William Trafford and sixteen choir monks received pensions; the six surviving lay brothers received nothing. Of the seventeen pensioners eleven were among those who swore to the Act of Succession in 1534. The others must have been newcomers to London from other Carthusian houses, as it is not conceivable that recruits would have been professed during the years 1534–8. Despite the existence of several lists of names and two or three precise statements by Chauncy, it is impossible to account exactly either for the full number of those known to have been in the house shortly before 1534 or for the subsequent arrivals and departures.[98]

When the monks had been ejected, the church, cloister, and buildings were almost immediately divided up into three portions.[99] The church and perhaps the chapter-house were given into the care of a Dr. Cave; the prior's cell and the new cells were given to the owner of an adjacent house, Sir Arthur Darcy; the residue of the fabric was, until March 1539, controlled for the commissioners of suppression by a certain William Dale. In June 1542, when the commissioners had ceased to be responsible, the whole place was turned over to the

[81] J. A. Froude, *Hist. of Eng.* ii. 350.

[82] *L. and P. Hen. VIII*, viii, pp. 213–14.

[83] K.B. 8/7/1/14 (Mdx. Sessions, Easter Term, 27 Hen. VIII).

[84] Thompson, *Carthusians*, 399–400.

[85] Cf. Bedyll's letter to Cromwell (B.M. Cott. MS. Cleop. E. VI, f. 259), printed in Thompson, *Carthusians*, 404–5.

[86] K.B. 8/7/3.

[87] The course of events may be followed in the relevant vols. of *L. and P. Hen. VIII*, and Thompson, *Carthusians*, 411–35, printing many letters. Many of the documents are in B.M. Cott. MS. Cleop. E. IV.

[88] Cf. letter in B.M. Cott. MS. Cleop. E. VI, ff. 172–4, printed in Aungier, *Syon*, 430–3.

[89] *L. and P. Hen. VIII*, viii, pp. 212, 260; Thompson, *Carthusians*, 457–8.

[90] B.M. Cott. MS. Cleop. E. IV, f. 247, printed in Aungier, *Syon*, 438–9; Chauncy, *Historia*, 113–14.

[91] B.M. Cott. MS. Cleop. E. VI, ff. 172–4; E. IV, f. 247.

[92] Chauncy, *Historia*, 115–16.

[93] *L. and P. Hen. VIII*, xii (1), pp. 337–8; B.M. Cott. MS. Cleop. E. VI, f. 208; B.M. Harl. MS. 6989, f. 69v. Their names were Richard Bere, Thomas Johnson, Thomas Greene (priests), John Davy (deacon), William Greenwood, Thomas Scryven, Robert Salt, Walter Peerson, Thomas Reddyng, and William Horne (lay brethren).

[94] C. Wriothesley, *Chron. of Eng.* (Camd. Soc. N.S. xi), 121; *L. and P. Hen. VIII*, xv, p. 484; Chauncy, *Historia*, 117. Chauncy, who was abroad, gives the wrong date of 4 Nov. 1541.

[95] *L. and P. Hen. VIII*, xii (1), pp. 337–8, 538.

[96] E 322/133; C 54/1/16.

[97] Commission of Suppression is dated 12 Nov.: E 117/12/22; Chauncy gives date in text: *Historia*, 119.

[98] Chauncy, *Historia*; E 315/233, ff. 63 sqq. Thompson, *Carthusians*, 487, gives a plausible explanation.

[99] Knowles and Grimes, *Charterhouse*, 36–38, 75–86; Thompson, *Carthusians*, 494–5.

king's servants, John Bridges and Thomas Hale, and used as a storehouse for tents, hunting-nets, and the like. It was thus for some years virtually derelict, save for the occupation of some of the cells by a family of Italian court musicians of the name of Bassano, and it was at this time that Maurice Chauncy seems to have revisited the place and seen the profanation of the church. Finally, on 14 April 1546, the whole place was sold to Sir Edward (later Lord) North. With its subsequent fortunes and the establishment of the school in 1614,[100] we are not concerned.

Of the monks, Maurice Chauncy, John Foxe, and the converse Hugh Taylor fled overseas in 1546–7 and joined the Charterhouse of Val de Grace at Bruges.[101] They were sent back to England in 1555, when Queen Mary was contemplating the refoundation of a Charterhouse. Foxe died before this could be accomplished, and it is noteworthy that of those who joined Chauncy at Sheen not a single monk came from the London Charterhouse.[102] The converse Hugh Taylor, however, was there, and shared Chauncy's exile in 1559; he died at the priory of Sheen Anglorum at Bruges in 1575; Maurice Chauncy, his prior, died on a journey at the Paris Charterhouse on 12 July 1581.[103]

The complex of buildings of a Carthusian monastery[104] can be considered as made up of three parts: first, the rectangular cloister of four alleys, giving access to the individual cells and gardens arranged along the cloister's external wall; next, the relatively small group of buildings serving the common need of all – church, chapter-house, prior's cell, sacristy, infirmary,[105] and refectory, grouped together at an angle (at London the south-western angle) of the cloister; and, thirdly, outside the claustral buildings, the guest-house, kitchens, offices, and lay-brothers' quarters, which at London were grouped round two courts, the 'Little Cloister' and the modern 'Washhouse Court'. Of these it may be said that at London the third group has in great part survived to the present day in use as the domestic and administrative offices of the North-Norfolk Mansion and its successor, Sutton's Hospital, while

the great cloister has disappeared save for portions of the external wall incorporating the entrance of cells A and B in the western alley, and T and V on the eastern.[106] As for the conventual buildings, these were partly destroyed soon after the Suppression, and partly incorporated in the mansion which later became the Master's Lodge, Gallery, chapel, library, and diningroom of the modern Charterhouse. These buildings have been described frequently and authoritatively, in particular by Sir William St. John Hope and Sir Alfred Clapham,[107] but as all these descriptions, with their accompanying plans and illustrations, have been largely superseded by more recent discoveries, it may be well to mention these latter briefly.

On the night of 10–11 May 1941, during a particularly heavy air-raid upon the City, the buildings of Charterhouse caught fire, and those that had formed the main parts of the Tudor mansion and Sutton's Hospital, partly covering the site of the conventual buildings, were entirely burnt out. When rebuilding became practicable a remarkable series of discoveries and deductions were made which made it clear that the existing chapel, hitherto considered to be identical with the choir and presbytery of the original monastic church, was in fact the monastic chapterhouse and that the original church must have occupied a site to the south of the chapter-house in Chapel Court, an hypothesis which received dramatic confirmation by the discovery of the tomb and coffin of the founder exactly in the recorded position[108] before the high altar of the original church. Consequently the south alley of the cloister was seen to lie considerably further to the south than had been supposed, which left space for the prior's cell at the south-west angle of the cloister, with the refectory adjoining it to the north as had been indicated in the waterworks plan, whereas hitherto it had been impossible to find room for it in this position.

All these discoveries were due to the research and investigations of the architects; subsequent excavations, besides confirming them, established the complete plan and disposition of the chapels in the monastic church, and also the dimensions of the Little Cloister, the exact dimensions and further details regarding the Great Cloister, and many details of the courses of the water-supply. Subsequent documentary research[109] made it clear that shortly before the suppression a 'new' prior's

---

[100] See *V.C.H. Surr.* ii. 196–8.

[101] Thompson, *Carthusians*, 495–9; cf. also Chauncy, *Passion*, ed. Curtis, 322–5.

[102] Chauncy, *Passion*, ed. Curtis, 500 sqq.; Knowles, *Rel. Orders*, iii. 439, 441.

[103] For Hugh Taylor see Hendriks, *Charterhouse*, 294–5; for Chauncy's death, ibid. 306–8. His age is there given as 68 in 1581; this must be an error for 72, as his age is given in an official deed as 57 on 8 Mar. 1566 (*Analecta Bollandiana*, xxii. 53, n.)

[104] For what follows see Knowles and Grimes, *Charterhouse*, 41 sqq.

[105] Normally a charterhouse has no infirmary, but there is a reference to one at London both before and after construction.

[106] The doorway and serving-hatch of cell B were revealed during reconstruction in 1958.

[107] Hist. Mon. Com., *West Lond.* 21–30.

[108] See p. 160.

[109] S.C. 12/36/26 (survey of Charterhouse made 18 Mar. 1545); *L. and P. Hen. VIII*, xiii (2), pp. 374–6; Hope, *Charterhouse*, 178–84.

lodging and three 'little' cells had been constructed, and enabled the excavators to indicate their position in the monastic plan, although the site where they had lain was covered by existing buildings. As a result of all this work, it was possible to draw a plan of the medieval monastery which, unlike previous plans, could be based securely upon visible and measurable remains.[110]

No catalogue of the library of the London Charterhouse is known to exist, but there are four lists of books[111] taken on loan or by gift: (i) books carried away from London by John Spalding, when returning to Hull, probably in the early 15th century; (ii) books lent in 1500 to Roger Montgomery on his departure to Coventry Charterhouse; (iii) an inventory of goods, including some books, taken to Mount Grace in 1519; and (iv) books taken *c.* 1530 by John Whetham to Hinton Charterhouse. The surviving books known to have belonged to the house have been listed by Dr. N. R. Ker.[112]

There is no direct information about the spiritual doctrine on the ascetical or mystical life given to the young monks. The lists mentioned above are interesting as showing the presence, as at Mount Grace, of copies of the mystical treatises current in England in the later Middle Ages. Thus there are two copies of *The Cloud of Unknowing*, two of *The Chastising of God's Children*, two of the English writings of Rolle and one of the *Incendium Amoris*, one of the enigmatic *Mirror of Simple Souls*, two of works of St. Bridget of Sweden, two of Ludolph of Saxony, one of the revelations of St. Mechtild, and one of Gerson's *De Contemptu Mundi*. Of the two copies of *The Cloud*, we know that one was written by William Exmew for the benefit of Maurice Chauncy.[113] A letter[114] of Prior Houghton to the vicar of the Cologne Charterhouse, written 23 July 1532, is chiefly concerned with the ordering of copies of the printed editions of Denis the Carthusian, whose writings 'appeal to us above those of all

other spiritual authors', and as he asks for ten copies of the complete works, twenty of a minor work, and twelve of any future work printed, he clearly has the needs of his community, and perhaps those of other houses also, in mind. The pages of Chauncy, as also those of the earlier chronicle, show clearly that members of the London Charterhouse at all periods were proficient in the ways of the spiritual life as traditionally presented by the medieval mystical theologians.

The commissioners for the tenth, early in 1536, returned the gross income of the house as £736, with obligatory rents and outgoings of £94, and a net income of £642.[115] Their list of properties tallies almost exactly with that given by the Suppression Commissioners of 1537.[116] This includes numerous tenements near the monastery and scattered about the City, pastures in Marylebone and Holborn, a 'messuage' (in the *Valor Ecclesiasticus* a 'manor') called 'Blumsburye', the manors of Rolleston (Leics.), Westfield (Norf.),[117] and rents from the manors of Ogbourne (Wilts.) and Cardones (Kent),[118] the rectories of Edlesborough (Bucks.),[119] Stockton Magna (Hunts.),[120] Braintree (Essex),[121] North Mimms (Herts.), and Cromer (Norf.); lands at Kingstonon-Thames (Surr.) and Higham (Kent), the 'Bull Inn' at Rochester (Kent), 'Atherley's lands' in or near the Lea valley, and a wood called 'Arnold's' in Middlesex.

*D. C. Knowles*

## Revised List of the Priors of the London Charterhouse[122]

This list has been updated using *Heads of Religious Houses*, vol. 2, p. 326 and vol. 3 (forthcoming).

John Luscote, 1371–1398
John Okendon,[123] occurs 1398; resigned 1412
John Maplested, occurs 1412–*c.*1440
John Thorne,[124] occurs *c.*1440; resigned *c.*1448
John Walweyn,[125] occurs *c.*1448; died 1449

---

[110] Knowles and Grimes, *Charterhouse*, plan facing p. 82. The architects responsible for the rebuilding were Messrs. Seeley and Paget.

[111] Thompson, *Carthusians*, 324–9.

[112] N. R. Ker, *Med. Libr. of Great Britain*, (2nd edn.), 122–3. In addition, Gonville and Caius Add. MS. 732/771, a collection of 14th–15th-cent. statutes and decrees of General Chapter, etc., written carefully in a beautiful hand later than 1526, and following the printed text of statutes in the edn. of J. Amorbach, Basle, 1510 (see f. 48v), may also with some probability be assigned to the Lond. Charterhouse.

[113] See *The Cloud of Unknowing*, ed. P. Hodgson (E.E.T.S., O.S. 218), introd., where the colophon reads *Liber . . . p[er] M. Chawncy quem exaravit sanctus Wille Exmewe* (i.e. which Exmew wrote). Previous writers (including Thompson, *Carthusians*, 377) read *secundum* for *sanctus* and found difficulty in interpreting the text.

[114] Letter printed in Hendriks, *Charterhouse*, App. VI.

[115] *Valor Eccl.* (Rec. Com), i. 430–1.

[116] S.C. 6/Hen. VIII/2396, mm. 28–41.

[117] *Cal. Pat.* 1377–81, 242 (1378).

[118] Ibid. 1476–85, 7 (1476).

[119] Ibid. 1391–6, 34 (1392).

[120] Ibid. 1381–5, 37 (1381).

[121] Ibid. 1413–16, 384 (1415).

[122] Names and succession of priors are uncertain; dates of those up to 1488 are taken from a list (L.R. 2/61, f. 15v; Hope, *Charterhouse*, 147) which gives length in years of term of office, without dates. Remaining notes on priors are from Hope, *Charterhouse*, 148–50, who gives no references.

[123] Died 14 Feb. 1418.

[124] Died 1453 or 1454.

[125] Formerly Prior of Coventry, died 6 Oct. 1449.

John Seman,[126] occurs 1449–69

Edmund or Edward Storer,[127] occurs 1469; resigned 1477

John Walsingham,[128] occurs 1477–*c*.1487

Richard Roche,[129] occurs 1487; resigned 1500

William Tynbygh (Tynbegh),[130] occurs 1500; resigned 1529

John Batmanson,[131] occurs 1529; died 1531

John Houghton,[132] occurs 1531; executed 1535

William Trafford,[133] occurs 1535–8

[126] Died 29 Dec. 1472.
[127] Later Prior of Hinton, died 1503.
[128] Formerly a Benedictine.
[129] Died 1515.

[130] Died 1531.
[131] Formerly Prior of Hinton, died 16 Nov. 1531.
[132] Formerly Prior of Beauvale.
[133] Formerly monk of Beauvale.

# HOUSE OF AUGUSTINIAN CANONS

## 3. BENTLEY PRIORY

### INTRODUCTION

There is little recent work on this priory or cell of Augustinian canons, which by the fourteenth century appears to have been annexed to the priory of St. Gregory outside Canterbury. Bentley was said to have been founded in 1171, *Heads of Religious Houses,* 2, p. 333, but see A. Binns, *Dedications of Monastic Houses in England and Wales, 1066–1216,* Studies in the History of Medieval Religion, I (Woodbridge, 1989), p. 120.

*Jessica Freeman*

Bentley was a priory or cell of Augustinian canons situated in Harrow, just inside the boundary with Great Stanmore parish.[1] It was dedicated to St. Mary Magdalen and in the patronage of the Archbishops of Canterbury.[2] It is said to have been founded in 1171 by Ranulf de Glanville, Justiciar 1180–89,[3] perhaps as a cell of the Priory of St. Gregory outside Canterbury. It was certainly dependent on St. Gregory's by the 14th century because in 1301 John de Bere, the former Prior, was said to have let the church at Wotton (Bucks.) to farm for twelve years without leave from his superior, the Prior of St. Gregory's, Canterbury, or from the diocesan.[4]

In 1255 the priory held 3 virgates of land in Wotton Underwood (Bucks.), two of which were in demesne and the third was held by Michael de Hamme at a rent of 4*s.* a year. One virgate had been given to the priory by Fredeshet de Wotton and the others by Alice de Ruppell.[5] The priory also held the advowson of Wotton church.[6] In 1291 the prior's goods at Stanmore were valued at 10*s.* and the lands and rents in Wotton at 13*s.* 4*d.*[7]

In 1243 the king pardoned the Prior of Bentley the interest on 60*s.* which he had borrowed from the Jews,[8] and in 1248 this prior, or his successor, died of suffocation under a load of corn which had accidentally fallen on him.[9] In 1318 Edward II sent John de Cotham to the 'abbot and convent of Binttlley', meaning presumably the priory

of Bentley.[10] A few years later John de Merston, a canon of St. Gregory's, Canterbury, was living at Bentley. Two others were sent there from the mother house as a punishment by the Prior of Christ Church, Canterbury, who had been appointed to inquire into irregularities at St. Gregory's. Within a few weeks, however, one of them was appointed coadjutor of the Prior of Bentley.[11]

In 1535 the farm of the lands of St. Gregory's at Bentley was valued at £4 10*s.* and at Wotton at £4.[12] According to the court rolls of the manor of Harrow St. Gregory's had ceased to maintain a separate cell at Bentley many years before, although it was still responsible for providing a canon to celebrate in the chapel of St. Mary Magdalen.[13] In 1546 the former priory was granted to Henry Needham and William Sacheverell, in so far as it had belonged to the Priory of St. Gregory, and later to the Archbishop of Canterbury.[14] There remain no traces of the buildings, which were eventually replaced by a large house called Bentley Priory, built by the Dukes of Abercorn.

*J. L. Kirby*

### Revised List of the Priors of Bentley

This list is taken from *Heads of Religious Houses,* vol. 2, p. 333.

Martin, occurs 1229
An unnamed prior was suffocated under a mow of corn in 1248

[1] Lysons, *Environs of Lond.* ii. 568.
[2] M.R.O., Acc. 76/2421.
[3] J. Tavernor-Perry, *Memorials of Old Mdx.* 11.
[4] *Cant. Reg. Winchelsey* (Cant. and York Soc.), 748.
[5] *Rot. Hund.* (Rec. Com.), i. 24.
[6] E. Lipscombe, *Hist. of Bucks.* i. 606; *V.C.H. Bucks.* iv. 133.
[7] *Tax. Eccl.* (Rec. Com.), 14, 46.
[8] *Close R.* 1242–7, 132.
[9] Matthew Paris, *Chronica Majora* (Rolls Ser.), v. 33.

[10] *Cal. Close,* 1318–23, 117.
[11] *Lit. Cant.* (Rolls Ser.), i. 337–9, 345.
[12] *Valor Eccl.* (Rec. Com.), i. 24.
[13] M.R.O., Acc. 76/2421.
[14] *L. and P. Hen. VIII,* xxi (2), p. 92.

John de Bere, predecessor of William of Carlton, occurs 1301

William de Carlton, occurs 1301

John Taleboth, occurs 1315

Robert, occurs 1321

John de Merston, occurs as canon of St. Gregory at Bentley, 1330; brother John de Hagh appointed coadjutor due to his old age, 1331

Adam, occurs 1334

Walter de Hancrisham, occurs 1337

No later priors are known.

# HOUSES OF AUGUSTINIAN CANONESSES

## 4. THE PRIORY OF ST. MARY, CLERKENWELL

### INTRODUCTION

Since the *V.C.H.* article drew on the priory's cartulary and original charters, it remains the substantive work. It fails, however, to mention the priory's chapel at Muswell Hill which was a local place of pilgrimage, particularly around the feast of the Assumption, see W. M. Marcham, 'New Facts Concerning "Clerkenwell Detached" at Muswell Hill', *T.L.M.A.S.*, n.s. 7 (1933–7), pp. 610–15.

The foundation of the nunnery and its subsequent links with its patrons and founders are discussed by Thompson, *Women Religious*, pp. 189–90, and the role of the prioress in Valerie G. Spear, *Leadership in Medieval English Nunneries* (Woodbridge, 2005).

For the century prior to the Dissolution, further information can be found on the identities not only of the nuns themselves but also of their staff, tenants, recipients of ecclesiastical patronage and others, as well as on the spiritual services the nunnery provided in Paxton, 'Nunneries', *passim*, and esp. pp. 312–23. This work also provides appendices listing chaplains, lay officials, graduate presentees in the London diocese and recipients of annuities and corrodies. Information on the library of the house can be found in Bell, *Nuns*, pp. 143–4.

More details are also now available on the extent and administration of the convent's urban property in Honeybourne, 'Property', pp. 78–81; Paxton, 'Nunneries', chap. 5; *Documentary Sources*, pp. 57–8. Excavations were recently undertaken on the site of the nunnery: see B. Sloane, *Excavations at the Nunnery of St. Mary de Fonte, Clerkenwell*, MoLAS Monograph series (forthcoming, 2007/8).

*Jessica Freeman*

The Priory of St. Mary at Clerkenwell was a house of Augustinian canonesses, although it is often described both by contemporaries and by historians as being of the Order of St. Benedict. It became one of the more important English nunneries, being twelfth in the size of its revenue at the Dissolution according to the *Valor Ecclesiasticus*. The priory lay immediately to the north of the house of the Knights Hospitallers of St. John of Jerusalem between the road to St. Albans and the Fleet river. It was founded *c.* 1145, shortly before its more famous neighbour and by the same founder, Jordan de Bricet.[1] During the last two years of his reign Stephen confirmed the gifts of both the founder and of Richard de Belmeis, then Bishop of London.[2] Several charters of Henry II between 1175 and 1182, one of Richard I in 1190, and a bull of Urban III dated 19 October 1186 show that within fifty years of its foundation the priory had widespread possessions in southern England, extending from Norfolk to Hampshire.[3] The charters of Stephen and Henry II were later confirmed by successive kings.[4] The bull confirmed the royal grants and also provided for the free election of the prioress, for the control of the chapter over the alienation of its property, and for exemption from certain tithes.

During the following three centuries the possessions of the nunnery, which owed much to the dowries of nuns who were members of landed families in the shires or of London merchant families, were concentrated nearer home. Ease of

---

[1] J. H. Round, 'The Foundation of the Priories of St. Mary and St. John, Clerkenwell', *Archaeologia*, lvi. 226; *Cartulary of St. Mary Clerkenwell*, ed. W. O. Hassall (Camd. Soc. 3rd ser. lxxi), p. viii. Dr. Hassall's edition of the early-13th-cent. Cartulary and his other writings are now the only important sources for the history of the priory. A number of the charters are also printed in Dugdale, *Mon.* iv. 81–86. For the site see *T.L.M.A.S.* xiv. 234–82.

[2] *Cal. Chart. R.* 1327–41, 398; *Clerkenwell Cart.* 1.

[3] *Clerkenwell Cart.* pp. viii, 1–13, especially nos. 2, 6, 8, 9, 10; W. O. Hassall, 'Two bulls for St. Mary Clerkenwell', *E.H.R.* lvii. 97.

[4] *Cal. Chart. R.* 1327–41, 398; *Cal. Pat.* 1399–1401, 541.

administration and the constant litigation in which, like all medieval property-owners, the nuns needed to engage simply to defend their lands, made such concentration an economic necessity. Whereas in the 13th and 14th centuries the revenues of the priory were drawn from sixteen counties outside London and Middlesex, by 1500 this number had been reduced to five, and even in some of these the property had shrunk. In London, on the other hand, the holdings of the nuns steadily increased. By 1190 they already held at least fourteen properties in the City,[5] and these were constantly augmented, partly by the dowries of the nuns and partly by the wills of London citizens.[6] In addition from time to time the nuns had money to invest in property, and London, where small parcels could be bought just outside their door, was the obvious place for this investment. Some of the money came from legacies from citizens of London,[7] some perhaps from the dowries of nuns, the sale of outlying properties, and savings from their income; the priory was not poor, although in 1314–15 they informed Queen Isabel in a petition that they were impoverished by the hard years, and sought licence to accept lands to the value of £20 yearly.[8] Whatever the source of their money, by the Dissolution they were drawing rents from sixty-four parishes in the City of London,[9] rents which by that time accounted for over three-fifths of the gross revenue of the priory.[10]

In Middlesex the first property was of course the site of the priory, given by Jordan de Bricet and Muriel his wife, with the lands and gardens nearby and the meadow beside the Holborn.[11] The lands given by the founder and his family in Clerkenwell, Stoke Newington, Steeple (Essex), and Wanstead (Essex) were described in detail in 1197 in a final concord between Lucy (Lecia) de Munteni, daughter of Jordan and the wife of Henry Foliot, and the prioress, Ermengarde.[12] Although the priory received substantial rents in Clerkenwell, no revenue from there is shown in the *Valor*, where their other Middlesex holdings were said to bring in over £50 a year, nearly a fifth of their gross income.[13]

The chapel and land of Muswell, or Muswell Hill, were held as the gifts of Richard de Belmeis, Bishop of London (1152–62).[14] In Tottenham a few years later Robert son of Sewin of Northampton gave the nuns 140 acres in Hanger and other property,[15] and in 1539 the pastures of the late priory there were worth £10 a year.[16] Between 1179 and 1189 William de Mandeville, Earl of Essex, granted 100s.-worth of land in Edmonton,[17] and John, son of Robert Blund, John White (*albus*), John Buchuinte, Gillian, daughter of William Renger, and Laurence de la Forde all added parcels to the priory's holdings in Edmonton before 1224.[18] At Bromley-by-Bow *c.* 1190 Roger de Pyrov granted land for which the priory had to pay a rent of 4s.,[19] and at Stepney a few years later Henry Foliot gave the land of Solomon son of Walter,[20] while at Hanworth Roger de Ginges gave a rent of 6d. from the marsh.[21] Towards Islington the nuns held two acres,[22] and later they acquired lands in Highbury, Holloway, Newington Barrow, and Tollington, all in Islington. Rents from Edmonton, Islington, Muswell, and Tottenham continued to be drawn until the Dissolution.[23]

The remaining counties in which Clerkenwell held property from the 12th to the 16th centuries were Cambridgeshire, Dorset, Essex, and Kent. In Sussex they held property only from the 14th century to the 16th. In Cambridgeshire the priory gained most of its income from the dowries of the eight nuns who came from the county in the 12th or early 13th century, but by 1300 some of the properties had been lost.[24] In Eversden Thomas de Andeville, William son of William of Eversden, Luke son of Warin, and Simon Luvel of Eversden gave small parcels in the late 12th or early 13th century.[25] In Kingston Eustace de Bancis gave the land and *mansio* of Lefeson with 80 acres of arable and 9 acres in the meadow, a gift confirmed by Henry II in 1175–6. William de St. George gave half a virgate on his daughter Mabel becoming a nun, William the bald (*calvus*) gave nine acres, and William de Bancis gave dowries for his daughters Avice and Margaret.[26] In Wimpole

[5] *Clerkenwell Cart.* 5–8.

[6] *Cal. of Wills in Court of Husting* (Lond.), ed. R. R. Sharpe, i. 8, 51, 98, 313, 445, 549, 585, 675.

[7] Ibid. i. 84, 460, 489, 615, 638, 650, 697; ii. 8, 37, 41, 47, etc.

[8] Eileen Power, *Med. Eng. Nunneries*, 179–80, quoting S.C. 1/36/201.

[9] S.C. 6/Hen. VIII/2396; *Clerkenwell Cart.* p. x.

[10] *Valor Eccl.* (Rec. Com.), i. 395–6.

[11] *Clerkenwell Cart.* 10.

[12] *Feet of F. 7 & 8 Ric. I* (P.R.S. xx), 101–3.

[13] S.C. 6/Hen. VIII/2118; S.C. 12/19/4; *Valor Eccl.* (Rec. Com.) i. 395–6. The failings of the *Valor* in the case of Clerkenwell, by omissions and confusion of counties, have been pointed out by Dr. Hassall. No doubt it understates the total value of the priory, but the details which can be checked are substantially accurate. S.C. 12/19/4 is a contemporary draft or copy.

[14] *Clerkenwell Cart.* 6, 12; B.M. Harl. Chart. 83 C 26.

[15] *Clerkenwell Cart.* 6, 11, 14–18; B.M. Campb. Chart. xxx. 2; Harl. Chart. 83 C 23; Add. Chart. 19909.

[16] *L. and P. Hen. VIII*, xiv (2), p. 371.

[17] *Clerkenwell Cart.* 24.

[18] Ibid. 18–19, 113–15; *Feet of F. Lond. and Mdx.*, ed. Hardy and Page, i. 52.

[19] *Clerkenwell Cart.* 96–98.

[20] Ibid. 40, 44, 56–57.

[21] Ibid. 61.

[22] Ibid. 30, 60, 73–74; S.C. 6/Hen. VIII/2118.

[23] *Valor Eccl.* (Rec. Com.), i. 395.

[24] For Cambs. see W. O. Hassall, 'The Cambs. properties of the nunnery of St. Mary Clerkenwell', *Proc. Camb. Antiq. Soc.* xlii. 33–40.

[25] *Clerkenwell Cart.* 86–89.

[26] Ibid. 79–86.

Roger de Bancis granted the nuns a small parcel of two acres.[27] All the lands in these three places came to be treated as a single unit, the manor of Beamont in Kingston. In 1254 it was valued at 30s.[28] and in the *Valor* at 40s.[29] The church of Fulbourn, granted by Jordan de Bricet and Muriel his wife, was confirmed by Henry II *c.* 1176.[30] At Hildersham Maud de Ros gave one mark yearly from the mill on her daughter becoming a nun.[31] William de St. George, whose endowment for his daughter has been mentioned, also gave a hide at Haslingfield for his sister Aubrey to become a nun. Robert de Beche gave half his mill in the same place, and in 1279 the prioress held there one hide of 120 acres worth 22s. a year in rent.[32] In Tadlow Alan son of Fulk gave 12d. rent on the mill to light the nuns' dormitory,[33] and at Wratting the grant of Margery de Buthlers was confirmed by Henry II in 1181.[34]

In Dorset Blandford St. Mary and the advowson of the church were granted to the nuns by Geoffrey Martel and confirmed to them between 1160 and 1176 by William his son; Aubrey, wife of Geoffrey and mother of William, became a nun at Clerkenwell. The rectory was retained until the Dissolution, when it was valued at 40s.[35] In 1303 Roger, then Rector, had licence to stay at the priory in the service of the nuns provided only that he was in his parish from Passion Sunday to the octave of Easter.[36] With the church the Martels also gave lands, which were valued at 100s. in 1488 and at £10 19s. 4d. in the *Valor*.[37] Alfred of Lincoln gave 20s. a year from the chapel of Broadway *c.* 1190. The chapel was temporarily in other hands, and until it became free the nuns were to draw their 20s. from the mill of Okeford Fitzpaine. Alfred's sister, also called Aubrey, became a nun. This 20s. was still received in the 16th century.[38]

In Essex Maurice de Totham gave the rectory of Great Totham with 15 acres there between 1181 and 1186.[39] Vicars were presented by the nuns until the Dissolution, when the income from the church was £6 6s. 8d.[40] In nearby Heybridge the nuns had a claim to the tithe, but surrendered it in 1237 to St. Paul's Cathedral.

The advowson of North Weald Bassett was given to the nuns by Cecily, wife of Henry of Essex, before 1181 and confirmed to them by her sons Henry of Essex and Hugh. The grant was confirmed by Pope Urban III in 1186, by Richard Fitzneal, Bishop of London, in 1194 and by William of Sainte-MereEglise, Bishop of London (1199–1221). In 1275 John Chishull, Bishop of London, assumed the advowson but the nuns continued to enjoy the revenue. This arrangement was challenged in the early 16th century and the appointment was then shared by the bishop and the priory. The vicarage was worth £7 5s. 4d., less outgoings of 24s. 8d.[41] In Bowers Gifford the priory held the marsh called Horshill, originally given by Simon son of Simon as a dowry for his daughter and confirmed in 1190. In 1490–1 and at the Dissolution it was worth 40s.[42] At Dunmow a collection of property, slowly built up between 1180 and 1340, eventually came to be known as the manor of Mynchyn Dunmow. The original was the gift of Roger son of Reinfrid, made on condition that the nuns should receive Alice his wife into their convent and take care of her burial. This property was increased by various grants and purchases so that by 1500 it produced a rent of about £5.[43] At Eastwood in the 16th century the nuns received a small rent of 4s. 8d., the origin of which is unknown.[44] Before 1179 William de Mandeville, Earl of Essex, granted certain assarts for a rent of 5s. in Hadley.[45] At Fyfield a small parcel of land was received *c.* 1180 from Richard the priest with the consent of Arnold de Curton, from whom he had acquired it.[46] In the Willingales the same Richard gave several holdings to the priory. William of Spain and his two tenants, Robert son of Menges, a knight, and Eustace of Willingale, a socman, William de la Mere and Agnes his wife, and the Prior of St. John of Jerusalem confirmed these grants. William of Spain's two tenants appear to have been in financial difficulties and to have disposed of lands to the nuns in return for their assistance. By the end of the 15th century the lands in Fyfield and the Willingales were accounted for together.[47]

[27] Ibid. 79.

[28] *Valuation of Norwich*, ed. Lunt, 225.

[29] *Valor Eccl.* (Rec. Com.), i. 395.

[30] *Clerkenwell Cart.* 11.

[31] Ibid. 20–21.

[32] Ibid. 77; *Rot. Hund.* (Rec. Com.), ii. 558.

[33] *Clerkenwell Cart.* 121.

[34] Ibid. 3.

[35] Ibid. 27–28; *Valor Eccl.* (Rec. Com.), i. 396; for Dorset see W. O. Hassall, 'Dorset properties of the nunnery of St. Mary Clerkenwell', *Proc. Dorset Nat. Hist. Soc.* lxviii. 43–51.

[36] *Salisbury, Reg. Simon de Gandavo* (Cant. and York Soc.), ii. 864.

[37] *Valor Eccl.* (Rec. Com.), i. 395.

[38] Ibid. 396; *Clerkenwell Cart.* 100–1.

[39] *Clerkenwell Cart.* 35–36, 38–39; B.M. Harl. Charts. 83 C 31, 83 E 1, 84 A 58; for Essex see W. O. Hassall, 'Essex properties of the nunnery of St. Mary Clerkenwell', *Trans. Essex Arch. Soc.* xxiii. 18–48.

[40] *Valor Eccl.* (Rec. Com.), i. 395.

[41] Ibid.; *Clerkenwell Cart.* pp. ix, 22–24, 251–4, 255; *V.C.H. Essex*, iv. 290.

[42] *Clerkenwell Cart.* 41–42.

[43] Ibid. 66–68; *Feet of F.* 10 Ric. I (P.R.S. xxiv), 193; Dugdale, *Mon.* iv. 87.

[44] *Valor Eccl.* (Rec. Com.), i. 395, wrongly listed under Mdx.

[45] *Clerkenwell Cart.* 34.

[46] Ibid. 96.

[47] Ibid. 47–50, 90–95; Hassall, *Trans. Essex Arch. Soc.* xxiii. 18–48.

A rent of 30s. in Langford was granted before 1176 by the three daughters and sons-in-law of Alice Capra, who became a nun at Clerkenwell. In 1534–5 quit-rents from Langford amounted to £6 3s. 1d.[48] Gillian of Latton gave 12d. rent in Latton, Robert de Leyborne a similar sum in Leyton, and Cecily de Crammaville 10s. in Thurrock, all probably after 1190.[49] In Mountnessing c. 1175 Robert de Munteni gave a rent of 3s. which, increased by another gift, was worth 5s. by the 16th century.[50] At Shoebury Reynold de Warenne's gift of 30s., made before 1176, was still worth 30s. in 1534–5.[51] At Steeple Reynold de Ginges and Emma his wife gave 2 acres, Henry Foliot and Lettice de Munteni 2 acres, and Brian son of Ralph 12 acres.[52] In Wanstead Abraham de Wanstead gave the mill of Wanstead before 1176, and Robert Brito de Aldewic gave a third part of Wanstead with the capital messuage. By 1181 the nuns were drawing a quitrent of one mark, which was still paid in 1490–1 and 1534–5.[53] Altogether the Essex properties were worth about £30 at the Dissolution, being next in value after those in London and Middlesex.[54]

In Kent the only important properties of the priory were in Sittingbourne, where the church was given to the nuns in the charter of 1175 and confirmed in that of 1190. In spite of some dispute about the tithes with Christ Church, Canterbury, the church was retained until the Dissolution, the prioress alone presenting to it. In 1384 it was said to be worth £23 6s. 8d., but by the end of the 15th century the value seems to have fallen to £15, the figure given by the *Valor*. The priory also collected a number of small holdings of land in the parish, valued at 40s. in 1384 but not afterwards mentioned separately from the rectory.[55] In Dartford the nuns had a rent of 6s. 4d., granted to them after 1190 by Thomas the clerk,[56] which eventually fell into arrears and was lost. In Sussex John Filliol had licence in 1318 to alienate to the prioress 40s. rent in Manxey, near Pevensey, which his daughters Joan and Katherine, possibly nuns, held for their lives. By the 16th century the value of this rent had fallen to

20s. It was leased in 1536 to John Sackville, perhaps a relative of the last prioress, Isabel Sackville, for 99 years, and eventually purchased by Sir Richard Sackville for £25.[57]

In eleven more counties the priory at some time held property but afterwards lost or alienated it. In no case was it very extensive. In Buckinghamshire 5s. rent in Cadmore End was granted by Elias and Lawrence de Scaccario, probably after 1181, and one virgate was granted by Miles de Beauchamp between 1190 and 1213.[58] In Cheshire Henry II confirmed a grant of Ranulf, Earl of Chester, and in 1186 Urban III confirmed the conventual church of the nuns of Chester, granted by the same earl.[59] In Gloucestershire Margaret, daughter of Robert son of Harding, gave the land of Baldwin de Nibley in North Nibley c. 1200 to provide an annual pittance for the nuns at Whitsun, and a few years later Maurice de Gant gave a rent in Dursley.[60] In Hampshire William Capra, Alice his wife, and William their son gave half a mark in Grately, and in Winchester Geoffrey Martel, donor of the church of Blandford (Dors.), gave one mark in rent.[61] In Croxley (Herts.) in 1218–20 Walter de Waunci, Robert de Amewill, and John de Seleford each gave 2s. 3d. quit-rent from one-third of the mill. Isabel Croxley gave a rent of 3s. in the same place for the nuns' kitchen. The mill was probably lost after a time to St. Albans Abbey. In Radwell Adam de Mandeville gave the land of Osmund c. 1180, and Ermengard his widow confirmed it. Agnes de Caune gave 13d. in rent c. 1190 in Reed. In Rushden in Henry II's reign Everard son of Ailwin gave some land called Longhecrof, and in Stanstead Abbots a rent of 10s. was given by Henry, son of Hugh, and Reynold de Ginges his brother. This rent was alienated to Waltham Abbey c. 1250.[62] In Lincolnshire the priory had in 1190 one seld in Boston, the gift of Robert of Leicester.[63] In Norfolk Michael Capra, his wife Rose, and Robert de Munteni gave 2s. rent in Burston, and Geoffrey

[48] Ibid. 26–27; *Valor Eccl.* (Rec. Com.), i. 395, wrongly listed under Mdx.

[49] *Clerkenwell Cart.* 78, 124, 121.

[50] Ibid. 52, 72.

[51] Ibid. 19.

[52] Ibid. 29, 39, 58, 59; B.M. Harl. Chart. 83 E 39.

[53] *Clerkenwell Cart.* 62–66; *Valor Eccl.* (Rec. Com.), i. 395, wrongly listed under Mdx.; *Feet of F. 7 & 8 Ric. I* (P.R.S. xx), 120.

[54] *Valor Eccl.* (Rec. Com.), i. 395. allowing for those properties wrongly listed under Mdx.

[55] For Kent see W. O. Hassall, 'Kent properties of the nunnery of St. Mary Clerkenwell and the Sackvilles', *Archaeologia Cantiana*, lxiv. 85 sqq.; *Clerkenwell Cart.* 9, 118, 194, 211–13, 218–19.

[56] *Clerkenwell Cart.* 122.

[57] W. O. Hassall, 'Sussex property of St. Mary Clerkenwell and the Sackvilles', *Suss. N. & O.* xi. 38–40.

[58] *Clerkenwell Cart.* 8, 106–7; W. O. Hassall, 'Bucks. properties of the nunnery of St. Mary Clerkenwell', *Recs. of Bucks.* xiv. 365–6.

[59] W. O. Hassall, 'Chester property of nunnery of St. Mary Clerkenwell', *Jnl. Chester and N. Wales Archit. and Arch. Soc.* xxxvi (2), 178–9; *Clerkenwell Cart.* 12.

[60] *Clerkenwell Cart.* 28–29, 104–6.

[61] Ibid. 119, 27; W. O. Hassall, 'Hants. property of nunnery of St. Mary Clerkenwell', *Proc. Hants. Field Club and Arch. Soc.* xvi. 288–9.

[62] *Clerkenwell Cart.* 103–4, 123, 89–90, 138–9, 106, 53–54; W. O. Hassall, 'Hertford properties of nunnery of St. Mary Clerkenwell', *Trans. East Herts. Arch. Soc.* xii. 100–4.

[63] W. O. Hassall, 'Note on Lincs. property of nuns of St. Mary Clerkenwell', *Lincs. Archit. and Arch. Soc.* N.S. iii. 137; *Clerkenwell Cart.* 8.

Capra gave the mill of Tittleshall.[64] In Oxfordshire Margaret Redvers gave 50s. rent from Heyford Warren and Newnham Murren c. 1240 to provide clothing for the convent.[65] In Suffolk Pain Baril and Hubert Baril gave land of the fee of the Earl of Clare in Cockfield, for which the nuns were to render 15s. a year. Reynold de Warenne c. 1178 confirmed the grant of the mill of Weston by Robert de Verli, whose sister Maud was to be a nun. In the same place at about the same time Clemency de St. Cler gave 3s. annual rent.[66] In Surrey John de Tanton gave 3s. 1d. quit-rent in Newington Butts for a pittance on his sister's anniversary.[67] From the farm of the same county King Stephen granted the nunnery a penny, but no trace of payment has been found.[68] Finally in Worcestershire the nuns had land in the market of Pershore by the gift of Margaret daughter of Roger, but this was perhaps sold before 1186.[69]

The size of the community is not known save for the rare occasions when all its members are named in contemporary sources. In 1379, besides the prioress, there were fifteen nuns and one sister;[70] in 1383 seventeen nuns were present at the election of the new prioress;[71] in 1387 six novices were professed of whom three had taken part in the election in 1383[72] and in 1388 another two were professed.[73] In 1524 eleven nuns took part in the election of the prioress.[74]

The priory evidently always had a sub-prioress, and in 1490–1 there was a treasuress, but no other obedientaries are known.[75] In 1527–8 Sir Thomas More was paid 53s. 4d. a year as steward, and the nunnery also employed a counsellor at 26s. 8d., a confessor for the like fee, an auditor at 53s. 4d., a number of chaplains, and a collector of rents from London, who was paid 40s.[76] In the 13th century one of the chaplains who resided in the priory was known as the master, the procurator, or even

the prior.[77] Besides the nuns themselves, their chaplains, and their servants, the priory also housed from time to time corrodarians, boarders, and even persons living in tenements.[78] With so many people coming and going, the priory, situated near London and beside one of the main roads leading out of the capital, can never have been a quiet place, but nothing is known of its relations with the outside world apart from the many lawsuits which the defence of its property involved. From Henry II the nuns received a number of gifts of money, mainly, in the later years, from the lands of Henry of Essex, one of their benefactors.[79] The Bishop of London was patron with the right of visitation, and the right to visit during a vacancy of the see was the subject of an agreement in 1262,[80] but there seem to be no records of visitation either by the bishops or by the Archbishops of Canterbury, except part of a letter which indicates that the Bishop of London visited the priory in 1433, 1439, or 1444.[81] In 1396 a chantry was set up in the church of St. Mary Woolnoth in London under the will of Thomas Noket, citizen and draper of London. The Priory of Clerkenwell was given responsibility for its oversight and received half a mark yearly, while the chaplain was paid 4½ marks.[82]

As one of the richer houses Clerkenwell survived until 1539. On 6 September of that year Richard Layton wrote to Cromwell 'we put the Duke of Norfolk's servant in custody of Clerkenwell and have fully dissolved it to the contentation of the prioress and her sisters'.[83] Within a year, however, the site of the priory had been sold back to the Crown by the duke, and it passed rapidly through a number of hands, the other properties being separately granted away.[84] The last prioress, Isabel Sackville, received a pension of £50, which she enjoyed for over 30 years, dying in 1570; she directed that she should be buried in the church of Clerkenwell.[85] Eleven other nuns, three of whom had also been present at the election of 1524, were receiving pensions in 1540.[86]

The nuns' church, which was already parochial before the Dissolution, stood partly on the site of the later church of St. James, Clerkenwell. The cloister of the nunnery lay on its north side. The

[64] *Clerkenwell Cart.* 119–20, 74–76; W. O. Hassall, 'Norf. properties of nunnery of St. Mary Clerkenwell and Capra family', *Norf. Archaeology*, xxviii. 238–40.

[65] *Clerkenwell Cart.* 129–30; W. O. Hassall, 'Property of St. Mary Clerkenwell in South Midlands', *Oxoniensia*, xiii. 73–74.

[66] *Clerkenwell Cart.* 124–5, 19–20, 121–2.

[67] W. O. Hassall, 'Surr. property of nuns of St. Mary Clerkenwell', *Surr. Arch. Soc. Coll.* i. 157; *Clerkenwell Cart.* 14, 183.

[68] *Clerkenwell Cart.* 14, 183.

[69] W. O. Hassall, 'Worcs. property of nunnery of St. Mary Clerkenwell', *Trans. Worcs. Arch. Soc.* N.S. xxiii. 75; *Clerkenwell Cart.* 3.

[70] E 179/42/4A.

[71] Guildhall MS. 9531/3, f. 267.

[72] Ibid. f. 346v.

[73] Ibid. f. 288.

[74] Ibid. 9531/10, f. 46.

[75] *Clerkenwell Cart.* p. xv, quoting S.C. 6/Hen. VII/396.

[76] S.C. 6/Hen. VIII/2118.

[77] *Clerkenwell Cart.* p. xii.

[78] Ibid. p. xv.

[79] *Pipe R.* 1159, 53; 1162, 73; 1182, 103; 1185, 43; 1186, 198; 1187, 19 (P.R.S. i, v, xxxi, xxxiv, xxxvi, xxxvii).

[80] Irene J. Churchill, *Canterbury Administration*, i. 172; ii. 49, 52.

[81] *Clerkenwell Cart.* 272.

[82] B.M. Harl. Charts. 53 H 15, 16, 40, 41; *Cal. Wills in Court of Husting* (Lond.), ii. 322–3.

[83] *L. and P. Hen. VIII*, xiv (2), p. 39.

[84] Ibid. xv, p. 220.

[85] Dugdale, *Mon.* iv. 78.

[86] *L. and P. Hen. VIII*, xv, p. 546.

church and other buildings survived into the 18th century; the church, by that time much changed by alterations and additions, was demolished in 1788 to make way for the present church of St. James. By 1815 a small piece of wall to the north of the church was all that was left of the priory, and this disappeared in the course of the 19th century.[87]

*J. L. Kirby*

### Revised List of the Prioresses of Clerkenwell

This list is taken from *Heads of Religious Houses,* vol. 1, p. 214; vol. 2, pp. 582–83, and vol. 3 (forthcoming).

Christina, occurs 1144, 1170

Ermengarde, occurs 1186, 1199

Isabel, occurs 1206

Alice (Alesia), occurs 1216, 1225

Eleanor, occurs 1221–3

Hawise, occurs 1231/2, 1244

Cecily, occurs 1245; 1248

Margaret or Margery, Whatvyll, Watevile, Watewyle, or Watervile, occurs 1251/2, 1264/5

Alice Oxeney, occurs 1270/1, 1276

Agnes or Anneys Marci, occurs 1283; died before 1305

Denise Bras

Margery Bray

Joan (de) Lewknore, occurs 1306/7, 1328

Joan (de) Fulham, occurs 1340, 1345

Idonea Let (Lewtier, Litier, Lutier, Lutiers, Lyter, Lyters, Lytier), occurs 1356, 1368. In 1376 Idonea was still alive, but described simply as a nun.

Katherine Braybrok, prob. successor of Idonea in 1379, occurs 1381; died 1384

Lucy atte Wod, elected 1384; resigned by 1389

Joan Vian, elected 1389; occurs 1403

Margaret Bakewell, occurs 1406, 1424

Isabel Wentworth, occurs 1425/6; probably the prioress Elizabeth in December 1446; occurs 1451

Margaret Bull, occurs 1456, 1464

Agnes Clifford, occurs 1469; died bef. 1473

Katherine Green, elected 1473; occurs 1487

Isabel (or Elizabeth) Hussey, occurs 1498; died before 1502/3

Rose Reygate, elected 1504 × 1507; died 1524

Isabel Sackville, elected 1524 to Dissolution; died 1570

---

[87] For description of site and conventual buildings, see W. O. Hassall, 'Conventual buildings of St. Mary Clerkenwell', *T.L.M.A.S.* xiv. 234–82.

# 5. THE PRIORY OF HALIWELL

## INTRODUCTION

The *V.C.H.* article covers most of the sources for this priory. However, for the century before the Dissolution, there is additional information in Paxton, 'Nunneries', pp. 60 and 62, 312–23 and *passim*, on the identities of the nuns themselves, for example the background of prioress Elizabeth Prudde, as the widow of a successful Westminster glazier, and of Elizabeth Arundell, who although she absconded from the priory, was later herself prioress. Further details are also given of the priory's staff, tenants, recipients of ecclesiastical patronage and others, as well as on the spiritual services it provided, and appendices list chaplains, lay officials, graduate presentees in the London diocese and recipients of annuities and corrodies. Books owned by Haliwell have a brief mention in Bell, *What Nuns Read*, pp. 10, 148–9.

There was a close relationship between the convent and the Fraternity of St. Nicholas of the Parish Clerks' Company, and four prioresses in succession were admitted as members between *c.*1456 and 1516, see N. W. and V. A. James (eds.), *Bede Roll of the Fraternity of St. Nicholas*, 2 vols. (London Record Society, 39, 2004), i, pp. 330, 578, 192, 193, 495. Dame Alice Hampton (died 1514–16), widow of a London alderman and a vowess of Haliwell, was also a member of the Fraternity (see G.L. MS 9171/9, ff. 5v–6). This association appears to be unique to the Haliwell house.

For material relating to the convent's lost cartulary, see *Monastic Research Bulletin*, 5 (1999), p. 26. Information on the convent's London property is to be found in Honeybourne, 'Property', pp. 92–3 and in *Documentary Sources*, pp. 57–8.

*Jessica Freeman*

The priory of St. John the Baptist at Haliwell, or Holywell, in Shoreditch, although often described both by contemporaries and historians as a Benedictine nunnery was, like the better-known priory of Clerkenwell, a house of Augustinian canonesses. It was one of the larger English nunneries, ranking ninth in wealth – three places higher than Clerkenwell – in the *Valor*; but as comparatively few records of the house or its property have survived it has been largely forgotten.[1] The founder was Robert Fitz Generan (or Gelran) the second known holder of the prebend of Holywell or Finsbury in St. Paul's Cathedral.[2] Robert's name occurs from 1133 to 1150. He gave the nuns the site for their monastery, being the 'moor' in which the spring called Haliwell rose; it was reckoned to contain 3 acres, and a rent of 12*d.* a year was payable for it.[3] The priory precinct lay within the area now bounded by Batemans Row, Shoreditch High Street, Haliwell Lane, and Curtain Road.[4]

The extent of the priory's possessions in the 12th century is shown by two royal charters of 1189 and 1195.[5] Two other royal charters dated 1235, the one confirming that of 1189 and the other confirming gifts received by the priory during the intervening half century, mark the end of the period of rapid expansion of the priory lands.[6] Edward III confirmed both charters of Richard I in 1336.[7] Besides the 3 acres already mentioned the nuns had in the 12th century another 3 acres, also owing a rent of 12*d.*, the gift of Walter the precentor, who followed next but one after Robert Fitz Generan as prebendary of Holywell. They held also the land of John Hilewit or Bylewit, given by Richard de Belmeis, Bishop of London 1152–62, a tithe of the household expenses of Walter Fitz Robert and his heirs, a tithe of William de Rochelle, the church of Dunton (Beds.), and lands in Bedfordshire, Essex, Hertfordshire, Surrey, and the City of London.[8] After 1195 they also gained possessions in Cambridgeshire, Kent, Norfolk, and Suffolk.

---

[1] An account of this house appears in L.C.C. *Survey of Lond.* viii. Extracts from its charters are to be found in B.M. Cott. Vitellius, F. 8, ff. 84–86, 189–91; these entries also appear in Bodl. Dodsworth Collections, cii. 90.

[2] Le Neve, *Fasti*, ii. 394; Hennessy, *Novum Repertorium*, 30.

[3] *Cal. Chart. R.* 1327–41, 372.

[4] L.C.C. *Survey of Lond.* viii. 153–84 and pls. 1 and 183.

[5] Ibid. 372–3; Dugdale, *Mon.* iv. 393.

[6] *Cal. Chart. R.* 1226–57, 200–1.

[7] Ibid. 1327–41, 372–3.

[8] Ibid.; Dugdale, *Mon.* iv. 393.

In Bedfordshire the nunnery first held the church of Dunton and two half virgates in the same place. One of these, formerly held by Gregory the priest, was given to the nuns by Geoffrey the chamberlain.[9] The other was the gift of Geoffrey de Mulneho, William his brother, and Emma their sister-in-law.[10] Towards the end of Henry II's reign Roger de Brahi, having bought this half virgate, sold it back to the nuns for six silver marks, a jewel, and a ring, to hold of himself and his heirs for an annual rent of 14*d*.[11] In 1203 one of the half virgates was held of the priory by Robert Fitz Alfred at a yearly rent of 6*s*.[12] Other lands in Dunton were added to the priory's holdings during the reigns of John and Henry III.[13] The priory presented to Dunton church in 1221, 1235, and 1277.[14] Lands in Hinxworth (Herts.) and Dunton were given to the priory in 1275 by Henry of Hallingbury.[15] In 1372 the prioress together with the Abbots of Waltham (Essex) and Warden (Beds.) held one knight's fee in Millow and Dunton.[16] The nunnery's holdings were eventually consolidated into a single manor known as Dunton Eyeworth. By 1535 the whole of the priory's revenue in Bedfordshire amounted to £13 6*s*. 8*d*., being the price of 80 quarters of malt drawn from this manor, but the nuns had to pay £3 9*s*. 10*d*. a year out of the rectory.[17]

In Essex at the end of the 12th century the nuns had of the gift of Robert Fitz Walter all the enclosed marsh in his demesne of Burnham, except the part of the Canons of Dunmow, and in 1201 the land of Leyton, the gift of Robert's wife, Gunnora de Valoynes.[18] In 1201 also Hugh de Marenny gave them an acre in 'Brumfeld' in Leyton, and a way by his wood called Ruckholt in order to reach their meadow called 'Sudmad'.[19] In 1256 they had lands in Farnham from Gunnora, widow of William Lovel, and in 1261–2 in Southminster and Althorne.[20] The marshes of Burnham, Southminster, and Althorne they retained to the end, when they formed one of the most valuable holdings, worth £39 a year. They also had a manor of Ruckholt in Leyton, worth £3

6*s*. 8*d*, and a watermill at Bromley or Stratford at Bow, worth £8.[21]

In Hertfordshire the nunnery's possessions were perhaps more varied, if less valuable. They began with the land of Gatesbury in Braughing of the gift of John of Gatesbury; the church of Welwyn, given by Gunnora de Valoynes; a virgate in Hinxworth, given by Theobald Fitz Fulc, and 6 acres there given by Elias de Essewell; 47 acres in Upwick in Albury and part of a pasture in 'Upwikesbrome' with the service and homage of Walter Bonesquiere, given by himself, and finally 12 acres in Upwick, given by Guy of Upwick.[22] It was found in 1201 that Henry of Furnell had disseised the prioress of her free tenement in Gatesbury.[23] In 1238 the prioress and convent secured a bull from Pope Gregory X confirming them in their possession of Welwyn church.[24] About the same time the priory had a further grant of land in Braughing, from Richard Langeford,[25] and in 1273 Henry of Hallingbury added to the nuns' holding in Hinxworth.[26] In 1303 the prioress, together with three other landlords, also held a fee in Alswick, in Layston.[27] This probably comprised both the land held by the priory in 1217 and that of Richard of Leftonchurch (Layston), acquired from the priory of Holy Trinity Aldgate in 1239.[28] In exchange for land in Cornhill in the parish of St. Mary Woolnoth, given by Alfred of Windsor, the nuns secured from Ralph, son of Ive, in Hertfordshire, his mill in 'Brambel' called Westmill with an acre of meadow between the Lea (*Luya*) and the house of Roger de Piro, and an acre upon the down.[29] At the Dissolution the priory drew revenues from Welwyn, Braughing, Layston and Wyddial, Albury, part of the tithe of Westbury in Ashwell, and Farnham and Roydon (both just over the border in Essex).[30] The holding in Hinxworth had become part of neighbouring Ashwell,[31] and all the other places except Roydon have already been mentioned.

In Surrey the priory's holdings lay principally in Camberwell. The Haliwell estate there was founded upon lands granted by Robert, Earl of Gloucester, to Robert of Rouen and Reynold Pointz and which

[9] Ibid.; *Cal. Chart. R.* 1226–57, 201; *V.C.H. Beds.* ii. 221–2; B.M. Harl. Chart. 83 A 50; *Cal. of Feet of F. Beds.*, ed. G . H. Fowler (Beds. Rec. Soc. vi), 119.

[10] Dugdale, *Mon.* iv. 393; B.M. Harl. Chart. 83 B 39; 83 B 40.

[11] Dugdale, *Mon.* iv. 393; B.M. Harl. Chart. 83 A 47; 83 A 49.

[12] *Cur. Reg. R.* ii. 146.

[13] B.M. Harl. Chart. 83 B 10; 83 B 45; 83 B 48.

[14] *Rot. Hug. de Welles* (Cant. and York Soc.), ii. 4; *Rot. Rob. Gravesend* (Cant. and York Soc.), 304; *Rot. Ric. de Gravesend* (Cant. and York Soc.), 210.

[15] B.M. Harl. Chart. 83 B 32; *Gent. Mag.* 1795, lxv (1), 369.

[16] *Cal. Inq. p.m.* xiii, p. 121.

[17] *Valor Eccl.* (Rec. Com.), i. 394–5.

[18] *Cal. Chart. R.* 1226–57, 201; *Feet of F. Essex*, ed. R. E. G. Kirk, i. 22.

[19] *Cur. Reg. R.* i. 454; *Feet of F. Essex*, i. 168 (1248).

[20] *Feet of F. Essex*, i. 213, 249, 251, 254.

[21] *Valor Eccl.* (Rec. Com.), i. 394, wrongly listed under Essex; S.C. 6/Hen. VIII/2396.

[22] Dugdale, *Mon.* iv. 393; *Cal. Chart. R.* 1226–57, 201.

[23] *Cur. Reg. R.* i. 400.

[24] B.M. Harl. Chart. 43 A 37; Dugdale, *Mon.* iv. 393; *Cal. Papal Regs.* i. 167, 191, 303.

[25] B.M. Harl. Chart. 52 I 12.

[26] Ibid. 83 B 32.

[27] *Feudal Aids*, ii. 431.

[28] Dugdale, *Mon.* iv. 394; H. Ellis, *Hist. St. Leonard Shoreditch*, 192.

[29] *Cal. Chart. R.* 1226–57, 201.

[30] *Valor Eccl.* (Rec. Com.), i. 354; S.C. 6/Hen. VIII/2396.

[31] Ellis, *Hist. St. Leonard*, 192.

they gave in whole or in part to the priory. During the 12th and 13th centuries the priory's holdings in Camberwell and its neighbourhood were augmented by further benefactions and by purchases and the priory successfully withstood challenges to its tenure of the Pointz lands. It would appear that from the early 14th century, if not before, these lands were leased. In 1322 the manor of Camberwell was held by John de Uvedale, who paid a rent of 12s. 8d. a year to Stephen de Bakewell, and 5s. to the Prioress of Haliwell.[32] At the same time John Abel held 34 acres and 40s. rent, paying 4s. a year to Stephen de Bakewell and 20d. to the prioress.[33] In 1369 John Adam held 30 acres of the prioress at a rent of 12s. a year in Homefield (in Hatcham or Camberwell).[34] The priory leased its manor of Camberwell in 1392 to Baldwin Cole, citizen and draper of London, for seven years at a yearly rent of £11 6s. 8d.[35] In 1472 the prioress held lands in Peckham in Camberwell[36] and in 1539 also in Deptford. In the *Valor* rents from Camberwell were valued at £13 6s. 8d.[37]

In Suffolk and Norfolk the priory's holdings were apparently short-lived. In 1235 the nuns had all the land of John the priest, son of Emma of Clare, of the fee of Richard John, knight, in Clare and 'Rembreg',[38] and c. 1261 Gillian, then prioress, made a grant of property in the parish of St. Sepulchre, Norwich, to Thomas Fitz Stannard, citizen of Norwich, for a rent of 2s.[39] In 1284 the priory had from John de Lovetot lands and the advowson of the church of Brampton (Suff.).[40] No more is heard of these properties.

Two counties into which the nunnery's possessions expanded after 1235 were Cambridgeshire and Kent. In the former the nuns acquired the church of Trumpington. The advowson of the church was given to them in 1343 by Simon, Bishop of Ely, whose sister, Elizabeth Montague, was Prioress of Haliwell at the time. The priory had royal licence to appropriate the church,[41] and presented to it at least in 1389 and 1395.[42] In 1400 papal letters authorized the augmentation of its value,[43] and in 1535 the farm of the rectory with the tithes was said to be worth £23 10s.[44] In Kent the priory obtained 180

acres of marsh in Elmley in Sheppey in 1248 from Cecily, daughter of Henry of Oxford. The grant was confirmed by Cecily and her husband, John of Durham, in 1254.[45] Rents in Ash were secured from Mabel Torpel in 1269,[46] and further property in 1275 and 1315.[47] At the Dissolution the priory drew £5 6s. 8d. from the farm of the manor of Ash, and £4 from the farm of the marsh, then called 'Feren' or Old Marsh, in Tunstall.[48] In Middlesex in 1539 the priory had lands in Edmonton, as well as the site of the house in Shoreditch.[49]

Extensive as these properties were in 1535 they were the source of little more than one-third of the priory's income, £222 out of a total of £347 coming from rents in London.[50] These holdings were already extensive in 1235. Serlo the Mercer gave his chief messuage in the parish of St. Antholin, his house in Milk Street in the parish of St. Lawrence, his share of a shop in the mercery in the parish of St. Mary le Bow, with various other shops and solars and 44s. rent in the parish of St. Alphage at Cripplegate, and his share of the land, houses, and shops which he and Solomon de Basing had in Honey Lane, and of the half of a 'seld' with its shops and solars which they had in Westcheap in the parish of All Saints, Honey Lane, and two shops which he had in the goldsmiths' area in the Cheap, and all his lands and houses in Coleman Street.[51]

Between 1259 and 1353 a large number of London citizens and their widows left small properties and rents in London to the priory.[52] In 1316 the prioress had a messuage near the 'Red Cross' rented to Joan de Bohun,[53] in 1318 a tenement and shop in St. Stephen's, Walbrook,[54] and in 1388 a shop called 'Haliwelle Croice'.[55] The nuns never received any great benefaction, but a very large number of small ones, so that gradually over the centuries they built up a large estate in the City of London. In the later 14th century bequests from London citizens in most cases took the form of sums of money, some of which may have been used for the purchase of City property. In 1331 the priory had a licence to acquire lands in mortmain to the value of £10 yearly,[56] but it is not known to what use it was put. In 1338, when

[32] Dugdale, *Mon.* iv. 393–4.
[33] *Cal. Chart. R.* 1226–57, 202.
[34] *Pipe R.* 1177, 196; 1182, 157–8; 1185, 238 (P.R.S. xxvi, xxxi, xxxiv).
[35] *Cur. Reg. R.* xi. 206, 327, 448; *Pedes Finium . . . Surr.*, ed. F. B. Lewis (Surr. Arch. Soc. extra vol. i), 12, 13.
[36] *Pedes Finium . . . Surr.* 23.
[37] *Cal. Inq. p.m.* v, p. 346; *Cal. Close*, 1313–18, 135.
[38] *Cal. Inq. p.m.* vi, p. 178.
[39] B.M. Topham Chart 11 *.
[40] *Cal. of Feet of F. Suff.*, ed. W. Rye, 84.
[41] *Cal. Pat.* 1343–5, 104.
[42] Ellis, *Hist. St. Leonard*, 188–9.
[43] *Cal. Papal Regs.* v. 280–1.
[44] *Valor Eccl.* (Rec. Com.), i. 394.

[45] *Cal. of Kent Feet of F.*, ed. Irene J. Churchill (Kent Recs. xv), 206, 410.
[46] Ibid. 357.
[47] *Rot. Hund.* (Rec. Com.), i. 235; *Plac. de Quo Warr.* (Rec. Com.), 2.
[48] *Valor Eccl.* (Rec. Com.), i. 394.
[49] S.C. 6/Hen. VIII/2396.
[50] *Valor Eccl.* (Rec. Com.), i. 394.
[51] *Cal. Chart. R.* 1226–57, 201–2.
[52] *Cal. Wills in Court of Husting* (Lond.), ed. Sharpe, i, *passim*.
[53] *Cal. Inq. p.m.* vi, p. 34.
[54] *Cat. Anct. D.* i. C 87.
[55] *Cal. Close*, 1385–9, 376–7.
[56] *Cal. Pat.* 1330–4, 216.

religious houses with holdings in the City were taxed for its defence, Haliwell was one of two houses paying the largest sum, 100s.[57] Most of the bequests of money were made not to Haliwell alone but to a group of religious houses in and around London, of which it was one.[58] After 1408 such bequests seem to have ceased, but this did not prevent the nunnery from having scattered holdings in 41 City parishes at the time of the Dissolution.[59]

In 1239 Henry III gave the nuns 300 tapers,[60] and in 1244 twelve marks for rebuilding their mills, which had been burnt down through the carelessness of the King's bakers.[61] In 1318 Edward II gave them six oaks from the forest of Essex.[62] But the priory owed very little to royal patronage, or indeed to any magnate before the reign of Henry VII when, according to Stow, Sir Thomas Lovell, Chancellor of the Exchequer, was a great benefactor of the priory. He is said to have undertaken much building at the priory, and certainly he built a chapel in which he himself was buried in 1524 and where an inscription enjoined the nuns to pray for his soul.[63] Finally in 1522 John Billesdon, grocer, left money to maintain chantries at Haliwell.[64]

In 1379 there were eleven professed religious in the priory.[65] At the election of the prioress in 1472 there were 7 nuns present and 10 novices,[66] and 13 professed nuns and 4 novices participated in an election in 1534.[67] Very little is known of the members of this house. Some were of London families and associations of this kind may have occasioned some of the bequests made to the priory by Londoners. An instance of this occurred in 1321 when Thomas Romeyn left to Haliwell the reversions of some London properties on the deaths of Alice and Joan, his daughters, and Christine of Kent, their aunt, all of whom were nuns there.[68] Others were from the country and they also brought lands and rents to the priory.[69]

There were also lay brothers attached to the priory. In 1275 Odo the smith (*faber*) gave rents in London to the priory for his son, Peter, a lay brother there and for Maud de la Cornere, one of the nuns.[70]

In 1314 Katharine de Cretinge complained that the prioress, two nuns, two lay brothers, and some other people carried off property of hers which was at Shoreditch.[71]

The most distinguished prioress was Elizabeth Montague. In 1334, when the Abbot of Westminster granted her, a nun of noble birth, 100s. a year because of the poverty of the house, the prioress and nuns gave permission for her to receive the pension, and undertook that she should herself dispose of it.[72] It was confirmed in the next year both by the Bishop of London and by the king.[73] Surviving receipts prove that it was paid in 1335 and 1351.[74] It is hardly surprising to find that within six years of this grant she had been elected prioress. She was the daughter of William, Lord Montague. Her brothers were William, Earl of Salisbury, Simon, Bishop of Ely, and Edward, Lord Montague, and her sisters, besides three married ones, included Maud, Abbess of Barking, and Isabel, a nun of the same house.[75] She was still prioress in 1355.

Of the life of the nuns and the government of the priory there seems to be no surviving record. The only known obedientaries are those mentioned at the elections of prioresses: sub-prioress, sacrist, subsacrist, precentrix, succentrix, and cellaress. No doubt the most important business was the collection of rents in London, but in this the prioress was assisted by male advisers and agents, clerical or lay, like Martin Jolliffe, upholsterer and citizen of London, who was described as 'the Steward and citizen of the house and Church of St. John Baptist of Holywell' and was feoffee of John Gayton who held the like position at Stratford.[76] In 1534 the Earl of Rutland was chief steward, John Newdigate, doubtless a relative of Sybil Newdigate, the prioress, understeward, William Berners, auditor, and Alexander Hamilton, receiver, drawing between them fees of £18, of which Hamilton took more than half.[77] In 1537 George Newdigate, '*generosus frater mei*', was appointed by the prioress to be chief steward, understeward, keeper of the courts, surveyor, and general receiver of the priory's lands.[78] With a gross income of about £300 from temporalities and £45 from spiritualities, and a net income of just under £300,[79] the priory was not poor.

[57] *Cal. of Plea and Mem. R.* (Lond.), 1323–64, ed. A. H. Thomas, 101.
[58] *Cal. Wills in Court of Husting*, ii. 37–398, *passim*.
[59] S.C. 12/11/35; S.C. 6/Hen. VIII/2396.
[60] *Cal. Lib.* 1226–40, 399.
[61] Ibid. 1240–5, 274.
[62] *Cal. Close*, 1313–18, 542.
[63] Stow, *Survey*, ii. 73; J. Weever, *Antient Funeral Monuments*, 211; Ellis, *Hist. St. Leonard*, 193–5.
[64] *Cal. Wills in Court of Husting*, ii. 535.
[65] E 179/42/4A.
[66] Guildhall MS. 9531/7, f. 5.
[67] Ibid. 9531/11, ff. 76–79.
[68] *Cal. Pat.* 1321–4, 11.
[69] Ibid. 1327–30, 388.
[70] *Cal. Wills in Court of Husting*, i. 26, 29.

[71] *Cal. Pat.* 1313–16, 146.
[72] W.A.M., 5885.3
[73] *Cal. Pat.* 1334–8, 93.
[74] W.A.M., 5884, 29856.
[75] *Cart. of St. Frideswide*, ed. S. R. Wigrams (Oxf. Hist. Soc. xxxi), ii. 9.
[76] Guildhall MS. 9171/6, ff. 234v–6v; see p. 157.
[77] *Valor Eccl.* (Rec. Com.), i. 394–5; S.C. 12/11/35.
[78] Dugdale, *Mon.* iv. 395–6.
[79] *Valor Eccl.* (Rec. Com.), i. 394–5; S.C. 12/11/35.

As early as March 1533 the prioress, Joan Lynde, was paying the tithe of Dunton to Cromwell,[80] and in 1537 her successor made an indenture for the sale of certain of the priory lands to the Lord Chancellor, Sir Thomas Audley,[81] but nothing could avert the coming end. No record of the actual dissolution has been found but in 1539 the disposal of the lands was proceeding apace. Thomas Pointz wrote to Cromwell that he desired the keeping of some suppressed house, such as Haliwell, to have an honest dwelling for his family.[82] In October Sybil Newdigate,[83] the prioress, had a pension of £50, Ellen Cavour, the sub-prioress, £6 13s. 4d., and twelve nuns pensions varying from 53s. 4d. to 93s. 4d. each.[84]

In 1544 Queen Katherine secured the site for Henry Webbe, her gentleman usher. The priory chapel was speedily demolished to make way for houses in a growing suburb of London. The remains were popularly known as 'King John's Palace', but by the end of the 18th century there was nothing left of the buildings except some fragments of walls and a doorway.[85]

*J. L. Kirby*

## Revised List of the Prioresses of St. John, Haliwell

This list is derived from *Heads of Religious Houses*, vol. 1, p. 215; vol. 2, pp. 583–4; vol. 3 (forthcoming).

Clemence (Clementia), occurs 1193, 1203
Magalen, perh. *c*.1203
Maud (Matilda), occurs 1224, 1225
Agnes, occurs 1237, 1246

Juliana (Gillian), occurs 1248, 1262
Avice, occurs 1268
Christi[a]na, occurs 1269, 1292
Alice, occurs 1293; died before 1295
Anastasia, occurs 1309
Christina, occurs 1314
Aubrey (Albreda), mentioned 1329 as former prioress
Lucy de Colney, occurs 1329, 1330
Mary de Stortford, occurs 1329, 1334
Tiffany (Theophania) la Bounde, occurs 1336, 1339
Elizabeth de Montagu (Montacute, Monte Acuto), occurs 1340, 1356; died before 1379
Ellen Gosham (Goshalm), occurs 1363; died before 1376
Anne, occurs 1381
Isabel Norton, occurs 1383, 1393, noted as immediate precedessor of Edith in 1400[86]
Edith Griffith (Gryffitz), occurs 1400, 1417
Elizabeth Arundel, occurs 1428; died 1432
Clemence Freeman, elected 1432; occurs 1447
Joan Littlecock (Litilkoc, Lytelcock), admitted to Parish Clerks' Fraternity as prioress of an unnamed house May 1456 × May 1457, probably on death of her predecessor; noted as deceased May 1462 × May 1463
Joan Sevenoke, elected by May 1463; died 1472; noted as deceased prioress of Haliwell in May 1473 × May 1474 when her successor, Elizabeth Prudde, was admitted a member of the Parish Clerks' Fraternity
Elizabeth Prudde (Prod), elected 1472; admitted to fraternity of Parish Clerks as prioress of Haliwell, May 1473 × May 1474; noted on the Bede Roll as deceased prioress of an unnamed house, May 1501 × May 1502; alive in 1492
Joan Lynde, occurs 1505; died 1534
Sybil Newdigate, elected 1534; surrendered the house, 1539; still alive 1549

[80] *L. and P. Hen. VIII*, v, p. 412.
[81] Ibid. xii (2), p. 359.
[82] Ibid. xiv (2), pp. 351, 354.
[83] *Mdx. Pedigrees* (Harl. Soc. lxv), 66–67; D. Knowles, *Rel. Orders in Eng.* iii. 226–7; see p. 166.
[84] *L. and P. Hen. VIII*, xiv (2), p. 115; xv, p. 545.
[85] Stow, *Survey*, ii. 73; Dugdale, *Mon.* iv. 392; Ellis, *Hist. St. Leonard*, 201.

[86] Paxton, 'Nunneries', 62; W.A.M., 30246; B.L. Add. Chart. 8444; *Heads*, 2, p. 584; Helena M. Chew, *London Possessory Assizes: a calendar* (London Record Society, 1, 1965), no. 199.

# 6. THE PRIORY OF KILBURN

## INTRODUCTION

To this comprehensive article may now be added an analysis of the origins and role of its founders and patrons and a discussion of the priory's foundation around a hermitage, see Thompson, *Women Religious*, pp. 25–6, 32–3, 63, 208. For the century prior to the Dissolution, Paxton, 'Nunneries', esp. pp. 312–23, has additional details about the nuns themselves, as well as about the priory's staff, tenants, recipients of ecclesiastical patronage and others, and the spiritual services the nuns provided. There are also appendices which list chaplains, lay officials, graduate presentees in the London diocese and recipients of annuities and corrodies. The books owned by Kilburn priory have been briefly mentioned in Bell, *What Nuns Read*, p. 20.

Information about the estates of the priory is available on the web site of the English Monastic Archives project, URL: http://ww.ucl.ac.uk/history/englishmonasticarchives/index.htm (accessed 28 February 2007). A 1446 rental at the Surrey History Centre (MS 3923) provides details of the estates of the priory at Leatherhead, Surrey. *Documentary Sources*, p. 83 has information about the priory's property in London.

*Jessica Freeman*

The priory of Kilburn was situated in the parish of Hampstead, between Edgware Road and the Kilburn stream at the top of what is now Belsize Road and close to Kilburn Station (B.R.). Excavations in 1850, which appear to have cut through part of the priory, revealed tiles and human bones.[1] A fragment of a funerary brass, found in the 1870's, was in 1965 in St. Mary's Church, Priory Road.[2] The priory was a small house of Augustinian canonesses, or possibly Benedictine nuns,[3] dedicated to St. John the Baptist and dependent on the abbey of St. Peter at Westminster which had held the manor of Hampstead from the 10th century.[4] The nunnery was probably founded *c.* 1130, although a foundation may have been contemplated some years earlier by Gilbert Crispin, Abbot of Westminster, for whose soul the nuns were obliged to pray.[5] The first nuns are said to have been three former

maids of honour to Maud, wife of Henry I, named Emma, Gunilda, and Christine. Herbert, Abbot of Westminster 1121–40, gave them 30s. out of the 60s. in alms which Sweyn, father of Robert of Essex, had given to Westminster, together with a rent of 2s. from Southwark and the site of the priory; over them he set one Godwin, who had formerly built a hermitage there. The abbey of Westminster and Gilbert, Bishop of London, consented to the grant.[6] The suggestion that the *Ancrene Riwle*, a guide-book for the spiritual and practical life of anchoresses, was written for the first nuns of Kilburn, is now discredited.[7]

A prioress eventually replaced the male head of the priory, but the house remained small, and its peculiar (but not unique) position as a priory of nuns dependent on an abbey of monks inevitably led to some friction with the bishop of the diocese. Bishop Gilbert had exempted the nunnery from his jurisdiction,[8] and this exemption was confirmed by Pope Honorius III in 1225.[9] In 1229, however, Pope Gregory IX found it necessary to appoint the Bishop of Rochester, the Prior of Dunstable, and Thomas, Rector of Maidstone, to hear a complaint of Westminster Abbey against interference by

---

[1] G. E. Mitton, *Hampstead and Marylebone*, 42; *Trans. Hampstead Antiq. & Hist. Soc.* (1904–5), 91–101.

[2] Pevsner, *Lond.* 187; *T.L.M.A.S.* vi. 276.

[3] It is usually assumed to have been Benedictine because of its dependence on the Benedictine Abbey of Westminster, but the very rare references to the Order call it Augustinian: J. J. Park, *Topog. and Nat. Hist. of Hampstead*, 175; *Cal. Pat.* 1350–4, 340; cf. F. G. Sitwell, 'The Ancren Riwle', *Ampleforth Jnl.* xxxvi. 161. For nuns the question was not of vital importance – compare Clerkenwell and Haliwell. Sybil Kirke, the last Prioress of the Benedictine nunnery at Stratford at Bow, but a former Prioress at Kilburn, was described in Tunstall's Reg. as Benedictine: Guildhall MS. 9531/10, f. 118.

[4] *Dom. Bk.* (Rec. Com.), i. 128a; Park, *Hist. Hampstead*, 87–90.

[5] J. A. Robinson, *Gilbert Crispin, Abbot of West.* 34.

[6] Dugdale, *Mon.* iii. 426; Westm. Liber Niger, f. 125; B.M. Cott. MS. Faustina A. III, ff. 325v, 326v.

[7] E. E. Power, *Med. Eng. Nunneries*, 528; *Ampleforth Jnl.* xxxvi. 153–67.

[8] Dugdale, *Mon.* iii. 427; Westm. Domesday, f. 636v.

[9] Dugdale, *Mon.* iii. 427; B.M. Cott. MS. Faustina A. III, f. 178; Westm. Domesday, f. 637.

Bishop Eustace of Fauconberg.[10] Proceedings were delayed by the death of the Bishop of London, but a settlement was finally reached in 1231 between the new bishop, Roger Niger, and his chapter, and Richard of Barking, Abbot of Westminster, and his abbey.[11] This settlement provided for both a secular priest to rule over the priory and for a prioress. The priest was to be presented by the abbey to the bishop, who would admit him to office. The prioress was to be instituted by the abbey and make her obedience to the bishop. The ordering, regulation, and correction of the house, including if necessary the removal of its head, were vested in the abbot, and only if he neglected his duties would the bishop interfere. From Westminster only the abbot or prior was permitted to visit the nuns and hear confessions. The bishop might enter the house when he wished to pray and hear confessions, but he was to bless or consecrate the nuns only by invitation of the abbot. These limitations on the bishop's authority no doubt explain the lack of records of visitations of the priory and of elections of prioresses. No more is known about the secular priests who presided over the early days of the priory.

After the foundation Abbot Herbert gave the nuns the land called 'Gara' in Knightsbridge, afterwards Kensington Gore,[12] and his successor at Westminster, Gervase (1140–60), confirmed this,[13] and gave the nuns two corrodies of bread, beer, wine, mead, and meat from the abbey.[14] These grants were confirmed by the next abbot, Lawrence (1160–76),[15] and his successor, Walter (1176–91), assigned the manor of Paddington to the almoner of the abbey to provide a feast on his anniversary, in which the nuns of Kilburn were to share without prejudice to their regular allowance from the abbey.[16] This anniversary feast was lost, but the regular corrodies continued until the Dissolution. Then the nuns were drawing a weekly allowance of 40 gallons of beer and 28 loaves of bread, which with annual money payments was worth altogether £16 1s. 4d. a year.[17] In 1290–1

and 1465 there were loans and transfers of money between the abbey and the priory,[18] which controlled its own estates and financial affairs, but there is no other information about their relationship. Brother Osmund, possibly a monk of Westminster, acted as the prioress's attorney in the King's Court in 1207.[19]

There is no further trace of the property in Knightsbridge and Southwark, but eventually the nunnery came to hold property in London, Middlesex, Buckinghamshire, Kent, Surrey, and Essex. In 1286 the nuns secured 13s. 4d. in rent from Falk de Wagefeud, known as Falk the Taverner, in the parish of Allhallows, Bread Street.[20] From the parish of St. Mary Somerset they had a similar rent in 1302,[21] and a rent of 20s. in St. Clement, Eastcheap, in 1303.[22] In 1338 religious houses with holdings in the City were taxed to put the City in a state of defence, and Kilburn paid 10s. on its property there.[23] In 1362 the priory drew 20s. and a mark towards a chantry for the soul of Adam de Blakeney from two tenements with cellars and five shops in Bow Lane in Dowgate ward,[24] and in 1423 a rent of 7s. from a tenement called 'le sterre on the hoope' in Allhallows, Dowgate.[25] In 1368 they had a rent of 33s. 4d. from a tavern with four shops in St. Bride Fleet Street,[26] and in 1419 a rent of 2s. in the same parish.[27] They had licence in 1375 to acquire from Thomas de Brandesby two shops with cellars in the parish of St. Nicholas in the Shambles.[28] In 1393 they held the tenements formerly of Thomas of Lincoln on the east side of 'Moynesokne' near 'Oldewich',[29] and these may have been identical with the 'Bell on the Hoop' and other property held in 1403 in the parishes of St. Mary le Strand and St. Clement Danes.[30] These properties were all small lots acquired gradually, so that by the Dissolution the nuns drew rents from 19 parishes, amounting to £16 gross or £13 net, the collector being paid 33s. 4d. for his work.[31]

In 1306 the nuns had a grant of rents in Kilburn to maintain the fabric of their church.[32] In Harrow

[10] Dugdale, *Mon.* iii. 427–8; Park, *Hist. Hampstead*, App. xvi–xviii; Westm. Domesday, f. 637; B.M. Cott. MS. Faustina A. III, f. 204.

[11] Dugdale, *Mon.* iii. 426; Park, *Hist. Hampstead*, 168– 70; W.A.M., 4843 and Chart. LIV; B.M. Cott. MS. Faustina A. III, f. 329.

[12] Dugdale, *Mon.* iii. 426; Westm. Liber Niger, f. 125; B.M. Cott. MS. Faustina A. III, f. 327.

[13] Dugdale, *Mon.* iii. 427; Westm. Liber Niger, f. 125v; B.M. Cott. MS. Faustina A. III, f. 328.

[14] Dugdale, *Mon.* iii. 427; Park, *Hist. Hampstead*, App. xiii–xiv; B.M. Cott. MS. Faustina A. III, f. 327v.

[15] Dugdale, *Mon.* iii. 427; Park, *Hist. Hampstead*, App. xiv; Westm. Liber Niger, f. 125v; B.M. Cott. MS. Faustina A. III, f. 328v.

[16] Park, *Hist. Hampstead*, 165.

[17] *Valor Eccl.* (Rec. Com.), i. 432; *L. and P. Hen. VIII*, xi, p. 130; xiii (1), p. 583; W.A.M., 5919* (a paper account of the corrodies, *temp.* Hen. VIII).

[18] W.A.M., 4848, 4861, 4863, 30399.

[19] *Cur. Reg. R.* 1207–9, 114.

[20] *Cal. Pat.* 1281–92, 225; *Cal. of Wills in Court of Husting* (Lond.), ed. Sharpe, i. 74.

[21] *Cal. Letter Bk. C*, 191.

[22] Ibid. 192.

[23] *Cal. of Plea and Memoranda R.* (Lond.), 1323–64, ed. A. H. Thomas, 101.

[24] *Cal. Inq. p.m.* xi. 322; *Cal. Letter Bk. C*, 192.

[25] *Cal. of Plea and Memoranda R.* (Lond.), 1413–37, ed. A. H. Thomas, 167.

[26] *Cal. Inq. p.m.* xii. 257.

[27] *Cal. of Plea and Memoranda R.* 1413–37, ed. Thomas, 73.

[28] *Cal. Pat.* 1374–7, 92.

[29] *Cal. Close*, 1392–6, 107, 110.

[30] B.M. Add. Chart. 5313.

[31] Park, *Hist. Hampstead*, App. xviii–xx; 22 pars. according to S.C. 6/Hen. VIII/2345.

[32] B.M. Harl. Chart. 53 E 17.

and Hayes they acquired lands in 1242–4 from William Huscarl[33] and four years later from the priory of St. Helen, Bishopsgate.[34] In Stanwell they received property from James of Haverhill in 1235–6,[35] and in Hampstead in 1243–4 from Robert son of Nicholas.[36] In Oakington (Tokyngton in Harrow) Ralph Tokyngton gave all his lands to the priory in 1246–7. One hundred and fifty years later a dispute arose over these lands. They had been leased by the priory to William Barneville for an annual rent of 30s. After his death his widow, Maud, and his son John refused to pay this rent, whereupon the prioress and convent took possession of the lands, but were disseised by Maud and John with the help of their neighbours. The Abbot of Westminster was appointed to arbitrate on the complaint of the priory and upheld the rights of the nuns. A settlement was reached in 1400 and 1401, when all the lands of the priory in Oakington were surveyed, the boundaries and area of each field being exactly described.[37] This Oakington property, with the other holdings in Harrow parish, apparently in Wembley, remained with the priory until the Dissolution, together with lands in Hendon, Stanwell, Tottenham, and West End (Hampstead).[38]

In Buckinghamshire the only holding of the priory was at East Burnham, where the nuns secured a virgate in 1207 from Henry son of Humphrey Tubelin,[39] and still drew a rent of 5s. for it in 1535. In Kent in 1376 the nuns were given an acre of land in Cudham, and the appropriation of the parish church, to enable them to find a chaplain to pray for the soul of Simon Langham, Archbishop of Canterbury.[40] In Surrey, lands in Milton (Middleton) in Dorking were given to the priory in 1248 by Philip de Frauncey and in 1269 by William le Corviser and Arlin atte Hache.[41] In 1273, 1283, and 1323 the priory was said to owe the service of half a knight's fee for the manor. John son of Roger de Somery, who gave the nuns some interest in it, died in 1321, and in 1323 his widow, Lucy, held the manor, then valued at 20s. a year, of the priory.[42] In 1349 it was described as a whole fee.[43] Also in Surrey

in 1365 the priory had from Roger de Aperdale a messuage, 30 acres of land, 8 acres of meadow, and 13s. 4d. rent in Pachevesham in Leatherhead and Mickleham,[44] in fulfilment of a royal licence to acquire lands and rents in mortmain.[45] In Essex the only holding of the priory was a pension from Aldham rectory, worth 6s. 8d. a year in 1535.[46]

From Henry II the nunnery received alms in money, 30s. in 1184 and 1185, and 15s. in 1186 and 1187.[47] The gifts of Henry III were more varied. In 1239 he gave them £4 to pay for robes for 20 nuns and two sisters,[48] in 1241 an Easter taper weighing 15 lbs.,[49] and in 1247 he pardoned them 14s. due at the Exchequer[50] and 10 marks.[51] In 1258 he gave them half the value of a ship forfeited as deodand,[52] in 1260 a thousand herrings,[53] and in 1265 cloth for their clothing and habits.[54] The charity of later kings consisted entirely of exemptions from the payment of taxation, tallages, and fifteenths and tenths. First granted by Edward III in 1352 for three years,[55] and made perpetual in the following year,[56] it was extended by Richard II in 1383 to cover their church of Cudham (Kent).[57] These grants were later confirmed, either for thirty years or indefinitely, by Henry IV, Henry V, Henry VI, Edward IV, and Richard III.[58]

Apart from lands and rents, many of which must have been given or devised to the priory, a large number of bequests were received, mainly from London citizens. In most cases these consisted of sums of money,[59] but occasionally there were other gifts, such as the red wine bequeathed by John of Oxford in 1340, or the basin and ewer from Alice Wodegate in 1387.[60] Usually Kilburn was one of a number of houses remembered by the testator, as in the cases of Robert de Pleseley, Rector of Southfleet (Kent), in 1368, and John Springthorp in 1425, both of whom left 20s. to the nunnery.[61]

[33] *Feet of F. Lond. and Mdx.*, ed. Hardy and Page, i. 27: C.P. 25 (1)/147/13/20.

[34] *Feet of F. Lond. and Mdx.* i. 32.

[35] Ibid. 22.

[36] Ibid. 28.

[37] *Feet of F. Lond. and Mdx.* i. 31; C.P. 25 (1)/147/15/266; *Cal. Close, 1399–1402*, 293–7, 299.

[38] *Valor Eccl.* (Rec. Com.), i. 432.

[39] *Cur. Reg. R. 1207–9*, 22, 114; *Feet of F. Lond. and Mdx.* i. 10.

[40] *Cal. Pat. 1374–7*, 391; J. Thorpe, *Registrum Roffense*, 264.

[41] *Pedes Finium . . . Surr.*, ed. F. B. Lewis (Surr. Arch. Soc. Extra vol. i), 31, 44. The former not 1232 as in *V.C.H. Surr.* iii. 147, but 32 Hen. III (1247–8).

[42] *Cal. Inq. p.m.* ii. 14, 495; vi. 256, 258; *Cal. Close, 1318–23*, 624, 630; Park, *Hist. Hampstead*, 171; B.M. Harl. MS. 6281.

[43] *Cal. Inq. Misc. 1348–77*, 8.

[44] *Cal. Pat. 1364–7*, 124; *Cal. Inq. p.m.* xii. 315; *Lists of Inq. a.q.d.* (Lists and Indexes xxii), ii. 547; *V.C.H. Surr.* iii. 297.

[45] *Cal. Pat. 1361–4*, 331.

[46] *Valor Eccl.* (Rec. Com.), i. 432.

[47] *Pipe R. 1182*, 98; 1185, 13; 1186, 177; 1187, 121 (P.R.S. xxxi, xxxiv, xxxvi, xxxvii).

[48] *Cal. Lib. 1226–40*, 432.

[49] Ibid. 1240–5, 37.

[50] *Close R. 1242–7*, 540.

[51] *Cal. Lib. 1245–51*, 150.

[52] *Close R. 1256–9*, 205.

[53] Ibid. 1259–61, 239.

[54] Ibid. 1264–8, 73.

[55] *Cal. Pat. 1350–4*, 250.

[56] Ibid. 539.

[57] Ibid. 1381–5, 283.

[58] Ibid. 1405–8, 470; 1413–16, 120; 1436–41, 486; 1461–7, 459; 1476–85, 510; B.M. Add. Chart. 63672.

[59] *Cal. Wills in Court of Husting*, i and ii, *passim*.

[60] Ibid. i. 460; ii. 271.

[61] *Cant. Reg. Langham* (Cant. and York Soc.), 356; *Cant. Reg. Chichele* (Cant. and York Soc.), ii. 306.

In 1239 there were said to be 20 nuns and 2 sisters,[62] but this is difficult to believe. It seems unlikely that the number of nuns ever reached that figure. In 1381, besides Alice, the prioress, there were only four nuns: Katherine, Emma, and two called Margaret; their surnames are unknown.[63] Some, if not all of the nuns brought dowries to the priory. Before 1317 a tenant in Westminster gave a rent of 3s. on his house in Kilburn, where his daughter was a nun,[64] and in 1343 William le Gaugeour, a London vintner, left an annuity charged on all his tenements to his daughter, Isabel, a nun.[65] In 1367 two nuns, Alice and Margery Pigeon, probably sisters, had a corrody or livery of food, with money for clothes, light, and fuel, for life from the Hospital of St. Giles-in-the-Fields.[66] (In 1352 a commission had been issued to arrest Margery Pigeon, an Augustinian nun of Kilburn, but then a vagabond in secular dress, and to deliver her to the prioress for punishment).[67] In 1366 Joan daughter of Alice and Richard de Worstede, a nun at Kilburn, figured in a dispute over property.[68] In 1374 Isabel Baudon, a nun there, was in receipt of an annuity from the property of her kinsman, James Andrew, draper of London.[69] In 1393 Maud Toky, the daughter of another London citizen, a grocer, received permission from the mayor and aldermen to become a nun at Kilburn, and in 1402 the prioress received Maud's share of her father's fortune, amounting to over £38, from the City chamberlain.[70] A few years earlier, in 1384, the Mayor of London paid 67s. to the prioress for maintaining the two daughters of the wife of John of Northampton, the famous mayor of London.[71] Clearly there was a close connexion with the City of London, and many of the nuns were daughters of the richer citizens. In 1391, however, it was said that one of the nuns, Margaret Lanney, who had worn the habit for 29 years, was a native of Normandy, and had to have a licence to remain in England, as all foreign religious had been expelled under the statute of 1377. In consideration of her age the licence was granted during good behaviour.[72]

The prioress in 1300 was probably a Londoner, for Jakemina Pountif, the orphan of a London citizen, was her niece and ward.[73] Most of the other prioresses are known, if at all, mainly by their first names alone. Emma de St. Omer (c. 1397–1403) was perhaps the nun Emma of 1381, but she can hardly have been born abroad like Margaret Lanney, her contemporary, or the fact would have been recorded. Probably the priory was too small to attract any great ladies. After the disappearance of the secular priest at the head of the priory there was doubtless always a chaplain. In 1297 one Thomas of Billingsgate was presented by Kilburn for ordination.[74] In 1391 the Pope granted relaxation of penance to penitents who on Midsummer Day, the feast of St. John the Baptist, visited and gave alms to the priory.[75]

Among the muniments of Westminster Abbey survives a small roll of payments made by John Glover, apparently the steward of the priory, for a period of 12 weeks from 18 August to 11 November.[76] The year is uncertain, but the handwriting suggests that it was written in the late 15th or early 16th century. During this period the nunnery spent 111s. on food and drink, of which the greater part was taken by meat, 49s., and fish, 24s. Most of the rest was spent on ale (12s.), beer (17s.), and wine and spice (4s.), leaving only 2s. 6d. for bread and 12d. for salt. Other foods were presumably grown by the priory itself. Another 44s. was spent on the wages of harvest men, the repair of farm implements, and such commodities as oatmeal, candles, and lamp oil. Servants' wages took another 46s., mostly for farmworkers, carter, ploughman, barleyman, thresher, and so on, but there were also three women servants and several men whose function is not stated.

In May 1535 the priory comprised the church, the hall, the chamber next the church, the middle chamber, the prioress's chamber, the buttery, pantry, and cellar, the inner chamber to the prioress's chamber, the chamber between the prioress's chamber and the hall, the kitchen, larder, brewhouse, and bakehouse, four rooms for the chaplain, confessor and hinds. The hall contained two tables, three trestles, three forms, one long settle, and two benches. It also had curtains and a cupboard. The chamber next the church was evidently the nuns' sitting-room, containing hangings, cushions, a little table, and two books of *Legenda Aurea*, one printed and the other manuscript, both in English. The middle chamber was their bedroom, with two wooden bedsteads, one feather bed, two mattresses, two old coverlets, three woollen blankets, and three bolsters. In the prioress's room was a fourposter and a trundle bed, eight pillows of down, and nine pairs

[62] *Cal. Lib.* 1226–40, 432.
[63] E 179/44/347.
[64] *Cal. Inq. Misc.* 1307–49, 71; *Cal. Close,* 1313–18, 503.
[65] *Cal. Wills in Court of Husting,* i. 470.
[66] *Cal. Pat.* 1364–7, 354.
[67] Ibid. 1350–4, 340.
[68] *Cal. Fine R.* 1356–68, 326; *Cal. to Escheat Rolls,* 105.
[69] *Cal. Wills in Court of Husting,* ii. 166.
[70] *Cal. Letter Bk. H,* 404, 405; H. T. Riley, *Memorials of Lond.* 535.
[71] *Cal. Close,* 1381–5, 494.
[72] *Cal. Pat.* 1388–92, 432.
[73] *Cant. Reg. Winchelsey* (Cant. and York Soc.), ii. 916.
[74] *Cal. of Early Mayor's Court R.* (Lond.), ed. A. H. Thomas, 76, 77.
[75] *Cal. Papal Regs.* iv. 398.
[76] W.A.M., 33287.

of sheets of linen and canvas. Also in the prioress's room were fire-irons and table-cloths for the tables both in the hall and the chamber next the church. The most valuable properties, however, were in the church – curtains, cloths, hangings, candlesticks, and silver vessels. Altogether the movables, including nearly £7 in ready money in the prioress's hands, were valued at £34, with £72 for the lead and bells.[77]

In 1535 the gross annual revenue of the priory was £86 7s. 11d., including nearly £8 from the leased demesne at Kilburn, £16 in corrodies from Westminster Abbey, over £20 from rents in the City of London, £11 10s. from other lands in Middlesex at Wembley, Oakington, Hendon, Stanwell, Tottenham, and Hampstead, £20 from Milton in Dorking and Leatherhead (Surr.), £9 from the rectory of Cudham (Kent), and small sums from Aldham (Essex) and East Burnham (Bucks.). The outgoings were comparatively small, £6 13s. 4d. for the stipend of the nuns' chaplain, 31s. 8d. for their receiver, 13s. 4d. for Robert Skynner, their steward their steward in Surrey, 6s. 8d. for Thomas Roberts, their steward in Wembley and Oakington, and some pensions, amounting in all to £12.[78] Very similar figures are found in accounts of the following year, except for a sharp fall in the revenue from Milton, which may possibly have been disposed of separately.[79] Being valued at less than £200 the priory was dissolved with the smaller houses,[80] and Anne Browne, the prioress, was given a pension of £10 a year.[81]

The site of the priory was first acquired by the Knights of St. John, by an exchange with the Crown, and afterwards in 1546 by the Earl of Warwick. Some subsequent owners were listed by J. J. Park.[82] He also reproduced an etching of a building which stood on the site in 1722,[83] although by 1814 when he wrote there was nothing left to see except a 'rising bank' in a field near the tea-drinking house called Kilburn Wells.[84]

*J. L. Kirby*

## Revised List of Prioresses of St. John, Kilburn

This list is taken from *Heads of Religious Houses*, vol. 1, p. 213; vol. 2, p. 575; and vol. 3 (forthcoming).

Alice, occurs 1208

Adelina occurs n.d. There is no clue as to her position in the sequence of prioresses

Margery (Margaret), occurs 1232; 1247/8

Joan, occurs 1248; 1258/9

Maud (Matilda), occurs 1268/9

Sabina, n.d. occurs mid-13th century

Cecily, occurs 1290

Agnes, occurs 1301; 1302

Maud (Matilda), occurs 1311

Alice de Pommesbourne, occurs 1339

Agnes, occurs 1345

Alice Pigoin, occurs 1352; 1381

Emma de St. Omer, occurs 1397; 1404

Alice, occurs 1423

Alice Pynchepole, occurs 1440; 1458

Matilda Reynold, occurs 1462; 1465

Katherine, occurs 1480; 1484

Sybil Kirk, occurs 1525; Prioress of Stratford at Bow 1528

Anne/Agnes Browne, occurs 1534; (formerly prioress) 1536–7

---

[77] Park, *Hist. Hampstead*, 179–85; Dugdale, *Mon.* iii. 424–5.
[78] *Valor Eccl.* (Rec. Com.), i. 432.
[79] Dugdale, *Mon.* iii. 329–30; S.C. 6/Hen. VIII/2345.
[80] *L. and P. Hen. VIII*, x, p. 515; xiii (2), p. 503.
[81] Ibid. xiii (1), p. 574.

[82] Park, *Hist. Hampstead*, 190–1, 196–7.
[83] Ibid. facing p. 202.
[84] Ibid. 202; Dugdale, *Mon.* iii. 425.

# HOUSE OF BRIDGETTINES

## 7. SYON ABBEY[1]

### INTRODUCTION

This account of the foundation and administration of the abbey still holds good, but much research has taken place, focused on the spiritual and intellectual life of its sisters, brethren and associated laypeople and patrons, and on the contents of its libraries in particular. For access to this research, see the bibliographies in: V. Gillespie (ed.), *Syon Abbey*, Corpus of British Medieval Library Catalogues, 9 (London, 2001). This includes an edition of the catalogue of the library of the brethren, including Thomas Betson's index and a list of donors. Bell, *Nuns* also contains a description and list of surviving books from the library of the sisters, and see also Christopher de Hamel, *Syon Abbey: The Library of the Bridgettine Nuns and their Peregrinations After the Reformation* (London, 1991).

For the religious life of the house see, for instance, Roger Ellis, 'Viderunt eam filie Syon: the spirituality of the English house of a medieval contemplative order from its beginnings to the present day', *Analecta Cartusiana*, 68 (1984). Useful articles are also published in the journal *Birgittiana* (1996 *et seq.*).

Several of the manuscripts of the regulations and liturgy of the abbey have been published, particularly under the editorship of James Hogg in *Analecta Cartusiana*. Note also *The Bridgettine Breviary of Syon Abbey, from the MS. with English Rubrics F.4.11 at Magdalene College, Cambridge*, ed. A. J. Collins, (London, 1969); *British Library. Manuscript. MS Claudius Bi: The liber celestis of St. Bridget of Sweden*, ed. Roger Ellis, Early English Text Society, Orig. Ser., 291 (Oxford, 1987).

Some research has been undertaken on the buildings and material culture of the abbey. See: R. W. Dunning, 'The Building of Syon abbey', *Transactions of the Ancient Monuments Society*, 25 (1981), pp. 16–26; Jonathan Foyle, 'Syon Park: rediscovering medieval England's only Bridgettine monastery', *Current Archaeology*, 192 (2004), pp. 550–5; C. M. Barron and M. Erler, 'The Making of Syon Abbey's Altar Table of Our Lady *c.*1490–96', in *England and the Continent in the Middle Ages: Studies in Memory of Andrew Martindale: Proceedings of the 1996 Harlaxton Symposium*; ed. J. Mitchell (Stamford, 2000), pp. 318–35.

Sources relating to the London property of the abbey are listed in *Documentary Sources*, p. 96.

*Stephanie Hovland*

The foundation of Syon Abbey at Isleworth in 1415[2] brought to fruition plans for the introduction of the Bridgettine Order into England that had been in the mind of Henry, Lord FitzHugh (d. 1425), Constable of England and King's Chamberlain,[3] for over ten years.[4] In 1406 he had visited the mother-house at Vadstena in Sweden and granted the Order his manor of Cherry Hinton (Cambs.) if some of the community could be sent to form the nucleus of

---

[1] *V.C.H. Mdx.* iii. 96–100

[2] B.M. Add. MS. 22285, f. 14v. This is the *Martiloge* of Syon, and will hereafter be cited as such. It has been edited in part for the Henry Bradshaw Soc. by F. Proctor and E. S. Dewick. Cf. also R. Dunning, 'The muniments of Syon Abbey', *Bull. Inst. Hist. Research*, xxxvii. 103–11.

[3] *Complete Peerage*, v. 422.

[4] Cf. Margaret Deanesly, *Incendium Amoris of Richard Rolle*, 91 sqq., and D. Knowles, *Rel. Orders in Eng.* ii. 176 sqq.; T. Nyberg, *Birgittinische Klostergründungen des Mittelalters*, 69–77.

a house in England.[5] Although two Swedish brothers came in 1408,[6] the project made little headway until Henry V became interested in it and, after himself laying the foundation-stone of Syon in the presence of the Bishop of London on 22 February 1415,[7] issued the foundation charter on 3 March.[8]

Syon was the only monastery of the Order of St. Saviour, commonly known as the Bridgettine Order from its foundress St. Bridget of Sweden (d. 1373), to be established in England before the Reformation.[9] The Order lived under the Rule of St. Augustine, with St. Bridget's Rule of the Saviour as its constitutions. There were also Additions for each house based on those drawn up for Vadstena from her *Revelationes Extravagantes*.[10] Many of the unusual features of the new Order were noted by Walsingham. The community was to consist of 60 sisters, including the abbess, 13 priests, 4 deacons, and 8 lay brothers, corresponding to the 12 apostles, the 72 disciples, and St. Paul; they were to use wool, not linen; there was to be a common church, with the nuns' choir above that of the brethren; the convents must have sufficient endowment to maintain them without begging, after which they were to accept no further gifts; an audit was to be held every year on the eve of All Saints, and any surplus was to be distributed to the poor; the abbess, with the consent of the community, must choose the confessorgeneral, whom all the brethren must obey; and no one save doctors or workmen might enter the nun's enclosure.[11] Further details of the work of the Order were given by St. Antoninus, who recorded that the sisters carried on lucrative work for the common good and provided both for themselves and the brethren, whose duties included preaching on feast days and hearing confessions.[12]

The habit was grey. The most distinctive part of the nuns' costume was a white linen crown with bands across the top in the form of a cross upon which five small pieces of red cloth were sewn in honour of the five wounds of Christ. The brethren wore a red cross on their habit over the heart.[13] In choir the brethren chanted the office according to the diocesan use, but the sisters had a special office in honour of the Blessed Virgin based on St. Bridget's *Sermo Angelicus* and known as *Viridarium Beate Marie*.[14]

Shakespeare has immortalized the legend that the abbey was founded in expiation for the murder of Richard II,[15] but there is no reference to it in the foundation charter. Henry V simply stated that he was dedicating the new monastery to the glory of the most high Trinity, the most glorious Virgin Mary, and all saints, especially St. Bridget. The nuns and brethren were to dwell in separate courts in the same monastery. They were to celebrate divine service daily for the king during his lifetime and for the salvation of his soul after death, and also for his ancestors and all the faithful departed. The abbey was to be on a parcel of land of the demesne of the king's manor of Isleworth within the parish of Twickenham. It was to be called 'The Monastery of St. Saviour and St. Bridget of Syon' and the community were to have one seal for business transactions. Maud Newton was appointed abbess and William Alnwick confessor-general. On the resignation or death of the abbess the nuns were to have custody of the abbey's possessions without interference from the king or his heirs. Until the revenues had been made up to 1,000 marks a year the balance was to be paid from the Exchequer. Provision was made for a permanent endowment, mainly from the lands of the alien priories, and many of them were to come to Syon when the leases lapsed, including widely scattered properties which had belonged to St. Nicholas, Angers; Caen; Fécamp; Loders; Marmoutiers; Mont St. Michel; St. Bertin; St. Omer; and Séez.[16]

Henry V also sought papal confirmation for his new foundation. His *supplica*, drawn up before 1418, stated that he had endowed the monastery of Syon, with Maud Newton and William Alnwick in charge. He asked the Pope to permit these two and other religious to transfer to the new abbey, and also to allow Syon to receive laity and secular clergy until the numbers laid down by their Rule were complete. He requested confirmation of the privileges of the Bridgettine Order as granted during the schism by Urban VI and asked that they should apply to Syon.[17]

In August 1418 Martin V issued two bulls concerning Syon. *Eximie devocionis* was addressed to the King and confirmed the appropriation of the churches of

[5] Diarium Vadstenense, in *Scriptores Rerum Suecicarum*, i. 123.
[6] Ibid. 125.
[7] *Martiloge*, f. 14v.
[8] Dugdale, *Mon.* vi. 542.
[9] *Dict. d'hist. et géog. ecclés.* x, col. 728.
[10] Ibid. Rule and Syon Additions are in Aungier, *Syon*, 294–404; critical edition in Veronica R. Hughes, 'Syon Additions to the Rule of St. Saviour' (Liverpool Univ. M.A. thesis, 1952).
[11] V. H. Galbraith, *St. Albans Chronicle 1406–20*, 32. Annual distribution to the poor noted by T. Fuller, *Church Hist.* iii. 276.
[12] *Divi Antonini Chron. tertia pars* (1586), 797; *Rot. Parl.* v. 551.
[13] *Rule of Our Saviour* (priv. printed, Syon Abbey, n.d.), caps. iii, xi; cf. Francesca M. Steele, *Story of the Bridgettines*, 15.

[14] H. Schück, 'Två svenska Biografier från Medeltid', *Antiqvarisk Tidskrift*, v. 127; a modernized version of the office is in E. Graf, *Prayers and Revelations of St. Bridget*. An edition of the Syon Breviary and a full account of the Bridgettine liturgy is being prepared by A. J. Collins for the Henry Bradshaw Soc.
[15] *Henry V*, 4, i; cf. Knowles, *Rel. Orders*, ii. 176.
[16] *Cal. Pat.* 1416–22, 34sqq.; *Rot. Parl.* iv. 141, 243 sqq.; Aungier, *Syon*, 31, 39.
[17] Deanesly, *Incendium*, 131 sqq.

Yeovil (Som.) and Croston (Lancs.) to the abbey.[18]
*Integre devocionis* was directed to the Archbishop of
Canterbury, the Bishop of London, and the Abbot of
St. Albans, and authorized them to amend any error
in the foundation of Syon and to admit to regular
profession those who wished to enter the monastery
so that an abbess and confessor could be elected.
Moreover, the Pope gave permission for any member
of an order of less strict observance to enter Syon.[19]
A third bull, *Sane sicut exhibita*, issued by Martin V
probably belongs to the same period, since some of its
provisions were embodied in the Additions to the Rule
drawn up for Syon about this time. Under its terms
the abbey and all its possessions were to be under
the protection of the Holy See and were to be free
from all centences of excommunication, suspension,
and interdict except by special mandate of the Pope.
However, the bishop of the diocese was to be the visitor
as prescribed in the Rule and was also to confirm the
election of the abbess and confessor-general. If the
ordinary neglected this duty, the abbess and confessor-
general might invite any bishop as visitor.[20]

These bulls were, indeed, issued at a time when
the future of the whole Bridgettine Order was in
considerable doubt,[21] but in 1419 the Pope decided
in its favour and also granted Syon the privileges
and indulgences conferred on the whole Order by
the bull *Mare magnum* of 1413.[22]

In the meantime work on the buildings was
proceeding. Safe conducts for the transport of stone
from Yorkshire were sought in 1417 and 1421,[23]
and some materials were brought from Sheen.[24]
Recruitment also continued, as is shown by a licence
for Margaret, anchoress of Bodmin, to enter Syon.[25]
Moreover, almost as soon as the foundationstone
had been laid, Henry V applied to Vadstena for
further brothers and nuns to come to England to
train the recruits. The mother-house agreed to
this request, which was supported by Philippa, the
King's sister and Queen of Sweden, and in May 1415
a party of four professed sisters, three postulants,
one priest, and one deacon left Vadstena to join
the two brothers already in England.[26] The task of

moulding the new community proved to be one of
great difficulty. Disputes arose over the performance
of manual work by the choir sisters and over the
claim of the English recruits to be fully professed.[27]
Consultations were held with distinguished
Benedictine and Cistercian theologians. One such
meeting in 1416 was attended by the king himself
as well as the whole community of Syon. This
conference refused to agree to the proposal that the
nuns should be released from domestic duties or
to support Maud Newton's claim to be obeyed by
the brethren.[28] Shortly afterwards Maud Newton[29]
and William Alnwick retired,[30] although before his
withdrawal Alnwick helped to draft the Additions to
the Rule for use at Syon.[31] Letters of advice were sent
from Vadstena in 1418. The brother who remained
with the sisters in England was commended for his
patience with their indiscipline. It was also stressed
that the English recruits were not yet professed
members of the Order.[32]

It was not until 1420 that the community was
ready and the first profession at Syon took place.
The Archbishop of Canterbury presided over the
ceremony, at which 27 nuns, 5 priests, 2 deacons,
and 3 lay brothers pronounced their vows.[33]
Immediately afterwards Joan North was elected
the first abbess and Thomas Fishborne the first
confessorgeneral. The Bishop of London blessed
and installed the abbess, and in the same year
granted the brethren the powers of minor papal
penitentiaries when hearing the confessions of the
community or pilgrims.[34]

The community had little peace in which to
settle into its routine. In 1422 the Pope again ruled
against double orders and ordered the Bridgettine
communities to separate.[35] Fishborne left at once
for Rome and with difficulty secured exemption for
Syon from this decree.[36] In England the accession
of Henry VI meant application for confirmation
of the abbey's charters. This was granted early in

[18] Dugdale, *Mon.* vi. 544.

[19] Deanesly, *Incendium*, 137 sqq.

[20] Copied in Guildhall MS. 9531/9, ff. 139–40; cf. Syon
Additions in B.M. Arundel MS. 146, ff. 25 sqq.

[21] Question discussed in W. Ullman, 'Recognition of St. Bridget's
Rule by Martin V', *Rev. Bénédictine*, 1957, pp. 190 sqq.

[22] T. Höjer, *Studier i Vadstena Klosters och Birgittinordens
Historia*, 179.

[23] *Acts of P. C.* (Rec. Com.) ii. 360 (1417); *Cal. Pat.* 1416–22.
397.

[24] E 364/56/B.

[25] Deanesly, *Incendium*, 136.

[26] *Scriptores Rerum Suecicarum*, i. 136. The priest was John of
Kalmar who had already organized a monastery at Reval
(ibid. 137).

[27] *Diplomatorium Suecanum*, iii, no. 2524. For similar disputes at
Vadstena cf. Höjer, *Studier*, 26, and for position of lay sisters, L.
Hollman, *Den heliga Birgittas Revelaciones Extravagantes*, 150.

[28] Deanesly, *Incendium*, 111.

[29] Her pension was granted in May 1417: *Cal. Pat.* 1416–22,
102.

[30] *Amundesham Annales* (Rolls Ser.), i. 27.

[31] Deanesly, *Incendium*, 111. The two surviving texts of these
Additions are late-15th-cent. MSS.: B.M. Arundel MS. 146
for sisters, and St. Paul's MS. W.D. 24 for lay brothers; cf.
Hughes, 'Syon Additions', xviii.

[32] *Dip. Suec.* iii, nos. 2521, 2522, 2524.

[33] *Martiloge*, f. 6v. For forms of profession cf. *York Pontifical*
(Surtees Soc. lxi), p. xli, and St. John's Coll. Camb., MS. 11.

[34] Ellis, *Original Letters*, ii (1), 91, giving the date as 1421.

[35] E. Nygren, *Lib. Privilegiorum Mon. Vadstensis*, 236. Text
also in *Revelationes Celestes S. Birgittae* (1624 edn.).

[36] *Scriptores Rerum Suecicarum*, i. 143; H. Cnattingius, *Studies
in the Order of St. Bridget*, i. 131–55.

1424, although without the exemption from taxes allowed by Henry V.[37] The community continued to grow, and in 1428 consisted of 41 sisters, 7 priests, a deacon, and 6 lay brothers.[38]

During the 1420s the abbess was occupied in gaining possession of the estates as leases lapsed or the grantees died. In 1424 lands at Isleworth and in Essex were handed over.[39] In 1428 the Prior of Lancaster died, and the abbess had to engage in long negotiations over the tithes and arrangements for the vicarage with the Archdeacon of Richmond before she finally secured possession in 1431.[40]

Further privileges were also obtained from Rome. In 1425 Martin V issued an important bull which, besides forbidding the abbess to alienate property without the majority consent and commanding her to see promptly to the needs of the brethren, granted the brothers the power to release penitents from vows of pilgrimage and to grant the *Vincula* indulgence to pilgrims visiting Syon.[41] In the same year the Pope also granted complete independence from Vadstena and freedom from the decrees of the general chapters of the Order, to which the abbey might send delegates or not as the abbess judged best.[42]

In 1426 the community decided that their original quarters on the site later known as Isleworth or Twickenham Park[43] were unhealthy and too cramped for their growing numbers. Preparations for a move began. The first stone of the new buildings was laid on 5 February in the presence of Cardinal Beaufort and the Duke of Bedford.[44] The duke also presented all the sisters of the first profession with rings and service books.[45] In June surveyors were appointed for the king's works at Isleworth with powers to requisition labour and materials.[46] The new buildings were ready for occupation by September 1431, when Syon petitioned the king for permission to move.[47] On 11 November the Archbishop of Canterbury solemnly re-enclosed the community, to which he also presented the vestments used during the ceremony.[48]

Although the buildings were occupied, repairs and improvements went on throughout the century. In 1443 the abbess obtained letters patent granting

her freedom for ten years from molestation by the king's purveyors, who were not to remove building materials on the site or interfere with them on the highways.[49] Again in 1468 letters of protection were issued for the *Mary* of Caen carrying Caen stone for Syon.[50] The scale of the operations may be judged from the fact that between 1461 and 1479 the sum of £6,226 was spent on church, cloister, dormitory, chapter-house, and smithy.[51]

The most important part of the work was the new church, on which £4,138 had been spent by 1480.[52] During the building a serious difficulty arose. Syon was apparently following the plan used at Vadstena where the altar had been placed at the west end on account of the slope of the ground.[53] A sign of papal approval was sought for this because it was contrary to the custom in England.[54] The new church was completed and consecration took place on 20 October 1488.[55] This was a day of rejoicing in an otherwise sad year for the community, which had suffered severely from the plague, losing seven sisters and three brothers, including the confessorgeneral.[56]

Very little remains of the abbey buildings, which have been thoroughly reconstructed by later owners.[57] It is thought that part of one of the two original cloisters remains in the courtyard, and part of the 15th-century undercroft of the west range is incorporated in the west range of the house.[58] A carved stone reputed to have been a pinnacle over the gatehouse is still preserved by the present community.[59] An inventory taken at the Dissolution lists many of the rooms: domestic offices and store houses, rooms for officials such as the butler, receiver-general, and auditor, and guest chambers including one for the king.[60] Of the few surviving vestments the Syon cope is of outstanding workmanship.[61]

During the 1440s Henry VI's search for funds for his new foundations at Eton and Cambridge caused Syon great anxiety. Stringent inquiries were made into the titles of grants of lands of the alien priories

[37] Höjer, *Studier*, 184.

[38] *Cal. Pat.* 1422–9, 205 sqq.

[39] *Cat. Anct. D.* ii. B 3819; i. B 1530.

[40] F. Madox, *Formulare Anglicanum*, f. 100; W. O. Roper, *Materials for Hist. of Church of Lancaster*, iii. 576.

[41] Cf. *Cal. Papal Regs.* xii. 340; Nygren, *Lib. Priv.* 277.

[42] Höjer, *Studier*, 193.

[43] Lysons, *Environs of Lond.* iii. 83; *V.C.H. Mdx.* iii, *passim*.

[44] *Martiloge*, f. 14v.

[45] Ibid. Dedication of Syon is noted in the Bedford Hours, cf. *B.M. Qrly.* iv. 63.

[46] *Cal. Pat.* 1422–9, 539.

[47] *Rot. Parl.* iv. 395.

[48] *Martiloge*, f. 10.

[49] *Cal. Pat.* 1441–6, 159.

[50] Aungier, *Syon*, 70.

[51] J. R. Fletcher, *Story of the English Bridgettines*, 28. This work, although published without critical apparatus, is based on full transcripts of sources now deposited at Syon Abbey, Devon.

[52] E. Power, *Med. Eng. Nunneries*, 92.

[53] J. Jorgensen, *St. Bridget of Sweden*, 233.

[54] *Cal. Papal Regs.* xiii. 789.

[55] *Martiloge*, f. 96.

[56] Thomas Westhaugh d. 1 June: ibid. f. 41 and *passim*.

[57] Lysons, *Environs of Lond.* iii. 87.

[58] *Hist. Mon. Com. Mdx.* 86.

[59] At Marley. Reproduced in A. Hamilton, *Angel of Syon*, 85, and Fletcher, *Eng. Bridgettines*, 35.

[60] L.R. 2/112.

[61] Now in V. & A. Mus. It was not made at Syon, cf. *Burlington Mag.* vi. 278 sqq.

made by Henry V.[62] As a result orders were given in June 1440 for an extent to be taken of St. Michael's Mount (Cornw.), as it was to be taken into the king's hands.[63] About the same time Syon also lost the manor of Tilshead (Wilts.), possessions in Spalding (Lincs.), and revenues of Corsham church (Wilts.). The abbey hastily sought confirmation of other possessions where there might be a flaw in the title, and in 1443 obtained letters patent concerning their property in Sussex and Gloucestershire.[64]

Henry VI showed his goodwill towards Syon in other ways. Complaints had been made in Rome that, owing to the conduct of the abbess, some of the brethren wished to leave the monastery and no recruits were coming forward to replace them. The Pope ordered the Archbishop of Canterbury to make inquiry, and, if necessary, take disciplinary action.[65] It was probably in connexion with this that the abbess complained that she had been wrongly cited before the archbishop's court, and she secured from the king exemption from the primate's jurisdiction.[66] Furthermore, in 1448 the king issued a charter granting extensive legal privileges to the abbey and its tenants. They were to be almost completely exempt from royal justice, the abbess holding all courts on her estates and taking all the profits of justice, whether administered in her own or in the royal courts, if any of her own tenants was concerned.[67]

Nevertheless Syon welcomed the accession of Edward IV, whose reign opened with the restoration of its lost estates. In 1461 the old charters were confirmed, with the exemption from taxes.[68] In 1463 the right to four tuns a year of Gascon wine, granted in the original endowment, was restored with arrears from the beginning of the reign.[69] In 1464 Parliament confirmed to Syon the charter of liberties of 1446–7, the letters patent issued in 1461–2, the Act of 1421–2 separating Isleworth from the Duchy of Cornwall, and all the privileges granted by Pope Martin V.[70] Finally, in 1465 the abbess procured a further charter confirming all her possessions and granting her licence to acquire further lands.[71]

Routine confirmations were obtained on the restoration of Henry VI in 1470, in 1486 after the accession of Henry VII, and from Henry VIII in 1512.[72]

In 1513 the right to appoint a coroner at Isleworth[73] and in 1520 the exemption of Syon tenants from all tolls were confirmed.[74] In 1503 a minor adjustment took place when Syon gave up the original site of the abbey at Isleworth to Henry VII and received in exchange the advowson of Olney (Bucks.).[75] The only set-back was at Wolsey's visitation under his legatine powers in 1523, when the abbey had to pay £333.[76] This visit, made 'wrongfully and suddenly', was one of the charges brought against the cardinal after his fall from power.[77]

The scattered possessions presented complicated problems of management, and the administrative staff of Syon may be taken as an unusually complete and elaborate example of the usual system adopted by nunneries.[78] The business affairs of the abbey were the responsibility of the abbess, who delegated the administration to the treasuress and undertreasuress.[79] The nuns were advised and assisted in their work by a lay staff whose functions may be most clearly seen in the valuation of 1535.[80] At the head of the central staff was the chief steward.[81] Two distinguished men held this post early in the 16th century. Sir Richard Sutton, a lawyer in the Inner Temple, probably carried out his duties in person, since he had a room at Syon and took great interest in the Order.[82] Some time after Sutton's death in 1524 Thomas Cromwell held the office, although the actual work was performed by Thomas Watson, steward of the household and stewardgeneral of all the lordships of the monastery.[83] The central staff was completed by a receiver-general and an auditor and a clerk.[84]

Apart from a home farm at Isleworth, which was controlled through a bailiff by the cellaress and provided her with supplies in kind as well as money, most of the lands were farmed through bailiffs.[85] The lands in Middlesex were managed by the steward of Isleworth, assisted by a steward of the courts and a bailiff. In most counties a steward was in charge and supervised the work of the minor officials for each manor, but in some counties, such as Devon where the lands were extensive, two

[62] Cf. Rymer, *Foedera*, x. 802.
[63] G. Oliver, *Mon. Exon.* 414.
[64] *Cal. Pat.* 1441–6, 234; cf. Aungier, *Syon*, 58, 68.
[65] Höjer, *Studier*, 258.
[66] Aungier, *Syon*, 58.
[67] Ibid. 60; *Cal. Chart. R.* 1427–1516, 91 sqq.
[68] Aungier, *Syon*, 68; Syon Ho., MS. D. xxiv. 2d.
[69] *Cal. Pat.* 1461–7, 175.
[70] *Rot. Parl.* v. 551 sqq.
[71] *Cal. Chart. R.* 1427–1516, 206.
[72] Aungier, *Syon*, 71; Hist. MSS. Com. *Exeter*, 433; *L. & P. Hen. VIII*, i, p. 567.

[73] Syon Ho., MS. D. xiv. 2 F.
[74] Hist. MSS. Com. *9th Rep. Plymouth Recs.* 273.
[75] Aungier, *Syon*, 531; *V.C.H. Mdx.* iii. 96.
[76] Fletcher, *Eng. Bridgettines*, 31.
[77] *L. & P. Hen. VIII*, iv (3), p. 2551.
[78] Power, *Med. Eng. Nunneries*, 99.
[79] *Rule of Our Saviour*, cap. xii.
[80] *Valor Eccl.* (Rec. Com.), i. 424 sqq.; Aungier, *Syon*, 439 sqq.; cf. Power, *Med. Eng. Nunneries*, 99–100.
[81] Aungier, *Syon*, 445.
[82] L.R. 2/112; *D.N.B.* He paid for the printing of *Orchard of Syon* for the nuns.
[83] Aungier, *Syon*, 445.
[84] Ibid. 446.
[85] J. E. Thorold Rogers, *Hist. of Agric. and Prices*, iii. 2; Power, *Med. Eng. Nunneries*, 99, 136.

chief stewards were appointed.[86] The abbess also needed legal advice and a few scattered references suggest the existence of such a staff. In 1455 Robert Kent B.C.L. was appointed proctor of Syon in all suits.[87] Three doctors of laws, Thomas Jan, Richard Lichfield, and Walter Knightley, were prayed for as special benefactors because they had acted as advocates for the abbey without fee.[88]

Expenditure was in the hands of the obedientiaries who, apart from the cellaress who had her own resources, drew their funds from and accounted for them to the treasuress.[89] At Syon the account rolls show that the Rule was followed strictly, no money being given to the sisters, but everything being provided by the officials responsible.[90] The chief of these were the cellaress, the chamberess, in charge of clothing for both the sisters and the brethren, and the sacrist.[91] The summary of the accounts drawn up for the fiscal year 1509–10 by the abbess and treasuress showed an income of £1,635 and expenditure of £1,275. The cellaress spent £974, the remainder going to the chamberess, sacrist, and 'various necessary expenses', leaving a surplus of £359.[92] The work of the cellaress, as revealed by her accounts, was of the most varied nature, partly farming, partly catering. She had not only to buy such items as bread locally and to deal with brewers in London, but also to send her agents to Oxford and Uxbridge to buy sheep and oxen. Livery had to be provided for the servants and payments had to be made for hedging and for attention to sick animals. Even the boats serving the ferry across the Thames came under her charge.[93] Among the officials helping her were the under-steward for the farm and the clerk of the kitchens for catering.

It was not only through its wealth and widespread lands that Syon became famous. The abbey was widely known for the *Vincula* indulgence and other pardons obtainable by pilgrims. The Pardon of Syon to be gained by pilgrims at Lammastide and Mid-Lent Sunday was publicized by the poet Audelay about 1426. His 'Salutation to St. Bridget' recounted how the saint originally obtained the indulgence for Vadstena and Henry V later gained the privilege for Syon.[94] Sermons at the abbey often mentioned these grants, and one composed by Simon Winter, one of the earliest members of the community, has been preserved. Expounding the text *Tibi dabo claves regni caelorum* (Matt. 16. 19) he first explained the doctrine of indulgences in general and then detailed those to be obtained at Syon.[95] An added attraction for pilgrims was the special faculty of the brethren for blessing rosaries, granted in 1500 by Pope Alexander VI.[96] The yearly offerings at St. Bridget's shrine were estimated at £6 13s. 4d. in 1535, the fourth highest in the country, although small compared with Walsingham's £260 or Canterbury's £32.[97] This, however, may have been a bad year, or else receipts were undervalued for the surveyors, as the figure in 1510 was nearly £29.[98]

Sermons at Syon were also an attraction. It was the duty of the brethren to expound the Gospel in the vernacular on Sundays and festivals,[99] and several of them must have been well fitted for this task since they held office as university preachers before entering Syon.[100] Several volumes of sermons composed by the brothers were in the library in addition to others which no doubt served as models.[101] Simon Winter himself composed a further book of sermons in English on indulgences as well as one on penance, besides sermons in Latin for Sundays and festivals. Thomas Bulde (d. 1476) wrote a similar work, and Brother Roger one in English.[102]

Besides sermons the brethren produced many spiritual treatises which, although primarily composed for the benefit of the nuns, enjoyed a wider circulation. The first of the authors among the brethren, Clement Maidstone,[103] formerly at Hounslow Priory, wrote on varied themes. His works included an account of Archbishop Scrope[104] and a volume of devotional works which was presented to Vadstena.[105] He also wrote several liturgical treatises, of which the most important was the *Ordinale Sarum sive Directorium Sacerdotum*. This proved to be a most useful work since, despite attacks by the Canons of Salisbury, nine printed editions were called for between 1487 and 1503.[106] Contemporary with Maidstone was

[86] Power, *Med. Eng. Nunneries*, 99, 136.

[87] Lancs. Rec. Off., DD. Cl. 1053.

[88] *Martiloge*, f. 72v.

[89] Power, *Med. Eng. Nunneries*, 136.

[90] Ibid. 137.

[91] Aungier, *Syon*, 392.

[92] S.C. 6/Hen. VIII/2184.

[93] Account for 1535/6 in S.C. 6/Hen. VIII/2283.

[94] 'Salutation to St. Bridget' in W. P. Cumming, *Revelations of St. Birgitta* (E.E.T.S.), pp. xxxi sqq.

[95] B.M. Harl. MS. 2321, ff. 17–62v.

[96] F. W. von Nettelbla, *Nachtricht von eigenem Klöstern der Heiligen Schwedischen Birgitte* (1764), 12.

[97] A. Savine, *Eng. Mon. on Eve of Dissolution*, 103.

[98] S.C. 6/Hen. VIII/2184.

[99] *Rule of Our Saviour*, cap. xiii.

[100] William Bond in 1509, cf. A. B. Emden, *Biographical Register of the University of Cambridge to 1500*, 72. Richard Reynolds in 1513, cf. Hamilton, *Angel of Syon*, 30.

[101] Mary Bateson, *Syon Mon. Libr. Cat. passim*. N. R. Ker, *Medieval Libraries of Great Britain* (2nd edn.).

[102] Ibid. 125, 126, 173, 181.

[103] Died 1456: *Martiloge*, f. 55. Cf. C. L. Kingsford, *Eng. Hist. Lit. in Fifteenth Cent.* 38.

[104] Printed in H. Wharton, *Anglia Sacra*, ii. 269 sqq. (of little historical value); cf. Kingsford, *Eng. Hist. Lit.* 38.

[105] Now Upsala Univ. Libr. MS. C. 159; cf. M. R. James, *Wanderings and Homes of Manuscripts*, 71.

[106] *Tracts of Clement Maidstone* and *Ordinale Sarum sive Directorium Sacerdotum*, both ed. by C. Wordsworth for Henry Bradshaw Soc.; *Short Title Cat.* nos. 17, 721–8.

the minor author Thomas Ismaelite, who wrote at least two devotional tracts, *Speculum humilitatis* and *De Ortu Virginis et Miraculis Christi*.[107] Two further works composed by brothers were a commentary on the Gospel of St. Matthew by Nicholas, deacon of Syon,[108] and a manual of instructions for novices in English by Thomas Prestius.[109]

The introduction of printing gave the brethren the opportunity of reaching a wider public, as contemporary taste favoured devotional literature.[110] The first published work from Syon seems to have been *A Profitable treatise to dispose men to be virtuously occupied* by Thomas Betson and printed by De Worde in 1500.[111] Amid the troubles preceding the Dissolution and probably while he was seriously ill, and confessor-general John Fewterer translated the *Mirror of Christ's Passion*, issued by Pynson in 1534.[112] He obtained his working copy from and dedicated his translation to Lord Hussey, an opponent of Henry VIII's religious policy and guardian of Princess Mary.[113] Already in 1530 he and Agnes Jordan, the abbess, had commissioned the printing of the *Mirror of Our Lady*, which was a commentary on the sisters' office composed by a brother of the house.[114] William Bond wrote the *Pilgrimage of Perfection*, published by Pynson in 1526 and reissued by De Worde in 1531, and a *Devout treatise for those that are timorous and fearful in conscience*, published posthumously in 1534 by Fawkes with a second edition in 1535.[115] An anonymous *Directory of Conscience* by a father of Syon was published in 1527.[116]

By far the most prolific of the Syon authors was Richard Whitford, who often signed himself 'The Wretch of Syon'.[117] Three translations and six original works which appeared between 1514 and 1541 have been attributed to him. All were concerned with the monastic or the spiritual life and some ran to several editions. The translations were of a *Commentary on the Rule of St. Augustine*, the *Martiloge*, and a volume

of extracts from the *Revelations* of St. Bridget. The original works were *Work for householders*, a treatise on the Eucharist which ran to seven editions, *Daily Exercise or Experience of Death, Fruit of Redemption, Divers holy instructions necessary for the Health of a man's Soul*, a version of the *Jesus Psalter*, and the *Pipe or Tun of Perfection*.[118]

There is a strong contrast between the type of literature produced by the brethren and the books available for study in their well-stocked library, although our knowledge of its contents is imperfect.[119] There were, however, more than 1,400 volumes of exegesis, theology, and canon law, kept up to date with printed works especially from continental presses, including Italian renaissance works.[120] Most of the books were gifts, many being brought by the brothers themselves on their profession and many being given by London clergy.[121] Five of the brethren gave 400 books between them and six others brought 30 to 40 each.[122] The value the community attached to its books may be seen by the good condition in which many are still to be found in their present homes.[123] Great precautions were taken against damage through age and use and arrangements were made for repairs and binding.[124] In gratitude to donors a special annual obit was decreed in 1471, when it was decided that the librarian should say a special office for the dead for Thomas Grant, his parents, and all donors to the brothers' and sisters' libraries.[125] Yet the brothers allowed others to use their books and possibly even to borrow them.[126] Certainly Thomas Gascoigne worked there and had a copy of St. Bridget's *Canonization Process*.[127] Occasionally indeed gifts of books were made. An *Horae* with Bridgettine additions was given to the Franciscans of Exeter[128] and in 1501 a printed volume of the *Revelations* was presented to John Doo of Fotheringhay College (Northants.) in return for prayers.[129]

This literary and intellectual activity was natural for the type of man who entered Syon. The brothers were more mature than the ordinary monastic

[107] Aungier, *Syon*; T. Tanner, *Bibliotheca BritannicoHibernica*, 447.

[108] Prob. Nicholas Peyntor, d. 1473, cf. *Martiloge*, f. 326, and Bateson, *Syon Cat.* 235.

[109] 'Formula Novitiorum', now Camb. Univ. Libr. MS. Dd. 33. 65; Bateson, *Syon Cat.* xxxvi. He was pensioned in 1539; Aungier, *Syon*, 89; and died at Stanwell in 154 (4), B.M. Add. MS. 22285, f. 57 (an erasure).

[110] P. Janelle, *L'Angleterre catholique* 15.

[111] *Short Title Cat.* no. 1978. He also drew up table of signs for use during times of silence, cf. Aungier, *Syon*, 405 sqq.; A. I. Doyle, 'Thomas Betsn', *Library*, 5th ser. xi. 115–18.

[112] *Short Title Cat.* no. 10838.

[113] Hist. MSS. Com. *4th Rep.* 410; G. Mattingly, *Catherine of Aragon*, 320.

[114] *The Mirror of Our Lady*, ed. J. H. Blunt (E.E.T.S.). Passages in text show that the author was a brother and not Thomas Gasgoigne as suggested by Blunt, cf. pp. ix, 164.

[115] *Short Title Cat.* nos. 3275, 3277.

[116] Ibid. no. 6904.

[117] *D.N.B.*

[118] *Short Title Cat.* nos. 13925, 17532, 23961, 25412– 26. The problem of the 'Jesus Psalter' is discussed by F. Wormald in *Laudate* (1936). For extracts from the Revelations see G. E. Klemming, *Heliga Birgittas Uppenbarelser*, 232.

[119] Bateson, *Syon Cat.* although earlier entries have been erased to make room for additions (*ex inf.* A. I. Doyle); Ker, *Medieval Libraries*, 184–7.

[120] Bateson, *Syon Cat. passim.*

[121] Ibid. pp. xv, xxiii sqq.

[122] Knowles, *Rel. Orders*, ii. 347.

[123] Opinion of N. R. Ker in notes now at Syon Abbey.

[124] R. J. Whitwell, 'An Ordinance for Syon Library', *E.H.R.* xxv. 121.

[125] *Martiloge*, ff. 4, 17v.

[126] Bateson, *Syon Cat.* p. x.

[127] *Loci e Libro Veritatum*, ed. J. Thorold Rogers, 170.

[128] Now Bodl. MS. Bodley 62.

[129] Lambeth Palace, 1500 91 (pr. bk.).

recruit, since they could not be professed under the age of 25.[130] The main recruiting ground seems to have been among the secular clergy, often men who had held benefices in the London area, and, in the 16th century, among Cambridge graduates.[131] Three cases have been traced of brethren leaving the Order. Two of these were for health reasons and the third entered a mendicant order more suited to his temperament.[132]

A common intellectual interest of the brethren and sisters lay in the study of the works of Richard Rolle, whose concentration on the affections of the Saviour provided suitable material for meditation in the Order. The brothers had thirteen volumes of his works in their library, including the exuberant *Melos*,[133] while the sisters had an unknown number. In the 16th century Joan Sewell owned a copy of the *Incendium*,[134] and at least eleven other sisters owned books, mainly the works of Walter Hilton and similar devotional writings.[135] Yet the evidence of the *Mirror of Our Lady*, the translation of the *Martiloge* into English by Whitford, and the insertion of English rubrics into the Processional, suggests that although the sisters were well read in vernacular spiritual literature they may not have been so familiar with Latin and may have had difficulty in understanding the liturgy.[136]

The social standing of the nuns was exceptionally high. The choir sisters were drawn from the nobility, the gentry, and London merchant families, whilst the few lay sisters probably came from the London area.[137] No scandal has come to light about the abbey, save the early disputes between the sisters and brethren over obedience, and the unreliable reports of the commissioners shortly before the Dissolution. This may well be due to the comparative maturity of the novices, who had to be eighteen on profession, and to the system of training under which the postulant had to be sent away for a year after her application to make sure of her vocation before entering the enclosure.[138] The rule of strict enclosure seems to have been well observed. In 1416 the Swedish sisters had to be released from a rash vow that they would make a pilgrimage to Canterbury in thanksgiving for a safe passage to England.[139]

The same mixture of aristocratic and mercantile families found among the choir sisters appears also in a list of special benefactors in the *Martiloge*,[140] which contains a hundred names made up chiefly of groups of the nobility, royal officials, and London merchants. The list reflects Syon's influence in court circles which was maintained up to the Dissolution. Beginning with many who had played a part in the founding of the abbey, such as FitzHugh himself, Clifford, and Chichele, the roll ends with Syon in exile. For the inclusion of some names no reason at all is given, but many were included for gifts of money, ranging from £200 from Margaret, Duchess of Clarence, to five marks from Sir William Banes. Two made valuable gifts – Thomas Chandler gave a jewelled reliquary and William Hemming a missal worth ten marks. Some were monastic officials – Henry Normanton, auditor, who also gave £100, John Sprotte, and Thomas Muston, steward.[141]

Although not included among the special benefactors, other names are mentioned in the *Martiloge* for gifts and favours, whilst others who left bequests to the abbey, including even such a famous lady as Margaret Beaufort, were not mentioned at all.[142] There were, however, obits for Edward IV 'who restored possessions which had been taken away unjustly', Thomas, Earl of Derby (1435–1504), benefactor, and Edward Courtenay, Earl of Devon (d. 1556), who gave £40 a year.[143]

In contrast to the lengthy list of benefactors, letters of confraternity seem to have been issued only rarely. The sole known case in favour of an individual was to John Talbot, 2nd Earl of Shrewsbury (1413–60).[144] Two other cases were of interchange of confraternity – in 1420 with St. Albans[145] and in 1455 with the Prior and community of Durham.[146] In 1536 the monastery of Syon was granted confraternity with All Souls College, Oxford, but there appears to be no record of a corresponding grant by Syon.[147]

Several devout lay people lived close to the enclosure in order to gain the spiritual ministrations of the brethren. In the early 16th century Sir Richard Sutton had as his confessor one of the brothers, Alexander Bell.[148] Lady Kingston, widow of the steward of Syon's manor of Minchinhampton (Glos.), occupied a chamber in the precincts.[149] At an earlier

[130] *Rule of Our Saviour*, cap. xix.
[131] Opinion based on *Martiloge* and Camb. Grace Bks.; cf. Knowles, *Rel. Orders*, ii. 347.
[132] *Cal. Papal Regs.* viii. 174; xi. 151, 638.
[133] Hope E. Allen, *Eng. Writings of Richard Rolle*, pp. ix, lvi.
[134] Deanesly, *Incendium*, 79; and see N. R. Ker's notes now at Syon Abbey.
[135] Power, *Med. Eng. Nunneries*, 253–4.
[136] Ibid. 4, 10; J. Bazire and E. Colledge, *Chastising of God's Children*, 77.
[137] Aungier, *Syon*, 51.
[138] *Rule of Our Saviour*, caps. ix, xix.
[139] *Reg. Chichele* (Cant. and York Soc.), i, p. lxvii.
[140] *Martiloge*, ff. 70–72v.
[141] Ibid.
[142] *Collegium Divi Johannis Evangelistae*, 121.
[143] *Martiloge*, ff. 15, 39v, 56.
[144] Clerk Maxwell, 'Some Further Letters of Confraternity', *Archaeologia*, lxxix. 209.
[145] *Reg. Abb. Johannis Whethamstede* (Rolls Ser.), ii. 372.
[146] *Durham Obituary Rolls* (Surtees Soc.), III, 118.
[147] J. Gutch, *Collectanea Curiosa*, ii. 268–72.
[148] Ibid. 532.
[149] L.R. 2/112.

date Margaret, Duchess of Clarence, specially sought the guidance of Simon Winter and indeed obtained permission from Rome for him to leave the enclosure to minister the sacraments to her.[150]

Before Syon was implicated in the case of the Holy Maid of Kent, the intellectual atmosphere seems to have been tolerant and the community ready to follow the official policy over the king's matrimonial troubles. Richard Pace, an Imperialist, was apparently confined by Wolsey at Syon because he opposed the annulment suit, and in 1527 wrote from the abbey saying that he had changed his mind.[151] In 1528 a London citizen, Humphrey Monmouth, when accused of heresy because of certain books in his possession, pleaded that he had shown the works to the confessor-general who had found little wrong with them.[152]

The position changed in 1533. At the trial of Elizabeth Barton, the Holy Maid of Kent, it was stated that her 'revelations' had been shown to many at Syon, including the abbess, confessor-general, and Richard Reynolds.[153] This would be natural, as she was alleged to have been influenced by St. Bridget's writings and to have been supplied with some of the material of her visions by the Syon community.[154] Moreover Sir Thomas More had been told of her visit, had seen her in the chapel there, and later discussed her visions with the brethren, warning them against her.[155]

Syon had attracted the attention of the government, and the precincts were frequently invaded by royal officials. In January 1534 Stokesley, Bishop of London, and Mores, surveyor of Syon and a supporter of Henry VIII, were very anxious to secure the signatures of the community on a document concerning the marriage question. The first draft was duly signed, but the wording was not sufficiently explicit to secure the approval of the Council. Mores produced a second draft, but this time the brethren refused to sign and advised the sisters to follow the same course.[156]

In 1535 a further crisis developed. The central figure was the most renowned of the brethren, Richard Reynolds,[157] who was charged with treason and suffered along with the Carthusian priors in April and May. Although they pleaded that there was no malice in their denial of the royal supremacy,

the prisoners were found guilty and sentenced.[158] Immediately after the verdict Cranmer wrote to Cromwell on 30 April marvelling that such a learned man as Reynolds should argue against the supremacy of the king and urging that, if this were the only issue, it would be better to convert him.[159] The plea was of no avail and on 4 May 1535 Reynolds and the other accused were executed.[160]

If Cromwell had hoped to secure submission by terror, he was disappointed. In July his visitor, Bedyll, reported that the sisters and most of the brethren were willing to conform but there were still two who refused and might have to be expelled.[161] By the end of the year opinion among the community had hardened against the government. Bedyll made a further visit in December and found opposition even among the sisters.[162] Many theologians were sent to persuade the brethren, but despite threats and promises, two of them, Whitford and Little, and a lay brother, Turlington, remained obdurate.[163] It may well have been about this time that another lay brother, Thomas Brownell, was imprisoned at Newgate. His death on 21 October 1537 is recorded as due to the squalor of the prison. Opposite his name the marginal note 'martyr' has been inserted in the *Martiloge*.[164]

In 1536, however, Syon was seemingly restored to favour, possibly because the disaffected had been expelled. In November the abbess was commissioned to take charge of Lady Margaret Douglas, later Countess of Lennox, who was bent on marrying against the wishes of the court.[165] Earlier in the year the brethren had been engaged in persuading the London Carthusians to agree to the royal supremacy, and Copinger reported to Cromwell that he thought he had been successful.[166] In September the secretary had a further opportunity of securing his grip on the abbey when he attended the election of Copinger as confessor-general.[167]

Again Syon's fortunes underwent a sudden change. In May 1538 Cromwell noted that Syon must be suppressed[168] and put into motion a scheme for gaining his object. The Bishop of London was charged with *praemunire* for using a papal formula at professions in 1537 and 1538 and with superstitious practices when blessing vestments at the abbey.[169]

[150] *Cal. Papal Regs.* viii. 63.
[151] *L. and P. Hen. VIII*, iv, p. 1472.
[152] Ibid. p. 83.
[153] Ibid. vi, p. 587.
[154] L. E. Whatmore, 'Sermon against the Holy Maid', *E.H.R.* lviii. 469.
[155] *Corresp. of Sir Thomas More*, ed. E. F. Rogers, 484, 486.
[156] *L. and P. Hen. VIII*, vii, pp. 8, 12.
[157] Cf. E. Graf, *Blessed Richard Reynolds*; Hamilton, *Angel of Syon*; Knowles, *Rel. Orders*, iii. 215.

[158] *L. and P. Hen. VIII*, viii, p. 213; *3rd Dep. Kpr's Rep.* 237–9.
[159] *L. and P. Hen. VIII*, viii, p. 229.
[160] Ibid. p. 249.
[161] Ibid. p. 441.
[162] Ibid. ix, p. 332.
[163] Ibid.
[164] *Martiloge*, f. 60v.
[165] *L. and P. Hen. VIII*, xi, p. 406.
[166] Ibid. p. 197. Cf. Knowles, *Rel. Orders*, iii.213 sqq.
[167] *L. and P. Hen. VIII*, xi, p. 202.
[168] Ibid. xiii, p. 322.
[169] Ibid. p. 398.

Stokesley replied immediately that since the statute he had used an amended formula and stressed the zeal he had shown in persuading the community to accept the king's supremacy. His plea was borne out by a Syon manuscript of the profession service which had the text amended with the formula 'quatenus illustrissimi regis et juribus regni non repugnat'.[170] Although the bishop was acquitted, Cromwell had made his point and was merely biding his time. Several times in 1539 he noted that Syon was to be suppressed by *praemunire*,[171] and more definitely in November 'among the houses to be suppressed is Syon'.[172]

The blow fell the same month. There is no surrender deed for the abbey and no official record of its suppression. Shortly beforehand many of the books in its library were removed.[173] In 1539 pensions were assigned for the community on a generous scale,[174] probably owing to the influential connexions of the sisters. Agnes Jordan, the abbess, was granted £200 a year,[175] but the confessor-general, Copinger, was already dead.[176] On the same day as the pensions were granted the community was expelled with its keys and seals.[177] Thus the 'most virtuous house of religion in all England'[178] was brought to a temporary end. With the exception of Amesbury (Wilts.), Syon was the last of the great nunneries to be dissolved.[179] In all, pensions were granted to 52 choir nuns (including the abbess), 4 lay sisters, 12 brothers, and 5 lay brothers.[180]

According to the *Valor Ecclesiasticus*, the principal possessions of the Abbey, besides its own site, were rents from Brentford, Heston, Isleworth, Sutton, Twickenham, Whitton, and Worton (Mdx.); the rectories of Chilham, Molash, and Throwley (Kent); rents and other payments from Aldrington, Brede, Charlton Ashurst, Ecclesden, Fishbourne, Littlehampton, Sompting, Steyning, Toddington, Warminghurst, Wiggonholt, and Withyham (Suss.); the manor of Cherry Hinton (Cambs.); the rectories of Martock and Yeovil (Som.); Olney rectory (Bucks.); rents and farms in Bothenhampton, Bradpole, Loders, and Upton (Dors.); rents and other incomes from Axmouth, Budleigh, Donnington, Harpford, Haderland (Otterton par.), Otterton, Sidmouth, and Yarcombe

(Devon); Poulton rectory and pensions from the vicarages of Croston and Eccleston and rents from Lonsdale (Lancs.); pensions from Boothby, Navenby, and Spalding and the farm of Aungee fee (Lincs.); tenements in the parish of St. Benet near Paul's Wharf, London; rents in Avening, Cheltenham, Slaughter, and the manor of Minchinhampton (Glos.); Felstead lordship (Essex); the lands of St. Michael's Mount (Cornw.); Corsham rectory and Tilshead manor (Wilts.). There were also sundry small rents and other payments. The total income was £1,944 11s. 5d., expenses were £213 5s. (*sic*) and the net income £1,731 8s. 4d. (*sic*).[181] Syon was the richest of the non-Benedictine houses and the largest and richest of the nunneries.[182]

Some of these lands, including the abbey buildings and demesne at Isleworth, remained in the king's hands, while the rest were disposed of in small parcels.[183] In Devon, for example, Otterton, Axmouth, and Haderland were leased to court officials, while the remainder stayed in the king's hands.[184]

The community did not disperse after the Dissolution but, apparently in the hope that the schism was only a temporary matter, remained in groups until they could return to Syon. Abbess Jordan rented a farmhouse near Denham (Bucks.), and with her went nine of the community.[185] Another group, led by Catherine Palmer, went abroad, staying first at Antwerp and later at Termonde in Flanders until the restoration.[186] The accession of Queen Mary brought the fulfilment of their hopes. Naturally it took some time to gather together the scattered community, but some were enclosed by Cardinal Pole at Sheen in November 1556.[187] The official re-establishment of Syon was confirmed by the cardinal on 1 March 1557,[188] and in April letters patent were issued granting the site and more than 200 acres of land at Isleworth.[189] The community then consisted of 21 sisters and 3 brothers, with Catherine Palmer as abbess and John Green confessor-general.[190] A further grant of lands at Isleworth was made in January 1558.[191]

---

[170] Ibid. p. 399; St. John's College. Camb., MS. 11.

[171] *L. and P. Hen. VIII*, xiv (2), p. 150.

[172] Ibid. p. 192.

[173] Bateson, *Syon Cat.* p. xvii.

[174] *L. and P. Hen. VIII*, xiv (2), p. 192.

[175] Ibid.

[176] See below p. 190, n. 40.

[177] Cf. *Gesammelte Nachrichten über die einst bestandenen Klöster der hl. Birgitta*, 161; E. L. Cutts, *Dict. of Church of Eng.* 96.

[178] *Wriothesley's Chron.* (Camd. Soc. N.S. xi), i. 109.

[179] H. T. Jacka, 'Dissolution of the English Nunneries', (Lond. Univ. M.A. thesis, 1917), 120.

[180] Aungier, *Syon*, 89. In 1518 the community included 56 sisters and 3 priests who were scrutineers at the election (ibid. 81).

[181] *Valor Eccl.* (Rec. Com.), i. 424–8.

[182] P. Hughes, *Reformation in Eng.* i. 2; Power, *Med. Eng. Nunneries*, 2.

[183] *L. and P. Hen. VIII*, xv, p. 53.

[184] J. Youings, *Devon Monastic Lands*, 9, 94, 108, 134.

[185] Abbess Jordan and several other nuns died at Southlands in Denham par. (Bucks.): *Martiloge*, ff. 25, 47, 58 (erasures). For Southlands see *V.C.H. Bucks.* iii. 257–8, and cf. R. H. Lathbury, *Hist. of Denham, Bucks.*

[186] Fletcher, *Eng. Bridgettines*, 37 sqq.

[187] *Cal. S. P. Ven.* 1556–7, 791.

[188] Original in muniments of Syon Abbey, Devon.

[189] *Cal. Pat.* 1555–7, 290 sqq.

[190] Ibid.

[191] Ibid. 1557–8, 295.

Meantime the work of refitting the buildings for monastic life had been going on, the cost being borne by Sir Francis Englefield who, through his wife, formerly Catherine Fettyplace, was related to two of the sisters.[192] The re-establishment was completed by the solemn enclosure of all who had rejoined by the Bishop of London, assisted by the Abbot of Westminster.[193] Both the queen and Cardinal Pole were rewarded for their favours by obits at the abbey.[194]

The community was not to remain long in enjoyment of its peaceful round. In May 1559 Parliament decreed the dissolution of the re-established monasteries, pensions being granted only to those religious willing to take the Oath of Supremacy.[195] Once again the community at Syon decided to continue its monastic life and it was arranged that the retiring Spanish ambassador, Feria, should take them and other religious abroad with him.[196] The community moved to Flanders, where it began a long exile in the Bridgettine house at Termonde.[197] Despite many difficulties and hazards it continued to exist in Flanders, France, and Portugal until its return to England in two groups, one in 1809 and the other in 1861, and it has been settled since 1925 at Marley, South Brent, Devon.[198]

*F. R. Johnston*

## Revised Lists of Syon Abbey Officers

For these institutions, see also the *Martiloge*, British Library Ms. Add. 22285, f. 1r.

### Abbesses of Syon to 1576
Matilda Newton[199]
Joan North, elected 1420;[200] died 1433[201]
Maud Muston, elected 1433;[202] died 1447[203]

Margaret Ashby, occurs 1448;[204] died 1456[205]
Elizabeth Muston, occurs 1457; died 1497[206]
Elizabeth Gybbs, occurs 1497; died 1518[207]
Constance Brown,[208] elected 1518;[209] died 1520[210]
Agnes Jordan, occurs 1521–2; died 1545/6[211]
Catherine Palmer, instituted 1557;[212] died 1576[213]

### Confessors-General of Syon[214] (to 1557)
William Alnewick, occurs *c.*1417–20[215]
Thomas Fishbourne,[216] elected 1420;[217] died 1428[218]
Robert Bell, elected 1428;[219] died 1460[220]
Thomas Westhawe,[221] occurs 1472;[222] died 1488[223]
Walter Fallden, died 1497[224]
Stephen Saunders,[225] occurs 1498;[226] died 1513[227]
John Trowell,[228] elected 1513;[229] died 1523[230]
John Fewterer,[231] died 1536[232]

---

[192] Fletcher, *Eng. Bridgettines*, 41.
[193] Aungier, *Syon*, 97.
[194] *Martiloge*, f. 63v.
[195] *Cal. S.P. Ven.* 1558–80, 79.
[196] Ibid. 95, 105.
[197] R. Persons, 'Preface to Hist. of Wanderings of Syon', in Hamilton, *Angel of Syon*, 194.
[198] Fletcher, *Eng. Bridgettines, passim*.
[199] Matilda Newton and William Alnewick were appointed as Abbess & Confessor-general respectively by King Henry V before the Syon community was properly set up, to oversee its initial development. They then returned to Barking Abbey & Westminster Abbey respectively, where they remained as recluses until their deaths, *The Incendium Amoris of Richard Rolle of Hampole*, ed. M. Deansley (Manchester 1915), pp. 91–130.
[200] B.M. Cotton MS. Cleo. E. II, f. 352.
[201] *Martiloge*, f. 58.
[202] Guildhall MS. 9531/4, f. 45.
[203] *Martiloge*, f. 57v.

[204] *Cal. Chart. R.* 1427–1516, 91.
[205] *Martiloge*, f. 43.
[206] Ibid. f. 36.
[207] Ibid. f. 52v.
[208] *Collectanea Topographia et Genealogia*, i. 325–6.
[209] Guildhall MS. 9531/9, ff. 128v–30.
[210] *Martiloge*, f. 46v.
[211] Ibid. f. 25; P.C.C., F. 4. Alen; *V.C.H. Bucks.* iii. 260 gives the date on her tomb as 1544.
[212] *Cal. Pat.* 1555–7, 290–2.
[213] *Martiloge*, f. 68.
[214] Ibid. f. 2..
[215] Alnewick is not included in the list in the *Martiloge* and has never been recognized as the first confessor-general by Syon, but see Knowles, *Rel. Orders*, ii. 179–80, 307–8; Dugdale, *Mon.* vi. 542; see p. 183.
[216] He was a monk of St. Albans who later became a secular priest; cf. *Amundesham Annales* (Rolls Ser.), i. 27; Cnattingius, *Studies*, i. 131–55.
[217] B.M. Cotton MS. Cleo. E. II, f. 352.
[218] *Martiloge*, f. 55v.
[219] Guildhall MS. 9531/5, ff. 69–72.
[220] *Martiloge*, f. 33.
[221] Emden, *Biog. Reg. Cambridge*, 630.
[222] T.N.A, PRO PROB 11/6, f. 163v.
[223] *Martiloge*, f. 41.
[224] Ibid. f. 55v.
[225] *William* Saunders, B.D., Confessor of Syon, is said to figure in a deed dated Syon, 1498 (Aungier, *Syon*, 110, n.), but the Christian name of Saunders, the confessor-general, seems certainly to have been Stephen.
[226] Aungier, *Syon*, 110, n.
[227] *Martiloge*, f. 33v.
[228] *BROU*, iii. 1910; T. Wright, *Letters relating to the Suppression of the Monasteries* (Camd. Soc. xxvi), 44–6.
[229] Guildhall MS. 9531/9, f. 40v.
[230] *Martiloge*, f. 35v. Aungier's reference to him as alive in 1536 is an error for John Fewterer: Aungier, *Syon*, 533.
[231] Emden, *Biog. Reg. Cambridge*, 226–7.
[232] *Martiloge*, f. 57; no year is given in this reference to Fewterer's death but an underlying entry which has been erased but is still partly legible reads... *vij Confessor generalis Anno dm* 1536; since he was accounted the 7th confessor-general the erasure clearly refers to Fewterer; *L. and P. Hen. VIII*, xi, p. 202.

John Copinger[233] occurs 1536;[234] died 1539[235]
John Green,[236] instituted 1557[237]

[233] J. Venn, *Alumni Cantabrigienses*, I. i. 396.
[234] *L. and P. Hen. VIII*, xi, p. 197. This letter, which is endorsed 'The confessor of Syon', is dated 23 Sept. 1536. Fewterer died 3 days later. He may already have resigned or the letter may have been endorsed after it was dated. It is also possible that Fewterer was incapacitated and that Copinger was acting in his place.
[235] *Martiloge*, f. 58. This notice of his death omits the year but an underlying erasure is partly legible and suggests that he died in 1539. The penultimate line ends '*ge =*' and the last line reads '(*neral*) *is Anno dni* 1539'; and cf. *Letters re. Suppression of Monasteries*, 44–46.
[236] His name is 'N. Grene' in the list in the *Martiloge* and the entry is in a different hand. His death is not noticed in the obituaries in that book. He was probably the same person as the John Green who at the Suppression was a priest in Syon and who received the highest pension (£10) after David Curson (£15). He was still in receipt of his pension in 1555–6: Aungier, *Syon*, 99.
[237] *Cal. Pat.* 1555–6; 290–2.

## *Prioresses*

From the Martiloge, British Library Ms. Add. 22285, transcr. by Dr. Virginia Bainbridge.

Katerina Neandester, died before 1428, f. 30v
Johanna Cobley, died 13 July n.d., f. 46v
Juliana Soklynge, elected by 1428; died 2 Dec. n.d., f. 66r
Emma Sevenoke, died 1470, f. 24v
Margaret Ashby, later 3rd Abbess, died 1456, f. 43r
Helen Eton/Eyton, died 1492, f. 67v
Anne Poole/Pole, died 1501, f. 36r
Elionora Scrope, died 1519 f. 34v
Margaret Windsor, died after 1539 f. 69r
Rose Pagett, died after 1557 f. 21v

# HOUSE OF TRINITARIAN FRIARS

## 8. THE PRIORY OF HOUNSLOW

### INTRODUCTION

The *V.C.H.* article for the priory of Hounslow is adequate rather than comprehensive, and there is a need for more detailed study of both this house and the Trinitarian order itself. George E. Bate, *A History of the Priory and Church of Holy Trinity, Hounslow* (London, 1924) provides a short history with several photographs.

There is evidence about the priory's property dealings to be found in L. Wright, *Sources of London English, Medieval Thames Vocabulary* (Oxford, 1996), p. 80 and also in *Documentary Sources*, p. 83. Excavations in the area in the 1990s are described in Robert Cowie, 'The Priory and Manor of Hounslow: Excavations at Hounslow Police Station, Montague Road, Hounslow', *T.L.M.A.S.*, 46 (1997 for 1995), pp. 125–35.

The priory attracted a wide range of support, from Londoners and Middesex gentry, as well as from further afield. See, for instance, G.L. MS 9171/1, f. 48, 5 f. 128v, and 6 f. 45v; Hertfordshire Record Office, MS 2AR27v; Westminster Archives, PCW Register Wyks, f. 68v; T.N.A. PROB 11/16, f. 204, and 17, f. 265. The house also granted letters of confraternity to prominent individuals in the locality, including William Chedworth, a Middlesex J.P. and Johanna his wife, in 1479: T.N.A. C270/32/32; C148/116. Sir (later Lord) Andrew Windsor (died 1543) of Stanwell, was steward of Hounslow (Paxton, 'Nunneries', p. 75). Lord Windsor, his wife and son George were all buried there, although by 1543 the priory church had become a chapel of ease for the inhabitants of Hounslow, T.N.A. PROB 11/29, ff. 179.

*Jessica Freeman*

The earliest mention of a religious house at Hounslow occurs in the charter roll in 1200.[1] Twenty-five years later William Longespée, Earl of Salisbury, included a gift of ten cows to Hounslow in his long list of bequests to religious houses.[2] In 1242–3 the 'Master' of Hounslow held one knight's fee of John de Neville, who held it of the king.[3] This fee was probably the manor of East Bedfont, which with the advowson was given by Neville to the hospital. His gift was eventually confirmed by Edward II in 1313.[4] Early sources give no indication of the order, if any, to which the hospital belonged. Later it was a house of the Friars of the Holy Trinity, an order founded in France in the closing years of the 12th century. It is possible that Hounslow belonged from the start to the Trinitarians, but it is more likely that it was given to them in the mid-13th century by Richard, King of the Romans, brother of Henry III. Richard founded a house of

Trinitarians at Knaresborough (Yorks. W.R.),[5] and at Hounslow he was the greatest benefactor, if not the second founder. To the friars there, whether newly-introduced or long-established, he gave his lands of Babworth in Isleworth, except the fishpond. These friary lands later comprised over 80 acres by or near the Crane above Baber Bridge, and in the enclosure cut out of Hounslow Heath further north.[6] In 1314 Richard's grant was confirmed by Edward II.[7] These lands of the friars were first described as the manor of Hounslow in 1296, when the minister and friars were granted a weekly market and an annual fair of eight days beginning on the vigil of the feast of Holy Trinity.[8]

Meanwhile in 1252 Henry III gave the minister and friars a silver cup for the eucharist, and also a silver thurible or censer, which second gift was confirmed in the following January.[9] Before 1275 Pain de Cleremont had given them 40 acres in

---

[1] *Rot. Chart.* (Rec. Com.), 98.
[2] *Rot. Litt. Claus.* (Rec. Com.), ii. 71.
[3] *Bk. of Fees*, 897.
[4] *Cal. Pat.* 1307–13, 578; 1313–17, 36.

[5] *V.C.H. Yorks.* iii. 297.
[6] *V.C.H. Mdx.* iii. 106.
[7] *Cal. Pat.* 1313–17, 78.
[8] *Cal. Chart. R.* 1257–1300, 463.
[9] *Close R.* 1251–3, 65, 306.

Stanwell and in the 14th century the friars acquired further property outside Hounslow.[10] In 1338 and 1358 this included lands in East Bedfont from William de Odiham and Thomas Lenee under a licence to acquire in mortmain, which had been granted in 1320.[11] Meanwhile, having secured the advowson, they had been allowed to appropriate the church of East Bedfont in 1314, and were pardoned the fine for the appropriation in the next year.[12] They presented vicars to East Bedfont from 1325 until the Dissolution.[13] In 1353 and 1428 the East Bedfont holding was still returned as one knight's fee.[14] In accordance with the will of John of Gloucester, Rector of Harlington, dated 1332, the friars received a tenement in the parish of St. Botolph without Bishopsgate so that they should celebrate for him and his family at Hounslow and Harlington; and after the extinction of a life interest they received a further messuage and three cottages in the same place in 1369.[15] In 1338 and 1358 the friars received lands in Stanwell and Harlington, under the licence of 1320 already mentioned.[16] In 1367 they were licensed to acquire in mortmain further property in Staines and Stanwell, namely a mill, 34 acres, and 5s. in rent, worth altogether 27s. 9d. a year, from the vicar of Heston;[17] and in 1353 they also held a fifth of a fee in Acton.[18] In 1358 William Fitzwaryn had licence to make them a grant in mortmain to the value of £10.[19] From the same vicar of Heston the friars received in 1362 a messuage, a mill, two gardens, two fisheries, 27 acres, an ait in the Thames, and 4s. 4d. in rent, all in Kingston-on-Thames (Surr.).[20] They secured the advowson of Littleton from Guy de Brienne in 1372, and presented to Littleton rectory from 1395 until the Dissolution.[21] In 1370 they also presented to Feltham.[22]

In 1376 some buildings were erected at Hatton Grange on the land of the friars of Hounslow, so that the king might stay there. These buildings were to revert to the friars after his death.[23] At the same time the friary was granted £20 a year at the

Exchequer that prayers might be said for the king, and to provide a chaplain to celebrate at Hatton Grange. In 1400 this grant was replaced by one of £10 a year from the fee farm of Kingston, which was confirmed at the beginning of the next two reigns and increased to £20 in 1462 but reduced to £10 again in 1468.[24] In 1382 the houses at Hatton Grange were leased to Richard II for his life at an annual rent of 50s. payable by the king's bailiffs of Kingston-on-Thames.[25] Hounslow was conveniently situated about half way between Westminster and Windsor, the most usual of all royal journeys, and from the time of Edward III, who gave them 10 marks to pray for the soul of Queen Philippa,[26] the friars enjoyed royal patronage. As late as 1530 they received 20s. in royal alms on Good Friday.[27] In 1349 Margery Barat bequeathed to the friars an ox and four bushels of corn, and in 1377 John Tornegold, merchant, bequeathed the reversion of certain sums of money to Hounslow and other religious houses.[28] In 1434 John Franks, Master of the Rolls, left 20s. for the repair of the fabric of their conventual church.[29] The friars had a brewhouse in Uxbridge which in 1523 was leased to Thomas Nicholas and figures in his will.[30]

The rules of the Friars of the Holy Trinity laid down that each house should have a minister, or prior, three clerks, and three lay brothers.[31] But, although occasional ordinations are recorded,[32] there is no evidence of numbers at Hounslow until 1537, when the minister, three friars, and one George Symson signed a lease.[33] Their revenues were supposed to be devoted to the relief of the poor and the redemption of captives. About 1352, when the Friars of the Holy Trinity at Oxford had died out, the Minister of Hounslow sent one of his friars to celebrate there.[34] The friars also seem to have provided a warden for the Hospital of St. Lawrence, Crediton, and a chaplain for Warland, near Totnes, both in Devon.[35] Fraternity was granted to prominent laymen, including, in 1508, Henry, Prince of Wales, who was to dissolve all the friaries thirty years later.[36] In 1406 the Minister was a

---

[10] V.C.H. Mdx. iii. 41.

[11] Cal. Pat. 1317–21, 453; 1338–40, 159; 1358–61, 56.

[12] Ibid. 1313–17, 210.

[13] Newcourt, Repertorium, i. 575; Lond. Reg. Gravesend (Cant. and York Soc.), 277; Lond. Reg. Sudbury (Cant. and York Soc.), i. 238, 264.

[14] Feudal Aids, iii. 374, 380.

[15] Cal. Wills in Court of Husting (Lond.), ed. Sharpe, i. 382; Cal. Pat. 1367–70, 250.

[16] Ibid. 1317–21, 453; 1338–40, 159; 1358–61, 56.

[17] Ibid. 1364–7, 380.

[18] Feudal Aids, iii. 375.

[19] Cal. Pat. 1358–61, 44.

[20] Ibid. 1361–4, 256.

[21] Ibid. 1385–9, 462, 478; Newcourt, Repertorium, i. 689.

[22] Lond. Reg. Sudbury (Cant. and York Soc.), i. 273.

[23] Cal. Pat. 1374–7, 256.

[24] Ibid. 401; 1399–1401, 290; 1414–16, 42; 1422–9, 71; 1461–7, 222; 1467–77, 67.

[25] Cal. Pat. 1381–5, 131; Cal. Close, 1381–5, 135.

[26] Issue Roll of Thomas de Brantingham, ed. F. Devon, 428.

[27] L. and P. Hen. VIII, v, pp. 749, 754.

[28] Cal. Wills in Court of Husting, i. 693; ii. 200.

[29] Cant. Reg. Chichele (Cant. and York Soc.), ii. 592.

[30] P.C.C. 11 Bodfelde.

[31] Dugdale, Mon. vi. 1558.

[32] Lond. Reg. Sudbury (Cant. and York Soc.), ii. 12, 97; Cant. Reg. Chichele (Cant. and York Soc.), iv. 322.

[33] Aungier, Syon, 490.

[34] Cal. Close, 1389–92, 472–3.

[35] Aungier, Syon, 492.

[36] B.M. Topham Chart. 48; Stowe Chart. 617.

collector in the deanery of Middlesex of the subsidy of 6s. 8d. granted by the clergy, and in 1440 of a half-tenth.[37] In the 15th century Robert of Hounslow, a friar of the house, became Provincial of the Order in the British Isles, and Clement Maydestone, who was a friar at Hounslow for a time before moving to Syon Abbey, wrote an account of the martyrdom of Archbishop Scrope.[38] It would appear from the will of Alice Lupton, who died in 1530/1, that Hounslow was at that time the residence of the minister provincial.[39] The will (proved in 1521) of John Gefferoy, a sergeant of the king, suggests that the house had a lay officer in some capacity and that he resided there.[40]

In 1535 the demesne of the house at Hounslow was said to be worth £5 2s. 6d. and other property there brought in £22 1s. 8d. Rents from other places were worth £34, the rectory of Bedfont £8 13s. 4d., and that of Hatton in the same parish £4. Altogether with the mill and the market the revenue of the friary was said to amount to £80, which was reduced to £74 by certain rents which it had to pay.[41] Nearly 200 ounces of plate were collected from Hounslow by the royal commissioners.[42]

In 1537 the minister and friars leased all their lands and possessions except the church and buildings of their convent but including the outhouses, gardens, and stables, to Robert Cheeseman of Southall for 80 years, at a rent of £26, of which £10 was to be paid to the minister and the remainder to the friars. The lease was signed by William Hyde, minister, three friars, and George Symson.[43] But the end was already at hand, and the lands in Hounslow, Heston, Harlington, East Bedfont, Littleton, Stanwell, Hatton in Hounslow, and St. Botolph, as well as the advowson and glebe of Littleton, the rectory of East Bedfont, the brewhouse in Uxbridge, and a water-mill at Kingston called 'Hogesmylle' were, with the perquisites of the courts, almost all annexed to the royal honor of Hampton Court,[44] Richard

Forster being appointed bailiff and collector.[45] The manor of Harlington was then valued at just under £15, of which 3s. came from the manor court and the remainder from rents.[46] Richard Layton had reported to Thomas Cromwell about the leasing of the friary to Robert Cheeseman. In 1539 he wrote again that he was going to Hounslow to pay the debts of the friars who, he alleged, 'drank weekly all the town dry'.[47]

Parts of the friary buildings with the chapel survived as the manor-house and parish church of Holy Trinity until 1816, when they were demolished to make way for a new parish church, later erected on the old site.[48]

*J. L. Kirby*

## Ministers of Hounslow

This list is from *Heads of Religious Houses*, vol. 2, pp. 532–3; and vol. 3 (forthcoming).

Nicholas, occurs 1256/7
Robert de Watford, occurs 1296, 1298
Ralph, occurs 1305
John de Staines (Stanes), occurs 1320
Bartholomew, occurs 1363
William, occurs 1369, 1381
Walter, occurs 1401, 1422
John Mulsey, occurs 1429, 1437
John Wodehalle (Wodehele), occurs 1446, 1460
Richard, occurs 1468
William Marchall, late minister, 1477
William Peerson (Pyerson, Peyrson), occurs 1478, 1479
John Fry, occurs 1493, 1506
Ralph Bekworth (Bekwith) occurs 1508–20; on 10 July 1510 John Fry, late minister, is called his predecessor
John Hammond, occurs 1520
William Beylbe (Beilbe), occurs 1522, 1524–5; he presumably resigned his office as he was still alive and a friar in 1538
William Hyde, occurs 1532 as minister and Provincial of the Order, 1538

[37] *Cal. Close*, 1405–9, 59; Aungier, *Syon*, 486.
[38] Ibid. 545; C. L. Kingsford, *Eng. Hist. Lit. in Fifteenth Cent.* 38.
[39] Guildhall MS. 9171/10, f. 161.
[40] P.C.C. 18 Maynwaryng.
[41] *Valor Eccl.* (Rec. Com.), i. 402.
[42] Aungier, *Syon*, 492.
[43] *L. and P. Hen. VIII*, xii (2), p. 268; Aungier, *Syon*, 489–90.
[44] S.C. 6/Hen. VIII/2396.

[45] *L. and P. Hen. VIII*, xii (1), p. 772.
[46] S.C. 12/19/17.
[47] *L. and P. Hen. VIII*, xiii (2), p. 185.
[48] *V.C.H. Mdx.* iii. 127.

# HOUSE OF KNIGHTS HOSPITALLERS

## 9. THE PRIORY OF ST. JOHN OF JERUSALEM, CLERKENWELL

### INTRODUCTION

One of the main developments since the *V.C.H.* account appeared has been the publication of an edition of the cartulary of the knights of St. John in England (B.L. Cotton Nero EVI 467): *Cartulary of the Knights of St. John of Jerusalem in England*, ed. M. Gervers, 2 vols., Records of Social and Economic History, n.s. 6 (Oxford, 1982, 1996). Another has been the recent publication of G. O'Malley, *The Knights Hospitaller of the English Langue, 1460–1565* (Oxford, 2005), which places the priory in the context of the Order's European networks. The priory's relations with its Scottish counterparts are dealt with in I. B. Cowan and A. Macquarrie (eds.), *Knights of St. John of Jerusalem in Scotland*, Scottish History Society (Edinburgh, 1983).

There is also more evidence of the priory's property dealings in London, and of descriptions of the site itself, *c.*1130–1185: see H. M. Chew and W. Kellaway (eds.), *London Assize of Nuisance 1301–1431* (London Record Society, 10, 1973); McHardy, *Church in London;* J. S. Loengard (ed.), *London Viewers and their Certificates, 1508–1558,* (London Record Society, 26, 1989); Honeybourne, 'Property', pp. 82–4; and J. K. Schofield, *The Building of London* (London, 1984), p. 50. Sixteenth-century material includes a survey of all the leases belonging to the priory, ministers' accounts for Sussex estates and enrolments of grants of the dissolved priory's lands: Surrey History Centre, Loseley MS 791; T.N.A. SC6/HenryVIII/2402–2403; LR/2/63; and see Davis, *Cartularies*, no. 857.

For the archaeology of the priory, see B. Sloane and G. Malcolm, *Excavations at the Priory of the Order of the Hospital of St. John of Jerusalem, Clerkenwell, London,* MoLAS Monograph series, 20 (2004).

Between 1462 and 1506, the priors were routinely appointed to the Middlesex Commission of the Peace, *Cal. of Pat.,* 1461–67, p. 567; 1467–77, pp. 621–2; 1485–94, p. 493, 1496–1509, p. 650.

*Jessica Freeman*

The priory of St. John of Jerusalem at Clerkenwell was the head house of the Hospital of St. John in England. This Order was closely-knit and also highly centralized and the history and function of Clerkenwell first calls for an account of the Order itself.

The Order of Hospitallers was founded in the 11th century and recognized by Pope Paschal II in 1116.[1] Centred upon the great hospital in Jerusalem, its original object was to provide succour for pilgrims to the Holy Places. But Raymond du Puy (master, 1119–24) permitted the Order to undertake military activities and these soon began to take precedence over the charitable work from which it took its name.[2] Upon the surrender of Jerusalem to

Saladin in 1187 the hospital there was lost and the Order became completely military. Its headquarters remained in the Holy Land until removed to Rhodes in 1310 and thence in 1530 to Malta.

The Order was divided into three categories, chaplains, knights, and *servientes*,[3] of which the first was, at least until 1236, accorded formal precedence. For their regulation statutes were drawn up by Gilbert d'Assailly (1162–70) and Roger des Moulins (1177–87). Those of the latter show us the administrative system when fully developed.[4] They lasted in this form until 1310.

---

[1] Delaville le Roulx, *Cartulaire Generale des Hospitalliers,* i. 29.

[2] Cf. letter (1178–80) from Alexander III to Rog. des Moulins: *Cartulaire*, i. 360. For Raymond's Rule see ibid. i. 62.

[3] This word probably had different meanings at different stages of the Order's development. It might here be translated as 'serjeant', which has a sufficiently wide connotation to include all the different shades of meaning.

[4] For a description of the Order's early constitution see le Roulx, *Les Hospitalliers en Terre Sainte*, vols. ii–iv.

Supreme authority was vested in the master,[5] appointed for life, and advised by a permanent body of counsellors – the Convent – resident in the Holy Land. In all legislative and disciplinary matters the general chapter (which met, in theory, every five years) was sovereign. It elected the master and the conventual bailiffs – the commander, marshal, hospitaller, draper, and treasurer. As endowments accumulated in the West, priories, with subordinate houses called commanderies, and smaller units, known as *camere* and bailiwicks, were established in various countries to facilitate the collection of arms and to further recruiting. The priors were appointed by the general chapter on the advice of the provincial chapters. They were responsible for sending to headquarters the annual 'responsions' which represented originally the entire revenue of the priory, after the deduction of necessary expenses. Later, responsions, although liable to fluctuate, were generally reckoned at a third of the net income. A valuable supplementary source of income was provided by the *frarie* contributed by the members of the fraternities attached to the various houses. They shared in the good works and spiritual benefits of the Order, and enjoyed the right, confirmed by papal privilege, of burial in its churches and graveyards in return for protecting its interests and contributing to its support.[6]

Each prior was assisted by a provincial (sometimes called a 'general') chapter which met annually, and which all bailiffs and commanders were in theory bound to attend. Its consent was required for all important decisions relating to the priory. The priors owed no homage or fealty to temporal authorities, and their temporalities were not taken in hand during voidances. Instead, the Convent claimed as a 'mortuary' the entire revenues of a priory from the death of a prior until the following 1 May, and as a 'vacancy' the net revenues of the succeeding year. In addition, the prior's effects were claimed as 'spoils' and shared between the master and the conventual bailiffs.[7] Priors were supposed to present themselves at regular intervals at the Convent to give an account of their stewardship, although in practice such appearances were rare. They were also subject to periodical visitation by the master or his representatives, and themselves had the duty of visiting, in person or by their accredited agents, the commanderies under their jurisdiction. All the brethren were liable to be called up periodically for service in the Convent, and from time to time a 'general passage' (*passagium*) involving the whole fighting force of the priory was ordered. The principle was early asserted that priors and commanders should normally be natives of the country in which their houses were situated.[8] Later it was found convenient to divide the entire Order into 'tongues' (*langues*). Of these there were at first probably only four, the English and Irish priories (the latter founded in 1174) being associated with the priories of France; but before 1300 the number had been increased to seven, of which the English and Irish priories, including the commanderies in Wales and Scotland, formed one.[9] In 1338 there were in England 41 commanderies, eight of which had been houses of the Templars.[10] Clerkenwell was the only one in Middlesex at that time while Hampton[11] and Harefield were *camere*, although the latter had been a commandery in the previous century.[12]

The constitution of the Order underwent further development after the conquest of Rhodes in 1310. The general chapter of Montpellier in 1330 organized the brethren there according to their respective tongues, to each being assigned as 'pillar' one of the conventual bailiffs. To the English tongue was allotted the Turcopolier, who had originally commanded the light cavalry recruited from the native population, which had formed a normal part of the Latin forces in Palestine.[13] The 'pillar' presided over the assembly at which the affairs of the tongue in Rhodes were discussed and was expected to provide the knights with an 'inn' or 'auberge' in which to live.[14] He was in theory perpetually resident in the Convent; but in practice frequently visited England, where he was from time to time employed by the master as a check on the prior – a proceeding which resulted, not unnaturally, in bad blood between them.

---

[5] The title of Grand Master is said to have been first assumed by Peter d'Aubusson (1473–1503).

[6] For conditions governing the enrolment of *confratres* see E. J. King, *The Rule Statutes and Customs of the Hospitallers*, 1099–1310, 194–5; A. Mifsud, *Knights Hospitallers of the Venerable Tongue of England in Malta*, 84–85. The Merchant Taylors' Co. of London, which, like the Hospitallers, had John the Baptist as its patron, was admitted to confraternity with the Hospital in the 14th cent.: C. M. Clode, *Early Hist. of the Merchant Taylors' Co.* i. 111–12; but the dating here is suspect.

[7] J. E. Nisbet, 'Treasury Records of the Knights of St. John', *Melita Historica* [Jnl. Malta Hist. Soc.], ii (2), 95 sqq.

[8] The earliest surviving deeds show that there was at first a large foreign element among the brethren comprising the English priory: *Cartulaire*, i. 851–2; iv. 319–27. As late as 1235 a German, Thierry de Nussa, was appointed prior.

[9] E. J. King, *Grand Priory of the Order of the Hospital of St. John of Jerusalem in Eng.* 49–50.

[10] *Knights Hospitallers in England*, ed. L. B. Larking (Camd. Soc. lxv), *passim*.

[11] *V.C.H. Mdx.* ii. 324–6. 327, 371.

[12] T. Hugo, 'Moor Hall in Harefield; a Camera of the Knights Hospitallers of St. John of Jerusalem', *T.L.M.A.S.* iii. 2–30; *V.C.H. Mdx.* iii. 238, 241, 243; S. E. Rigold, 'Two Camerae of the Military Orders', *Arch. Jnl.* cxxii. 86–132.

[13] On the Turcopolier and his office see Mifsud, *Hospitallers in Malta*, 87 sqq.

[14] The English 'auberge' in Rhodes is still in existence. It was bought by a member of the English Order in 1919, and carefully restored.

Under the new constitution commanderies were reserved to the use of the tongue to which they belonged and after 1354 commanders were normally nominated by the tongue. The master could appoint to one commandery in each priory (in England West Peckham (Kent) enjoyed this 'magisterial' status); and every five years he might also appoint to one other commandery in every priory. Each prior was also permitted every five years to appoint to one commandery in his own priory. When a commander had served for fifteen years, ten of which had been spent in the Convent, he became eligible, if a knight, for a conventual or capitular bailiwick or a priory, carrying with it the title of 'crucifer' or Grand Cross. In the English tongue there were four Grand Crosses – the priors of England and Ireland, the Turcopolier, and the bailiff of Eagle.[15]

From the first recognition of the Order successive Popes granted it a number of privileges. Its members were exempted from the authority of the local ordinaries and from payment of tithes, and enjoyed extensive rights of sanctuary. They were authorized to maintain in all their houses, in addition to secular clerks, as many lay servants as were needed to care for the poor and the sick. All were subject to the exclusive jurisdiction of the Hospital.[16]

The process by which the English priory was established is obscure. Such early grants as have been recorded are difficult to date; but the Order had received some endowments before the foundation of Clerkenwell. The appearance in surviving lists of benefactors of the names of, for example, Gilbert, Earl of Hertford (d. 1152),[17] Robert, Earl of Derby (d. 1139),[18] Adeliza de Clermont,[19] wife of Richard fitz Gilbert, (d. 1123), and mother of the Earl of Pembroke (d. 1148) suggests the reign of Stephen or possibly Henry I.[20] Before 1154 the Templars were a more favoured Order than the Hospitallers; they received generous benefactions from Stephen and his queen. With the accession of Henry II, however, the fortunes of the Hospitallers began to improve, and in 1155[21] and 1177–8[22] they were granted charters. It was the mission of the master, Roger des Moulins, to England in 1185, in company with the Patriarch of Jerusalem, to seek help for the Latin Kingdom,[23] that brought the Order to the fore. The Master of the Temple, who had been the third member of the embassy, died in Italy on the way, leaving Roger without a rival.

Richard I, who held the Order in affection as a result of services to him on Crusade, granted the English Hospitallers a charter in 1194 enlarging their privileges, and handed over to their care hospitals at Worcester and Hereford.[24] John, too, extended his patronage to them.[25] His relations with the Order remained amicable throughout, although, like other religious orders, they suffered from his exactions. They rallied to the support of Henry III against Louis VIII of France[26] and frequently undertook financial and diplomatic business for him.[27] Edward I appointed Prior Joseph de Chauncy as Treasurer of the kingdom (1273–80),[28] but in 1295 financial stringency encouraged the king to sequestrate the revenues of both the English and the Irish priories, although under pressure from the Pope he later restored them.[29] The subordination of the priory to the Crown began in the 14th century, when, as the sequel to the appointment of an alien prior, the king twice took the temporalities into his hands and compelled the newly-appointed prior to take the oath of fealty.[30] Philip de Thame, elected in 1335, secured from the king a formal recognition of the exemption of the Hospital from all such feudal obligations,[31] but they were in fact constantly reimposed and in the later Middle Ages it became normal procedure for newly-elected priors to perform fealty, although they always did so under protest. Obstacles were also frequently placed by the Crown in the way of the payment of responsions, and communication between the priory and the Convent suffered many interruptions.

The numbers and social status of the brethren at the different stages in the history of the priory are not easy to determine, although it is probable that the total was never large. The extent of 1338[32] gives 119, of whom 34 can be identified as chaplains, 34

[15] Eagle (Lincs.) had been given to the Templars in Stephen's reign. It passed to the Hospitallers in 1312.

[16] For these, and other privileges, see *Cartulaire*, i. 95, 107, 173, 350, *passim*.

[17] Ibid. 298.

[18] Ibid. 236.

[19] Ibid.

[20] Cf. Dugdale, *Mon.* vi (2), 802–3, 804, 834. All these datings are open to question.

[21] *Cartulaire*, i. 180.

[22] L. Delisle and E. Berger, *Recueil des Actes de Henri II, roi d'Angleterre et duc de Normandie*, ii. 258–60.

[23] *Gesta Hen. Sec.* (Rolls Ser.), i. 335–6.

[24] Dugdale, *Mon.* vi (2), 839; *Cartulaire*, ii. 604; W. Rees, *Hist. of Order of St. John of Jerusalem in Wales*, 22.

[25] *Cartulaire*, iv. 271; Dugdale, *Mon.* vi (2), 808–9. For the early foundations see D. Knowles and R. N. Hadcock, *Medieval Religious Houses in Eng. and Wales*, 241 sqq.

[26] *Pat. R.* 1216–25, 291.

[27] Ibid. 1225–32, 558; *Cal. Pat.* 1232–47, 126, 130, 220–1, 432, 465, 490–1; 1247–58, 326; 1266–72, 459; *Close R.* 1237–42, 52, 190–1; 1251–3, 108; 1253–4, 191.

[28] *Cal. Close*, 1272–9, 32; *Cal. Pat.* 1272–81, 382. For his activities as treasurer see Close and Pat. Rolls *passim*.

[29] Rymer, *Foedera*, i (2), 817; *Cartulaire*, iii. 666.

[30] On the death of Prior l'Archer in 1330, and of his successor, Leonard de Tibertis, formerly Prior of Venice, in 1335: *Cal. Close*, 1330–3, 67, 154–5.

[31] Ibid. 1333–7, 363, 453, 501–2.

[32] *Hospitallers in England*, *passim*.

as knights, and 48 as *servientes*; the status of 3 others is unknown. There were in addition 4 *donati*. No mention is made of those resident in the Convent or of those still unprofessed. In general the English knights seem to have been recruited from the country gentry rather than from the aristocracy. Moreover, the same names recur from time to time, frequently place-names – often of property belonging to the Order – and they can safely be accepted as indicating a family relationship.[33]

After the dissolution of the Templars the English tongue was supposed to contribute 28 of the 200 men comprising the enlarged establishment at Rhodes.[34] Although, however, the numbers resident in the Convent were later increased on several occasions, and in 1514 reached a total of 550, the English contribution remained unchanged, and there is good reason to believe that it often fell below the prescribed total. There is no direct evidence of the toll taken by the several visitations of the plague in the 14th century, but it is significant that in 1361 the complement of clerks and chaplains at Clerkenwell was well below strength,[35] and that sixty years later only two or three brethren were resident there.[36] That a general decline in numbers had long been in progress is, moreover, strongly suggested by the fact that in the later Middle Ages the commanderies were frequently grouped together in twos and threes under the control of a single individual,[37] despite statutes to the contrary. While this can undoubtedly be ascribed in part to economic causes, it suggests also a shortage of men eligible for the rank of commander. The growing practice of leasing commanderies points in the same direction.[38]

In the later Middle Ages the priors sat in parliament as 'premier barons' of England,[39] and were members of the king's Council,[40] while from time to time they held ministerial and military office under the Crown. They were directly and disastrously involved in the civil disturbances of the 15th century, but recovered their social and political prestige, although not their independence, with the accession of the Tudors.

It was the loss of Rhodes in 1522 that first seriously shook the stability of the Order in England by enabling the king to bring pressure to bear both on the priory and on the Convent. He was popularly credited with a plan to 'nationalize' the priory and utilize the knights for the defence of Calais. A personal visit to England by the master, de Lisle Adam, in 1528 temporarily saved the situation,[41] but the raising next year of the 'great matter' of the king's divorce sealed the fate of the English priory. In 1538 Henry, as Supreme Head of the Church in England and Protector of the Order – a title first conferred by the master upon his predecessor – took over control of the English Hospital. He licensed the prior to receive English subjects to the habit, provided that they had previously taken the oath of allegiance. Brethren appointed to commanderies must obtain royal confirmation, and formally repudiate papal authority and jurisdiction. The first year's revenue in such cases was to go to the Crown; the second year's to the Convent, after deduction of the new tenth. The collection of alms, save by express royal warrant, was forbidden. Offences were to be dealt with in the first instance in provincial chapter, with right of appeal to the Crown.[42]

The King's demands were submitted to the general chapter in September 1540 and rejected. The master wrote to the King expressing the views of the general chapter, but the English tongue had already been dissolved by statute five months earlier on the ground that the brethren had 'sustained and maintained the usurped power of the Bishop of Rome … '.[43] The possessions of the priory, valued at some £2,385, were conferred on the Crown. This sum was exclusive of Clerkenwell itself but it included London rents worth £241 and an annual revenue of £163 from the Temple.[44] Pensions were awarded to the four Grand Crosses, and a total of 22 English knights, and four chaplains.[45] To Prior Weston was

[33] William Tong, Turcopolier in 1433, Robert Tong, Turcopolier in 1468; William Middleton held Eagle in 1366, Hugh Middleton, Turcopolier, 1422–29; John Weston, Prior of England, 1476–89, William Weston, Prior of England, 1527–40. Two members of the Newdigate family (cf. p. 166) and four of the Babington family were Knights of the Order in the 16th cent.

[34] King, *Grand Priory in Eng.* 37.

[35] Dugdale, *Mon.* vi (2), 832.

[36] Ibid. 839.

[37] Cf. the list of Commanders in the provincial Chapter held at Clerkenwell in 1417: Mifsud, *Hospitallers in Malta*, 153; Knowles and Hadcock, *Med. Religious Houses*, 241–9 on Beverley, Carbrooke, Mount St. John, Skirbeck, Temple Grafton, Willoughton.

[38] *Valor Eccl.* (Rec. Com.), i. 404–5; Knowles and Hadcock, *Med. Religious Houses*, 242; *V.C.H. Mdx.* ii. 525.

[39] A. F. Pollard, *The Evolution of Parliament*, 382; O. Pike, *Constitutional Hist. of the House of Lords*, 162–3, 218, 346–7.

[40] J. F. Baldwin, *The King's Council during the Middle Ages*, 122–3, 129, 165, 197, 202.

[41] E. Galea, 'Henry VIII and the Order of St. John' *Jnl. Arch. Assoc.* xii (1949), 59 sqq.

[42] Mifsud, *Hospitallers in Malta*, 200, n. 1; *Book of Deliberations of the Venerable Tongue of Eng.* 1523–67, ed. H. P. Scicluna, preface, p. ix. In Aug. 1539 Thos., Lord Audley, reported to Cromwell that Prior Weston had applied to him for Commissions to gather 'the frary': *L. and P. Hen. VIII*, xiv (2), p. 10.

[43] Act concerning lands of St. John's Hospital, 32 Hen. VIII, c. 24.

[44] *Valor Eccl.* (Rec. Com.), i. 206, 403; M. C. Rosenfield, 'The Disposal of the Property of London Monastic Houses' (Lond. Univ. Ph.D. Thesis, 1961).

[45] *Stats. of the Realm*, iii. 779–80. The pensions were proportioned to the declared net value of the commanderies held, and fees of office were continued.

assigned the handsome sum of £1,000 a year, but he died on the very day of the dissolution.[46] Most of the brethren in England appear to have acquiesced without protest in the changed situation, and the sub-prior, John Mablestone, who had recently built himself new quarters at Clerkenwell, was even allowed to retain possession of them for life.[47] Four, perhaps five, ventured to oppose the King, and paid the penalty with their lives.[48]

Mary's accession in 1553 created a new and more promising situation. The Queen at once sent an agent to Malta to open negotiations for the restoration of the priories of England and Ireland. In April 1557 she authorized Cardinal Pole, as papal legate, to reinstate the Order, and restore it to such of its former possessions as had not been alienated. The next month he issued a decree restoring the priory at Clerkenwell and the bailiwick of Eagle, with eight of the former commanderies.[49] Richard Shelley became Turcopolier and Thomas Tresham prior.[50] Neither had been professed before their appointment as Grand Crosses, but a number of Henrician knights who had been pensioned in 1540 now rejoined the Order. The death of Mary in 1558, however, meant the end of the high hopes raised by the Catholic restoration. Elizabeth I's accession was followed promptly by the confiscation of the property of the reconstituted priory,[51] although a dwindling number of knights remained in Malta until the final extinction of the English tongue in 1631.

The hospital's house at Clerkenwell appears to have been founded some time in the reign of Stephen. Rejecting earlier theories, J. H. Round showed that the founder was Jordan de Bricet, younger son of Ralph fitz Brian, a tenant of the Bishop of London and of the honor of Peverel.[52] Jordan married Muriel de Monteny, a member of the prominent Essex family, from whom he probably obtained his land. The documents relevant to the foundation of Clerkenwell are two deeds preserved in the cartulary of St. Mary's, Clerkenwell, of which Jordan was also the founder. In the first (*c.* 1148) Walter, 'prior of the brothers of the hospital who are in England', quitclaimed to the nuns his rights in the ten acres of land in dispute between them, in return for the grant to him of five acres by Jordan, '*dominus eiusdem fundi*'.[53] In the second (1184–5) Arnold, Prior of Saint-Gilles (Gard) upon which the English priory was then dependent, ratified Walter's act.[54]

Clerkenwell was a commandery; it was also the headquarters of the Order in England and the residence of the prior, a combination which complicates the task of unravelling its particular history. The prior occupied private quarters in the close, and in the early 14th century received an allowance of 20*s.* a day except on the 121 days when he was supposed to be on visitation and in receipt of a similar sum as procurations.[55] In the later Middle Ages he was also assigned an 'appanage', comprising a group of commanderies, of which Clerkenwell was one, together with their 'members' and a number of appropriated churches.[56] An annual sum was allotted him for the robes of his household and dependants.[57]

He was assisted in the work of administration by the provincial chapter, which met annually at Clerkenwell or Melchbourne (Beds.) usually about the feast of St. Barnabas (11 June)[58] or the Nativity of St. John the Baptist (24 June).[59] A provincial chapter held at Melchbourne in 1328 is described as composed of 'commanders, proctors and syndics', but the only commanders named are those from Ansty (Wilts.), Clerkenwell, Dinmore (Herefs.),

[46] Weston was already reported dangerously ill in Oct. 1538. The Grand Master wrote to Cromwell begging him, in case of a vacancy, to do his best 'for the honour of the Religion': *L. and P. Hen. VIII*, xiii (2), p. 277.

[47] *Stats. of the Realm*, iii. 779–80. A similar concession was in fact made to all four chaplains, who were to retain their fees, together with the houses they occupied, 'for the term of their natural life'.

[48] They were Adrian Fortescue, Thomas Dingley, Weston's nephew, David Gunstone, and John Forest. H. W. Fincham, *The Order of the Hospital of St. John of Jerusalem* (2nd edn.), 23, adds the name of Marm. Bowes (cf. W. Porter, *Hist. of the Knights of Malta*, 574). Sir Wm. Salesbury, described in the *Bk. of Deliberations* as 'the poore knyght', is commonly thought to have died in prison; but it seems that he died on the way to Malta in 1539, while bringing letters from the Prior to the Grand Master: *L. and P. Hen. VIII*, xv, pp. 232–4, 237–8, 321.

[49] 'Six Documents relating to Queen Mary's Restoration of the Grand Priories of England', ed. E. J. King (Libr. Cttee., Order of St. John of Jerusalem, Hist. Pamphlets, no. 7).

[50] M. E. Finch, 'The Wealth of Five Northants Families', *Northants. Rec. Soc.* xix, *sub.* the Tresham family.

[51] *Stats. of the Realm*, iv. 527.

[52] J. H. Round, 'The Foundation of the Priories of St. Mary and St. John, Clerkenwell', *Archaeologia*, lvi (2), 223 sqq.

[53] *Cartulary of St. Mary, Clerkenwell*, ed. W. O. Hassall (Camd. Soc. 3rd ser. lxxi), no. 205.

[54] Ibid. no. 206. Cf. the reference, in a grant by Bricet to Robt. the chaplain of land in the field adjoining 'the Clerkenwell', to the acre given by him to the Hospitallers in the same field in lieu of 13*d.* which he had promised to give yearly as alms to the Hospital of Jerusalem: *Cartulaire*, i. 1–2. The deed has been dated to 1144.

[55] *Hospitallers in Eng.* 211.

[56] *Cal. Papal Regs.* ix. 3; King, *Grand Priory in Eng.* 83.

[57] *Hospitallers in Eng.* 211.

[58] e.g. in 1338 a chapter was held at Melchbourne on Tues. before the feast of St. Barnabas (9 June), and in 1339 on Tues. after (16 June): *Cal. Pat.* 1338–40, 303–4, 330.

[59] In 1335 there was a meeting at Clerkenwell on Tues. after Midsummer (27 June): ibid. 1334–8, 351. Cf. ibid. 1340–3, 224, 230. In 1336 the chapter met on Tues. before the feast of St. John (18 June): ibid. 352.

Hogshaw (Bucks.) and Stavely (Derb.).[60] In 1338 one hundred and twenty marks were allowed for the expenses of the chapter held on the feast of St. Barnabas, and the 'assembly' held at the end of Lent.[61] The chapter which met at Clerkenwell in 1417 to elect the new commander of Buckland (Minchin Buckland or Buckland Sororum, Som.) included, besides the prior, the sub-prior, thirteen commanders, and five other brethren.[62] The weekly chapters originally held in the individual houses seem to have fallen into abeyance with the decline in the number of the brethren in the later Middle Ages, but the custom may have survived at Clerkenwell, where some kind of community life was probably maintained until the end.

The financial affairs of the priory were normally in the hands of the treasurer, an official who often played an important role in the affairs of the kingdom, as well as of the Order, since, especially in the 13th century, the treasury had frequently to provide safe custody for the jewels and treasure of the king.[63] Robert the treasurer who was prior between 1204 and 1214 had previously been 'treasurer of the Hospital in England'.[64] Gilbert the treasurer, who appears in 1226,[65] certainly held that office, and so did Benet, who occurs in 1232.[66] In 1269 Stephen de Fulbourne seems to have doubled the roles of commander of Clerkenwell and treasurer,[67] as did an unnamed brother who is mentioned with Prior Hanley in 1286;[68] but in the early 14th century, which was a time of grave financial crisis, supreme control appears to have been exercised by the prior,[69] and the treasurership to have been temporarily in abeyance.[70]

The only reasonably full description we possess of the composition and organization of the medieval community at Clerkenwell is that provided by the extent made in 1338 by Prior Philip de Thame for the information of the master.[71] The head of the house was the commander. Next in rank was the prior of the church, commonly called the sub-prior to distinguish him from the Prior of England. He controlled the clergy, who in 1338 included three brother-chaplains, ten secular priests, a deacon, a sub-deacon, two chaplains serving newly-founded chantries, and a third ministering in a quasi-parochial capacity in the chapel assigned to the use of the lay members of the household. The secular chaplains were paid by the sub-prior from the issues of a church specially appropriated for the purpose. Since most of them served chantries, their numbers increased as new foundations were made. In 1242, for instance, three were added in pursuance of bequests by Andrew Bukerell (Mayor of London, 1231–7) and Peter de Elilond, bringing their number to seven.[72] In 1361 the master reminded the prior that there should be at least fifteen secular chaplains, as well as a number of clerks, on the establishment.[73] Some of the latter, like the deacon and sub-deacon in the extent, would no doubt be ordained to the title of the priory church, while others filled various administrative posts. In 1338 three were employed in collecting the *frarie*, and one, with two *garciones*, assisted Master William de Whiteby, who is described as *procurator generalis privilegiorum* of the priory.[74] A *serviens* acted as general proctor to the hospital, assisted by a clerk who represented the interests of the brethren in the Exchequer, and an attorney who was 'continually present' on their behalf in the Common Pleas. One of the brothers filled the office of cellarer (*claviger*) to the community. A knight, William Brex, who had earlier been commander of Yeaveley (Derb.) and had been granted for life the *camera* of Harefield (Mdx.), but is not otherwise described in 1338, brought the total of the professed members of the Order resident in Clerkenwell up to seven.[75]

The resident lay servants of the house (*liberi servientes, servientes officii*) included two serving in the store-room (*dispensa*), a porter, a cook, a brewer, and the chamberlain of the commander, all of whom were entitled to robes and wages. Of lesser rank were the two millers, a 'killeman', a bolter, a groom, a door-keeper, kitchen-boy, and a washerwoman, who received a daily livery and an annual stipend. Meals were taken in common in the great hall of the priory; but a careful distinction was drawn between

[60] *Hospitallers in Eng.* 215.

[61] Ibid. 211.

[62] Mifsud, *Hospitallers in Malta*, 153.

[63] e.g. *Close R.* 1237–42, 190–1; 1253–4, 191; *Cal. Pat.* 1232–47, 220–1, 432; 1272–81, 215. Cf. E. F. Jacob, *The Fifteenth Century*, 204.

[64] *Cartulaire*, ii. 344.

[65] *Pat. R.* 1225–32, 24, 27.

[66] Ibid. 490–1.

[67] *Cal. Pat.* 1266–72, 348.

[68] Ibid. 1281–92, 244.

[69] Cf. the statement in the 1338 extent that any deficit in the annual account is made good by the prior from the treasury: *Hospitallers in Eng.* 101.

[70] In the report on the finances of the priory in 1328 references occur to 'thesaurarius nuper defunctus', 'bone memorie dictus thesaurarius', etc.: *Hospitallers in Eng. passim*. The office had been restored by 1341. In 1502 Thos. Newport is described as treasurer: *Cal. Pat.* 1494–1509, 285. In 1526 John Babington held the office: *Bk. of Deliberations*, 9. The sub-prior, John Mablestone, is called at the Dissolution 'assistant treasurer'.

[71] *Hospitallers in Eng. passim*.

[72] *Cartulaire*, iv. 348 sqq.

[73] Dugdale, *Mon.* vi (2), 832.

[74] Whiteby is described elsewhere as *procurator generalis Hospitalis in Curia Christianitatis* (*Hospitallers in Eng.* 178) and as being given a robe 'de secta clericorum' at Christmas (ibid. 206).

[75] Ibid. 44, 79, 207.

the *mensa conventus* or *mensa fratrum*; the *mensa liberorum servientium* at which the upper servants ate; and the *mensa garcionum* or 'Danysbord'. The numerous corrodarians were normally entitled to eat at the *mensa fratrum*, or to receive the equivalent allowance of food and drink, if unable for any reason to take their meals in hall. The women and married couples who were included among them were usually supplied for private consumption with an allowance of bread and ale. They included superannuated servants of the hospital and of the king, but also many lay persons who had given land or money on condition that they should be provided by the brethren with bed and board for life. The provision made for them varied with the amount of their 'investment'. The most lavish was that made for William Langford, who had served as steward under three successive priors during the financial crisis of the early 14th century, and undoubtedly merited the title bestowed on him by the brethren, '*servitor religionis nostre precipuus*'.[76]

Clerkenwell was near enough to the court and the centre of government to be favoured with frequent visits from the king and the magnates, distinguished foreign visitors, and royal officials. It had also to keep open house for brethren in, or passing through, London on business, and for agents of the master crossing to England on the affairs of the Order. In 1185 it was at Clerkenwell that a council of magnates met to consider a reply to the appeal of the Patriarch of Jerusalem for support for the Latin Kingdom. In 1212, although excommunicate, John spent March at Clerkenwell, and knighted the heir to the King of Scots there on Easter Day.[77] Henry of Lancaster was a guest for the fortnight preceding his coronation in 1399[78] and the Emperor Manuel was entertained there on his visit to England in 1400.[79] The Turcopolier's frequent visits were a constant drain on the resources of the priory, as well as a source of irritation to the prior; and in 1440 Prior Botyll, while recognizing his right and that of all commanders to hospitality, required them to contribute to the cost of their maintenance. The Turcopolier was assigned special quarters '*in parte vocata turcoplerisside*', with stabling, hay, and straw for one horse, but was to pay for his keep and for that of his servants and grooms. Commanders were charged for their board and for that of their servants. A commander wishing to provide his own accommodation was to be offered a site, and supplied with timber for building purposes.

Hospitality to wayfarers in all houses of the Order was placed under the supervision of a 'wise and discreet knight'.[80] Nothing is known of any such supervisors at Clerkenwell but in the 16th century 20s. a week was expended on alms bestowed at the door and in the hall of the priory, *ex antiqua fundacione et consuetudine accustumata*, besides 6s. 8d. given to the poor on Prior Docwra's anniversary, and £4 4s. 5d. distributed on Maundy Thursday in money, food, woollen and linen clothing, and shoes among thirteen poor persons.[81]

The plan of the hospital cannot be reconstructed with any certainty, since few traces of the buildings remain.[82] It was probably roughly rectangular, the boundary wall of the precinct running east from the gate-house to St. John's Street, then north almost to the corner of Aylesbury Street, where it turned west to Clerkenwell Green. Loseley's 'Survey of Lead',[83] compiled at the time of the Dissolution, mentions besides the church with its two chapels, Docwra's chantry, vestry, and 'steeple', the gate-house, the 'priests' dorter' (which has been identified with the dormitory of the knights, but which was much more likely the sleeping quarters of the secular priests attached to the priory); the 'yeoman's dorter' (possibly where the *liberi servientes* slept); the armoury, distillery, and counting-house; 'my lord's chamber' and other 'chambers' (many probably formerly occupied by lay corrodarians); the great chamber door and the great stairs; and the hall, the length of which is given as 105 ft. In 1546 there are mentioned the church and burial ground, three gardens, an orchard with a fishpond – traces of which have been discovered – the sub-prior's lodging and garden, the 'schoolhouse' adjoining it, the great and little courts, the Turcopolier's garden, the wood-yard, the slaughter-house, plumber's house, woolhouse, laundry, counting-house, the porter's house, and the gate-house, with the conduits, water pipes, and springs,[84] which were supplied by leaden pipes running from the meadows at Barnsbury known as 'Commandry Mantells'. None of the buildings can be precisely located, but it is probable that the main block, including the prior's lodging, lay immediately north of the choir of the church. In St. John's Lane lay the house of the bailiff of Eagle, and on the west side of the river Fleet were the two water-mills belonging to the priory.

[76] Ibid. 96–97, 205; *Cal. Pat.* 1334–8, 352; *Cal. Close,* 1333–7, 708.

[77] Fincham, *Order of St. John* (2nd edn.), 16.

[78] King, *Grand Priory in Eng.* 63.

[79] Ibid. 63–64.

[80] Mifsud, *Hospitallers in Malta*, 47, n. 1.

[81] Dugdale, *Mon.* vi (2), 832.

[82] A. W. Clapham, 'St. John of Jerusalem, Clerkenwell', *Trans. St. Paul's Eccl. Soc.* vii. 37–49; brought up to date by Fincham, *Order of St. John* (2nd edn.), 25–31, 47–53, 60–70, 71 (plan).

[83] 'The Surveye of Lead belongyg to Seyent Joens in Smythfeild': *Trans. St. Paul's Eccl. Soc.* vii. 47–49.

[84] Fincham, *Order of St. John* (2nd edn.), 27–28.

The first church, which had a round nave, was consecrated by the Patriarch of Jerusalem in 1185.[85] During the next hundred years a number of additions and extensions were made to it. Prior Joseph de Chauncy built the prior's chapel before 1280[86] and his successor, William de Hanley (c. 1281–90), left as his memorial the cloisters on the south side of the church.[87] In 1381 the whole priory was sacked and set on fire and, according to Stow, burnt for three days.[88] It is not clear how soon the devastation was repaired. Clapham considered that most of the buildings shown in Hollar's drawings, published in 1661, suggested the 15th century,[89] but under Priors Redington (1381–95) and Grendon (1396–1417) the work must have made considerable progress, since Henry of Lancaster stayed in the priory in 1399.[90] Redington was probably responsible for rebuilding the church, in which the original round nave was replaced by a rectangular one with three aisles; but it is possible that the great tower at the west end of the north aisle, so much admired by Stow, was begun by Prior Weston (1476–89) or Prior Kendal (1490–1501) and completed by Prior Docwra (1502–27), or at least embellished by him.[91] Docwra was certainly responsible for many improvements and for new work, including the great gate-house which is still *in situ*.[92] There are several references to the chapter-house in 15th-century Close Rolls.[93] In 1439 Prior Robert Mallory dedicated a chapel at Clerkenwell to St. Catherine, St. Margaret, and St. Ursula.[94] The ecclesiastical ornaments and other goods belonging to the church had been carried off by the rebels in 1381. They were, however, recovered by the Crown and restored by Richard II to the prior in 1393.[95] It may have been Prior Mallory who presented the church with a fine silver processional cross,[96] now in the possession of the English Order of St. John at Clerkenwell Gate. Later, Prior John Weston (1476–91) presented a triptych of Flemish workmanship, of which two panels still survive.[97]

In 1546 the Crown granted the site of the Hospital to John Dudley, Viscount Lisle, later Duke of Northumberland. Under Edward VI the nave of the church and the great tower were blown up to provide material for Somerset's house in the Strand; but the buildings were granted, in accordance with the will of Henry VIII, to the Princess Mary, and so could be restored to the Order in 1557.[98] In Elizabeth I's reign the priory became the headquarters of Edmund Tylney, Master of the Revels.[99] Later it came into the possession of William Cecil, Lord Burghley, and passed from him to the Earl of Aylesbury.[100]

In considering the landed endowments of the English Hospital, it is necessary to distinguish those belonging to the priory as a whole, and thus subject to the general supervision of the prior, and those held by him as his appanage, from those belonging immediately to the commandery of Clerkenwell. The greatest single accession of territory by the priory as a whole followed the suppression of the Templars in 1311, when, by order of the Pope, all the possessions of the suppressed Order were transferred to the Hospitallers.[101] The enforcement of their claim cost the priory dear, however, and, combined with the financial stringency caused by the loss of Rhodes and the administrative inefficiency of Prior l'Archer (1321–9), resulted in an acute financial crisis in the twenties and thirties of the 14th century. The sequel was the compilation in 1338 by order of Prior Philip de Thame (1335–53) for the information of the master, of the extent, already referred to, which remains the most important single source for the history of the Order in England.[102] In it the income of the Clerkenwell commandery is estimated at £400 a year.[103] This comprised, in addition to the revenue from Clerkenwell itself, property in Middlesex at Cranford, Edgware, Friern Barnet, Hackney, Hampstead, Hampton, Harefield, Harrow, Hendon, Kingsbury, and 'le Boys' (? Edgware); as well as at St. John's Wood (? the Lokeswode of the 1338 return)[104] and Ficketts Fields,[105] and from lands and tenements at Wycombe (Bucks.), Chingford, Ingatestone, Rainham, and West Hanningfield (Essex), Broxbourne (Herts.),

[85] Dugdale, *Mon.* vi (2), 805.

[86] King, *Grand Priory in Eng.* 23.

[87] E. J. King, *Knights of Malta in the British Empire*, 38.

[88] Stow, *Survey*, ii. 84.

[89] *Trans. St. Paul's Eccl. Soc.* vii. 37. See illustration facing p. 189.

[90] Fincham, *Order of St. John* (2nd edn.), 16.

[91] Ibid.

[92] For details of Docwra's career see *D.N.B.* and F. Duncan, 'Sir Thomas Docwra, Prior of England', *Gent. Mag.* 1881, ccl (1), 102 sqq.

[93] e.g. *Cal. Close*, 1447–54, 173; 1476–85, no. 734.

[94] King *Grand Priory in Eng.* 49.

[95] *Cal. Pat.* 1391–6, 236–7, 241; Dugdale, *Mon.* vi (2), 839.

[96] *Ex inf.* Order of St. John of Jerusalem, Clerkenwell.

[97] Fincham, *Order of St. John* (2nd edn.), 58.

[98] Stow, *Survey*, ii. 84–85; Fincham, *Order of St. John* (2nd edn.), 30.

[99] Fincham, *Order of St. John* (2nd edn.), 30–31.

[100] Ibid. 31.

[101] For the results of the suppression see C. Perkins, 'The Wealth of the Knights Templars in England and the Disposition of it after the Dissolution', *American Hist. Rev.* xv. 252–64; 'The Knights Hospitallers in England after the Fall of the Order of the Temple', *E.H.R.* xlv. 285 sqq. Cf. A. M. Leys, 'The Forfeiture of the Lands of the Templars in England', *Essays presented to H. E. Salter*, ed. F. M. Powicke, 155 sqq.

[102] See *Hospitallers in Eng.* for a complete transcript of the extent, with an introduction, now somewhat dated. It contains also the financial report sent to the master in 1328, when the finances of the priory were at their lowest ebb.

[103] Ibid. 95.

[104] *P.N. Mdx.* (E.P.N.S.), 139.

[105] C. W. Heckethorn, *Lincoln's Inn Fields*, 48–50.

North Ash (Kent), Addington and Merrow (Surr.), Sodington (Worcs.) and elsewhere, together with the income from appropriated churches at Bisham (Berks.), Roydon and Thurrock (Essex), Standon (Herts.), and Rodmersham (Kent), and from five mills. The *frarie* in London, Middlesex, and Surrey contributed an estimated total of 40 marks a year.

*Helena M. Chew*

## Commanders of Clerkenwell

Stephen de Fulbourne, occurs 1268[106]
Thomas de Enderby, occurs 1297[107]
Robert de Somerdeby, occurs 1328[108]
Alan Macy, occurs 1338[109]
Nicholas de Hales, occurs 1351[110]
Miles Skayff and Marmaduke Lumley, occur together 1469, 1470;[111] Lumley occurs 1473[112]

## Priors of England

This is a corrected version of the list from *V.C.H. Middlesex*, i.

Walter, occurs from 1142 to 1162[113]
Richard de Turk, occurs before 1173[114]
Ralph de Dive, occurs 1178[115]
Garnier de Nablus, occurs c.1184 to c.1190[116]
Alan de St. Cross, occurs 1190, 1195[117]
Gilbert de Vere, occurs 1195[118]
William de Villiers, occurs c.1199, 1202[119]
Robert the treasurer, c.1204 to c.1214[120]
Henry of Arundel, occurs 1215, 1216[121]
Hugh d'Aunay, occurs c.1216 to 1222[122]
Robert de Dive, occurs 1223 to 1234[123]
Thierry de Nussa, occurs 1235 to 1246[124]
Robert de Manby, occurs 1249[125]

Elias de Smetherton, admitted 1253; occurs 1256[126]
Robert de Manby, occurs 1267 to 1265[127]
Roger de Vere, occurs 1267 to 1272[128]
Joseph de Chauncy, occurs 1275 to 1280[129]
William de Hanley, occurs 1281 to 1290[130]
Peter de Hagham, occurs 1293 to 1297[131]
William de Tothale, occurs 1297 to 1315[132]
Richard de Pavely, occurs 1315[133]
Thomas l'Archer, occurs 1321 to 1329[134]
Leonard de Tibertis, appointed 1330; died 1334[135]
Philip de Thame, occurs 1335 to 1353[136]
John de Pavely, occurs 1354[137]
Robert de Hales, occurs 1372; slain 1381[138]
John de Redington (Radyngton), occurs 1381, 1395[139]
Walter Grendon, occurs 1396, 1415[140]
William Hulles, appointment confirmed 1417; dead by 1433[141]
Robert Mallory, occurs 1435, 1439[142]
Robert Botyll, occurs 1444, 1467[143]
John Langstrother, knight, appointment confirmed 1468; occurs Feb. 1471; executed 1471[144]
William Tournay, occurs 1472, 1473[145]
Robert Multon, occurs from 1473 to 1475[146]
John Weston, 1476–89[147]
John Kendal, occurs 1490; died 1501[148]

[106] *Cal. Pat.* 1266–72, 190.
[107] Lond. Rec. Soc. i. 85–86.
[108] *Hospitallers in Eng.* 215.
[109] Ibid. 101.
[110] *Cal. Papal Regs.* iii. 380.
[111] *Cal. Pat.* 1467–77, 231–2.
[112] *Cal. Close,* 1468–76, no. 1377.
[113] *Cartulaire,* i, 120–1; iv. 247.
[114] Ibid. iv. 333; i. 685–6 is a charter of this prior wrongly attributed to c. 1200–4.
[115] Ibid. iv. 364–5.
[116] Ibid. iv. 321–7, 329.
[117] Ibid. i. 570; Bp. of Bangor, 1195.
[118] *Cartulaire,* iv. 332.
[119] Ibid. 318, 334.
[120] Ibid. 334–8.
[121] Ibid. 338–9, 339.
[122] Ibid.
[123] Ibid. 341–3.
[124] Ibid. 347–9.
[125] *Close R.* 1247–51, 251.

[126] *Cal. Pat.* 1247–8, 171; *Cartulaire,* iv. 350, 351.
[127] *Close R.* 1256–9, 62; *Cartulaire,* iv. 288–9; Manby may still have been prior in 1266; cf. *Close R.* 1264–8, 274.
[128] *Cartulaire,* iv. 253; *Close R.* 1268–72, 590.
[129] Ibid. 1272–9, 32; *Cal. Pat.* 1272–81, 382.
[130] *Cal. Pat.* 1272–81, 424; Ibid. 1281–92, 403.
[131] *Cartulaire,* iii. 619–20; *Cal. Pat.* 1292–1308, 256; H. M. Chew, ed., *London Possessory Assizes: A Calendar,* (London Record Society, 1, 1965), no. 202 (where William de Hampton was described as prior of the church of Clerkenwell).
[132] *Cal. Pat.* 1292–1308, 312; Ibid. 1313–17, 277.
[133] Ibid. 345.
[134] Ibid. 1317–21, 575; B.L. Cott. Nero E VI 467; *Cal. Close,* 1330–3, 154–5 names him as dead by 4 Sept. 1330.
[135] *Cal. Close,* 1330–3, 154–5; Ibid. 1333–7, 563.
[136] Ibid.; *London Assize of Nuisance,* no. 436; B.L. Cott. Nero E VI 467, f. lxiiii (66).
[137] *Cal. Close,* 1354–60, 54.
[138] *Cal. Pat.* 1370–4, 188; C. Oman, *The Great Revolt of 1381,* 67.
[139] *Cal. Close,* 1381–5, 208; *Cal. Pat.* 1391–6, 622. He was described as immediate predecessor of Grendon, *London Possessory Assizes,* no. 202.
[140] *Cal. Pat.* 1396–9, 112; *London Possessory Assizes,* no. 202; *London Assize of Nuisance,* no. 658.
[141] *Cal. Papal Regs.* vii. 59; *Cal. Pat.* 1429–36, 296.
[142] Ibid. 452; Ibid. 1436–41, 290.
[143] Ibid. 1441–6, 260; Ibid. 1461–7, 567.
[144] *Cal. Papal Regs.* xii. 234–5; T.N.A. C 67/44, m. 4; King, *Grand Priory in Eng. 73.*
[145] *Cal. Pat.* 1467–77, 306; *Cal. Papal Regs.* xiii (I), 216.
[146] *Cal. Close,* 1468–76, 380, 386.
[147] *D.N.B., sub* Sir Wm. Weston; But Hennessy, *Novum Repertorium,* 243, has 'vacates, 1485'.
[148] *Cal. Papal Regs.* xiv. 273; T.N.A. KB 9/422, m. 85d; Dugdale, *Mon.* vi (2), 799.

Thomas Docwra, 1502–27[149]
William Weston, knight, occurs 1527–40[150]

[Thomas Tresham, appointed 1557; died 1559][151]

[149] Ibid.; *L. and P. Hen. VIII,* iv (2), p. 3208.
[150] Ibid.; T.N.A. E 24/23/17; Dugdale *Mon.* vi (2), 799.

[151] *Cal. Pat.* 1557–8, 313; cf. *V.C.H. Middlesex* i, p. 96 n. 65.

# ALIEN HOUSES

# 10. THE PRIORY OF HARMONDSWORTH

## INTRODUCTION

There is little to add to this account of the small cell at Harmondsworth, which belonged to the alien priory of St. Catherine, near Rouen in France, apart from some material which relates to the manor of Harmondsworth between 1232 and 1450, to be found in L.M.A., Deeds ACC/0446/M/098, L/001.

*Jessica Freeman*

In 1069 William the Conqueror gave the land and church of Harmondsworth to the Benedictine Abbey of Sainte-Trinité du Mont, by Rouen, afterwards known as St. Catherine's.[1] In 1086 the abbey held this manor of the king in chief.[2] Two years later a priory dependent on this abbey was founded at Blyth (Notts.). This house became a conventual priory and owing to its size escaped dissolution in 1414, surviving until 1536.[3] Blyth was not entrusted with the administration of the rest of the abbey's property in England, and no doubt a cell, consisting of a prior with one monk as his companion, was very soon established at Harmondsworth for this purpose, although no mention of a prior has been found until 1211.[4] This property was soon widely scattered. About 1090 Ilbert de Lacy and his wife gave their manor at Tingewick (Bucks.) with the land, waters, meadows, and wood belonging to it to the Abbey of Holy Trinity and the priors of Harmondsworth were often called lords of the manor of Tingewick.[5] In 1209 Gilbert de Finemere quitclaimed to the abbey his right in the manor of Tingewick, and Richard de Cruce his rights in Harmondsworth.[6] The rectory and demesne of Saham Toney (Norf.) with rents and services were given to the abbey in John's reign.[7] Later the abbey acquired the church of St. Leonard's by Hastings (Suss.) and it was attached to Harmondsworth.[8] In 1246 both this abbey and

the priory of Bradenstoke (Wilts.) claimed the patronage of the church of Easton (Wilts.), but St. Catherine's, which said that the church was a gift from Anselm, Earl of Pembroke, who had died in the previous year, failed to establish its right.[9] Eudes Rigaud, the indefatigable Archbishop of Rouen, carried out several visitations of St. Catherine's Abbey in the years 1265–8. Each time he found that the abbey had about 30 monks at Rouen, 14 at Blyth, and 2 at Harmondsworth. He had no faults to find, but suggested that the abbot should visit his priories more often, a suggestion which he also made to other abbots.[10]

Like other landlords the abbey began to have trouble with its tenants in the 13th century. In 1233 the abbey experienced difficulties in exacting customary dues from its free tenants in Harmondsworth.[11] In 1275 the tenants impleaded the prior that he should not exact from them customs and services other than those which were due when the manor was held by the Crown.[12] Next year one Richard le Taylor, probably one of the abbey's tenants, was killed at Harmondsworth, whereupon the manor and that of Tingewick were taken into the king's hands. The manors were restored to John de Walemond, the prior, as proctor of the Abbot of St. Catherine's, for a fine of £20.[13] The abbey was pardoned this fine, or a similar one, in 1280.[14] While the manors were in the king's hands certain muniments were stolen by the tenants,[15] but despite the loss of his records the prior apparently won his case, being able to show from Domesday Book that the manor was not ancient demesne, and

---

[1] *Cartulaire de l'Abbaye de la Sainte-Trinité du Mont de Rouen*, ed. A. Deville (Coll. de Documents Inedits, Coll. de Cartulaires de France, iii), no. lxvii, p. 455; *Cal. Doc. France*, ed. J. H. Round, 21; *Regesta Regum AngloNormannorum*, ed. H. W. C. Davis, i. 9.

[2] See p. 109.

[3] D. Matthew, *The Norman Monasteries and their English possessions*, 44–51; *V.C.H. Notts.* ii. 83–84; Dugdale, *Mon.* iv. 620–5.

[4] *Pipe R.* 1211 (P.R.S. N.S. xxviii), 136.

[5] *Early Yorks. Charters*, ed. W. Farrer, iii. 176; *V.C.H. Bucks.* i. 212; iv. 249–50; *Arch. Jnl.* iv. 249–51.

[6] *Pipe R.* 1209 (P.R.S. N.S. xxiv), 37.

[7] F. Blomefield, *Hist. of Norf.* ii. 321.

[8] *V.C.H. Suss.* ix. 27.

[9] *Sarum Charts. and Docs.* (Rolls Ser.), 301–2; *V.C.H. Wilts.* iii. 324.

[10] *Reg. Visitationum archiepiscopi Rothomagensis*, ed. T. Bonnin, 530, 568, 611.

[11] *Close R.* 1231–4, 294; M.R.O., Acc. 446/98/4.

[12] *Cal. Close*, 1272–9, 247.

[13] *Cal. Pat.* 1272–81, 166.

[14] *Cal. Close*, 1279–88, 70.

[15] *Cal. Pat.* 1272–81, 236.

quoting the rolls of William de Raleigh, a justice of Henry III, to show that the tenants could be tallaged at will by the abbot.[16] The public record had triumphed. The Domesday entry was so important to the abbey that in 1341 the prior paid for an exemplification of it, a copy which still survives among the muniments of Winchester College.[17] But the tenants still held the prior's own records, and threatened to burn him in his house. Apparently they defied the sheriff's attempt to carry out the judgement of the royal courts.[18] In 1279 the next prior, Richard, was complaining of similar troubles at Tingewick,[19] and in 1281 twelve persons, including the widow of Richard le Taylor, were in gaol, charged with burning the houses of the priory at Harmondsworth.[20] Perhaps it is not surprising to find that the prior had incurred several heavy debts.[21]

The Abbot of St. Catherine's secured a confirmation in 1285 of a charter of Henry II granting the abbey all liberties and free customs in its possessions, which were not specified.[22] No doubt the confirmation was a precaution following the troubles of the previous decade, and it was to be used nearly a century later in 1372, when the prior was accused of failing to distribute a weekly dole of bread to the poor. It was alleged that he was bound to do this under the terms of the original grant of the church and land at Harmondsworth, but he produced the charter to show that he held in free alms.[23]

In 1291 the goods of St. Catherine's at Harmondsworth were valued at £48 and the church at £20, while the rents and mill at Tingewick were valued at £15 10s. and the church there at £7.[24] Three years later when Edward I seized alien priory lands in consequence of the French war the manor of Harmondsworth was valued at over £60. Of this sum more than one-third came from rents and services, a little under one-third from tithes, and the remainder from the profits of the demesne, the court, and two water-mills. At the same time the stock, including the prior's palfrey, the farm animals, and the furnishings of the priory were valued at £25. Tingewick manor was said to be worth £25, made up of £16 for the annual value and £9 for the stock.[25] Under Edward II the priory was again taken into the king's hands, and restored to the prior in 1324, when a detailed

inventory of its stock and goods was again made. There was a large store of grain, some thirty head of cattle, a few pigs, and an assortment of poultry. Inside the priory were the bare necessities for the lives of the monks: two beds, three tables, chests, cloths, silver vessels, two cups, pewter pots, a wash-basin, fire-dogs, a pestle and mortar, and other utensils.[26] An inquisition of 1340 found that the manor of Harmondsworth was worth nearly £26 a year, the church £20, and Tingewick £8 – perhaps an example of the tendency of such inquisitions to undervalue.[27] There is a note of about the same date of the names of deceased tenants from whom the prior should have heriots.[28]

In the 14th century all alien priories were constantly taken into the king's hands on account of the war with France. The priors of Harmondsworth seem to have retained control by paying a rent to the Crown, which remained unchanged at the very high figure of £80 a year from 1338 to 1369, and was then reduced to 80 marks.[29] The king, however, usually kept the advowsons belonging to the priory in his own hands, presenting at various times to Harmondsworth, Tingewick, St. Leonard's by Hastings, and Saham Toney.[30]

The last prior was Robert Beauchamp, who held the office for almost forty years from March 1352. In 1371 there was at least one other monk, John Hawnsevyll.[31] In 1390 William of Wykeham, Bishop of Winchester, secured both papal and royal authority to acquire the lands of alien priories for his colleges,[32] and in the following year he obtained from Richard II a licence for St. Catherine's Abbey to sell him all its possessions in England, apart from the Priory of Blyth. These possessions comprised the manor of Harmondsworth with the advowson of the church and vicarage, the manor of Tingewick with its advowson, the advowsons of Saham Toney and St. Leonard's, and certain yearly pensions.[33] Meanwhile Wykeham sent a member of his household, Richard Altryncham, to Rouen to negotiate with the abbey. The sale was agreed, the price being fixed at 8,400 gold francs, which were paid in 1392 through a firm of Genoese bankers. The bishop also undertook

[16] Ibid. 290.

[17] Ibid. 1340–3, 253; Winchester Coll., 11338 (Harmondsworth 5).

[18] Cal. Pat. 1272–81, 292.

[19] Ibid. 346.

[20] Ibid. 467.

[21] Cal. Close, 1279–88, 44, 139.

[22] Cal. Chart. R. 1257–1300, 302–3; the original charter is in Winchester Coll., 11335 (Harmondsworth 2).

[23] Winchester Coll., 11337 (Harmondsworth 4); T. F. Kirby, 'Charters of Harmondsworth, Isleworth, Heston, Twickenham, and Hampton-on-Thames', Archaeologia, lviii. 341.

[24] Tax. Eccl. (Rec. Com.), 14, 17, 20, 32, 47.

[25] E 106/2/1.

[26] E 106/7/18 (8).

[27] Cal. Inq. Misc. ii. 418, 455.

[28] Winchester Coll., 11438 (Harmondsworth 74b).

[29] Cal. Pat. 1338–40, 56; 1343–5, 547; 1388–92, 434; Cal. Close, 1337–9, 336; Cal. Fine R. 1337–47, 28, 262; 1347–56, 314, 325; 1369–77, 22; 1377–83, 24.

[30] Newcourt, Repertorium, i. 633–4; London Reg. Sudbury (Cant. and York Soc.), i. 281; Blomefield, Norf. ii. 320; Cal. Pat. 1330–4, 534; 1343–5, 41, 537; 1345–8, 216, 348, 364; 1348–50, 263; 1370–4, 154, 344; 1374–7, 35–36, 201; 1377–81, 63, 286; 1381–5, 20; 1385–9, 241; 1388–92, 190.

[31] C 76/61, m. 6.

[32] Archaeologia, lviii. 342–5.

[33] Cal. Pat. 1388–92, 374, 434.

to provide for Robert Beauchamp and for John le Cellier, his companion, all such things in the way of wine, food, clothing, and lodging as befitted religious of their estate for the rest of their lives. He would also furnish a chapel for the abbey.[34] The property became part of the endowment of his two colleges at Winchester and Oxford.[35] The priory stood to the west of Manor Farm and the tithe barn.[36]

*J. L. Kirby*

## Revised List of Priors of Harmondsworth Priory

This list is taken from *Heads of Religious Houses,* vol. 2, p. 165.

William, occurs 1260

John, mentioned in 1279 as predecessor of prior Richard[37]

---

[34] *Archaeologia,* lviii. 343–5.
[35] *Cal. Papal Regs.* 1362–1404, 441.
[36] *V.C.H. Mdx.* ii. 6.
[37] However, *V.C.H.* list has John de Walemond, occurs 1276, *Cal. Pat.* 1272–81, 166.

Richard, occurs 1279

William de Bosco *alias* de Yvelont, occurs 1296, 1300

John de Ibelound, occurs 1305 as proctor of St. Catherine

Humphrey *dictus* le Contepoyntour, occurs as general proctor in England of the abbey of St. Catherine, 1317

John de Fraunkevyle (Frankavilla, Frankevill), occurs as prior 1314; as proctor of the abbey of St. Catherine, 1318; as general proctor in England of St. Catherine, 1321

William de Pestlamore, occurs *c.*1324, 1326, as general proctor of St. Catherine 1329

John Busott(is), 1332, proctor of St. Catherine at Harmondsworth

Roger Sorel, occurs 1342, 1345; died before 1351

John Cibe, 1351 Master of St. Catherine; ceased to hold priory by 1352

Robert de Bello Campo (Beauchamp), Master of St. Catherine, granted keeping of priory 1352; occurs 1391; 'lately prior' 1392.

The priory was dissolved 1391 and granted to Winchester College.

# 11. THE PRIORY OF RUISLIP (OR OGBOURNE)

## INTRODUCTION

There is little to add to this account of the priory at Ruislip, which was a small cell of the Abbey of Bec in Normandy, except to draw attention to the existence of a collection of thirteenth- to fifteenth-century deeds, manorial and estate records and material relating to the prior acting as proctor for the Abbot of Bec, to be found at Eton College (Eton College, ECR 7, 26/21, 26, 28, 63/3).

*Jessica Freeman*

The manor of Ruislip was given to the Abbey of Bec by Ernulf de Hesdin shortly after the making of Domesday Book, and his gift was confirmed in a general charter granted by William I between June 1086 and September 1087.[1] No conventual priory was ever founded there. The bull issued by Lucius III in 1144, which contains a general confirmation of English property, lists Ruislip among the manors of Bec and does not describe it, like St. John of Clare, St. Neots, and Goldcliff, as a priory,[2] and it was still classed as a manor in another confirmation of Honorius III in 1223.[3] It became, however, an important administrative centre for the English lands of the abbey, and for a time in the late 12th and early 13th centuries a prior and probably one companion were sent out from the mother house to form a tiny cell.[4] A Prior of Ruislip is first named towards the end of Henry II's reign;[5] he acted as representative of the abbot, presenting to churches in his gift,[6] and frequently acting as attorney in legal proceedings. Between 1200 and 1230 priors of Ruislip appeared in suits concerning land and rights in Ardleigh (Essex),[7] Knotting (Beds.),[8] Milborne (Dors.),[9] Blakenham (Suff.),[10] Ruislip,[11] Steventon (Berks.),[12]

Weedon (Northants.),[13] Atherstone (Warws.),[14] and Swyncombe (Oxon.).[15] Other representatives also acted from time to time on the abbot's behalf; in the late 12th century various monks of Bec are mentioned without ascription to any particular cell, and from 1206 the Prior of Ogbourne (Wilts.) appears in the public records as a proctor of growing importance. For a time the priors of Ogbourne and Ruislip acted together and shared the administration of all the estates of Bec directly dependent on the abbey and not assigned for the support of any one of its subject priories.[16] When John seized the goods of the abbey after the death of Abbot William in 1211 the priors of Ogbourne and Ruislip jointly offered a fine of 700 marks to have custody of the lands and churches belonging to their priories.[17] Royal protection was issued to the two priors jointly in 1234,[18] and when the Prelates' Aid of 1235–6 was collected the Prior of Ogbourne paid 50 marks for himself and the Prior of Ruislip.[19]

The English property of the Abbey of Bec included 24 manors widely scattered over southern and eastern England, and a very great number of tithes.[20] During the early part of the 13th century there seems to have been a rough grouping of manors so that dues were collected at both Ruislip and Ogbourne. According to a custumal made in the mid-13th century the Prior of Ruislip then received, amongst other dues, 20 marks for the tithes of Chaureth (Broxted parish, Essex), 6 marks for the manor of Broughton (Bucks.), 22s. for tithes

---

[1] See p. 126; H. E. Salter, 'Two deeds about the Abbey of Bec', *E.H.R.* xl. 74–75; M. Chibnall, 'Relations of St. Anselm with Eng. Dependencies of Abbey of Bec', *Spicilegium Beccense*, i. 521–30.

[2] J. Ramackers, *Papsturkunden in Frankreich*, neue Folge, ii (Normandie), no. 21.

[3] A. A. Porée, *Histoire de l'Abbaye du Bec*, ii. 570–1.

[4] M. Morgan, *Eng. Lands of Abbey of Bec*, 23–24; *T.L.M.A.S.* viii. 203–4.

[5] *Select Documents of Eng. Lands of Abbey of Bec*, (Camd. Soc. 3rd ser. lxxiii), 8.

[6] Newcourt, *Repertorium*, ii. 230, note *a*.

[7] *Cur. Reg. R.* i. 311, 443, 477.

[8] Ibid. ii. 313 (here, however, the representative is described as 'Adam, monk of Ruislip').

[9] Ibid. x. 186.

[10] *Rot. Litt. Claus.* (Rec. Com.), i. 411; ii. 43.

[11] C.P. 25(1)/146/7/70.

[12] *Cur. Reg. R.* xiii. 97–98: the Prior of Ruislip here acted on behalf of the Priory of Pré, a French cell of Bec.

[13] *Pat. R.* 1225–32, 288.

[14] Ibid. 167; *Cur. Reg. R.* xiii. 117–18.

[15] *Cur. Reg. R.* xiii. 518.

[16] *V.C.H. Wilts.* iii. 395.

[17] *Pipe R.* 1211 (P.R.S. N.S. xxviii), 136. The pipe roll begins 'Prior de Okeburne et de Resleppe' and then continues in the plural; the chancellor's roll more accurately states 'Prior de Okeburne et Prior de Rislep'.

[18] *Cal. Pat.* 1232–47, 69.

[19] *Bk. of Fees*, 563.

[20] Morgan, *Eng. Lands of Bec*, 138–50.

of Westcliff-by-Dover (Kent), 44 marks from the Abbot of Cleeve (Som.) for the prebend of Cleeve, 25 marks for the tithes of Glynde (Suss.), and 14 marks from the Prior of Wilsford (Lincs.) for the farm of Hykeham (Lincs.).[21] The same custumal shows that carrying services from manors as far away as Swyncombe (Oxon.) and East Wretham (Norf.) might be to Ruislip.[22] But already by this date the abbots of Bec were reducing the number of their monks charged with administrative duties in England. Their motives seem to have included concern for discipline in the cells; in 1210 Abbot William sought and obtained from Innocent III permission to recall the two or three monks settled in any cell where the Rule was not properly observed and to unite its lands with those of another cell.[23] He does not seem to have availed himself of this permission immediately in England, but there is no evidence that a separate Prior of Ruislip was ever appointed after 1236. Temporal considerations also prompted the centralizing of administration in the hands of a single man; increased litigation made the appointment of separate attorneys in every suit inconvenient, and in 1225 a proctor-general of the Abbot of Bec is mentioned for the first time.[24] In February 1242 brother William de Guineville, proctor-general of the abbot, was admitted as general attorney in all suits concerning the abbey's lands and rights in England;[25] he was plainly a man of energy and organizing ability, and there is no doubt that during his term of office the amalgamation of the 'priories' of Ogbourne and Ruislip became complete. His normal title was 'Prior' or 'Proctor' of Ogbourne,[26] but he was called 'Proctor of Ruislip' in one charter concerning land in Swyncombe;[27] and this ambiguity of title persisted into the time of a later Proctor of Ogbourne, Richard de Flammaville, who was described in one judgement of 1259 as 'Prior of Ruislip'.[28] Thereafter the English proctor of the Abbot of Bec was normally known as Prior of Ogbourne.

Ruislip manor, however, remained an important administrative centre, and the Prior of Ogbourne frequently resided there. Its size, wealth, and proximity to London no doubt helped to account for its importance. Of the 907 acres in demesne in 1294, 675 acres, comprising nearly three-quarters

of the total, were under cultivation.[29] The land appears to have been fertile and was exploited for market production as well as the support of a large household. London provided an additional and attractive market, where both corn[30] and timber[31] might be sold. During the 13th century cultivation increased: the demesne was enlarged, and peasant assarting took place in the wooded region round the park.[32] Active exploitation of the demesne with a large paid labour force[33] continued well into the 14th century,[34] and after it ceased to be a monastic cell Ruislip retained many of the features of a prosperous home farm in a good marketing region. At no time had it any conventual buildings. An inventory made in 1294 mentions a chapel in the manor-house;[35] another inventory of 1435 shows that the house was a spacious one, containing a hall, chamber, countinghouse, prior's chamber, lord's chamber, forester's chamber, and chapel, as well as bakehouse and scullery.[36] The site of this building was possibly on the lawn of the present Manor Farm at Ruislip, where early masonry has been dug up.[37] Other evidence from an earlier period suggests that it supported a sizable household. The food supplies sent to the larder in 1289–90 included 20 cattle, 22 sheep, 36 roebuck, and 418 quarters of wheat for bread;[38] among the servants named in 1294 were a mace-bearer, a door-keeper, a cook, a baker, a gardener, and a carpenter.[39] Table silver to the value of £17 9s. and two beds worth £2 were mentioned in an inventory of 1324, and at the same date the account of the guardians of alien property in Middlesex for the nine weeks they had held the manor shows that the Prior of Ogbourne and his companion monk, with their horses and grooms, had resided at Ruislip throughout that period.[40] Towards the end of the 14th century the audit of manorial accounts from the Abbot of Bec's property seems to have been held at Ruislip.[41] Up to that date the economic evidence suggests that it remained a

---

[21] *Docs. of Eng. Lands of Bec*, 81–82.

[22] Ibid. 89, 115.

[23] *Regesta Pontificium Romanorum*, ed. A. Potthast, i. 358; *Patrologia latina*, ed. J. P. Migne, ccxvii. 275 (no. 236).

[24] *Rot. Litt. Claus.* (Rec. Com.), ii. 67.

[25] *Cal. Pat.* 1232–47, 272, 291.

[26] Ibid.

[27] King's Coll. Camb., MS. Q. 7.

[28] Ibid. Q. 4.

[29] Morgan, *Eng. Lands of Bec*, 47. A very high proportion of leguminous crops was grown: ibid. 52; *Docs. of Eng. Lands of Bec*, 140.

[30] Ibid. 74.

[31] King's Coll. Camb., C. 7.

[32] Morgan, *Eng. Lands of Bec*, 86, 93.

[33] *Docs. of Eng. Lands of Bec*, 82–83. Labour dues were potentially heavy, but comparison of rents owed by working tenements *c.* 1248 with rents collected in 1289–90 indicates that at that date most works were sold: ibid. 75–81, 130.

[34] Morgan, *Eng. Lands of Bec*, 113–15. The subsidiary manor of Northwood in Ruislip was farmed out before 1384.

[35] E 106/2/1.

[36] S.C. 6/917/26.

[37] *T.L.M.A.S.* viii. 205; *V.C.H. Mdx.* ii. 9.

[38] *Docs. of Eng. Lands of Bec*, 130, 140.

[39] E 106/2/1.

[40] S.C. 6/1126/5.

[41] Morgan, *Eng. Lands of Bec*, 59.

centre of administrative importance, and may well have been the normal residence of the Proctor of Ogbourne when he was not travelling about the country attending to his numerous duties. When in the early 15th century the demesne began to pass into the hands of the peasantry[42] this is a sign that the function of the manor had changed, and it was ceasing to be an important centre even as an estate office.

After the death of the last Prior of Ogbourne in 1404 the dispersal of the manors of Bec in England began, and Ruislip was one of the group that ultimately made up the endowment of St. Nicolas (later King's) College, Cambridge.[43] John, Duke of Bedford, enjoyed the custody of all the manors until his death in 1435; in 1437 Ruislip, then worth £60 yearly, was assigned to John Somerset for life.[44] A year later, however, the king granted the reversion of the manor to the chancellor, masters, and scholars of the University of Cambridge;[45] and finally on 12 February 1441, with their consent,

it was regranted to the rector and scholars of the king's new foundation, St. Nicolas College.[46] In spite of disturbances to the endowment after the deposition of Henry VI, Ruislip was regranted to the provost and scholars of the College by Edward IV, and remained thereafter in their possession.[47] It is noteworthy that although the royal letters patent granting the properties sometimes refer to the 'manor or priory of Ogbourne' Ruislip is never, at this date, called anything except a manor.

*Marjorie M. Chibnall*

## Revised List of the Priors of Ruislip

This list comes from *Heads of Religious Houses*, vol. 1, p. 107; vol. 2, p. 188; and vol. 3 (forthcoming).

Richard de Coleliva, occurs 1179, 1198
William, occurs 1224; probably died 1225
Ralph, occurs 1226, 1230
Michael, occurs 1230, perhaps the Michael de Turnebu, who occurs as proctor of Bec in 1232

---

[42] Ibid. 118.
[43] *V.C.H. Wilts.* iii. 396.
[44] *Cal. Pat.* 1436–41, 46.
[45] Ibid. 187.

[46] *Cal. Pat.* 1436–41, 521–2.
[47] Ibid. 1461–7, 74; *V.C.H. Cambs.* iii. 379–80.

# HOSPITALS[1]

## 12. ALDERSGATE HOSPITAL

### INTRODUCTION

Nothing further has been discovered about this hospital, and it remains among the more obscure of the Middlesex foundations.

*Christian Steer*

Two 16th-century authorities[2] refer to a medieval hospital for the poor outside Aldersgate. This Cluniac foundation was suppressed by Henry V as an alien house, and its lands and goods granted to the parish of St. Botolph, Aldersgate. In place of the hospital William Bever founded a brotherhood of the Holy Trinity, which was in turn suppressed by Edward VI. The endowments, consisting of property worth £18 16s. a year in the parish of St. Botolph Aldersgate, were granted at an annual rent of 13s. 4d. in 1548 to William Harvye or Somerset, one of the king's heralds-at-arms.[3]

*Marjorie B. Honeybourne*

### Master

Alexander Chapman, master of the guild, occurs 1547[4]

---

[1] For more detailed accounts of the hospitals in this section see Marjorie B. Honeybourne, 'The Leper Hospitals of the London Area', *T.L.M.A.S.* xxi (1), 3–61. See also the 'Note on the Middlesex Leper hospitals', above p. 241.

[2] J. Leland, *Collectanea* (1770 edn.), i. 113–14; Stow, *Survey*, ii. 80, 144, 395.

[3] *Cal. Pat.* 1547–8, 271; 1548–9, 99.

[4] Ibid.

# 13. THE HOSPITAL OF THE VIRGIN MARY AND THE NINE ORDERS OF HOLY ANGELS, BRENTFORD

## INTRODUCTION

This account may now be supplemented by the detailed investigation of the guild and the hospital by Anne F. Sutton and Livia Visser-Fuchs, 'The Cult of Angels in Late Fifteenth-Century England: An Hours of the Guardian Angel presented to Queen Elizabeth Woodville', in *Women and the Book*, ed. Lesley Smith and Jane H. M. Taylor (London, 1996), pp. 230–65. Dame Joan, widow of Thomas Luyt, a lawyer and MP for Middlesex, kept certain household items at the Hospital in 1497, and her chaplain, John Bromfield, may also have acted as the guild's chaplain (T.N.A. PROB 11/11 f. 28).

*Jessica Freeman*

Before 1446 the main Bath road at Brentford End had been diverted to the north when a stone bridge over the Brent was built here. Between the old and new roads stood this hospital, just inside the parish of Isleworth and not far east of Syon Abbey. The hospital, founded in 1446 by John Somerset, the royal physician and chaplain, and Chancellor of the Exchequer, incorporated a wayside chapel already built by Somerset. The hospital community consisted of a chaplain and his clerk, nine poor afflicted men, and two servants. A guild, called the Guild of the Nine Orders of Holy Angels by Syon, and consisting of a master, brethren, and sisters, was set up to administer the hospital and chapel, and this corporate body was empowered to hold land in mortmain to the value of £40 a year and to have a common seal. Each year a guildsman was to be elected master of the guild, chapel, and hospital.[1]

The original endowment consisted of 260 acres at Northwood in Ruislip parish and nearly 500 acres in the parishes of Isleworth, Brentford, and Heston.[2] By a curious arrangement made in 1463 most of this property was transferred to new feoffees under a twelve-year agreement to pay ten marks a year to the chaplain celebrating divine service in the chapel at Brentford Bridge, four marks a year to the chapel clerk, and 7½ d. a week to the five poor persons in the almshouses. In addition, every second year, at Christmas, each resident was to receive two cartloads of fuel, and the five poor persons were each given a robe. The new owners were to keep the chapel and houses in repair, and fill any vacancies among the fraternity.[3] Arrangements after the expiration of the

twelve-year term are not recorded, but in 1479 John Saverey, the master, obtained an exemplification of the letters patent setting up the hospital in 1446.[4]

By 1498 much of the endowment had been alienated.[5] Early in the 16th century, however, the manors of Osterley and Wyke were returned to the hospital.[6] They had been purchased by Hugh Denys, a London citizen,[7] who bequeathed them in 1511 to Sheen Priory (Surr.) in trust to enlarge, or perhaps refound, the Hospital of All Angels beside Brentford Bridge for seven poor men, and to found a chantry for two secular priests. The foundation was to be called 'the chapel and almshouses of Hugh Denys'. The priests were to be resident and hold no other benefices, and they were to receive nine marks a year and free fuel. The poor men, all resident, were each to have 7½d. a week, free fuel, and a gown worth 4s.[8] In 1530 the Prior and Convent of Sheen transferred the manors of Osterley and Wyke to the Abbess and Convent of Syon under a covenant to administer these estates for the hospital's benefit.[9]

The hospital was suppressed in 1547, and the site and its other lands were granted to the Duke of Somerset,[10] who also received Syon Abbey. On Somerset's fall in 1552 the property reverted to the Crown, and in 1557–8 the hospital precinct, including the chapel and eight almshouses, was

---

[1] Ibid. 1446–52, 29; 1476–85, 138. The foundation charter is printed in Aungier, *Syon*, 215, 459–65.
[2] *Cat. Anc. D.* v. A 13445; *Cal. Close*, 1441–7, 147–8.
[3] *Cat. Anc. D.* v. A 13416.
[4] *Cal. Pat.* 1476–85, 138.
[5] *Cal. Close*, 1485–1500, 334.
[6] For details of the descent of these manors see *V.C.H. Mdx.* iii. 109, 110.
[7] He is sometimes identified with Hugh Denys, verger of Windsor Castle (d. 1511): *L. and P. Hen. VIII*, i, p. 483.
[8] Syon Ho., MS. A. xv. 5. a (the 1608 survey of Syon); Lysons, *Environs of Lond.* iii. 91–92, 96; Aungier, *Syon*, 221–2, 465–78.
[9] *L. and P. Hen. VIII*, iv (3), p. 2818.
[10] *Cal. Pat.* 1547–8, 172; 1549–51, 431.

granted to the newly-restored convent of Syon.[11] The bulk of the original endowment, including the manors of Osterley and Wyke, had already been alienated.[12]

After the second dissolution of Syon Abbey Elizabeth I leased the chapel and the hospital with its appurtenances to Richard Burton, and he or his successors demolished the chapel and two of the almshouses and converted the site into a garden.[13] In 1608 five almshouses were being used for the poor of Isleworth. Some of these were still there in 1649 but are said to have been rebuilt about four years later.[14] In 1729 they were again rebuilt as the parish workhouse.[15]

No detailed description of the hospital has survived. The premises were of brick[16] and in the 16th century comprised two priest's houses, with small gardens, and seven 'bedehouses' or almshouses with similar gardens. The almshouses adjoined the south aisle of the chapel,[17] which had a 'steeple'.[18] Within the precinct was a small pond called the Chapel Pool, and, adjoining the almshouses to the west, were two messuages called 'the Sprottes' and the Rose Inn.[19]

*Marjorie B. Honeybourne*

## Master

John Saverey, occurs 1479[20]

[11] Ibid. 1555–7, 290–2, 444; 1557–8, 295, 450. The number eight may imply an extra bedesman, or be an error for seven.

[12] For details see *T.L.M.A.S.* xxi (1), 57.

[13] Syon Ho., MS. A. xv. 5. a. For the subsequent history of the chapel site see *T.L.M.A.S.* xxi (1), 57–58.

[14] Seven almshouses were apparently still standing and in use in 1576: *V.C.H. Mdx.* iii. 120.

[15] Ibid.

[16] J. Leland, *Itinerary*, ii, f. 1, *s.a.* 1542.

[17] Syon Ho., MS. A. xv. 5. a.

[18] Aungier, *Syon*, 470.

[19] Syon Ho., MS. A. xv. 5. a. For 17th-cent. plans and descriptions of the site see *T.L.M.A.S.* xxi (1), 58.

[20] *Cal. Pat.* 1476–85, 138.

# 14. HAMMERSMITH HOSPITAL

## INTRODUCTION

Nothing has since been published which gives more information about this hospital. John Brytt, who described himself as the 'cheyff of the spyttillhouse' at Hammersmith, referred to the implements and household stuff of the hospital in his will in 1521 (G.L. MS 9171/9, f. 187v) and was probably keeper at the time.

*Patricia Croot*

The only medieval mention of this leper hospital occurs in the will, dated 1500,[1] of Joan, wife of Sir Thomas Frowyk of Ealing. Lady Frowyk left 4d. each to every leper in Hammersmith and in four other lazar houses so that prayers might be said for her soul.

In 1549 Hammersmith Hospital came under the care of St. Bartholomew's Hospital,[2] and in 1555–6 the inmates shared in the 26s. 8d. paid by St. Bartholomew's to the poor of the lazar houses under their control.[3] In 1558–9[4] and again in 1560[5] patients were transferred from St. Bartholomew's to Hammersmith.

A proctor of 'the poor house or hospital of Hammersmith' is recorded in 1578 and 1581. This proctor was John Payne of Hammersmith, who was licensed to collect alms in Buckinghamshire and Northamptonshire. He promised to hand over the sums collected to the 'guider' of the hospital.[6]

The hospital received a few private contributions for patients between 1590 and 1608,[7] and each year from 1602 to 1620 the 'guider' of Hammersmith received at irregular intervals from the governors of St. Bartholomew's sums, varying between £5 13s. 4d. and £13 10s., towards the cost of the patients

and his own expenses. These varying amounts were replaced in 1621 by a yearly allowance of about £9 10s., which was continued until 1623. Payments to the hospital then ceased.[8] The last known reference to Hammersmith Hospital occurs in 1677,[9] and thereafter the house seems to have fallen into gradual decay.[10] By 1705 no trace of the building remained.[11]

Norden's map of 1593 shows the hospital south of Palingswick (now Ravenscourt Park), on the north side of the western road (King Street), and just west of the Creek.[12] The irregular south-eastern boundary of Palingswick suggests that the hospital stood near the highway opposite the northern end of Rivercourt Road.

*Marjorie B. Honeybourne*

## Revised List of Keepers or Proctors

This is a revised version of the list in the *V.C.H.*

John Brytt, died 1521[13]
John Golsyngper, occurs 1560[14]
Robert Bray, occurs 1574[15]
John Payne, occurs 1578, 1581[16]

[1] P.C.C. 2 Moone.
[2] See p. 154. St. Bart's, never owned Hammersmith Hosp., which was on copyhold land of Fulham manor: *T.L.M.A.S.* xxi (1), 15.
[3] N. Moore, *Hist. of St. Bart's. Hosp.* ii. 219; St. Bart's. Hosp. Ledger, Hb 1/1, f. 277v.
[4] Ibid. f. 370v.
[5] Ibid. Journal, Ha 1/1, f. 221v.
[6] B.M. Harl. Ch. 86, B. 11, B. 25. A transcript of the 1578 bond is printed in T. Faulkner, *Hammersmith* (1839), 264.
[7] For details see *T.L.M.A.S.* xxi (1), 14.

[8] St. Bart's. Hosp. Ledgers, Hb 1/3, ff. 279v, 572; Hb 1/4.
[9] Lysons, *Environs of Lond.* ii. 421; T. Faulkner, *Fulham*, 342.
[10] Faulkner, *Hammersmith*, 264.
[11] W. Bowack, *Antiquities of Mdx.* (1705), 43.
[12] A Fulham court roll of 1616 confirms this location: L.C.C. *Survey of Lond.* iv. p. xvi.
[13] T.N.A. PROB 11/11, f. 28.
[14] St. Bart's. Hosp. Journal, Ha 1/1, f. 221v.
[15] L.M.A., DL/C/615, pp. 44, 57. Said to be 'not licensed'. *Ex inf.* Jessica Freeman.
[16] B.L. Harl. Ch. 86, B. 11, B. 25.

# 15. THE HOSPITAL OF ST. ANTHONY, HIGHGATE (OR HOLLOWAY)

## INTRODUCTION

There is little to add to the present account apart from noting that the hospital drew the occasional bequest. John Hill of Haringey (or Hornsey) left a small sum in 1500 to an unnamed lazar house, presumably that at Holloway in the adjoining parish of Islington (G.L. MS 9171/8, f. 228v), while in 1528 Sir William Butler included Highgate in his testamentary gifts to six London lazar houses, see *Bedfordshire Wills Proved in the Prerogative Court of Canterbury 1383–1548*, ed. M. McGregor, Bedfordshire Historical Rec. Soc. 58 (1979), no. 112. The use of the hospital as a poor-house can be documented from at least 1531 when Johanna, widow of Master Henry Redmayne, of West Brentford, chief mason of the king's works, left a pair of coarse sheets to each of five 'poor houses', one of which was Highgate: G.L. MS 9171/10 f. 171.

*Jessica Freeman*

Highgate leper hospital stood facing Whittington Stone (once a wayside cross) on the west side of Highgate Hill, the highway between Highgate and Holloway.[1] The hospital was founded in 1473 by William Pole, sometime yeoman of the Crown and himself a leper.[2] As the hospital site was given to Pole by Edward IV, the Crown always appointed the master, and on Pole's death in 1477 the appointment went to another leper, Robert Wylson, a London saddler, in return for war service.[3]

The administration of the London lazar houses was taken over by St. Bartholomew's Hospital in 1549,[4] but four patients had been sent from St. Bartholomew's to Highgate in 1548.[5] In 1550 two governors of St. Bartholomew's were sent to view Highgate spital and next year submitted a report and inventory.[6] The revenues were small and, apart from occasional sums paid for the upkeep of patients,[7] the only substantial donation recorded was the 40s. bequeathed in 1565 by Sir Roger Cholmeley, founder of Highgate School.[8]

From about 1550 patients other than lepers were being sent to the hospital,[9] which henceforth until its closure in 1650 seems to have resembled a poor house rather than a hospital.[10] In 1650 the premises, covering two roods and worth £9 a year, consisted of a timber building with a tiled roof, containing a hall, a kitchen, three small rooms on the ground floor, and five small rooms above, and an orchard and garden.[11] The government sold the property in 1653 to Ralph Harrison of London.[12] The site was built over in 1852.[13]

*Marjorie B. Honeybourne*

## Revised List of Governors, Keepers, Proctors, or Guides

William Pole, founder, occurs 1473–7[14]
Robert Wylson, appointed 1477[15]
John Gymnar and Katherine his wife, appointed 1498[16]
Simon Guyn, appointed 1533[17]
John Stafford, occurs 1551–2, 1557[18]
William Parker, occurs 1560, 1561[19]
William Storye, appointed 1563; died 1584[20]
John Randall, appointed 1584; died 1590[21]
Thomas Watson, appointed 1590; occurs 1593[22]
William Stockwell, appointed 1605[23]
John Harbert, dead by Sept. 1650[24]

---

[1] For details of the site see *T.L.M.A.S.* xxi (1), 16–18.

[2] *Cal. Pat.* 1467–77, 373.

[3] Ibid. 1476–85, 48.

[4] See *T.L.M.A.S.* xxi (1), 9.

[5] St. Bart's. Hosp. Ledger, Hb 1/1, ff. 55, 110.

[6] Ibid. Journal, Ha 1/1, ff. 4, 15.

[7] Ibid. ff. 122, 277.

[8] P.C.C. 24 Morrison.

[9] St. Bart's. Hosp. Journal, Ha 1/1, ff. 122, 196, 196v, 205 (*bis*), 277, 330v.

[10] T. E. Tomlins, *Perambulation of Islington* (1858), 137, 212 n; *T.L.M.A.S.* xxi (1), 17.

[11] Survey printed in Tomlins, *Islington*, 139.

[12] Ibid., from Close R.

[13] See *T.L.M.A.S.* xxi (1), 18.

[14] *Cal. Pat.* 1467–77; 1476–85, 48.

[15] Ibid. 1476–85, 48.

[16] Tomlins, *Islington*, 135.

[17] *L. and P. Hen. VIII*, vi, p. 87.

[18] *Cat. Anc. D.* vi. C 6891; St. Bart's. Hosp. Ledger, Hb 1/1, f. 277; Journal, Ha 1/1, f. 224.

[19] St. Bart's Hos. Journal Ha 1/1, f. 221 v.

[20] Tomlins, *Islington*, 139.

[21] Ibid. 138–9.

[22] Ibid. 137–8.

[23] Ibid. 138.

[24] Ibid. 139.

# 16. THE HOSPITAL OF ST. GILES-IN-THE-FIELDS, HOLBORN[1]

## INTRODUCTION

This article remains the best account of the history of this hospital, which was also known as St. Giles 'of the Lepers', and St. Giles 'without the (bar of the) Old Temple'. There is, however, much useful information in D. Marcombe, *Leper Knights: the Order of St. Lazarus of Jerusalem in England, c.1150–1544* (Woodbridge, 2003), esp. pp. 161–71. Although pre-dating the *V.C.H.* article, C. L. Kingsford, *The Early History of Piccadilly, Leicester Square, Soho* (Cambridge, 1925), contains information about the lands held by the hospital in relation to the Plan of 1585 (see pp. 5–12), and corrects (pp. 32–5) J. Parton, *History of the Hospital and Parish of St. Giles* (London, 1822). Sources for the London estate of the hospital may be found in *Documentary Sources*, p. 82, and there were several quitrents due to the hospital and to the Master in 1548: see Kitching, *Chantry Certificate*, pp. 11, 51, 56.

*Jessica Freeman*

This leper hospital, dedicated to St. Giles, the patron saint of cripples, was founded in the fields of Holborn in the early 12th century[2] by Maud (Matilda, d. 1118), wife of Henry I. The hospital, with an oratory, was on the south side of the old Roman road from London to the west, on the curve of St. Giles's High Street near the present Charing Cross Road (formerly Hog Lane). The parish church of St. Giles probably occupies the site of the hospital chapel.

Queen Maud endowed her foundation with 60s. yearly rent from her perquisite of Queenhythe,[3] and this rent-charge was specially noted when in 1246 the customs on this public landing-stage passed to the City.[4] Further gifts from London citizens raised the annual endowment to over £100, and it seems that one citizen, a leper, gave so much that in *c.* 1354 the citizens claimed that he had founded the hospital.[5] The queen had granted the supervision of the hospital to the City,[6] and for most of the Middle Ages the mayor and commonalty regularly appointed two wardens or overseers for this and the other London leper houses.

Henry II confirmed Maud's endowment[7] and added a further 60s. a year to buy habits for the lepers

and 30s. 5d. to provide lighting. A second charter of Henry II indicates that St. Giles's was a royal free chapel exempt from the bishop's jurisdiction. During the Interdict (1208–14) Pope Alexander IV granted the hospital his special protection.[8] His bull reveals that the lepers were trying to live as a religious community and that the hospital precinct included gardens and 8 acres of land adjoining the hospital to the north and south. This and other land near the hospital formed the home farm, worked by the hospital itself. In 1321 there were at the hospital farm horses, carts, and two ploughs; and in 1391 at least 8 horses, 12 oxen, 2 cows, 156 pigs, 60 geese, and 186 domestic fowl. Two years later brushwood, hay, and straw are mentioned. White and brown loaves, peas, and porridge formed part of the diet.[9]

During the 13th century disputes arose over the administration of the hospital. The Crown had appointed the two wardens or overseers in 1246;[10] but in 1261–2 the citizens of London secured a patent[11] stating that they had always been accustomed to appoint, by consent of the hospital brethren and by royal mandate. The citizens, having made their point, then selected the royal nominees, two Londoners. The citizens next attempted to secure the right to appoint the master, but the Crown's claim was confirmed in 1287 on the ground that the hospital had been founded by the king's ancestors.[12] The king then had to defend his position against the Bishop of London, who claimed the right of

---

[1] The chief sources for the hospital's history are given in *T.L.M.A.S.* xxi (1), 20, n. 1.

[2] The foundation date is discussed in L.C.C. *Survey of Lond.* v. 117.

[3] H. A. Harben, *Dictionary of Lond.* 492–3.

[4] *Cat. Anc. D.* iv. A 6684; *Cal. Letter Bk. C*, 15; *Chronica Maiorum et Vicecomitum Londoniorum*, ed. H. T. Riley (Camd. Soc. xxxiv), 12, 20.

[5] *Cal. Letter Bk. G*, 27.

[6] L.C.C. *Survey of Lond.* v. 117; Moore, *Hist. of St. Bart's. Hosp.* ii. 146.

[7] B.M. Harl. MS. 4015 (St. Giles's Hosp. Cart.), cited by Dugdale, *Mon.* vi (2), 635–6, and translated in J. Parton, *Hist. of Hosp. and Par. of St. Giles* (1822), 6–7. Other property confirmed to the hospital is listed in *T.L.M.A.S.* xxi (1), 20.

[8] *Cal. Letter Bk. G*, 29; Parton, *St. Giles*, 8–11.

[9] *T.L.M.A.S.* xxi (1), 21, 23–24.

[10] Williams, *Early Holborn*, ii. 1033.

[11] *Cal. Pat.* 1258–66, 201.

[12] Ibid. 1281–92, 271.

visitation. At an inquisition held in 1293[13] it was asserted that the hospital was a royal free chapel, that the hospital advowson had always belonged to the Crown, and that upon appointment the master had at once exercised spiritual jurisdiction both in the parish and precinct of St. Giles's 'without any intermeddling' by the bishop. Of all the hospital's property only the church of Feltham was subject to the bishop; and the king alone had the right to visit St. Giles's.

The hospital soon felt the weight of the king's power, for in 1299 Edward I suddenly granted the revenues and administration of St. Giles's to the Master and Brethren of the Order of St. Lazarus of Jerusalem,[14] who had their English headquarters at Burton Lazars (Leics.).[15] St. Giles's thus became a cell to this house (which by 1299 provided not for lepers but for the poor, aged, and sick) and the head of Burton Lazars became ex officio Master of St. Giles's.[16]

The hospital's affairs did not improve, partly owing to internal quarrels and waste, and in 1303 some of the inmates broke the locks off the gates and allowed Robert Winchelsey, Archbishop of Canterbury,[17] to enter and usurp the office of visitor. Some muniments were carried off, and the master complained to the king.[18]

Further trouble was caused by the practice, commonly employed by officers of the royal household, of sending to the hospital non-leprous decayed domestics and others. In 1315 the master, brethren, and sisters petitioned in Parliament against this usage, contending that the hospital had been founded for lepers only.[19] Edward II's ruling in their favour was incorporated in a new charter.[20]

In 1347 Edward III ordered the mayor and sheriffs to see that all lepers left the City within fifteen days.[21] The City authorities had by this time set up their own leper hospitals, but they naturally wished also to utilize St. Giles's Hospital, to which they had always laid claim. The citizens therefore in 1348 complained to the king that since the Master and brothers of Burton Lazars had taken over St. Giles's the friars had ousted the lepers and replaced them by brothers and sisters of the Order of St. Lazarus, who were not diseased and ought not to associate with those who were. After an inquiry it

was agreed in 1354 that henceforth the mayor and commonalty should for ever present to the warden of the hospital fourteen lepers from the City and suburbs, or, if there were not enough there, from the county of Middlesex. If the citizens made further gifts, the number of lepers was to be increased in proportion.[22] Shortly before this settlement, in 1349, the Chancellor, John Offord, who was ex officio royal visitor to St. Giles's, had drawn up new rules for the management of the hospital.[23]

The affairs of the hospital still did not prosper, and in 1367 Edward III took the hospital under his protection, appointing as master Geoffrey de Birston, one of the brothers of the house, with instructions to straighten matters out and put the care of the lepers first.[24] In 1384 Richard II required the aldermen of London to make returns of the yearly value of all the hospital's tenements and rents in the City.[25] Next year the king appointed some of his clerks as visitors to inquire into defaults in the books, vestments, ornaments, and buildings and into the dissipation and alienation of the hospital estates.[26] Four years later the king appointed another commission[27] to visit the hospital, with instructions to reform abuses and remove incompetent officials. Despite the efforts of the Master of Burton Lazars,[28] the king took the hospital under his special protection and in 1389 appointed as warden or master for life John Macclesfield, one of the royal clerks,[29] who removed his predecessor, Nicholas of Dover, Master of Burton Lazars.[30] In 1391 Robert Braybroke, Bishop of London, usurped the right of visitation and jurisdiction by collusion with Richard de Kynble, a 'brother' of the hospital, and his brother Hugh. Macclesfield reported the intrusion, which was recorded on the Patent Rolls.[31] In the same year, for a large financial consideration, Richard II ignored the rights of Burton Lazars and granted St. Giles's Hospital, advowson, and lands in frankalmoin to his grandfather's Cistercian foundation, the abbey of St. Mary Graces on Tower Hill.[32] Legal proceedings[33] were soon instituted by the Master of Burton Lazars, who complained that the Abbot of St. Mary Graces had dispossessed St. Giles's of live stock, grain, carts, furniture, books,

---

[13] Not enrolled until 1391: *Cal. Pat.* 1388–92, 458.

[14] Ibid. 1292–1301, 404.

[15] Dugdale, *Mon.* vi (2), 632–4.

[16] He sometimes appointed a deputy; e.g. *Cal. Pat.* 1381–5, 463.

[17] In place of the Bp. of London, that see being vacant.

[18] *Cal. Pat.* 1301–7, 189.

[19] *Rot. Parl.* (Rec. Com.), i. 310.

[20] *Cal. Pat.* 1313–17, 300; see also ibid. 1334–8, 231; 1377–81, 117; Parton, *St. Giles*, 16.

[21] Deed printed in ibid. 17–18.

[22] *Cal. Letter Bk. G*, 28–29.

[23] Ibid. 30–31. These rules have not survived.

[24] *Cal. Pat.* 1364–7, 388. Parton, *St. Giles*, 13–14, prints the full text of the patent but misdates it.

[25] *Cal. Letter Bk. H*, 155.

[26] *Cal. Pat.* 1381–5, 596.

[27] Ibid. 1388–92, 143.

[28] Ibid. 1385–9, 309.

[29] Ibid. 1388–92, 115.

[30] Deed printed in Williams, *Early Holborn*, ii. 1637–8.

[31] *Cal. Pat.* 1388–92, 458.

[32] Ibid. 1396–9, 47–48; see also Parton, *St. Giles*, 22.

[33] Deed printed in Williams, *Early Holborn*, ii. 1638–9.

vestments, and ecclesiastical ornaments worth more than £1,000.

The City authorities doubted the legality of the grant to the Abbot of St. Mary Graces and held back various rents in the City until commanded by the king in 1393 to hand over money.[34] Further action was taken by Walter Lynton, the dispossessed Master of Burton Lazars, who in 1399 entered St. Giles's with an armed band, turned out the abbot's representatives, and occupied the premises.[35]

During these disturbances the lepers were 'in want of maintenance' so in 1401 Henry IV ordered[36] the mayor to collect 100s. from the hospital's city tenants. This sum was duly handed over to five lepers, and a few months later a similar collection and distribution took place.[37] In the same year Walter Lynton instituted proceedings against the Abbot of St. Mary Graces,[38] and in 1402 the abbot's grant of St. Giles's Hospital was revoked and Lynton was restored to legal possession.[39] It was probably at this time that Lynton compiled the hospital cartulary.[40] In 1414 he had the chief royal grants of St. Giles's Hospital to Burton Lazars inspected, confirmed, and enrolled.[41]

During the legal proceedings the Abbot of St. Mary Graces had accused Walter Lynton of reducing the number of lepers, dismissing the chaplain, clerk, and servants, and replacing them by sisters, contrary to the foundation statutes. At an inquiry in 1402 it was found that in case of necessity the number of lepers was often reduced from fourteen to nine or fewer.[42] About this date the city gallows were moved from West Smithfield to a site just northwest of the hospital precinct, at the gate of which condemned prisoners were given a large bowl of ale, called 'St. Giles's Bowl'. There were also gallows at Tyburn.[43]

During the 15th century leprosy, although dying out elsewhere, was still rife in the London area, and St. Giles's continued as a leper hospital until at least 1500.[44] By 1535–6, however, the fourteen inmates were described simply as 'paupers'.[45]

In 1539 the priory of Burton Lazars, with its dependent house of St. Giles's, was dissolved.[46]

Three years earlier Henry VIII and the Master of Burton Lazars had agreed upon an exchange of land under which St. Giles's lost much without compensation.[47] The remaining possessions, excluding St. Giles's church, were granted by the king in 1545 to John Dudley, Lord Lisle.[48]

The hospital premises originally comprised the oratory or church, very soon partly parochial, wherein burned 'St. Giles's light',[49] the houses of the lepers, the master's house, and rooms for the chaplain, a clerk, and a messenger or servant. By 1224 other brothers and sisters had been introduced to carry on the administration and to help the sick; and between 1224 and 1292 the master and three other chaplains and clerks are mentioned, as well as a sub-deacon and proctor.[50] A chapter-house had been built by 1321.[51]

Much of the hospital's landed property lay around the precinct and constituted the home farm. This land extended eastward almost to Holborn Bar. Within the City there were houses and rents in many parishes, as well as the 60s. due annually from the customs of Queenhithe. Other hospital property was concentrated in the west of Middlesex at Feltham, Heston, and Isleworth.[52]

*Marjorie B. Honeybourne*

## Revised List of Masters of the Hospital of St. Giles in the Fields[53]

John the chaplain, occurs 1118 or earlier[54]
[Osbert FitzGodwy, ?occurs *ante* 1186][55]

[34] Ibid. 1632.
[35] Ibid. 1635 (deed).
[36] *Cal. Letter Bk. I*, 13–14
[37] *Cal. Letter Bk. I*, 14.
[38] Deeds in Williams, *Early Holborn*, ii. 1637–9; *Cal. Pat.* 1401–5, 120.
[39] Procs. printed in Parton, *St. Giles*, 26.
[40] B.M. Harl. MS. 4015.
[41] *Cal. Pat.* 1413–16, 248.
[42] Procs. printed in Parton, *St. Giles*, 22–26. There were never, as is often asserted, 40 lepers.
[43] Stow, *Survey*, ii. 91; Parton, *St. Giles*, 38; R. Dobie, *Hist. of... St. Giles*, 10.
[44] P.C.C. 2 Moone.
[45] Dugdale, *Mon.* vi (2), 635.
[46] Ibid.
[47] Statute printed in Parton, *St. Giles*, 29–32.
[48] *L. and P. Hen. VIII*, xix (1), p. 371.
[49] Parton, *St. Giles*, 55–57.
[50] Ibid. 5, 55–57.
[51] B.M. Harl. MS. 4015, f. 125.
[52] *T.L.M.A.S.* xxi (1), 20–21. For illustrations of the buildings within the precinct and the land surrounding it see Clay, *Medieval Hospitals*, 71; *Lond. Topog. Soc.* pubn. 17 (plan of *c.* 1560); ibid. pubn. 54 (plan of 1585).
[53] Until 1299 the heads of the house were normally called 'master', although 'proctor', 'warden', and 'keeper', terms so far as can be judged of equivalent meaning, are also used. After the hospital was granted to Burton Lazars, 'warden' was the commoner title, whether for the Master of Burton Lazars, his Deputy, or the king's nominee. Any term other than 'master' is given in the footnotes to the list. For the City's 'wardens' or overseers of the hospital see *T.L.M.A.S.* xxi (I), 10–11. Since the Master of Burton Lazars was from 1299 *ex officio* Master of St. Giles's, all the known masters of that hospital are entered in the list below with (B) behind their names. The list of Masters of Burton Lazars is taken from *V.C.H. Lecis.* ii, 38–9, but with a few amendments. Where a Master of St. Giles's occurs some time before he is known to have been Master of Burton Lazars the fact has been noted in case he should have been deputy-master of St. Giles's at the time. Royal nominees are distinguished by (C).
[54] Hen. II's confirmation charter has 'ubi Johannes bone memoria fuit capellanus'; *Cal. Chart. R.* 1327–41, 192.
[55] Williams, *Early Holborn*, ii. 1622.

[Ralph son of Adam, ?occurs 1186][56]

[Robert, ?occurs 1186][57]

Walter of Oxford, occurs 1200[58]

Roger of St. Anthony, occurs 1201–2[59]

William de Cokefeld or the chaplain, occurs ?1206–7,[60] 1211–24[61]

[Edward, ?occurs 1218][62]

Gerard, occurs from 1217–18,[63] 1223[64]

Walter the chaplain [?or of Thame], occurs 1226–7;[65] 1260–1[66]

William the chaplain, occurs ?1260–1,[67] 1272[68]

Roger de Clare, occurs from 1275–6,[69] 1278–9[70]

Geoffrey (or William) de Setfountaine, *temp.* Henry III[71]

Ralph de Seinfontains (Septem Fontibus), occurs 1281;[72] resigned by 1286[73]

Henry of Durham (C), appointed 1286;[74] confirmed 1287[75]

[Robert de Stapul, ?occurs 1287][76]

William de Wytheresfeld (C), appointed 1291[77]

Walter de Clerkenwell (C), appointed 1293[78]

[Henry de Cateby, ?occurs 1297][79]

[ ], Master of Burton Lazars, grantee 1299[80]

[Walter Christmas, ?occurs 1302][81]

John Crispin (B), occurs as 'keeper' of St. Giles's 1303,[82] 1305;[83] as Master of Burton Lazars, 1316[84]

William de Werefeld, ?deputy, occurs ante 15 Feb. 1316[85]

Richard de Leighton (B), occurs?;[86] occurs as Master of Burton Lazars, 1319[87]

William de Aumenyl (B), occurs as Master of Burton Lazars, 1321[88]

William de Ty (B), occurs?; occurs as Master of Burton Lazars, 1323, 1327[89]

Hugh Michell (B), occurs?;[90] occurs as Master of Burton Lazars, 1336–9[91]

Richard (B), occurs as Master of Burton Lazars, 1345[92]

Thomas de Kirkeby (B), occurs, ?as deputy, 1341;[93] as 'warden' and as Master of Burton Lazars, 1347[94]

Geoffrey de Chaddesden (B), occurs 1354[95]

Robert Halliday (B), ?occurs;[96] occurs as Master of Burton Lazars, 1358[97]

Geoffrey de Birston or Briston (C), appointed 1367;[98] occurs 1370[99]

[56] 'Warden'; Parton, *St. Giles,* 42 (deed).

[57] Williams, *Early Holborn,* ii. 1622.

[58] *Cur. Reg. R.* i. 372.

[59] 'Proctor': B.L. Harl. MS 4015, f. 35v; 'master and *custos*': ibid. f. 166v; Rector of St. Antholin's: ibid. f. 55v. Richard of St. Anthony, 'proctor', is perhaps the same man: ibid. f. 44v.

[60] B.L. Harl. MS 4015, f. 156. This deed was witnessed by Roger FitzAlan and Serlo the mercer, both described as sheriffs. They were not, however, sheriffs together, for the former was in office in 1192–3 and the latter in 1206–7.

[61] Parton, *St. Giles,* 42.

[62] 'Proctor': ibid. 46.

[63] 'Proctor': B.L. Harl. MS 4015, f. 12v.

[64] 'Proctor': ibid. f. 41v.

[65] *Cat. Anc. D.* ii. B 2355. This is a conjectural date, but he was certainly master by 1229: *Cur. Reg. R.* i. 372.

[66] B.L. Harl. MS 4015, ff. 27v–28. For the suffix 'of Thame', see Williams, *Early Holborn,* ii. 1571, 1643. Called 'proctor' in B.L. Harl. MS. 4015, f. 10, 'rector' ibid. ff. 171, 172v, and *commagister,* ibid. f. 167v.

[67] B.L. Harl. MS 4015, f. 50v. The deed is headed 45 Hen. III (1260–1), but is witnessed by William FitzRichard, 'warden' of London. The description given to FitzRichard seems to relate to his being from 1246 onwards the City's 'warden' or overseer of the leper hospitals rather than to his later (1265–6) post as 'warden of the City', a new post created by the king in a time of stress to supersede that of mayor: *T.L.M.A.S.* xxi (I), 10; *Chronica Maiorum et Vicecomitum Lond.,* ed. Riley, 90–3.

[68] B.L. Harl. MS. 4015v, *[sic, but probably an error]* f. 102v. William de Kirkes (Parton, *St. Giles,* 43) is possibly Wm. the chaplain.

[69] Williams, *Early Holborn,* ii. 1572 (deed).

[70] *Cal. Lond. & Mdx. F. of Fines,* i. 55. For the suffix 'de Clare', see B.L. Harl. MS 4015, f. 147. For proof that it was applied to this Roger see ibid. 180v–81. Called 'master and warden' (*custos*), ibid., f. 148.

[71] 'Warden': H.M. Chew, ed., *London Possessory Assizes: A Calendar,* London Record Soc. 1965), nos. 188–9 (Geoffrey), 235 (William). It is very likely, since the assizes in question were held in 1411, 1412 and 1427, that the warden in question was in fact Ralph *Septem Fontibus*.

[72] *Cat. Anc. D.* i. C 765.

[73] *Cal. Pat.* 1281–92, 252; *V.C.H. Essex,* vii, p. 111.

[74] To the 'custody': ibid.

[75] Ibid. 271.

[76] Williams, *Early Holborn,* ii. 1622.

[77] He was presented to the bishop by the Crown on 20 Jan. (St. Pauls MS. A, box 60, no. 46) and appointed as 'warden' to 'sustain' the master and others on 20 Feb. (*Cal. Pat.* 1281–92, 423). He occurs as 'master' on 12 and 28 Mar. (B.L. Harl. 4015, ff. 151–1v, 176v) and as 'warden' on 13 Mar. (Williams, *Early Holborn,* ii. 1653).

[78] To the 'custody' during pleasure: *Cal. Pat.* 1292–1301, 22.

[79] Williams, *Early Holborn,* ii. 1622.

[80] See above.

[81] Williams, *Early Holborn,* ii. 1622.

[82] *Cal. Pat.* 1301–7, 189.

[83] Ibid. 357.

[84] *V.C.H. Leis.* ii. 38.

[85] Williams, *Early Holborn,* ii. 1578 (deed).

[86] B.L. Harl. MS 4015, f. 119.

[87] *V.C.H. Leics.* ii. 38.

[88] *Cal. Close,* 1318–23, 498; 1330–3, 327.

[89] Ibid. The surname Tytnt, appearing in earlier lists, is inaccurate.

[90] Parton, *St. Giles,* 47.

[91] *V.C.H. Leics.* ii. 38. His apparent recurrence as Master of Burton Lazars in 1347 (ibid.) is probably erroneous.

[92] Ibid.

[93] B.L. Harl. MS 4015, f. 10.

[94] *Cal. Close,* 1346–9, 388.

[95] Ibid. 1354–60, 83; *V.C.H. Leics.* ii. 38.

[96] Parton, *St. Giles,* 47.

[97] *V.C.H. Leics.* ii. 38.

[98] A brother of house, appointed by the Crown as 'keeper': *Cal. Pat.* 1364–7, 388; 'master', 1368: B.L. Harl. MS 4015, ff. 136v, 137.

[99] *Cal. Pat.* 1367–70, 336.

William Croxton, deputy, appointed 1371;[100] occurs 1381 and 1382;[101] confirmed 1384

Nicholas of Dover (B), occurs as Master of Burton Lazars 1364;[102] confirmed as 'warden' of St. Giles's 1387;[103] dispossessed 1389[104]

Richard Clifford (B), appointed as Master of Burton Lazars in 1389[105]

John Macclesfield (C), appointed 1389;[106] occurs 1391[107]

Richard Crowelegh (C), appointed 1390[108]

[William de Warden], Abbot of St. Mary Graces (C), appointed 1391;[109] dispossessed 1402[110]

Walter Lynton (B), occurs as Master of Burton Lazars 1401–1421;[111] occurs as master of St. Giles's, 1403,[112] 1417[113]

Geoffrey Shrigley (B), occurs as Master of Burton Lazars 1421 to 1445[114]

William Sutton, knight (B), occurs as Master of Burton Lazars 1450 to 1482[115]

George Sutton (B), occurs as Master of Burton Lazars 1484 to 1504[116]

[Thomas Harringwold, ?deputy, ?occurs 1493][117]

Thomas Honyter (B), occurs as Master of Burton Lazars, 1506[118]

Thomas Morton, knight (B), occurs as Master of Burton Lazars 1509 to 1524[119]

Thomas Ratcliffe (B), occurs as Master of Burton Lazars 1526 to 1537[120]

Thomas Leigh, knight (B), occurs as Master of Burton Lazars 1537[121] to 1543–4[122]

[Robert Barker, ?deputy, ?occurs 1542][123]

[100] A brother of the house; appointed by the Master of Burton Lazars and confirmed by the Crown in 1384: ibid. 1381–5, 463.

[101] 'Master': *London Possess. Assizes*, nos. 157, 159.

[102] *V.C.H. Leics.* ii. 38.

[103] Williams, *Early Holborn*, ii. 1637.

[104] Ibid.

[105] *V.C.H. Leics.* ii. 38. Later Bp. of Worcester (1401) and London 1407.

[106] 'Warden': *Cal. Pat.* 1388–92, 115.

[107] Ibid. 458.

[108] 'Warden': ibid. 288.

[109] Ibid. 1396–9, 47–8; and see above.

[110] Ibid. 1401–5, 120; and see above. For his name see *V.C.H. Lond.* i. 464.

[111] *V.C.H. Leics.* ii. 38.

[112] B.L. Harl. MS 4015, f. 133v. 'Warden', 1404; Williams, *Early Holborn*, ii. 1640.

[113] 'Master': PRO, KB9/207/1, m. 5, 'warden': C67/37, m. 33.

[114] *V.C.H. Leics.* ii. 38. 'Warden': *London Possess. Assizes*, no. 235; 'warden': *Cal. Plea and Mem. R.* (Lond.), 1413–37, 168.

[115] *V.C.H. Leics.* ii. 38. 'Warden': *Cal. Pat.* 1452–61, 359; PRO, KB9/413, m. 31, 431, m. 70.

[116] *V.C.H. Leics.* ii. 38. The later date is not given in this list but is taken from *Cal. Pat.* 1494–1509, 391, where he is called 'warden'.

[117] Parton, *St. Giles*, 49.

[118] *V.C.H. Leics.* ii. 38.

[119] Ibid. 'Keeper': *L. and P. Hen. VIII*, i (I), p. 221; 'warden', 1522: *Cat. Anc. D.* iii. D 1108.

[120] *V.C.H. Leics.* ii. 39; Parton, *St. Giles*, 49.

[121] *V.C.H. Leics.* ii. 39.

[122] Williams, *Early Holborn*, ii. 1673 (deed).

[123] Ibid. 1622.

# 17. KINGSLAND (OR HACKNEY) HOSPITAL[1]

## INTRODUCTION

No additional research on the hospital has been published since the above account. The *V.C.H.* histories of Islington and Hackney give information about the hospital's location and surroundings, see *V.C.H. Middlesex*, viii (1985), p. 41; x (1995), p. 28. The Hackney account, which includes the hamlet of Kingsland, also mentions local use of the hospital in the seventeenth century and gives a brief history of its chapel, which continued in use after the hospital closed: *V.C.H. Middlesex*, x. pp. 109, 123.

*Patricia Croot*

Kingsland leper hospital was founded by the citizens of London in about 1280. It stood just over two miles from the city on the west side of the Roman road to the north and at the south end of the hamlet of Kingsland in the manor of Newington Barowe.

The first recorded 'guide' or governor of the hospital, in this instance called 'forman', was William Walssheman, who in 1375 took an oath to prevent lepers from entering the city.[2] Kingsland was one of the group of leper houses supervised by the two wardens appointed by the City.[3] In 1545 the 'guide' of Kingsland petitioned the City for rules for his house.[4] Four years later Kingsland, together with the other five London leper hospitals, was transferred to St. Bartholomew's Hospital.[5] Subsequently the hospital records give particulars of several patients sent to Kingsland.[6] In 1555–6 Kingsland received a quarter share of the 26s. 8d. paid by St. Bartholomew's to four of its 'outhouses'.[7] Further occasional payments were made by St. Bartholomew's and by private persons for the upkeep of patients sent to Kingsland.[8]

During the early 17th century the costs of Kingsland Hospital mounted rapidly. In 1602 repairs to the house and barn cost approximately £150, and in the following year fourteen bedsteads were bought for £14.[9] At this period the 'guide' was receiving at irregular intervals sums usually amounting to about £8 a year, to which extra sums were added in 1611 and 1612 for the Christmas diet of the inmates.[10]

In 1613 the hospital was enlarged by the building of a new 'sweatlie ward' at a cost of £6 4s. 7d.,[11] and in 1625 and 1627 the 'guide' requested more money for fuel and food for the inmates. In 1643 and 1644 he had to be given £10 extra for winter fuel alone.[12] John Topcliffe, surgeon, who had probably been guide for fifty years, was in 1646 granted a fixed yearly salary of £8, together with £16 'for the poor that are admitted into diet'.[13] His successor, John Kent, another surgeon (appointed 1649), was soon in difficulties over the cost of medicine, special diets, and fuel. The hospital building had also been enlarged and so a further £20 was needed for drugs, physic, sheets, straw for beds, and burial charges. During Kent's tenure it was laid down that a candle was to be burned in each of the six wards every night in winter, and that a detailed diet was to be drawn up for each day.[14] The practice of admitting only women patients to Kingsland and only men to the Lock may also have begun at this time.[15]

The Great Fire of 1666 so depleted the revenues of St. Bartholomew's Hospital that all the patients at Kingsland had to be discharged before Christmas 1666. The 'guide' continued in residence to look after the premises, and in 1667 was allowed to take patients whose friends agreed to pay for everything except special diet.[16] By 1680 conditions had returned to normal and Kingsland was to have 20 patients, maintained by St. Bartholomew's. After 1682 the 'guide' was to receive £30 a year, together with a further £3 for washing the patients' sheets, for coals and candles, and for hemp for maintaining

---

[1] 'Kingsland' only became the established usage in the 16th cent. The chief authorities for the history of the hospital are listed in *T.L.M.A.S.* xxi (1), 36.

[2] Riley, *Memorials of Lond.* 384; *Cal. Letter Bk. H*, 9.

[3] *Cal. Letter Bk. H*, 343; *I*, p. 184; *K*, pp. 142–3.

[4] Corp. Lond. Rec. Off., Repertory 11, ff. 173, 177.

[5] See *T.L.M.A.S.* xxi (1), 9.

[6] For details see ibid. 32.

[7] See ibid. 9.

[8] See ibid. 32.

[9] St. Bart's. Hosp. Ledger, Hb 1/3, ff. 287v, 357v.

[10] Ibid. ff. 512, 542.

[11] Ibid. ff. 547v, 548v.

[12] Ibid. Journal, Ha 1/4, ff. 150, 164, 276v, 286v.

[13] See *T.L.M.A.S.* xxi (1), 33.

[14] St. Bart's. Hosp. Journal, Ha 1/5, ff. 48v, 72, 187, 194v, 195, 318v, 320, 321v. The weekly diet is given in Ha 4/1, ff. 12v–18v.

[15] This division had taken place by 1657: Ha 1/5, f. 136.

[16] Ibid. Ha 1/6, ff. 28, 36, 39; G. Whitteridge, 'The Fire of London and St. Bart's. Hosp.', *Lond. Topog. Record*, xx. 47–78.

the sheets. Each patient was given 4d. a day to buy his own food.[17]

Services in the hospital chapel are recorded from 1638, when Jeremiah Gosse was chosen as minister at Kingsland and the Lock in place of a Mr. Powell, who had received £10 a year.[18] Many persons from outside the hospital attended the chapel services and in 1716, after a disturbance in the chapel, curtains were provided to shut off the patients.[19] These patients were suffering from ague, fever, dropsy, jaundice, and diarrhoea amongst other diseases.[20] In 1754 many had venereal disease, but the statement that the Kingsland and Lock outhouses had always been used by St. Bartholomew's for such patients[21] is not borne out by extant records.[22]

In 1725 St. Bartholomew's made a survey of Kingsland. This revealed that all the wards were on the ground floor, were 'very ancient and very defective', and were now three feet below the level of the road outside the hospital. It was decided to rebuild and enlarge these wards. The rebuilding programme provided for thirty beds, a bath-house, a couch-room, a surgery, and other amenities. The coach-house and stable were next rebuilt, and in 1727 the surgeon's house was to be repaired.[23] Other minor repairs and innovations were effected during the 1730's,[24] but evidently the cost of maintaining the outhouses was becoming too great. In 1754 a sub-committee of the governors of St. Bartholomew's reported on both Kingsland and the Lock. It was found that the 'guide' or surgeon of Kingsland was receiving as well as a house and his salary of £30 an additional £50 for medicines. The other staff consisted of a chaplain with a salary of £12 and a gratuity of £8, and a sister, a nurse, and a helper, each receiving 3s. 6d. a week. Since the two outhouses together were costing more than £700

a year to maintain, it was recommended that both should be dissolved and their patients transferred to two special wards at St. Bartholomew's.[25] This proposal was rejected, but in 1760 the decision was reversed and Kingsland Hospital was closed.[26]

*Marjorie B. Honeybourne*

## Revised List of Guides

This is a revised version of the list in the *V.C.H.*

William Walssheman, occurs 1375[27]
John Nyk, occurs 1543[28]
— Lawson, d. by 19 Mar. 1552[29]
— Lawson (his widow), governess and matron, occurs 1552[30]
Cuthbert Harrison, occurs 1557, 1560[31]
John Dyconson, occurs 1589–90; d. by 1595–6[32]
William Moore, occurs 1601–2[33]
John Topcliffe, occurs 1625; dismissed 1649[34]
John Kent, occurs 1649, 1666[35]
John Bignall, occurs 1669; resigned 1682[36]
Richard Berry, occurs 1682, 1689[37]
Nicholas Field, occurs 1708; died in office 1720[38]
James Dansie, occurs 1720, 1734[39]
Joseph Webb, occurs 1749[40]
Robert Young, appointed 1755;[41] not in office by July 1761[42]

---

[17] St. Bart's. Hosp. Journal, Ha 1/7, ff. 95v, 122v, 185v; Ha 4/1, f. 54v.
[18] Ibid. Ha 1/4, f. 246.
[19] Ibid. Ha 1/9, f. 142v.
[20] Ibid. f. 149.
[21] St. Bart's. Hosp., J 12, p. 488.
[22] *Lond. Topog. Record*, xx. 54 n.
[23] St. Bart's. Hosp. Journal, Ha 1/10, ff. 54, 63, 65v, 97, 133, 138, 138v, 141v, 154v.
[24] Ibid. ff. 154v, 229, 284v, 290, 301v.

[25] St. Bart's. Hosp., J 12, p. 488.
[26] Moore, *Hist. of St. Bart's. Hosp.* ii. 372, 376. For the subsequent history, and illustrations of the site, see *T.L.M.A.S.* xxi (1), 35–6.
[27] *Cal. Letter Bk. H*, 9.
[28] Corp. Lond. Rec. Off., Repertory 10, f. 303.
[29] St. Bart's. Hosp. Journal, Ha 1/1, f. 39.
[30] Ibid.
[31] Ibid. f. 221v., 224.
[32] Ibid. Ledger, Hb 1/3, ff. 33, 131v.
[33] Ibid. ff. 235–56v.
[34] Ibid. Journal, Ha 1/4, f. 150; Ha 1/5, ff. 33v., 58v.
[35] Ibid. Ha 1/5, f. 33v.; *Lond. Topog. Record*, xx. 54.
[36] St. Bart's. Hosp. Journal, Ha 1/6, f. 76; Ha 1/7, f. 125.
[37] Ibid. Ha 1/7, ff. 125, 325.
[38] Ibid. Ha 1/9, f. 5v.; Ha 1/10, f. 14v.
[39] Ibid. Ha 1/10, ff. 14v., 301v.
[40] Moore, *Hist. of St. Bart's. Hosp.* ii. 633 n.
[41] St. Bart's. Hosp. Journal, Ha 1/12, f. 530.
[42] Ibid. Ha 1/13, f. 217.

# 18. KNIGHTSBRIDGE HOSPITAL[1]

## INTRODUCTION

This account is still useful for the mid-sixteenth century onwards, drawing on the more detailed article published by Honeybourne in 1963. However, recent research by the V.C.H. indicates that a 14th-century foundation by the City of London cannot be correct (see 'Note on the Middlesex Leper Hospitals', above p. 241) since the Knightsbridge lazar house and chapel were founded by two lepers, William Thomson and his wife Agnes, shortly before 1474. A chancery case of *c.*1485 (T.N.A. C1/52/274–7) states that Agnes had a leasehold plot by the highway at Knightsbridge, acquired by her previous husband, John Simond, from Westminster Abbey for a term of years. Since she and Thomson wished to build a small chapel on the land to pray for their benefactors, they asked Henry Clowe or Clough, tailor of London, to negotiate with the abbot for a longer term. Clough was said to have obtained an eighty-year term for the use of William, Agnes and their son Richard, to remain after their deaths to Clough to use the property to house the sick. This seems to be the eighty-year lease of 1473 granted by the Abbey to Thomas Clowgh and Richard Thomson, yeomen of Knightsbridge (*Survey of London*, XLV, *Knightsbridge* (2000), 40). In his will of 1474 Thomson bequeathed his house called the 'Spetill house' at Knightsbridge to his wife for life and then to Richard, to be a home for sick men forever, making Clough executor with Agnes, and giving Clough control of maintenance and choice of occupants of the hospital after Agnes's death (G.L. MS. 9171/6, ff. 254v.–5). By *c.*1485 both Agnes and Richard were dead and Clough was in charge of the hospital and chapel. In his will of 1512, Clough left his house at Knightsbridge called the lazar house to his sons-in-law Robert Ellington and William Campton for the remaining forty years, paying 10*s.* a year for an obit for him in the church of St. Gregory. He specified that he paid the 4*s.* rent to the Abbey for the property, from which he received 40*s.* a year, though it is not clear how this was derived (T.N.A. PROB 11/17, f. 62v.). There is a gap in the hospital's history until 1549 when it was under the supervision of St. Bartholomew's, but some of those subsequently named as wardens or governors of the lazar house also paid the rent to the Dean and Chapter of Westminster (the Abbey's successors as ground landlord), so it is clear that neither St. Bartholomew's nor the City of London ever owned the hospital as such. The hospital was not endowed, and after contributions from St. Bartholomew's ceased in 1623 it was dependent on private donations.

The Survey of London's account of the hospital's buildings and activities until it ceased in the early eighteenth century augments the *V.C.H.* account. The chapel continued in use as a local chapel of ease, being rebuilt several times (*Survey of London*, XLV, *Knightsbridge* (2000), pp. 4, 19–20, 40–1).

*Patricia Croot*

Little is known[2] of Knightsbridge leper hospital before 1549 when it was one of the six lazar houses handed over by the City to St. Bartholomew's Hospital. The earliest reference to Knightsbridge occurs in 1475,[3] but the hospital was probably among those set up or taken over by the City in the 13th or 14th century.[4]

---

[1] Knightsbridge Hosp. was anciently in the par. of St. Margaret Westminster; from 1536 in the par. of St. Martin-in-the-Fields; and ultimately, from 1725, in the par. of St. George Hanover Square.

[2] For 15th- and early-16th-cent. references to Knightsbridge, see *T.L.M.A.S.* xxi (1), 38.

[3] Clay, *Medieval Hospitals*, 103.

[4] See *T.L.M.A.S.* xxi (1), 5, 7.

After St. Bartholomew's assumed control a number of patients were sent from St. Bartholomew's to Knightsbridge.[5] In 1555–6 the keeper received from St. Bartholomew's 6s. 8d. for 'keeping the poor'.[6] In 1582 John Glassington was the 'guider'. An annual rent of 4s. was paid to the abbey church of Westminster,[7] and St. Bartholomew's paid 45s. for nine 'sore poor people'.[8] Subsequently Glassington received frequent and increasingly large amounts.[9] In 1595 he submitted a report on the state of his hospital.[10] He said that there were no lands nor endowments; that he had spent during his tenure more than £100 on repairs; and that there were 36 or 37 patients, supported wholly by voluntary contributions. Food alone had cost £162 in 1594, and candles, linen, bandages, and medicine had also been bought. Glassington claimed to have cured 55 patients, some of whom had been dismissed as incurable from other hospitals. Some patients were made to work, and all attended prayers in the chapel twice daily.

Regular financial assistance from St. Bartholomew's ceased in 1623,[11] and although the vestry of St. Margaret's, Westminster, made occasional grants,[12] by 1629 the hospital chapel (by then an official chapel-of-ease to St. Martin's-le-Grand) had fallen into serious disrepair. The chapel was rebuilt at the cost of the inhabitants of Knightsbridge, and from 1634 pew-rents were charged to maintain the chaplain, repair the chapel, and relieve the poor in the hospital.[13] In 1699 the chapel, now separately administered, was again rebuilt at the expense of Nicholas Birkhead, a London goldsmith.[14]

The Knightsbridge lazar house and chapel were still standing in 1708,[15] but the chapel only was mentioned in 1720.[16] The hospital stood on one of the main roads out of London, about a quarter of a mile west of Hyde Park Corner, between Piccadilly and Kensington. The buildings were north-east of the ancient bridge over the Westbourne Brook, marked since 1845 by Albert Gate.

*Marjorie M. Honeybourne*

## Revised List of Governors, Keepers, Proctors

The *V.C.H.* list does not distinguish between governors and proctors, but in the 1570s and 1580s at least there was both a governor or warden and a proctor, and the designations have therefore been added to the revised *V.C.H.* list below. The proctors, appointed by royal letter patent, were responsible for receiving alms given to the lazar house and for delivering them to the governor when required.

William Thomson, founder, *c.*1473 to d. 1474[17]
Agnes Thomson, widow, from 1474, d. by 1485[18]
Henry Clough, governor until d. 1512[19]
Richard, goodman of the lazar house, buried 1546[20]
Hugh Fabyan, proctor, occurs 1549–50[21]
Thomas (or Jasper) Fabyan, keeper, occurs 1555–7[22]
Henry Fryer, keeper, occurs 1560[23]
Henry Roberts, appointed proctor Aug. 1577[24]
Edward Brambletonne, appointed proctor Oct. 1577[25]
John Glassington, warden or governor, also guider, occurs 1577 to 1598[26]
David Morrice, appointed proctor 1582[27]
William More, *prefectus*, buried 1620[28]
Daniel Bissell, guider, occurs 1622[29]
John Glassington, surgeon, appointed governor 1654[30]

In 1649 James Winter paid the 4*s.* rent for the lazar house and 4*d.* for a piece of ground leased with it,[31] and may therefore have been warden that year.

[5] St. Bart's. Hosp. Ledger, Hb 1/1, ff. 55, 110, 277v, 339v; Journal, Ha 1/1, f. 221v.
[6] See *T.L.M.A.S.* xxi (1), 39.
[7] Dugdale, *Mon.* vi (2), 766.
[8] St. Bart's. Hosp. Ledger, Hb 1/2, f. 282.
[9] Ibid. Hb 1/3, ff. 33, 46v (*bis*), 51, 53, 63v.
[10] Lysons, *Environs of Lond.* ii. 179.
[11] St. Bart's. Hosp. Ledger, Hb 1/4.
[12] M. E. C. Walcott, *Westminster* (1849), 301; E. Walford, *Old and New Lond.* v (1872–8), 23.
[13] Newcourt, *Repertorium*, i. 694.
[14] Lysons, *Environs of Lond.* ii. 180; J. McMaster, *Short Hist. of St. Martin's-in-the-Fields*, 332.
[15] Newcourt, *Repertorium*, i. 694.
[16] J. Strype, *Survey of Lond.* (1720), ii (6), 67, 78. For the later history of the hosp. site see *T.L.M.A.S.* xxi (1), 40–41.

[17] G.L. MS. 9171/6, ff. 254v.–5.
[18] Ibid.; T.N.A. C 1/52/274–7.
[19] G.L. MS. 9171/6, ff. 254v.–5; T.N.A. PROB 11/17, f. 62v. (Hen. Clowght).
[20] J.V. Kitto, *Accounts of the Churchwardens of St. Martin-in-the-Fields, 1525–1603* (1901), 112.
[21] St. Bart's. Hosp. Ledger, HB 1/1, F. 56; Journal, Ha 1/1, list of dismissed patients.
[22] Ibid. Ledger, Hb 1/1, f. 277v.; Journal, Ha 1/1, ff. 223, 224. There appears to have been some confusion over his Christian name since the clerk first wrote Gabriel (f. 223).
[23] Ibid. Journal, Ha 1/1, f. 221v.
[24] B.L., Harl. Ch. 85 F.33.
[25] B.L., Harl. Ch. 84 I.23.
[26] Ibid.; B.L., Harl. 85 F. 33; St. Bart's. Hosp. Ledger, Hb 1/3, f. 176.
[27] B.L., Harl. Ch. 86 A.16.
[28] *Register of St. Martin-in-the-Fields, 1619–36* (Harl. Soc.), 159.
[29] St. Bart's. Hosp. Journal, Ha 1/4, ff. 127v., 130.
[30] Lysons, *Environs of London*, ii. 179.
[31] *Acts and Ordinances of the Interregnum*, ii. 262–71.

# 19. MILE END HOSPITAL[1]

## INTRODUCTION

The *V.C.H.* account is still useful for the sixteenth and seventeenth centuries, but there is no evidence for the thirteenth-century foundation, nor that the City was ever involved in running the hospital before 1549, and all indications are that it was privately founded in the 1470s (see above p. 241, 'Note on the Middlesex Leper Hospitals'). The earliest known reference to a lazar house at Mile End occurs in a will proved in 1473, one of three making bequests to the hospital between 1473 and 1485, suggesting it was founded not long before, and probably by a local resident since all but one of the known bequests to the hospital were by residents of Stepney and Stratford Bow (*ex inf.* Jessica Freeman).

Supervision of the hospital was apparently in the hands of the bishops of London in 1532 and 1540, possibly as lords of the manor of Stepney, as the hospital stood on manorial waste on the north side of the main highway, just east of the hamlet at Mile End: see *V.C.H. Middlesex*, xi (1998), p. 16. However, in 1548–9 St. Bartholomew's Hospital paid a surgeon to amputate the leg of a patient at Mile End (N. Moore, *Hist. of St. Bartholomew's Hosp.* ii (1918), p. 204), and by 1549 Mile End was one of the six lazar houses around London supervised by St. Bartholomew's and the City of London, but the means by which supervision was transferred to St. Bartholomew's is not known.

*Patricia Croot*

Mile End leper hospital, said to have been founded before 1274,[2] stood within the demesne of the Bishop of London's manor of Stepney.[3] The hospital was on the main road to Essex,[4] to the north of the present bridge over the Regent's Canal and about two miles east of Aldgate.[5] The hospital stood between the hamlets of Mile End and Stratford at Bow.[6] In 1529 it consisted of a group of houses with six beds, a suite of rooms apparently intended for the overseer, and a chapel dedicated to Our Saviour and St. Mary Magdalen.[7] Appointment of the overseer appears in 1529 to have been by a lay proprietor,[8] but in 1532 Bishop Stokesley appointed Richard Wade,[9] and in 1540 Bishop Bonner appointed John Mills.[10] The day-to-day running of the hospital was transferred by the City to St. Bartholomew's Hospital in 1549, and henceforth patients were sent to Mile End and occasional sums were paid for their support.[11] The Spital House is mentioned once or twice in the later 16th century,[12] and was still standing in the 17th century, when the property was conveyed to the Drapers' Company.[13]

*Marjorie B. Honeybourne*

### Revised List of Governors, Proctors, Keepers or Masters

[?John Gymer, died 1522][14]
Richard Wade, appointed 1532[15]
John Mills, appointed 1540;[16] occurs 1557[17]
John Stafford, occurs 1560[18]
John Lyddington, died 1574[19]
Henry Smith, occurs 1589[20]

---

[1] This account has been augmented by Dr. K. G. T. McDonnell's researches into the manor of Stepney.

[2] Clay, *Medieval Hospitals*, 46–47.

[3] Guildhall MS. 9531/11, f. 14v.

[4] Stow, *Survey*, ii. 146.

[5] W. Archer-Thomson, *Drapers' Company: History of the Company's Properties and Trusts*, section 47.

[6] Stow, *Survey*, ii. 146.

[7] Guildhall MS. 9171/10, ff. 137–8.

[8] Ibid.

[9] Ibid. 9531/11, f. 14v.

[10] Ibid. 9531/12, f. 18v.

[11] For details see *T.L.M.A.S.* xxi (1), 43–44.

[12] Guildhall MSS. 9171/16, f. 178; 9171/17, f. 217; *T.L.M.A.S.* xxi (1), 44.

[13] Archer-Thomson, op. cit. section 47.

[14] G.L. MS. 9171/10, ff. 137–8.

[15] Ibid. 9531/11, f. 14v.

[16] Ibid. 9531/12, f. 18v.

[17] St. Bart's. Hosp. Ledger, Hb 1/1, ff. 54v., 55, 170v., 277v., 336; Journal, Ha 1/1 ff. 146v., 159, 169; Strype, *Eccl. Memorials* (1822 edn), ii (2), 248; Lysons, *Environs of Lond.* iii. 483 (from the par. reg. of Stratford at Bow).

[18] St. Bart's. Hosp. Journal, Ha 1/1, f. 221v.

[19] G.L. MS. 9171/16, f. 178.

[20] Lysons, *Environs of Lond.* iii. 483.